REL

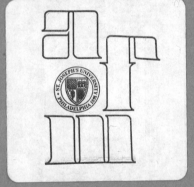

THE ULTIMATE GUIDE TO EXPORT MANAGEMENT

THE ULTIMATE GUIDE TO EXPORT MANAGEMENT

Thomas A. Cook

AMACOM

American Management Association

New York • Atlanta • Boston • Chicago • Kansas City • San Francisco • Washington, D.C.
Brussels • Mexico City • Tokyo • Toronto

Special discounts on bulk quantities of AMACOM books are available to corporations, professional associations, and other organizations. For details, contact Special Sales Department, AMACOM, a division of American Management Association, 1601 Broadway, New York, NY 10019.
Tel.: 212-903-8316. Fax: 212-903-8083.
Web site: www.amacombooks.org

This publication is designed to provide accurate and authoritative information in regard to the subject matter covered. It is sold with the understanding that the publisher is not engaged in rendering legal, accounting, or other professional service. If legal advice or other expert assistance is required, the services of a competent professional person should be sought.

Library of Congress Cataloging-in-Publication Data

Cook, Thomas A.
  The ultimate guide to export management / Thomas A. Cook.
    p. cm.
  Includes bibliographical references and index.
  ISBN 0-8144-0581-9
    1. Export marketing—Management. 2. Export trading companies—Management. 3. Foreign trade promotion—Management. I. Title: Export management. II. Title.

  HF1416.C665 2001
  658.8'48—dc21

                                    2001016122

Printing number

10 9 8 7 6 5 4 3 2 1

Dedicated to my mother… Muriel Cook, who was always an inspiration to me

Contents

1   Identifying the Risks of Global Trade   1

International business means opportunity, but with this comes a certain degree of risk. International businesspeople need to be able to know when these risks are present, develop systems for identification, and understand how these exposures affect global business strategy.

4   Freight and Logistics Issues for Import/Export Managers   65

A critical aspect and cost of selling goods overseas is freight. This
chapter reviews many of the factors affecting the decisions importers
and exporters must make when dealing with freight. It also provides
comprehensive options for reducing cost, negotiating better rates,
and obtaining the best service contracts.

5   Specialty Logistics Issues for International Trade   83

Many U.S. corporations facing unique challenges to their import/export operations use specialized solutions to ship freight and meet customer satisfaction objectives. This section reviews these nuances of global trade logistics.

8   Trade Finance, Banking, and Letters of Credit   139

A key issue to increase export sales is to arrange competitive and creative approaches to finance transactions and protect overseas receivables. This chapter reviews the financial and accounting concerns of exporters and provides the fundamental details of international banking, terminology, and various payment options.

9   Cargo Loss Control   147

More than 70 percent of cargo loss in transit could be eliminated if goods are properly packed for transit. This chapter addresses the concerns that shippers face and presents ideas, solutions, and options for loss-free imports and exports.

13 Global Personnel Deployment and Structure   247

The cost-effective use of personnel in export sales and operations can make or break a new or mature global trade program. The author offers a survey of the issues with specific recommendations spanning more than 25 years of review.

14 Obtaining Export Assistance   253

This chapter identifies and outlines the options an exporter can use from an array of resources in sales, marketing, operations, and banking.

Foreword

I am continually impressed with the scope of knowledge and expertise Tom Cook has demonstrated in international business. As Executive Director of the World Trade Institute, I know many practitioners of global trade skills in import/export management, insurance, logistics, compliance, documentation, banking, law and tax. Tom's knowledge encompasses the diverse areas of the field, and we are fortunate to have him demonstrate his expertise in various seminars that he presents on our behalf. I am proud to write the foreword for *The Ultimate Guide to Export Management* as it seemed to be an inevitable by-product of Tom Cook's teaching prowess.

The future for the export executive is multifaceted. We know this from much of the market research we do in establishing the course agendas and programs for our School of International Trade and Commerce at Pace University in New York City. We have learned that the export executive of the future will have to master numerous skill sets to be successful. In reading this text it is clear to me that Tom has addressed all of these skill sets, not only from an academic perspective, but also from the hands-on practical perspective that is critical to communicating this subject area in education and training.

Tom Cook has always received rave reviews for his seminars at Pace University, as well as other venues, such as the AMA where he also has an affiliation. After reading this ultimate guide, I could envision him in front of his class, lecturing, teaching, and mentoring the students on the many aspects of export management and global trade.

Students; traffic managers; and export executives in sales, customer service, operations, and finance will all benefit from the contents. The intense details that every person involved in exporting should know, to better serve their companies and at the same time, enhance their skill set are well articulated. The section on "compliance management," which is a "hot" topic at the World Trade Institute is of particular interest. Tom has covered the subject well. He guides the reader through the maze of issues involved to grasp the necessity of understanding export compliance and offers solutions that deal with this subject relative to protecting a company's interests.

Having come from the commercial side of international logistics, I know the difficulties that executives face in finding resources and answers to all the dilemmas, questions, and problems they encounter day to day.

The Ultimate Guide to Export Management is a one-stop shop for the global executive. A "wherewithal" for the exporter. Not only is every subject covered in-depth in the text, but additional information is provided in the appendix, which is one of the best resource libraries in the business. The appendix includes a listing of web sites, which will be extremely helpful. It also includes government resources, a listing of various periodicals, key telephone numbers, and a host of other important information in more than 200 pages. I know it will be utilized regularly here at Pace and will be recommended to others.

The style, format, and pace of the book are excellent. It is easy to read, has a logical sequence, and presents all the particulars in an intelligent and personalized manner.

The book also provides what Tom refers to as "connectivity" in global trade, meaning that everything is connected, like links in a chain. I know this to be very true in exporting. One must cover all the bases and that is just what this book does.

Read it, follow the guidelines, and you will do well in exporting.

Donna Sharp
Executive Director
World Trade Institute at Pace University
New York City, New York

Preface

Competing Effectively in Global Trade

There is a significant amount of intelligence, resources, and detail necessary for companies to do well in exporting. This "ultimate guide" provides hands-on, comprehensive advice and counsel at the most basic functional level for export executives to use to achieve success in the world of exporting.

Those individuals and corporations that develop a broad and extensive mind-set for global sales and operations will be more likely to succeed. International competition is fierce. Americans are already behind the eightball even as they begin exporting. This is largely due to the fact that our foreign competitors are better prepared. They start learning about export at an earlier age–their training begins in grammar school. They can speak, read, and write several foreign languages. The more affluent have traveled to, gone to school in, or worked in the United States, Great Britain, or Germany. A greater percentage of their GNP is involved in exporting, sometimes as much as three to four times greater, compared to the United States. Exporting to the world is the lifeblood of these countries, whereas for many U.S. interests it is only an alternative market.

Americans do have quality products that are in global demand. Once we master the skill sets of global trade, we will be in a position to assault the competition. Obtaining the skill sets of foreign marketing and sales; understanding letter's of credit, trade finance, export compliance management; choosing and picking freight forwarders and carriers; learning INCO Terms; dealing with cultural issues; and avoiding political and economic eventualities are but a few of the stealth/precision/cunning capabilities that we need to excel in exporting.

So whether you are in operations, sales, marketing or finance–if you are involved in global trade, you need a foundation of technical skill sets that allows you to conquer all the issues of exporting.

The key is to understand the risks and mitigate them. Exposures loom in global trade. Risks in the areas are economic, political, documentation, cultural issues, carriers, distances, customs, compliance, duties and taxes, regulations, language, legal, weather, handling, and more. Learning what the risks are and dealing with them successfully will lead to the greatest opportunity for maximizing profits.

This book outlines export risk management, offers the basics for training and education, elaborates evaluations and comments, and outlines numerous resources to deal with these export exposures. The book provides detailed hands-on information to allow one to learn the skill sets necessary to mitigate the typical problems associated with global trade.

When product is exported overseas, we need a wealth of information. What are the export compliance rules for goods being shipped from the United States? What are the import regulations and import compliance standards our product will face in the country it is being exported to? How should the goods be packed, marked, and labeled? What are the documentation requirements? How will you be paid? How do you protect our foreign receivable? How will you choose the forwarder and carrier? These are a few of the questions surrounding exports from the United States. The more detailed your product is, the more countries you export to will complicate the export process. Make the freight time-sensitive, perishable, or Haz-mat and the difficulty factor increases exponentially.

All of these questions are answered in *The Ultimate Guide to Export Mangement*. Insight into all the issues, options, and choices that the exporter will encounter is provided and solutions and resources are offered. All of this will allow you to be a more astute exporter and purchaser of global services.

The exporter of the new millennium must be able to work all day and all night, speak several languages, negotiate global contracts, manage international customer service with flair and style, purchase international services with great value, and be a risk manager of corporate interests and profits. Yes, there are many hats. There are many responsibilities.

The key to export success is to manage from an informed position, develop resources, and learn the skill sets. This book, like no other, provides the total base of knowledge, preparing you to be the most prepared and most knowledgeable exporter.

1

Identifying the Risks
of Global Trade

This chapter reviews much of what will be covered in this guidebook. It is critical for export executives to understand all the risks that are involved in global trade. Once those are understoood, the options to eliminate the risks or reduce their consequence can be thoroughly reviewed.

To minimize the exposures and maximize the profits, is an excellent export strategy that is emphasized throughout this book. This chapter provides the reader with the background of how this strategy comes into play in developing a sound and profitable export program.

Facing the Challenges of World Trade

U.S. companies engaged in global trade need to rise to the occasion and directly meet the challenges of competing in world markets. American companies are up against significant competitive pressures from trading giants such as Japan, England, Germany, and China who are attempting to challenge U.S. penetration and growth in foreign markets.

Competition from these nations, many with unfair trading practices, presents several obstacles to American interests. This forces U.S. companies to climb to the top using four critical steps for global success: **creative marketing, improved logistics, cost savings**, and **key resources.**

Using Creative Financing as a Marketing Tool

One excellent creative approach for U.S. companies is to offer credit terms on a transactional basis in lieu of the letter of credit (L/C) or requiring payment in advance. The cost of an L/C in some countries can be as high as 13 percent, which puts the landed cost of the U.S. product at a disadvantage, even before it is shipped. Despite this, U.S. exporting companies have typically been unwilling to risk overseas collections—an arrogant and costly position.

Export credit insurance can be obtained that will protect you from foreign receivables losses. Export credit and political risk insurance are available from many private and governmental entities. One of the best and leading options is available through the Export-Import Bank in Washington,

D.C. Receivable protection combines the better of two worlds. You create sales that would not exist without the coverage, and you protect your receivable assets in the event of commercial default or political eventuality.

Improving Logistics

Logistics is often a secondary consideration, which is used after a sale or transaction is negotiated. **However, when logistics is part of the sales and negotiation process, it offers another potential competitive tool to gain global advantage.**

"Foreign competition makes international business increasingly price-sensitive."Bringing cost-effective supply chain management tools into the international sale results in less costly exports. For example, a foreign trade zone (FTZ) or custom-bonded (CB) facilities allow you to hold your product in foreign entry gateways in secure storage and offer timely availability of products to your customers overseas. Instead of taking three to four weeks for delivery, you can clear and deliver your product in two to three working days. To some customers, this can be a critical factor in selecting a supplier. In addition, the FTZ or CB will defer the costs of duties, taxes, value-added taxes (VAT), and clearance costs until the goods are cleared and shipped to the customer. (This is discussed in more detail in Chapter 15.)

Providing Export Cost Savings

Foreign competition makes international business increasingly price-sensitive. Steps must be taken to reduce the landed cost to overseas customers. Five integral actions can ensure success:

1. **Identify all the components of the landed cost and act on each one individually.** The small price considerations will add up to favorable savings.

2. **Identify the correct harmonized tariff code (HTSUS), which is sometimes referred to as the Schedule B number.** Duties are calculated on the HTSUS. Sometimes a different HTSUS will produce a different classification, and therefore lower duties.

3. **When shipping, look for consolidators.** Though sailings or flights are less frequent, depending on availability, consolidators often save as much as 20-50 percent on freight costs.

4. **Proper documentation, marking, and labeling will assure safe, timely, and competitively priced shipments.** When done incorrectly, freight will be held up in customs, resulting in clearance delays and additional handling and demurrage charges.

5. **Analyze ways to reduce weight and dimensions to lower freight costs.** Proper packing is important, but more often than not, lightweight cartons, pallets, and alternative shipping materials can be used.

Developing Key Resources

The complications of global trade are difficult at any level. But to achieve the pinnacle of success, an American company needs to devote the time and money necessary to accumulate and propagate intelligent, responsive, and comprehensive sources of support and resources.

Read global trade publications. Participate locally in international trade associations. Develop integral networking contacts with consultants, bankers, insurance executives, freight forwarders, accountants, and international carriers and spend at least 5 percent to 10 percent of your time developing these contacts. Ultimately, they will provide options in reducing the cost of international services. This is another way to reduce the landed cost and make you more competitive in global sales.

Stepping up to face the challenges and stepping forward wisely will minimize the risks and maximize the profit opportunities in global business.

Shipping to a New Market—Potential Exposures

American companies are increasing their export markets and adding new countries to their list of ultimate destinations. Many companies ship to more than thirty destinations, spanning five to six continents.

Traditional export markets of Western Europe have now grown to include the newly formed CIS countries, Latin America, the Middle East, and Asia. The information superhighway cannot keep up with this rapid growth and cannot meet the need to develop the information and capabilities necessary to service the needs of U.S. exporters that would assure them successful and profitable international transactions.

The American exporter must be more disciplined when entering a new market to reduce risk and maximize trade profits. The following five guidelines will help the exporter accomplish this goal:

❖ Establish a network of resources.

❖ Carefully manage the terms of sale and payment.

❖ Execute preplanned logistics.

❖ Know the document requirements.

❖ Know the export insurance issues.

The exporter needs to integrate all of these areas because one area can be directly affected by the others. Care should be taken before acting on any one matter. The information that one would require to profile the world is not available in any one source. The exporter must rely on a vast network of contacts and sources of timely data and intelligence.

Establish a Network of Resources

The Department of Commerce in Washington, D.C. is one of the best places from which to start when entering a new market. The Department of Commerce provides various means of critical support. It provides timely commercial data on most countries in the world. In addition, country desk officers are available who maintain daily communication with the U.S. Foreign Commercial Offices and the Department of State, U.S. embassies around the world, foreign consulate offices here and abroad, and many commercial contacts worldwide. Individuals within the department are experts on specific countries. State and local government, freight forwarders, bankers, international marketing consultants, accountants, marine insurance companies, local world trade associations and port authorities also can be important networking sources for local market and country information.

Export-Import Bank, Foreign Credit Insurance Association, National Customs Brokers and Forwarders Association, American Institute of Marine Underwriters, U.S. Small Business Administration, U.S. Department of State, and the National Institute for World Trade are important network resources. Major companies involved in international support services such as Price Waterhouse Coopers, AT&T, Sprint, American Express, Federal Express, KPMG, and Citibank are also sources for international trade data in various countries. They often have direct experience, or know someone who does, and can readily provide the required information.

Carefully Manage the Terms of Sales and Payments

Banks, freight forwarders, and friendly competitors are often excellent resources for determining the best terms of sales. A new market can present a significant exposure here, as each country will have a different set of laws, regulations, and practices that have different meanings for terms of sale. *INCO Terms,* a book published by ICC Publishing, New York City, outlines what countries subscribe to the INCO standards and terms of sale, offers common and agreed upon meanings for the exporter and importer. If a country does not subscribe, specific knowledge of local laws and practice must be obtained and understood in the event a dispute arises.

New emerging markets of Eastern Europe and Latin America should be watched carefully and surveyed before an international transaction is closed and the terms of sale finalized. The key to making a transaction successful in a new market is getting paid, which makes the terms of payment critical. A new market does not necessarily require prior trading experience. Banks may provide sources for customer credit worthiness through their local branch networks. International credit agencies, such as D&B and Graydon America, are good alternatives at a price.

Initially, selling on more secured payment terms, such as L/C and payment in advance, may be viable options before selling on more relaxed terms. Should competitive pressures force you to sell on an open account, purchasing export credit insurance may transfer your risk to a third party.

The U.S. Government, through the Export-Import Bank, will provide options and commercial insurance. Companies such as the FCIA (Great American), Continental, CNA, and the American International Group (AIG) also provide options.

Keep in mind that once the goods are shipped, you will have little influence on the exposures affecting the shipment, which makes the wording of terms of sale and payment critical to finalizing the transaction and obtaining your dues. INCO Terms are covered in greater detail in Chapter 6.

Execute Preplanned Logistics

New markets challenge the best of logistics professionals. New markets present a different geography, different physical profile, and an infrastructure that may not be matured. Your prior modus operandi of shipping 40-feet ocean containers may not work in certain countries where the roads are small and narrow. They may only accept 20-foot containers or less than container load (LCL) freight only. This change in container size may increase unit costs and hamper your competitive edge. Some landlocked countries may best be reached by air and truck only. Some emerging markets such as Mexico are undergoing a major internal enhancement of their transportation infrastructure. This makes long-term planning obsolete.

Packaging, labeling, and unitization become critical factors. Materials handling methods in certain countries may be inadequate for handling large unitized pallet loads, forcing the exporter to ship several smaller units that can be handled manually by human labor. Warehousing and distribution systems could be lacking, causing the U.S. exporter to reconsider issues such as packaging, unitization, and timing of the shipments and protecting the freight for longer inventory cycles in exposed areas. "Just in time" (JIT) inventory management takes on new meaning in global trade. **The U.S. exporter must review and scrutinize the entire distribution chain from point of packaging and shipping to the time it is received by the consignee.**

Know the Documentation Requirements

The responsible exporter understands that the document requirements for countries around the world vary greatly. The freight forwarders or shipping agents are typically the best sources for this information. Another great source is your customer's clearance agent in the importing country. Always obtain the names and communication numbers for your customers.

The typical documents required are an invoice, a packing list, a bill of lading, and a certificate of origin. Other documents include import/export license, insurance certificates, inspection certificates (SGS), NAFTA certificates, consolidation bills, and health and sanitary certificates.

Poor document handling is the chief cause of customs delay and late deliveries to customers. Exporters must know what the needs are before shipping, and execute the paperwork or have their freight forwarders handle it on their behalf.

Know the Export Insurance Issues

The marine insurance policy, which would typically provide an "all risk," "warehouse to warehouse" coverage, should be controlled by the exporter. In some foreign countries, such as Venezuela and Nigeria, this coverage must be purchased in the local markets. There may be another twenty to thirty countries that have similar provisions. Your local insurance brokers and marine underwriters can advise on the local requirements and assist in arranging the coverage.

In local purchase situations or when the importer is controlling the coverage, contingent insurance should be secured in case the other policies fail.

When entering a new market, coverage should be extended or started in the following areas: life and health, disability, workers' compensation, property and inventory, inland transit, general liability, and automobile. Many times policies written in the United States will give extension privileges for writing coverages abroad. All types of insurance claims occur for which no coverage exists. Review the scope of coverage before the claims occur. The insurance companies can assist in providing coverage in host countries.

The U.S. Exporter has vast marketing potentials in new and emerging markets. The opportunities are endless, but they pose an array of exposure problems. By following the guidelines outlined in this chapter, the exporter can minimize the exposure and be a successful international trader.

Staying Competitive while Reducing Exposure

Years ago, when U.S. corporations were selling particular products overseas with little or no competition, they could demand that their foreign customers pay cash up-front or with an L/C. Today, U.S. corporations are in intense competition with companies from countries all over the globe. One of the standard business practices now required in international trade is for companies to give their foreign buyers thirty-, sixty-, and ninety-day credit terms. In some cases, credit terms can extend to 120 days or more. In Brazil, for example, importers expect to receive up to 360 days.

Credit is not just a way of doing business overseas. Attractive credit terms can provide the competitive edge needed to close the deal. However, as the international activity of U.S. companies increases, the overseas exposure also increases from commercial and political risks. One of the biggest concerns of U.S. companies is whether their foreign customers will pay for the goods and services provided. U.S. companies have an estimated annual overseas exposure of more than $40 billion—and that's serious potential jeopardy.

Various international service providers offer consulting services to companies on how to conduct business overseas and minimize exposure. Banks, insurance brokers, customhouse brokers, freight forwarders, consultants, accountants, and attorneys are a few of the professionals who can assist you with export trading activity.

The question is how can America's global traders remain competitive against companies from Asian and European countries while protecting their exposure? Exposure for a U.S. company venturing offshore is sitting in the United States with a liability in accounts receivable while having a product or service delivered abroad. What happens if the local customer in that country just doesn't pay for whatever reason—legitimate or not? The lines of recourse the American company has are limited. The more third world or developing nations you get, the more limited the recourse.

Problems can arise from a variety of sources. A foreign currency can be devalued or, if the customer pays in the local currency, the government may not have the foreign exchange to transfer the money into U.S. dollars. Companies must also worry about political risks such as foreign confiscation, embargoes, and expropriations as well as wars, strikes, and riots overseas.

This is part of the fear factor that is making many U.S. companies hesitate to trade offshore.

In other countries, government agencies and industry associations back private transactions, which guarantees payment and enables the company to offer attractive credit terms with minimal exposure. This permits America's competitors to compete abroad more effectively.

"We lack that thrust in the United States," There are programs available in the United States to help companies compete offshore. . . **"What the government has been unable to do is make all of these programs available to all of the companies that would like to trade overseas."** We estimate that 85 percent of the money available to promote overseas trade is consumed by about 15 percent of the U.S. companies trading abroad. "In other countries, it is made very simple to get things done. So, U.S. companies are left at a disadvantage."

Larger corporations have the expertise to evaluate country risk and write comprehensive contracts overseas, but small to mid-size U.S. companies lack the experience and staffing to evaluate how to do business overseas. These companies also have more of a risk because a greater percentage of their business is involved in a foreign transaction.

There are numerous government and private programs available for U.S. companies to finance their overseas transactions and protect their exposure. The Export-Import Bank of the United States and the Foreign Credit Insurance Association offer a variety of programs to assist U.S. companies.

Professional service providers work with the people who are going to do business overseas and measure and evaluate their exposure. They then provide options for transferring exposure to third parties, such as banks, insurance companies, or another trading company. Professional service providers provide quality information and various options to reduce the risk and make it easier to export. In addition, they are networked into the international business community to connect the right people to get the deal or transaction done.

Facing the Risks of Global Trade

American firms face new challenges when competing in world markets that present an array of exposures that are different from traditional domestic trade problems. However, with these new challenges come opportunities for greater market share, export success, and profit potentials.

The first challenge is understanding the competition. Every major nation in the world, led by countries such as Japan, Germany, Great Britain, and France are professional exporters and international entrepreneurs. Export activity represents more than 50 percent of these countries' gross national product (GNP) and is the focus of new business development. In addition, the export role of the governments of these countries is substantive and very supportive.

U.S. firms are not competing on equal terms. Recognizing that, we must employ a greater sense of creativity to combat competition where we are at a disadvantage.

For example, offer better payment terms: sales that were traditionally done on a letter of credit now need to be offered on open account, sixty days site draft, ninety-day consignment, etc. The additional receivable exposure can be mitigated by securing export credit and political risk insurance that allows transfer of the exposure to a third party.

The cost of transporting the goods to destination and maintaining a competitive advantage is an additional challenge. This is very visible in a sale to a European buyer when we are competing directly with a European supplier. Geography provides the European a natural advantage.

Creatively using distribution warehouses located at strategic points close to the point of sale can reduce this disadvantage. Freight can be sourced in bulk in less costly modes and distributed directly to customers from these distribution facilities at competitive transportation prices.

Another potential solution rests in scrutinizing some of the components of total transportation costs and taking steps to reduce the expense of those components. For example, marine insurance is a transportation expense. Send out competitive bids. The insurance market currently is "soft" and rate reductions of 10 to 25 percent can be achieved. Assuming higher deductibles or limiting policy terms and conditions are other options for reducing marine insurance rates.

Packaging is another cost of transportation and for some product lines can be a large part of the total expense. Options are to seek competitive bids from packaging suppliers, with incentives for these vendors to reduce costs of your export packing. Keep in mind that transit rates are typically predicated on weight or volume. If these two variables are reduced by 20 percent, the freight charges will be reduced. In analyzing packaging options, one must review materials handling considerations. For example, if pallets are used that might add up to 15 percent of the total transit weight, one might consider using slipsheets to replace the pallets and reduce the gross weight by 12 to14 percent. Cargo safety and ease of handling should be considered before making this change. Other options might be to use less heavy plastic or fiberboard pallets and determine if over packing is necessary.

Another cost of transportation is the mode and carrier selected and the rates they charge. Shipping is very competitive. When was the last time you reviewed their rates? When was your forwarder last challenged to reduce freight rates by 10 percent and their fees by 5 percent? Have consolidators been looked at? Have nonvessel operating common carriers

(NVOCCs) been considered as a less costly shipping option? The bottom line to reducing shipping costs is to present several options that need to be reviewed thoroughly for cost-effective results to be achieved.

Another option in evaluating distribution costs is reviewing the time element issues. Air freight is a faster means to transport cargo faster and is typically more expensive. Is shipping by air necessary? However, ocean freight usually requires preshipment warehousing. Perhaps air freight would be less costly when the cost of warehousing and the ancillary costs associated with storage such as insurance, security, accounting, inventory management, etc. are considered. All of these issues need to be considered when evaluating total transportation costs. Carefully scrutinizing these areas and effecting some changes will result in savings in 75 percent of most situations.

Another area for American firms to consider is providing "value-added," that is, provide more than just the product. Provide additional services or benefits from you rather than a competitor. An example might be to offer technical assistance in the use of the product or service you are selling. This can come in several forms. For example, you can bring your clients to your offices for education and training. Send you own technicians to their sites. Provide better technical manuals and training aids, etc. Structure an ongoing update and modernization program; provide credits for upgrades and repurchasing, etc. This will be appreciated, and it assists in building and enhancing longer term relationships with your clients.

Another option is to offer an ongoing system for providing spare parts and supplies that is easier and less expensive than the system the customer is currently using.

A clear example of this "value-added" concept are the automobile retailers in the United States who, in addition to selling the car, provide an array of services that differentiates one dealer from another, and at the same time provides opportunities for additional revenue and excellent customer rapport!

The final area of action is product and service adaptation. The exporter needs to meet the needs of the international customer in lieu of the expectation that they will compromise and accept a product or service that is less than adequate. Too often Americans take an arrogant attitude and force customers to accept a product or service adapted for the American market.

All that is needed is a little market research and some refinements in the design and manufacturing stages to provide a product that will meet or surpass customer expectations. Areas such as sizes, use of the metric system, alternative languages, made-to-order sales, variation of ingredients, compliance with local regulations, consideration of religious and ethnic issues, environmental, weather-related concerns, politics are but a few of the elements that can make products and services sell overseas in greater abundance and with higher profit potentials. The key is to be aggressive, competitive, creative, and ultimately to mitigate risk and maximize the opportunity for profit potential.

All of the factors, steps, and details required for successful exporting are presented in this book, affording an excellent resource to determine the opportunity and the means to be "export wise."

The Future Holds Perils for Smaller Exporters: Potential Deregulation Issues and Tips on How to Survive

Look out small shippers! Peer out your window, view the horizon, because there is a new ship coming into harbor, and its payload holds little value to the small or new exporter.

Congress has passed new legislation to change the current face of ocean transportation in the United States. In principal the new legislation will reduce the authority of the Federal Maritime Commission (FMC) and allow "free trade" to take over the current pricing guidelines and controls put forth by government regulation.

While many steamship lines and ocean carriers—as well as very large shippers—are for deregulation, the small shipper is bound to suffer. The current regulatory system, governed by the FMC, puts tight controls on how a large-volume shipper can negotiate rating tariffs with ocean carriers. While larger shippers will always have the best rates, the regulations controlled the disparity to "acceptable" tolerances, so the smaller shipper, who might pay more, would not pay "a lot" more. In that the cost of transportation becomes part of the cost of goods being sold, this new change could greatly increase the competitive advantage of larger companies, potentially threatening the smaller exporter with demise.

Some carrier and shipper circles contend that steamship lines, which handle large exporters' business, will compete aggressively for that business—in some cases with "loss leader" pricing. This presents two dilemmas for smaller exporters. It will provide large exporters lower transportation costs, and it is feared that smaller exporters with little volume and less clout will pay even higher rates to make up for the lowered revenues generated by cut-rate pricing offered to the larger competitors.

The FMC not only influenced pricing but also governed all regulatory affairs between shippers and ocean carriers, becoming a forum for the rights of all size shippers and a legal entity to handle disputes and problems. It also authorized the operating rights through licensing of freight forwarders and nonvessel operating common carriers (NVOCCs). Both of these matters were in the best interests of all shippers, but more particularly smaller exporters who have fewer resources and money available to deal in the world of international trade.

Some insiders believe that the FMC will not be totally eliminated, but instead made substantially smaller and will work under the direction of the Department of Transportation (DOT). However, most see the lobbying efforts of the larger shippers, carriers, and their trade organizations (National Industrial Transportation League) to have been successful in eliminating what they view as laws, regulations, and bureaucracies that impede free trade. The bottom line is that the smaller shippers potentially will be big losers in the arena of international trade if the current direction of government deregulation takes place.

Usually there is opportunity in the face of disaster, but I am not certain that in this instance there is any opportunity. The best strategy may be to dig the trenches, put up the camouflage, prepare for the incoming, and make the very best of what will be a difficult circumstance, which began showing effects in 1998 and continued into 2001.

My recommendations are as follows:

1. The final dismemberment of the FMC and regulatory issues has not yet occurred. While the ship is taking on water quickly, it has not yet sunk. This means you might have some effect by contacting your federal legislators. If individuals, companies, and trade organizations lobby diligently, it might be possible to mitigate the final legislation and future acts. While it is certain that the FMC as we know it is over, its future role and structure are not yet shaped.

Explain your concerns about the small exporter and ask legislators to modify the current direction to secure "stopgaps and assurances" to protect the smaller shipper.

2. Use caution for all future pricing structures of export sales where the cost of transportation is a factor, particularly on long-term contracts. Although it is not certain, it is likely that any exporter with less than 50-100 container loads a year (or the equivalent) is likely to pay higher ocean freight rates.

3. Join common trade associations that use their clout to negotiate with ocean carriers.

4. Start communicating with your freight forwarder and/or NVOCC to obtain the best possible pricing. It is possible that their size and overall frequency of shipments will give them some competitive advantages, which you can use.

5. Be creative. Look to every potential opportunity to gain clout, such as massing your business with one carrier, instead of two or three. Meet with your buyer, who may have certain advantages because of size, location, political clout, etc. to negotiate a better tariff; or start networking to develop resources and contacts that might prove beneficial in this new ocean marketplace. Alternative sourcing or varied logistical patterns might prove to be better options.

6. Beef-up your negotiating skills. Free trade means the best negotiators will get the best deals. There are many classes, seminars, and programs available to assist one in enhancing negotiating skills. Look at any airline magazine for a handful of choices.

My last recommendation and probably the most important: Do not wait until the increases come before reacting. Be proactive now. Take any or all of the six recommendations and act now. Mitigation in 2001 and beyond will reduce risk and increase the potential for export success.

Navigating the Obstacles of Global Trade

Most shippers face poor service and high freight rates that ship on an LCL—and the less frequently they ship, the worse the situation is. Their "unit cost" for shipping, whether it be per pound, per kilo, per cubic meter, per container load, etc., will be much greater than shippers with a high frequency of exports.

The reduction in the scope of authority of the FMC potentially makes matters worse for the smaller shipper/exporter as larger shippers will have greater clout in carrier negotiation on the "backs" of the less frequent and LCL shipper. This means higher ocean rates for shippers with less than 500 trailer exchange units (TEUs) annually and even more so for shippers with less volume. The new to-export company will have a hard time obtaining competitive ocean freight rates.

The following recommendations might afford the best value for your transportation dollar and offer service and freight rates that are competitive. The cost of transportation and the ability to deliver product on a timely basis is critical to the U.S. exporter. These suggestions can provide the competitive advantage you need as they help mitigate the competitive advantage of larger shippers.

1. Know your options. Dealing direct with carriers is limited as most do not accept LCL freight. Your best options are freight forwarders, consolidators, and NVOCCs. They already have volumes of freight on particular trade routes with prenegotiated freight rates with carriers and discounts of which a portion can be passed on to you.

They also can provide an array of logistics services that can assist you in completing your export trade:

- Inland transit options

- Warehousing

- Consolidation points

- Documentation and banking

- Export packing

For those shippers with LCL freight, in the long run a relationship with a quality forwarder, consolidator, and NVOCC will be the difference between profit and loss, success or failure. Some traditional trucking companies also are now offering LCL ocean freight services, such as Yellow Freight, APA, Roadway, and CFI. Potential savings may be available from these trucking options.

2. Maximize clout with your forwarder, consolidator, and NVOCC. Give them as much "of the pie" as feasible, then negotiate all your transportation costs inclusive of loading, storage, handling, and freight. This could easily provide an additional savings of 10 percent to 15 percent.

3. Work with your overseas buyers to time your shipments to take advantage of larger orders. Potentially reaching the size of even 20-feet containers would greatly decrease your freight costs on a "unit cost basis."

Know your "break-even point" in shipping LCL versus FCL. There will be some point where it is cheaper to buy a container than to ship LCL. Depending on product, dimension, weight, trade route, etc., this can range from 40 percent to as much as 80 percent of container capacity. In some circumstances, you may be better off paying a little more and buying the container. This provides the following:

- Exclusive utilization of space

- Control over stowage, blocking and bracing

- More security

- Less exposure to multiple handling and diverting of freight

- Potential for more direct routing

Your freight forwarder, NVOCC, and carrier can work with you in this regard to determine the break-even point for your specific situation.

4. Look to trade associations that offer membership and clout in the purchasing of freight services for the smaller exporter. Many associations are trade-specific, including forest products, wine and distillers, citrus growers, to name a few. The Small Business Exporters Association (SBEA) based in Washington, D.C., recently secured a program for the small exporter for all different types of freight. Two other groups are the North American Association of Export Companies (NEXCO), Long Island Import/Export Association (LIEXA), and the LTD Shippers Association, which focuses on imports from the Far East.

The key to export success in logistics for the smaller, less frequent, and LCL exporter is knowing the options and establishing strategic relationships and alliances with forwarders, NVOCCs, and trade associations.

International trade by itself is competitive enough without logistics becoming an obstacle. By using a little smarts and playing all strokes to your advantage, the obstacle can be mitigated and competitiveness maintained.

Exposures in Today's Foreign Market

U.S. corporations are experiencing an increase in the export of their products and services, as well as augmenting their investment in foreign countries; most international economists agree that the survival of the U.S. corporation depends on the ability to expand successfully into foreign markets. With this expansion, however, U.S. companies also face more exposure related to foreign economic and political climates. To trade successfully abroad, American companies must be familiar with the available options that will reduce these international trading exposures.

The exporter faces a myriad of risks such as war, strikes, riots, civil commotion, terrorism, embargos, and currency inconvertibility. Of these examples, currency inconvertibility is typically considered the most serious.

Take for instance, the Long Island manufacturer that lands a contract to provide its product to a company based in Brazil. The terms of sale are freight on board (FOB) in New York, but the payment terms are 360 days sight draft (these conditions mean the risks are transferred to the buyer in New York, but the buyer does not pay until one year after delivery). The Long Island manufacturer has no choice but to sell on these terms because the company knows that the competition in Japan, Germany, and Great Britain would welcome the opportunity to step in and assist the Brazilian Corporation. At the end of the year, the Brazilian company pays its invoice to the Long Island manufacturer in local currency, however, the Brazilian government bank is unable to produce enough U.S. currency to transfer the amount into American dollars. As a result, the Long Island company must wait another ten to eleven months for payment. The cost to the manufacturer in terms of time, effort, and depreciation of funds has reduced its profit margin to zero.

Had the manufacturer purchased political risk insurance to protect itself from the currency inconvertibility exposure, this problem could have been significantly reduced. In only thirty to sixty days after default, the seller could have been indemnified by an insurance company for the full value of its loss plus interest.

Another risk associated with the case described is that of the local buyer refusing to pay its obligation to the producer. This exposure, called *credit risk*, can also be insured through various governmental and private insurance companies.

The U.S. company making a fixed investment overseas also faces the risk of losing its investment, profit, and personnel through such exposures as civil commotion, terrorism, nationalization, confiscation and war. Take the example of the California-based trading company that decided to build a packaging and distribution warehousing facility in the Philippines to provide a product that will eventually be sent back to the United States. To assist with this project, the company sent ten management personnel overseas and spent $2.3 million in materials and supplies. It anticipated $1.5 million of gross revenue per annum, which will produce annualized profits of $300,000. This company can protect its personnel against terrorist attacks through several kidnap and ransom insurances that not only provide indemnification in the event of a loss, but also attempts to prevent losses from occurring at all and mitigate losses if they do occur. Fixed investments can be protected with various insurance policies designed to protect against these type of overseas exposures. Lastly, the California company can protect its anticipated revenue and profit base through policy endorsements and specialized wordings.

Another significant exposure the American exporter faces abroad is related to product liability and how the politics/laws of a particular country determine its handling of foreign companies transaction occurring within its borders.

U.S. trade abroad sometimes includes the "dumping" of a product not sold in the United States or shipping goods of lesser quality or standard. In these cases, the American company often stands to lose thousands of dollars through fines, penalties, and legal liabilities. Other risks include the possibility of developing a poor trading reputation and the potential for personal fines and imprisonment for the employee representing the company's interests. Even products of superior quality might not meet certain national standards, or local customs and laws might be restrictive causing considerable exposure.

International Freight Shipments—Avoiding the Major Pitfalls: Where Did My Shipment End Up?

Documentation. It makes all the difference. Just a simple mistake can cause substantial delays in obtaining clearance in a foreign country. It can also mean additional costs to complete customs clearance. Lost time and money makes for unhappy customers and adds to your aggravation.

Start with the Correct Documents

Some of the many documents that may be required include:

- Invoice
- Packing list
- Export declaration
- Health/sanitary certificate/quality
- Certificate of origin
- Export/import licenses
- SGS inspection certificates
- Bills of lading
- Carnets
- Import customs documents

Complete Those Documents

Take the time to be sure you have the correct answers to the following questions:

- ✔ What language should be used?
- ✔ Is the spelling totally accurate?
- ✔ How many copies are required?
- ✔ What is the proper format?
- ✔ Does the form require notarization or consularization?
- ✔ Does it get shipped ahead or travel with freight?
- ✔ Who must sign?

Obtaining Support

Even the experienced exporter occasionally needs the support of an expert. When venturing into new territory, you should check with several sources to make sure you have the latest data. Laws, customs, politics/economics, and local regulations can change swiftly and completely.

Sources you can turn to include the following:

- Your own professional freight forwarder
- Your customer who probably has resources and relationships with the local authorities that will cut down on the cost and hassle
- Department of Commerce country desk officers
- International Trade Reporter, Bureau of National Affairs
- *Export Yellow Pages*
- *Official Export Guide*
- Council for International Trade
- *Shipping Digest: International Trade Desk Manual*
- Bureau of National Affairs

An Important Tip: Fax samples of the documentation ahead of the shipment to your customer or the customer's agent. This will assist in preclearance and confirm that all documents are in order.

Accurate Documents = Prompt Payment

An important function of the documentation can be to make sure the exporter gets paid and that collection is available under the agreed terms of sale and payment. One example is a L/C transaction, where the exporter expects to receive payment once the goods are shipped. In reality, once the goods are loaded and an original bill of lading is available, a presentation of all the required documents is made to the bank, typically by the freight forwarder.

> **Accurate Documents =
> Prompt Payment**

The bank never sees the freight, but compares the documents presented with the requirements of the L/C. The bank is actually making payment on the "quality" of the documentation. The paperwork is scrutinized carefully and must be in perfect order to avoid payment delays, additional costs, and penalties if discrepancies are found. Don't avoid going into new territory because the process is intimidating. Your freight forwarder will help you avoid the pitfalls.

Chapter 1 provided an overview of all the risks and issues for the exporter. It also began the process of outlining the steps in mitigating these risks and exposures, assuring export success. The foundation has been established leading to the balance of comprehensive detail, resources, and knowledge necessary for the exporter to know and to follow.

Concluding Remarks

The reader can now understand the magnitude of risks and exposures involved in exporting. However, these should not be detrimental if they are managed successfully. This chapter presented an overview of options for the exporter and specific solutions and resources available to help them deal and manage the exposures to a successful conclusion. The balance of this book will now discuss in detail specific solutions and export strategy for managing export development, sales, and operations.

2

Gaining Entry into World Markets

The exporter needs to develop a plan of action and strategy to answer the following questions: Should I export? How should I start? What do I need to be concerned about? This chapter provides detailed information that will assist the export executive making these decisions. It outlines the initial process, identifies resources, and provides "handholding" tips for execution.

Too many American companies enter the export arena and go through very difficult learning curves that could have been avoided with better initial preparation as outlined in this chapter.

Global Overview

The global marketplace is perfectly positioned for aggressive U.S. companies to grow and develop by exporting. Political and economic events have opened doors and created opportunities for those involved in all product lines entering world markets. Mature markets in the West and emerging markets in South America, Africa, and Asia present significant opportunities. With these opportunities, however, comes risk. This chapter presents the resources and skill sets that are necessary to minimize the risks and maximize the opportunities for profit potential in global markets.

This chapter will also help U.S. corporations determine if exporting is a viable and potentially profitable option. The chapter begins by helping you evaluate the exportability of your company's products or services and identify the factors within your company that can enhance your chances of international success.

This chapter addresses all of the issues that are critical to success as an exporter:

- Developing an exporting plan

- Market research

- Methods of getting your product to market

- Pricing considerations

- Financing your export operations

- Reducing the associated risks and liabilities of international expansion

The United States is the largest exporter in the world and its products are in global demand. American exporters from the 1950s to the 1980s enjoyed a position in trade with less competition and more control of overseas markets. Strong competition primarily from Western Europe and Asia dramatically changed the flow of goods in the world, which had a great effect on the U.S. domestic market. This affected imports into the United States, which has now affected exports and global reach into the new millennium. As a result, American manufacturers confronted the dual needs to compete domestically to retain their traditional market and to look abroad for growth opportunities. They have risen to the challenge: According to the U.S. Department of Commerce, exports have become a significant factor in the growth of the U.S. economy. Between 1986 and 1999, U.S. exports added more than 40 percent to the rise in Gross National Product (GNP). In 1995, almost 85 percent of U.S. GNP growth was due to exports, representing a record high of more than $400 billion. The numbers for 2000/2001 are not yet available, but the trend is continuing.

Reasons to Become Involved in Global Markets and Export

New opportunities and the benefits of diversification are the key reasons to become involved in global markets and export. Corporations and manufacturers based in the United States need to strategize business plans that offer stability, growth, and contingency opportunities. Exporting presents an answer to all three strategies.

Global changes in infrastructure, communications, technology, and transportation systems have pushed the boundaries of the marketplace around the world, making a larger customer base accessible.

Export markets in numerous countries offer increased profits and can result in greater sales stability. Overseas sales can also hedge against a U.S. recession, a decline in domestic demand, and seasonal fluctuations in domestic sales.

International sales may result in higher profits and enhanced cash flow compared to domestic sales after setup costs due to favorable overseas tax incentives.

Domestic markets may pose certain limitations that international sales can counter or expand.

Exporting may be an effective strategy to combat a foreign competitor who has begun selling in the United States. By attacking your competitors on their home turf, you may mitigate their threat in your domestic market.

Inventory management and deployment of domestic production can often be better balanced with the opportunity to shift into export markets.

Exports may prove to be a testing ground in which to test market future domestic sales at lower costs. This has worked well in the food, chemical, and pharmaceutical industries—all of these industries often test their products on foreign soils first.

Changing technology is often a reason to look to foreign markets whose technology advance may not have caught up to the West.

Exporting may make better use of a company's resources, which might be more cost effective when operating in foreign markets.

Exporting creates synergies with its counterparts overseas. These synergies often have a life of their own creating mutual benefit and long-term opportunities.

Effectively Developing a Global Strategy

Any size company can export. Yes, it does take time, resources, and expense, but these factors can be managed effectively. One should not be afraid to look to foreign markets. The following six steps can be used to develop an export marketing strategy:

1. **Commitment.** Make sure the commitment is there from senior management. Without it, once costs and exposures rise, senior management will be quick to abandon the effort.

2. **Competitiveness.** Determine the competitiveness of your product or service in overseas markets.

3. **Costing.** Determine the price you must charge to cover your "total costs" for getting your product to the market and the potential market price.

4. **Marketing.** Identify your target customers and establish a business plan or strategy to reach and attract them.

5. **Geographic Areas.** Determine the markets on a country- and region/city-specific basis and the best distribution and logistics to get to that market.

6. **Risk Mitigation.** Identify the risks and exposures and the steps to effect mitigation.

There are comprehensive and difficult issues involved in selling a product or service in a foreign market. However, once you have developed a comprehensive strategy to deal with all of these issues, the exporting process is reasonably straightforward. Each exporter will determine the benefits to move forward—market expansion and lucrative profits lead the charge.

It is critical to understand that in export trade, there is opportunity. Where there is opportunity there is risk, and potential reward. This handbook of exporting will help you mitigate the risk, thereby maximizing the return on investment.

Should Your Company Enter the Global Arena and Begin to Export?

International marketing is not all that different from domestic marketing. While there are nuances that we will cover, the basic principle of quality, creativity, and price are consistent. If your product sells well domestically, it is likely to sell well overseas. If your product sold well in the United States, but is now "getting old," it might still sell well in foreign markets who have yet to catch up to the technical or new product advances in the U.S. domestic market.

The following ten questions will assist you in determining the export readiness of your products:

1. Do you know if this type of product or service is currently sold in an existing foreign market from a local or export source?

2. Do any of your domestic customers turn the domestic purchase into an export sale?

3. Is the product successful domestically? If so, do similar conditions exist internationally? Do international users of the product already exist? Are the same marketing conditions in those opportunities?

4. What protections exist, such as trademarks, patents, proprietary rights, etc.?

5. What is the overall capability for a foreign competitor to take your product and duplicate it?

6. If the product is becoming technologically "prehistoric", are there global markets that do not require the most modern technology?

7. What modifications may be required to meet the laws, engineering criteria, or cultural needs of other countries?

8. Are your U.S.-based competitors involved in export sales?

9. What is the size potential of the foreign market?

10. What value added makes your product better?

Initial market review and analysis begins in your own facilities and not in your potential global markets. The type of customer to target in global markets can be determined by what is happening in the U.S. market. Survey your domestic clients and look closely for those who may be purchasing your product and then exporting it. It may have already determined that there is a global market for your product.

I have been involved in numerous projects and studies in the last five to seven years that have identified huge opportunities for U.S. products in all markets over the globe, particularly in Europe, Latin America, and Asia. The growing populations and their lack of a manufacturing infrastructure leaves voids that U.S. corporations can take advantage of. When carefully approached and managed, secondary markets in Africa, the Middle East, and Southeast Asia present export potential.

Analyze your domestic competitors and their export activities. You can obtain significant data from U.S. Trade Statistics from the Census Bureau provided by several companies, one of them being PIERS, a subsidiary of the *Journal of Commerce*. This data can tell you who is exporting similar products to where. These databases are great tools for gathering competitive marketing information on similar industries.

Following this initial review, you will need to determine who will take ownership of the export development. You may want to look for outside consultants and export management expertise to provide support.

Your chances for successful exporting depend on your company's commitment from senior management. The costs and the utilization of resources demand attention and approval from the "top."

Senior Management Issues

Entering exporting requires sound reasoning and a common-sense approach to the decision-making process.

> *I cannot emphasize enough. . . . A commitment from senior management is critical to the success of an export program.*

- Does senior management understand the costing and resource utilization and drain on the internal infrastructure?

- Are all personnel committed to exporting? Are you in it for the long haul or set up for a short-term gain?

- Will your commitment continue despite initial difficulties and financial requirements?

- Time frame for exporting to generate positive returns?

- Returns on investment and profitability?

- What export experience do you or your management team have?

- Who will have ownership and be responsible for establishing the export business?

- How much time is being alloted for overseas operations?

- What personnel and organizational structure would be required to ensure that export sales are adequately served?

Additional considerations:

1. What competition do you face from foreign shores?

2. Do your domestic sales end up in foreign markets?

3. What previous experience do you have?

4. Do you have a general understanding of the local laws, culture, and business customs of the countries with which you expect to be involved?

5. What effect will international sales have on domestic production?

6. Do you have capital available to commit to international expansion?

7. How will you meet the demand for new orders?

8. Has someone figured out "landed cost" to determine actual pricing, margins, and competitiveness?

9. Can you develop the internal infrastructure to manage export order processing?

10. Will you integrate an export-compliant operation?

Your service providers network of international offices and export professionals can bring knowledge of local markets worldwide and of the sometimes complex start-up processes to your export assessment and planning process. The right service providers can review your current business and operating history to help you answer the questions in this chapter and determine if exporting is the next best step for your company. They can also provide market and product analyses to assess the viability of your product in overseas markets.

Aligning with Export Professionals

One of the most critical steps exporters can take is to align themselves with experienced professional service providers of global trade. Bankers, accountants, customhouse brokers, freight forwarders, insurance brokers, consultants, lawyers, to name a few, are integral to mitigating the risks and maximizing the opportunities in export trade.

One of the most frustrating learning curves the new exporter will face is identifying reliable and skilled partners/service providers. Once identified, investing the time to develop a close working relationship should be a priority. Throughout this book, I identify all the necessary international service providers and how to choose them and manage their services.

Structuring an Export Program

Market Research

Knowledge of the marketplace, and your own overseas/export capabilities are the starting point of analysis in developing an export program. Markets that appear to have exporting potential at first blush may not be suitable for your company. Quality market research can help you evaluate the true potential. Market research is a critical step in developing export potential.

Export trade opportunity information can be gathered through interviews, commissioned surveys, and direct contact with potential customers or representatives. Export market research delivers high value information, but can be time consuming and expensive. This approach should be geared to your company's needs and resources to minimize costs. International trade shows held in the United States are an excellent example. These shows are an affordable way to gain your first exposure to foreign markets and offer an excellent networking opportunity. In recent years, there have been more and more shows attracting numerous exhibitors and visitors from around the world.

Other export marketing options use data from compiled sources, such as government trade statistics for a country or product.

Five steps will assist you in this regard:

1. **Learn what resources are available.** A number of web sites to assist you in this regard are listed in the appendix and a schedule of periodicals/magazines that would be very useful.

2. **Stay current on world political and economic events that affect the international marketplace.** A change in the political makeup of a country or significant economic activity may open a market that was closed. There have been recent changes in Asian and Latin American markets where domestic economic challenges have opened doors and created opportunities for those that are prepared to make long-term investments.

3. **Review and scrutinize trade and economic statistics available through the Census Bureau.** Trade statistics are usually available by product and by country and provide information regarding shipments of products during specific periods of time. In addition, population, household income, consumer spending, and production statistics provide useful information to assess your market potential.

4. **Work all your resources: private, multiple service providers (freight forwarders, bankers, insurance brokers, major accounting firms, consultants, etc.), and government agencies, e.g., the U.S. Department of Commerce in Washington, D.C.** All serious exporters should visit Washington, D.C. to see their support options and meet with potential private and government professionals who have programs and services to offer. Various service providers' personnel can assist you in making connections in Washington, D.C. from the Department of Commerce, the U.S. Department of Agriculture, the Food and Drug Administration, Export-Import Bank, the Small

Business Exporters Association, the National Association of Machine & Tool Builders, and an array of other entities who have the capability to assist exporters with their overseas analysis.

5. **Collect and review research data to isolate the markets that present the best opportunity for your product and company culture.** Identify countries around the world by using the following:

   ✔ Worldwide background data on demographics, production, GNP, trade policy, political climate, consumer profiles, and general trends for all countries.

   ✔ Country data, once you've identified viable exporting targets for product or economic and political conditions. Reports in this group include information on trade barriers and trade leads and contacts.

   ✔ Product/industry data to select foreign markets for a specific product or industry by indicating potential market size and the largest competitors.

Scrutinize all marketing and trade statistics. They are historical trends that may not reflect future events. In addition, there are factors that may skew the numbers. A market that appears to be a large importer may not be consuming the imported goods, but instead re-exporting to other destinations. Alternatively, an apparently untapped market may be untapped because country restrictions prevent imports of your product.

The Internet has provided an entire world of access to export marketing and operations data. A list of exporting and industry web sites are listed in appendix B: Important Web Sites.

Market research will serve as your road map for exporting. Consultants and market research companies are excellent resources for these efforts, particularly for new-to-export companies.

Utilizing Third Party Assistance

Many companies chose third party companies to provide export expertise. These are known as export trading companies, export management companies, purchasing or trading cooperatives or trading intermediaries.

Export Management and Trading Companies

While export management companies (EMCs) and export trading companies (ETCs) have declined in the last ten years, they still serve a useful purpose in global trade. These can be great options for a company that is new to export. They offer immediate expertise and less start-up cost. The experience, contacts, and resources they provide can prove invaluable.

An EMC acts as the export department for one or several manufacturers of noncompetitive products. Typically, it is a U.S.-based company that solicits and transacts business for a commission, or a retainer and a commission, or an agreed to markup.

Typical EMCs will specialize by product, foreign market, or both and have established distribution networks. Immediate access to a foreign market and the ability to set the price for your product are the two principal reasons for using an EMC.

Depending on how you structure the relationship, you may lose control over the sales process, which could be a major drawback of using an EMC. Careful selection, negotiation, and regularly maintained communication can reduce this drawback. Delaying commission payments until you have received payment for shipped goods also can increase your control.

ETCs are broader in scope than EMCs. They are driven by opportunity more than long-term relationships. They also can represent an association or an industry.

ETCs are useful for projects in which economies of scale can be achieved through joint effort and where risk can be better managed when spread over a greater volume of activity. An ETC usually takes title to the goods and sets the resale price.

The Export Trading Company Act, passed in 1982, was intended to encourage the formation of ETCs, stimulate U.S. exports, and reduce the uncertainty regarding the application of U.S. antitrust laws to export operations. The act allows banks to make equity investments in commercial ventures that qualify as ETCs and authorizes the U.S. Export-Import Bank to make working capital guarantees to U.S. exporters.

Export agents, merchants, or foreign trading companies purchase products directly from the U.S. company and then resell under their own names. The remarketer takes on the risk of the overseas sale. In this type of exporting arrangement, the U.S. company relinquishes control over the product. Be aware, however, that you are still liable for the quality of the product. This type of indirect exporting is best used for private branded merchandise. The major advantages of using a remarketer are reduction of risk and guaranteed distribution.

Foreign Distributors or Sales Agents

Most exporters eventually establish a network of foreign distribution sales agents. This is an excellent low-cost option for entering a new market.

Exporters will retain commission agents to purchase U.S. goods on their behalf. The commission agents typically are compensated by the foreign company and, therefore, are motivated to acquire the product at the best terms and the lowest possible price. Commission agents may be foreign government agencies established to find and acquire desired products.

An exporter's agent is the equivalent of a manufacturer's representative in the United States. Using the company's product literature and samples, the agent presents the product to potential buyers. The foreign agent usually works on a commission basis, assumes no risk, and is under contract for a definite period of time. Remember that the term "agents" is legally defined and, therefore, any contract with an agent or representative should specifically state if the representative or agent has the legal authority to obligate your company. Local laws, rules, and cultural issues will come into play in this regard.

A foreign sales agent or distributor will purchase merchandise from a U.S. manufacturer for resale at a profit. Distributors normally carry noncompetitive but complementary products. Foreign distributors are the likely choice if your product requires postpurchase servicing because they carry an inventory of products and spare parts and maintain facilities and personnel for support and warranty service. Payment terms and length of association between a company and a foreign distributor are established by contract.

U.S.-based manufacturers will usually sell through distributors, as a first-step entry into a new market. This will typically lead to a long-term relationship or eventual independence by the U.S. exporter.

The following are recommendations for choosing agents or distributors:

1. **Execute substantial research.** Check the agents and distributors out thoroughly.

2. **Do not enter initial contracts long term.** Use monthly contracts until you are satisfied with their performance.

3. **Clearly spell out your expectations and performance standards.**

4. **Use U.S. counsel with global expertise and local presence in that market.**

5. **Address all patent, trademark, and proprietary issues.**

6. **Bring dispute relief to independent arbitration in a neutral country.**

Evaluating your choices of the best distribution option for your particular situation is the major element of your exporting strategy. Each option has corresponding risks and degrees of managerial or financial involvement.

Sometimes utilizing various choices is your best strategy—a direct sales approach in one country, agents or distributors in others, and the less direct option of an ETC in yet a third. Various levels of a multifaceted strategy approach is perfectly reasonable and may well be the most cost-effective.

Every effort to research and learn as much as possible about your export partners should be reviewed. Turn over each and every stone. Take the time necessary to visit with your customers and gain knowledge of their supply chain. Secure Dun & Bradstreet reports or "World Traders Data Reports" (WTDRs) from a Department of Commerce district office and check references. Make sure your choice of a domestic intermediary is bonded or take out bonding or political risk insurance yourself. In some countries, dealing only with incorporated agents or distributors reduces the risk of foreign taxation.

Potential foreign partners can be chosen using the following criteria:

• Prior success in export/import transactions.

- Ability to establish a functional, well-founded working relationship.
- Synergy with your business.
- Personal qualities of those engaged in international sales and operations.
- Language skills and cultural identity of the staff.
- Number of field salespeople they employ.
- Short- and long-term growth plans, if any.
- Logistics expertise.
- Expansion capability and willingness to expand to meet your needs if necessary.
- Consistency of sales growth.
- Adequate storage and warehouse facilities.
- Method of inventory control.
- Adequate equipment and qualifications to service your product if necessary. If equipment and qualifications are not adequate, willingness to acquire the needed resources and training. (Note: to what extent will you have to share in such costs?)
- Territory they cover.
- Number of product lines they represent.
- Compatibility of product lines with your product.
- Conflict of interest.
- Other U.S. companies they sell for.
- Type of customer with which they work.
- Compatibility of foreign partner's interests with your product line.
- Their key accounts and what that means to your efforts.
- Percentage of total gross sales these key accounts constitute.
- Ability to compile market research information to be used in forecasting.
- Advertising budget.
- Promotional costs you will share and how the amount will be determined.
- Number of exporters they represent.
- Evaluating that you are their largest supplier or principal source of activity.

Typically foreign agents and distributors will require contracts, which are best done by an attorney. All details of the contract should be explicit and all terms clear and concise. The contract should include the following:

1. Parties and legal entities clearly defined.

2. Responsibility for marketing, selling, or promoting the product.

3. Territory within or out of the country.

4. Terms of sale and payment.

5. Required product specifications or modifications.

6. Estimated sales forecast.

7. Product service and warranties.

8. Involvement in logistics and distribution, if applicable.

9. Compliance issues outlined.

> *Protection of manufacturer's proprietary rights is also an essential part of any agreement, so expressly state the rights and obligations of each party.*

Clauses that address choice of law, arbitration, and compliance with both countries' laws can avoid disputes later. Each country will have certain terms and conditions for doing business, as well as exclusivity arrangements and currency restrictions. Retain an attorney well-versed in international law with local representation to help you draft and review your agent/distributor contract.

Developing Your Costing Structure

Your ability to offer competitive pricing structures will be criticial to your ability to enter a new market and sustain growth. As in the U.S. domestic market, the cost of getting the product to the consumer is a significant factor in the pricing formula. In exporting, there are costs that may be added as the product enters the destination country, such as tariffs, customs duties, and import or value-added taxes. If you discount the effect these costs have on your final price, you may miss an important facet of your pricing equation.

Many importers will utilize a "landed cost" valuation in comparing various overseas suppliers. The bottom-line cost will determine your competitiveness.

Some additional areas that need to be reviewed when starting to export are as follows:

- Currency conversion
- Customs, clearance, duties, taxes, and VAT
- Personnel travel and entertainment
- Translation expenses
- Market research
- International postage and communications
- Legal expenses

- International commissions

- Consolidation

- Freight forwarding

- Product modifications

- Packing, marking, and labeling revisions

- International cargo insurance

- Foreign inland freight and warehousing

Ultimately you will determine the "landed cost," which is the final cost to the importer of bringing your product to their market.

You will need to identify your margins and costs by product. The export price cannot be the Ex-works price (the cost of the goods at your plant prior to export) plus the cost of export. The price will be determined by a mix of factors such as your excess production capacity, order quantity, profit margin goals, and desired market share. You will need to learn about the INCO Terms, which are discussed in chapter 6.

Payment in U.S. dollars may not always be possible because some foreign countries impose restrictions on currency transactions. If the market you have chosen looks particularly profitable, you should carefully evaluate the currency alternatives available.

You may choose to complete the transaction in the local currency. If you choose this route, first ensure that your bank will handle the exchange. In addition, your final payment terms and the letter of credit terms should fix a transaction value for the currency in one of four ways:

1. Based on what works best to complete the transaction for both parties.

2. Based on the exchange rate at a particular time.

3. Based on an average over specified periods of time.

4. Based on the fixed rate of the country.

Fixing the transaction value ensures accurate pricing. This is why alignment with a quality, experienced international bank and loan/account officer will be critical to your export success. Depending on where you are located, you may need to find a bank in a major gateway city, such as New York City, Los Angeles, or Miami as smaller city banks have less expertise on site.

Many export situations will determine that payment is made in a currency other than the U.S. dollar. When this occurs, accounting conventions require the sale to be reflected in your records at the exchange rate on the date that title to the goods passed. Subsequent changes in the exchange rate through the date of payment will result in transaction gains or losses.

Exporters may want to analyze the option of using a third currency. If you decide to take this route, experience in currency markets is critical and having a quality/experienced international banker as a partner is an advantage in this situation.

As your exporting operations grow and your currency transactions become more complex, you may want to consider hedging. Hedging is a mechanism that allows you to take a position in a currency to protect against losses due to wide currency exchange fluctuations. It is a futures contract in which you invest your dollars to take a high or low position relative to the current exchange rate. Successful hedging requires a practiced knowledge of the currency exchange market.

This is one of the key reasons that you need to have quality international accountants and bankers as one of the export professionals available to guide you through the maze of payment options.

Preparing Your Product for Foreign Sale and Distribution

This subject is complicated because you are dealing with a subject that requires an intimate knowledge of all your potential foreign markets—packing, marking, labeling, legal, ingredients, electrical requirements, etc. What

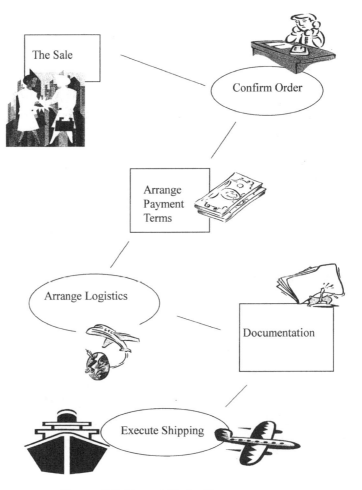

Figure 2-1. Export Order Process.

it requires, ultimately, is a separate set of SOPs for each country to which you export. This is burdensome and detail oriented. But it cannot be missed. Generalizations will not work. The i's must be dotted and the t's crossed.

There may be a need to re-engineer or modify your products to conform to government regulations, climate conditions, local standards of living, and buyer preferences. This then becomes an important consideration when estimating sales potentials and associated profits.

Foreign regulations are common in international trade and may become more prevalent in the future. These rules and regulations can take the form of significant duties and tariffs or of nontariff barriers like product regulations or specifications. These regulations are imposed to protect local industries from competition, require importers to comply with environmental controls, and regulate the number of products originating from certain countries.

Detailed information on regulations imposed by foreign countries is available from the country desk officers of the Department of Commerce. The web site address is listed in the appendix.

It is potentially less expensive to make the modification at your plant than at a third party facility in a foreign port. If your product is successful in your domestic markets, it may well thrive abroad. Nonetheless, look at your target market to ensure that native tastes or cultural differences, local safety and security codes, import restrictions, or even practical applications do not dictate product modifications.

If modifications are in order, your market potential must be significant enough to justify the direct and indirect expense involved. Your company should complete a cost/benefit analysis of product adaptation. Consulting and accounting firms can provide support in these areas.

This is all particularly true for exporters of consumer products, food, and chemicals/pharmaceuticals.

Logistics of Export Distribution

Logistics and distribution are a key aspect of marketing. Generally, an exporting company must find the most expedient way to enter foreign markets. You can choose alternative methods once you have gained a foothold.

> *For some products and raw materials, the cost of logistics is the greatest element of the "landed cost" to the importer or your customer overseas.*

For some products and raw materials, the cost of logistics is the greatest element of the "landed cost" to the importer or your customer overseas.

In serving foreign markets, you must determine what level of demand you can sustain. If production capacity is limited and you have identified a number of foreign markets, the best course of action would be to plan a staged entry. Select a member of a common market with easier access to its neighbors rather than an independent country to facilitate your stated entry plan.

Foreign Tax Considerations

Coordination must occur with international financial accounting to determine the implication of tax laws on your export both here in the United States and in the country of importation. There could be serious ramifications depending on how the distribution or agency relationship is structured.

Most major accounting firms can:

- Assist you in evaluating tax ramifications to both you and your trading partner by establishing the best INCO Terms and payment methods.

- Assist you in understanding all the tax incentives available to you, structuring your foreign operations to achieve the maximum benefit of these incentives, and completing the required tax returns.

- Assist you in selecting international counsel and inform you of local legal restrictions such as countertrade laws.

- Introduce you to consultants who will assist you in obtaining validated export licenses.

- File for refund claims under customs drawback programs, even if you were not the original importer.

- Help you prepare the application for the establishment of a free-trade zone and assist you in meeting operational requirements.

Foreign Sales Corporations

The U.S. Government has regulations in place that afford larger exporters certain tax advantages by having overseas payments forwarded through a foreign sales corporation or a Domestic International Sales Corporation (DISC).

These entities afford certain tax relief on U.S. exports for all U.S. companies. Currently, these tax advantages are under attack from the rest of the world as they provide a form of export subsidy. **As of January 2001, the fate of these corporations is uncertain.** All exporters should consult with their accounting, consulting, or banking firms to determine the feasibility and worth of using them.

Finding and Managing Export Service Providers

The following guidelines are recommended to help you find and manage your export service providers:

- Network with world trade associations and attend international seminars and functions as the first steps in exposing your needs to export service providers.

- Work with friendly competitors and colleagues who can provide references, share experiences, and suggest options.

- Find service providers that specialize in your industry and companies that are of like size to yours.

- Identify service providers who have experience in your markets and offices or agents in your target countries.

- Treat the service providers as partners in your business to obtain the maximum benefits, including long-term "partnerships" that will work to service both of your needs.

- Clear communication of your goals combined with full disclosure of pertinent product, trade, and logistics data will allow the service provider to represent you fully and accurately.

- Review performance annually, and perform stewardship reports to assure consistent and high level performance.

- Consider value when comparing price. The lowest bid is not always the best.

Most service providers belong to national associations, such as the National Association of Customhouse Brokers and Freight Forwarders, the National Association of Purchasing Managers, Banker's International, Treasury Management Association, the Association of World Trade Associations. Take advantage of these resources.

Identifying the Costs of an Export Shipment

Companies engaged in exporting often need to determine the costs associated with the international transaction. This step affords proper allocation of expenses and determines the exact profit gains on the export sale. It also assists the export marketing and sales effort with determination of competitiveness.

Rest assured that the importer, the foreign customer, distributor, or agent is factoring in all the export/import costs, eventually leading to a "landed cost," to shop comparatively.

The first step is to learn the basic INCO Terms, published by the International Chamber of Commerce (ICC). These internationally accepted trading definitions set the global standard for "terms of sale." Whether it be CIF, FAS, CPT, or DDU, these terms will be part of all export sales and identify the responsibilities, risks, liabilities, and more importantly, the "costs" for both the exporter and importer. The terms are outlined in a reference guide, which is updated every ten years. There is a new edition, *INCO Terms 2000*. It can be obtained from the ICC, 156 Fifth Avenue, New York, New York 10010. It costs approximately $35.00 and is a critical reference source for all serious exporters.

The INCO Terms are considered the foundation of the export sale. For example, in the simplest of explanations, if you were selling to a customer in Frankfurt, Germany, from your plant in Cleveland, Ohio, and the INCO Term that was agreed to was "FOB Baltimore" (ocean freight mode), this would mean that the exporter would deliver the freight and bear all costs associated with the export to the vessel in Baltimore. Once the freight passes the ship's rail, the title, liability, risks, and costs would be passed to the importer/buyer. This means that the exporter would be responsible for the inland transit and insurance costs to the point of loading onto the vessel, the costs of document and export license processing, and potentially some of the freight forwarding costs. These "total costs" would then be identified and factored into the export price as a line item or part of the invoice total to properly protect profit margins.

If the terms of sale for the same transaction were "CIF Rotterdam," the exporter would bear all costs to get the freight to the inbound gateway in Europe, i.e,. the ocean freight, insurance, and forwarding costs. This would greatly increase the costs to the export transaction, as it is typical that the highest expense associated with the export supply chain would be the international logistics/transportation costs. The importer, however, would be responsible for clearance, duties, taxes, and VAT.

Particular to many exporters who ship perishables, time-sensitive, or project business; the "international leg" expense is a major factor, consideration, and cost to the overall transaction. It is the terms of sale that determine who is responsible to pay; but at the end of the day, it will become a cost of the overall "landed cost" to the buyer in the overseas market.

The following lists outline the itemized costs that could be part of an export transaction:

Export Costs

- Invoice value (typically on an Ex-works basis).
- Warehousing, if applicable.
- Inland freight and forwarding.
- Document preparation and forwarding.
- Handling.
- Export compliance.
- Consularization or legalization. (Note: Some countries, such as, but not limited to Saudi Arabia, Turkey, and Argentina require that the commercial export documents for certain goods and/or values be stamped by their local U.S. consulate office before entry into their country. This is determined by specific products, values, and utilization. This adds cost and time to the export transaction.)
- Ocean, air, truck, or rail transportation and forwarding (the international leg).

Import Costs

- Temporary or permanent storage.

- Import license.

- Product registrations.

- SGS inspection. (Note: Some countries, such as, but not limited to Peru, the Philippines, and Nigeria require that some products over certain values be inspected, at their expense prior to export out of the United States or elsewhere. This inspection must be completed successfully before entry into their country.)

- Taxes, duties, GST, and VAT.

- Import clearance, handling, and courier.

- Import compliance.

- Inland freight.

- Handling or document processing.

Other Potential Costs

- Insurance.

- Terminal handling/wharfage charges.

- Carrier surcharges and demurrage.

- Commissions or agents fees.

- Export packing, marking, and labeling.

- Translation.

- Legal fees.

No matter how the costs are outlined, what the terms of sale are, or who is to be responsible to pay directly or indirectly; the culmination of these costs become part of the "landed cost" in the export transaction for the buyer/importer. **It ultimately determines the competitiveness in export sales and markets.**

Exporters who pay attention to these costs and work with the buyers in better supply chain logistics for the purpose of reducing these costs will be more successful in their international endeavors.

An Export Case Study

At a recent trade show in Chicago, a mid-size public pharmaceuticals company had identified that their product had some potential in foreign markets. Numerous foreign buyers had approached the booth and made various inquiries regarding handling distribution of the product in their markets.

One potential distributor in Brazil approached them by visiting them in their Pennsylvania offices two weeks after the show. Over several days of meetings, they developed what appeared to be an excellent working relationship. Four weeks later a three-year exclusive distributor agreement was signed between both parties.

Shipments started six weeks later. First some sample shipments, followed by some airfreight, and then small LCL ocean freight orders. Initially no credit was extended to the Brazilian company and all sales were paid-in-advance, then eventually through letters of credit. Transportation was controlled by the buyer, as the exporter was instructed to "drop ship" in Miami at their forwarder's warehouse.

The sample shipments went well and were favorably received. The first two or three small airfreight shipments went well. Then problems began. The first LCL ocean freight shipment was to be paid for through a letter of credit, freight shipped to Miami. Terms of the sale were FOB Miami, but no one at the shippers plant in Pennsylvania understood exactly what FOB Miami meant in terms of transfer of title, liability, assumed costing, or risk.

The freight arrived in Miami OK and was shipped successfully to Sao Paolo. The first problem encountered was the handling of the letter of credit. No one at the exporter's facility had processed one before, so they worked out a deal with the consignee's forwarder in Miami to help them prepare and make the presentation to the bank. Two days later the nightmare began and lasted some four months. The documents were given to the bank after the expiration date. It took the shipper three weeks to have the letter of credit amended by the Brazilian customer. The bank then found out that the bill of lading was issued improperly and it took the consignee's forwarder in Miami another four weeks to make the necessary changes.

Simultaneous to the shippers' problems, when the freight arrived in Sao Paolo, the customer was unable to clear the freight because the documents were not prepared correctly. The shipper who prepared the commercial invoice did not put the import license or product registration numbers on it. To their defense, they did not know they had to, nor did anyone advise them that it was necessary. Eventually, the documents were corrected, but the clearance process ended up taking three weeks in lieu of the four to five days planned for. Demurrage costs (carrier late pickup charges), which were charged to the consignee, amounted to $1130. The consignee demanded the exporter pay the cost, as it was generated from their error in creating bad documents.

The exporter relied on the consignee's forwarder to advise them on preparing the correct documents and in the execution of the letter of credit. The exporter soon found out that it had little control over the freight forwarder in Miami because the freight forwarder was picked by the consignee and their interests were severely jeopardized by having the freight forwarder so intimately in the export "loop."

A costly lesson, but a good one. They were bleeding, but not down for the count. The exporter had now begun its painful export learning curve, with some wounds, but nothing considered life threatening. The exporter now knew to utilize it's own forwarder in handling letter of credit shipments, to be more careful regarding accountability on the letter of credit expiration dates, and how to pay better attention to detail on the export documentation for shipments to Brazil. All future shipments to Brazil were difficult, but were handled successfully.

Concluding Remarks

There is a substantial amount of information and criteria needed to determine if your company is ready to export and just what the initial steps are. This chapter addressed these concerns with analysis of all the issues and specific steps to follow to come to sensible, understandable answers to the questions: Should I export? How I should start? What do I need to be concerned about?

This chapter provides the initial perspective for establishing the foundation of export success.

3

Meeting International Customer Sales and Service Demands

Servicing global customers is as much an art as it is a science. While it can be said that "Customer service is customer service in any business," in international customer sales and service there is a completely different set of skill sets required for managing this area successfully.

Cultural, language, legal and foreign infrastructure issues all come into play, with great consequences, if not handled properly.

This chapter addresses all the customer service concerns with the best options for avoiding costly errors.

Skills Needed to Succeed in International Trade

The 1990s have seen a dramatic expansion in the number of U.S. corporations engaged in world trade. With this growth has come the problems of entering a new world—one that has language barriers, political risks, difficult transit hazards, credit and payment dilemmas, and insurance headaches.

However, with these barriers comes opportunity. The American business that can master the skills of world trade will gain new markets, high profit potentials, and the advantages of successfully doing business in the international market place.

Success in transacting business internationally means acknowledging that most of the work has to be done up-front, before the shipment is expedited because most control is lost at point of shipment. From that time forward, the fate of your cargo, ability to get paid, and ultimate delivery is in the hands of others. **A mistake in documentation, labeling, or packaging could be fatal.** An error in the commercial paperwork, such as the letter of credit, will hold up payment. Not knowing local customs and laws can hold up the shipment and add hidden costs. Those personnel involved in world trade must master a number of basic trading skills to be successful. Each skill interfaces with others, which necessitates a basic understanding of all the skills to mitigate the risks of world trade and increase profits. The following guidelines should be considered for export transactions.

The exporter must be focused on a specific marketing strategy, more so than in a domestic sale, primarily because the opportunity for something to go wrong is great and the margin for error is even greater. And when something goes wrong, the consequences could be very harsh.

Specific markets and a well thought-out marketing strategy are keys to success. An array of factors must be considered such as politics and culture, legal ramifications, distribution complications, collection problems, communication difficulties, insurance concerns, and the additional "hidden" costs involved in world trade.

The international trader should align with quality professionals in three key areas: BANKING, TRANSPORTATION/FORWARDING, and INSURANCE. The quality of these individuals will have a direct influence on the viability and profitability of the international sale. They will identify exposures to you and offer workable options for resolving them before they become insurmountable obstacles that are costly and time consuming.

Maximize resources from friendly competitors, trade associations, government entities, foreign trade associations, consultants, and the media. The world is changing swiftly and dramatically. A continual flow of up-to-date information is critical. Spending at least 5 to 10 percent of one's time in maximizing resources and networking will "pay off in spades."

Paying attention to detail is absolutely vital. The international sale requires an inordinate amount of detail work. There is no room to cut corners. The i's must be dotted and the t's crossed. Understanding the terms of sale, currency implications, political environment, legal ramifications, etc. is tantamount to failure or success. Every detail must be reviewed, checked, and rechecked. Nothing can be left to chance.

Understanding the documentation requirements for foreign trade in itself can be a full-time, frustrating job. International transactions are burdened with paper. Not only is it complicated, but it is continually changing. No one person or source can provide all the answers. The answers are typically gray, not black and white. This causes confusion and discomfort leading to arbitrary decision making, with experience as the leading factor. This is where networking and resources with experienced freight forwarders, various bankers, accountants, service providers, etc. . . can pay off tenfold.

Risk transfer can be a necessary evil as well as a necessary tool in avoiding disaster and profit potentials. The import/export business should find a specialized insurance broker and underwriting company that can assist them through the international maze of insurance, claims handling, and local insurance requirements in the country where the export transactions are occurring. Most insurance in foreign countries is treated differently than in the United States. For example, health and medical benefits, along with workers' compensation policies, would not typically extend to employees traveling overseas unless the policies are specially endorsed. Product liability coverage is increasingly becoming an issue as more and more countries become litigious in the handling of their claims. Proper insurance plays a major role in transferring risk and increasing opportunity for protection of assets.

Marine insurance provides protection of goods during transit, where the greatest probability of loss and damage occurs. The policy should be tailor-made to conform to the terms of sale and the terms of payment for each shipment where exposure exists. Typical policies in today's market are "ALL RISKS" and cover the goods from point of origin to final destination.

Another major risk facing the exporter is the ability to get paid. Political and export credit exposures face all exporters who sell on terms where a receivable is created. The following risks present a physical and financial hazard: protracted default, currency inconvertibility, contract frustration, confiscation, nationalization, war, strikes, riots, and civil unrest to name a few. All these risks can be insured through various government and private sources.

Freight forwarders can assist in this area by affording access to their "house" marine insurance policies and their international shippers, with broad insuring terms and competitive pricing.

Intermodalism is playing a greater role in international transits where combinations of more than one mode occur in the overall shipment. While ocean transit enjoys the largest market share of international transportation, air freight is growing. It is becoming a viable option in just-in-time (JIT) inventory management and with certain product lines and trade routes.

Transit times, packaging needs, warehousing and inventory management, and insurance concerns are just a few of the variables involved in the overall decision-making process. The freight forwarder is usually an excellent source for transportation consultation and advice. Most forwarders work within close proximity to major airports and seaports and there is an array of forwarders and customhouse brokers to choose from.

Packaging needs to be designed to handle the rigors of international transit. Shock, vibration, condensation, excess water, extremes in temperature, storage heights, and multiple and rough handling are but a few of the hazards facing the design and packaging engineers.

Consideration must also be given to ultimate destination, the availability of materials handling equipment, logistics, and other factors to develop successful packaging. **If one notes that 30 percent of all transit losses in international trade are due to a controllable cause, the importance of packaging in providing a sound product and satisfying the customer to protect future orders and reduce competition is clear.**

Labeling and proper marking are also important packaging considerations. The movement of hazardous and labeled cargoes present serious regulated and legal issues that have strict penalties and consequences when not followed correctly. There are many sources to assist the international trader in these matters such as forwarders, consultants, and the Department of Transportation.

The last step is an acknowledgment that one must master all of these international trading skills to be successful in importing and exporting. A decision on packaging will affect storage, shipping, and insurance cost factors. A decision on terms of sale will affect competitiveness, modes of transit, and insuring responsibility. A decision on documentation could affect packaging needs, insurance viability, and carrier acceptance for transit.

These examples are but a few of the scenarios that show the interdependency of the various considerations in international shipping that must be well thought-out before practice and execution. Any decision could have great as well as devastating consequences. The individual and company that "can put it all together," "address all the issues," will begin the process of mitigating risk and maximizing profit.

Excellence in Customer Service in Global Trade

Many American companies have begun to master the skills of customer service as the backbone of profitability and continued growth and most certainly competitive advantage!!! These skills must be applied to global trade but will need to be modified, adapted, and enhanced for the complexities and unique persona of international business.

The U.S. exporter will grow and prosper in direct proportion to the quality of customer service. And this will hold true for small and large business, alike. One certain factoid in global trade is that business is "relationship" driven and the quality customer service dictates the quality of the relationship. This section presents an overview of the "competitive advantage" issue and "quality communication" as the starting point of global effectiveness.

Competitive Advantage

American exporters face stiff competition in global markets due to many factors, including the proximity of competitive sourcing, pricing after cost of logistics, political and cultural differences, currency fluctuations, communication and infrastructure imbalances, and trade finance incapabilities.

Those American export companies that show creative talents, exalt patience and persistence, ally with key vendors, and master the skills of global trade and international customer service will be staged for competitive advantage.

This not only refers to providing a price which is competitive, while a critical issue, may be only one of many issues that determines who a foreign buyer purchases from. Look at your own personal buying habits. Some, but not all individuals buy with only price in mind. All experienced businesspeople know that following that guideline only can be deadly.

We sometimes pay a higher price for a multitude of reasons: convenience; positive relationship with the people we buy from; the service attached to the purchase; the sales and marketing factors tied into the transaction; the technical and knowledgeable sales/customer service personnel; responsive, timely communication and follow-up; and more.

I believe that the majority of purchasing decisions brings an array of factors into play. As a general rule, if the pricing from one company to another is within a reasonable range, the company with the higher price will win eight out of ten times if many of the other attributes are offered with greater advantage. I have found this true time and time again in my own global sales efforts and have been witness to it within my clients' activities. A critical factor for making all these issues work for you is communication.

Quality Communication

Quality communication can be broken down to three key disciplines:

- The art of communicating
- Responsiveness
- Persistence

In the art of communicating one must recognize that different cultures have different means of communication. How to address a written fax, letter, or e-mail to when to send it, whether to use first or last names, who to copy all will play an important role in how the customer will respond, how seriously they will take your company, or how mad they will get if you have insulted them.

While most foreign buyers speak some degree of English, commit yourself to know the basic rudimentary and business language of your buyer's country. You will be respected for the effort, and it will provide a definite advantage in understanding what is going on in negotiations and trade meetings. I maintain a little "cheat sheet" next to my phone. It provides the basic "hello," "good-bye," thank-you," etc in a number of key foreign languages. It goes a long way in developing a better relationship with my overseas customers.

All written communication should be typed. Foreign communication is difficult enough without having to decipher poor handwriting. It also expresses your professional commitment to doing the job correctly, which sends conscious and subliminal signals with positive impressions.

Responsiveness can be a major factor that will provide immediate favorable "feelings" on the part of foreign buyers. This means following up in a timely fashion and acknowledging all communication, even if it's just to say, "We're working on it." Meet all time frames promised. If you need more time...communicate that and request an extension when necessary.

A complaint I hear time and time again is how poor response can sour a deal, and ultimately, long-term relationship opportunities. As world communication becomes more high-tech, there will be numerous options presented, including the Internet, Intranet, EDI, international fax, e-mail, cell phones, mobile telecommunications, satellite capabilities to assure timely and quality communication to gain global advantage.

A timely response and quick decisions are generally characteristics of the American culture. This can be bad and good news, depending on which side of the table you sit on and the expected results. Regardless, our culture looks to an immediate response to inquiries and rapid decision making. Unfortunately, most of the world operates using a different frame of reference. Many American individuals and companies lose patience and walk away from lucrative opportunities in the process. The key to overcoming this obstacle is persistence.

The steps in being persistent must be tailored to the particular culture you are exporting to. Decisions in Japan are typically lengthy and made by management groups in lieu of individuals only. Being too diligent and persistent will cause aggravation and probably loss of the opportunity. In the Middle East, persistence is considered a good quality when intermingled with developing a personal relationship with the buyers. In Latin America too much follow-up too soon will elicit a lack of response and frustration on your part.

Knowledge of local cultures can be achieved by researching the culture. There are numerous reference books in the library and business book stores that outline the "do's" and "don'ts" of all trading cultures. The country desk officers at the Department of Commerce, consulates, and embassies are excellent sources of information. The Chamber of Commerce, international service providers, and trade associations are often good references as well.

No matter what the culture is, one must have a system of follow-up/persistence to accomplish the sale. The persistent effort that follows local customs must be organized and focused, while using all the powers of influence and networking with a balance of patience to obtain the order. Persistence is well served when accompanied by a developing personal relationship.

Building Personal Relationships

In many countries, developing a close personal relationship exudes confidence in both parties that will result in long-term partners in trade. If you have a product that is in high demand with no competition, then being an "order taker" is the method of operation. However, most of us deal with intense foreign competition, and we must maximize our opportunities.

A key strategy is to develop the personal relationship. This works in most cultures and becomes a necessary tool in developing the sale and maintaining future activity. A personal relationship will facilitate the negotiation process and make the transaction easier to accomplish. It also opens the door of mitigation. "Breaking bread," an expression for a business lunch or dinner is often a necessary part of developing sound global business and personal relationships. Foreign buyers often "buy" from the individual first—the company second.

Problems are likely to occur in an international trade. Shipping the wrong product, logistics delays, government intervention, and cargo claims are all going to happen if you are in this business long enough. The strength of the personal relationship, the trust and bond that parallels this, will carry you through the difficulty of the problem to a favorable resolution. International litigation generally is not a workable option. It is costly, difficult to achieve, and a favorable settlement is dismal at best. A good working relationship, cultivated by the personal relationship is a much better option.

Strategic partnerships were a method of survival in the late 1990s and will follow into the new millennium. These require a lot of good faith between the partners, which is fostered in the development of the personal relationship. Most parties have to "like" the other party before doing business. Breaking the bread or the pasta, sushi, knishes, tacos, or whatever and doing all the other things necessary to facilitate the personal relationship become key to all the other factors in developing your export business.

Negotiating Problems with International Customers: Three Key Steps

Probably nothing has the potential to frustrate a customer more than their perception of how they are treated when a problem occurs. Poor treatment during a problem is probably the number one cause for a customer to go elsewhere. For any global business this means lost revenue with little opportunity for regaining a client's business.

We all have and know of unreasonable clients, but in reality most customers are reasonable. They understand that mistakes occur and certain things happen that are out of everyone's control. With the reasonable client, which is the majority of our fold, how we respond in a difficult situation or when a problem occurs is how we will be ultimately judged.

The following three steps are guidelines to follow when faced with the inevitable problems in the transportation business we all earn our living in.

Be in Their Face

The worse thing you can do is to hide or not face up to the problem. The customer knows when you are avoiding the issue and so do you. Think of a scenario from your own personal circumstances—the mechanic who was fixing your car, the bank teller sorting out your account, the store clerk attempting to rectify your purchase. When something went wrong in any of the scenarios, you would be more upset, more frustrated, fighting mad, when they would not return your calls, were unavailable to take your call, were suddenly not available, etc., etc. The "hiding" becomes more frustrating than the initial problem itself. Remember what you said, when faced with these situations, "I will never use this mechanic again," "I will never shop in this store again," "I am finding a new bank tomorrow."

Well, our customers can feel the same way. The best course is to face the problem head on. Don't hide. Be up-front and demonstrate a willingness to be honest and open with all potential solutions.

Mitigation Is Key

In the sales dialogue with potential global customers, I often use the terminology, we are the best "mitigators" in the business. I further explain that in this business things will go wrong. It is inevitable. Most experienced importers and exporters know this. I then let them know that we will advise them immediately and begin the steps necessary to "mitigate" the problem ASAP. This might mean calling the receiver and advising of the revised ETA, rerouting the freight to catch the next flight, finding a new carrier that can meet the delivery requirements, send the sales or customer service manager over personally to look for the freight, etc., etc.

The experienced shipper appreciates this attitude in the sales process. More importantly, they appreciate it when reality shows its ugly head and a problem occurs. Then they see our customer service and operations personnel do everything possible to mitigate the problem and make a bad situation turn out to be a molehill instead of a mountain. They also appreciate honesty and acknowledgment when a mistake is made, however disheartening or frustrating this may be.

Follow-Up and Communication Are Critical

Follow-up and communication is critical following the disaster. Make a phone call or make a visit. Apologize again and again if necessary. Make sure you communicate that you are aware of the problem and how it affected their operation and how much you care about the chain of events and the circumstances that occurred. Timely communication and reaction can turn around the worst situation.

Emphasize the positive. Demonstrate how you mitigated the problem. Sometimes creative dialogue will allow you to show how the actual blame was someone else's responsibility. This is when "band-aids" can prove effective. Eliminating the invoice or reducing the costs or charges may prove a good course of action. This is sometimes referred to as "dancing," but it works.

Outlining what steps will be taken to make sure this will not happen again usually will bring on a favorable reaction from the client. Providing an outlet for their frustration and having them participate in the solution can also prove beneficial.

The key is responding quickly, facing the problem head-on with an honest and responsible approach, offering solutions for the future, and, most importantly, creating the perception that you care. Treat them as you wish to be treated by your vendors.

The bottom line is that the export business has certain inherent problems associated with it. How we deal with these problems with our customers will determine not only our ability to maintain a client but our profitability and opportunities for long-term success.

The Growing Need for Third Party Logistics in Exports

Export transportation costs are on the rise. This is true for all types of companies, those with 10,000-pound machinery to ship and those moving fifty pieces of small packages express, and for all modes of transit anywhere in the world.

The boards and senior operating management of many corporations have to come to recognize that long-term survival could hinge on the structure of the logistics costs and control systems. The more "international" a company is, the more involved in exporting, the more serious this challenge. Foreign competitors in Europe and the Far East have mastered certain shipping techniques and acquired a competitive advantage. To meet the competition, some U.S. companies have elevated the traditional role of "traffic manager" to vice president of logistics and/or director of distribution. Others have turned to third party logistics providers.

Though the concept of third party logistics has existed for more than twenty years, it has now come into vogue and is at the forefront of transportation technology. The industry is still young and evolving, but the basic concept involves part of a late 1980s trend toward downsizing. As part of this phenomena, corporate management evaluated the cost of maintaining in-house capability against the cost of outside vendor services. In many cases it served the company's best interest to reduce staffing and look to outside third party support.

In the field of transportation this was called "third party logistics" or TPL. As we begin the new millennium, it has grown into a diverse range of transportation and logistics services provided to corporations by third party vendors. The field challenges every aspect of export business in professional, creative, and comprehensive worldwide transportation services. Major transportation companies such as Maersk, Ryder, Yellow Freight, UPS, Roadway, Airborne Express, Federal Express, and the Hub Group have started third party logistic service divisions.

Reasons for Downsizing in Corporate Transportation

The two major reasons for companies to downsize in transportation are cost and control.

When companies expand export distribution operations, they often build large internal infrastructures of personnel, equipment, warehousing, computers, and systems to service the expansion. The cost of such infrastructures can be enormous, particularly for small to medium-size exporters. In many cases, large and mid-size companies are reducing the size of these in-house entities to just a few management and operating personnel and transferring their functions to third party logistics companies.

These companies have decided that an outside vendor could do the job in a more cost-effective way and with a wider range of service capabilities, potentially higher quality, and with greater access to professional talent. In addition, it is typically easier to terminate a vendor than in-house personnel, who may be tenured, unionized, or "just too difficult." This offers management more flexibility.

Cost and Benefits of Third Party Export Logistics

Each industry, company, and export manager must evaluate the individual situation and determine the best direction to fit the needs of the company. Such an evaluation will have a lot to do with the direction the company is heading, the mission statement, and the position regarding in-house versus third party. Many companies are quite clear in this regard. Many have no interest in increasing corporate staff or empires within their newly downsized management teams. Others believe firmly that it can best be done by in-house staff that is fully controlled, trained, and managed. Every situation is unique.

In the simplest form, the current and future cost of in-house export logistic operations must be compared with bids from potential third party providers. Evaluation guidelines will need to be established to allow equal comparison of the bids from the third party compared to in-house operations. Cost and scope of services should be the bottom-line guidelines for the decision making process The current trend strongly suggests that most of these matrix comparisons favor the export third party option.

Potential benefits of the third party option include:

- Immediate savings in direct personnel and overhead costs as well as in long-term costs, such as tenured employee benefits

- Access to quality and experienced personnel

- Access to vast transportation support resources

- Ease of setting goals, performance standards, and ultimate termination

- Savings in export transportation costs can be achieved when the logistics provider can place you in group purchasing networks (GPNs)

Following are two examples of these benefits at work. The first is a situation where a retail company with stores around the country needs to position certain inventory at various key points. In terms of space, however, its needs may be small—one to three trailer loads at any one time. It has access to many options, but costs are high. Through a third party logistics company who may be involved with other retailers, such a company might enter the third party logistics company network and purchase the space at the same cost as a much larger buyer, and therefore pay much less. Savings can vary in every situation, but our review has shown potential savings of 5 to 25 percent.

Another example. A large domestic shipper enters a new market overseas, using small, less-than-container load ocean shipments. Initially transport rates are high, but through a relationship with a third party logistics company who purchases ocean freight through a subsidiary non-vessel operating common carrier (NVOCC), such a shipper could buy into a much larger purchasing network and obtain lower rates than if approaching the ocean carriers directly. Potential savings could range from 5 to 30 percent.

One of the major advantages of an association with a third party logistics company is access to a quality, professional export support team. Their skill level, combined with years of trial and error produce more cost-effective transportation. They can analyze any set of current shipping systems and bring many other options to the table.

Intermodalism in Exports

TPLs bring a diverse background of integration that typically can provide better service and lower transportation costs at the same time. Integration can mean intermodalism. Intermodalism is the use of several modes of transit or distribution systems to accomplish transportation goals. A good example of intermodalism is the mini land-bridge combination of rail and ocean shipments in the United States.

A Northeastern U.S. exporter shipping to the Far East traditionally will load the shipment in Port Newark. It will take six to eight weeks for delivery. Another cost-effective option is to put the shipment on a rail car to Long Beach, then transfer to an ocean vessel. This could reduce transit time by half and, depending on volume, could cost the same or only slightly more. If time is money, the overall savings could be significant.

TPLs are becoming increasingly supportive of intermodalism to accomplish transportation objectives. Rail, air, ocean, and truck combinations are on the rise and when the connections are properly constructed, can provide more timely deliveries at cost-effective pricing.

TPLs recognize that there is an entire supply chain for most export companies that needs to be linked to meet all the needs of the company it is serving. Areas of sales, customer service, manufacturing output, raw material and supplies purchasing, inventory management, distribution, and collection of funds are all integral in this process.

Any one factor or any set of circumstances can affect any or all parts of the entire supply chain. The TPL staff understands this issue and can matrix all factors relative to one another to find the best solution.

Electronic Data Interchange (EDI) and Management Information Systems (MIS)

An integral resource in TPL performance is their computerized information capability. Use of EDI and MIS can reduce the duplication of export shipping documents, which could be extensive on an international transaction. It can link carriers with export banks, customs, and other government agencies. It can also link export sales with inventory control, tie inventory to production, and so on.

The goal is paperless transportation. Many carriers and government agencies, along with all transportation service providers, are currently working together and testing out paperless international shipments. By 2003 to 2005, they may reach their goal. The use of EDI in exporting is vast. We have only scratched the surface, but we know it to be integral in bringing together all facets of third party logistics.

Almost every export trade magazine and journal is touting third party logistics. Advertising of vendor services has increased, evidencing the growth of TPLs. Intermodalism has played an integral part in the development of TPLs. Integration of many aspects of the export supply chain process: trucking, international freight, inventory management, and sales all become synergistic with common goals of:

- Cost-effective export distribution
- Cohesive EDI networks
- Successful transportation purchasing management

This development holds many challenges. Many transportation companies are at the cutting edge of this technology. Those that do not move quickly or chose to ignore this trend will be at a serious disadvantage. Exporters must study their own shipping profiles to determine if TPLs make sense for them. Shippers who do not take an investigative look may be leaving a very cost-effective logistics option for the competition to master.

Setting Up Quality Control Procedures for Exports

To gain a competitive advantage, U.S. exporters must ship in a timely fashion, be accurate, and communicate intelligently and responsibly. Foreign competitors gain ground against their U.S.-based rivals due to better logistics management. They export on schedule. They ship what they're supposed to. Their methods for quality control and mitigation of problems and systems for communication are simply better.

U.S. exporters generally have a superior product or service. Combining this with a higher form of logistics management, the result is a winning duo that can't be beat. Accomplishing this is as much an art as a science. I will outline some of the considerations, that the U.S.-based exporter can follow. This is the "science" part. The "art" part is more subtle, accomplished over time, mostly through a learning curve, experience, and diligence.

Ship Timely

When our foreign plants, distributors and customers buy from us, it is typically planned around their needs to meet inventory, production or sales requirements. JIT (just-in-time) inventory systems require "tight" and intensive scheduling standards.

While international shipping has numerous variables that can play havoc on scheduling, most carriers represented by the ocean, air, rail, and trucking companies can count on 90% on-time performance, within reasonable parameters, for their international interests. That's not bad for global trade.

Therefore, the exporter can have a reasonable expectation that their goods, if shipped on time will arrive on time. The key words, being "shipped on time." This calls for the exporter to make sure that sales and customer service are communicating in a timely fashion to operations and that inventory and production commitments that are required can be maintained.

Export intermediaries and export management companies that typically buy from third parties, in lieu of their own production sites, must maintain even tighter relations and communications with these suppliers to assure timely availability.

Good coordination with freight forwarders and international carriers rounds out the steps necessary to ship timely. Realistic utilization of shipping schedules and building schedules and building in "hedges" and "leeways" for potential short delays will go a long way in assuring timely shipping.

The use of third party logistic companies is popular today. These third party service providers can assist greatly in providing systems for management to follow and execute to coordinate the meeting of export shipping schedules.

Ship Accurately

Ship quality product and the amount you're supposed to export and you will have completed a second "third" of the puzzle. Tie that in to shipping timely and you've won 66 percent of the battle.

Internal operating systems and methods for accountability will typically address this concern. Export management companies must utilize reliable suppliers who have these systems of control, or they will need to have a facility to bring the freight into a pre-export location for checking prior to export. This is usually a more expensive option than dealing with reliable suppliers.

The loading dock in most plants and warehouses is where freight will be staged prior to export. It is typically at this point where operating systems can be set up for maximum control. Count, check, weigh, and document—then recount, recheck, reweigh, and document again. Have the person sign off who did the checking and a supervisor sign off on the recheck. All of this should be documented to a file for access and qualification in case it is needed at some later date.

Automation and technology offer ease of this process, but at some point a person who physically checks is usually necessary. If technology is used, the documentation to the EDI file must be made in a timely manner with internal checks for accuracy and personnel accountability.

The product, the count, and the systems for quality control must be part of the export documentation chain, whether it be the invoice, the packing lists, the bills of lading, or other documentation.

International shipping is an expensive cost in the export transaction. For some products and destinations, the cost of shipping exceeds the value of the goods. Mistakes that occur can be costly, if not deadly. It is better to take some extra steps before the goods leave, even allocate a small amount of funds, than handle the additional unknown and potentially greater costs in lost or stolen merchandise to mitigate a problem, reship at a later date or deal with a dissatisfied customer, which in the long run will result in a loss of business. Keep in the mind that it can take years to gain a customer and only moments to lose one. Time and money spent up-front is a known factor. At the other end, is an unknown potentially greater hazard.

Communicate Intelligently and Responsibly

To ship timely and accurately is critical, but to complete the last "third piece" of the puzzle, one must communicate the status of the shipping in an intelligent, a "foreign articulate," and responsible process. This starts with the negotiation and completion of the sale. Be honest, up-front, and exact on realistic production, inventory, and shipping schedules. Don't promise something that can't be delivered, "it will bite you in the butt," at a later date.

Keep the customer updated on the status of future and current shipments. Problems and delays do occur. If you report these responsibly and in a timely manner, the customer will appreciate the information and may be able to replan accordingly, mitigating your delay.

The key is timely communication that is honest and direct. Customers usually react favorably to this. More often than not, you can make a good impression from a poor situation. Offer options. Be creative. Make sure the client feels that you are doing everything possible to mitigate the problem. Their perception of what you are doing will often dictate how they will handle future orders.

Technology can make the communication chain work more effectively. Use of e-mail, the fax, the Internet, etc. can prove to be cost-effective options. In many countries, the communication infrastructure does not work well. You must then be creative and use several methods to make sure the communication gets through. Cell phones in some countries work better than direct line systems.

However, don't rely only on impersonal technology. Pick up the phone and call. This might mean a late evening or early morning wake-up to accommodate global time zones, but often hearing your voice will go a long way toward making the client feel more comfortable, even if some abuse comes with the call. Keep in mind that export sales is relationship driven and personalized, caring service is the best antidote to potential shipping difficulties. In most countries export sales is "relationship driven". So make the most of the relationship and be honorable in the communication process. Your foreign customers will even favor the relationship with more trust and enhancement for the long term.

Controlling the Terms of Sale

The INCO Terms, published by the International Chamber of Commerce, advises on and provides definitions for terms of international trade. They include CIF, FOB, FAS, all acronyms for potential terms of sale that the U.S. exporter needs to understand and conduct successful international trading. An exporter can obtain a copy of the INCO Terms booklet, which should be part of every exporter's library, from any International Chamber of Commerce Office or ICC Publishing Corporation, Inc., 1212 Avenue of the Americas, New York, NY 10036.

In attempting to understand who should control the terms of sale and what the parameters are in the decision-making process, several critical factors must be reviewed.

Overview: Sales Terms

The various terms of sale have significant consequences regarding responsibilities, liabilities, costs, and profits/loss confronting both the importer and exporter. The INCO Terms are European in foundation, reflecting a different mind-set. The terms combine documentary and transactional requirements for passage of title and payment terms. There are many hidden costs involved in international trade that the INCO Terms help to define. The exporter should be aware that terms of sale directly affect costs and could affect an exporter's competitive advantage. The more responsibility assumed, the higher the price. For example, the price might be $4,500 from the plant dock, $4,800 to the U.S. port of export, and $5,800 delivered to the customer's door in Oslo, Norway.

The INCO Terms advise who is responsible for arranging transportation services, freight charges, insurance, etc., but freight forwarders, banks, carriers, and experienced shippers are the best resource for figuring out what they are all about.

Name the Terms and the Point of Shipment

When using the terms, a point of destination or a site must be named. For example, if you were selling FOB (free on board), the question is "FOB at what point?" According to the definitions of the terms, once the goods are loaded on board the transportation conveyance, title passes to the buyer. But does this occur at the plant or at the port?

If you sell FOB plant, the title will pass once the freight has been loaded on board the inland conveyance. This means that the buyer will arrange to pay for the inland transportation. They will also assume responsibility for loss or damage to the freight during transit.

Choosing to sell FOB port of loading requires that the exporter arrange for the inland freight. The exporter will then assume all transit liabilities until the freight is transferred to the international carrier. If it is an ocean shipment, the risk transfers once the freight passes the rail of the vessel, illustrating the extent of the definition of the terms.

If you had an international transaction in France that called for a CIF (cost, insurance, freight) sale with a named point, such as Paris, and the shipment was by air, the exporter would be responsible for arranging the transportation. The shipper would assume all transit liabilities and provide marine insurance up to the point of pickup from the Paris airport. In such a case, the exporter has taken on a great deal of responsibility and with it an equal amount of risk. This is when the exporter needs to be a good traffic manager and/or have a quality freight forwarder. The marine insurance, the underwriter, and the claims systems must be in place to deal with potential losses in an international transaction.

Terms of Payment

At the time the export sale is being consummated, the terms of payment need to be decided as this will have great effect on the decision making for the terms of sale. Assume, for example, that you complete the transaction with all i's dotted and t's crossed, with the terms of sale as FOB/NY.

The shipment is made with the terms of sale calling for a payment from your buyer in Paris in sixty days. The shipment arrives missing three of ten pieces. They represent approximately $12,000 of the total invoice value, for which your buyer discounts your bill. You argue that the "risk" passed in New York; therefore the insuring responsibility, with a clean bill of lading, was with the buyer from the time the freight was received on the international conveyance.

The buyer argues that the shipment showed up short and that under no circumstances—if the U.S. exporter is to keep the account—will he/she contribute to the loss, holding the exporter fully responsible. According to this scenario, while the terms of sale "appeared" to offer less exposure to the exporter, the terms of payment that allowed sixty days provided greater exposure. The position of the importer was both unreasonable and incorrect, but it is a common path when the buyer holds the advantage of not yet having paid for the freight.

Without *contingency insurance or unpaid vendor protection*, the exporter may have to sue to collect— at the cost of losing a customer, unnecessary aggravation, and great expense.

Additional Considerations

A very general conclusion that can be drawn is that in most export situations, the exporter should control the terms of sale as well as the terms of payment. Every factor must be considered in this evaluation, such as, but not limited to the following:

- Price and payment terms
- Competitive pressures
- Forwarder and carrier options
- Opportunities for loss and damage
- Previous experience with buyer
- City and country of destination
- Customs clearance in buyer's country
- Current economic and political situation in buyer's country

An additional consideration in controlling terms of sale offers the exporter short- and long-term options for maintaining competitiveness. If you choose to sell on terms—where all the basic shipping, documentation, insurance, and freight choices are in your control— then you have the ability to affect the CIF costs. You are not forced to accept a particular insurance company whose marine rates may be higher than you can obtain in the open market. If you are free to choose steamship lines, you have the option to look at possible nonconference carriers that might offer lower shipping costs. Each variable must be evaluated. Controlling the option to evaluate will afford the more competitive choices that will work to the exporter's advantage.

Another important consideration in determining the terms of sale is to look at the pitfalls of attempting a "door to door" sale, if required to do so, particularly in certain countries where customs law and practice work to the disadvantage of the exporter.

As "importer of record" in door to door sales, you assume certain liabilities in the import country that you might want to reconsider.

In certain countries, such as Mexico (though this situation is changing), U.S. exporters have found it preferable to sell FOB port of entry such as Laredo, in lieu of a CIF sale point of destination. Mexican customs (their trade and practice) have afforded the importer a better opportunity to arrange clearance than with the exporter's agent. This is also true in other countries such as, but not limited to Thailand, Algeria, and Iraq. Each situation must be carefully evaluated on its own merits. The exporter's freight forwarder's local relationship with foreign clearance agents plays a vital role in this regard.

The current political and economic situation in the buyer's country is critical. Take the situation in certain parts of the new Eastern Europe. While there is a big demand for U.S. products, payment is difficult at best. In order to make the sale, the U.S. exporter may not be able to sell completely on secured terms but may be willing to sell on a collect or sight draft basis. This arrangement might meet the need of the importer and reduce some of the exporter's exposure.

The key word is "reduce" not "eliminate." The exporter will need to make arrangements through the freight forwarder or the carrier not to release the freight until the payment is made to the local representation. Good communication and tight monetary controls will be critical to successful execution of this option.

Equally important is attention to the minutia of transactional detail for the passage of title and payment terms. Although title may transfer, responsibility, particularly fiscal responsibility, may not end.

Quality marine insurance affords protection to the exporter in all situations. The marine insurance contract should have features that protect the exporter regardless of who is responsible to insure and where title passes. "Unpaid vendor" or "contingency" insurance can be part of any successful export program. It will afford the exporter full transportation insurance in cases where they are not responsible for insurance, but may be exposed to payment or contract terms.

It is also critical when letters of credit are used for international transactions that the term of the sale conform to INCO practice as well as Uniform Customs and Practice (UCP) 500 for payment terms.

The bottom line is that the exporter must evaluate many issues in determining the best terms of sale for a particular export transaction. In any case, the exporter should negotiate a controlling advantage that will mitigate potential loss and maximize protection of profits.

Increase Your Export Sales through Credit Insurance

U.S. exporters are in an excellent position to utilize a tremendous resource in developing a significant increase in export sales activity. Export credit insurance has been around for more than twenty years, but is now becoming increasingly available for all U.S. companies. It has become easier to access and obtain and is more competitively priced and flexible in design to meet the various and specific needs of individual corporations.

Accepting a foreign receivable is risky business. Some U.S. companies see it as obstacle in doing international export business. But the reality is that our foreign competition is offering terms and, more often then not, selling on terms, which makes the difference between getting the deal or losing it.

However, what we see as an obstacle is really an opportunity, when managed creatively and responsibly.

There are numerous insurance entities, both government and private that offer U.S. companies insurance policies to protect their export sales from receivable exposures, as well as political risk exposures, such as those seen most recently in India and Pakistan. U.S. Government programs, such as with Ex-Im bank and Overseas Private Investment Corporation (OPIC) are designed to encourage U.S. companies of all sizes and makeup to export, and if a receivable is created, offer insurance as a "safety net."

The export credit insurance tool is often used in conjunction with banks to obtain favorable trade finance for the funding of the international transaction. This becomes a significant side benefit.

The bottom line being that the export credit insurance is leveraged as collateral to obtain trade finance. When the cost of borrowing in foreign countries can be as much as 30 percent, letters of credit costing as much as 7–15 percent, offering terms can provide competitive advantage in export sales. Export credit insurance can be considered the assurance of payment, when all else fails.

The cost of credit insurance varies, depending on spread of risk, commodities, countries of destination, specific terms offered, limits, deductibles, etc., but typically costs less then 1 percent of the values at risk. This amount could easily be absorbed into gross profits or transferred to the customer in the cost of the sale.

The U.S. Government entities that provide these coverages are doing so to promote export trade from the United States in consideration of creating jobs and reducing the deficit. Most of their decisions have political influence and consequences.

Private companies such as FCIA, CNA, AIG, Fidelity & Deposit that offer these export credit and political risk insurance's are motivated by profit and sometimes are a more expensive option. However, they will insure risks in certain countries that are off limits to the government options. They also can be more flexible in the underwriting terms and conditions from one insured to another. The policies insure such exposures as confiscation, nationalization, expropriation, deprivation, embargoes, transfer and currency risks, contract frustration, unfair calling of letters of credit, protracted default.

Policies can be obtained after an extensive application process. You obtain terms and conditions at a set premium charge. Deductibles, coinsurance, and waiting periods are all applicable to individual accounts.

We recommend that exporting companies utilize consultants and/or qualified insurance brokers to review your risk profile and to evaluate what options might best suit your specific needs. Professionals in export credit insurance can easily cut through the "red tape," expedite the whole process, and be available to `handhold" through the underwriting cycle. They are also available to assist with claims handling and renegotiating policy terms when warranted.

The Asian crisis has clearly identified a need to extend terms. Export credit insurance is available to most Asian countries and will allow you to maintain market share, open new doors—even in the face of these challenging times.

Export credit insurance managed properly can be an important tool for the exporter in protecting foreign receivables and increasing international sales.

Worldwide Shipping: Know, Name, and Control the Destination

Having been involved in many aspects of international trade for more than 21 years, the consistent mistakes that exporters make in selling their goods and services to global markets never cease to amaze me. Two years ago I wrote about the importance of understanding and controlling the terms of sale. One great source for this information is INCO Terms. A key element of the terms of sale is specifically naming a point where you as the exporter are responsible to tender the freight to the customer and potentially also transfer certain obligations, responsibilities, and risk at that time.

To understand the importance, it might be best to review a specific example. I met an exporter based in Philadelphia, who had an opportunity to sell used machinery for shoemaking to a manufacturing company just outside Mexico City. The sale was very price-sensitive. When the order came through, the Philadelphia company had to ship some 39,000 pounds of used equipment, crated, by truck from a point in Camden, New Jersey to Mexico City. The buyer was under the impression that the sale was made contemplating a delivery to site. The exporter was under the impression that he was to get the freight to Mexico City and did not take the time to determine where in Mexico City the client wanted the product delivered. Negotiations took some nine weeks and no one asked the "where" question. Mexico City is just that—a city, not a point to receive freight. Particularly for the inexperienced international trader, such as both the U.S. exporter and the Mexican consignee were in this case.

Well, it turned out that the trucker who was used to ship the freight had indeed provided a quote for shipping the used equipment to Mexico City, but only as far as their depot on the western side of the city (U.S. side of Mexico City). The consignee or importer was on the southeastern corner of Mexico City. As it was to be known, the distance between truck depot and ultimate destination was just over fifty-five miles. The consignee would be charged an additional $580 to have the freight delivered to the final destination.

To digress for a moment, I often run into this situation when someone is shipping to a local point in the New York metropolitan area, only to find out that the freight will arrive at JFK Airport to be trucked to a local point, called Parsippany, some forty miles plus in distance through some of the worse congestion in the world. This can occur in any major metropolis, such as Los Angeles, Jacksonville, Paris, Moscow, or Sydney. While fifty miles may be "local" in the panhandle of Texas, it most certainly is not in most major cities on this small, and getting smaller, planet we trade on.

Getting back to Mexico City. This is a typical example of poor planning, bad communication, and not paying attention to detail on both sides of the export. Irrespective of who is legally liable, a disgruntled customer makes for an unsuccessful deal. In this case, if the exporter sold CIF Mexico City or under newer or similar terms, then the carriers depot would be an acceptable final destination to conclude the transaction. It would have had to name a specific point in the terms of sale, with an address, for it to go anywhere else.

On a transaction worth $280,000 with a 20 percent profit margin, $550 may mean very little. But in a $12,000 sale, it is almost 4 percent, which could be all or part of the entire profit. I have born witness to many a faux pas that have cost one party or the other tens of thousands of dollars in additional expenses, such as in this Mexico City example.

Quality freight forwarders, logistic executives, and the international consultants who are working for you should be able to point these issues out and cause you to take the necessary precautions to mitigate the potential pitfalls, but they need to be advised of just what you are and how you are completing the transaction. They can be excellent partners in keeping you out of trouble.

Awareness; common sense; and taking the time to check, review, and check again are all essential ingredients to prevent this type of error. Visualize the trade and act accordingly. When you buy furniture and have it delivered, you do not expect to pick it up at the local gas station—you expect it to be delivered to your door, brought in, unpacked, and put next to your bed. You envisioned it, agreed on it, signed the bottom line, and it happened. Well, when you're completing the next global trade, visualize the trade and make sure that both yours and your client's expectations are going to be met when it comes to the delivery point.

Another issue to keep in front of you when determining the point of delivery is to make sure you know what all the additional costs are and who will pay them. If you are required to go "door to door," sometimes referred to as a "free domicile delivery," then issues such as who will pay for inland trucking, customs clearance, duty, taxes, and other local costs need to be identified before the freight is shipped.

Freight held up at point of clearance while a debate is going on as to who pays will be more costly, bring on excessive delays, and expose the cargo to additional potential for loss and damage. The best advice is to know, name, and control the delivery point in agreement with your customer. You will minimize future headaches and secure the best opportunity for successful global trade.

Gaining Competitive Advantage: Customer Service and Logistics

The subject of international logistics is considered by many executives involved in world trade to be somewhat the "dirty" part and certainly one of the more difficult aspects in this global arena. In an attempt to simplify the discussion and address all the areas in detail, a review of the information will be presented in four parts: *(1) the difficulty of world trade, (2) the relationship of transportation to the whole picture of global business, (3) eight steps toward competitive advantage, (4) a summary, focusing on the concept of competitive advantage.*

International Transportation and Logistics: Potentially the More Difficult Part

While there are many reasons why transportation and logistics can be the most difficult part of the export business, they can be summed up as— once something goes wrong and the goods are already on their way, there is very little you can do to mitigate the potential problems you will face.

That time to mitigate, the cost to mitigate, and the opportunity to mitigate become dismal realities in the face of a global logistics problem. When compared to a domestic shipment—you can always turn the truck around, make a phone call, and deal with the problem. However, I'd like to see you turn around the 3800 TEU SS Sealand Houston on its way to the Dominican Republic or a Lufthansa 747 freighter half way across the Atlantic on its way to Frankfurt. I'd like to see you call the Mexican customs inspector in Neuvo Laredo and tell him that the NAFTA certificate of origin can be in English and does not have to be in Spanish...are you loco or something???? Or attempt to negotiate the SGS inspection requirement with an Indonesian government official "on the take" in Jakarta. Or attempt to get freight through customs in Moscow, which is now about at the top of the list in the world for corruption.

The risks and complications involved are numerous. The distance involved, legal issues, difference in language and customs, changes in documentation requirements, variations in transportation infrastructure, differences in time, third world politics, war and terrorism, compliance management, people issues, and so on, and so on is what makes it difficult. But what we really are saying is the all of these come under the category of lack of control or influence once the freight leaves the point of origin.

Some True and Interesting Sea Stories (slightly modified to protect the innocent)

All of these stories emphasize the importance of transportation in global business.

It is the nature of the beast or is it the beasts involved?! In 1988, a major U.S.-based truck manufacturer delivered 288 trucks to an Indian consignee in Port Chittagong only to have the trucks arrive the same week the monsoon season started and the longshoreman went on strike. The trucks are still sitting in the port yard rusted to the ground that they came ashore on twelve years ago. Now they're a tourist attraction!

A mid-size apparel importer brought 300 leather jackets into the United States from Brazil only to find out after the boxes were opened that all the jackets were infested with a weevil-type critter found in Brazilian sisal crops. The importer then learned that to cut shipping costs their Brazilian exporter had used a consolidator who coloaded the jackets in a 20-foot container with three pallets of sisal rope. I wonder where the bugs came from?

A southern-based chemical company exported $1.5 million worth of pharmaceuticals to their Mexican subsidiary two days before the devaluation. To this day only 30 percent of the pre-export value has been repatriated to the U.S. parent. How would you like to be the export manager explaining his excellent sense of timing?

A New York exporter shipped $3 million worth of glass making machinery to Spain. The carrier dropped the single container during vessel discharge in Barcelona. The damages sustained and confirmed by appointed marine surveyors fixed the loss at $2.1 million or almost 60 percent of the value. The carrier who was sued hid behind the $500 limitation of liability per package defense, (read the small print on an ocean bill of lading!) on the basis that the container was the "export package." The exporter claimed negligence, hoping to supersede the limitation of liability argument.. But in the end, the courts held in favor of the defense, claiming negligence was not proven, an accident was the cause, and that the $500 held up as the goods as they had been packaged would not survive the international transit without the benefit of the steamship container. The traffic manager was assigned to duty in an Anchorage plant that year. He wasn't sure why. Need we illustrate more?

The illustrations demonstrate that the importance of transportation and logistics in global trade is twofold. It affects capability to perform and it *affects price.*

If we cannot perform at a certain price then we will not be competitive with the Canadians, British, French, Germans, Japanese, Koreans, or the Chinese. Foreign competitors are breathing down our necks and we need every competitive advantage we can muster. Control all the aspects of international transportation and you control a very important aspect of your competitive profile. The product, your service, and where in the world you operate, could make logistics as important as the FOB Fort Wayne price.

> *Foreign competitors are breathing down our necks and we need every competitive advantage we can muster.*

Control all the aspects of logistics: warehousing, pre-export inventory management, export packing, documentation, mode of transit, EDI capabilities, choice of forwarders and customhouse brokers, the marine insurance coverage, the ocean and air carriers, and so forth and you begin to control all the factors that have a direct and indirect relationship to your competitive advantage.

Eight Steps Toward Competitive Advantage

Following are eight steps to gain a competitive advantage.

1. **Identify what your capabilities are in-house and then what your needs are**. Once these are determined, you can focus on

the carriers and service providers that best suit your needs. One of the advantages of being in the United States is the close proximity to a significant transportation infrastructure and major gateways, where the selection of carriers and service providers is the best in the world. The options to find specialists in your areas of need is great indeed.

2. **While you may leave the logistics job to third party professionals, learn the basics and become familiar with the terminology, your options, and the mechanics involved in moving freight from Cleveland to Durban.** Develop a grasp of the basic knowledge of shipping, its components, and what your resources are and how to use them. It is the two thirds of the iceberg you don't see that will kill you. Gain knowledge for knowledge helps you navigate around the icebergs!

3. **Choose your forwarders, customhouse brokers, warehouseman, truckers, etc. by those that meet your needs and specialize in your product, your countries of origin or destination and have compatibility with your operating requirements.** There is nothing wrong with having one or two carriers working for you. One might have the bulk of work, but the other works as a safety measure or in a specialty capability. No forwarder or carrier is all things to all people.

4. **Get competitive pricing.** You may want to favor a particular carrier, but keep them honest by getting bids and working with them to keep pricing and servicing in line. Loyalty is important and should always be factored in, but subtle competition can have advantages.

5. **Group your purchasing clout when you can.** Savings could be achieved by offering a more capable and comprehensive carrier or service provider most of the work. By having them handle the trucking, the warehousing, the clearance, and the freight, savings of 15 to 40 percent can be obtained.

6. **A quality international transportation program is supported by a quality insurance program that provides protection from many of the risks involved in global trade.** Marine insurance, political risk, export credit, foreign products liability are just a few of the exposures that can be transferred to third party insurance companies to reduce your overseas exposure.

7. **A quality international transportation program includes attention to detail in areas such as packaging, stowage, marking, and labeling—all known as cargo loss control.** Monies spent up-front will have favorable long-lasting effects in better product outturn, more satisfied customers, and more orders.

8. **Look to your transportation service providers as partners in your business with common goals and a team approach to getting the job done.** Having a positive attitude of being on

the same side of the fence will go a long way in achieving successful international buying or selling, importing or exporting—and ultimately profitable results.

The Concept of Competitive Advantage

Successful purchasing of international transportation services begins with the understanding of the risks and difficulties of global trade. Knowledge and information is a critical ally in managing your purchasing process and tying this to long-term team relationships with partners in your carriers and service providers who at the end of the day will provide you with the best opportunity to mitigate risk and maximize profit to give you the best opportunity for a competitive advantage.

4

Freight and Logistics Issues for Import/Export Managers

Until we have a *Star Trek* capability and can move things through space electronically, all freight will have to move physically from point A to point B. And that is what we call "logistics."

Managing logistics in export trade is critical because the bottom-line competitiveness of the export trade will be determined by shipping costs and shipping efficiency. This chapter dissects all the material one needs to know about managing export logistics and obtaining great value for all the external services necessary to move products internationally.

Export Trade: Five Key Areas to Get the Best from Your Forwarder

The quality of your freight forwarders and the delivery of the international services they provide can make or break your export operation. Even though they sometimes seem to be nothing but a necessary evil, forwarders can be your best ally in mitigating the hazards of world trade and assuring successful and profitable international transactions.

Like other key vendors, freight forwarders need to be managed and treated as partners with mutual goals, common direction, and a full understanding of what each party brings to the relationship and ultimately the benefit to each other through the association. Five key points in this regard are presented in this chapter:

1. Selection

2. Logistics consulting

3. Pricing

4. Value-added services

5. Setting performance standards

Selection

There are several resources to help you determine what forwarder to choose:

- Go to other shippers for referrals.

- Ask carriers for recommendations.

- Go to the National Association of Customhouse Brokers and Forwarders.

- Check the *Export Yellow Pages.*

- Check the American Export Register.

Potentially, there are another dozen resources to turn to such as another shipper who has first-hand experience. To determine if the freight forwarder is suited to meet your needs, you must set up selections criteria.

For example, a large shipper may have a fully staffed traffic department and may be fully capable of executing documentation and negotiating freight rates. In this case, a freight forwarder might be needed for a niche type activity, special tasks, and overall logistics consulting.

On the other hand, a small shipper may require the freight forwarder to execute every document, from the pro forma invoice, the export declaration, the certificate of origin to the bill of lading, etc.

It is essential to note that even some very large shippers have decided to purchase all services of a freight forwarder in lieu of establishing a fully staffed traffic department. At the same time, some qualified small shippers prefer to do much of the work themselves. You need to survey your needs, which then become the criteria for the selection process.

Freight forwarders vary greatly from one another in skills, capability, and delivery of services. Some forwarders are specialists on certain trade routes, specific commodities, degree of value-added services, etc. Some shippers use two or more forwarders for different areas.

We suggest that shippers create a list of criteria, which would be a reflection of the shippers' needs. This should be given to the forwarder in order to obtain a proposal from him. The proposals from various forwarders will serve as a gauge for evaluation of their services in the areas you have identified to be important. For example:

- Documentation, rating, carrier selection

- Postselection, packaging, insurance, warehousing, EDI

- Knowledge of your product

- Logistics consulting

- Customs clearance, labeling, hours of operation, rate negotiation

- Export compliance management

- Inhouse education and training

Logistics Consulting

One of the most important services a forwarder can provide is advice and counsel. Most shippers would probably tell you that the single most important factor in freight forwarder selection is their experience, resources, and general working knowledge of international trade. The freight forwarder can make significant contributions to your overall sales, marketing, pricing, and distribution choices. If you typically sell on Cost, Insure, Freight (CIF) basis and are now venturing into a totally new market, your freight forwarder, based on previous experience, may advise you that the claims experience is horrendous in the importer's airport of entry or port facility and that you should amend your terms to a Cost & Freight (C&F) basis. This obviously will affect pricing and may be a key factor in making the transaction profitable in the long run.

Another example may be that you are experiencing a frequency of damage claims via a particular mode of transit. The forwarder might guide you to changes in packaging that would better protect your cargo and lead to an improved loss experience and more satisfied customers.

Pricing

Pricing can vary among different forwarders. We suggest that pricing always be obtained up-front. In some situations, it may be impossible to estimate costs exactly, but in most cases a forwarder can provide a fairly accurate estimate. Two basic elements of a freight forwarder's charges are fees and carrier costs.

For ocean freight, you will typically pay what the forwarder pays to the carrier except for consolidations, nonvessel operating common carriers (NVOCCs), and project work where certain discounts or surcharges may apply. The forwarder will typically earn a commission in ocean freight and will charge handling fees.

In other modes of transit, such as by air, you will pay what the forwarder charges you and not necessarily what the forwarder pays the carrier. This is why the rates in international airfreight tend to be more evenly priced.

Fees will vary among forwarders. Obtaining shipping information, contracting overseas agents, following up, faxing, negotiating rates, and preparing documentation all have costs attached. Following is a shipping cost breakdown checklist.

Domestic Invoice Total—Additional Domestic Costs (may be part of the forwarder's fee)

- Warehousing

- Inland freight

- Export packing

- Loading changes

Shipping and documentation

- Consularization/notarization

- Export declaration

- Export license

- Certificate of origin
- Packing list
- Bills of lading
- SGS inspection
- Insurance certificates
- Health/sanitary certificates
- Miscellaneous

Banking and finance

- Letter of credit
- Sight draft
- Miscellaneous

Freight forwarding fees

Insurance

Freight

- Foreign import costs
- Customs clearance
- Local delivery
- Import license
- Miscellaneous

Value-Added Services

A forwarder can provide an array of services that may be considered standard or value-added. For example, you may be entering a new market in a different country. In your analysis, you will need to be supplied with a significant amount of data. Your forwarder may be in a position to review your needs and provide feedback in areas such as:

- Export shipping and mode options
- Costs of shipping
- Documentation requirements
- Packaging considerations
- Warehousing and inland transit options (third party logistics)
- Legal and government restrictions
- Labeling requirements
- Distribution systems
- Compliance management

Another potential value-added service is providing EDI capability. This basically entails the retrieval of manual shipping data in an automated format, production of documentation, and tracking in an automated mode. The range of data, equipment availability, report formatting may vary, but the bottom line is that the EDI capability needs to reduce costs and provide shipping data in a timely manner and comprehensively to be considered value-added.

Other examples of potential value-added services are:

- Capability to handle hazardous materials
- Export packing expertise
- Warehousing capabilities
- Expertise in marine exposures and coverages
- Comprehensive office and agency system

Setting Performance Standards

> *We are strong advocates of making sure that freight forwarders keep their promises and maintain high quality standards leading to cost-effective service and on-time performance.*

Following are five steps that can be used to maintain the forwarder's performance:

1. Keep all commitments, quotes, proposals, promises, etc., in writing.

2. Allocate time frames to all jobs. Maintain a diary and follow-up schedule to determine responsiveness and accuracy.

3. Have all jobs quoted. If there is no time to quote, then have pricing made available as soon as practical.

4. Have your forwarder submit annual stewardship reports and bring in competitors from time to time.

5. Demand regular meetings with your forwarder. Gain access to senior management. It is also recommended that you meet with all staff and operating personnel and make sure they are familiar with your account, your needs, and the promises made by the salespeople. Knowing who the operation personnel are is key, as they sometimes become far more important to you than the salesperson.

The effectiveness of the forwarder will partially depend on how the exporter manages this valuable vendor relationship. The forwarder should be viewed as a partner who can be part of or comprise your entire logistics management team. When used effectively, the forwarder can maximize profit, mitigate risk, and spearhead you into successful exporting.

Following is a comparison checklist for choosing freight forwarders. Establish criteria that is specific to your operation and prioritize the salience and importance.

- Service areas.
- Scope of expertise.
- Ocean, air, truck, and rail.
- Quality of sales and operations personnel.
- Location nearest your main office.
- Pricing.
- Insurance availability and fees.
- Warehousing and fulfillment capability.
- Your own or third party trucks.
- EDI capability.
- Imports and exports and domestic.
- Export documentation.
- Tracking capability.
- Handles small packages.
- Handles time-sensitive freight.
- Consulting services.
- Import/export compliance capabilities.
- In-house training and education.
- Packaging, marking, and labeling.
- Payment terms.
- Will lay out duties and taxes.
- Are you a "small fish in a big pond"?
- Who will service your account/from what office?
- Sales versus operations personnel.
- Office and agency network.
- Years in business.
- REFERENCES.

Use of "Consolidators" in Export Trade: A Viable Option for Ocean and Airfreight

Larger ocean shippers, those with over 100 TEUs (20-foot equivalent unit. . . 20-foot container) per annum are typically at the lower end of the scale but have minimum clout to negotiate directly with steamship lines for rating discounts and relief from standard tariffs. The more volume, the more clout you will have in reducing ocean shipping costs. Large exporters with more than 1,000 TEUs are in a great position for favorable ocean tariffs.

Many ocean carriers will only price shipping starting at 20-feet and 40-feet units. Many will not even look at less than container load (LCL) freight. This places the smaller, less frequent shipper at a disadvantage to larger more frequent shippers. Those shippers with small shipment (LCL) sizes have less options and will typically pay more. Sometimes an LCL shipper will pay more for a third of a container worth of freight than for the whole container at a full container rate. A good example: A shipper from San Francisco has 12 metric tons of dried vegetables to ship from Port of Oakland to Prague. The LCL rate is $242 per megaton or $2,904. The 20-foot container rate holding approximately 22 megatons is only $3,900 or a difference of $1,000. Add another 3 megatons and it would be better to buy the full container. Of course. dimensions would play a role but this example is for demonstration purposes only.

Shippers need to investigate this as it may be more cost effective and certainly less risky to ship the full container load (FCL) in certain circumstances. The shipper must become an "educated consumer."

The more practical option is to develop a relationship with a forwarder who accesses an NVOCC or one that is an NVOCC. Those NVOCCs licensed by the Federal Maritime Commission (FMC) act as consolidators, accept LCL freight, and can offer savings to smaller, less frequent shippers that often are not available dealing directly with the actual carriers.

The NVOCC is able to take the volume of "all its shippers" and negotiate with the clout of "many." It can then predict greater volumes with the steamship lines arranging for tariff relief. These discounts can then be passed off in proportion to the small shipper. The NVOCC becomes like a buying cooperative or purchasing group that works on the concept of clout in negotiation. The clients of the NVOCC benefit as the membership grows and the management becomes stronger.

Three quality NVOCCs are Direct Container Line, Sea Lion Shipping, and Rose Container Line.

One must be very careful when choosing NVOCCs, as there are many "fly-by-night operators" in the industry. NVOCCs become a direct extension of the carrier, offer their own bill's of lading, and accept certain liabilities, as if they were the actual steamship line.

When choosing an NVOCC:

- Make sure you get referrals and credit references. Many NVOCCs have expertise in certain commodities or trade routes. Make sure the one you chose meets your needs.

- Make sure they carry the proper liability insurance.

- Get all pricing and quotes in writing.

- Identify the specific routing. To save money many NVOCCs will divert freight causing delays and adding unnecessary risk to export cargo.

Sea Lion Shipping, Rose Container Line, and Direct Container Line have good reputations and offer competitive pricing and quality service.

NVOCCs can often provide inland warehousing, documentation, and logistics/fulfillment services directly or in conjunction with their forwarding entities or other carrier relationships. NVOCCs and consolidators who specialize in various commodities, specific geographic regions, or trade routes can be valuable in providing export transportation advise and counsel. SeaLion Shipping, for example, has expertise in chemicals, perishables, contract freight, and cargo with special needs. EconoCaribe Consolidators specializes in consolidations to the Caribbean and Latin America.

Most ocean gateways, such as New York, Miami, Los Angeles, Houston, are homes to many Consolidators/ NVOCCs. Local port authorities, freight forwarders, world trade Clubs, and international associations can be excellent referral sources for NVOCC options.

Some value-added services that these entities can provide are as follows:

- Inland trucking
- Warehousing
- Pick and pack/fulfillment
- Marking labeling
- Consolidation/repacking
- EDI, exchange of information, and tracking of freight
- Access to freight forwarding services
- Worldwide agency network
- Hazardous material or perishable capability

The concept of consolidation and NVOCC services also extends to airfreight. Companies such as ACI and Air Consolidators International, based in New York and Los Angeles with satellites in other cities can offer airfreight shippers competitive pricing, particularly to smaller shippers and those who ship less frequently.

Typically these air consolidators will receive freight at air gateways such as New York, Miami, and Los Angeles and certain days of the week will move freight to a particular city in a foreign country. Their move is typically an airport-to-airport basis, with the terminating airport city being a major inbound gateway to that country, not a smaller inner city point. Examples would be: in Australia. . . Sydney, in Germany. . . Frankfurt, in Brazil. . . Sao Paulo, in China. . . Beijing or Hong Kong. U.S. importers use airfreight consolidators on inbound imports frequently and with success.

Airfreight consolidators will typically book space in advance based on prior experience of freight volumes. They will usually obtain competitive rates. This space then becomes available to the clients of the airfreight consolidator as required with some portion of the rate discount passed back to them. Often freight forwarders with high volumes of airfreight will arrange their own consolidations as needed or prearrange consolidations for predictable clients and trade routes.

Consolidation and the effective use of NVOCCs can be a lucrative method to control exporting costs.

Ocean Freight Rates: Some Unsettled Seas for Small Shippers

The next twelve to twenty-four months will set the course for ocean freight rates for the next twelve to twenty-four months. All indications point to an average rate increase of 5 to 10 percent for large and medium shippers and potentially double digit increases for smaller shippers with less the 100 container loads per year. LCL rates will increase some 3 to 4 points higher than FCL rates.

There are many identifiable reasons for the increase. There is a worldwide increase in demand on vessels and equipment as world trade continues to expand. On certain trade routes, such as the Far East to North America, demand is up some 30 percent. Other routes are up more than 60 percent and others only in the single digits. For certain steamship lines, capacity has reached maximum. Freight is being accepted with a very small chance of making the intended voyage. Many shippers and forwarders are experiencing their worst delays in more than ten years.

Positioning of containers, chassis, and other freight handling equipment in areas in the United States such as the South and Midwest is becoming more difficult with increasing delays. [Typically, the more specialized the equipment, such as liquid bulk containers, high tops, extended units, and so on is more rare than the standard dry 20-foot and 40-foot containers.] When incorporated into a traditional supply and demand diagram, the result of all of this is as expected: increased ocean freight rates.

Another significant factor is the instability of currency exchange. In past years, steamship lines often could predict how exchange rates would fluctuate, and price accordingly. Over the last 24 months, worldwide exchange rates, with the U.S. dollar leading the pack, have been unstable and difficult to predict.

Over time, the shipping industry has developed what are known as conferences. The best known of these, which affects all importers and exporters in the United States, is the TransAtlantic Conference for Trade in the Atlantic (TACA) between the U.S. East Coast and Europe. The traditional conference has participating steamship lines that agree to and offer identical rates, tariffs, and service guidelines. While many see this as unfair competition, it has lead to some stability in pricing. The conference does allow larger volume shippers to arrange for discounting of standard tariffs through negotiation. The typical shipper must have at least one hundred full container loads to qualify for a discount. Freight forwarders and/or NVOCCs who have large volumes on certain trade routes make their money by negotiating large discounts and then, through consolidation points, attracting smaller volume shippers, passing on a percentage of the discount, and keeping the difference. This is an excellent service for smaller volume shippers and offers the option of competing with the "big boys." However, most feel that conferences will be in the distant past as we now have the Ocean Shipping Reform Act, discussed later in this chapter, that will eliminate most conferences as we know them.

Some steamship lines are "nonconference." They typically charge a few points less than the conference carriers and usually can be more flexible. However, one of the benefits of working with the conference rather than nonconference shippers is more regular shipping schedules and better service options. Taking that into consideration, each situation must be weighed on its merits.

The TransAtlantic Conference recently adopted some changes, including allowing larger volume shippers to negotiate independent tariff discounts. Most trade professionals believe that this will be to their advantage and to the detriment of smaller volume shippers and those shippers who ship on an LCL basis.

While all of this is somewhat concerning, there are still some options available to smaller volume shippers. They can enter into trading contracts with freight forwarders and NVOCCs who have larger volumes and can negotiate favorable rates. While you may be small to Sealand or Maersk Line, you are likely to mean more to an NVOCC such as Votainer, Direct Container Line, or Sea Lion Shipping. And as a result you could obtain more competitive pricing.

Look to associations. There are some trading associations, typically with similar products, that have large memberships that take advantage of bulk purchase agreements arranged through these associations, such as the wine and distillers, fruit, rubber, and specialty chemical industries, among others. If your industry association does not have bulk purchasing agreements in place, one can be established. This writer is one of many key executives in the international shipping industry with experience in association business and can assist all interested parties. It is also possible to contact the conferences directly, all of whom are accessible through the *Journal of Commerce* in the "Shipcards" section in each daily issue.

LCL shippers should work with overseas customers to accept larger orders and full container loads. The unit cost would come down dramatically and provide better pricing. Other advantages are better security, less handling, and less opportunity for loss and damage.

Negotiate "now" with your carriers, before the pricing increases. You might have a 365-day window.

Look to transportation service providers, such as freight forwarders, NVOCCs, third party logistics companies, and integrated carriers who can view your entire account and provide freight economies by "grouping" inland/domestic, warehousing, packing, documentation, and ocean freight services. By handling all the work, they can provide savings via a larger purchasing dollar and their expertise in logistics management.

The Ocean Shipping Act of 1998, which took effect in 1999, provided significant advantages to larger shippers. The principal benefit was the confidentiality of rating agreements. A secondary benefit was the willingness of carriers to amend service contracts to provide value-added capabilities.

Many smaller shippers thought the act would hurt their ability to compete against larger shippers. As of January 2001, smaller shippers have yet to be adversely affected.

The bottom line is that for most shippers and particularly those with smaller volumes, ocean freight increases should be in their 2001-2002 budgets. Taking some of the steps we have outlined may help mitigate additional costs to an acceptable level and help maintain your competitive advantage.

Potential Increases in Airfreight Rates

In the late 1990s, many exporters saw a decline in the cost of shipping goods by airfreight. Competitive pressures afforded such a situation and benefited those needing to move international freight by air.

However, the scenario is quickly changing. Many exporters in 2000 saw increases from 4 to 8 percent in the first three months of 2000, and all indications point to a continued rise of up to 12 percent, depending on trade routes and carriers. Many U.S. carriers such as American, Northwest, Continental, United, and Delta have taken steps to initiate rate increases on certain of their international trade routes. Foreign carriers such as Alitalia, Lufthansa, British Airways, Air France, and KLM have hardened their pricing structures, and the trend will continue during the next 12 to 18 months. Integrated carriers such as UPS, Airborne, DHL, and Federal Express have also responded with higher rate structures and tariffs.

It is important to note that most airlines have formed "alliances" with synergistic carriers and increased their overall freight capabilities. The size of commercial aircraft has been downsized, and this has been a factor in the overall freight market.

Freight forwarders who often act as the intermediary between exporters and the actual airfreight carriers are witnessing increases of 3 to 6 percent—higher in some areas. In consultation with their clients, they are preparing for this trend to continue well into 2001. Following is a discussion of the reasons for this expected increase.

There is a global increase in airfreight utilization that stresses current airfreight capacity. Some trade routes—the United States to Europe and the Far East are two good examples—are experiencing rate increases because of supply/demand issues. Why such demand? There are many factors. One factor is the growing need for speed. Everyone wants everything today. As the world shrinks, so does the supply chain process. UPS used to deliver from the United States to major European cities on a two- to three-day basis. Five years ago, this was acceptable. Now clients want it delivered the following day by 8:30 A.M., and many carriers can now respond to this demand.

The practice of JIT or "just in time" purchasing, production, and inventory management will sometimes reduce the inventory and distribution process, which will result in a demand for quicker shipping requirements that only airfreight can provide.

World trade is on the rise, and all modes of transit are benefiting, particularly airfreight. The elimination of tariffs (GATT), the creation of new trading alliances (NAFTA, Mercosur, Euro, etc.), and the strength of the U.S. dollar all have been favorable for exports for U.S. companies.

U.S. products are in great demand in overseas markets. Contrary to popular opinion and a misguided media, most international businessmen know that U.S. products do well in overseas markets. Airfreight has benefited from this, placing a greater demand on airfreight services, and in the meantime causing backlogs, delays, and increased tariffs.

Some airfreight analysts point to the reduction in cargo capacity as another reason for rate increases. The reality is that the airline industry, being "passenger oriented" first, and "cargo oriented" second, has reduced the size of fleets and the individual carrying capacity of the planes. There used to be more than twenty 747 jumbo jets from JFK to Europe each night. Now there are fewer than twelve, a 40 percent reduction. Newer planes also carry less cargo than the jumbo 747s.

During the last five years, airlines, along with some dedicated freighters, have reduced their fleet size and cargo capacity, causing the system to stress. Many airlines have recently upgraded their aging fleets, which has caused significant capital expenditures. They are now attempting to recapture these costs.

The additional cost of fuel, which has increased over 15 percent in the last twelve months, will cause carriers to pass on these increases through direct price increments and surcharges. In conjunction with this, many trucking companies have passed on their fuel cost surcharges. Keep in mind that these factors will affect airfreight, because there is typically an inland leg to all international airfreight shipments.

All of these factors have shared in causing airfreight rates to rise. Those who have been planning or budgeting responsibilities should be prepared for increases ranging from 6 to 15 percent through 2001. But all is not lost. As in all global trade issues, there will be some exporters who might see airfreight decreases or at least stability and fare better than others. There are things one can do to minimize the effects of this global airfreight rate increase trend.

Market your shipping needs. Bring in competition. You will be amazed by the results. While loyalty and service are critical components of international partnerships, they can always be factored into the negotiation process.

Look to maximizing your clout with one or two carriers. Many of the worldwide carriers such as United, Continental, Delta, Lufthansa, British Airways, and Air France can service the world through their main hubs, if not directly, then through their line haul carrier agreements with other airlines. Placing all your business with a "main" air carrier will provide clout in the negotiation process. Many carriers have formed partnerships to enhance their service parameters. Examples of such arrangements include Northwest and KLM. Now the shipper in Chaska, Minnesota can route cargo with Northwest to Bombay. Northwest does not go to Bombay, but will forward the freight to Detroit (one of its hubs), then through its partnership agreement with KLM will forward the freight to Amsterdam for eventual on-forwarding to Bombay. It's a "win-win" for everyone. The shipper can drop in Chaska and have his freight move all the way to Bombay, under one bill of lading, with one source for track-ing and tracing. Another example: the exporter in Detroit, Michigan ship-ping freight to Jakarta, Indonesia, can now drop his freight in Detroit with Northwest Airlines. Northwest will route it to Minneapolis where it will be transferred to its worldwide partner, KLM, who through its hub in Amsterdam, will on-forward to Jakarta. Such arrangements work out well for both unsophisticated and more experienced exporters.

Work with airfreight consolidators who can often provide competitive rates not available directly with the carriers, particularly for smaller ship-pers. Consolidators typically target particular markets and trade routes—you need to know this—your freight forwarder holds the key to these con-tacts.

Look to specialized airfreight forwarders who will allow access to their airline contracts, typically at better rates than you might be able to obtain on your own. Keep in mind that larger forwarders maximize their clout with carriers based on commitments of the "total business" of their clients' exports.

Combine your total freight purchasing with third party logistic providers. Combining all your transportation purchasing with these providers might provide greater strength in negotiation, as well as economies in the entire distribution process.

Manage inventory, purchasing, and international sales in such a way as to take advantage of other modes of transit, such as truck, rail, or ocean, that might provide lower freight pricing. Airfreight for shipments in ex-cess of 500 pounds should always be a last resort and saved for occasions when no other options exist.

Analyze option "gateways," such as Miami and Dallas, that might pro-vide lower airfreight rates than other gateway cities, such as Los Angeles, New York, and Chicago. Sometimes the cost of moving the freight by truck to the gateway, plus the airfreight rate will be less than dropping at the nearest local airport or international gateway.

These are but a few of the options to consider when dealing with the problem of potential increasing airfreight rates in 2000 and 2001. Keeping these options in mind as rates rise will provide the best hope for dealing with the problem while maintaining profitability and growth.

Negotiating International Freight Rates

Achieving the Skills to Negotiate Global Transit Costs

Exporters who face the reality that the better they negotiate their freight rates, the more competitive their products, and the result will be greater opportunities to make higher profits.

Rate negotiation is an art. It usually takes years of experience. Viewed as a purchasing management function, it can control the ultimate success or failure of any export operation.

Regardless of who pays directly for the freight costs in an export sale, the customer will eventually pay for it. By controlling the cost, you will favorably affect customer satisfaction. Because you get what you pay for, let us consider the first step.

There is an array of services that transportation service providers and carriers will provide:

- Documentation
- Export packing
- Door to door
- Inland transit
- Licensing
- Insurance
- Routing
- Storage
- Consolidation
- Loading/unloading
- Rate negotiation

As the exporter, you must decide what services you require, what services you will keep in-house, and which ones you will have your carriers provide. Once these are determined and you have let the carrier know, then you have taken the first step in the negotiation process.

Determine the Field of Vendors/Suppliers

The second step is a difficult one because personal and long-term relationships will come into play. We suggest you chose one or two forwarders and give them access to the market. You may want to bring one consolidator and/or nonvessel operating common carrier into the bid process. And you may want to go to one or two carriers directly. This will afford you access to the broadest canvassing spectrum of the available market.

Keep in mind, however, that all this requires an allocation of resources, time, and effort. If you have a limited availability of all three, you may want to only go to one or two forwarders affording them, with direction, the access to all market options.

Experience has shown that all these options will maximize your opportunities for the best rates.

Provide Quality Information

It is key that you provide both quality and up-to-date shipping information. We recommend the following as basic data:

- Specific descriptions of products (provide schedule B numbers).
- Advise points of origin and times of availability.

- Identify packaging and unitization (pallets, slip sheets, D containers).

- Give net, tare, and gross rates.

- Give dimensions, including unitization pieces, i.e., pallets.

- Identify all shipping needs, who is to prepare documents, insurance required, clearance needed.

- Advise on any tangible information, e.g., perishable, fragile, hazardous.

- Provide all pertinent consignee and delivery information, e.g., address, telephone number.

- Any special documentation requirements.

- Advise terms of sale and payment.

Taking the time and making the effort to provide good shipping information will pay off in multiples as vendor efforts will not be wasted in renegotiations or correcting misdirected quotes.

Put Everything in Writing

It can be very frustrating to have billing disputes between exporters and carriers after freight has been shipped. For this reason alone, we recommend that all quotes be put in writing. This prevents future headaches and can limit litigation potential when disputes occur.

In the best scenario, it is recommended that a "quote sheet" be established between the exporter and the transportation vendor, whether it be a carrier, forwarder, or otherwise. What this entails is to have a profile of all the shipping data, as outlined previously, provided to the carrier by the exporter. This immediately begins the process of vendor accountability because it cannot be argued as to what the carrier based the quote on. We also recommend that this is transferred via EDI, e-mail, fax, or other electronic means. This affords timely and cost-effective communication, as well as ease of inventorying the massive amounts of "paper" associated with an export transaction. It should also contain a reference number for both current and future identification and tracking.

The transportation vendor should have a system in place to acknowledge the quote request and advise the time frame for response, ask additional information, if required, or obtain edification on any area requiring it.

The carrier would then send the quote back electronically. **This closes the circle of accountability,** as the exporter has the quote in "black and white," as does the carrier. The room for error or misunderstanding is minimized. The billing should match the quote.

While setting up these systems causes pain at first, has a learning curve, and usually comes with employee reluctance, in time they usually work well and provide richer rewards than the efforts expended.

Contingency Plan

In international shipping, no matter how well you prepare or plan, there are always going to be some variables that will come into play for which you will have difficulty budgeting. After years of experience in international trade, one learns about new variables every day. It is one of the things that makes the field challenging.

An example of a cost that might show up after the shipment has been dispatched that would not have typically been budgeted for is "waiting time." Trucks or inland carriers dropping off containers at the pier or freight at the airline terminals will give the exporter about one hour to accomplish this. If they are held up by the carrier, they will pass off waiting charges in the range of twenty to eighty dollars per hour. Delays of an entire day could greatly increase the cost of shipping.

Discrepancies might arise from negotiating letters of credit, and a bank will charge fees and penalties to correct the documentation or the letter of credit. There is additional expense in the communication and time delays as the discrepancy is being corrected.

Changes in duties, taxes, reclassification of cargoes, all can lead to unexpected costs in international shipping.

Not figuring the differences between actual and dimensional weights causes discrepancies. In LCL freight, the carrier will have a right to charge the tariff rates against the actual or the dimensional weight. If you have an item with a low weight that has bulk, you may be budgeting in the 1,000-kilo actual weight, when in fact the dimensional weight is 1,500 kilos, adding approximately an additional 30 percent to the shipping charges. This is where total and quality information with pieces, weights, and dimensions must be given to the carrier to minimize the opportunity for this to occur.

In all these areas, it is almost impossible to budget for the expenses. It is recommended that regular shippers develop a slush fund and put 1 percent of international sales into it to handle any potential or unexpected costs. If the money from the fund is not used, it can be cleared out periodically and used in the regular flow of operating expenditures.

The Ocean Shipping Reform Act of 1998 (OSRA)

Lower pricing is the "silver" medal, but service can be the "gold"!

We can only assume that by now everyone is aware of the Ocean Shipping Reform Act (OSRA) signed into law in 1998 and effective as of May 1999 that affects all ocean shippers into the new millennium.

Many international shippers have already achieved significant benefits in lowering their shipping costs as a result of the confidentiality features that the new law provides. While saving freight costs is critical to better competitive global sales, there is a secondary benefit of OSRA, which is the ability to freely negotiate service parameters from the ocean carrier and the terms agreed to within the tariff and bills of lading. Gaining competitive advantage in global sales is not only achieved through direct savings in freight costs but now can be achieved through an array of flexible issues afforded under the OSRA, including:

- Carrier liability: terms and amounts

- Positioning of containers and availability

- Payment terms

- Pricing exclusive of accessorial charges, such as the terminal handling charge (THC) and bunker adjustment factor (BAF)

- Long-term contracts

- Collect freight arrangements

- Logistics services

Carrier Liability

Ocean carriers limit their liability in the wording on the bills of lading and tariffs and by law, e.g., COGSA, etc, which usually is $500 per package. In addition, when you analyze the exposures or risks for which they are liable, it is evident by these factors along with legal precedence that the carriers are actually "liable" for very little.

This area can now be negotiated with carriers toward them assuming greater risks or limits. While it is still unclear how litigation might be affected, this entire area is subject to modification and change by the ocean carriers for the benefit of shippers. Holding the ocean carrier to a higher standard of accountability and liability will help to make them perform better because they will not be able to hide under prior defenses. This potentially affords the shipper significant commercial advantages.

Container Positioning

Shippers will be able to negotiate ocean service contacts that will enable them to have containers available where and when needed for better control of inventory and supply chain management timing. World trade is increasing. The ocean carrier capacity to maintain internal support infrastructures of equipment has not kept up with demand. This sometimes stresses the demand requirements of shippers, particularly exporters, to have containers positioned at their facilities on a timely basis.

The more "inland and away from outbound gateway centers" the more difficult the situation. You may have to arrange container positioning a week in advance or as little as 2 to 3 days ahead of loading. With the new law this can be easily negotiated as part of the overall carrier agreement and containers positioned on a basis that serves your need and availability and not the supply/demand facility of the carrier.

This could greatly improve the management of your outbound export supply chain process.

Payment Terms

Carriers typically held short leashes on exporters' payment terms, typically due on a cash basis in 7 working days and rarely as much as 30 days.

Today, with OSRA, you can negotiate the payment terms as part of the overall carrier agreement and obtain terms that meet your internal cash flow needs. Thirty days is a given, and depending on volume and pricing, there is a potential for forty-five to sixty days with more flexible carriers, NVOCCs, and forwarders.

Accessorial Charges

I have witnessed some exporters obtain all-inclusive pricing structures that eliminate the individual surcharge accounted for by certain carriers on a line item basis, such as bunker/fuel adjustment factor (BAF), currency adjustment factors (CAF), Panama toll charges (PTC), container service charge (CSC), and THC. Instead, the carrier provides a pricing structure without these potential additional costs on a line item basis. This assists with standardization and affords more consistency in establishing shipping costs on specific trade routes.

Long-Term Contracts

Some exporters with long-term projects or lengthy sales contracts might want to look into the possibility of negotiating ocean freight costs for more than a year. Commitments can be obtained from ocean carriers, NVOCCs, freight forwarders, and logistics providers that expand contracts for up to three and five years. Most will allow some flexibility for annual price adjustments, but they are preagreed at fixed or standard terms and levels based on reasonableness.

Collect Freight Arrangements

Many exporters struggle when ocean freight terms are collected, as many carriers are reluctant to provide the capability to all service areas or charge exorbitant fees. This is a serious point of negotiation. Carriers now, more then ever, are willing to provide collect capabilities throughout their service network and the "collect fees" are negotiable and can be kept at reasonable terms.

Logistics Services

The increased flexibility offered carriers under OSRA allows ocean carriers to become better partners in providing third party logistics services. Areas such as pick 'n' pack, fulfillment, packing, warehousing, domestic distribution, bonded capabilities are but a few of the value-added capabilities being offered more easily.

Ocean carriers within their own infrastructures and with establishing close vendor ties are capable of offering an array of third party logistics services completing a very important aspect of integrating the international supply chain process.

Overall, exporters benefit with OSRA in that carriers can now price competitively and offer an expansion of services. That is where the "gold" is won—with competitive pricing the more easily the ocean carrier also can add value.

5

Specialty Logistics Issues for International Trade

International trade has some very specific nuances, depending upon the destination, the products shipped, and the circumstances surrounding the needs of the transaction. This chapter presents the most important and frequently used specialized logistics needs for U.S. exporters engaged in global trade and reviews of the issues and how best to manage them proactively.

Controlling Shipping Issues in the Entertainment, Communications, and Broadcast Industries: Six Key Practices

The entertainment, communications, and broadcast industries have a unique set of requirements for their logistics needs. Perfection is a priority. Tolerance for late deliveries is nonexistent. Damages must be few and far between. Time sensitivity is critical. The potential loss of revenue for late deliveries is serious and has consequences. Only a handful of logistics service providers are available to handle the delicate needs of these industries.

1. Use experienced reputable carriers.

Handling the shipping needs of the entertainment, communications, and broadcast industries is both an art and science. Above all it requires experience. Experience can best be determined by a quality reputation, which is obtained through the following:

- Consistent performance
- Safe secure deliveries
- 'Round-the-clock service
- On-time pickups and deliveries
- Worldwide capability

- Personalized service
- Flexible service parameters
- Competitive pricing
- Tenure in business

When determining your transportation carrier, seek out referrals from quality sources. Firsthand experience is often your best guide. Bigger is not always better. More so than in other industries, the entertainment and related businesses require a lot of attention, often not available in large transportation carriers where you are just "one small fish in a very large pond." This industry also requires a lot of flexibility, again not typically available in more structured, rigid larger carriers.

The key is a happy medium in finding a carrier that is large enough to provide the necessary resources and capabilities, but structured with flexibility and personalized service enhancements.

Time is typically critical in this industry. Carriers with an understanding of that issue with systems in place to make pickups and deliveries at any time in any place are rare commodities, but there are a limited number of companies that do specialize in this area and can respond to those specific needs. The entertainment industry is global, therefore the transportation company used must have capabilities that encompass every corner of the world.

2. Make sure the shipment is insured.

A shipment that is lost or damaged and is not insured can be a total nightmare and provides the potential for financial ruin. Carriers typically limit their liability. The limit can be determined by reading the service contracts, tariffs, or the bills of lading. These limits will usually fall far below the value of the goods shipped and the agreed-upon terms will often limit exposures that fall out of their control, such as "acts of God and inherent vice."

Shippers have options to protect their interests. The best is to purchase an independent transportation policy that covers all shipments, worldwide at the broadest insuring terms available, that is, "all-risk."

Carriers will also afford you the ability to declare higher values and/or purchase insurances through them. They will charge additionally for this service and coverage availability.

It is critical for you to know first where you stand, then arrange for the necessary coverage. There are specialized insurance brokers and underwriters "geared up" for the entertainment, film, broadcast, and communication companies that have the knowledge and the expertise to provide competitive options and assist and mitigate in the recovery of claims.

You should have all the necessary information with you, particularly when off-site, for the purpose of mitigating a loss or processing a claim. This insurance will prove to be money well spent and will save lots of dollars in the long run.

3. Pack and label the freight.

Improper packing and labeling can account for almost 70 percent of all losses in transit. It is the shipper's responsibility to make sure the freight is properly protected for the intended journey. The more remote the ultimate destination, the greater the need to provide adequate levels of packing, marking, and labeling.

Proper Packaging Is Key! And Is Typically the Shipper's Responsibility

If you are unable to take care of this, specialized carriers will often provide these services and charge you accordingly. The bottom line is, as the shipper, whether you package or pass it onto a third party, you must make sure the freight is addressed.

Carriers and freight forwarders are often good sources for packing advice. The fragile and expensive nature of communications and broadcast equipment requires the need for a high standard and level of packing. Once your shipping needs are known, the case manufacturers can provide packing that conforms to international standards.

Because equipment will be handled repeatedly, sometimes with degrees of carelessness, shipping globally will require enhancements to handle these increases in exposure. Airfreight is often the mode of transit. Though typically safer than by truck, rail, and ocean forms of transit, handling and abuse can often occur. Equipment must be protected from shock through the use of cushioning mediums that have high degree of resilience. Outer casings must be rigid and provide protection against handling, stowage, and transit exposures.

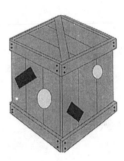

Fiberboard is often a packing choice. We recommend minimal standards of double wall, with moisture protection additives and at least 200-pound plus in bursting strength. For international shipments, triple wall will offer better results.

Unitization, palletizing, consolidation and containerization should be considered when practical. Stretch and shrink-wrapping are excellent enhancements. This will prevent loss and damage by reducing access to freight (larger units are more difficult to pilfer) and will afford handling by forklift rather than manual movement. Often you can load containers or unit loads at origin, then secure the unit until it reaches the ultimate destination. This maximizes security, reduces opportunity for loss and damage, and usually will provide the best potential for freight arriving in the intended condition.

In addition, unitization will often reduce shipping costs as carriers will provide rating discounts. In airfreight and ocean freight, the use of LD3 containers or 20-foot and 40-foot steamship containers will reduce shipping costs as much as 30 percent over standard "loose and break bulk" modes.

Labeling all pieces with the shipper's name, address, contact names, and telephone numbers is critical. Even when you unitize/consolidate several pieces as one shipping unit, it is important to label each piece in the event, by mistake or otherwise, that the consolidation unit is broken down.

Product names sometimes have value, but more often than not, it is best to keep product or brand name identifiers secluded. Advertising during transit provides little public relations but does call out to potential thieves.

We recommend that all boxes and cases provide some barrier to moisture and contaminants. Once the goods leave your care and custody, you lose control. Carriers could leave your freight out in open areas while awaiting transfer and expose the cargo to the elements. Stretch and shrink-wrapping provide excellent loss prevention measures. Opaque wrap will also cover brand names.

Using the proper packaging and adequate unit loads will increase up-front costs slightly, but in the long run will always reduce the cost of shipping and all its related and intertwined expenses.

4. Competitive bidding.

There is absolutely nothing wrong with obtaining two to three bids from competitors in the transportation services area. There are many integrated carriers, transport providers, and freight forwarders who will be more than willing to provide competitive bids. Even if you are satisfied with your current carrier, it pays to keep that carrier honest and/or reconfirm that your deal is a good one.

Having said that, certain guidelines should be followed in the bidding process:

- Long-term relationships and favorable track records should always be given certain advantages in the proposal process.

- Price is important, but if the freight is lost or arrives damaged, then the best price has little value. We recommend that you find a balance between service and price. To accomplish that determine the best carrier by service, then negotiate the pricing. Even go as far as to request a proposal that only outlines services. Once you have reviewed all of the proposals, choose the best one or two, then work on the pricing.

- Stick to the bid deadlines.

- Make sure you compare "apples to apples."

- Get the opinions of others in your organization. Particularly those who interface with the shipping function sector.

Following these guidelines will maximize the bid process to get a good price and "the best value for your transportation dollar."

5. Form partnerships with your carriers.

There is no better way to maximize carrier performance and control shipping costs than to form partnerships with the transport management team handling the servicing of your account.

Bring them into your management thought process. Afford them access to the same information and future planning you have. You will be surprised to see how by treating them as a "partner," their performance will increase and they will start affecting the pricing favorably acting as if it was their own dollars expended.

It requires a lot of trust, usually accomplished with an existing relationship or a highly recommended one. The following are necessary for it to work successfully:

> *The buzzword of the 1990s and the new millennium is "third party logistics," meaning to purchase the services of a third party transport carrier to work on your transportation needs. Taking this concept to a more enhanced state is to have that relationship on a higher level or "partnership."*

- Payment for services must be adequate.

- Communication must be excellent.

- Trust factor must be absolute.

- Dialogue must be straightforward, no-nonsense.

- Goals must be clearly defined.

- Time frame for goal completion must be realistic and doable.

- Carrier be made part of budgetary process.

The smaller shipper may not need such a comprehensive relationship, but larger and more frequent shippers will find that this is an excellent option to have when seeking to maximize carrier performance and control shipping costs.

6. Dealing with time-sensitive and specialized freight needs.

The communications industry has specialized needs. Often the shipments are time-sensitive and arrangements for pickups and deliveries have unique times and features. The pickup could be in Oslo at midnight, following the broadcast of the Olympics with delivery the following day in Los Angeles. Or the pickup could be at 5 AM outside an arena in Las Vegas for 800 pounds of anvil cases to be delivered the same day to New York City for retooling..... then out again for next-day delivery in San Juan, Puerto Rico.

The shipment may be transiting overseas on a temporary basis and require an international carnet to assist the clearance, duty, and tariff issues. You may require local assistance in a city on foreign shores. You may need counsel and support on foreign documentation needs.

The transport companies you use must be able to handle these special needs and have experience in all these matters, along with a network of foreign offices and/or agents.

The bottom line is that while the shipment of freight and equipment may sometimes be frustrating, and we accept that there are certain things we cannot control, the process can be controlled to certain acceptable tolerance levels and the costs can be managed.

Shipping Equipment Internationally on a Temporary Basis

Many individuals and companies who operate on a global scale from time to time have the need to move equipment, samples, or trade show material on a temporary basis to and from countries overseas and then back to the United States. These situations often can lead to mass confusion, shipping uncertainty, additional costs, and delays at customs. Ignorance of workable options in conjunction with improper preparation is usually the cause. The shipper has the following three options available:

- Carnet (ATA)
- Local leverage
- Temporary import bonds (TIBs)

Carnet (ATA)

The carnet is usually considered the best option in shipping goods worldwide on a temporary basis. It affords shippers the opportunity to temporarily import goods without having to pay duties and taxes in the countries of destination and upon its return to the United States. It also eases customs entry and formality and will reduce the overall cost of customhouse services.

Carnets are classified for issuance in the following categories:

- Professional equipment
- Commercial samples
- Exhibitions and fairs
- Consumable items, gifts, goods for sale are not acceptable for carnet application

The United States Council for International Business, with offices in various U.S. cities, is part of a worldwide association, the International Chamber of Commerce, that administers the issuance of the carnet. In the

Carnet Members Countries and Their Territories

Algeria	Andorra	Australia	Austria
Canada	Canary Islands	Ceuta	China
Denmark	Estonia	Faroe Islands	Finland
Greece	Greenland	Guadeloupe	Guernsey
Ireland	Isle of Man	Israel	Italy
Lebanon	Lesotho	Liechtenstein	Lithuania
Malta	Martinique	Mauritius	Mayotte
Namibia	Netherlands	New Caledonia	New Zealand
Reunion Island	Romania	Russia	Senegal
Spain	Sri Lanka	St. Barthelmey	St. Martin (Fr. Side)
Tahiti	Taiwan	Tasmania	Thailand
Balearic islands	Belgium	Botswana	Bulgaria
Corsica	Croatia	Cyprus	Czech Republic
France	French Guiana	Germany	Gibraltar
Hong Kong	Hungary	Iceland	India
Ivory Coast	Japan	Jersey	Korea
Luxembourg	Macao	Macedonia	Malaysia
Melilla	Miquelon	Monaco	Morocco
Norway	Poland	Portugal	Puerto Rico
Singapore	Slovakia	Slovenia	South Africa
St. Pierre	Swaziland	Sweden	Switzerland
Tunisia	Turkey	United Kingdom	United States
Wallis and Futuna Islands			

Nonmember* Areas Caribbean Islands

Anguilla	Antigua	Aruba	Bahamas
Barbados	Barbuda	Bermuda	Cayman Islands
Dominica	Grenada	Jamaica	Netherlands Antilles
Roadtown	St. Croix	St. John	St. Kitts-Nevis
St. Lucia	St. Thomas	St. Vincent	Grenadines
Tortola	Trinidad and Tobago	Turks and Caicos Islands	

Others

Fiji Islands	Guam	Indonesia	Philippines
South and Central American Nations			

*ATA Carnets may be accepted here, however, the USCIB will not guarantee their acceptance.

process of obtaining the carnet, there is a bonding requirement that the council also administers.

The fees vary for carnets, but average around $250. The bond costs will vary depending on the value of the equipment but are approximately .4 percent of the total value. Other factors that might affect the overall availability and cost of the carnet include the following:

Financial integrity of the applying company

Time available to process the carnet application

Number of countries to be visited

Time frame overseas

An application form is easy to complete. The general list that must accompany the application is a bit more detailed, requiring the following information:

Description of all equipment

Manufacturer's name, serial, and/or model number

Quantity and weight of each item

Value of each piece listed

One should allow at least five to seven days to process a carnet. However, for an additional fee, some carnets can be processed the same day or overnight, but this is the exception and not the rule. You are better off allowing as much time as possible for processing.

For frequent users of the carnet, arrangements can be made with the U.S. Council for Ease of Applications, Expedited Carnet Processing and Surety Arrangements.

Not all countries are carnet available. Recently Russia and the Baltics were added to a list that includes the United States, Algeria, Australia, Austria, Belgium, Bulgaria, Canada, Cyprus, Czechoslovakia, Denmark, Finland, France, Germany, Gibraltar, Greece, Hong Kong, Hungary, Iceland, India, Israel, Italy, Japan, Korea, Luxembourg, Malaysia, Malta, Mauritius, the Netherlands, New Zealand, Norway, Poland, Portugal, Romania, Senegal, Singapore, South Africa, Spain, Sri Lanka, Sweden, Switzerland, Turkey, the United Kingdom, and Yugoslavia.

The country list is fluid and always changing due to a number of political reasons, economic events, and forces involved in the international arena. One should always check with the U.S. Council for updates.

The U.S. Council is always looking to improve service. Fax and online services are now available for carnet processing, and they are continually working to add countries that are carnet approved. The period of the carnet can vary slightly, but usually is for a period of one year, but the surety can remain open for as long as thirty months.

The carnet document travels with the equipment and is signed in and out of the countries upon entry and departure. Among European Community countries, it only needs to be signed in and out once. The carnet document, once utilized, is returned to the U.S. Council, and if all papers (vouchers and counter foils) are completed, the carnet is closed out. The premium for the bond is nonrefundable, but the bond may remain open until a later date to assure there will be no claims following the return. **The Carnet headquarters of the U.S. Council for International Business is located at 1212 Avenue of the Americas, New York, NY 10036. Phone: 212-354-4480; fax: 212-944-0012; Website: www.uscib.org; e-mail: atacarnet@uscib.org.**

Local Leverage

When carnets cannot be used, a good second option is to obtain local leverage in the country of destination by working with the local customs office to afford temporary entry. Often the best circumstance is when your local contacts can provide influence over their local customs officials.

For example: You are planning to exhibit in a trade show in a noncarnet country. Often in these circumstances the local management group handling the show, sometimes the hotel where the show is being held, has made prior arrangements with customs to afford ease of entry and a reduction or elimination of duties and taxes.

Another example: You are sending show equipment to a "shoot" in a noncarnet country. Often the managers of the shoot can influence the local customs officers, prior to the equipment arriving, by approaching the local agency involved with the promotion of the entertainment business. Many countries have favorable methods for handling temporary imports when it can be demonstrated to benefit the local economy.

Many times the answer lies in maximizing local clout and resources in the country of destination. It is amazing what can be accomplished with a little creativity and effort.

Temporary Import Bonds (TIBs)

These are typically a last resort and could be quite expensive. Local customhouse or insurance facilities often can provide third party access to financial guarantees to local authorities in the country of destination. Typically, these need to be arranged up to 60 days ahead of arrival and can cost up to 20 to 30 percent of the value of the goods. Certain Latin American countries have 100 percent surety requirements. Many times the surety guarantee is not refundable, proving to be quite expensive.

Often your U.S. insurance broker or underwriter can assist in arranging for the TIB along with the customhouse broker in the importing city of destination.

The high cost of the TIB, along with the timing and difficulty of arranging it makes the TIB a last resort option.

When utilizing the TIB or other noncarnet means, one must consider the return to the United States. All equipment should be registered with U.S. Customs before the original departure. This is usually done hours before the equipment is loaded aboard the international transit conveyance. There is a specific U.S. Customs form for registration. Similar to the carnet list, it identifies piece count, value, origin/manufacturer, serial numbers, etc., accompanied by export bill of lading details.

The equipment is subject to inspection by customs officials requiring you to have the freight available for inspection when customs signs the registration certificates. Some U.S. Customs officers will require you to drop the equipment at the exporting carrier before signing off. All export points in the United States are manned by customs officers who will be able to assist you in the registration process.

If many pieces are shipped, all boxes, packages, etc. the contents as it relates to any of the lists or information provided to authorities should be clearly identified. This will greatly ease the inspection process if officials chose to do the same. All pieces should also be clearly labeled with the destination address, contact names, and telephone numbers for communication purposes.

Exporting equipment temporarily can be done easily when you know the options and prepare in advance. Your freight forwarders, customhouse brokers, foreign agents, and U.S. Customs are excellent resources for assistance. The U.S. Council with qualified and responsive staffing can also provide assistance.

Shipping Perishable Freight

Shipping ice cream isn't that different from shipping computer parts, it's just that the temperature range variance is narrower and failures are more immediately obvious. Fresh meat, ice cream, frozen dough, medicine, milk, and candy are but a few of the many products shipped globally that will spoil if not handled under the almost perfect standards for shipping perishable freight. Perishable products have more critical tolerances than general cargo, but the principles apply to both.

The exposures to perishable freight include the following:

- Time

- Weather

- Adverse handling

- Poor documentation and labeling

- Poor communication

- Bad insurance

The shelf life of most perishables is reduced when the product is handled out of the required environment. Ice cream may be sellable within a year of manufacturing, but only if it is kept frozen. A maximum operating temperature range must exist for the product to hold its value. Too warm, it will melt. Too cold, it will freeze. It is as important for the frozen product to be maintained in the correct temperature within the appropriate range.

This goes for just about any product shipped, in that there is a maximum and safe operating temperature for it to be handled and stored in. That range is typically the smallest for perishables. But having said that, any extreme in temperature will most likely cause harm to the majority of international freight.

Depending on the time of year and the course of transit, the parameters of temperature fall between zero and 100 degrees Fahrenheit. Obviously this can change by 20 to 30 percent depending on the variables of the season and location: New Delhi in August is hot.

For most shippers utilizing that guideline will determine the exposures to their freight. Shippers in consultation with their forwarders, carriers, customers, and government weather resources can identify the specific needs surrounding the distribution and supply chain requirements. Once identified, these details will provide the necessary steps to be taken to provide safe transport.

Any issue that will delay delivery will cause potential harm to perishable freight. While all perishable freight may not be specifically time-sensitive, it does by its very nature have a conflict with time.

Therefore, perishable freight must be shipped with time in mind, i.e., the most expeditious and safe method possible, with obvious cost efficiencies in place. Always keep in mind what happens when things go wrong.

Perishable freight could adversely affect the conveyances in which it is carried. This brings in an additional consideration to the transport company, as well as a potential liability to the shipper. Melting butter in the hold of a 747 freighter, could cause damage to the airplane, at great expense. Decaying meat in a 40-foot ocean container could cause great harm to the container in cleaning, fumigation, and recouping expense; hassles with customs, food and agricultural authorities; and total loss of freight to the "unhappy" importer.

Adverse handling will negatively affect perishable freight. Temperature-sensitive cargo usually will require special handling. An example would be an airfreight shipment of frozen ice cream samples packed in dry ice. During terminal stays and particularly if a flight is delayed, the freight should be kept in refrigerated or frozen reefer space when available. This requires the carrier to accomplish an additional physical movement. With certain carriers and certain carriers personnel, this is an easy task. In many instances, however, it is a burden and difficult to accomplish. The bottom line is the difference between the ice cream melting or staying frozen.

A 20-foot steamship container loaded with chocolate and shipped at ambient temperatures will provide a safe haven for the freight. However, place that container on the deck of a vessel, under direct sunlight, with no steps taken for ventilation, in ambient temperatures of 80 degrees Fahrenheit and the internal temperature of the container could exceed 110 degrees Fahrenheit. At that temperature, the chocolate could spoil. Think about your car in the parking lot during summer months. Keep the windows closed, return a few hours later, and you're set for a "hot to sit in" car with the air conditioning blasting. That's how hot it will be inside that ocean container.

Following is a discussion of recommendations that should be considered when shipping perishable freight.

1. **Samples should be shipped with the same urgency and quality operational procedures of commercial freight.** Just because a small quantity is shipped does not mean it is not susceptible to harm or customs scrutiny. A lot of this sample freight is shipped by Integrated carriers, such as UPS, Federal Express, or DHL. On certain trade routes consideration should be given to alternative options in dealing direct with forwarders carriers or courier companies. Samples are a test for regular shipments as well. Don't "nickel and dime" the sample shipment, because it has low value. The sample is an extension of your operation, and it's safe, timely arrival will increase your opportunity for concluding a much larger order. Therefore, use the best method of shipping, which may mean paying a fair transportation cost.

2. **Communicate with all parties involved in the shipment.** Use your resources and learn all the shipping, documentation, and handling requirements before executing the order. Make sure all parties understand the shipping requirements.

3. **Set up a system that affords ease of tracking the status of the shipment and allows all potential problems to be communicated as soon as possible so mitigating steps can be enacted quickly.** When structuring the details of the shipment logistics, communication lines must be included as a priority. All parties involved in the storage, handling, forwarding, and transport must be advised to communicate shipment status and problems as soon as possible. Use of written communication is key. Fax, e-mail, and letters of instruction should all be utilized. Telephone and fax numbers, key personnel, and emergency response actions need to be communicated and documented in the process.

The bills of lading, which become the contract of carriage between you and the carrier, are an excellent source to communicate the special shipping requirements associated with perishables. For example, keep away from heat, dry ice required, maintain temperatures between 10 and 40 degrees Fahrenheit, use ventilated containers only, sensitive to extremes or sudden changes in temperature, product must be stored in freezers during terminal stays are but a few of the clauses that would be placed on bills of lading. By doing so, two things are accomplished: (1) Special needs are communicated, which hopefully the carrier will comply with, and (2) by including these clauses you establish a line of accountability to hold the carrier liable in the event the freight is damaged due to their lack of or incorrect actions.

Besides communicating to the carrier via the bill of lading, calls should be made to operating personnel, which help to make sure on a more personal basis that directions are understood and will be complied with. While all this sounds logical, you would be surprised at how many times these simple steps aren't followed because many shippers take the approach "out of sight, out of mind."

4. **Exporters need to identify carriers and staff that have the expertise and previous operating experience to handle perishable freight.** There are independent companies and individuals within the trucking, warehousing, freight forwarding, steamship lines, and air carrier industries

that are specialized in the care and handling of perishable exports: trucking: Glacier Express, air: Lufthansa, sea: Sealand, warehousing: Christian Salveson, and freight forwarder: American River Logistics are just a few of these companies. They all have offices and agents in major U.S. gateway cities, with sales and operating personnel to assist you with your shipping needs. To obtain freight orders, many carriers will misrepresent their perishable capabilities. You will need to discern this. Ask for referrals and follow up diligently. A review of carriers capabilities must include the quality of their tracking and overseas office and the agency network to mitigate the potential problems that will occur over time.

5. Keep current with government and overseas customs regulations to assure accurate documentation requirements and timely clearance and delivery. While sources exist in booklet form to identify export documentation, these are not acceptable to this author as the information is usually outdated by the time it is published and certainly not current at the time of your shipment. Rules, regulations, and local practices vary greatly from country to country, city to city, and import customs officer to officer.

Instead, communication with your customer and your freight forwarders office/agent in the country of importation to identify not only the documentation requirements, but also the rules and regulations for packaging and labeling just prior to shipping is recommended. This will offer the most current information and provide the greatest opportunity to reduce import problems.

At the same time identify local nuances that might affect your perishable export by asking the following questions: Are cold store facilities during terminal stays and clearance delays available? Are there better carriers to utilize into that particular port or airport facility that will work better than others? As the exporter is there anything you can do prior to shipment that will make it easier for your customer to facilitate import, etc.? Perishable exports that involve food and medicines are typically under some degree of scrutiny by government officials in every country. This may involve interaction with many different government agencies in the importing country. Foreign equivalents of U.S. Customs; Food and Drug Administration; Department of Agriculture; and federal, state, and local health agencies will all be factors affecting the perishable export. Many times the entire process will be in a gray area and certainly confusing. Countries in the Middle East will bring religion into the equation. Certain countries such as Mexico, which is still evolving NAFTA rules, are not absolutely clear on packaging and labeling requirements and show inconsistencies at various border crossings. Western European cultures are becoming more Americanized in their product liability concerns, and this will directly affect U.S. perishable food and medicine exports. Eastern European countries are still reorganizing under all the democratic changes and some countries such as Poland, Russia, and Czechoslovakia do not have clear and concise regulations for perishable imports and are struggling with their transportation infrastructures, causing logistical problems for safe and timely deliveries.

6. Insure all shipments on an "all-risk, warehouse to warehouse" basis to cover any of the potential risks and exposures you will face in exporting perishables. This includes refrigeration breakdown. Many marine insurance companies will provide full coverage, but will have amendments to the policy restricting coverage for perishable freight. One such clause, "24-Hour Reefer Breakdown," implies that the conveyance, such as a steamship 20-foot container, can retain the required temperature for at least 24 hours once the temperature control unit has broken down. This may or may not be correct. As the insured, you need to determine if these policy amendments/endorsements exist and how they might affect your ability to get paid if a loss occurs. For a premium to be agreed upon, most underwriters will provide a tailored marine policy to cover your specific needs.

Another factor affecting underwriting perishable exports is that of preshipment conditions. Marine insurance coverage is designed to cover insured risks during transit. It is presumed that the goods are sound prior to export. For example, an export of frozen meat upon defrosting at destination is discovered to have an awful "taint." When all the documentation is reviewed by underwriters, on presentation of a claim, if they do not identify anything that shows how the loss occurred during transit, they will deny the claim on the basis that the goods were probably not sound prior to shipment—what is sometimes referred to a preshipment condition.

Some underwriters, for a consideration, will provide terms that give "prima facie" evidence that the goods were sound prior to export, upon issuance of certain plant or third party inspection certifications. One such certificate, the MID Certificate, is provided by the Department of Agriculture, Meat Inspection Division. Inspectors from the MID will inspect shipments prior to export and plant departure and certify the quality and status for export. Upon the issuance, the marine underwriter, who extends this coverage, is acknowledging that the goods were sound prior to export and this in return will make it easier to negotiate on a concealed damage claim.

This is an important consideration for all perishable exports and an essential ingredient in a complete export strategy. The marine underwriting community is professional, competitive, comprehensive, and accommodating to the needs of U.S. exporters and are prepared to tailor policies, terms, and conditions to meet some of the demanding needs of perishable exporters.

Insurance companies such as Great American, Continental/MOAC, CIGNA, Fireman's Fund, AIG, Hartford, and W.H. McGee are just some that have quality staff and capabilities to insure perishable exports. John Rowney is President of Great American, Marine Division, which I have great respect for as one of the best marine underwriting sources for insuring U.S. perishable exports.

7. Certain precautions should be taken in the shipping process. For airfreight shipments, make sure that samples are packed with enough dry ice to accommodate the tenure of the flight—5 pounds of dry ice for each 20 pounds of product per transit day is a guideline. For a 40-pound shipment going from Chicago to Hong Kong with an estimated transit time of two days plus adding one day for something to go wrong, one would need $3 \times 5 \times 2$ or 30 pounds of dry ice. Specific product requirements will need to be considered, as well as what packing is utilized.

Styrofoam boxes covered on the exterior by fiberboard provide adequate protection. Keep in mind that dry ice is preferable to blue ice and regular water ice, but product and time considerations need to be evaluated. All flaps, corners, and openings should be sealed with tape. The exterior of the box should be haz-mat labeled DRY ICE CLASS 9, identified as a perishable, and any special handling requirements should be clearly outlined. It is also well advised to use the language of the importing country.

Dry ice is classified as a haz-mat and requires "haz-mat" labeling and will have certain restrictions and limitations on carriage and handling. New technology is developing with experimental chemicals and "blue ice" that can hold temperatures for longer periods of time than dry ice, but another 1-2 years for experimentation is needed before this author will make any recommendations for consideration. CROYPAK Corporation in San Diego, California has some new products available to replace dry ice.

For airfreight shipments, make sure that the specific airplane is not booked to carry live animals. The carrier cannot combine a shipment with dry ice with live animals, which means that the perishable will get bumped at the time of loading. Dry ice rapidly absorbs oxygen when exposed to air, opening the opportunity for less air to be available to the live animal. In a small space, such as a cargo hold, this could prove deadly to any living thing in the cargo hold.

Use airfreight carriers with capabilities to store product in reefer areas during terminal stays and customs delays. Direct flights are preferable, when available.

For ocean shipments use only reputable carriers with the most direct routing. Transfers of perishable freight are often a cause of spoilage claims. In evaluating ocean carriers of perishable goods, look to their perishable equipment capability and inventory. How old are the insulated boxes and the refrigeration units that keep them cool? What is their maintenance program? Do they have a game plan when reefers break down on route. Can they replace broken units quickly?

Time, which is the biggest enemy of the perishable exporter, is always adversely affected by weather. While this is almost impossible to specifically control by shipment, it can be generally controlled by the overall strategy of supply chain management. If you know that airfreight becomes crowded from Thanksgiving to New Year's Day, then attempt to ship before or after this time frame. For ocean shipments from the United States, the winter North Atlantic can provide havoc and potential delays. When possible, you may want to limit the volume of shipments at this time.

Perishable exports can reap high awards and profits when the risks are mitigated. The steps outlined in this chapter are all feasible and can be easily followed. The recommendations are critical to the safe and timely delivery of all perishable exports.

Use Specialized Carriers and Forwarders for the Best Service and Rates

No international forwarder or carrier can be all things, all the time, to all parts of the globe. More typical is that there are common traits among forwarders and carriers that tend to specialize in certain trade routes, commodities, and service levels. Knowing who these forwarders and carriers are and having some level of working relationship with the sales and/or operating management will show results in the long run. Larger shippers often will have their international business split among several carriers and forwarders to take advantage of individual areas of expertise. While one may not want ten transportation vendors to contend with, having two to four may prove workable with beneficial results.

In this evaluation, consolidators and nonvessel operating common carriers (NVOCCs) should be brought into the profile of options as they tend to "specialize" in certain geographic zones and or commodities. They also can bring competitive rates to the table, particularly for less frequent shippers and all less than container load (LCL) exporters.

Develop Relationships with Your Carriers and Forwarders

All carriers and forwarders have sales or account representatives. Get to know these people well. They usually can bring a significant amount of resources to your favor. They are often the critical link to operations, which ultimately will be responsible for how the carrier services your account. Know who the key operating personnel are in case you have to reach them directly. Know who the general or senior manager is for those more difficult or time-sensitive problems.

Visit the carrier operations offices to meet the operating personnel personally. Face-to-face meetings will bring about a better working rapport. Operations personnel, who can be inundated with problems on any given day, will work harder for you when they know who you are, have "broken some bread" with you, and there is some basis of friendship.

Knowing the key players, their strengths and weakness, their idiosyncrasies, etc., will better enable you to maximize utilization of their services, particularly at critical transportation times, which occur frequently.

Know Your Commodity Classification

Ocean transportation rates are controlled by many key factors of which one is the commodity. Often subtle differences in how you "describe" the commodity will affect the freight rates. While you do not want to be dishonest, you do often have room to offer a different commodity classification that will enable you to obtain a better freight rate. Your sales agent and/or freight forwarder can assist you in determining the correct, best option.

Review the Logistics

The typical ocean move will have several legs of the journey. Minimally you will have two inland transits and an ocean leg. When the freight rates are being quoted, have them quoted with and without the inland transit. The reason being that you may be able to obtain better land rates on your own, depending on an array of factors.

Check Out Intermodalism

Sometimes combinations of rail (piggyback or container or flat car [COFC]), truck, and ocean will provide better rates than more direct modes.

Develop Negotiating Skills and Bring Them into Practice

In any purchasing management function, developing skills that afford greater control of vendor prices will prove cost effective, particularly with carriers and forwarders. Once you have received a rate proposal from your transport vendors, unless you know absolutely that the rates quoted are the best, go back and ask for better pricing. Even if you get nowhere, you are better off for asking. The most likely result is that you will get pricing anywhere from 5 to 20 percent better for just taking the time to ask.

Compromise on Little Things to Win Bigger Issues

Be persistent and have persuasiveness. Do not give in. Be stubborn and maintain your demands. It may take several meetings to bring in the results you want.

Many times in the proposal stage, the transport vendor might ask for you to divulge what rates you are looking for or what rates you currently are paying. This must be faced with severe scrutiny and discretion used when responding. Divulge this information only in the best of long-term relationships. You would be better off telling the carrier to give its best rates. Once this has been done, you can always work with the carrier to bring them in line with what you need if the rates quoted are higher. The downside, however, might be in the case where your current rates or expectations are high, and the carrier knowing this, will provide rates just low enough to beat the competition, even though the capability exists to offer even lower rates. You lose.

Remember that negotiation is as much an art as a science. It takes a great deal of effort, skill, and persuasiveness to be on the winning side consistently. In exporting, having the best rates gives you a significant competitive advantage, resulting in more satisfied customers, increased sales, and higher profits.

The Choice of Transportation: Air vs. Ocean

Exporters are always being confronted with making shipping decisions for which the choice between air and ocean is a critical factor. The many factors affecting the decision-making process are:

- Cost
- Time sensitivity/delivery requirements

- Nature of product and size of orders

- Customer needs, origin, and destination locations

Cost

Ocean shipping is generally less expensive than airfreight. This would be true whether determining calculations by volume or weight. Most shippers consider shipping by air a "premium service" left for high priority and urgent shipments only.

Shipping 20,000 pounds of electronics from New York City to London might cost $3,500 by ocean compared to $11,000 by airfreight—a 68 percent cost savings. Obviously one would have to acknowledge that the air transit on a door-to-door basis might be two to four days compared to twelve to twenty days by ocean. Also the ocean leg might bring on greater exposure for damage during transit as well as all the hazards associated with vessel transit across the North Atlantic Ocean.

The savings on a cost comparison basis only is diminished as the size of the shipment lessens. In other words, an LCL by ocean transit does not produce as great a savings compared to airfreight. There is no exact size to determine that the savings/benefit issue balances itself out as all trade routes and commodities have wide variables; however, once the shipment weighs less than 1,000 pounds or 454 kilos, one needs to take a serious look at airfreight pricing, as it would probably, on a door-to-door basis, be very close to ocean transportation costs.

It is important to keep in mind that the commodity, its density, dimensions, and the trade route will all have an affect on the breakpoint for a responsible comparison of air versus ocean.

It is also important to look at the trade route at particular points, such as the United States/South American corridor. Currently, there is a heavy amount of airfreight that comes from cities such as Bogota, Rio de Janeiro, Buenos Aires, and Caracas to various American cities through gateways, such as Chicago, Miami, and New York. There is also a lot of competition among airfreight companies. The effect of all this is that a shipper can negotiate favorable airfreight rates for higher and lower weight breaks. In comparison with ocean freight, this would bring up the potential breakpoint to weights as high as 5,000 pounds or 2268 kilos, or less.

Time Sensitivity/Delivery Requirements

Airfreight will always provide a better option on time-sensitive freight. Major cities in the world can all be reached within one to four days from all gateway points in the United States. Depending on outlying points of final delivery and the infrastructure of the importer's country, you may need to add another one to four days for local clearance and delivery. Ocean freight can take up to as much as seven to forty-five days to reach most port cities, not including time for clearance and inland transit.

A vendor filling orders on a just in time (JIT) inventory management basis may only have two to three days to move the inventory supplies from their Chicago manufacturing plant to the customer in Brussels. Ocean transit provides no option. Airfreight becomes the only answer and is very doable.

More exporters are considering airfreight, even with its increased transit expenses, as a lucrative overall logistics option because savings can be had that outweigh the additional freight expenditure. These savings include the following:

1. Reduced cost of inventory, storage and insurance costs

2. Less expensive packaging and handling outlay

3. Lower transportation (marine) insurance

4. Greater productivity of manpower and use of time

Nature of Product and Size of Orders

The size of the shipment will dictate carrier options. In simplest of terms, it does not pay to send a 10-pound package by ocean. The economy of small packages is in airfreight. Integrated carriers, along with the U.S. Postal system, have numerous options for small packages less than thirty pounds.

Integrated carriers such as UPS, Airborne, DHL, and Federal Express and freight forwarders are excellent options on midrange freight from 30 to 500 pounds. Once 500 pounds is reached, one would need to review ocean freight as a potential option. Most shippers, however, make the "break" at 1,000 pounds.

However, larger freight by weight and dimension pose several logistical problems to air carriers. The size of the aircraft plays a key role in determining service availability. The openings in the cargo hold are an important element. For instance, a 737 passenger carrier that takes freight in the belly will typically restrict the weight of one piece to 300 to 350 pounds and the height or width to no more than 42 inches.

Compared to a 747 freighter that can handle up to 35,000 pounds per piece, the actual determining factor would be density per square foot. The 747 has forward lower door openings of 104 inches by 64 inches and a front nose loader with 7- by 10-feet capability.

There are commercial aircraft in the Hercules class that can handle up to 100,000 pounds per piece. The actual determining factor would be density per square foot—with nose opening in excess of 20 by 30 feet. There is an array of carriers and forwarders that specialize in heavy lift cargoes. One would have to look at the air carriers, their aircraft, and their trade routes to determine just how large a piece they could carry. It is also important to understand that the larger aircraft, particularly one with heavy weights on board, needs plenty of runway to land safely. Not all airports have this capability. You may be able to get the cargo on the plane in JFK/New York but there may be no capability to handle the larger aircraft in Durban with shorter runways.

The nature of the product will also determine carrier options. One would not ship scrap metal by air. Its value against a high density and volume affords only ocean freight as a competitive option. If you are moving an entire oil platform, its size restricts you to the vessel mode. One would not ship precious artwork with very high value by ocean. The risks and time frame are too great. News and media communications, films, and tapes that are old the next day are only newsworthy when delivered the following morning, making airfreight the only choice. These are but a few of the examples involved when considering the options.

Needs, Origin, and Destination Issues

The customer may dictate carrier options. These options may be part of the sales negotiations and ultimately part of the sales contracts being clearly identified in the commercial documents, such as the letters of credit. In certain developing countries, the importer may require shipments by ocean to be with their national carriers. In this case you may have little option as to the carriers used once the mode is agreed upon. The customers' inventory and purchasing management systems may dictate need. The location of the shipping point and the origin point will dictate mode of transit. For example, an exporter to Latin America, located near Miami, will have lots of less expensive airfreight options compared to an exporter located in Pocatello, Idaho. Shipping to Guam makes all modes expensive because of its remoteness. The closer an exporter is to port cities such as New York City, Los Angeles, Seattle, New Orleans, the lower the inland costs. The river system presents potential lower inland costs than trucking, but still, the closer you are to the port, the lower your overall transportation costs. As the Eastern Block opens up, exporters are finding new opportunities in Russian ports, such as Moscow, Irkutsk, Omsk, and Igarka. They are finding out that there are high transportation costs into these areas, great risk of theft, pilferage, and damage and very few options by air and ocean with reasonable and consistent delivery schedules.

Exporters to the Caribbean find ocean and air viable options on smaller shipments. There are many LCL carriers with ocean consolidations at competitive prices. Airfreight to the Far East is expensive compared to ocean freight where there is a high volume of traffic and many competitors. The transit times are continually being improved with faster vessels, better scheduling, and new intermodal methods, such as miniland bridge, which moves freight by rail from eastern and central points to the west coast and then onto vessels destined for the Far East.

The bottom line is that there are many factors, which must be considered when deciding the best options. Forwarders, carriers, transportation consultants, traffic clubs, and international trade organizations, along with several key transportation periodicals are usually the best resources for gathering data to make informed decisions. Informed decisions lead to better shipping and greater profits in exporting.

Dealing with Strikes in Purchasing Transportation Services: The 1998 United Parcel Service Disaster Teaches Us a Few Lessons

The freight forwarding, trucking, and air carriers industry was never so busy once the teamsters led strike was activated against the leading small package carrier—United Parcel Service (UPS).

The effects on shippers and carriers will be long-lasting. The small package industry will never be the same. Many exporters, importers, and domestic shippers were greatly affected. They will not operate on a similar basis again, although some never learn from their mistakes!

On reflection, five suggestions have been identified that exporters and, for that matter, all shippers should consider in lieu of a revisit to an equally grand fiasco as witnessed in the UPS strike.

Don't Put All Your Eggs in One Basket

Having sold freight services for many years, I often came across the traffic manager who had no reason to see me as, "He was very happy with his current carrier." Hogwash! While I fully recognize that it is not necessary to see every freight vendor who calls on you, the UPS strike clearly demonstrated the need to have and continually develop relationships with several providers.

You may decide to have one primary vendor, but you should have options and/or at least relationships with potential vendors so you can act quickly if necessary.

Many diehard UPS shippers frantically called Federal Express, Airborne, DHL, or their friendly freight forwarder looking for a last minute option only to find out that they were first servicing existing accounts, reluctant to open new accounts, or charging retail plus prices, leaving you with a significant disadvantage. Too bad!

Maintain a Portfolio of Options

Spend at least 5 to 10 percent of your time meeting new vendors, attending networking sessions, visiting trade associations/trade shows, etc. While they might not have short-term advantage, they will provide long-term advantages so when options are needed, they are just a call away.

While we all have busy schedules and are expected to accomplish more with less, an integral ingredient to success in global trade is to network oneself with an array of service providers, friendly competitors, and exporting colleagues to maintain a dossier of options for potential future needs. The effort will pay off in spades and prove a successful ingredient in your overall export operation.

Develop a Contingency Plan

The UPS strike proved that the inevitable can happen. We should not wait until it happens again before planning a contingent strategy. The UPS strike could have been foreseen. The media started to report the potential problem more than six months before the strike started—more than enough time to seek alternatives.

Many companies were crippled by the strike. UPS who allegedly carries 80 percent of all small package freight in the United States would never be replaced in the short term, in the best of circumstances. This strike affected all modes of transit, strained the entire transportation infrastructure both within the United States and for our exports. No one alternate carrier or group of alternates could totally replace the shipping requirements of the UPS client base.

This called for strategies that reach into:

- ✔ Manufacturing

- ✔ Production

- ✔ Inventory management

- ✔ Corporate planning

This now calls for a very intensive organized effort for larger companies and a focused charge for smaller organizations, which goes way beyond just thinking of freight movements but instead of "total global logistics."

The worse case scenario must be predicted and alternate plans found that offer some degree of fail-safe.

A company would best be served by meeting with key operating and sales staff, forming a committee that would review the consequences of a potential UPS strike, and developing a strategic PLAN B to prevent a potential disaster from occurring.

Maintain Quality Communications

The disruption this strike caused for many companies strained vendor-client relations. Timely, accurate, and quality communication between the shipper and the consignee could help.

- ✔ The consignee being made aware of the problem early on might have considered other options for shipping or alternate supply sources.

- ✔ The consignee might adapt to the situation and have you ship only critical goods in the short term.

- ✔ The consignee will feel better knowing you are doing all you can and are keeping them informed.

- ✔ The cost of shipping potentially increased—let the consignee know ahead of time and work out options to share the additional costs.

All this will go a long way in maintaining client relationships for the long term.

Change the Logistics

Many exporters of small packages found an option by retiming their shipments and sending larger orders. This opened the door for a host of options with consolidators, freight forwarders, and specialized integrated units to deal directly with air, truck, rail or ocean carriers.

Keep in mind that there are small package carriers—and those that carry heavy weights (from 100 pounds to 20 tons and more). By increasing your shipping weights, you now have an array of options, competitors, and vendors who can move your freight.

The strike proved fruitful for some companies who thought UPS was the only option. Many shippers found numerous choices by common carrier, freight forwarder or by integrated competitors.

Often what appears to be a disaster can offer many long-term benefits. Being forced to search for choices now opens the door for potentially better shipping methods and logistics that can prove more cost effective to the exporter.

6

Export Documentation: Practice, Compliance, and Procedures

The engine of export trade is documentation. This chapter encourages the reader to understand the importance of export documentation, packing, marking, and labeling in export trade. Failure to complete documentation correctly is the number one reason for export problems to occur and the beginning of customer dissatisfaction. Managing export documentation is very much a science that has strict rules and procedures. This chapter provides a vast amount of detail on export documentation. Specific examples of export documents are provided in the appendix.

INCO Terms: Utilization in Export Trade/Name the Shipping Point

The INCO Terms, published by the International Chamber of Commerce, advises on and provides definitions for terms of international trade. They include CIF, FOB, FAS, all acronyms for potential terms of sale that the U.S. exporter needs to understand to conduct successful international trading.

An exporter can obtain a copy of the INCO Terms booklet, which should be part of every exporter's library. It can be obtained from any International Chamber of Commerce Office or ICC Publishing Corporation, Inc., 1212 Avenue of the Americas, New York, New York 10036.

In an attempt to understand who should control the terms of sale and what the parameters are in the decision-making process, several critical factors must be reviewed.

Overview of INCO Terms

The various terms of sale have significant consequences regarding responsibilities, liabilities, costs, and profits/losses confronting both the importer and exporter. The INCO Terms are European in foundation, reflecting a different mind-set. The terms combine documentary and transactional requirements for passage of title and payment terms. There are many hidden costs involved in international trade that the INCO Terms help to define and set out. The exporter should be aware that terms of sale directly affect costs and could affect an exporter's competitive advantage. The more responsibility assumed, the higher the price. For example, the price might be $4,500 from the plant dock, $4,800 to the U.S. port of export and $5,800 delivered to the customer's door in Oslo, Norway.

The INCO Terms advise who is responsible for arranging transportation services, freight charges, insurance, etc., but freight forwarders, banks, carriers, and experienced shippers are the best resource for figuring out what they are all about.

Name the Terms and the Point of Shipment

When using the terms, a point of destination or a site must be named. For example, if you were selling FOB (free on board), the question is FOB at what point? According to the definitions of the terms, once the goods are loaded on board the transportation conveyance, title passes to the buyer. But does this occur at the plant or the port?

If you sell FOB plant, the title will pass once the freight has been loaded on board the inland conveyance. This means that the buyer will arrange to pay for the inland transportation. They will also assume responsibility for loss or damage to the freight during transit.

Choosing to sell FOB port of loading requires that the exporter arrange for the inland freight. The exporter will then assume all transit liabilities until the freight is transferred to the international carrier. If it is an ocean shipment, the risk transfers once the freight passes the rail of the vessel, illustrating the extent of the definition of the terms.

If you had an international transaction in France that called for a CIF (cost, insurance, freight) sale with a named point, such as Paris, and the shipment was by air, the exporter would be responsible for arranging the transportation. The shipper would assume all transit liabilities and provide marine insurance up to the point of pickup from the Paris airport. In such a case, the exporter has taken on a great deal of responsibility, and with it an equal amount of risk. This is when the exporter needs to be a good traffic manager and/or have a quality freight forwarder. The marine insurance, the underwriter, and the claims systems must all be in place to deal with potential losses in an international transaction.

Terms of Payment

At the time the export sale is being consummated, the terms of payment need to be decided as they will have a great effect on the decision making for the terms of sale. Assume, for example, that you complete the transaction with every i dotted and t crossed, with the terms of sale as FOB/NY. The shipment is made with the terms of sale calling for a payment from your buyer in Paris in sixty days. The shipment arrives missing three out of ten pieces. They represent approximately $12,000 of the total invoice value for which your buyer discounts your bill. You argue that the title passed in New York, therefore the insuring responsibility, with a clean bill of lading, was with the buyer from the time the freight was received on the international conveyance.

The buyer argues that the shipment showed up short and that under no circumstances—if the U.S. exporter is to keep the account—will the buyer contribute to the loss, holding the exporter fully responsible. According to this scenario, while the terms of sale appeared to offer less exposure to the exporter, the terms of payment, allowing 60 days, provided greater exposure. The position of the importer was both unreasonable and incorrect, but it is a common path when the buyer holds the advantage of not yet having paid for the freight.

Without contingency insurance or unpaid vendor protection, the exporter may have to sue to collect at the cost of losing a customer, unnecessary aggravation, and great expense.

A very general conclusion that can be drawn is that in most export situations, the exporter should control the terms of the sale as well as the terms of payment. Every factor must be considered in this evaluation, such as, but not limited to the following:

- ✔ Price and payment terms
- ✔ Competitive pressures
- ✔ Forwarder and carrier options
- ✔ Opportunities for loss and damage
- ✔ Previous experience with buyer
- ✔ City and country of destination
- ✔ Customs clearance in buyer's country
- ✔ Current economic and political situation in buyer's country

An additional consideration in controlling terms of sale offers you, the exporter, both short- and long-term options for maintaining competitiveness. If you choose to sell on terms where all the basic shipping, documentation, insurance, and freight choices are in your control then you have the ability to affect the CIF costs. You are not forced to accept a particular insurance company whose marine rates may be higher than you can obtain in the open market. If you are free to choose steamship lines, you have the option to look at possible nonconference carriers that might produce lower shipping costs. Each variable must be evaluated. Controlling the option to evaluate will afford the more competitive choices, which will work to the exporter's advantage.

Another important consideration in determining the terms of sale is to look at the pitfalls of attempting a "door to door" sale, if required to do so, particularly in certain countries where customs law and practice work to the disadvantage of the exporter.

In certain countries, such as Mexico (though this situation is changing), U.S. exporters have found it preferable to sell FOB port of entry such as Laredo, in lieu of a CIF sale to point of destination. Mexican Customs (their trade and practice) have afforded the importer a better opportunity to arrange clearance than with the exporter's agent. This is also true in other countries such as, but not limited to Thailand, Algeria, and Iraq. Each situation must be carefully evaluated on its own merits. The exporter's freight forwarder's local relationship with foreign clearance agents plays a vital role in this regard.

The current political and economic situation in the buyer's country is critical. Take the situation in certain parts of the new Eastern Europe. While there is a big demand for U.S. products, payment is difficult at best. To make the sale, the U.S. exporter may not be able to sell completely on secured terms but may be willing to sell on a collect or sight draft basis. This arrangement might meet the need of the importer and reduce some of the exporter's exposure.

The key word is "reduce" not "eliminate." The exporter will need to make arrangements, either through the freight forwarder or the carrier, not to release the freight until the payment is made to the local representation. Quality local representation, good communication, and tight monetary controls will be critical to successful execution of this option.

Equally important is attention to the minute transactional detail for the passage of title and payment terms. Though title may transfer, responsibility, particularly fiscal responsibility, may not end.

Quality marine insurance affords protection to the exporter in all situations. The marine insurance contract should have features that protect the exporter, regardless of who is responsible to insure and where title passes. Unpaid vendor or contingency insurance can be part of any successful export program. It will afford the exporter full transportation insurance in cases where they are not responsible for insurance but may be exposed to payment or contract terms.

It is also critical when letters of credit (L/C) are used for international transactions that the terms of the sale conform to INCO practice, as well as Uniform Customs and Practice (UCP) 500 for payment terms.

The bottom line is that the exporter must evaluate many issues in determining the best terms of sale for a particular export transaction. In any case, the exporter should negotiate a controlling advantage that will mitigate potential loss and maximize protection of profits.

Additional reference sources are available from INCO Terms for Americans, International Projects, Holland, Ohio 43528; Uniform Rules of Contract Guarantees, ICC Publishing Corporation, 1212 Avenue of Americas, New York, New York 10036; Document Instruction, Unz & Company, Central Avenue, New Providence, New Jersey 07974-1139. A particularly outstanding reference source for INCO Terms is *INCO Terms for Americans* by Frank Reynolds. The author has mastered the subject and provides excellent details in his book.

A Review of the Thirteen Standard INCO Terms

The International Chamber of Commerce's *INCO Terms 2000* includes thirteen trade terms that specify the buyer's and seller's responsibilities, risks, and transfer of title and costs when those terms are made part of the international transaction.

EXW EX WORKS (named place): Any mode of transport; seller makes goods available to buyer at seller's premises or other location, not cleared for export and not loaded on a vehicle. The buyer bears all risks and costs involved in taking the goods from the seller's premises and thereafter.

FCA FREE CARRIER (named place): Any mode transport; seller delivers goods, cleared for export, to the carrier named by the buyer at the specified place. If delivery occurs at the seller's premises, the seller is responsible for loading; if delivery occurs elsewhere, the seller must load the conveyance but is not responsible for unloading.

FAS FREE ALONGSIDE SHIP (named port of shipment): Maritime and inland waterway only; seller delivers when the goods are placed alongside the vessel at the named port of shipment. The seller also clears the goods for export.

FOB FREE ON BOARD (named port of shipment): Maritime and inland waterway only; seller delivers when the goods pass the ship's rail at the named port. The seller clears the goods for export.

CFR COST AND FREIGHT (named port of destination): Maritime and inland waterway only; seller delivers when the goods pass the ship's rail at the port of export. The seller pays cost and freight for bringing the goods to the foreign port and clears the goods for export.

CIF COST, INSURANCE, AND FREIGHT (named port of destination): Maritime and inland waterway only; seller delivers when the goods pass the ship's rail at the port of export. The seller pays cost and freight for bringing the goods to the foreign port, obtains insurance against the buyer's risk of loss or damage, and clears the goods for export.

CIP CARRIAGE AND INSURANCE PAID TO (named place of destination): Any mode of transport; seller delivers the goods to a carrier it nominates but also pays the cost of bringing the goods to the named destination. The seller also obtains insurance against the buyer's risk of loss or damage during carriage and clears the goods for export.

CPT CARRIAGE PAID TO (named place of destination): any mode of transport; seller delivers goods to carrier it nominates and pays costs of bringing goods to the named destination. The seller also clears the goods for export.

DAF DELIVERED AT FRONTIER (named place): Any mode of transport to a land frontier. Seller delivers when goods are placed at the buyer's disposal on the "arriving means of transport" (not unloaded), cleared for export but not cleared for import before the customs border of the destination country.

DES DELIVERED EX SHIP (named port of destination): Maritime and inland waterway only. Seller delivers when goods are at the buyer's disposal on board the ship not cleared for import. The buyer pays discharging costs.

DEQ DELIVERED EX QUAY (named port of destination): Maritime and inland waterway only. Seller delivers when the goods are placed at the buyer's disposal, not cleared for import, on the dock (quay) at the named port of destination. The seller pays discharging costs, but the buyer pays for import clearance.

DDU DELIVERED DUTY UNPAID (named place of destination): Any mode of transport. Seller delivers the goods to the buyer not cleared for import and not unloaded from the arriving means of transport at the named destination, but the buyer is responsible for all import clearance formalities and costs.

DDP DELIVERED DUTY PAID (named place of destination): Any mode of transport. Seller delivers goods to the buyer, cleared for import (including import license, duties, and taxes) but not unloaded from the means of transport.

Obstacles to Export Documentation

One of the major pitfalls in an international sale is the quality of the documentation supporting the transaction. A mistake in spelling, execution, language, or number of copies will cause substantial delays in obtaining clearance and require additional expenditure to complete the process. Wasted time and money cut into profits, producing dissatisfied customers and additional aggravation to export staff.

Many potential exporters shy away from exporting due to the fear of the potential headaches caused by export documentation. In reality, while the process is complicated and has a steep learning curve, with the right approach and support from several resources the process can be simplified and the inherent obstacles lifted. Most of the necessary documents required for an export transaction are included in the following list:

- ✔ Invoice
- ✔ Packing list
- ✔ Export declaration
- ✔ Bill of lading
- ✔ Certificates of origin

Other documents that may be required include:

- ✔ Payment instruments (L/C, sight drafts)
- ✔ Health/sanitary certificates
- ✔ Export/import licenses
- ✔ SGS inspection certificates
- ✔ Carnets
- ✔ Certificates of insurance
- ✔ Required import documents

In addition to knowing the specific documents, the exporter will need to know:

- Language
- Number of copies
- Copy recipients
- Required signatories
- Format
- Notarization
- Consularization
- Shipping instructions

There are two excellent sources of information. The first source is your customer or customer's agent. The second is your freight forwarder. In both cases, if they do not have the answers immediately at hand, they have the means and the sources to find them. Additional resources include the following:

- Country Desk Offices in the U.S. Department of Commerce
- Export Yellow Pages
- *Official Export Guide*
- World trade centers and clubs
- U.S. Chamber of Commerce
- U.S. Council for International Trade
- *Shipping Digest*
- *North American Export Guide*
- *International Trade Reporter (BNA)*

Five Helpful Hints

1. Check with several sources for documentation requirements. This double-check will assure correct compliance.

2. Documentation files should be set up for each country to facilitate compliance on repeat or future sales. These files should be updated regularly as laws, customs practice, and regulations change frequently.

3. Fax all documents ahead of export execution to give your customer an opportunity for review. If changes are necessary, this will permit sufficient time to manage the modifications.

4. Develop systems to check and recheck the original documents before they leave your premises.

5. Make sure that at least one complete and legible set of documents is left behind and accessible for the unlikely event that the originals are lost.

Documentation and Letters of Credit

An important function of export documentation is to assure that collection proceeds according to the agreed terms of the sale and that payment is received by the exporter.

In a typical L/C transaction, the exporter anticipates receipt of funds once the goods are shipped. While this may be true in theory, in practice the exporter will only receive payment once the required documentation is received and approved by the confirming bank. This process can be difficult if mistakes are found, the document set is incomplete, the i's are not dotted or the t's not crossed.

The bank scrutinizes the documentation so closely because it never sees the freight. Discrepancies in documentation cause extra expense, payment delays, and aggravation. Following is a list of ways to minimize L/C problems:

Select banks with which you have a working relationship.

Construct L/C checklists that detail the necessary documents, their format, and all pertinent information. This list must be reviewed and managed as part of the export process to ensure accuracy and compliance.

Before a deal is completed make sure that all the requirements of the L/C can be met, all costs of compliance have been taken into consideration, and responsibility has been assigned regarding payment for changes or discrepancies in the L/C.

For L/Cs from third world countries that are confirmed by their banks in the United States, you should make sure that you understand not only the L/C requirements, but also the interpretations of potential gray areas, as these can prove to be problematic.

While documentation can be a hurdle for exporters, it also represents an opportunity. Those who can master the details and demonstrate the diligence needed to do the job correctly will show greater profits and have more time to execute bigger and better export sales.

Power of Attorney

Freight forwarders, customhouse brokers, agents, etc. all have to sign documents on the exporter's/importer's behalf and make statements/declarations to authorities and the U.S. Government.

The device utilized to provide authorization is the "power of attorney." The appendix, within the export documentation section, includes a standard power of attorney.

Because of all the new complications in export compliance, I am recommending that the format in the appendix be considered. Of course, this should be reviewed and edited by corporate counsel, but it is a good starting point.

Harmonize Tariff Schedule of the United States (HTSUS)

The HTSUS is a classification resource used for the classifications of commodities for either importation to or exportation from the United States. There are many different commodities entering or exiting the commerce of the United States. Government agencies, such as the Bureau of Export Administrations and the U.S. Customs Service, govern the reporting regulations related to the international movement of such commodities. The HTSUS is used to clarify an identification number of all commodities that are either being imported or exported.

The harmonize number consists of a ten-digit numerical format composed of a four digit heading, a four digit subheading, followed by a two-digit statistical suffix. The HTSUS reference is structured as a reference for rules of interpretation established by the U.S. Customs Service. The resource provides a structured guideline to assist any interested party in the task of a commodity classification number assignment. The resource guide consists of three key areas of reference for classification purposes: the general rules of interpretation, the general notes, and individual chapter notes.

The HTSUS reference guide is separated into 99 chapters. Chapters 1 to 97 deal specifically with types of commodities. Chapters 98 and 99 deal with circumstances of importation or exportation. Each chapter is preceded by the chapter notes that include details of inclusions to and exclusions from individual chapters.

Classification is not an exact science and requires interpretation rules and guidelines as established in the HTSUS for clarity and definition. Customs and the Bureau of Export Administration (BXA) have structured their reporting requirements around the HTSUS system for the purposes of linking direct commodity identification to a particular number. Other government agencies, such as the Food and Drug Administration and the Fish and Wildlife Service, are also linked to U.S. Customs through the commodity classification reporting HTSUS number. It is crucial to establish the correct reporting HTSUS number so as not to circumvent the regulatory involvement of these other government agencies.

The HTSUS can be accessed on line through the U.S. Customs web site, HTSUS.gov or in hardcopy format. All guidelines defined in the HTSUS reference must be clearly understood prior to the ultimate selection of any commodity classification code. Industry expert advice from a customs consultant, customhouse broker, or customs attorney specializing in customs operational procedures can be helpful in this regard. U.S. Customs can also assist in the selection of a binding classification ruling if requested to do so by the importer or exporter of record.

Unsettled Seas Ahead for Many Exporters: Government Regulations and Posture Is Changing

Exporters will need to pay close attention to the many changes coming from Washington, D.C. over the next two years—starting now.

Bureau of Export Administration (BXA)

Those exporters with products requiring BXA control an/or export licensing are facing changes that were enacted as of April 1996, with final compliance in November 1996.

The new rules are supposed to make compliance easier to manage, but anyone with exports controlled by BXA regulation must be aware of all the changes, modifications, and editions to assure compliance for the years 2000 and beyond.

Some of the positive changes are easier more accessible instructions, a decrease in license types from twenty-three categories to seven, consolidation of definitions, etc. The BXA can be reached for assistance.

Federal Maritime Commission (FMC)

The process of reducing the power base and scope of the FMC has begun. The major concern of smaller shippers is that larger shippers will be able to negotiate more freely regarding ocean rates, giving them a competitive advantage over smaller shippers who have less volume to negotiate with.

Also, regulations concerning the differences and controls over carriers, NVOCCs, and freight forwarders will be diminished making them more alike, providing similar and crossover services to their import/export clients.

Automated Export System (AES)

Exporters eventually will need to make arrangements either directly or through service providers to declare and report shipping export declarations to customs, BXA, and the Census Bureau via an electronic interface. The days of manual reporting are numbered. This will highlight the importance of automation in exporting and have numerous positive side effects in automating the entire export process of documentation, payment, and execution of the actual shipment.

The government needs to regulate the flow of goods from the United States and have a method for accurate export data.

The AES, also referred to as Pass, has already begun automation in several cities and with various exporters and service providers. It is expected to come into full compliance in a transition period from 2000 to 2002.

The exporter who pays attention to these changes and adopts operating procedures to accommodate these issues will mitigate future problems and allow smoother sailing for international sales.

Export Compliance: "You Can't Look the Other Way"

Various government authorities, including U.S. Customs, BXA, the Department of Transportation (DOT), and the Federal Aviation Administration (FAA) are beginning to crack down on exporters. In conjunction with this, there have been numerous changes to INCO Terms from the 1990 edition to the new 2000 series, as well as changes in practice for the International Traffic in Arms Regulations (ITAR), the AES, and the Census Bureau in respect to the definition of the "exporter" for completing the Shippers Export Declaration (SED).

Exporting, which has always been associated with intense documentation, bureaucracy, and lots of nonsense is now inundated with lots of government scrutiny. This results in additional aggravation that can come in the form of:

- More paperwork
- The need to automate
- Fines and penalties
- Intensive recordkeeping
- Adherence to more legal issues
- Prevention from exporting together

I have most recently followed numerous cases where exporters have received significant fines for not complying with various export regulations. These are on the increase as various government agencies gear up for enforcement through technology, manpower, and mandates for stricter controls take priority.

> *As a 25-year veteran of international trade, I never spent as much time on export controls as I do now in all three areas of my practice: consulting, education and training, and logistics management.*

Many corporations—both mom and pop and Fortune 100s—are just not paying attention to these export compliance matters as seriously and diligently as is necessary. The consequences are becoming serious and costly. Serious exporters who have learned to pay attention to these important issues, such as export packing, marine insurance, quality documentation, and successful logistics will now be spending time, money, and resources on compliance issues to survive in global trade. The appendix contains an outline of many export compliance case profiles.

The SED

Years ago this was considered a nuisance document. Not many exporters or their forwarders took its accuracy or it being forwarded quickly as a very important issue. We now know accuracy and timeliness in reporting is a critical and integral component of export compliance.

The SED is one of the very few documents required by the U.S. Government. Most exporters create a shipper's letter of instruction (SLI), which is a cover page or starting point to the SED. It provides very basic data on what makes up an export and the key details for shipping.

Historically the SED gets dropped off with the international carrier at the time the shipment is dropped. Many years ago, if this was done after the fact and that was OK. Today it must be with the carrier on or before it is dropped, or the carrier cannot accept the freight.

The SED is what the federal government desires to be reported electronically through the AES. Only 15 percent of all exports into 2000 are reported electronically. The government, specifically customs, the BXA, and Census would like to see this mandated to all exports over the next few years.

A number of issues are typically raised when processing SEDs. One being: I am the manufacturer, but I am selling Ex-works, so therefore I am not the exporter. Therefore I do not prepare the SED. This has created a quandary. Recent efforts to tighten this issue up gives the "exporter" several options. The manufacturer could show as the exporter. If the importer has an official presence in the United States with it's own EIN number (corporate social security number. . . . Unique to each legitimate corporation), they could show as the exporter. If the freight is NLR (no license required), the elected freight forwarder could show as the exporter.

The issue relating to the SED indirectly, and irrespective of who completes it, is that the manufacturer, irrespective of the terms of sale, still has certain responsibilities regarding export compliance that are particularly related to who the importer is, where they are, and what the goods will be utilized for.

U.S. Government Requirements for the SED

Filing proper SEDs is a major compliance issue for the federal government and specifically the BXA, Customs, and Census Bureau. The rules are changing frequently for SEDs. I recommend that all exporters pay close attention to the various web sites for the BXA, Customs, and Census, as outlined in the appendix for any changes affecting their export sales and operations.

Significant efforts should be made by shipper's, exporters, freight forwarders, and carriers to comply with the requirements for completing the Shipper's Export Declaration. Accuracy, completeness, and timeliness are critical.

Federal authorities have the authority to fine carriers up to $1,000 for filing late SEDs and can detain shipments for noncompliance of SED requirements, which may result in difficulties far greater than a penalty fine.

Highlights of Exporter and Freight Forwarder SED Requirements

- Must provide accurate and complete information on the SED. The exporter is responsible even if the SED is prepared by an authorized agent.

- Exporter must provide the forwarder with a formal power of attorney or the less formal written authorization as stated on the SED.

- The forwarder must submit the SED to the exporting carrier prior to exportation—there is no delayed filing for freight forwarders.

- Forwarders must provide the exporting carrier with statements or citations when an item or shipment is exempt from SED requirements.

- Exporter or forwarders must report corrections, cancellations, or amendments to information reported on the SED to customs at the port of exportation as soon as the need for such changes is determined.

- Exporter or forwarders must maintain all records relating to the exportation for a period of three years.

Key Exporting Carrier Requirements

- Must receive SEDs or exemption statements or citations from exporter prior to departure.

- Must file manifest (vessel and aircraft) and all required SEDs with customs prior to departure unless a bond is filed with customs. The manifest must include exemption statements or citations in all cases where an SED is not required.

- If a bond is filed with customs, the carrier must file a complete manifest and all required SEDs within four business days after clearance or departure—carriers are subject to fines up to $1,000 per violation if the SEDs are filed late.

2001 Changes for SEDs and Principal Party in Interest (PPI)

The Foreign Trade Statistics Regulations and the Bureau of Export Administration have now changed the way SEDs are completed. Some changes began in the fall of 2000; new ones are taking place in 2001.

One of the key changes, or better "qualifications" is that the party responsible for completing and filing the SED for an export transaction varies with the responsibility of the export clearance. Should a U.S. exporter assume export clearance responsibility, the exporter or the forwarding agent is responsible for completing and filing the SED.

Under the new regulations, an exporter must insure the accuracy of all the export information on the SED, sign it, file it manually or electronically (AES) with U.S. Customs. When an exporter utilizes a freight forwarder, authorization is provided through the power of attorney and the ability to substantiate any data provided on the SED. Many exporters have freight routed via their import clients through their own agents or forwarders. They must then provide written authorization to that forwarder to create and file the SED. However, the exporter must cooperate and provide information necessary for the forwarder to prepare the SED.

A new field and term has been developed by the Foreign Trade Statistics Regulations (FTSR) called U.S. Principal Party in Interest (USPPI) (Figure 6-1, shaded area). The USPPI is the entity that receives the primary monetary benefit from the export transaction, typically the manufacturer, distributor, order party, or a foreign buyer located in the United States. The forwarding agent cannot be the USPPI, unless acting as the order party or agent for the importer. Under BXA rules, in a routed transaction the forwarder can apply for export licenses.

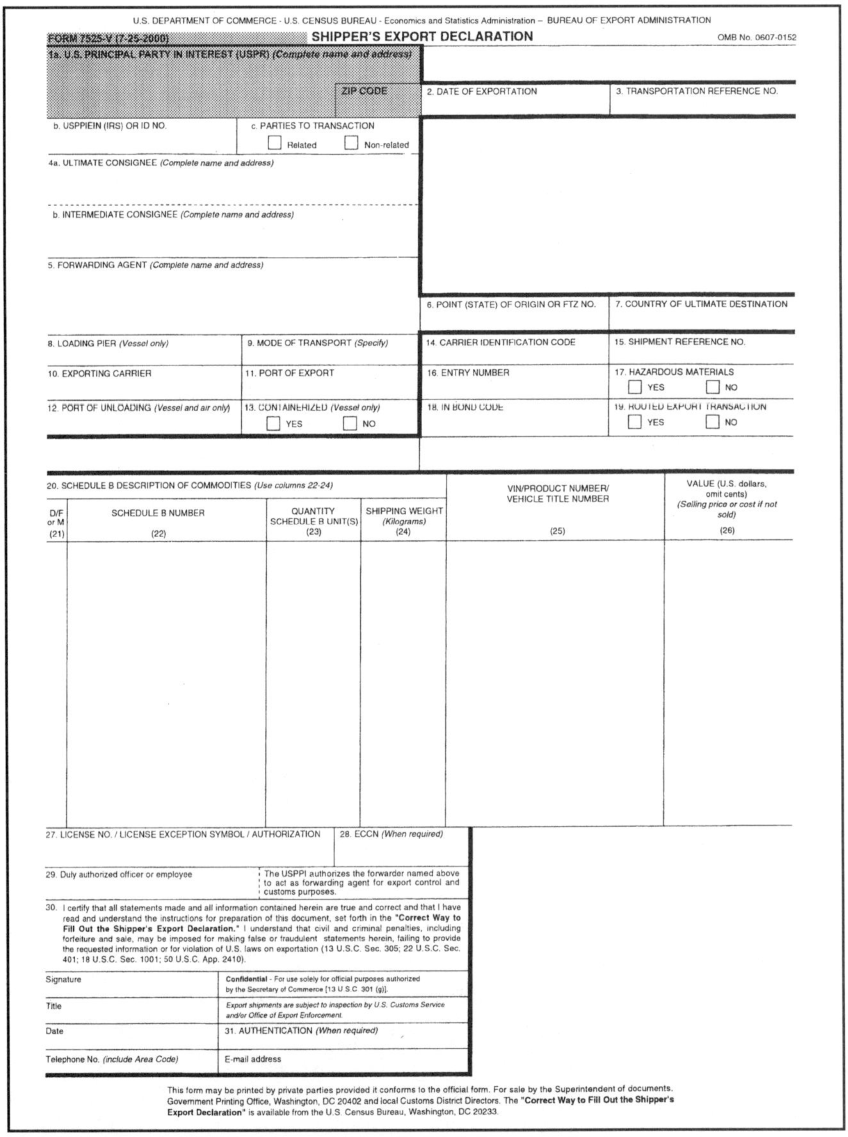
U.S. DEPARTMENT OF COMMERCE - U.S. CENSUS BUREAU - Economics and Statistics Administration – BUREAU OF EXPORT ADMINISTRATION

FORM 7525-V (7-25-2000) **SHIPPER'S EXPORT DECLARATION** OMB No. 0607-0152

1a. U.S. PRINCIPAL PARTY IN INTEREST (USPPI) *(Complete name and address)*

ZIP CODE

2. DATE OF EXPORTATION

3. TRANSPORTATION REFERENCE NO.

b. USPPIEIN (IRS) OR ID NO.

c. PARTIES TO TRANSACTION ☐ Related ☐ Non-related

4a. ULTIMATE CONSIGNEE *(Complete name and address)*

b. INTERMEDIATE CONSIGNEE *(Complete name and address)*

5. FORWARDING AGENT *(Complete name and address)*

6. POINT (STATE) OF ORIGIN OR FTZ NO.

7. COUNTRY OF ULTIMATE DESTINATION

8. LOADING PIER *(Vessel only)*

9. MODE OF TRANSPORT *(Specify)*

14. CARRIER IDENTIFICATION CODE

15. SHIPMENT REFERENCE NO.

10. EXPORTING CARRIER

11. PORT OF EXPORT

16. ENTRY NUMBER

17. HAZARDOUS MATERIALS ☐ YES ☐ NO

12. PORT OF UNLOADING *(Vessel and air only)*

13. CONTAINERIZED *(Vessel only)* ☐ YES ☐ NO

18. IN BOND CODE

19. ROUTED EXPORT TRANSACTION ☐ YES ☐ NO

20. SCHEDULE B DESCRIPTION OF COMMODITIES *(Use columns 22-24)*

D/F or M (21)	SCHEDULE B NUMBER (22)	QUANTITY SCHEDULE B UNIT(S) (23)	SHIPPING WEIGHT *(Kilograms)* (24)	VIN/PRODUCT NUMBER/ VEHICLE TITLE NUMBER (25)	VALUE (U.S. dollars, omit cents) *(Selling price or cost if not sold)* (26)

27. LICENSE NO. / LICENSE EXCEPTION SYMBOL / AUTHORIZATION

28. ECCN *(When required)*

29. Duly authorized officer or employee

The USPPI authorizes the forwarder named above to act as forwarding agent for export control and customs purposes.

30. I certify that all statements made and all information contained herein are true and correct and that I have read and understand the instructions for preparation of this document, set forth in the **"Correct Way to Fill Out the Shipper's Export Declaration."** I understand that civil and criminal penalties, including forfeiture and sale, may be imposed for making false or fraudulent statements herein, failing to provide the requested information or for violation of U.S. laws on exportation (13 U.S.C. Sec. 305; 22 U.S.C. Sec. 401; 18 U.S.C. Sec. 1001; 50 U.S.C. App. 2410).

Signature

Confidential - For use solely for official purposes authorized by the Secretary of Commerce [13 U.S.C. 301 (g)].

Title

Export shipments are subject to inspection by U.S. Customs Service and/or Office of Export Enforcement.

Date

31. AUTHENTICATION *(When required)*

Telephone No. *(include Area Code)*

E-mail address

This form may be printed by private parties provided it conforms to the official form. For sale by the Superintendent of documents. Government Printing Office, Washington, DC 20402 and local Customs District Directors. The **"Correct Way to Fill Out the Shipper's Export Declaration"** is available from the U.S. Census Bureau, Washington, DC 20233.

Figure 6-1. The New Shipper's Export Declaration (SED) for 2001.

HTSUS

The SED section #20 on the new form is for declaring the harmonized tariff code. One will need to determine the official description of the commodity to be exported by obtaining a copy of the U.S. Government publication, *Harmonized System/Schedule B Statistical Classification of Domestic and Foreign Commodities Exported from the USA.* Determining just what 10-digit code to use is as much an art as a science. The government purports to all exporters that most logistics/sales/operations executives will require technical assistance from inside experts (scientists/engineers/technicians) to determine the proper classification. Freight forwarders, consultants, customhouse brokers, and commodity specialists at customs are all available to assist with these efforts.

When to Use and How to Value the SED

Many exporters confuse this concern. All exports of any value require an SED when the goods are covered under an Individual Validated Export License (IVL). All mail or parcel post shipments over $500 and other modes over $2500, including replacement parts, repairs, fulfillment, in-house, COMAT fall under SED guidelines. Many exporters fail to report company-to-company shipments that are exported.

The value, which is stated on the commercial invoice, is the value for the SED. Many exporters fail to report the correct value on the commercial invoice, particularly for samples, repairs, and COMAT. The value stated has to have a resemblance to real market value. Other affirmative statements can be made on the commercial invoice to make sure foreign customs deal with the matter responsibly, such as: *Value stated for customs purpose only; Goods are not for sale or resale; Goods are samples only for testing and evaluation purposes; Goods for trade show for promotion only. No foreign exchange involved; Goods being returned for repair.*

These are all examples of affirmative statements for foreign customs. But the value stated must have a resemblance to market value. Do not assume that because you are not billing for it, that it has zero value. Each country has its own set of standards regarding market valuation. You will need to know these country by country when setting up SOPs for exports.

For SED purposes, the key is that an SED will be required for those types of exports if the value exceeds $500 for mail or parcel post shipments or $2500 for other modes. The BXA has stepped up its enforcement activity. Many exporters are getting warnings and fines when SEDs are filed incorrectly. Keep in mind that someone is signing the SED, making a statement that all information is *True and Correct.* The real question . . . is it?

INCO Terms

I have always held the position that INCO Terms are the foundation of global trade and that most exporters misunderstand them. Following is a discussion of how the thirteen options that INCO Terms represent are misunderstood from a practical standpoint.

INCO Terms fundamentally tell an importer and an exporter (to a certain extent, not absolute) what their responsibilities are, their potential liabilities, their potential risks, when title transfers, and who is responsible for certain costs in the international transaction.

INCO Terms are universal in that they apply to all trading nations, under all circumstances and times. They transpose language, cultural, and legal issues local to all countries and peoples. This does not mean that an exporter does not take into account local issues when completing the transaction but can feel comfortable that, for the most part, an INCO Term in the United States will have the same meaning to the customer in South Africa, Brazil, or the Netherlands.

In most U.S. Corporations, a salesperson or sales division, agent, or distributor begins the sales process. This is also where the terms of sale are generally concluded. It has been my experience that most international sales representatives, although they have the responsibility, do not understand the ramifications of INCO Terms, particularly as they relate to who is responsible for various transportation costs associated with the export and who is responsible to manage the execution of the export documentation.

The consequences of not comprehending the INCO Terms can sometimes lead to internal aggravation among operations, finance, and sales due to the potential of additional or unaccounted transportation expenses. For example, an export salesperson in Cincinnati has an internal Ex-works base price of U.S. $30,000 and is asked to deliver the freight to an ocean gateway, such as Baltimore. Technically the sale has now changed to FOB Baltimore in lieu of Ex-works Cincinnati. This now puts the burden of the transportation costs of the inland leg back to the exporter. Unless this has been figured into the base costing or as a line item surcharge, it will be difficult after the fact to account for or recover the cost from the buyer or importer, unless it was identified up-front. This is where the internal strife will begin and escalate.

Most exporters do not realize that FOB and CIF terms are being replaced by FCA and CIP, respectively, and that FOB and CIF are really designated for ocean freight transportation only. I regularly see FOB USA Airport and CIF Destination Airport, which technically is not correct.

The other issue with INCO Terms is that an INCO Term, such as CFR, by itself is not complete. An INCO Term is complete when tied in with a place, i.e., FOB Port Elizabeth, CFR Oakland, CIP Rotterdam, DDP Tokyo. An international sales person who offers FOB, CIF, CPT terms without the named place is only addressing part of the equation and leaving out a very integral component, leading to confusion and much frustration.

A critical issue is that INCO Terms are the standard terms of sale to describe what would be considered a "typical international transaction." There are thirteen standard options. However, normal trading practice will afford variations of the thirteen options, leading to countless options and some combinations, which challenge the senses.

For example: You could have an export sale via ocean freight . . . FOB Charleston, but sales agrees to prepay the ocean freight to the importers domestic gateway, say Copenhagen, Denmark, billing the ocean freight charges back to the importer through the Ex-works invoice cost. On the surface, this might not make sense. It could be accomplished via any agreement reached between the two trading parties. For tax or sales or inland distribution reasons, the importer might best be served by incorporating the international freight costs, so the exporter accommodates the client by formally selling FOB Charleston, but functionally selling CIF Copenhagen. The paperwork shows one thing, but a side agreement creates another. One must always be careful when doing side agreements or extensions not to create an illegal transaction or a future compliance headache. The reality is that international salespersons, agents, and distributors are always agreeing to provisions in the export transaction that will alter the ramifications, liabilities, and costing as determined by the actual INCO Terms.

INCO Terms are terms of sale that run in conjunction with a related but completely different subject—the terms of payment. That could be a source of confusion and potential pitfalls. For example: An exporter sells FCA O'Hare Airport in Chicago. Basically the exporter is accepting responsibility to the point at which the goods are loaded onto an aircraft at the designated airport. They pass liability, title, and costing once the goods are loaded on board the plane. But, the terms of payment are Sight Draft 60 days. The plane crashes. According to INCO Terms, technically the risk of the international leg was for the account of the buyer. Now the buyer having not received the goods is still obligated to pay. Will they? What will it cost you to collect? The more third world the transaction, the less likely your opportunity to collect? These are all true, very serious everyday issues. So international sales and operations must pay attention to the potential conflicts that arise in exports between the terms of sale and the ultimate terms of payment.

By the way, the exporter could have arranged for contingency/unpaid vendor insurance, which would provide "all-risk" protection if they were unable to collect from the buyer.

Overview of the BXA

In all my export educational seminars and corporate export facility reviews, I never have spent as much time as I do now reviewing and analyzing export compliance issues that U.S. corporations face in managing export compliance. The reality is that the government through the BXA has stepped up its enforcement efforts, not only on issues typically engaged in national security, but now with our mainstream exporters in areas such as the accuracy of the SEDs; the overall consistency, conformity, and trueness of the exporter's invoice, packing list, certificate of origin, etc.; overall recordkeeping; and the due diligence process in determining what can be exported, to whom, and where.

The BXA is complicated. Understanding the regulations in detail is cumbersome and arduous. It would take a full-length monograph to review all the issues in detail. Following is a discussion of the very basic parameters of what each exporter should know about export compliance with the BXA.

The BXA asks five questions:

- What are you shipping?
- What quantity/what value?
- Where?
- To whom?
- For what utilization?

In the simplest of explanations, this is what I believe the BXA is requiring each exporter to answer before they can be compliant in their export operations. A key factor here is that the BXA requires that in each transaction, each export relationship, etc. that there is an SOP, starting with proper due diligence, accountability, recordkeeping, and compliance before an exporter can successfully export.

Ignorance of the rules and regulations is not an acceptable excuse. The fines and penalties can be severe and harsh, with civil and personal prosecution, suspension/revocation of export privileges, and imprisonment as potential consequences. One just needs to read the export chronicles to see the recent rash of enforced compliance by the BXA in a proactive mode to catch potential noncompliant individuals and corporations.

- Corporations showing different values between the SED and the commercial invoice or showing a lower value on the commercial invoice than was the transaction actually accounted for have been fined by the BXA.

- Corporations shipping freight to destinations knowing that a potential transshipment or third party sale will occur to a prohibited country have been penalized.

- Corporations shipping to individuals or corporations on the Denied Persons list have had their export privileges revoked or suspended, either temporarily or permanently.

- Corporations had their goods seized for showing that the goods are of U.S. origin on the export documents, when they were originally imports into the United States. Technology companies appearing to export innocuous software only to learn that their products require export licenses in that the technology has applications for national security exposures.

- High-tech companies finding out that their products are licensable because through minor retooling, such as with laser equipment for alarm systems, the product could be retooled for laser weaponry.

The bottom line is that there are really hundreds of reasons that the exporter must pay attention to the new level of scrutiny that the BXA is executing on export compliance. This is to avoid serious fines and penalties; prevent export privilege suspensions; prosecution of the corporation and individuals; and to avoid the expense associated with litigation, mitigation, and the inability to export successfully.

I have observed many corporations ignore their export compliance requirements and/or procrastinate on dealing with them. For many, this delay or inaction has been very costly.

The activity of the BXA is not waning. It is growing. From the actual outbound ports through to the corporate transaction files, there is stiff review and scrutiny. The BXA has established a 29-step process outlined on pages 126 and 127, that the exporter must go through to make sure that they can export the product to a particular country. . . to a specific entity. . . for certain utilization. The process must be documented, maintained for at least five years, and totally retrievable under any potential audit.

The BXA has established "red flags" or potential occurrences or observations made to the export company from the potential foreign buyer that are supposed to cause the exporter to raise their level of diligence until the inquiry/diligence is successfully mitigated, closed out, or favorably rectified. For example:

- The foreign buyer wants to pay cash.

- The foreign buyer uses freight forwarder for the delivery sight.

- The foreign buyer is in a completely different business.

- The foreign buyer purchases a product that requires installation and training, but tells you not to provide it.

- The foreign buyer is not cooperative with details, delivery sights, dates, etc.

There are numerous other red flags that the BXA has identified that the U.S. exporter must learn to understand and react to before completing the export transaction. Corporate management would be shocked to learn how much of the onus is on them in the execution and diligence of their foreign sales.

Exporters must learn the regulations, maintain and update the changes, and have SOPs in place to deal with all the export compliance issues. They must employ specialists on staff or delegate the responsibilities to third parties under contract who are qualified to provide the export compliance management response necessary. Law firms, freight forwarders, and consultants are the three major types of third party service providers that can offer export compliance expertise.

When OSHA was developed and expanded in the 1970/1980's, many corporations resisted this new government intrusion. Some twenty years later, it is well entrenched into corporate America. I view what happened with health and safety issues in corporate America back then similar to what is happening now with export compliance. We can argue about it, we can fight it, but it is here now, apparently here to stay, and we need to deal with it constructively like a necessary evil. I firmly believe that those corporations and individuals who embrace export compliance proactively will benefit immensely, and those that defer will be at a loss with export operations that are handicapped.

The BXA also requires that individual exports to foreign parties be reviewed by a checking process to determine the suitability of the importer. These include the following:

Department of Commerce: Restricted parties list; end-users requiring a license.

Department of State: Debarred list, chemical/biological weapons concerns, missile technology list, designated terrorist organizations.

Department of Treasury: Specially designated nationals, narcotic traffickers, designated terrorists.

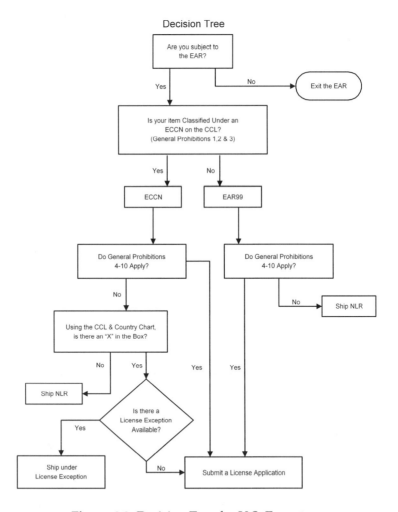

Figure 6-2. Decision Tree for U.S. Exporters.

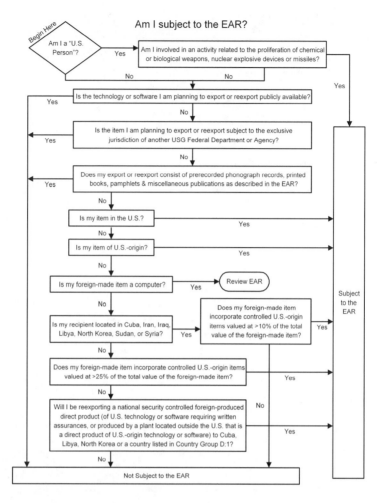

Figure 6-3. The 29-Step Process of U.S. Export Regulations.

ITAR stands for the International Traffic in Arms Regulations. The Arms Export Control Act authorizes the President to control the export and import of defense articles and defense services. The president shall designate which articles shall be deemed to be defense articles and defense services.

License or other approval may be granted only to U.S. persons and foreign government entities in the U.S. Application for license or requests for other approval will generally by considered only if the applicant is registered with the Office of Munitions Control.

Defense articles are technical data recorded or stored in any physical form, models, mockups, and other such items which reveal technical data relating to items such as:

Significant military equipment	Missile technology
Firearms	Artillery projectors
Ammunition	Launch vehicles

Explosives, propellants	Vessels of warer and special naval equipment
Aircraft and associated equipment	Tanks and military vehicles
Military training equipment	Protective personnel equipment
Military electronics	Optical and guidance control equipment
Toxicological agents/equipment	Radiological equipment
Spacecraft systems	Auxiliary military equipment, i.e.: cameras
Submersible vessels	Nuclear weapons, design and test equipment

Defense services:

- Furnishing assistance to foreign persons, whether in the United States or abroad in the design, development, engineering, manufacture, production, assembly, testing, repair, maintenance, modification, oepration, demilitarization, destruction, processing, or use of defense articles.

- Furnishing to foreign persons any technical data such as classified information, software, information for the design, development, production, including blueprints, drawings, photographs, plans.

U.S. person: lawful permanent resident, also means any corporation, organization, trust, entity, that is incorporated to do business in the United States.

Foreign person: not a lawful permanent resident, also means any foreign corporation, organization, trust, entity that is not incorporated or organized to do business in the United States.

Export:

- Sending or taking a defense articles out of the United States.

- Transferring registration, control, or owndership to a foreign person of any aircraft, vessel, or satellite covered by the U.S. Munitions List whether in the United States or abroad.

- Disclosing/transferring in the United States defense articles to an embassy, agency, or diplomatic mission.

- Disclosing/transferring technical data to a foreign person whether in the United States or abroad.

- Performing a defense service on behalf of or for the benefit of a foreign person whether in the United States or abroad.

How Does ITAR Affect Exports? (Registration with Office of Defense Trade and Obtaining an Export License)

Any person in the United States who engages in the business of either manufacturing or exporting defense articles or furnishing defense services is required to register with the Office of Defense Trade Controls. Manufacturers who do not engage in exporting must nevertheless register. Registration is a means to provide the U.S. Government with necessary information on who is involved in certain manufacturing and exporting activities. Registration does not confer any export rights or privileges. It is generally a precondition to the issuance of any license or other approval.

Exemptions:

- Officers and employees of the U.S. Government acting in an official capacity

- Persons whose pertient business activity if confined to the production of unclassified technical data only

- Persons all of whose manufacturing and export activities are licensed under the Atomic Energy Act of 1954

- Persons who engage only in the fabrication of articles for experimental or scientific purpose, including research and development

Any person in the United States who intends to export or to import temporarily a defense article must obtain the approval of the Office of Defense Trade prior to the export or temporary import, unless the export or temporary import qualifies for an exemption.

- Applications for export or temporary import to be made as follows:

  - Applications for permanent export (Form DSP-5)

  - Applications for licenses for temporary export (Form DSP-73)

  - Applications for licenses for temporary import (Form DSP-61)

  - Applications for export or temporary import of classified defense articles or classified technical data (DSP-85)

Applications for Department of State export licenses must be confined to proposed exports of defense articles including technical data.

Office of Defense Trade Control requires all pertinent documentary information regarding the proposed transaction and proper completion of the application form, also including:

- Attachments and supporting technical data or brochures.

- Freight forwarders lists.

- Certification letter signed by an empowered official must accompany all applications submitted.

- Purchase order, letter of intent, etc.

The Best Sources for Export Documentation

There are numerous options for all exporters in determining what the documentation requirements are for various countries. The first issue one needs to tackle is the three "Cook" principals of export documentation:

1. Export documents are import documents. The U.S. Government only requires that we complete the SED for exports. It does not require that we cut any other documents, i.e., the commercial invoice, packing list, certificate of origin, etc. The conclusion is that the documents we prepare for exporting are really designed to facilitate the import in the foreign country we are shipping to in order to assist the customer in complying with their customs clearance procedures.

2. Documentation is the engine of customs clearance worldwide. They determine product identity and origin, consignee, value, quantity, and utilization, which are all the components of customs in determining the correct duties, taxes, VAT, etc.

3. Documentation is a critical component of "landed cost" pricing and is key in affecting the competitiveness of an exporter's access to global markets.

With that understanding, exporters need to develop a dossier of resources in export documentation requirements. The best is your freight forwarder. You ride on the back of their experience and worldwide office/agency network to provide documentation requirements in every gateway.

The next best resource is your customer. They usually will have the responsibility to deal with customs clearance issues and typically will have previously imported. Therefore, they can be an excellent resource, as they will directly benefit from the ease of providing accurate and timely information.

U.S. consulates in foreign gateways can be good sources. In the web site listing in the appendix is the site for the Department of Commerce. At this site one can find contact information for all our consulates worldwide.

While these written sources are good; they should be only considered starting points, as the information contained is only as good as the last publishing date. In international trade, documentation, packing, marking, labeling, and legal issues change quickly. Knowing the status and options will ease the pain. The appendix includes a detailed listing of sources for export documentation.

Societe Generali Surveillence Inspections

Societe Generali Surveillence (SGS), based in Switzerland, is a general inspection company with global reach. They have cargo-surveying and inspection capabilities on six continents, mostly centered in major gateways. On behalf of any company or request, they will send out a qualified cargo inspector to certify a cargo for count, accuracy, meeting quality specifications, documentation, or other issues related to a foreign importer's purchase order.

There are many countries in the world that require preshipment SGS inspections, such as Peru, Oman, Nigeria, and Argentina. The Philippines had the requirement up to April 2000, but did away with it, as it was no longer necessary. What these countries required was for the importer to arrange an SGS inspection of product they purchased from an overseas source, prior to export from the supplier's country. This was part of their import licensing process and a necessary evil in their import documentation. The arrangements and costs would be the responsibility of the importer. The exporter would only need to contact the local SGS office once the goods were ready for export so they could inspect and approve before the goods were shipped. For the exporter, documentation, time, and freight availability were the only issues.

A different criterion for when and at what value an SGS inspection was necessary was set for each country. Products, utilization, ultimate consignee were secondary criteria. The SGS inspector would issue an approval statement and forward the originals to the correspondent office in the importers country. A copy would remain with the shipper (exporter) for their records and typically another copy to be forwarded with the export documents.

Basically, the SGS inspection process deals with the concern of the importer's government that a legitimate import/export transaction is occurring and that there is a market value relationship between the products being shipped and the commercial documentation. Quality, count, purchase order confirmation, documentation, etc. are all SGS issues as well. The SGS can be reached in the United States.

Concluding Remarks

Paying attention to detail with proper packing, marking, labeling, and documentation is one of the most critical areas of export trade and a direct determinate of success or failure in the global arena. Having personnel on staff and/or access to proper resources as outlined in this chapter is an integral component of successful export management.

7

What Exporters Should Know about Importing

Almost all exporters import. Almost all exporters have returned merchandise. For these reasons it is very important for the exporter to understand what U.S. Customs regulations are for imports, all government compliance regulations, and the best in-bound supply chain options.

Import Compliance: A Necessary Evil!

The Customs Modernization Act of 1995 put a much greater onus on importers than had existed previously. U.S. Customs spent the next five years in a program called informed compliance. They set out to educate the importing public—what the rules were and how to administer their import responsibilities.

Since 1999, U.S. Customs has now entered into a new phase—enforced compliance—which is an aggressive effort to hold importers responsible and accountable for import compliance, with severe fines, penalties, and consequences.

Under a mandate from Congress, the Customs Modernization Act, outlined strict interpretations of U.S. import rules and regulations and a procedure for strict enforcement. They also funded the enforcement effort. As a side note, many industry analysts see this whole effort as a way for customs, who has steadily been losing tax and duty revenue due to worldwide treaties and agreements eliminating them, to maintain it's revenue flow through new fines and penalties.

Regardless of the rhyme or reason, exporters need to understand this new customs policy because many exporters are also importers, they have returned goods, and circumstances often arise where goods are being brought into the United States.

Customhouse Brokers

These companies are typically part of freight-forwarding organizations and/or international transportation service providers. They are licensed and sanctioned by U.S. Customs to clear goods through the border for a fee on behalf of importers.

They are required to be an extension of customs, upholding import law and regulations and collecting duty and taxes on their behalf.

Brokers do not have to be utilized in clearing your goods, as a company can do this itself, but it typically makes commercial sense to employ a broker to work on your behalf. They should know the laws, common practice, and functionality of the clearance process to assure timely and accurate release of your product from customs. Although they charge for their services, they are usually a cost-effective option in the long run.

There are large customhouse brokers: Fritz companies, Circle Freight, Schenkers, Expeditors, Tower Group in addition to many small and mid-size brokers. Some smaller-size, but quality brokers include: Newage, American River Brokerage Service, and Northeastern. It is imperative for you to find a broker that is conducive to your size and needs.

You certainly want a broker that is automated broker interface (ABI) compliant, meaning they have an automated relationship with customs and can interface with your automated systems for ease of clearance and less paperwork.

Friendly competitors, carriers, international trade organizations, and U.S. Customs in your inbound gateway can all be sources used to assist you in making the right selection.

While customhouse brokers help you manage the clearance, and you will certainly delegate many of the clearance responsibilities to them, you cannot defer all liability associated with proper compliance to them because U.S. Customs does not allow you to delegate ultimate control and supervision of their activity. Thus, it is important that all importers understand the basics of import law and how it applies to their specific inbound activity.

Duties and Taxes

All duties and taxes must be remitted to customs within ten days of clearance. These are determined by two key factors: the origin of the goods and the description as identified by the appropriate Harmonized Tariff Code (HTC). Secondary issues might be utilization of goods, such as in the case of samples or promotional items; the value; and who the ultimate consignee might be.

Through various web sites, publications and resources available through customs, one can obtain the tariffs to determine the applicable duties and taxes. This information also can be obtained form a customhouse broker or local customs office.

Selecting a Customhouse Broker

Customhouse brokers are considered to be industry experts in the customs business. There are considerable risks involved in the selection of a customhouse broker. A broker is required by customs law to maintain a valid customs power of attorney to conduct any and all customs business on behalf of the importer. This power of attorney legally authorizes the customhouse broker to act on behalf of the importer legally binding the importer to many legal obligations. Extreme care needs be exercised in this selection process. U.S. Customs purports that many brokers are operating below the reasonable care and compliance standard that is legally expected of them. This lack of reasonable care and compliance equates to fines and penalties for both the importer and broker. It is essential to carry out the following points when choosing a customhouse brokerage service:

- Verify that the brokerage operation has qualified customs brokerage personnel with more than five years of operation experience on all levels of customs entry processing.

- Verify that the key licensed person in charge of brokerage operations has licensed support personnel within the brokerage office conducting your customs business.

- Verify that the operations staff has proper and exact experience in valuation issues.

- Verify that the operation staff has proper and exact experience in classification issues. Often they will utilize the wrong HTSUS classifications, based on information the importer has supplied. This will cause potential fines and penalties for both parties and delay the import process.

- Verify that the brokerage operations has representation in all ports in which they claim to conduct customs business. It is important that your entries are not being processed by a third party broker to which the importer has not issued a power of attorney to act on its behalf. Importers are to make the decision of who conducts their customs business, not an intermediary broker.

- Verify compliance knowledge with the brokerage operations.

- Make personal visits to the broker's office to note working conditions and automated capabilities.

- Always select an ABI broker who has an operating software package that is not more than five years old. Many changes have taken place in the automated arena of customs business, which makes it crucial to keep pace for clearance advantages.

- Monitor brokerage communications procedures related to "shared" information being given to and received from customs by your broker. All communications need be forwarded to the importer. Verify the procedures in place to accomplish this goal.

What You Should Know about "Drawback"

Drawback is a privilege granted by U.S. Customs, which allows an importer to collect 99 percent of duties previously paid by exporting the merchandise from the United States or destroying the imported goods under customs supervision. It is important to note that drawback is a "privilege" that can be taken away if customs considers the drawback claimant in constant fraudulent violation concerning their drawback claims for refunds.

There are three main types of drawback:

Unused Merchandise Drawback. A 99 percent refund of duties paid on imported merchandise that is exported in the same condition as when imported and remains "unused" in the United States. The importer may claim a drawback for three years from the date of importation.

Rejected Merchandise Drawback. A 99 percent refund on imported merchandise that is received not conforming to the importer's standards of approval and/or the standards of any government agency (i.e., FDA, Department of Agriculture, FCC, Fish and Wildlife Service, U.S. Customs). The importer may claim a drawback for three years from the date of importation.

Manufacturing Drawback. A 99 percent refund of duties paid on imported merchandise that is received and is to be further processed or manufactured in the United States. Customs will allow a 99 percent refund of duties paid on the imported merchandise for a period of up to five years from the date of importation.

It is key to note that unless given prior permission, all merchandise must be examined by U.S. Customs prior to export to qualify for the drawback privilege. A filer notifies customs of their intent to file a drawback claim in reference to a drawback by filing a "Notice of Intent" CF 7553.

An importer must allow at least five working days prior to the export of the merchandise. Customs will notify the drawback claimant within two working days of their intent to examine or waive the examination.

Drawback is a fantastic opportunity to recover previously paid duties on exportation and/or destruction. Careful attention must be paid to time limitations and correctness of information declared to customs.

Customs can pursue costly fines and penalties against a drawback claimant for incorrect claims submitted for refund. It is automatically reviewed as a fraudulent act, punishable by a penalty up to the domestic value of the merchandise.

A frequent drawback claimant needs to consider a complete drawback program, containing adequate recordkeeping procedures for proper filing.

Necessary Drawback Documentary Requirements

Following is a list of necessary drawback documents:

- Letter requesting a drawback claim to be filed on behalf of exporter
- CF 7501 entry summary

- Import commercial invoice
- CF 3461 entry/immediate delivery
- Import packing list
- Export invoice
- Export packing list

Careful consideration for drawback eligibility must be maintained by industry experts. This is a very trade-specific area of expertise. Assistance from specialized brokers and consultants is a necessity.

Returns and Repairs: The Most Cost-Effective Options

Many exporters have merchandise returned for repair with the intention that once it is repaired, it will be re-exported. The best situation to be in as an exporter in this circumstance is to control the entire export/import process from beginning to end. Because certain documentation has to be presented to customs at both ends, to prevent duplication of payment of duties and taxes one party should handle both transits to ease the process. One forwarder/carrier has the export and the same entity handles the import and then the re-export of the repaired piece. This will provide the best economies of scale, ease of document/clearance handling, and the lowest costing.

Too often, returned freight just shows up at the border. The exporter is alerted late, has to pay demurrage, and the whole process gets complicated. The use of one forwarder/carrier eliminates most of the problems. Returned freight still has to be cleared through customs, but if handled properly; one will not have to pay duties and taxes.

The key is to provide communication and shipping instructions to your overseas customer so they will know who to contact for shipping instead of just sending it by any means available. For merchandise that is just being returned, one must go through a clearance process and no duties or taxes will have to be paid if the documentation and clearance is processed correctly. Using qualified forwarders and customhouse brokers will make the return process run more smoothly and protect your need for competitive pricing.

Quality logistics becomes an integral component of your customer service capability and provides a competitive advantage.

Concluding Remarks

Some exporters export successfully, but then fail when the merchandise has to be returned to the United States or they become involved in reverse logistics. Hopefully, this chapter has raised awareness of all the import issues and presented the best resolutions to manage import compliance and inbound supply chain effectiveness.

8

Trade Finance, Banking, and Letters of Credit

This chapter presents all the mechanics and options involved with getting paid. This important aspect of exporting should be negotiated at the front end of the sale and not as an afterthought. All of the frequently used payment methods, how best to interface with a bank, how to insure receivables, and the important details associated with letters of credit are discussed. The skill sets of trade finance take numerous years to master. This chapter expedites the knowledge learning curve and summarizes all the factors that the exporter needs to capitalize on.

Trade Finance

Getting paid is a critical aspect of the export business. This often "critical component" of the export sale is often forgotten until the receivable becomes an issue. Trade finance is often an integral part of being able to close an international deal. American exporters find that foreign firms often have advantages in selling to export customers because they offer terms. This forces the U.S. exporter to sell on an open account or provide some means of providing extended payment options. Often this is the factor that will make or break the deal. Relationships with trade finance professionals and often the export credit insurance professional is another important factor in succeeding on the financial side of international trade. The appendix includes a detailed section on options for getting paid on exports.

Options in Global Finance and Banking

Exporters need to develop options for how they receive payment for foreign transactions. These choices increase competitiveness.

Export payment tools such as acceptances and drafts for collection and letters of credit are common options for reducing the risk of nonpayment between you and your customer. In both cases, while you must ship before payment, the buyer must pay before taking delivery of the goods.

In an export trade, the payment option can be designed so that you make a draft payable to you that is drawn on the buyer. This draft, with the bill of lading documenting the shipment of the goods, is delivered to a third party, typically a bank in the buyer's country. This is accomplished by courier and offers a degree of control over access to the goods. The bank notifies the buyer that it has received the documents. Upon payment of the draft by the buyer, the bank will release the bill of lading, enabling the buyer to gain access to the freight. The exporter will then receive the funds through the banking system. If the exporter desires to extend credit to the buyer, a time draft allows the buyer to take delivery of the goods and pay the draft within a specified period of time. This type of draft is often referred to as a trade acceptance, which can be held to maturity or sold at a discount to a bank.

Dating back to the 1200s, letters of credit have been an excellent option in global trade. Letters of credit mitigate the risk for the exporter and the importer and utilize a bank as the third party intermediary in the transaction. Letters of credit are described in detail on page 133. They typically use documentation requirements to assure compliance before payment is made.

When an export sale requires secured financing, such as with a letter of credit transaction, the buyer and seller agree on the terms of the sale and the buyer structures the letter of credit with an opening bank. The buyer's bank forwards the letter of credit, which includes all the instructions and shipping conditions the exporter requires to receive payment at the beneficiary U.S. bank. The exporter must review and scrutinize all conditions in the letter of credit carefully and ensure that all the terms can be met. This process requires detailed communication and accountability within the exporter's office.

Once the export is shipped overseas, all the documents are presented to the U.S. bank for review. Once all the conditions have been met, the beneficiary bank pays the exporter and forwards the documents necessary for the importer to take delivery.

Letters of credit may have advantages over other options in that the exporters should get paid upon shipping the goods in compliance with the stated requirements. All letters of credit should be confirmed and irrevocable. This nullifies the political and economic risks and makes the letters of credit binding until both parties agree to change or amend it.

Relationship still drives letters of credit. Both parties will need to cooperate through amendments and discrepancies. This requires good faith and a willingness for compromise on various issues to make the export deal happen.

When evaluating the use of letters of credit, keep in mind the cost to the importer. These costs might be significant enough to make the deal too expensive for the importer.

Export trading companies (ETCs) and export management companies (EMCs) are often very aggressive in arranging financing of export transactions. They often have various means to collateralize overseas sales. In addition, many ETCs have an export credit insurance policy in place to protect foreign receivables. In addition, ETCs are sophisticated in evaluating credit risk and knowing just how far to "push the envelope."

As in the domestic market, factors are available to purchase export receivables. Typically, the interest rate on this financing option is much higher, because the risk passed on is higher. If you choose this option, go back to your pricing estimates to determine if there is enough margin in the product to pay for factoring. Two areas of gain through factoring are: (1) immediate payment frees cash that would otherwise be tied up for months; (2) collection risk can be reduced.

Exporters who approach this subject with creativity have options through financial services called "confirming" and "forfeiting." An independent company confirms an export order in the seller's own country and makes payment for the goods in the currency of that country. These options are designed to help exporters and importers expand their markets, improve cash flow, and create greater profit leverage. Confirming coordinates and pays for, with terms, the entire export transaction from factory to end-user. Forfeiting represents the selling, at a discount, of a longer term receivable or promissory note of the buyer. These instruments can include the guarantee of the foreign government.

Many U.S. banks do not have international capabilities. The exporter needs to spend considerable time finding banks with a global reach. Quality international loan officers are an integral part of the exporters' business. Banks have been faulted for being so slow and resistant to "new" deals that the exporting opportunity is missed.

Export-Import (Ex-Im) Bank, SBA, and the DOC are examples of government agencies at the federal level with programs that encourage local banks to assist you. Government programs, especially at the state level, are increasing. Some states now offer direct financing as part of their state export assistance programs.

During the past twenty years there has been a great willingness of foreign-based banks to be more accommodating and offer greater expertise on behalf of U.S. exporters. Standard Chartered, Bank of New York, Chase Manhattan, HSBC, and ABN-AMRO are a few quality foreign banks.

Export-Import Bank

The Ex-Im Bank of the United States is an independent U.S. Government agency that helps finance the overseas sales of U.S. goods and services. Ex-Im Bank will finance the export of all types of goods or services, including commodities, as long as they are not military-related (certain exceptions exist). The Ex-Im Bank offers direct loans for large projects and equipment sales that require long-term financing. It also offers guarantees on loans made by cooperating U.S. and foreign commercial banks to U.S. exporters and their customers.

Ex-Im Bank programs reduce the amount of collateral required to finance a loan and generally make financing more available. Four programs that are helpful to the beginning exporter are discussed in the following paragraphs.

Working Capital Guarantee Program

The Working Capital Guarantee Program covers 90 percent of the principal and interest on commercial loans to creditworthy small and medium-size companies that need funds to buy or produce U.S. goods or services for export. Exporters may apply for a Preliminary Commitment. This is a letter from Ex-Im Bank outlining the terms and conditions under which it will provide a guarantee that can be used to obtain the best financing terms from a private lender. The lender also may apply directly for a final authorization, or guarantees may be for a single transaction or a revolving line of credit. Guaranteed loans generally have maturities of twelve months and are renewable. Certain lenders experienced in the program have been given delegated authority that enables them to commit the Ex-Im Bank's guarantee.

Intermediary Lending Program

The Intermediary Lending Program is offered through intermediary U.S. banks. These medium-term fixed-rate export loans have the lowest allowable interest rates, which reduces the bank's risk and increases your chances for financing. The purchaser is required to make a minimum 15 percent cash payment and the bank loan covers up to 85 percent of the export contract on terms ranging from one to five years. At the time of commitment, the interest rate is fixed according to the classification of the country to which the export is shipped.

Export Credit Insurance

Various underwriters such as the Foreign Credit Insurance Association (FCIA), CNA, and others will issue credit insurance covering 100 percent of losses for political reasons (war, expropriation, currency inconvertibility, etc.) and up to 95 percent of commercial losses (nonpayment by the buyer due to insolvency or default). This kind of insurance encourages banks to extend credit on the basis of covered accounts receivable and enables the exporter to be more competitive by extending credit or extending more favorable terms to foreign customers. The FCIA is now a private entity, part of The Great American Insurance Company, based in New York City.

Small Business Administration (SBA)

The Small Business Administration (SBA) has several financial assistance programs for U.S. exporters that meet the SBA's size standards. The International Trade Loan Program makes more credit available—up to a $1 million SBA guarantee per borrower for facilities and equipment, plus $250,000 of working capital.

The Export Revolving Line of Credit Loan proceeds can be used to finance labor and material needed for manufacturing, to purchase inventory to meet an export order, or to penetrate or develop foreign markets.

Regular Business Loan Guarantees guarantee loans to pay existing obligations or to purchase fixed assets, enabling the new exporter to increase or modify production capacity. Loans may have maturities of up to 25 years, with a maximum guarantee of $750,000.

Overseas Private Investment Corporation (OPIC)

Owned by the U.S. Government, the Overseas Private Investment Corporation (OPIC) is a self-supporting entity charged with encouraging U.S. private investments in less developed countries. OPIC offers insurance programs for investors in foreign projects and specialized insurance for U.S. contractors and exporters operating in developing countries. OPIC also offers financing services in the form of direct loans of up to $6 million per project and will guarantee bank loans of up to $50 million. Its financing and guarantee programs are designed to protect the small contractor.

Commercial Banks

Because getting help at the federal or state level requires that you work through a commercial bank, it is important to select one that sees the profit potential in serving a company of your size in the area of exports. Before giving a bank your business, the Department of Commerce recommends that you ask these questions:

- How is the bank's international department? Can they hold your hand?
- Will the bank provide the appropriate level of financing?
- Does the bank have foreign branches or correspondent banks where you want to do business?
- Does the bank confirm letters of credit directly? What are the charges for confirmation, processing drafts, and payment collection?
- Can the bank provide buyer credit reports? At what cost?
- Does the bank have experience with state and U.S. Government financing programs that support export transactions?
- What other services can it provide (e.g. trade leads)?

Reducing Risk through Insurance

Insurance is an export tool to transfer risk. Any form of risk transfer has an associated cost that has to be figured into pricing calculations. Remember that risk is in direct proportion to potential profit. The more money you can lose, the more you can make. All business, including exporting, involves risk, but your exposure in export markets ultimately should be no greater than in domestic markets.

There are some simple ways to reduce exporting risk to an acceptable level. One way is to reduce the risk of collecting money due you on your exported product or service, thus minimizing your financial exposure. The letter of credit, for example, is an inexpensive and efficient form of insurance because it dictates levels of credit risk, shipment terms, and merchandise quality. Insurance programs have evolved that hedge against risk. Basically, insurance is needed to cover three areas of risk: shipping risk, political risk, and credit risk.

Marine insurance transfers a portion of the transportation exposures to a third party insurance company to protect from the risks of export logistics and distribution. It covers against loss or damage in transit and includes shipping by any mode, such as but not limited to ocean, air, courier, foreign parcel post, rail, or truck. It is available in two forms: special cargo, which covers a single specified shipment, and open cargo, which is continuous and thus covers all cargo moving at the seller's risk. A special cargo policy is more expensive because the insurance company's risk is not spread over a large number of shipments. Because volume is the key, the cost of insurance for someone in the business of shipping—export broker, shipper, or freight forwarder—can be less expensive than it is for the small exporter.

Other physical and financial risks can be covered by an array of political and credit policies issued by both government and commercial entities for war, strikes, confiscation, and money transfer exposures. All transactions should have some form of insurance for credit, damage during shipping, and political risks.

Export Credit Check Information

There are numerous sources available for developing creditworthiness information on foreign corporations. Following is a list of recommended credit agencies:

- Veritas Group of Companies
  121 Whitney Avenue
  New Haven, CT 06510

- Kreller Business Information
  817 Main Street, 3rd Floor
  Cincinnati, OH 45202

- Credit Report Latin America and World
  PO Box 3972
  New York, NY 10163

- Status Credit Report
  21 Whitechurch Road
  Cardiff, Wales
  CF14 3 JN
  United Kingdom

- Dun & Bradstreet
  www.dnb.com
  Offices countrywide

- Owens Online
  6501 North Himes Avenue
  Suite 104
  Tampa, FL 33614

- FCIB-NACM
  www.fciglobal.com

- Graydon America
  116 John Street
  New York, NY 10038

- J.I. International
  PO Box 26
  699 Terryville Avenue
  Bristol, CT 06011

As an alternate source one can contact the U.S. Consulate or Foreign Commercial Service (outlined in the appendix) in the buyer's country for additional background and credit information.

Key Issues in Managing Letters of Credit

The principal concept behind Letters of Credit is to introduce a bank as a third party to act as an intermediary in the collection of funds for the exporter and provide certain assurances to the importer that the exporter has honored their obligation, before payment is authorized.

Many exporters use letters of credit in their payment programs. While they are somewhat complicated, the risks can be mitigated by following these eight steps:

1. Letters of credit are not guarantees. They still require the good faith and cooperation of both parties. If one party wants to rip off the other, through fraud or misrepresentation, it is easy to do. Remember, the bank in a letter of credit pays against documents. They never see the freight. One could easily create a bogus set of documents and "ship rocks." However, the bank pays against accurate documents that are presented in a timely fashion. The exporter might meet all the shipping requirements of the right product, but a mistake on the documents or presenting them after the expiration date might make it difficult to receive payment if the importer and the bank involved do not cooperate.

2. A letter of credit gets negotiated. Don't roll over when presented with a letter of credit that is not acceptable. Demand terms that you can live with and more importantly that will meet the requirements.

3. Make sure you have staff that is detailed. Letters of credit are a dot the i's and cross the t's paperwork. If you do not have the staff, then make sure your service providers do.

4. Control the freight on letters of credit. The last thing you want to do is have someone handling the shipment who works for the other guy and not you.

5. All letters of credit should be confirmed and irrevocable. Irrevocable makes it a contract that cannot be altered without the consent of both parties. Confirmation removes the political risk and credit exposure, passing it off to the bank, at a fee to the exporter.

6. Letters of credit have a cost associated with them. In some places, the cost will be as high as 15 percent, and for the exporter to confirm, the cost will be anywhere from 0.50 percent to 3 percent. Your product may lose its competitiveness when a letter of credit is the instrument of payment.

7. Develop checklists when preparing letters of credit. The following should be included:

- Name and address of beneficiary and applicant.
- Conditions and terms are doable.
- Shipping and expiration dates are checked.
- Proper INCO Terms are used.
- Correct carriers, ports, and trans-shipments are utilized.
- Proper insurance arrangements have been made.
- Drafts drawn correctly or payment arrangements.
- Documentation requirements are met.
- Paperwork is checked, checked again, and rechecked before presentation to the bank.

A more complete list of all types of export payment options, including letters of credits, is available in the appendix.

Concluding Remarks

Having export sales without payment has no value. The key to getting paid is to understand the risks and the options and to have a specific trade finance strategy as outlined in this chapter. This area must be taken very seriously as many U.S. companies have not collected payment on a timely payment and sometimes not at all.

Addressing these issues in advance and managing the foreign receivable and utilizing quality banks and insurance companies will go a long way in assuring profitable export sales.

9

Cargo Loss Control

Seventy percent of all cargo losses are controllable. If the exporter takes steps prior to export transit to work with quality forwarders and carriers and to insure suitable export packing, proper marking, labeling and documentation, there will be a dramatic reduction in the incidence of loss and damage claims.

Loss control is a science utilizing technology, experience, and good common-sense to bring about proactive actions to achieve desired results favoring loss-free exports. This chapter reviews this material in detail with recommendations for packing, materials handling, stowage, choice of carriers, etc.

Export Packing: A Mystery, an Art, and a Science

More than 70 percent of cargo losses in global trade can be attributed to loss or damage from controllable sources. The remaining 30 percent of losses from sources such as a force majeure, acts of God, etc. are uncontrollable. Water, marking/labeling, and handling damage make up most of the cargo losses that would be considered controllable. This means that actions taken by the shipper or the designated freight forwarder prior to the international journey could prevent the loss from occurring.

The key words are "actions. . . prior to the international journey." The exporter or shipper only can control what happens when the freight is in their custody, care, and control (prior to shipping). Preshipping actions greatly influence what happens to the cargo during the global transit.

We all acknowledge that international transit is subject to all kinds of impediments, including:

- Salt and fresh water hazards (including condensation)
- Multiple handling, dropping, and racking
- Conveyance stress (truck, rail, ocean, and air)
- Shock and vibration
- Cultural and language differences
- Customs and shipping delays

- Pilferage and theft deterioration

- Contamination and inherent vice

- Acts of God and forces majeure

Prudent shippers typically purchase marine cargo insurance policies to protect their interest in the cargo on an "all-risk," "warehouse to warehouse" basis. However, court precedence has dictated, and many cargo insurance underwriters warrant, that the cargo must be properly packaged for the international transit. This means that the packing the shipper uses must be able to stand up to all the hazards and impediments listed previously. If not, the ability to obtain favorable settlement on a cargo claim is severely diminished. This can mean consequential damages, as well as direct financial loss, dissatisfied customers, and the loss of future orders in addition to a big heap of aggravation, frustration, and stress.

However, there are numerous options available to exporters and shippers to manage the export packing process to maximize the opportunities to move freight in a timely manner and safely through the international transit. This is often referred to as "cargo loss control management." The necessary steps in cargo loss control management are as follows:

- Management policy

- Packing guidelines

- Carrier arrangements

- Development of resources

Management Policy

Management must recognize the value of cargo loss control and set policy for all of the operational staff to follow. It is widely recognized that money spent up-front in better packaging, labeling, and handling systems will have future financial benefits that eventually outweigh the up-front expenditures by a ten-to-one ratio.

In addition, money expended up-front is a known, budget-oriented number versus the potential uncertainty of future losses. The effort can be managed by building the costs into the sales pricing. Successful shipping to overseas consignees will justify the costing in long-term relationships.

While all companies are attempting to cut corners in expenses to make their products sell in the most competitive of global markets, packaging is rarely an area that can be traded off. Management must then set policy guidelines to instill a sense that all must be done, within cost-effective reasonableness, to assure quality outturn in export sales.

More often than not, steps in "cargo loss control" overall can become more cost-effective options for shipping, which ultimately reduce the overall expense of an international shipment. An example of this is with unitization or consolidation.

Unitization is the tying together of a smaller number of units into one handling unit. Such as putting twenty small cartons on one pallet. The pallet causes an additional expense, but goes a long way toward reducing the handling of the individual cartons. Stretch or shrink-wrap the unit load and you provide protection from moisture, contaminants, and pilferage. Carriers often provide rating discounts for unitized loads because cost of handling is reduced. These discounts negate the additional handling and material cost.

Another example is the use of master shipping cartons that are standardized in the freight industry, such as E, EH, or D containers. Smaller cartons or shipping units can be repacked or consolidated in these standard master cartons, which prevents multiple handling and pilferage and creates a barrier to moisture and contaminants. Carriers offer rating discounts for these master shipping containers that offsets the initial outlay of money.

The moneys spent up-front result in a future payback that includes more satisfied customers, better cargo outturn, reduced shipping and insurance costs, and most importantly, a continuation of more export orders. Management, once committed should:

- Set packing guidelines.
- Set carrier arrangements.
- Develop resources.

Set Packing Guidelines

Management must coordinate packing with sales, marketing, engineering, and legal in concert with logistics. Packing that is "export-ready," but does not conform with the marking and labeling requirements in the country of export might get the freight there, but it will not go to market. Packing that has a sales orientation, meets all the legal requirements, and works in the American market may not hold up well in an export logistics process that involves numerous handlings with great exposure to theft and pilferage.

The bottom line is that export packing must take all the issues into consideration. This means tight coordination to the many interests involved in the packing process from sales to marketing then to traffic management. Once the coordination occurs, export managers need to set packing guidelines and standards. These standards must be practical and cost effective. Lines of accountability between all the vested interests need to be established to assure consistent compliance.

Any export packing guidelines need to be flexible, with standards that change from mode to mode, country to country, commodity to commodity, and all the variables that could affect product outturn.

Standards should be committed to writing. It is recommended that the packing be part of the quoting process on export pro forma orders. This makes for a better sale and more clearly advises the overseas prospect of just what they are buying.

Carrier Arrangements

Packing needs to be thought-out in respect to mode and carrier. There are many issues, including:

1. The environment the freight will pass through

2. The number of multiple handling

3. Exposure to theft and pilferage

4. The various aspects of ocean versus air versus rail versus truck, etc

5. Protection from the elements

6. The nuances of the cargo

There is a tendency to choose the mode of transport based on cost. Many times that causes more expense when all the hidden costs that could be associated with a poor choice of carriers are added.

The exporter needs to know if the carriers utilize consolidation centers, where freight could be handled poorly and with greater exposure to theft and pilferage. Do they cut corners on security? Do they utilize their own operated facility or is it leased to third parties? Do they have measures of performance and accountability? Did they take the most direct route or use various substations and transfer points?

Many times by using quality and more reliable carriers that have better answers to all those questions reduces the need for additional expense in export packing. In other words, the choice of carriers and mode will influence how the goods are ultimately packed for export.

Choosing responsible, higher end carriers can be a science. Develop the options, know who the carriers management team is, obtain numerous references, and call them all!!! How long have they been in business? How long have they serviced that trade route? What is their loss record?

Export Packing: Learning Your Reference Sources

Many marine insurance cargo policies and international bills of lading refer to "adequate or proper export packing." When these entities are challenged to define proper or adequate, the response is never black and white. The reason is that there are no set guidelines that advise just what is considered adequate export packing. What constitutes adequate export packing is ultimately the judicial system that becomes involved when the issue is challenged legally.

However, there are numerous resources that can be used to assist exporters in developing proper export packaging guidelines. In general, some ocean, truck, rail, and air carriers provide certain assistance. Insurance companies, freight forwarders, surveying firms, and consultants also are available. The U.S. military has some reference material.

The best sources are surveying firms, freight forwarders (who have qualified staff), and larger carriers who have developed the expertise.

A list of some of recommended written reference material includes the following:

A Shipper's Guide to Stowage of Cargo in Marine Containers (U.S. Department of Transportation, 1982

Cargo Stowage Manual (Sea-Land Service, Inc., 1980)

Handbook of Package Engineering (McGraw Hill, 1971)

Principles of Package Development (Avi Publishing, 1972)

Stowage: The Properties and Stowage of Cargoes (Brown, Son & Ferguson, 1979)

Cargo Work (Brown, Son & Ferguson, 1981)

Packing, Volumes 1 and 2 (Defense Supply Agency, 1974)

Methods of Loading, Blocking, and Bracing (E.I. Dupont, 1988)

Cargo Handling (Work Saving International, 1984)

Containerized Transport and Marine Insurance (Munchener Ruckversicherungs-Geselschaft, 1977)

Marine Cargo Loss Prevention (Munich Re, 1985)

Ten Steps to Cargo Loss Control (American River International, 1999)

Fibre Box Handbook (Fibre Box Association, 1976)

Ports of the World (Cigna, 1990)

Cargo Loss Prevention Recommendations (International Union of Marine Insurance, 1991)

This list of references is an excellent starting point for those interested in export packing guidelines that are in print. Much of the material is available through the Internet by accessing the publisher's web sites.

Export packing usually is not an issue until it becomes an issue: a claim, a poor outturn, a dissatisfied customer right after they start screaming. It needs to be part of the overall international sales and operations thought process from the time the sale is made, through to planning, manufacturing, inventory, and shipment to the overseas customer. Moneys spent upfront have a favorable effect on the headaches, frustrations, and problems caused once a shipment goes awry.

Yes, export packing is a little bit of a mystery—an art—and science, but there are considerations to take into account and actions that can be taken by the exporter before the shipment leaves to maximize the opportunity for a successful journey.

Cargo Loss Control in International Trade

Once freight is shipped, once it is under way, once it is in the hands of international carriers, there is very little the shipper or consignee can do to prevent loss or damage. Cargo loss control is the art and science of preventing loss and damage through actions prior to shipping freight. Taking steps prior to shipping helps the importer/exporter reduce the exposures of international trade, thereby increasing the opportunity for protection of assets and future profits.

These are a few basic principles to follow in cargo loss control in international trade to reduce the opportunity and frequency of transit losses. One should be aware that over 70 percent of transit loss is due to water, theft, and handling damage, all of which could be seriously mitigated or prevented by steps taken prior to freight being shipped.

The Right Attitude

Management must develop a policy and credo that loss and damage can and will be kept to a minimum and that all steps must be taken to have products arrive in a safe, sound, and customer-satisfied condition. Study after study has proven that an ounce of prevention is worth a pound of cure. Any dollars spent up-front to better package freight or ship with a more quality carrier, etc., come back in spades in loss-free shipping, lower insurance costs, and more satisfied customers. Management needs to be committed to this concept. It requires cost in money, time, and resources that must be allocated to achieve desired results.

Packaging and Labeling

It cannot be said enough that one must "export pack" all international freight shipments. This means that the packaging must be able to stand up to the rigors of international exposure, principally water and handling. Packaging used to move freight from Lake Ronkonkoma, New York to Columbus, Ohio is not the same as packaging used to move freight from Cleveland, Ohio to Tokyo, Japan. There are different, more severe exposures, which means different, more stringent criteria.

Fiberboard cartons, the most frequently used shipping container, should be at least double-wall and of a bursting strength of not less than 275 pounds; triple wall for high value and breakable items. The product should be adequately protected with cushioning and padding. Plastic coating and wax impregnation assist in waterproofing, along with strength- and shrink-wrapping.

Blind product identification also reduces theft. There is usually no reason to advertise what's inside the package in international transportation.

Marking and labeling of freight is as critical as the packaging. In every freight terminal there are areas "to the side" that hold freight for which the destination or point of origin cannot be identified. Lost freight is a frequent and serious problem.

Packages should have secure, multiple labels with the consignee clearly identified. Use of foreign languages can be helpful. Return shipping addresses with telephone numbers are important. The labeling should be waterproof and secure enough to deal with the multiple handling of global transportation. Freight forwarders, carriers, insurance companies, and the U.S. Government are excellent resources for specific packaging guidelines for international trade (Figure 9-1).

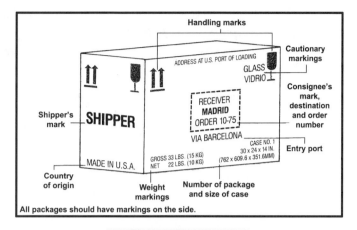

Figure 9-1. Packaging Guidelines for International Trade.

Documentation

All international freight needs a passport to travel through the maze of global obstacles, hazards, and barriers. The passport is the documentation that precedes or accompanies cargo in international shipping that allows the carrier to move the freight and customs to clear it for ultimate delivery to the overseas customer. It is imperative that the documentation be timely, accurate, and meets all the needs of all the parties requiring the paperwork to complete the trade.

Typical international documents such as, but not limited to, bills of lading, dock receipts, commercial invoices, packing lists, certificates of origin, and import and export licenses must all work together to affect a successful international transaction. Poor documentation many times is the reason for loss and damage. This causes delay and undue handling and sometimes inspection that opens the "Pandora's Box" to greater loss potential. Delays in customs in some foreign countries can result in serious problems. While the cargo waits for clearance, there is the potential for increased handlings and exposure to the elements. Foreign surveys often have determined that the greater opportunity for loss on international shipments occurs during the clearance process.

Other considerations in documentation are the language it is written in, legalization and notarization requirements, number of copies, who needs to receive it, and how it ultimately appears. Freight forwarders, custom-house brokers, chambers of commerce and consulates can assist you in the preparation of all international documents.

For shippers to remain competitive in international trade they must have satisfied customers who receive sound product on a timely basis with the most cost-effective transportation and logistics services. Cargo loss control is a method to accomplish this now and for the long-term.

Minimizing Cargo Losses in the Transport of Bulk Liquids

An increasing number of distribution managers are being asked to show better profits and reduce costs on transportation movements. Losses associated with transportation movements cut sharply into accomplishing these goals. One area of significant concern is the problems inherent in the movement of bulk liquids.

Bulk liquids movements involve two inherent dangers that can reduce profit: shortages and contamination.

While many losses occur as a result of shortage and contamination that are due to forces majeure, or reasons beyond the control of the shipper and carrier, it is estimated that at least 80 percent of these types of losses are caused by action or inaction of the shipper and the inland or international transportation companies.

Losses: Real or Imagined?

Determining the quantity of bulk liquids at any given point in the distribution channel from seller to buyer is a difficult task. The area in which shippers and carriers fall down most consistently is accountability and its documentation at each carrier interface between the shipper and consignee. One method of determining accountability through an independent source is using surveyors who can certify in a test or inspection the quality and quantity of the product. Typically, the surveyor utilizes an outside agency or testing laboratory to assist in measuring the quality and determine the quantity or count on his/her own. In a transportation movement, particularly over a long distance or on an international basis, this poses a continuing problem. The survey and techniques utilized to determine the quantity loaded are often not the same as the techniques used to measure the quantity at discharge. For example, one surveyor may round off at decimal point .000 while another may round off in whole numbers. When dealing with hundreds and thousands of tons, a small variation in rounding-off could result in a 1 percent to 2 percent loss in weight or volume. Differences between U.S. and metric standards cause problems. Differences in the way measurement is made by using ullages, draft surveys, or weight measurements also lead to quantity variations.

Why Measurements Fail

Gauging and sampling of bulk liquids is an art, not a science. Because the volume and density of a liquid are continually changing with ambient temperatures, measurement with gauging equipment varies. Calibrating tables are dependent upon the dimensional stability of the containment tank, which will also vary.

For example, a barge that is considered to be a certain volume in its internal dimensions may be considerably dented on the outside from collisions with various tugs, docks, etc., and therefore its internal measurement may be off quite consistently. One may assume that the vessel is full and therefore holds a certain amount of product. If there is considerable denting inwards along the structure of the hull of the vessel or conveyance tank car, etc., the total amount of product assumed to be in the conveyance will not actually be there.

During transit or pumping it is often necessary to heat, agitate, or vent the cargo. With pipeline distances and the variable tank configurations, this process may not allow a homogeneous distribution of temperature throughout the liquid, further complicating the gauging and sampling process. This is particularly true of older conveyances and storage points.

Finally, there are human variables that are influenced by environmental factors, condition and calibration of measuring equipment, international and domestic trade, differences in language, and customs and trade procedures.

If a conveyance is being loaded in Michigan during the winter months and a terminal operator is asked to take an ullage when the temperature is 30 degrees below zero with winds as high as 70 miles per hour, the quality of the work will be diminished. There may also be circumstances where somebody will not leave the comfort of a warm terminal house and will just estimate or use the last figure for his ullage.

Passing the Bulk

The problems associated with determining the amount and quality of liquid at arrival is further complicated by the fact that the liquid could be transferred up to seven or eight different times during transit and at each carry interface, the art of gauging and sampling is required.

This is true particularly on international shipments where there may be four or five different conveyance or transportation companies involved. On such a shipment cargo transfer could occur from five to seven times, with opportunities for additional storage or transfer exposure with transshipments.

These carrier interfaces could also bring about changes of mode from barge to tank car, tank truck to pipeline, temporary storage at the port of loading or discharge, as well as the loading and discharge of the vessel or barge. There are normally acceptable trade loss or clingage allowances involved in each of these transfers, further complicating the problem of determining the quantity to be expected on arrival.

Clingage is the amount remaining in the conveyance or pipeline due to the normal adhesion of the product, also referred to as trade loss. This should be the amount anticipated by the buyer that will be unavailable at discharge.

Survey, which is the traditional manner by which the quality and measure of cargo placed into transit by the seller is determined, is an area that can be improved. Surveys should be required at all carrier interfaces where the goods change transportation companies or mode to provide a trail of documentation for accountability. When transportation and storage companies are aware that they will be held accountable, their interest in caring for the cargo increases in direct proportion to their involvement with complaining shippers or receivers presenting documented claims.

Due to many environmental and human variables that are involved in the art of gauging and sampling bulk liquids, through various trade associations buyers are striving towards requiring standardized survey and procedures and gauge and equipment tables of measure to control the gauging and sampling process as completely as possible. Standardization would facilitate review of the trail of accountable documents in each carrier interface to determine responsibility for loss or contamination during transit. On the individual level, the shipper can use the following ten action steps as a guide for minimizing loss and damage during bulk cargo movements:

1. **Product Control.** The first step is in-house controls to insure proper preparation and shipping of the product. This requires quality control standards governing the handling of the product before it is loaded into the transit conveyance of pipeline, as well as proper procedures to document the process.

2. **Trading Control.** This entails making sure the traders and sales personnel are aware of limitations in the distribution channels, which will control the sales function. They must know the product, the mode of transportation, distribution times, etc. They must also be aware of the appropriate level of trade loss, which is typically standardized within an industry.

3. **Surveying Firms.** Personal and professional relationships must be established with surveying firms that have established, favorable track records. But while a long-term relationship based on past performance is an excellent idea, complacency on the

part of service companies can lead to a decline in performance. Therefore, occasional changes in business arrangements with surveyors should be arranged to insure their competitiveness and quality. Insurance brokers and underwriters are excellent sources for leads on qualified surveyors.

4. **Survey and Procedures.** Guidelines must be established, implemented, and monitored for standardizing surveying practices and procedures throughout all the interfaces a bulk cargo will transit. The methods for surveying and establishing lines of accountability from beginning of transit to final destination must be harmonious and in total synchronization to eliminate spurious deviations.

5. **Documentation.** In conjunction with establishing surveying practice and procedure, documentation is vital to obtain prudent lines of accountability. Just accomplishing the survey is only half the job—it must then be documented. Shippers and operators should require that certain documents be completed prior to acceptance or transfer of cargo.

6. **Selection of Carriers.** In today's world of price cutting and rate slashing, a shipper may be prone to choose a cheaper carrier. However, a less expensive carrier may be one who in the long run increases the shipper's loss exposures. There are particular carriers who have very successfully handled bulk liquids and have excellent track records. These are the ones who should be considered if they are available.

7. **Selection of Terminals.** This is as important as carrier selection. If the wrong terminal or storage facility is used, it can lead to significant exposures, particularly in regard to contamination. There are many terminals whose higher storage rates are actually the favorable rates due to their records of loss experiences.

8. **Action Loss Steps.** A plan of action should be developed regarding what steps should be taken in the event of a loss. Sending backup material, preparing new replacement orders, arranging for temporary storage, surveys, and documenting insurance claims are all among the considerations that should be addressed by these contingency plans. Preparing in advance the steps that will be taken helps to mitigate the loss and satisfy the customer's needs at an earlier date. Designed action plans and claims management manuals, providing step-by-step procedures, should be included in insurance brokerage services.

9. **Representation.** Shippers should make a habit of visiting the various carrier facilities and storage terminals where the cargo will be handled. It has been determined that when a transportation or storage company is aware that it will be held accountable

and the client shows a personal interest in the operations and the way the cargo is being handled, the service company's interest in caring for the cargo increases proportionately.

10. **Insurance Programs.** Even in the best of circumstances, there will be losses to cargo as a result of quality or count. An insurance program covering against all losses from fortuitous causes provides protection. The basic insurance policy provides "all-risk, warehouse to warehouse" protection. Special insurance can also be arranged, including "guaranteed outturn," that pays for claims also noted as "paper shortages," where there is a difference between shipped and outturned weights and no evidence of physical loss or damage from an external cause. A shipper or receiver of cargo responsible for insurance should enlist the services of a sophisticated marine broker and insurance company to ensure that the broadest coverage at the most competitive price has been obtained.

Paper Handlers Move to Cut Insurance Costs

According to a recent survey of industry experts, 70 to 80 percent of cargo losses for U.S. paper and pulp exporters are controllable. In addition, for shippers, insurance has become a significant cost factor for transportation. The market has turned and prices have jumped substantially. Anything that a shipper can do to reduce insurance costs is going to greatly enhance the competitive sales price in global markets.

In the area of pulp and paper exports, there are several recommended loss control measures, particularly with respect to improper handling and stowage and water damage. Steamship companies and terminal operators who are dictated to by time, available space, vessel/port rotation, high stevedoring expenses, and other factors often lose sight of common-sense approaches to proper pulp and paper stowage and handling.

Industry experts have provided these recommendations to insured's since 1981 with positive results. Marine underwriters and brokers are often a source of expertise for loss control assistance.

Affecting the Bottom Line: Marine Cargo Loss Control in the Pulp and Paper Industry

"Affecting the bottom line," refers to reducing transportation expenses and increasing sales. Two simple facts must be agreed to: a cost of transportation is insurance, and lower prices and better product outturn increase sales.

The key to accomplishing the two goals is marine cargo loss control. Specific examples, case studies, and effective loss control management principles of marine cargo loss control follow. The topics of marine insurance, distribution hazards, and recommendations are presented in depth with background material and, ultimately, the combined effect of these areas is presented.

Definitions of key terms follow.

Marine Insurance. Coverage by contract whereby one party (marine underwriter) undertakes to indemnify or guarantee another against loss by a specific peril while in marine transit; usually for a consideration referred to as a premium.

Outturn. The element of time cargo arrives at final destination, which may or may not be the port area.

Loss Control. Any intentional action directed at the prevention, reduction, or elimination of the pure risks of business.

Cost Effective. Resultant benefits outweigh the costs to attain those benefits.

Controllable Losses. Losses that can be reduced through action in packaging, materials handling, stowage, and other distribution functions, such as rough handling, improper stowage, water damage, etc.

Loss Audit. The act of evaluating past loss experience so that trends can be documented and measured to lay the groundwork for loss control actions. Detailed loss audits also study claims files for accuracy and performance of underwriters, brokers, surveyors, and claim-settling agents.

Marine Insurance

Exporters buy marine cargo insurance for various reasons, including bank requirements, letters of credit, contract requirements, customer needs, claims settling facilities, etc. However, the major reason for buying cargo policies is to protect insurable interests whether they be material, financial, good faith, or some other interest.

Keeping that in mind, marine underwriters provide a financial tool: the cargo policy, for protection of that interest. Marine underwriters, like other companies, are looking for a reasonable profit. Too often they are viewed as adversaries instead of business partners. A good insurance broker matches exporters with underwriters that establish a good relationship that makes for effective, sound business partners.

The marine underwriter has a vested interest in your company's well-being because as you prosper and grow, so will the underwriter. Therefore, they are more than willing to cooperate with exporters to provide adequate and reasonable protection, fair rates, settling and surveying facilities, claims statistics, and loss control expertise. Underwriters are experienced loss and damage professionals and should be considered sources of loss control talent.

Brokers provide intermediary services and are an additional source of underwriting, claims, and loss control expertise. Many marine insurance companies, such as CIGNA, AIG, Great American, and Chubb, have ex-merchant marine officers on staff to help evaluate packaging, stowage. and materials handling functions.

Unfortunately, pulp and paper exporters suffer a frequency of losses resulting from improper handling and stowage and water damage. An exporter has two sound choices to lower insurance costs in the face of frequency of handling, stowage, and water damage claims:

1. The exporter, through the broker/underwriter, should evaluate loss frequency and magnitude to choose levels at which deductibles are warranted. Small dollar losses (for general purposes, $500 or less) often mean assureds are trading dollars with underwriters for losses under this amount. This is a dollar for dollar program. Surveying expenses and settling fees often are larger than actual loss estimates. There comes a point when it is less expensive for the exporter to pay for losses under certain dollar amounts than it is to insure these losses. Underwriters could still handle the small loss and provide first dollar coverage to foreign customers through "buyback" arrangements and bill the U.S. exporter for under-deductible losses.

2. The exporter can take measures to reduce losses to levels where the operation will be more competitive. Seventy to 80 percent of marine cargo losses are controllable. Studies of pulp and paper exports of major U.S. export accounts document that figures of 70 to 80 percent are accurate. Brokers and underwriters are more than willing to provide loss control studies to document problem areas and offer recommendations to management with viable and cost-effective alternatives.

Distribution Hazards

Rough handling is a major contributor to loss for pulp and paper exports. It begins in the United States at the ports of loading through railcar, truck, and barge off-loadings to warehouse handling, and finally, to loading of the merchant vessels.

Stowage as an extension of handling is another major contributor of cargo losses particularly in break bulk vessels. Steamship companies and terminal operators who are controlled by time, available space, vessel/port rotation, high stevedoring expenses, and other factors often lose sight of common-sense approaches to proper pulp and paper stowage and handling methods.

Rough handling is typically most significant during vessel loading where, for example, rolls of paper are jammed and crushed into stowage positioning. Rolls are often torn and chaffed by handling "dogs" improperly aligned, stevedores moving too quickly, rolls bumping into the vessel's protrusions, and the use of improper equipment. More severe damages such as core deformation or excessive ply damage are a result of outright abuse as in the case of rolls dropping onto the pier apron or vessels deck from heights of 20 feet plus.

Stowage is a problem to vessel owners who have to stow rolls of linerboard with different heights and circumferences into odd shape holes.

Adding to the problem is additional cargo with completely different shapes such as pulp, lumber or plywood which are typically "room-mates" to linerboard exports. Vessel's owners attempting to maximize vessel efficiency try to decrease the ship's "turnaround" time, and in doing so, hurriedly handle and stow cargo, resulting in further damages.

Water damage is another significant loss contributor. Shipments by LASH Barges are often riddled with water damage claims. With many older barges the LASH system has difficulty in maintaining adequate watertight integrity, which often means leaking hatch covers.

In lash barges, vessel holds, steamship containers, condensation presents additional water hazards that are typically underestimated but account for frequent and large water claims. For example, warm, moist air in a U.S. Gulf Coast vessel loading will condense onto the vessel's overheads and bulk-heads as the vessel transits to cooler latitudes. This condensation accumulates on the deck where the cargo is laying or will drip onto cargo directly.

Keep in mind certain cargo losses are not controllable— sinking, stranding, fire, etc. but statistics have demonstrated these catastrophe losses typically only account for less than 20 percent of cargo losses leaving approximately 80 percent of losses that can be controlled. The next section of this chapter addresses specific solutions for controlling losses.

Vessel discharge is dictated by stowage and improper stowage often leading to difficult unloading that causes additional cargo damage. Inland warehousing and transit particularly in third world countries is less than adequate and presents severe exposures for cargo. In some countries, the inland transit is more severe than the ocean leg. A quality insurance broker, based with CNA in New York City is Michele Milone, who is considered a seasoned professional in credit insurance.

Loss Control Recommendations

The following eleven recommendations are offered to the pulp and paper industry for exports of linerboard and pulp. The recommendations are generalized, and discretion should be utilized by each exporter to weigh the merits of the recommendation for his/her own facility as well as tailor it to meet specific distribution operation.

1. Marine Underwriters and Brokers. Marine underwriters and brokers are often a source of expertise for loss control assistance. Utilize their services as your premium dollars are paying for their time and labor. Marine underwriters and brokers usually can provide local talent overseas for difficult claims settling, surveying, and interpretation of local laws/regulations/customs, etc.

2. Pre- and Postshipment Surveys. On a regular basis or by spot checking these surveys are often an excellent source for setting up proper handling and stowage; as well as having someone there who could document the accountability of the stevedores and steamship company. Surveyors, particularly with a maritime background, lend practical experience and often can be considered extensions of corporate traffic and warehousing functions.

3. Preparing Loss Audits. Audits will document loss trends and weigh problem areas. Once problems are identified, studies can be made to evaluate alternative solutions and cost-effective actions. Remember that marine underwriters and brokers are excellent sources for loss information. Utilization of EDI formats assist in auditing volumes of loss data and often can provide reports by mill, nature of loss, vessel name, ports of loading/discharge, etc.

4. Strapping and Roll Packing Linerboard.
   A. All wood plugs should be placed securely and flush to the roll's end in the core.
   B. Consider using three straps around the roll's girth in lieu of two (one at each end and one in the center).
   C. Many times rolls have straps with tails of 1 to 3 feet hanging loosely off the roll. The end strap should be placed as close to the end as possible without overhanging it, approximately 1/2 inch to 1 inch.
   D. Straps should be a minimum of 1/2 inch, preferably 3/4 inch in lieu of the current 3/8- inch strap.

5. Trucks, Container, and Railcars for Linerboard Transport.
   A. Only rolls that can stand vertically in the inland conveyances should be loaded. The procedure of placing rolls on their bilges (horizontally) in the second tier should not be followed. Stevedores have difficulty, particularly with low overheads, in grabbing the top tier, horizontally stowed rolls and many times when grabbing is impossible will pull the roll out until it falls to the deck of the railcar and then pick it up with the clamps. This can cause the roll's core to be deformed.

   This difficulty in obtaining the top tier rolls is common and only a few shippers stow rolls on the bilges in the second tier.
   B. Make sure access to removing rolls from transit conveyances is attainable. Often shippers should utilize "key" rolls that allow ready access by longshoremen. If access is difficult, longshoremen will damage cargo attempting to discharge the stows.

6. Warehousing: Vessel Loading.
   A. Terminal operators should be required to take exceptions as soon as the cargo comes out of the inland conveyances in lieu of typical procedures where exceptions are taken once the cargo is moved into the transit shed.
   B. Cargo handling should terminate when there is precipitation.
   C. Terminal operators should consider placing dunnage on the transit shed deck to keep the cargo away from areas where moisture and contaminants collect.
   D. Terminal operators should be required to maintain clean decks and storage spaces. At some terminals, debris, broken wires, dirt, rubber tire residue, etc. are on the deck, particularly on the pier apron. This can stain and/or cut into the cargo ends.

E. Terminal operators should be required to close all openings of the transit shed during rain showers. At certain ports, precipitation causes puddles of water that enter shed openings and run into contact with the cargo. Cargo will at times remain in these puddles until vessel loading, which can be more than a day away.

7. Vessel Loading.
   A. Steamship companies should be forced into being more conscientious about management and supervision during the vessel loading. Usually there is little supervision or direction of the longshoremen, which is a primary reason for the frequency of pulp and paper damages during loading.
   B. Steamship companies should maintain a tight stow reducing the frequency and size of void areas as much as possible. We are confident this can be accomplished by the following: (1) supervising the longshoremen; (2) allowing more time to place the rolls tightly rather than rushing to stow; (3) better management of prestowage plans; (4) using dunnage in void areas such as with 2-inch or 4-inch wood pieces or experimentation with air bags.
   C. When spreader bars are used to handle cargo, a lanyard should be placed to allow the longshoremen to control the swinging of the spreader bar as it is being brought onto the vessel. This would prevent the cargo from hitting against the sides of the bulkhead and adjacent cargo and would allow faster and easier handling.
   D. On all conveyances, particularly vessel's holds, the deck should be dunnaged with pallets prior to loading so as to put an area of separation between the rolls and the deck where water and contaminants will collect.

8. Prestowage Plans for Linerboard.
   A. To facilitate prestowage, an inventory list should be sent to the pier prior to arrival so that pier personnel may coordinate the transit shed stow when the linerboard arrives for staging at the pier. This would eliminate a step in roll segregation as well as reduce some of the damage occurring to the rolls during handling. This procedure would allow the rolls to be brought to the vessel in size order, facilitating stowage within the vessel thereby reducing the uneven tiers, a cause of damage.
   B. Color code cargo for easier segregation and identification.

9. Moisture Proofing. Shrink-wrapping and stretch-wrapping offer inexpensive methods to individually shroud rolls of paper or bales of pulp. Additionally, the wrapping offers a level of protection against dirt and contaminants. If individual bales and rolls are not shrouded, then consideration should be given to laying shrouds over complete stows draped down to the deck to shed water away from the cargo.

Conveyance decks should be dunnaged with pallets to put distance between the deck and cargo where moisture and contaminants will collect.

10. Claims Management. Maintain tight control over cargo claims activity by having overseas claims processed through one central location, such as your insurance brokerage or underwriting facility. These companies process, adjust, and manage all overseas claims so control and accountability are centralized. This centralization offers substantial benefits such as positive cash flow thru expedient claims settlement, continuity of claims adjustments, and a source for EDP loss statistics.

11. Foreign Warehousing. Exporters should consider the advantages of utilizing overseas distribution center warehousing where they have frequent sales. These warehouses would store U.S. product overseas prior to final transit to foreign customers. This step would segregate damaged from sound product and allow only sound product to be sold to customers. The warehouse could also serve as a recoopering and salvage facility. These facilities have provided a competitive edge over northern European pulp and paper distributors.

Summary

Pulp and paper exporters can look to marine underwriters as a source of cooperation and expertise in evaluating marine transit exposures and applying appropriate deductible levels. They will also be a source for claims management systems and loss control professionals. Underwriters and brokers should be viewed as partners in business affairs rather than as adversaries.

Marine insurance professionals can be keys to an effective loss control program.

Exporters must identify and measure distribution hazards and their effect on cargo outturns. This chapter highlighted the most severe hazards of handling, stowage, and water damage, but each shipper must use discretion as a shipper's distribution system may produce or amplify hazards not previously identified as major loss contributors.

Once distribution hazards are identified, specific loss control recommendations can be applied to reduce the opportunity for loss and damage. Eleven specific loss control actions that have produced positive results when applied in pulp and paper exports for shippers who have utilized them were outlined in this chapter.

Insurance is a cost in moving cargo. Minimize the cost, and you reduce the transportation expense and become more competitive. Unfavorable cargo outturn is not a desirable result. Enhance cargo outturn, and the likely result will be satisfied customers and more sales. Marine cargo loss control is an important method that will affect the bottom line.

Containing Losses on Ocean Shipments

Intermodal containers are now the primary mode of transportation for shippers in most parts of the world. As the advantages of containerization have been more clearly identified, distribution managers have moved away from the traditional breakbulk mode to the point where some firms' imports and exports are 100 percent containerized.

One of the most important factors contributing to the popularity of the intermodal boxes among shippers and carriers alike is that they help prevent losses. The *Handbook of Package Engineering* (McGraw Hill, New York, 1971) noted throughout the 1900s that "Damage, shortage, and pilferage losses have been reduced from ten to less than one percent, insurance rates are almost cut in half, and delivery time reduced by one-third," through the use of ocean containers.

However, the picture is not entirely rosy. Containerization has its own unique hazards. It has even amplified some of the traditional problems associated with marine transportation. There are basically six hazard areas associated with containerization: weight restrictions, stowage on the vessel, cargo packing, moisture and condensation, mode, and stowage.

A fine line governs weight restrictions that must be defined by the shipper or consolidator. The governing local, state, federal, and international mandates must be adhered to and identified. An intermodal shipment may come under any or all of these jurisdictions, and the person preparing that shipment must be aware of which apply.

Stowage on the vessel is not a direct concern of the shipper. Shippers have little control once the container leaves their premises. One thing a shipper should do, however, is alert the carrier or forwarder to all factors affecting the cargo. These include hazards, stowage needs under deck or on deck, temperature and climate restrictions, etc.

It is sometimes incorrectly assumed that containerization replaces export packing. Each shipment must be judged separately before the decision is made to export pack or use standard domestic packing. Part of this process is to determine whether or not the shipment moves in a house-to-house, house-to-pier, pier-to-house, or pier-to-pier mode. A house-to-house mode gives the shipper maximum control over how the freight will be handled, otherwise packaging should be designed to survive the toughest leg of the journey.

Packaging should provide containment, restraint, cushioning and moisture, and odor barriers where needed. Remember, a container is like a "minihold" on the vessel. It is subject to the same strain, stresses, and movements as the vessel.

Manual handling is the major cause of damage. In container shipments other than house-to-house shipments, handling during loading and unloading is out of the control of the shipper and is typically of a rough nature. But there are some things a shipper can do to better protect the cargo.

Unitizing on pallets and securing the cargo with stretch or shrink film definitely helps. Reducing the number of exposed surfaces in a unit load helps prevent stowage and handling damage and pilferage too. Outer packages offer protection to inner units. Unit loads store more uniformly within the container and usually cost less to block and brace.

Overall, handling of unit loads will be easier and safer at each stage. Inventory and count control will be easier, transportation equipment can be turned around faster, and the film can provide a barrier against moisture and contaminants.

Bags, Cartons, and Drums

Kraft multiwall paper bags, which are used widely, stow well in containers. In an international movement where bags are subject to various handlings and marine exposures, the shipper may be well advised to consider increasing the number of plies, using a poly liner or laminate. Stretch or shrink film will also provide added protection. Multiwall kraft or synthetic bags, which have a high level of tear resistance, are good moisture barriers. Cross-tier stacking helps prevent shifting and maximizes stowage capacity.

In house-to-house movements, the most popular shipping container probably is the fiberboard carton. When properly palletized and shrink or stretch wrapped, domestic grade fiberboard will hold up well. However, should the shipment be other than house-to-house, the strength of the fiberboard may have to be upgraded. A double- or triple-wall may be necessary, and moisture-resistant properties ought to be considered.

When containers are broken down and individual cartons are stored in transit sheds or warehouses out of the shipper's control, the strength of the corrugated cartons should be considered carefully. This is necessary because stacking heights are likely to exceed package restrictions. In addition, all seams and closures should be secured with waterproof tapes. Strapping should be used to reinforce cartons.

Drums are also widely used in international distribution. They are generally fiber drums or 55-gallon steel drums and usually hold bulk powder and liquid chemicals. A large percentage of products shipped in drums have special requirements or hazardous qualities covered by the Department of Transportation's Code of Federal Regulations Title 49 or by local regulations in the destination country. The handling environment and possible excessive roughness also should be kept in mind when specifying drums.

How Dry It Is

A main function of containers is to protect the cargo from the elements. The key offender is precipitation. Containers do have leak-through holes and weak seals, causing millions of dollars in cargo damage annually.

Containers should be inspected for holes prior to loading freight. However, a box may be punctured during handling. There are four sources for this type of damage. The container may receive a puncture from an exterior force when racked against the ship's superstructure or from pier equipment. It may receive a puncture from the cargo itself or from dunnage breaking loose. Another opportunity for punctures occurs when transit locks or the lifting frame come down into the corner castings to handle the container. If not properly aligned, they may puncture holes in the container ceiling. Finally, the roof of the container may be punctured by a longshoreman walking on it during stowage or off-loading.

When cargo is loaded in a warm, moist atmosphere and transits to cooler latitudes, water vapor in the air will condense on the cooler surfaces of the container walls and ceiling. It will accumulate into droplets and then drip onto the cargo. This is known as container sweat.

In the same manner, cargo sweat occurs when the surface of the cargo is cooler than the atmosphere in the container. This causes condensation on the cargo itself.

These condensation processes could interchange intermittently throughout the length of the voyage, particularly when containers are stowed on deck. The containers on deck are warmed by direct sunlight during the day and cooled during evening hours. Possible cures for the condensation problem include packaging methods such as: using vented containers to reduce internal temperatures and vent moisture vapor, insulating containers, or using dunnage or pallets to keep cargo away from the deck and walls where moisture collects.

Other methods include draping a polyethylene shroud over the cargo; using desiccants to control moisture; using moisture absorbent liners and paints to prevent droplets from forming on the container walls; predrying the product; or using kiln-dried lumber in packing, pallets, and dunnage.

The Mode Sets the Mood

The mode of transportation also affects the cargo. The different stresses associated with the various modes must be considered. Typically, a pier-to-pier shipment uses only one mode—the vessel. However, as industry moves further into intermodalism, containers encounter additional modes that amplify old hazards as well as introduce new ones.

A container moving inland in an intermodal move may move over the road as a trailer exchange unit, by rail as a container on flatcar (COFC) movement, or possibly by barge or coastal carrier. Forces affecting the over-the-road leg of the journey include acceleration, deceleration, vibration, retardation, and centrifugal force. The COFC experiences the same forces, but they are greatly modified. Especially critical on the rail movement are acceleration and deceleration during switching and humping.

Shipboard transit subjects the container to the vessel's six basic motions: pitch, sway, heave, yaw, roll, and surge. A combination of these movements may affect the container at any time. Barges and feederline vessels may be more prone to extremes of these forces because the crafts are smaller than deep sea ships.

Many different products and package types, each with different transit requirements, may be stowed in a container. It is nearly impossible to define with 100 percent accuracy what the stowage requirements will be for all products.

General Packaging and Stowage Considerations for Marine Containerization

Twenty years ago containerization was an innovative mode of transit. Today, it is a proven and successful mode of transport comprising a significant part of the marine shipments for compatible breakbulk type cargoes. Damage, shortage, and pilferage losses have been reduced from 10 percent to less than 1 percent, insurance rates are almost cut in half and delivery time is reduced by one-third.

As the advantages and uses are more clearly identified, distribution managers are selecting the intermodal container in lieu of the traditional breakbulk mode. In some corporate distribution plans containerization already represents 100 percent of the shipment mode for their imports and exports.

However, with its advantage and benefits, it has its own unique hazards and has sustained and amplified some of the traditional exposures in the marine environment. The following discussion outlines these marine exposures and offers viable considerations to reduce loss and damage.

Hazards

Hazards encountered in shipping of marine containerized cargo are similar to those shipping breakbulk cargo: weight restrictions, stowage on vessel, moisture and condensation, mode, vessel motion and stowage, packaging, and containerization.

There is little the shipper can do in regard to weight restrictions and stowage on vessel. These are primarily the carrier's responsibility. However, there is a fine line in weight restrictions that must be defined by the shipper and/or consolidator and be adhered to according to local, state, federal, and foreign mandates.

Stowage on vessel is not necessarily a direct concern for the shipper who has little control over this function once the container leaves the premises. Nonetheless, the shipper should alert the carrier to all factors that affect the cargo, e.g., hazards, stowage under deck and on deck, temperature restrictions, dangerous goods, inherent natures, etc. These factors affect stowage onboard but are primarily the concern of the carrier rather than the shipper. Shippers should also be sensitive to "hazardous qualities" of cargo in transit as public awareness is paramount and government regulations are predominant here and abroad.

Moisture and Condensation

A significant form of moisture in containers that causes problems is condensation. Loss control consultants see condensation as a problem area often overlooked by distribution personnel. When cargo is loaded in a warm, moist atmosphere and transits to cooler latitudes, water suspended in the air (water vapor) will condense on the cooler surface of the container walls and overhead and will accumulate into droplets that will drip down on the cargo surfaces and cause damage. This is known as container sweat. Cargo sweat is when the surface of the cargo is cooler than the atmosphere in the container and water vapor condenses on the surface of the cargo. These condensation processes could interchange intermittently throughout an entire voyage, particularly when containers are stowed on deck that would be warmed by direct sunlight during the day and cooled during the evening hours.

General considerations for moisture protection in containers include the following:

1. It is important that the exterior packing material, e.g., barrier wrappers, shrouds, coatings and laminating, etc., provide a barrier to moisture so that the product can be suitably protected.

2. Vented containers can be used successfully to reduce internal temperatures of the container and to vent moisture vapor. Insulating containers maintain internal temperatures by controlling and limiting the effect of the external ambient temperature.

3. Follow strict guidelines when inspecting and documenting the condition of the container prior to loading and when a loaded container arrives prior to unloading. These procedures are outlined under "Containerization—General Considerations."

4. Cargo should be dunnaged off the deck such as with pallets to put a distance between the cargo and the deck where moisture may collect.

5. A polyethylene shroud should be placed over the cargo draping down the sides and to the deck at the container doors to shed moisture away from the cargo.

6. Use of desiccants has some but little effect on the controlling of moisture vapor in the container's atmosphere.

7. Utilization of moisture absorbing liners and water vapor absorbing paints that sponge up moisture in the air, rather than allow it to form droplets on the surface.

8. A source of moisture can be the product itself or its packaging. For many commodities, such as coffee and cocoa beans, fiberboard and corrugated materials will hold up to 75 percent of their weight with water. Green lumber used in box, crate, pallet, or dunnage construction material can hold up to 70 percent moisture. Utilization of kiln-dried lumber reduces this. Predrying the product and limitation of moisture content prior to exporting should be maintained.

Containerization Mode

The word "mode" means the method of transport of the container itself. Thus, a pier-to-pier container typically has only one mode—the vessel. However, as industry progresses with intermodalism, the container is transiting several additional modes that amplify hazards as well as introduce new ones. The container that moves inland in a house-to-house or pier-to-house mode will transit over the road as a twenty-foot equivalent unit (TEU); via rail, known as "piggy backing" or containers on flatcar

(COFC); or via barge or small feeder vessels across narrow waterways, intercoastal, or up rivers.

Over the road forces that affect the TEU are acceleration, deceleration, vibration, retardation, and centrifugal forces. COFC movements will be affected by those same hazards. The acceleration and deceleration forces will be amplified, particularly during the humping and switching operations in rail yards. On long rail movements, the spacing of ties could develop a negative resonance that could loosen internal blocking and bracing and internal packing restraints or affect the product directly.

Vessel Motion and Stowage

There are six basic ship motions that affect containerized cargo: pitch, sway, heave, yaw, roll, and surge (Figure 9-2). It is likely that a combination of these movements will affect the container at one moment in time.

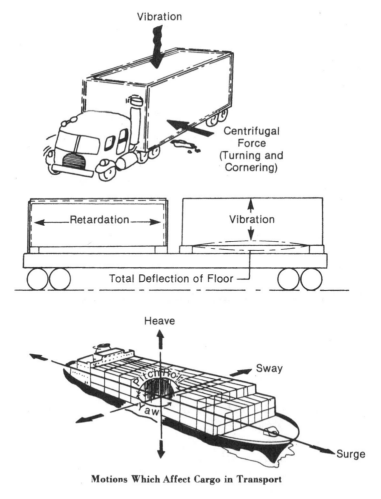

Motions Which Affect Cargo in Transport

Figure 9-2. Six Basic Ship Motions that Affect Containerized Cargo.

Barge shipments or feeder vessel movements have similar forces that affect the container. However, because the barge or feeder typically is smaller than the seagoing vessel and could be affected more readily or more severely by wind, sea, and wave action, the effects of these forces could be more prominent.

Because different products and package types have different transit requirements, it is almost impossible to define 100 percent the stowage requirements for all products. General guidelines and principles must be developed and then adapted to meet the specific requirements of the product and its package. Following are some examples of helpful guidelines:

1. Attempt to distribute the weight of the cargo throughout the container deck. Load the container evenly with the weighted items distributed over the length instead of concentrated at either end or the middle. A good idea is to use pallets or spreader bars to distribute the weight of concentrated items.

2. Stow heavier goods on the bottom and lighter units on top.

3. Dunnage all voids. Wood is useful, but air bags are useful where wood dunnage is not feasible, such as in small space or oddly configured areas.

4. Block and brace all heavy loads. The loads can be better secured with diagonals, either nailed to the deck or up against the container rails or corner posts. Never use the container sidewalls for heavier items. The strength of the container is along its framing.

5. Never rest cargo up against the container doors.

Packaging Considerations for Container Shipments

Containerization can sometimes replace export packing. However, each shipment has to be judged on its own merits before the decision is made to export pack or use standard domestic packing. Too many times claims adjusters see survey reports referring to use of domestic packing for an international transit.

An important factor in determining the method of packaging is whether or not the shipment moves in a house-to-house, house-to-pier, pier-to-house, or pier-to-pier mode. If it is the latter three, it will be subjected to the environmental hazards, handling, and stowage of a breakbulk move, and the packaging must be able to withstand these hazards.

A container is like a "minihold" on the vessel subject to the same strains, stresses and movements as the vessel. The package should provide a medium for containment, restraint, cushioning, handling, stowage, and any other factor that would be considered relevant to the cargo's arrival, i.e., moisture, odors, leakage, etc. If the container transits less than a house-to-house mode, one should package for the toughest leg of the journey.

Manual handling, which is the major cause of damage, becomes apparent in container shipments with cargo handled in the loading and unloading. Particularly when in a less than house-to-house container mode, handling is out of the control of the shipper and is typically of a rough nature where losses to cargo will occur.

Bags. Kraft multiwall paper bags, widely used in international and domestic transportation, stow well in containers. In an international transit where the bags are subject to various handlings and marine exposures, the shipper should consider increasing the number of plies, using a polyliner, laminating or applying films to provide moisture resistance, and/or using synthetic bags that have a high level of resistance to tearing and are water-resistant. Cross-tier stowage is recommended to prevent shifting and maximize stowage capacity.

Fiberboard Cartons. Probably the most widely used shipping container in international distribution is the fiberboard carton. If the shipment transits house-to-house in a palletized, shrink/stretch wrapped mode, domestic grade fiberboard is likely to hold up well. If the shipment is less than house-to-house, the strength of the fiberboard carton should be upgraded to a double-wall or triple-wall with weather-resistant properties.

When containers are broken down and the fiberboard cartons are stowed in transit sheds or warehouses out of the shipper's control, the strength of the corrugated materials must be considered carefully because stacking heights are likely to exceed package restrictions. All seams and closures should be secured with waterproof tapes and the cartons reinforced with strapping.

Drums. International distribution makes wide use of the fiber drum and the 55-gallon steel drum. Typically, drums are used to transport bulk powder and liquid chemicals that may have special requirements or hazardous qualities covered under DOT regulations and Code of Federal Regulation, Title 49.

When developing drum packaging, remember that the handling environment in less than a house-to-house mode will be severe. The drums may be dropped, dragged, and rolled on their sides excessively and storage heights could be higher than designed strengths.

Drums with rolling hoops should be stowed with alternating rows raised by wood dunnage on the deck so that the hoop's mesh is flush against the drum sidewall of adjacent drums and the stow becomes tight.

Wood Boxes/Crates. Wood is a favorite packing material utilized heavily by export packers and consolidators who know the marine environment well.

When the container transits house-to-house, shippers could consider reducing their packaging to tri-wall or double-wall fiberboard from wood because handling and stowage would be less severe, but all factors relating to this change must be considered.

When wood is used in container moves that are less than house-to-house modes, it should have the same quality and design requirements as in breakbulk moves.

The wood skids, boxes, crates, etc., when stowed in containers should be blocked and braced heavily. If they shift, they could cause considerable damage to adjacent cargo, the containers, or the product contained.

Containerization—General Considerations

Inspections. Containers should be inspected for watertight integrity and soundness prior to utilization in the following areas:

1. The floor, sidewalls, ceilings, doors, corner castings, and underframing should be visually inspected. A good idea is to have someone enter the empty container and close the doors behind themselves. If there are any spots of light, the holes can be considered sources of water entry.

2. Nails, banding clips, staples, and other securing materials should be removed to prevent damage to product during loading and unloading.

3. The container should be cleaned and swept free of all residuals. If odors remain, the container should be aired and vented prior to stowing and if necessary, treated with appropriate deodorizers to protect cargo from being tainted.

4. A container inspection report should be filed with the shipping documents.

Some companies photograph the container (identifying the container number) and final stowage to demonstrate the adequacy of packaging and stowage for insurance purposes. The photographs are filed with the shipping documents.

When a loaded container arrives, it should be inspected for any apparent causes of damage to the cargo and to document any possible causes for concealed damages to cargo that may be found later. This will be important if it is necessary to file claim against the carrier in the event of a loss.

Seals. Seals should meet the following criteria:

1. Be adequately sound to prevent accidental breakage in normal handling and stowage conditions.

2. Forcible removal must destroy its essential parts for opening and closing.

3. Must be tamperproof so that it cannot be opened without some indication that it was opened—or that there was an attempt to open it.

4. Has serial numbers, preferably embossed.

Container Yard Security

Container storage yards should be well lighted with limited access by unauthorized personnel. Containers should not be stowed against fences or other areas where there is easy access. In storage, containers should be placed so the doors face one another to make opening difficult without moving the container. Finally, containers with high value cargo should be placed in upper tiers until ready for transit.

Through common-sense practices and technical guidelines, importers and exporters need not face loss and damage to cargo on a regular basis. The bottom line of loss control practice is twofold: protection of corporate assets and assuring corporate profit. This chapter provides a means of affecting the bottom line for containerized cargo shipments.

Shipments by Air Need Cargo Loss Control

Many exporters and even many freight forwarders believe that shipping via air is safer than by water. In some instances, this may be true; however, many air distribution systems pose greater hazards to cargo than comparable marine choices. Export shipments via air warrant the same attention as marine shipments.

Marking, Stowing, and Packing

A major problem with air cargo is that it is usually loaded individually. In too many cases, this breakdown into unitized loads has caused cargo loss. Typically, only one exterior unit is marked or labeled and the remainder of the cartons get lost or damaged during transit.

Think ahead about cargo access and storage area heights. Shippers can learn the aircraft specifications carriers from the carriers. For example, aircraft cargo hold openings have limited access heights. Cargo standing upright will be placed on its side when it cannot be loaded vertically. Unitized shipments are particularly vulnerable to loss when air carriers run out of room in air transit sheds and stow cargo in airport perimeter storage locations that have no security and are exposed to the elements.

To avoid having your air cargo scattered. Label and mark all units in the cargo load. However, the burden is not exclusively yours.

Demand top service. You want your cargo given priority handling, prime stowage locations, and maximum security at all times. To get this service, ask for "special handling" and require documentation on stowage and security procedures.

When packing, shippers should provide internal restraints to prevent shifting, with the stages of aircraft motion in mind. These stages are take-off, lift, drag, thrust, gravity, and landing. Some airlines offer tri-wall consolidation boxes for unitizing, handling, and packing. Take advantage of these!

Airlines are sensitive to hazardous cargo regulations and some carriers refuse hazardous cargoes altogether. Consult with your carrier/forwarder prior to shipping. Choose airlines well in Third World countries, where air services are limited and can be rougher on cargo than marine transit services. Cargo can be susceptible to unusually rough handling, poor storage, and long tie-ups for clearances, pickup, and delivery.

Air Cargo Containerization

Containers should be inspected for their watertight integrity and soundness prior to use. Following are some inspection guidelines:

> Visually inspect the floor, sidewalls, ceilings, doors, corner castings, and underframing. A good idea is to have a person enter the empty container and close the door behind themself. If there are any spots of light, the holes can be considered sources of water entry.

> Remove nails, banding clips, staples, and other securing materials to prevent damage to product during loading and unloading.

> Clean the container and sweep it free of all residuals. If odors remain, the container should be aired and vented prior to stowing and if necessary treated with appropriate deodorizers to protect the cargo.

> File a container inspection report with the shipping documents to document the inspection.

> Keep documentary proof of container adequacy. Some companies photograph the container (identifying container number) and final stowage to demonstrate the adequacy of packaging and stowage for insurance purposes. Photographs should be filed with the shipping documents.

> Consider using air containers on a house-to-house basis. Many shippers have the volume and airline carriers are more than pleased to cooperate with surface transportation.

Sealing

Seals on air cargo should meet the following criteria:

- They should be strong enough to prevent accidental breakage in normal handling and stowage conditions.

- When removed forcibly, the opening and closing function must be destroyed.

- They must be tamperproof, that is, sealed or closed in such a way that any attempt to have opened them will be obvious.

- They should carry serial numbers, preferably embossed.

- Seal records should be maintained by shippers, carriers, and transit yards to set up lines of accountability through all carrier interfaces.

Security Areas

Frequent users of certain air cargo areas can have an impact on security. Here are some principles exporters should insist on:

- Fencing is placed away from buildings and high enough to prevent broaching.

- Barbed wiring or stakes at the top of fencing to provide additional protection.

- Prompt repair of damages and regular scheduled inspections.

- Gates are guarded at all times and the flow of traffic kept to a minimum and controlled.

- Drivers change truck stops frequently during inland transport.

- Advance notice procedures whereby the consignee is notified at least 24 hours prior to the arrival of sensitive shipments. Alter intermediate points as well.

- Periodic review of carrier performance to identify those with a record of a high instance of loss or damage.

- Adequate lighting throughout the terminal, particularly those areas where cargo is worked and stored.

- Additional lighting on high poles, covering wide areas and reducing shadowing in access-wanted or unwanted areas.

- Don't forget the other end!

Overseas customers and subsidiaries receiving your goods have a responsibility to you to process them efficiently and safely. Following are some guidelines for assuring safe reception of your goods:

Receiving should notify purchasing when cargo arrives and contact suppliers immediately when cargo has not arrived.

Only specified personnel should be authorized to check cargo.

Once checked, cargo should be moved immediately from receiving areas to storage areas.

Freight bills should be totaled and compared to the number recorded on the manifest.

All pickup drivers should tender positive identification.

Prepare legible documentation, with clearly written signatures.

Security cribs should be maintained with thorough inventory control.

Remove loose or broached cargo to cooperage stations as soon as possible.

Insist on piece counts at all cargo handling interfaces.

Segregate shipping from receiving areas.

Restrict access to cargo documentation to a need-to-know basis.

Maintain a "tight" ship—good housekeeping, minimal congestion, unrestricted movement, etc.

Consider shipping component in various stages in lieu of sending finished or fully assembled cargo.

Container Yard Security

Container storage yards should be well-lighted with limited access by unauthorized personnel. Containers should not be stowed up against fences or other areas where easy and simple access can be completed. In storage, containers should be placed so the doors face one another, making opening difficult without moving the container. Containers with high value cargo should be placed in upper tiers until ready for transit.

Air Cargo Receiving Procedures

Do not sign delivery carrier receipts without inspecting the exterior packaging of each unit, noting any marks or stains, dents, scratches, or other signs of exterior force on the delivery receipt. If there is exterior damage to the packaging, photograph the overall conditions (including pallets, containers, etc.) as well as the specific damage to the packing. Open damaged packages as soon as possible after receipt (especially items with long replacement times), photograph the damage to the contents, and separate and preserve the damaged goods and materials until surveyed by insurance company representatives.

Claims Procedures

If there is damage, shortage, or loss to a consignment, immediately notify the underwriters, local surveyors, and agents; and file claims in writing against air, ocean, and inland carriers.

This procedure must be followed regardless of whether the full extent of loss is immediately apparent or it appears that some time will lapse before an accurate or final determination of loss can be made. Early notice to the surveyor is required under typical marine policy terms and affords the insured party access to counsel and guidance from underwriters representative of who, in turn, will advise underwriters if the loss is serious.

If it appears that final resolution of the survey may be delayed, the surveyor should nonetheless immediately and clearly establish that the losses occurred in transit. The surveyor can then pursue the matter until the full extent of the damage is established.

Airlines, railways, and ocean carriers may automatically decline liability claims under the terms of carriage printed on their bills of lading. This is usually an initial form of declaration that may be revised upon further examination of their delivery records. However, once the insured has held the carriers liable, the insured is not normally required to pursue further action against them, regardless of their remission or denial of liability.

When you notify the delivery carrier and insurance company representatives that you or your buyer received damaged goods now available for surveying, state that you are filing claims and are holding the delivery carrier liable for the damage. Whatever your feelings about the damage, cooperate during the survey, which is meant to determine objectively the extent and the approximate cause of damage. Cooperation does not mean volunteering information. Discretion is advised.

Once the packing is opened, the protection it provided for the contents during storage after arrival has been reduced. Steps should be taken to compensate for the packing being opened to insure that the contents are protected from the elements.

Keep in mind that with intermodalism, air cargo may transit several modes before destination. All advice can be "containerized" in a phrase: Think ahead!

Concluding Remarks

The shipper must be proactive in cargo loss control before the shipment leaves. Following all the recommendations outlined in this chapter will go a long way in accomplishing loss-free exports.

Money spent up-front will affect the potential for unknown loss and damage at the other end.

Cargo loss control is another necessary discipline of export trade to keep exports safe and achieve satisfied customers, which will, in turn, increase sales and long-term successful international relationships.

10

Risk Management in International Business

Understanding the exposures of international business is a skill set required for export executives. This chapter explores the risks associated with exports: receivables, loss and damage, political risk, etc. and discusses various insurance products and services available to transfer the exposures to third parties. Private and government insurance concerns are readily available to provide various products for exporters to use to reduce risk and make them more competitive in world trade. In addition, this chapter provides insight into the skill set of risk management, which is vital for the continuation and growth of export trade.

The Logistics of Political Risk Management in Exporting

As exporting continues to make the world smaller, it can make it more complicated. The more complicated it is, the greater the risks. U.S. companies are increasing investment and trade activities in all parts of the world. Where there is certain political instability, i.e., Israel, Lebanon, Russia, Argentina, Haiti, Nigeria, and Korea, to name a few "hot spots," there is a growing demand for corporations to analyze exposure, adopt risk transfer options, and provide loss control alternatives; in other words, do "political risk management." When we consider the "realities of political risk management," "what are we saying?" or, in better terms, "what are we asking?"

These risks and exposure questions are germane to all size companies and must be considered by the most experienced and the new to export company. Political risk management must become a function of the overall logistics management responsibility. Following are seven areas that should be reviewed thoroughly when evaluating the risk management functions of "political risk" before goods are shipped.

1. Limited Marketplace. There are only a handful of markets here and abroad that can provide political risk coverage. The U.S. Government through the Overseas Private Investment Corporation (OPIC) Ex-Im Bank, along with private companies such as the Foreign Credit Insurance Association (FCIA), American Insurance Group (AIG), and CNA are definite options, which can be explored through a corporate insurance broker.

2. Terms and Conditions. Boilerplate policies are not adequate. The policy must be written to follow the nature of the trade, transaction, or contract occurring in the foreign market.

3. Analysis. Risk managers must consider the social, economic, political, and financial situations of the foreign buyer or partner, the host country, and the world situation in general. This is key to determining exposure!

4. Loss Control Options. One must look at options to minimize loss through engineering, contract wording, transaction planning, etc. In many instances the purchase of insurance can be avoided by executing other options that are more secure and less costly.

5. Retention. Political risk covers financial loss. Typical exposures such as confiscation, nationalization, expropriation, and deprivation (CNE & D), contract frustration, unfair calling of financial guaranties, etc. require the risk manager to consider a coinsurance factor and a substantial waiting period that become the retention levels for the corporation.

6. Corporate Communication. The nature of overseas sales, the bureaucracy of a large corporation, and the time and distance involved, often leave "risk management" as an afterthought. The realities typically have the risk manager review a contract—after its been signed, sealed, and delivered. The risk manager needs to communicate to its operating divisions (1) what the exposures are, (2) what the risks are, and (3) how to access the terms before goods are shipped! This is key to a "total approach" effort for successful risk management.

7. Brokerage Selection. The reality of who your political risk broker should be is a difficult one. The specialization of political risk requires not only basic insurance knowledge, but knowledge of international trade, political science, banking expertise and contract analysis. There are only a handful of specialized brokers in political risk who are spread throughout some of the major brokerage houses, as well as some small specialty facilities. Marsh (merged with Johnson & Higgins), Frenkel, and Willis Faber are but a few of the experienced and qualified brokerage organizations.

These seven areas provide an overview for the exporter to consider before merchandise is shipped. It is key to remember that the U.S. Government is committed to promoting exports and investment abroad; thereby reducing the deficit and enhancing our economic stability on foreign shores.

Through finely tuned risk management the exporter now can deal with the realities of political risk exposure worldwide. Taking steps as part of the logistics process is significant to the U.S. exporting industry successfully competing in world markets.

Political Risk Insurance Update: 2000 and Beyond

As the twentieth century comes to a close, U.S. companies are increasing their overseas trade and investment activities. However, the recent wars in Bosnia, the Persian Gulf, the Caribbean, and Central America (Panama) heightened executives' concerns over the risk of political instability. During the last decade, Bosnia, Argentina/England, the Tiananmen Square incident, the Panama invasion, instability in Indonesia, the turmoil in Central and West Africa, and similar events have caused many a sleepless night for senior corporate executives.

Political risk insurance is available to ease these concerns and provide stable international activity and investments. There are a host of willing brokers and underwriters anxious to manage and deal with political risk exposures. This chapter reviews the insurance options.

History

To understand the current political risk insurance arena, it is helpful to understand some of the history of this relatively new line of insurance. The first modern political risk policies were written in the early 1960s. Over the years, political risk policies have become clearer and more specific regarding the intent and scope of coverage. In some instances, these changes broadened coverage, while they made the policies more restrictive in others. The marketplace has also undergone changes over time. Ten to fifteen years ago there were many insurers and reinsurers participating in the political risk insurance marketplace; today there are only a handful.

Perhaps the greatest change in political risk insurance since its inception is the underwriting approach used. Today, underwriters have strong skills in international trading, finance, and banking combined with underwriting expertise in international insurance. A political risk insurance underwriter must understand international trade first and underwriting second. To underwrite the vanilla-type of political risk policy, such as one covering confiscation and nationalization, a basic understanding of international trade is necessary. For more complicated risks, such as counter trade, currency inconvertibility and contract frustration, the underwriter must be well educated in the art and science of international trade. Knowledge of banking, letters of credit, foreign contract negotiation, and international law is a prerequisite for successful underwriting. Because there are no formal schools that provide training in political risk insurance, insurers have developed their own training and education programs, and many of them are excellent.

Today's highly educated underwriters require much more information than did their counterparts ten or more years ago. They ask hard, detailed questions. They also review copies of contracts and terms of trade in order to completely understand the transaction before binding coverage.

While the political risk insurance marketplace has waxed and waned over the years, the future looks bright. The insurers are positioned for effective underwriting and creative marketing to respond to the needs of U.S. companies engaged in international trade.

Spread of Risk

As with any line of insurance, it is important for insurers to achieve a spread of risk in their insurance portfolios in order to offer stable pricing and policy terms. Unfortunately, however, the buyers of this insurance have a natural tendency toward adverse selection, i.e., corporations with sales or assets in a variety of markets or countries tend to insure only the political risks associated with those areas of the world that present current political instability. The tendency of exporters/insureds to retain "easier" risks while transferring "hot spots" to insurers frustrates insurers' attempts to maintain a diverse spread of risk.

However, there is an inherent flaw in this philosophy of insuring only the difficult risks and retaining the less risky exposures. If an underwriter is provided with a broad spread of risk, a reduction of rates and more liberal underwriting terms may be obtained. The greater the spread of risk presented to an underwriter, the lower the rate that will be used to develop premium, up to a point. This may allow the insurance of more risk for the same premium than would be charged to cover only those countries, projects, or products that present the most exposure to the exporter.

There are several ways an exporter/insured can provide insurers with a spread of risk when buying political risk insurance, including the following:

Diversification of Countries. Consider insuring all export sales, even sales to countries with a tradition of political and economic stability.

Diversification of Products. Insure all products and not just those presenting the highest risk of loss.

Terms of Sale/Payment. Some methods of sale and payment present greater exposure than others. The most secure type of sale is one that has some form of guarantee, security, or collateral from an independent third party facility, such as a letter of credit where a third party banking facility guarantees the financial aspects of the transaction. However, a significantly higher exposure is presented to the exporter/insured when sales are done on an open account, site draft consignment, or other terms whereby the customer in the third world country is likely to receive the merchandise before being obligated to pay. By insuring secured sales along with those that have no third party guarantee, the spread of risk is increased.

Timing. Spread of risk can be increased by making shipments over an extended period of time as opposed to adhering to a compact shipping schedule. This approach allows time for some shipments to be paid for before other shipments are delivered. Adjusting the timing in this manner avoids exposing the entire value of the transaction at one time. Shipping schedules encompassing a one- to three-year period are viewed favorably by many underwriters, but some types of transactions will benefit from a longer period (e.g., seven years).

Political Risk Coverages

There are several types of political risks:

- Confiscation
- Currency inconvertibility
- Nationalization
- Devaluation
- Expropriation
- Unfair calling of financial guarantee
- Deprivation
- Trade disruptions
- War, strikes, riots, and civil commotion
- Terrorism
- Contract frustration

There are a number of different types of political risk coverages. In many respects, political risk insurance is similar to export credit insurance (and some people might include export credit insurance in the list); however, there are some distinct differences between these two categories of insurance. Basically, a political risk loss results from a peril originating out of a political or government eventuality, whether the consignee is a sovereign or private entity. An export credit risk, on the other hand, is typically defined as the credit exposure emanating solely from the actions or inactions of the private buyer.

The main distinction is that credit exposures emanating solely from private buyers are inherently more volatile than those that depend on the action of a governmental entity. This results in fewer insurers willing to write export credit coverage. When it is provided, a substantial volume of underwriting and credit information is required, the rates are high, and the coverage terms are restrictive.

Incidents such as the Gulf War and Bosnia caused many people to focus on war and terrorism coverage. Virtually all property insurance policies contain war exclusions, making it clear that damage caused by a war between two or more countries is excluded. The application of a property insurance policy to terrorist acts may not be so clear-cut, but some form of basic coverage is provided for terrorist acts by many property insurance policies. The approach used in the war exclusion of the latest Insurance Services Office, Inc. (ISO) is that commercial property forms is commonly used even in nonbureau forms. Such policies exclude only damage from war, rebellion, revolution, civil war, or warlike action of a military force. Property policies containing exclusions of this nature would typically be deemed to cover damage caused by most terrorist acts. However, some property insurance policies also exclude damage caused by a hostile or warlike action of an agent of a foreign government. Under this language, an insurer might be justified in excluding coverage if the terrorist act were proven to be inflicted by an agent of a foreign government.

ISO War Risk Exclusion

The ISO will not pay for loss or damage caused directly or indirectly by any of the following:

War and military action.
1. War, including undeclared civil war
2. Warlike action by a military force, including action hindering or defending against an actual or expected attack, by any government, sovereign or other authority using military personnel or other agents
3. Insurrection, rebellion, revolution, usurped power, or action taken by governmental authority in hindering or defending against any of these

Coverage for the excluded property damage exposures is available in the political risk insurance marketplace in the form of a war risk, civil commotion, and terrorism policy. The need for this coverage is dictated largely by the stability of the regions in which the insured's facilities are located and the scope of the war risk exclusion in the insured's property insurance policy. Of course, war risk exclusions can vary considerably from policy to policy and must be carefully analyzed when evaluating the need for separate coverage.

Confiscation, nationalization, expropriation, and deprivation (CNE&D) are the most commonly purchased political risk coverages. They are needed by organizations with assets, such as refineries or manufacturing plants, that are permanently located in other countries. The policies respond when these assets are taken over by governmental action, as recently occurred in Libya, Iraq, and Nicaragua and, in the more distant past, Chile, Vietnam, and Iran.

Nationalization takes place when the host government simply takes over an asset. Deprivation is said to occur when the host government interferes with the foreign entity's access to or utilization of its asset without actually taking possession of it. In either situation, the property owner can suffer a substantial financial loss. Confiscation and expropriation are similar actions; the host government takes over the foreign asset with the intent of returning it to the owner in the future. However, the time frame is usually not specified and often extends over several years, causing financial loss to the foreign-based property owner. Because of the similarities between these exposures, the best approach to structuring CNE&D coverage is to insure all four perils in a single policy. This approach minimizes the problems that could otherwise result from disputes with insurers as to whether a particular action falls into one category or another.

Another common political risk for which insurance is available is contract frustration. This entails the nonperformance or frustration of a contract with a host government entity or private buyer in a third world country as a result of an invalid action. An invalid action is an activity detrimental to the U.S. interest that would be considered inappropriate or illegal in the United States. It can be further defined as an action that wrongfully invalidates an overseas transaction in such a manner that the exporter is unable to obtain payment for its product or recoup its assets.

As an example of the contract frustration exposure, assume a U.S. company has a contract with a third world government to supply custom-designed parts for the construction of a factory. However the third world government cancels the contract without a valid reason prior to delivery of the product. In such a situation, it would be common for the firm to have spent a substantial sum on the initial design and preparation to manufacture the parts. Because the project involved a custom design, it is unlikely that another buyer for the parts could be found, and the exporter would suffer a financial loss.

Currency inconvertibility is an increasing concern for U.S. exporters, particularly those that sell on open account or provide open terms of payment. This type of loss occurs when the insured's customer pays in local currency, and the local government is unable to exchange the local dollars into foreign currency. Examples of countries where this can be a problem are Columbia, Brazil, Nigeria, the Philippines, and Mexico.

Currency inconvertibility has become a particular problem in countries that underwent a tremendous expansion in the 1960s through to the year 2000 because of foreign oil sales and the growth of foreign direct investment. When oil sales began to decline in the 1980s and OPEC could not agree on pricing and sales quotas, affected countries suffered a trade imbalance, causing more hard dollars to leave the country than were arriving. This made it difficult for the national banks of these countries to convert the local currency into the currency of other countries because the banks were not able to purchase foreign dollars, yen, Swiss francs, etc. with hard currency. In other words, the banks may not possess an adequate amount of U.S. dollars or other currencies to make the exchange. Ultimately, what typically occurs in these situations is a rescheduling of the country's debt over a multiyear period, implementation of strict economic controls internally within that country, and involvement by various international entities, such as the IMF, World Bank, and General Agreements on Trade and Tariff (GATT).

When insuring a trading activity in a country that commonly has problems converting its currency, underwriters typically will write the policies with a waiting period that corresponds with the time frame over which the conversion will occur. This waiting period ranges anywhere from 60 to 720 days. The purpose of the waiting period is to ensure the coverage applies only to fortuitous loss.

An often overlooked exposure of many companies doing business overseas is the risk of an unfair calling of a financial guarantee. This risk usually arises with large transactions that take many months or years to complete. In such a situation, it is common for the buyer to make a down payment (e.g., 15 percent of the contract price), followed by periodic installment payments as the project progresses. The buyer would typically require the seller to post a letter of credit or other financial guarantee against these payments, and the buyer would be able to draw down on that letter of credit in the event something occurred that caused the supplier to default. The unfair calling of this financial guarantee is an exposure to the exporter/supplier, and unfair calling insurance protects the exporter against this risk.

Trade Disruption

Another exposure that companies involved in international trade often overlook is the business interruption exposure, caused not by physical damage to a plant or other facility, but by a political event. Both importers and exporters face this loss exposure. For example, assume a manufacturer relies on a single supplier in a third world country to provide raw material that it imports for its U.S. manufacturing plants. A political occurrence, such as a war, strike, change in government, confiscation of the supplier's assets, change in politics, or change in law occurring in the source country, could disrupt the flow of that raw material into the United States. The manufacturer's ability to produce the finished product would be impaired, and a substantial financial loss may occur if an alternative source of the raw material could not be found. In a similar fashion, an exporter can experience a loss when the product is not delivered on time because of some event beyond the control of the exporter. Such exposures are insurable in the political risk insurance market.

It is important to understand that most executives tend to view their potential loss as the value of the physical product, failing to consider the potential loss of earnings, extra expense, loss of profits, and loss of market in the event a physical and/or political eventuality occurs. Trade disruption coverage can provide protection for these losses.

Markets

The political risk insurance marketplace can be divided into two basic categories: government markets and private markets. In the United States, the principal government market is the FCIA (now part of the Great American Insurance Company), which was authorized through the U.S. government via Ex-Im Bank. With headquarters in New York City and satellite offices throughout the United States, the FCIA provides many types of political risk coverage as well as export credit insurance for U.S. exporters shipping U.S. products to approved countries. Most non-Communist countries in the world that have favorable trading status with the United States are considered approved.

In the past, the FCIA was considered bureaucratic and unresponsive to the needs of most exporters. However, in recent years, this has changed, and the FCIA has become more responsive by offering competitive and comprehensive programs, such as the bank letter of credit and new-to-export buyer programs.

OPIC is the other U.S. government-sponsored market for political risk insurance. OPIC insures U.S. nonmilitary investment exposures, such as confiscation and nationalization, in developing nations throughout the world. Its terms and conditions are broad, and the rates are as competitive as the FCIA's. However, only assets located in nations having favorable trade relationships with the United States qualify for coverage with OPIC.

There are two drawbacks to the U.S. government programs. First, they are subject to U.S. diplomatic and trade policies. When the U.S. government is following a restrictive trade policy with a particular country, the Ex-Im Bank and other government facilities tend to follow suit, thus reducing the availability of coverage or restricting coverage terms for that country. Likewise, when the government eases trade restrictions with a country, coverage availability and terms will increase.

While this may be good politics, it sometimes restricts coverage availability for transactions with countries that, while not on favorable trade terms with the United States, might present good business opportunities and be excellent credit risks for individual businesses. For example, a number of U.S. companies have been very successful in trading with the Soviet Union over the last few years and have been paid regularly and responsibly. Because, however, of its unfavorable trade relationship with the United States, transactions with the Soviet Union are generally not eligible for most of the U.S. government's insurance programs.

The second drawback to U.S. government markets is that they only cover U.S. companies and/or products. As an example of how this restricts availability, consider a firm located in New York City staffed by U.S. personnel that exports Canadian products into Europe on an open account basis, thus creating an exposure that could be covered by export credit insurance. This company would not be eligible to buy credit insurance from the U.S. government facilities because the product is not manufactured in the United States.

Of course, this limitation of coverage availability is fundamental to the underlying purpose for which Ex-Im Bank and OPIC was created: To encourage and support the exportation of U.S. products and services. These facilities are not always profitable, but provide an indirect means of subsidizing U.S. business interests overseas. At this time, the U.S. government will only subsidize activity that directly benefits U.S. interests, products, or services.

Most other Western nations also have established facilities similar to the Ex-Im Bank and OPIC to insure export sales to other countries. U.S.

companies with divisions domiciled in these nations can often access these local government programs.

The private insurance market provides coverages that are not available from the government markets, and it is not bound by the diplomatic policy of any one nation. This market is basically made up of some U.S.-domiciled insurance companies and London markets. The principal U.S. companies that write political risk insurance are Chubb, CNA, and American International Underwriters (AIU), but there are a handful of other insurers that occasionally write various types of political risk coverage. Most U.S. insurance companies with marine capability will write war, strikes, riots, and civil commotion coverages on overseas transactions. Along with Chubb and AIU, other underwriters include MOAC (Continental), CIGNA, Fireman's Fund, and Great American.

Being commercially driven, U.S. insurers will write insurance in those areas where there is an opportunity for profit. The natural downside of this tendency is that it is difficult to obtain insurance from these insurers in countries where the possibility of loss is significant. In general, however, U.S. insurers offer broad policies and competitive rates and are willing to write on a spread of risk basis affording the exporter a complete program covering all overseas sales.

The London market is composed of Lloyd's of London, Institute of London Underwriters (ILU), and other insurers. This marketplace is as competitive as its U.S. counterpart. In addition, the London insurers typically are willing to put out more capacity and are more agreeable to manuscripting policy forms. London underwriters also have different perspectives on certain areas of the world than their U.S. counterparts and may provide coverage in areas where U.S. insurers are reluctant to do so.

Care should be taken in choosing an agent or broker to access the marketplace. The broker should be large enough to bring a substantial number of international resources to the table and have a staff that is knowledgeable in international trade and the political risk marketplace.

Loss Control

There are a number of loss control tactics that U.S. companies doing business overseas should consider using. These measures will help reduce exposure and secure more competitive pricing and more comprehensive terms from political risk insurers.

Political risk exposures are heavily influenced by the contracts underlying the business transaction. All too often contracts are executed on overseas transactions without review by insurance advisers. Knowledgeable insurance advisers often can suggest alterations that will substantially reduce the exposure, making the transaction easier and less costly to insure. For example, underwriters view the inclusion of arbitration clauses favorably because such clauses substantially increase the likelihood that the exporter will get a fair hearing in the event of a dispute, as opposed to arguing its case in the local courts. Consider a situation in which an exporter is fighting the government of a third world country on an unfair calling of a financial guarantee in that country's court. There would be a serious disadvantage to the U.S. firm in that situation compared to an arbitration proceeding in Zurich, London, or some other city outside that government.

Another consideration is to give the local government an interest in the overseas venture. For example, assume a U.S. firm builds a plant in a third world country.

> *By including the country's government as a minority partner in the venture (e.g., a 25 percent share), the government is given a strong incentive to support the venture rather than take any actions that would adversely affect it.*

Involving local personnel in the management and operations of a local venture can also reduce the political risk exposures. When a foreign-owned facility employs many local citizens, the government is less inclined to cause a disruption of its operations.

Careful consideration should be given to the currency transactions specified by the contract. A transaction that runs into problems because it requires that local currency be converted into U.S. dollars might flow more smoothly if some other currency, such as yen or marks, could be used to complete the deal. The alternative currency might then be used in other international trades or converted to U.S. dollars.

It is also important to set up contingency plans to follow in the event a political eventuality occurs that would disrupt the venture or transaction. This involves developing specific strategies for dealing with potential political problems.

Conclusion

In the last few years, there has been a dramatic increase in U.S. exporting and importing activity. More U.S. companies than ever are making investments overseas and importing raw material or finished products from their overseas subsidiaries. These activities present substantial risks not faced by organizations operating solely in their home country. Once these exposures are identified, they can be insured by government-sponsored facilities or in the domestic and London insurance marketplaces.

Political Risk: Not for the Fainthearted

In the last twenty years, the primary market for political risk insurance had many players, most of them new. Reinsurance capacity was adequate. The demand for coverage was great and rates were high. Then the marketplace changed dramatically.

In the mid-1980s insurers encountered significant losses. "Hot" areas such as Lebanon, Nicaragua, Libya, Iraq, and Iran produced frequent and large claims in underwriting exposures such as war, terrorism, confiscation, nationalization, expropriation, deprivation, and currency inconvertibility.

In addition, the worldwide debt problem brought substantial and numerous claims in currency inconvertibility, devaluation, and contract frustration. Because of claims in countries such as the Philippines, Brazil, Argentina, Mexico, and Nigeria, insurers experienced an increase in loss frequency. As a result, many private insurers withdrew or significantly restricted coverage in certain geographic areas.

In the early 1980s through the late 1990s, insurers had written broad policies containing terms that should have been black and white but that actually were gray. One of these areas was related to currency devaluation. However, it didn't take too many losses before underwriters made it clear that this exposure was to be excluded under their insurance terms.

Ultimately, as a result of the losses that hit the marketplace and fears of more in the future, the marketplace sorted itself out. There are a number of new underwriters, including those who write niche policies under speciality banners, that can be accessed through corporate insurance brokers.

Some major players, such as Lloyd's, AIG, and Chubb, provide substantial capacity, although these insurers now write the risks in a more detailed and comprehensive manner than they did earlier in the decade. Lloyd's has undergone a changing of the guard. Many Lloyd's leaders that were in this business in the early 1980s through to the end of the 1990s remain today, but others who attempted to write political risk insurance have abandoned it.

In addition, although the efforts were minimal, many marine underwriters in London did attempt to extend their policies to cover certain types of political risk. And war risk underwriters in London were, and still are, major players in CNE&D risks.

One cannot discuss political risk insurance, which is part of the system of international trade, without including institutions in trade finance and banking, which play a major role in the whole process. For example, during the last ten years banks have attempted to enter this market as insurers, brokers, or major assureds. In examining political risk insurance in the 1980s, the major role played by government facilities must be considered. Most westernized trading nations have some sort of government agency that provides insurance on export sales. Typically, these programs are designed to promote export trading and foreign investment. Often they are politically motivated.

The United States has OPIC and the Ex-Im Bank. OPIC primarily responds to fixed investments in third world countries, while the Ex-Im Bank responds to all U.S. exports worldwide. The Ex-Im Bank is more inclined to help U.S. trading or exporting company and provides a full range of political risk and export credit insurance programs.

Another quality insurer is the FCIA. At one time the FCIA was underwritten by a consortium of private insurance companies, but sometime between 1980 and 1982, because of poor loss experience, the programs became completely underwritten by the U.S. Government through Ex-Im Bank in Washington, D.C. The FCIA offers an array of programs and services through a professional staff of marketing, underwriting, and claims executives. It is now a private underwriter that is part of the Great American International Companies.

In the early 1980s, the Ex-Im Bank was accused of being just another government agency with lots of red tape and bureaucracy. But recently it has upgraded its staff, streamlined its procedures, and modernized its programs and is becoming a lucrative option for exporters. FCIA's programs are designed for large and small companies, first-time exporters, and financial institutions.

It is important to note that banks in Ex-Im Bank programs can receive their funds promptly when losses occur and not get caught in trade dispute problems that curtail cash flow. Consequently, the Ex-Im Bank should become an even more important player in the new millennium as the U.S. Government continues to emphasize U.S. exports and provides the resources to promote them. The agency's challenge is to meet the needs and demands of the U.S. exporter and to make its programs known and easily accessible.

The demand for political risk insurance will grow in the year 2001, primarily because U.S. companies will increase their exports to both westernized and third world countries. To compete with foreign and domestic suppliers, U.S. companies will sell on extended terms, increasing their credit exposures.

The political risk underwriter will need to extend coverage to commercial credit risks. Currently, only a handful of underwriters will provide the export credit cover. Other markets willing to provide political risk exposure cover should step up to the plate and provide some sort of protection for sales to private buyers, as well as the accompanying credit risks. Government insurance programs, which must meet requirements for "American" content, will have to be modified to address the need for "foreign" content as well.

Because of these particular needs, the development of appropriate underwriting skills in credit analysis, political risk review, and international trade also must proceed. The political risk underwriters of the future must be multifaceted and have talents beyond those required by "normal" underwriting. They must also be well versed in letters of credit, foreign banking practice, and current events on a multinational basis and should have an eye for hidden exposures covered by international trade terms.

Because political risk insurance is a unique exposure, special relationships exist. Numerous markets that may be involved in this area but do not make that information public make accommodations to suit their clients.

In addition, the seriousness of the political risk exposure calls for more of a partnership between the insured and the underwriter than do more traditional forms of insurance. The contract of sale between the exporter and the foreign buyer becomes the building block of the policy, ensuring terms and conditions. The insured and the underwriter must communicate openly, develop a complete understanding, and make certain that the "intent" of the policy is made clear. This is essential because the intricacies of international trade are not always black and white.

U.S. and some major foreign banks, which have played a functional role in political risk insurance, will also continue to be an integral part of the market. Many of the banks that have set up export trading companies to become directly involved in international transactions will attempt to become first party insurers as well. Because banks continue to face legal challenges to their right to become involved with insurance, this development process will be tedious and slow, but definitely will continue to evolve. Banks first will attempt to buy and control brokers that can handle these risks, eventually becoming direct underwriters themselves.

Other Players

Europe, Hong Kong and Japan will supply other players, in addition to the United States and London. For example, in the late 1980s Pan Financial, a company formed in London as a result of a triventure of Skandia, Yasuda, and Continental, would underwrite certain classes of political risk and credit exposures. The trading nations of the world recognize the need to provide insurance for exports, and both government and commercial resources will respond to this need.

Foreign markets will be particularly important for reinsurance because domestic capacity for these risks will remain limited. (The U.S. reinsurance market appears to have determined that the class is too difficult and that it has tremendous loss potential.) Reinsuring this class of underwriting calls for a different mentality from that required for reinsuring commercial covers. Political risk insurance has no set underwriting guideline rules or rating structures. It does not have decades of loss tables or loss experience to measure trend on. It is a totally free market that depends solely on capacity and negotiation.

Insurance against Political and Credit Risk Exposure for the Small and Medium-Size Enterprise

In order to grow and expand their worldwide market share and continue to have a high degree of profitability, U.S. small and medium-size companies must increase their activity in the world market. This increase in activity will heighten the exposures faced by these trading enterprises, which can be broken down into four basic areas: export sales activity, personnel, corporate liability, and financing.

Overseas Sales Activity

U.S. companies are also selling more of their product abroad. In fact, just in the last quarter, American companies demonstrated the highest increase in over four years in exporting activity. A considerable amount of this business consists of exports to our Western friends, however, we have also seen an increase in sales to secondary trading partners and third world countries. Many small and medium-size companies make up this increase.

Another exposure facing companies involved in foreign trade is that of the buyer not honoring the terms of a payment, thereby extending the accounts receivable. Whether or not a product is sold to a Western and/or third world country, the buyer, being a private organization, may not uphold its obligation to the seller. If this situation occurs, it is very difficult, if not impossible, for the seller to collect on the account receivable as the means available to do so are extremely limited. The less economically advanced the nation is, the more difficult it is to collect. American companies can insure these accounts receivable exposures, referred to as export credit risks, through various government and private resources. For smaller companies, the FCIA or Ex-Im Bank is a favored option. Larger risks can approach private sources such as CIGNA, AIG, and Chubb.

Particularly in third world countries, one of the major exposures to U.S. sales activity, primarily in accounts receivable situations, is that of currency inconvertibility. This risk becomes reality when a private organization honors its obligation and pays for goods in local funds, but a foreign government is unable to transfer these funds into U.S. dollars. Numerous losses of this type have occurred in countries such as the Philippines, Nigeria, Mexico, Brazil, and Venezuela due to the tremendous debt-related problems of these countries. Slow currency convertibility in Russia and other former Soviet (CIS) countries is becoming a major detriment to trade to these nations as this problems grows into a serious dilemma for U.S. exporters.

For example, companies who need to do business in Russia often have no alternative but to sell on terms that create an account receivable. (Typically, this requirement means site draft sixty or ninety days.) Following the arrival of goods and clearance through Russian customs facilities, the Russian customers pay in rubles. Most exporters wait six months to a year for the Russian government to transfer the rubles into U.S. dollars. In some cases this conversion has taken more than three years.

Exporters with export credit insurance policies have been able to receive their funds just ninety days after the default has occurred. In these instances, the insurance company will subrogate against the host government and wait for the funds to be transferred. Under typical third world moratorium debt conditions, underwriters are likely to see the funds in two to seven years, thereby suffering only a cash flow loss.

Personnel

With the increased activity of companies doing business overseas, there are more and more American personnel traveling to foreign countries. They are exposed to damage and/or loss of life. Statistics show that in the last ten-year period almost 40 percent of all worldwide terrorism has been directed at American interests. The U.S. company can provide some level of protection through kidnap and ransom insurance. This insurance provides a third party indemnification for any kidnap and ransom money that may need to be expended, but more important, it allows insurance company professionals to intervene and mitigate any loss that may occur.

When a U.S. national traveling on business was kidnapped in a South American country two years ago, the company appealed to the US government to intervene. Government agencies, however, were unable to provide timely and/or comprehensive assistance, and the firm did not know how to proceed. At this point, the professional staff of the insurance company providing the kidnap and ransom insurance stepped in and obtained local talent who understood the situation and were able to negotiate the employee's release. Approximately sixty days after the event, the employee was released, upset and emotionally damaged, but in good physical condition. The employee later remarked that it was specifically the insurance company's intervention that enabled the crisis situation to be resolved as smoothly as it was.

Another issue concerning personnel traveling overseas is that of the health insurances they require. Companies must ensure that their insurance policies extend indemnification and support services to foreign countries. Companies must also ensure that related insurances such as workers' compensation, disability, and life insurance cover employees' travel abroad. The question is: If an employee goes to the hospital, who pays, and how? Clearly these kinds of risks increase the more the exporter travels in areas with specific problems. The use of a specialized facility that assists U.S. nationals abroad called SOS Assistance Corporation in Philadelphia, Pennsylvania is highly recommended.

Liability Insurances

In the United States, companies are familiar with the exposures they face in the U.S. court and litigation system for third party liability, especially as it relates to their product liability exposures for domestic sales. American companies in particular have experienced a dramatic increase in product liability lawsuits. With augmented sales of American products overseas, more and more domestic companies are exposed to legal action either in local litigation systems abroad or in the United States. As a result, American companies must ensure that general liability policies extend coverage to overseas sales. Small and medium-size companies can lose substantial amounts of money that will affect bottom line results.

American companies must also consider the fact that foreign governments often take highly unfavorable stands on questions of the U.S. company's liability when doing business in their country. In certain nations, executives can be held personally liable and subject to heavy fines and imprisonment for the activity of their company in that country.

Companies must be are aware of local law and legislation and that their insurance policies provide indemnification in the instances to which the laws apply. It is just a question of asking a few questions.

Financing

Small and medium-size companies typically have difficulty finding financing for their export activity, particularly financing with extended payment terms and for trade with third world countries.

By using insurance as a tool, exporters can structure trade finance situations to expand their business. Once the bank or financing facility develops a comfort level achieved through insurance as a fallback, they become more willing to extend financing for export transactions.

The banks can become "named insureds" or "loss payees" as their interest appears. Export trade financing for $25,000 to $25 million has been arranged for an array of small and medium-size trading companies, enabling them to successfully complete transactions and compete in world trade. While the asset base is important, the comfort level and the exporter's trade finance experience become an important part of determining how much new business the exporter can take on.

Basic Steps to Protection

In general, trading companies have many types of exposures when they conduct business on a multinational basis. There are three basic steps a company should follow to protect its interests overseas:

1. Companies should acquire in-house expertise or retain it. Acquiring expertise on a transaction-by-transaction basis is possible as an alternative to having in-house staff spend more time than is currently warranted. Some transactions carry the full cost of the expertise. For others, consultants with fees independent of the transaction may be needed.

2. American companies must remain fully apprised of all possible options available to minimize or transfer risks abroad through government programs and private organizations. Knowing which government program to approach or how the balance shifts between government and private sector programs as conditions change means staying on top of the market.

3. Corporations operating multinationally must practice loss control measures such as, but not limited to: Contract review, use of local services in foreign countries, monitoring currency exchange laws and international trade trends, and being aware of political activities worldwide. Through these means of gauging the climate of the international marketplace, some forecasting can be accomplished that will reduce the risk of a political event damaging successful world trade activity.

Although the many exposures inherent in world trade complicate the trading environment, most transactions are completed, and for those companies that have prepared in advance, the responsibility for the problem items can be shifted to experts who are prepared to resolve them.

Basics of Insuring against Political and Credit Risks

To grow and increase global market share while maintaining a high degree of profitability, corporations around the world must increase global scale activity. But of necessity this also heightens the exposures faced by such multinational enterprises in the areas of fixed investments, sales activity, personnel, and corporate liability.

Numerous companies are purchasing or building factories, offices, and other operational facilities overseas. The major exposure such companies face abroad, particularly in third world countries, is the possibility of the host government's confiscating, nationalizing, expropriating, or depriving the venture of its interest. Many Western companies have witnessed this in Iran, Libya, Peru, Nicaragua, and some African nations.

For example, prior to the fall of the Shah, a company had a contract with the Iranian Government to establish facilities to provide local telephone and related communication services to the Iranian people. Following the shah's demise, and with it the fall of the pro-Western regime, the government confiscated all of the company's supplies, equipment, and fixed property for its own use. The company was uninsured at the time and lost between $10 and $15 million, which had to be absorbed internally. Had this client taken advantage of an option to insure such overseas exposure, the loss could have transferred to an insurance company and been indemnified for 100 percent of the loss.

With an increase in the number of governments worldwide that are unfriendly to foreign interests, including nations in Latin America, the Middle East, Asia, and Africa, the multinational with fixed investments overseas should take steps to provide political risk insurance against these exposures.

In addition to making fixed investments in the world market, foreign companies are also selling more of their product abroad. In particular, in the 1990s to now in 2001, U.S. companies demonstrated the highest increase in exporting activity. And while a considerable amount of this business consists of exports to Western friends, there has also been a significant increase in sales to secondary trading partners and third world countries.

Exporters from various countries also encounter other types of exposure, including embargo by the exporting government or the government of the country to which the merchandise is being shipped. For example, a company arranged to sell its product to Nicaragua when the U.S. Government suddenly declared an embargo on trade activity with that country. This client had developed a product line specifically designed for a customer in Nicaragua, and all the sales literature, packaging, etc. had been designed specifically for this firm. The goods were not shipped because such a shipment would have broken U.S. trade law at the time. The product had to be retooled and repackaged for shipment elsewhere. The expense exceeded $1 million. The company submitted a claim under the embargo provisions of its political risk insurance policy and received full indemnification.

Political Risk Coverage Analyzed: Ten Critical Steps for Risk Managers

With more corporations making direct investments overseas, increasing foreign sales activities, and dealing more frequently with third world countries, the political risk exposure has increased, creating a need for risk managers to direct attention to this subject area.

Political risk exposures generally refer to losses emanating from government or political sources. They include confiscation, nationalization, expropriation, and depravation of assets by foreign governments; import/export license cancellations; currency inconvertibility; war; strikes, riot, and civil commotions; embargo; contract cancellation/repudiation; and boycott. Losses emanating from business dealing with private entities abroad are generally classified as export/credit exposures. Insurance can be purchased against one or all of these risks. Following are ten critical steps that a risk manager should take when purchasing political risk insurance:

1. Selecting a Broker/Underwriter. The choice of a broker is perhaps the risk manager's most important concern, because the broker is the first line of contact. There are many brokers who can talk around the subject of political risks, but there are few who can perform adequately in a limited insurance market.

There are few options in the choice of underwriting market today, but the number is increasing rapidly as more insurance companies enter the political risk arena to meet the demands of American businesses.

A properly selected broker/underwriter combination will maximize risk management effectiveness. Establishing broker/underwriter rapport will help accomplish mutual understanding, reliable service, continuity of coverage, and increased opportunities for competitive pricing.

2. Service Requirements. In the process of selecting a broker and underwriter, an analysis must be made of what the corporate entity is looking for in the relationship. Aside from arranging the protection of assets, other services available include:

Export financing

Filing of applications

Political risk intelligence

Loss control and claims handling

Contract and exposure review

Communication of coverage to divisions, subsidiaries, etc.

The servicing area for political risk varies greatly among brokers, underwriters, and specialty consultants. Commissions and fees that affect the bottom line should reflect the services provided and the ultimate decision in a choice of broker and market.

3. Combining Risks. Risk managers should combine various political risk exposures under one policy. This will maximize underwriting clout in obtaining favorable terms and conditions and will greatly help to reduce premiums. Underwriters will favor a spread of risk and react positively toward being the corporation's only political risk market.

Because of the limited number of markets, minimal capacity, and a small underwriting/brokerage political risk community, it makes good risk management sense to concentrate risks into one market and not continually seek competition.

Risk managers also should combine other international risks in the coverage such as kidnap and ransom, difference in conditions, business interruption, marine, construction all-risk, etc. Underwriters favorably view combining these insurances in a package policy, because they typically are more stable and predictable than other political risks and help provide more reasons for the market to perform.

4. Communication. Because political risk insurances are unique and cannot be explained to the layman as easily as other conventional property/liability coverages, there is an absolute need to establish comprehensive communication channels between the risk manager's office and operating units such as international sales, treasury, corporate finance and credit, and legal to name a few. The following actions are recommended:

- Set up in-house seminars to educate and inform employees.

- Establish formal communication systems, including updates and weekly status reports.

- Appoint local coordinators to become familiar with the subject area and operating plan if, because of distant operating units, logistics present problems.

- Consider having brokers communicate directly with the divisional/operating personnel. This might expedite information transfers and provide additional support. However, the risk manager should always be kept informed of activity.

5. Contract Review. The typical method of providing underwriting data to the market is through questionnaires. This is an excellent starting point; however, a thorough review should always include analysis and review of the contract, terms of sale, terms of payment, and other documents relating to the exposure. This will help assure that the proper coverage is obtained, the underwriter thoroughly understands the risks, and any questions as to intent are answered clearly.

Changes often can be obtained by altering contract wording, terms of sale, etc., which could greatly reduce exposure and/or increase underwriting ability.

6. Political Risk Intelligence. Political risk insurance focuses on economic, social, and political events. To assess the need for coverage, the exposures must be understood, and understanding the exposures requires information. There are numerous sources of international intelligence including the U.S. State and Commerce Departments, private information services, banks, trade associations, embassies, and the media. As part of brokerage services, qualified facilities will assist in the area of information support and provide up-to-date intelligence on world conditions.

7. Rates, Terms, Conditions. Consider that each market's standard policy is different and that manuscripting is a necessity if proper coverage is to be provided. The exact exposure should be explicitly defined, and coverage should be tailored to meet the risk, whether it be for nationalization, currency inconvertibility, license cancellation, war, etc. Other areas that should be addressed are:

- Deductibles and coinsurance.

- Waiting period.

- Rescheduling.

- Warranties and exclusions.

- Method of reporting of exposures.

- Coverage for business interruption and protection of profits.

- Loss of market, delay.

- Changes or fluctuations in currency, which is an area for which it is becoming more difficult, if not impossible, to arrange coverage.

- Currency for claims payments.

- War risks.

- Cost, which appears to be controlled by market conditions, current economic and political situations, and quality of presentation, is typically a significant corporate expenditure.

- Premiums vary greatly with each risk, but one must be assured that apples are not being compared with oranges. Compiling checklists comparing quotas is a good method for fair evaluation.

8. Export Credit. Most political risk coverages exclude export credit (the proximate cause of loss emanates from the private buyer). Risks such as nonpayment and contract frustration are significant exposures that exist when dealing with private buyers. It is important to determine whether the ultimate buyer is private or governmental as interests may be jointly held. The time to make this determination is before the policy is secured and not after a loss has occurred.

Markets for export credit coverage are more limited than for political risk, requiring specific underwriting details about the creditworthiness of the buyer and the payment track record. Obtaining this insurance is often a tool for increasing foreign sales, because account receivables are protected and banks are more apt to provide lucrative export financing.

9. Loss Control. Insureds should seek measures to minimize opportunity for loss and to entice the interest of local businesses. Such measures include:

- Utilization of local management, personnel, etc.

- Development of sales that require continuing support, like providing service, maintenance, spare parts, accessories, etc.

- Development of rapport with local officials by joining business associations, trade groups, etc.

- Review of opportunities for local financing of the import or project.

- Analysis of the contract to further protect interests or secure favorable treatment from the host country.

All of these will help control the fate of your venture in the event of a loss.

10. Claims Procedures. Before a loss, written procedures should be developed addressing the who, what, when, where, and how of handling claims. List all personnel of the broker and the underwriter and include their home phone numbers. Contingency plans should be developed to provide options in the event of loss so that business will stay on track with little interruption. Run drills and have meetings with key personnel. Procedures should be agreed to ahead of time to arrange for arbitrators in the event of contractual and/or claims disputes.

Use a Specialist to Arrange International Protection

The Export Trading Act of 1982 made it easier for the small to medium-size company to do business overseas. To be competitive, these companies have to sell on terms where credit is extended beyond transfer of title or alternative credit/financing terms are offered. This poses two significant exposures: contingent marine and political/export credit. The inexperienced exporter typically overlooks these exposures until there is a loss. Additionally, U.S. exporters are selling on terms where the importer is controlling insurance, i.e., cost and freight (C&F), free on board (FOB), free alongside (FAS) etc. and has terms of payment extended beyond the ocean voyage or after arrival at the ultimate destination.

The marine insurance problem arises when a loss occurs that is discovered at the final destination, and the buyer refuses payment or partial payment based on the fact that not all the merchandise has arrived or is not in 100 percent sound condition.

The exporter will advise the buyer that the full quantity of a sound product was shipped, and that the buyer should seek payment from its insurance company. However, the buyer may never have arranged insurance or may have limited terms and conditions not covering this type of loss or the policy may have a huge deductible. Whatever the reason, the buyer has the merchandise and has not paid for it. Other than litigation, there are few other means to seek indemnification from the loss. This is where the marine insurance policy can play a strategic role.

There are numerous insurance brokerage companies that specialize in managing these exposures.

An exporter who sells on terms where it does not control insurance and can sustain a financial loss as a result of physical loss or damage can arrange a "contingency cover" that will respond to the loss as if the exporter was insuring the cargo as a primary interest. This insurance is known as "unpaid vendor" cover and can be easily arranged as part of the master cargo policy or on an independent special risk basis. This area is where most exporters leave the door open for exposure and most brokers and underwriters miss the boat. It takes a unique and specialized understanding of marine cargo logistics to do it well.

Specialized insurance brokers highlight other exposures such as political risk/export credit that may even be more significant as it is a primary and direct source of loss, not "contingent."

The risks faced come under a multitude of titles: import export license cancellation, private buyer guarantees, currency inconvertibility, confiscation, expropriation, war risk debt rescheduling, contract frustration, letter of credit drawdown, consequential damages, nationalization, deprivation, strikes, riots, and civil commotion.

Increasing those exposures is the U.S. exporter's need to deal with the third world political events in Iran. Afghanistan, Lebanon, Mexico, Nigeria, and Brazil have increased the demand for facilities to allow exporting corporations to transfer their risks.

There are numerous government and private insurance companies available to underwrite the political and export credit exposures. Lloyds of London underwrites a multitude of U.S. exporter exposures.

An increasing number of U.S. companies are participating in foreign government purchases and investments. The contracts involved have inherent political risk exposures. What if a foreign government, after placing a $3 million order and after 10 months of production (generating expenses of $1.5 million), experiences a coup d' état? The new government cancels the contract. Because of the nature of the sale, only $250,000 of the $1.5 million already expended can be salvaged, bringing the net loss to $1.25 million. This risk could have been insured.

What about the U.S. exporter who sells on consignment to Central America and ninety days after arrival the private buyer has not paid or, the customer has paid, but because of a trade deficit the state bank is unable to convert currency? Where does that exporter turn for collection? These risks are insurable.

Political and export credit insurance can be expensive and developing underwriting data is time consuming, however, the exposure warrants the effort and expense because of the protection it provides from potential disaster.

Policies typically have deductible and coinsurance levels with long waiting periods between time of default and underwriters claim payment. These terms should be negotiated in accordance with your contractual obligations.

Terms and conditions vary from underwriter to underwriter and competent brokerage support is mandatory to negotiate the most comprehensive coverage for a particular client's needs. There are only a handful of competent insurance brokers. When choosing a broker the exporter should review the broker's capability to place the coverage and also provide a country risk analysis, analyze sales contracts, work with international marketing executives, service the account daily, and assist in claims settlement.

Many U.S. exporters have used their policies in conjunction with export financing facilities to arrange lucrative export financing and have found this transfer of risk to be an avenue to increased foreign sales.

An exporting executive has the responsibility to protect the corporation's assets. The application of contingent marine insurance and political risk/export credit covers are prudent steps in the overall functions of exporting management. The bottom line is protection of assets and profit and the opportunity to become more competitive in international sales.

Transporters and Exporters Need Political Risk Coverage

Political risk is an issue of rising concern for the transportation industry. As world trade becomes more extensive, especially with third world countries, the need for political risk insurance is obvious. Although the political risk insurance market is tightening, with rising rates and shrinking capacity, coverage is available.

Shippers and transportation companies should be very aware of the fact that there are exposures, and that there are ways to transfer or minimize those exposures. Most companies doing business overseas are exposed to political risk and in need of coverage, from Fortune 500 companies to one-man trading companies. There are many companies unaware of the need for or the availability of political risk insurance.

Traditionally, the U.S. Government has had export insurance programs, but those programs are not the only options. U.S. private markets and Lloyd's of London also provide protection. The most pressing political risk coverage needs are fixed assets exposure and accounts receivable exposure. As an example, the exposure to political risk for a steamship company with overseas operations can be far-reaching. Terminals, cargo handling equipment, and other overseas terminal area assets may be at risk if the political climate in the country in which the company is operating changes. Industrial mishaps or political revolutions can leave an overseas company with substantial losses.

CNE&D coverage is available for such an exposure that will reduce losses that threaten an international company.

Fixed assets coverage for assets on land in an unstable or politically turbulent foreign country is largely unavailable. Companies managing to obtain on-land fixed assets coverage will meet with limited terms and very high prices.

Coverage is available by any mode of transit, and underwriters limit terms in most cases and prices vary considerably. However, insurance is always available at a price.

Underwriters have suffered tremendous losses during the last twenty years. As a result, there has been a tightening up of the market with insurance contracts becoming more detailed. The political risk market has incurred losses in such countries as Iran, Mexico, the Philippines, Brazil, Lebanon, Nicaragua, Russia, Korea, and El Salvador with similar areas indicated as "potential hot spots."

In addition to fixed assets exposure, companies doing business overseas, especially exporters and transporters, are subject to accounts receivable exposure. Export credit insurance is available for those political risks.

When a company exports goods or services to a country with an unstable economy, receiving payment is often a problem. The shipper can become a victim of inconvertibility of foreign currency. In countries where foreign exchange is controlled by the local government conversion can take many months or, in some cases, years. If a foreign government makes a decision to hold back on its foreign exchange of currency, an exporter can suffer a substantial loss. When the proximate cause of a loss emanates from a government or a political eventuality it becomes a political risk exposure.

An exporter of goods or services also can suffer losses due to an action on the part of the U.S. Government, thus creating a political risk exposure. An example would be a company that had contracted to build a telecommunications system for Libya, and due to political conflicts, the U.S. Government cancelled all export licenses to that country causing a loss for the telecommunications company. Because that loss was the direct result of a political decision on the part of the U.S. Government, political risk insurance was needed to cover the loss.

In dealing with political risk, a specialized insurance broker is essential. A political risk expert who is able to determine what coverage is needed, where a risk may be placed, and what kinds of loss control measures are needed to minimize political risk exposure is needed.

There are numerous brokers and underwriters who are prepared to provide extensive loss control advice for political risk customers. In the case of an accounts receivable exposure, a company may be advised to bill through a foreign subsidiary where the foreign exchange climate may be more agreeable than that between the United States and the country to which goods are being exported. It may be easier to convert the local currency of a third world country into Swiss or British currency than into U.S. dollars. Billing through a third country could, in some cases, minimize a risk.

There should also be loss control measures in place for political risk clients with fixed assets exposure. A variety of measures are available. Exposure can be reduced by involving local management in the operation of an overseas facility. If a plant is run by nationals, rather than by foreigners, the company is in a whole different ballpark.

Additionally, if a local government has an interest in an operation within its borders, political risk is lessened. It is recommended that corporate contingency plans for companies operating overseas to insure against loss of a plant or loss of future production be put into place.

While political risk capacity is shrinking due to recent losses, the need for coverage is growing. As the globe continues to shrink with more and more third world countries becoming part of the international commerce scene, the growing need for political risk insurance for shippers and transporters will continue.

Getting More from Marine Insurance

U.S. corporations in international trade are expanding their activity to increase overseas market share. Companies previously involved only in domestic sales are looking to foreign markets to increase greater growth and productivity. With this heightened activity, the requirements for comprehensive marine insurance programs are increasing, and the distribution manager's role in arranging these programs is becoming more vital.

When buyers aren't buying, when capital is scarce, when profits dwindle to a fraction of their former selves, distribution managers are put in a tough position. To put it more bluntly, it becomes time for them to cut their costs or pack their bags. When budgets must be trimmed to realize short-term economies, consideration of long-term benefits (other than job security) often goes out the window. One of the first casualties of these spontaneous purges is insurance. When people are forced to cut in any area they can, one of the first things they do is shop around for a cheaper insurance program, and they may end up leaving an insurance company they've been with for thirty years to go with a new agent who doesn't know them as well. While this may result in lower premiums, it also results in having an agent who won't cooperate as well when there is a large claim or doesn't have fifty years of premium payments to support paying the big claims. That means there's a better chance of foot-dragging when claims service is needed down the road.

Another favorite budget-trimming technique used by under-the-gun exporters is changing transportation packaging to take advantage of cut-rate carriers. If the exporter has used a U.S. flag conference carrier, a third world carrier with which the opportunities for claims recovery are minimal may be considered. Once again, from an insurance standpoint, the short-term savings may be far outweighed by the procedural problems that are likely to crop up down the road.

The shipper must recognize that insurance is not designed to yield short-term dividends. That's not what insurance is for. It's not meant to be used that way. Manipulating insurance coverage to milk savings for the short run will defeat the ultimate goals of the best-laid insurance plans.

The mission of the distribution manager in the current market with regard to marine insurance should not be one of concentrating on the reduction of premiums or on downgrading packaging and carrier standards that protect cargo from the need for a claim in the first place. **Rather, the emphasis should be on customizing insurance programs to take advantage of the opportunities to protect corporate assets, and therefore affect the bottom line of transportation costs.** Cost effectiveness can be improved not only by cutting initial costs, but by getting a greater return on the money companies have been investing all along.

Clearly, there are a number of steps an international shipper can take to help achieve both the short-term and long-term insurance objectives of its company.

Terms and Conditions

All-risk and "warehouse to warehouse" are standard conditions offered in marine insurance policies.

You have inland transit lanes that are brutal to the cargo, justifying the need to insure the cargo from door to door. When you're moving cargo to, say, South America, a major market in the new millennium, the most severe leg of the entire journey is the inland transit on the import leg.

Overland movement subjects cargo to a different set of stresses than does an ocean leg that many shippers overlook as they design packaging to protect their cargo for an ocean shipment.

While the majority of loss and damage comes from rough handling, most shippers must protect their goods against more exotic causes of damage. All-risk insurance coverage provides a broad base of protection, but does have exclusions including delay, inherent vice, willful misconduct of the assured, and loss of market. For example, if an electronics manufacturer is shipping high-technology equipment overseas and the anticipated voyage includes outside storage and the product becomes rusted or deteriorated as a result of outside storage, underwriters could take the position that the loss is uncovered because it would inherently happen if the cargo was stored outside and was not properly protected against the environment. Distribution managers should make sure that product lines that are susceptible to an inherent-type loss travel under policies that are properly endorsed to provide that kind of protection.

Another type of risk is loss of market, which is covered by loss of profits or business interruption insurance. It provides coverage for cargo that is lost at sea, delayed, or damaged at the time of arrival with the result that the shipper loses a sale, is unable to complete a project, has an installation delayed, etc. Under this policy, the shipper can still recoup its financial losses.

Brokers and Underwriters

There are plenty of insurance brokers and underwriters around, but very few of them are specialists in international transportation insurance. The search for such a specialist is one of the essential tasks distribution managers must undertake when insuring assets.

If a company is shipping overseas, it should deal with a forwarder that specializes in overseas shipments. When dealing with a claim that originates overseas, the company will them be dealing with an attorney who's a specialist in international law. In the same way, when insuring an international shipment, a specialist is needed.

Corporate insurance and finance departments are good sources of advice on the selection of brokers and underwriters. It is important that the distribution manager carefully select the broker who will place and arrange insurance programs, and that the underwriter is a well-established marine agency with worldwide servicing capabilities and a staff of professionals for in-depth backup and expertise.

Insurable Interests

On an FOB New York export sale, according to international trade definitions as interpreted by INCO Terms it is the buyer's responsibility to insure the cargo once it has been placed on the vessel. The terms of sale dictate the insuring responsibility.

However, the terms of payment can also come into play and determine insuring responsibility. A corporation could have an FOB New York sale, and terms of payment could be site draft sixty days. The U.S. corporation's insurable interest would be up until the day it receives payment.

The vessel could sail from New York destined for Rotterdam and sink three days out. When the corporation attempts to collect payment from the buyer who was responsible for insuring the merchandise, it may discover that the buyer did not insure, has limited terms and conditions, high deductibles, or other factors that will retard the company's opportunities to collect full or partial payment.

Third world nations are having an increasing effect on the insuring responsibilities of foreign shippers by implementing local regulations that require shippers to insure their cargoes in the local market. Failure to do so can result in fines or even seizure by government authorities. This necessity often burdens U.S. shippers with insurance policies that are characterized by high premiums and narrowly defined terms. In that case, a contingent or difference in conditions policy, which sits above anything that has to be purchased locally, should be obtained. This provides protection in case the policy purchased locally falls short or if the buyers did not purchase the required insurance .

Contingency coverage is particularly useful when a shipper's products have been sold on an accounts receivable basis. In this case, the risk is not only that merchandise will be lost, but also that payment will never be received. The potential problem for shippers with this type of sale is that if part of the shipment is lost or damaged on its way to the buyer, the buyer may rightfully refuse payment. However, because the exporter shipped sound goods, it will expect payment and will advise the receiver to recoup the loss from the insurer. The buyer, however, may not be sufficiently insured or may be carrying a huge deductible. Apart from legal action, the only way for the exporter to recover its loss in the event of such standoffs is through contingency insurance. The underwriters will expect you to seek payment from the buyer or the buyer's insurance company and will only pay for the loss on a loan basis, but if settlement cannot be made, the loan becomes a final settlement.

The bottom line to the dilemma—insurable interests versus insuring responsibility—is to attempt to control the insuring function at all times, whether you are selling or buying merchandise to or from overseas.

Competitive Markets

Shippers who feel compelled to reduce their premiums should be able to do so without sacrificing the relationship they've built with their current insurance company. Most of the worldwide marine insurance market continues into the year 2001 to be in a soft posture, which means that extremely competitive rates, terms, and conditions can be achieved at this time. This phenomenon has occurred during the past decade, and while it is always expected to tighten up, it is still a soft marketplace. This could be beneficial to the distribution manager who is trying to reduce transportation costs. In other words, lower premiums may be there for the asking while insurance companies struggle to maintain their customer base.

The marine insurance market may harden in the near future if conditions follow the "harder" probability/liability market of 2000/2001.

Reduced Paperwork

Computerization of insurance reporting has not been among the most vigorously waged campaigns in the computer revolution. In most cases, the technology is ready for action, but shippers haven't applied computer technology to more than a few specific tasks. Unfortunately, insurance reporting is not one of those tasks.

There are so many companies, including some of the biggest in the world, who duplicate and reduplicate paper for the reporting of insurance. Some have import/export order entry systems, and all the information they need is in those computer systems. The same information included on invoices is also needed for insurance reports, but many companies are taking this information, which is computer-generated for billing, and are copying it by hand into their insurance reports instead of generating those reports by computer as well.

One bright spot on the international documentation front has developed with regard to certificates of insurance that are often used to meet commercial banking and customer requirements. Much has been done to eliminate the requirements for these certificates through the use of preprinted invoices and/or preprinted "sticky-backs" which affix to the commercial documents that serve as proof of insurance.

Settling Fees

Marine insurance typically is rated by the shipper's experience, meaning that actual claim experience will determine what premium rates the shipper will pay for marine coverage. Thus, the greater the claims activity of the shipper, the higher the premium rate will potentially be. There are ways to minimize costs in advance of actual losses that can save cash in the short term on individual loss settlements and in the long term in the form of lower premiums.

An expense associated with claims activity is overseas settling fees for agents of the underwriter who handle the claim, as well as survey fees incurred when ascertaining the nature and degree of loss or damage. Some studies have indicated that these expenses range from 5 to 25 percent of claims dollars. That means that for every $100 of claims paid, $20 of that amount could be associated with just handling or settling the claim. Many times a small claim overseas, say $100, will have a $150 survey fee attached to it.

The opportunity exists to prenegotiate settling fees with overseas agents through U.S. brokers or underwriters on a reduced-account or bulk basis. The old saying, "If you don't ask, you won't get," holds true. There's no reason not to ask for a consideration on reducing settling fees. Limits also can be determined, such as for losses under $500, for which surveys can be waived and claims can be paid with the processing of a few documents.

Buy-Back Deductibles

Many shippers dislike the idea of deductibles on principle. They note that many claims are for relatively small losses. Without first-dollar coverage, the shipper pays for the entire loss out of it's pocket and never recovers anything through the expensive insurance programs.

The insurer's side of this is that a deductible program is more cost-effective and mitigates nuisance claims and costs.

Airshippers Beware—Be Warned: Recent Air Disasters Cause New Regulations

The freight-forwarding industry, along with the entire nation, mourned the tragic disaster of TWA flight 800, off the Long Island shoreline. Our thoughts and prayers are with the victims, the families, and all those parties associated with this most unfortunate and devastating event.

In light of this incident, along with the SwissAir and ValueJet tragedy, there is an increased awareness regarding the need to protect the vast population who travel by air, as well as international freight. Because of this, the Federal Aviation Administration (FAA) has implemented new security measures that will affect all shippers, direct carriers (e.g., airlines), and indirect carriers (e.g., freight forwarders).

It is necessary to increase the awareness of all shippers regarding these new regulations to minimize the effect it will have on the movement of freight. There are three important matters to consider.

First, there is a specific form to complete at the time of shipping, in addition to the already numerous documents required. With cooperation from the shipper, this will not be an issue or affect the overall movement of cargo.

Second, the shipper must allow more time for the consignment to reach its final destination. There is an increase in waiting time at the airlines when tendering cargo, mainly because the air carriers must scrutinize each and every driver and shipment. Once the cargo has been accepted, the air carrier has the right to retain the cargo for an indefinite period prior to the actual loading. The air carrier also has the right to X-ray and/or physically inspect the cargo for a visual check of the contents. Indirect air carriers can exercise this right as well.

Pilferage

The third and possibly most significant effect of these new regulations is Exposure to Risk! By giving direct and indirect air carriers the authority to open cargo for inspection, the risk of damage and pilferage is increased. The following steps should be followed to help reduce this risk:

1. While these new rules are being strictly enforced, the shipper should strongly consider insuring all consignments. If the shipper cannot insure the goods by its own means, the freight forwarder can assist. A reputable freight forwarder will have insurance options available.

2. The shipper should advise the freight forwarder that if inspection is intended, it should be performed at the point of origin, the container should be resealed prior to departure from the shipper's facility, and all should be done in the presence of the shipper.

Following is an outline of what is required by the shipper in order to comply with these new regulations.

Shippers Security Endorsement Form

No trucker will be permitted to receive cargo from a shipper without the Shipper's Security Endorsement signed at the time of the pickup. This form should be provided by the trucker.

If one employee is tendering numerous packages for either the same destination or multiple destinations at the same time, only one form is required to be completed.

However, if one employee tenders a consignment and the trucker is then asked to proceed to another department or dock in the same facility for additional packages, the truckers must have a Shippers Security Endorsement signed from each and every person in that company who tenders the cargo.

The shipper will be required to fill in their company name, original signature, printed name, and date.

In addition and absolutely mandatory, the shipper (or more specifically the employee who is tendering the cargo) must present two forms of valid identification (ID), one of which must be a picture (e.g., driver's license) ID . The shipper ID information will be recorded on the Shippers Security Endorsement and the original will be held on file by the forwarder for presentation to the FAA upon request. A copy is given to the airline at the time of tender.

Please note that these rules can change at any time and all shippers must keep informed of any such changes.

To reduce the amount of delays in movement of cargo, the shipper should take the following steps:

1. Marking and Labeling. Ensure that the cargo is properly marked and labeled before it leaves your facility. This is especially critical for IATA classified "Dangerous Goods by Air." When shipping dangerous goods, it is most important that proper documentation and labeling are in strict accordance with the rules and regulations of shipping dangerous goods by air.

2. Cooperation. Cooperation with the trucker when asked to fill out the endorsement at the time of pickup will ease the process. The person releasing the cargo to the trucker should have ID ready, as per the outline presented previously.

3. FAA Approval. Confirm that the freight forwarder has FAA approval to operate as an indirect carrier. A freight forwarder who is approved is given an assigned number that will be indicated on all air waybills, domestic or international. If the forwarder is not FAA approved, it will delay the movement of your cargo.

4. Centralize. If there is more than one package, attempt to have all packages available at a central location within your facility so that only one shipper's security endorsement will require completion.

5. Photo ID. Shippers should consider utilizing a photo ID system for all employees who handle freight. Many gateway airports and airlines have installed procedures for photo ID requirements.

These new rules will increase delays in transportation, especially in the international arena. Compliance with these new regulations must become standard operating procedure. In time, with mutual understanding, cooperation, and patience, this new obstacle in shipping can be overcome. It is our common goal to reduce transit time, and most importantly, to secure safety during air travel.

The SwissAir Disaster: Makes You Think Twice about the Perils of Global Trade

Our hearts go out to the passengers, crew, families, and friends of the SwissAir flight that went down off the coast of Halifax, Canada. All of us who travel internationally as part of our work in exporting feel this tragedy, very close to home. It makes you think twice about international travel and the risks we face when doing our job in global markets. One risk often overlooked, until doom raises its ugly head, is that of the individual risks and personal needs of personnel.

Many years ago, I encountered my first client situation where an executive was kidnapped in a major Latin American city. The call came into my California client's office. Their agent advised that their salesman did not show up for a meeting, was not in his hotel, and they just had received a call from kidnappers who wanted $60,000 by tomorrow, or else.

My client called the local police , who referred them to Washington, D.C.—the FBI, CIA, and the State Department. They were nice and to a certain degree helpful, as was the American embassy in the Latin American city where the abduction took place. Even the local police were helpful. But it took several days for everything to be organized, and some ten days later, the client was released, stressed and at a loss, but unharmed.

This was my client's first management exposure to international terrorism. They realized how vulnerable they were. Fortunately, it turned out well but an executive, colleagues, family, and friends were at odds for a week plus three days.

With our assistance the company decided to review it's overall exposures to the many personnel that travel overseas.

> **They discovered numerous loopholes in their overseas practice and procedures and the various insurance policies they thought would respond.**

They realized that their standard workers' compensation policy, as well as their health plan ceased once the employee began to travel overseas. They made arrangements quickly to endorse these policies to include international travel. They modified the policies for life and disability coverages as well, taking foreign travel into consideration.

They purchased kidnap and ransom insurance. This not only protects against kidnap and ransom, but offers the company a place to call to begin the process of investigation, recovery, and mitigation. The government process alone can be bureaucratic, frustrating, and slow. The kidnap and ransom underwriters have teams set up in advance to deal with foreign terrorism.

Terrorism spreads beyond specific acts of kidnap. Executive's caught up in the middle of war, civil strife, and global disasters are also at risk. Just look at some recent events in Jakarta, Kuwait City, Bosnia, and the embassy bombings in Africa.

These serious eventualities are not the only issues for concern. More mundane events, such as the need for a dentist while traveling in Beijing, the need for emergency financial assistance while in Jeddah, the need for immediate legal defense in Frankfurt, etc. etc. Just what would you do, who would you call???

There are some options in assisting you with these international exposures. There are various consultants who can work with you in evaluating your global exposures and providing mitigation options. One firm based near Philadelphia, International SOS Assistance Corporation can be very helpful in this regard. They provide twenty-four, seven day a week direct assistance with U.S. companies engaged in international trade. Some of the services they provide include:

- Emergency medical and security evacuation services
- Worldwide alarm centers
- Access to lawyers and interpreters
- Medically supervised repatriation
- Travel assistance
- Insurance benefits
- Pretrip reports
- International telecommunication services

The first step in dealing with overseas exposures is identifying the risks and the problem areas and then develop contingency plans to provide options and mitigate the consequences. There are consultants; insurance companies, such as AIG, Chubb, CIGNA; and companies like SOS Assistance that can provide hands-on services to protect a company's most valuable asset—its employees.

Concluding Remarks

Those exporters who transfer risk are more likely to produce profitable export sales and sustain high levels of new business development in foreign markets. The recommendations outlined in this chapter provide sound advice for the exporter to analyze overseas exposure, find methods for risk transfer, and provide insurance products for professional risk management and sound export strategy.

Keep in mind that the underwriting market is a "fluid" one. It changes often and swiftly. All exporters need to watch market conditions on a regular basis to verify markets, terms, and conditions.

11

Technology in Global Trade

The future of international trade lies with greater utilization of technology. The execution and management of e-commerce sales, fulfillment, logistics services, payment options, and more through technology is discussed in this chapter.

Export transactions handled totally by technology is here now. It is not a pipe dream. Those companies that are not spending time, money, and resources on automating export operations will not be in export trade for long. The efficiencies gained in export automation will make one company substantially more competitive then another. Guidelines and options for the use of technology in global trade are outlined in this chapter with an emphasis on documentation, tracking, and information management.

Using Technology to Gain a Competitive Advantage in Global Trade

U.S. importers and exporters can gain significant competitive advantage in global trade through the use of technology. Access to new markets, more cost-effective sales efforts, and less costly logistics are but a few of the immediate benefits.

Global technology as it relates to international trade is changing and growing every day. There are many options available to the large, medium, or small import/export firm. Hook up a PC, secure a modem, and you are ready to go for less than U.S.$2,000. An in-depth review of global technology reveals more than thirty specific tools available in this technological era.

Many software and service providers provide extensive data on businesses overseas. These resources are both government and commercial based. Using electronic data interchange (EDI) or the Internet, one can log in and find an array of information on the following:

- Market data on overseas opportunities

- Names and contact data on overseas companies

- Names and contact data on resources, support services, and service providers

- Research profiles on products, services, and demographics

- Specific product and prospect opportunities

Many of these data providers, such as Trade Compass based in Washington, D.C., have become serious information providers. Others, such as the Department of Commerce, AT&T, and Dun & Bradstreet, have been providing the service a long time, but have greatly expanded their individual capabilities.

More progressive companies have developed their own web pages to advertise the products and services they sell. This can be accomplished by the smallest of companies for under U.S.$25 per month. Very extensive and more elaborate web sites can cost tens of thousands of dollars and have electronic commerce capabilities that offer the customer the ability to place an order through the web site, among other services.

E-mail affords cost-effective, timely communication between sellers and buyers. It can replace the fax or enhance it. It has "broadcast" capability that allows the user to form one message and send it to a wide audience automatically at times when usage rates are the lowest, allowing very cost-effective communication.

It allows marketing and sales pieces to be forwarded without the expense of overnight mail and express services. It allows more flexibility and "tailorability" to individual client needs, in different languages, or with different presentation designs to allow for cultural, ethnic, and religious nuances.

Letters of credit, which are heavily used in global trade can be transacted via automation without the need for all the historical paperwork. Wire transfers, sight drafts, and other means of documentary credit devices can now be accommodated via EDI. Many of the world's leading financial institutions have begun various initiatives independently and in conjunction with various banking service providers to establish:

Common EDI means of communication

Secure methods of protecting confidential data

More timely paperless transactions

Global links between foreign firms in an array of countries with local and international banks

Successful logistics providers now view their role as information/communication providers as well as companies that move freight.

The integrated carrier, the freight forwarder, the customhouse broker, the ocean and air carriers, etc. who are making the investments in technology will be the only ones who will survive into the twenty-first century.

The logistics industry is enhancing its use of technology by:

- Developing defined EDI or Internet interfaces with its customers' import/export order entry systems
- Providing linkage into warehousing, inventory management, and shipping functions

- Establishing systems for tracking freight and to deal with customer service issues

- Becoming an integral partner with its clients as an information resource

- Having programs that ease the knowledge of preparation of and execution of international documentation

- Affording access to government reporting requirements and export licensing matters

The integrated carriers such as Federal Express and United Parcel Service along with the larger freight forwarders and air/ocean carriers have generally taken leadership positions offering various competitive products.

Many logistics providers are expanding the array of services they are providing because technology has afforded options not previously available.

Automation Takes the Pain out of International Trade Documentation

Within five years, exporters and importers will be exchanging their arduous, painstaking, transactional documents via the Internet or some other EDI capability.

> *Today, these same exporters and importers need to determine if they are going to react now and be at the forefront of this technology or wait until they are behind the eight-ball.*

International documentation typically proves ownership, facilitates transportation, and reacts with customs for entry into the buyers country. Some documents are used for other purposes, such as an insurance certificate in case of loss or damage.

For many international transactions and the accompanying documentation, much of the detail is the same from document to document. Pieces, weight, commodity description, value, from/to, commercial and pro forma invoices, certificates of origin, shippers export declarations, bills of lading are the key export/import facts and documents—all with loads of repetitive data.

Automation affords the most cost-effective approach to creating these documents and managing their distribution and utilization.

The U.S Government is taking an aggressive approach to import/export trade automation. For more than ten years the government's import initiative, the Automated Brokerage System (ABS) has been very successful, basically automating the import transaction for both customs brokers and U.S.-based importers. While the system still has numerous bugs that are being worked on, it can be declared a success.

Most recently, a combined effort of U.S. Customs, the Census Bureau, and the Bureau of Export Administration (BXA) has resulted in Automated Export System (AES). The AES is designed to automate the exporter's requirement to send a shipper's export declaration to the government. This is now done primarily manually at the time a shipment is dropped off with the outbound carrier.

At some point in 2001, all exporters, their forwarders, or agents will have to be online with U.S. Customs in order to report export SED data. While the details of the process, timing, and substance of the transfer of this data are still being negotiated, the responsibility to report some SED information by 2001 will be happen. This will lead exporters to automate other aspects of their export operation, which will have immediate, as well as long-term favorable effects.

Automation allows cost-effective export administration and an EDI-based tracking capability. It affords ease of transfer of export data between various company units (export to accounting to shipping) and allows interface with forwarders and carriers.

Eventually, it will allow transfer of data directly to customers, their overseas agents, and their host customs entity. This will do away with "hard copy,"which is expensive and difficult to manage successfully.

Keep in mind that many individuals and companies shy away from exporting because of the problems associated with managing export documentation.

Technology in the documentation supply chain creates the opportunity to ease this task, facilitating import/export activity. It also provides numerous benefits in reducing the cost of the transaction, tracking the logistics/transportation, and providing useful data for future management utilization.

As we progress into 2002, technology will be an excellent foundation for export compliance management.

EDI—What to Expect from the Carrier

Exporters searching for timely information, tracking capabilities, and methods of reducing the cost of exporting are depending increasingly on carriers with EDI facilities. What products or services is EDI offering? What methods is EDI using to deliver these products and services to customers?

Some exporters consider forwarders an extension of the cargo carriers. In this case, the forwarder will be considered a carrier. Forwarders also have taken a leadership role in maintaining a competitive advantage through the use of technology.

Basic EDI Services the Carrier Provides

- Automated bills of lading
- Routing and booking
- Pricing
- Tracking
- Documentation information

Most carriers provide electronic bills of lading. This readily reduces the cost of executing shipments, particularly for frequent or repeat exports. Integrated carriers, such as UPS, Airborne, DHL, and Federal Express have responded to exporters by providing automated processing of bills of lading associated with export transactions. Most larger freight forwarders and steamship lines can also provide this service. Some air carriers have a limited capability. Others, such as United Airlines, American Airlines, Delta, and Lufthansa have updated their capabilities for this service.

Many carriers have enhanced their services to assist a shipper to find out about levels and routing options. These advanced carriers allow easy booking—another cost-saving measure.

Shipping rates are available online with some carriers, with the exception of integrated carriers, on a limited basis.

Tracking is critical to the overall evaluation of a carrier's performance. Airlines and integrated carriers have taken the leadership role in this area. Steamships have made great strides but are behind in providing automated data. Compared to airfreight, ocean freight is more complicated to track.

Carriers, particularly freight forwarders, are required to adhere to documentation procedures for export transactions. Integrated carriers such as Federal Express have automated the process with newly developed software programs for IBM and Apple PCs.

While there are government and private written sources on documentation procedures, these are often outdated. Automation facilitates the ability to update changes in a timely manner.

Delivery Systems

The means used for communication is as important as the information provided. Many carriers, particularly major ocean and air carriers who often provide 800 telephone numbers, are automated internally. A customer service representative at a computer terminal should answer questions based on information in the computer. This is an acceptable option for small shippers.

This does not work for frequent shippers, who should have the capability to obtain information online.

Some forwarders and carriers with in-house EDI systems deliver the data via fax. This may work in some cases, but direct interface is more cost-effective. Most carriers allow limited access via modem, which is a quick and reliable means for transferring data between carrier and shipper. From the carrier's perspective it also allows control over access to the entire system.

Some systems provide interface from mainframe to mainframe. This system is more expensive, but provides quick detection of viruses, which could have devastating effects if undetected. Many companies use third party facilities (called "firewalls") that interface between carriers and shippers. This slows the process of data interchange but the trade-off guarantees security. Many of the third party facilities act as conduits for carriers before the transfer to the shipper. Teledyne Brown is one such third party facility that interfaces with various air carriers and feeds the information to forwarders and shippers. The direct interface includes bills of lading, booking, tracking, billing, payment transfers, exchange of documentation information, costing and rating data, and e-mail.

What one expects from the carrier is governed by need and competition. Carriers are being forced to respond to the need to provide extensive data and services on a direct interface basis with its shippers and exporters.

EDI is expanding quickly, and over the next two to five years will become state-of-the-art for carrier/exporter communication and services provided. The exporter should demand the services afforded by technology and keep the pressure on during this revolution that is taking place in international trade.

Where's My Export Freight?

You have completed a $225,000 transaction with a buyer in Thailand and shipped the freight via an air carrier just three days earlier for delivery on Thursday. You walk into your office at 0845 on Friday morning and find a fax from an irate new customer screaming, "Where's my freight?"

You call your freight forwarder or integrated carrier and it takes all day Friday to track the shipment. You find out that it had arrived on Wednesday, but it has been delayed in customs, awaiting documentation from the shipper, and you knew nothing about it. Customs is closed in Bangkok on Saturday, so you have to wait until Monday to begin to resolve the problem. In the end, the freight is delivered on Tuesday—five calendar days after the scheduled date. Not a great scenario, but also not atypical.

In the better scenario, you ship the freight on Monday, as before. On Tuesday, you look in your computer, which is directly linked to your air carrier and note that the shipment is confirmed on a flight to Tokyo to meet a transfer flight to Bangkok. On Wednesday, when you come into the office, you have a message from the air carrier or forwarder, advising you that the freight arrived last night, but the invoice was missing from the pouch of documents attached to the master air waybill. Your agent in Bangkok advises you to fax a copy, and he will clear with that document. You do as advised. On Thursday, you receive a confirmation from your computer that the freight was out for delivery at 1500 local time in Bangkok. On Friday the fax from your new client advises that all has arrived and he appreciates that all was in order and delivered on time.

Obviously, the second scenario is one that quality exporters would prefer. With certain international carriers, forwarders, and integrated transportation companies, this can be a reality. The carriers that have this capability will survive into the twenty-first century. Those that do not get onto the bandwagon and cannot provide quality, proactive tracking and tracing will not be in business in the year 2002. Many smaller and unresponsive, nonforward thinking companies have already fallen by the wayside because they have not participated in the race for the information superhighway. EDI is here to stay and will become the measure of the more qualified, service-oriented transportation companies. There are three key areas that EDI will play a role in:

1. Transfer of shipping information to organize and execute international exports

2. Tracking and tracing shipments

3. Management information and reports

Transfer of Shipping Data

Everyone involved in export understands the voluminous documentation reports involved with export orders. Much of the information is repetitive and the time required to produce these documents could easily be reduced through electronic interface.

Freight forwarders have taken the lead in this regard. Many large and medium-size freight forwarders have spent the time and money and made the effort to link their in-house computer systems with their customers' systems. This affords ease of communication and allows electronic transfer of data that would normally travel by fax, mail, courier, or other means. This speeds up the documentation turnaround time, provides greater accuracy, and may provide other ancillary benefits such as control of inventory, accountability systems, and easier quality control management.

Because of the repetitive information in an export order, such as the shipper and consignee address, having information in a system's memory to access if one is preparing an invoice, a packing list, an export declaration, a house bill of lading, or other document could speed up the execution of these documents. With a specialized export document program, many additional variables, such as pieces, weights, product codes, clearing agents, and shipping instructions also are readily available and reproducible in all the various required documents.

In elaborate systems, many documents can be forwarded ahead of the shipment via an EDI database, affording the foreign clearance agent the opportunity to clear the goods before arrival. This expedites delivery and makes customers happy.

The banking, government, and shipping communities entered this arena long ago through such organizations as the NCITD, attempting to standardize shipping EDI needs and to speed up document transfers and payments.

Tracking and Tracing

Integrated carriers such as UPS, Federal Express, and Airborne have taken great strides in this regard. Their efforts still are evolving, but are light years ahead of where these companies were two or three years ago.

Steamship lines and air carriers, including United Airlines, American, Continental, Sealand, Maersk & NYK Line are but a few of the carriers that have set up 800 numbers to give clients the capability to track and trace their shipments.

Airlines maintain exact data because of the more time-sensitive nature of their shipping clientele. Steamship lines have quality systems that afford basic tracking and updates of ETAs around the world. The problem with both airlines and steamship lines is that they depend on people to input data in a timely and accurate fashion. They all could utilize better input quality control management and systems.

In addition there is a syndrome that the people who utilize the computer to track and trace develop that I have named "the ugly track face syndrome." What happens is that they depend on the computer 100 percent and forget that the computer is tracking something physical. For example, a shipper calls the 800 number of an airline to find out why the freight has not shown up in Brussels. The shipper gets the pat answer, "Well it must be there because the computer says it is so." By that time, the shipper would like to reach through the phone and strangle someone. The shipper needs someone at the airline or the integrated carrier to find out why the computer is wrong and to do a physical search. This always becomes a struggle and is one of the reasons many shippers turn to forwarders, who will usually do this arduous work for them.

The computer, which was supposed to resolve the problem, can become the bone of contention and cause more harm than good. Many carriers are looking to more modern methods of tracking and tracing. UPS, ABX, and Federal Express drivers have coding devices to provide up-to-the-minute data. They are good examples of companies that are using the latest in technology to stay ahead of the competition.

Steamship lines and long-haul trucking companies that enter Mexico and Canada are utilizing satellite tracking devices to locate containers and trailers. Many transport companies are bar coding freight to track its position as it passes through the various checkpoints in the transit cycle.

High-tech carriers on specialized reefer transport loads are using sophisticated equipment to monitor the performance of refrigeration units and measure the temperature of the stow. Some have limited capability to make changes necessary to protect the cargo from loss or damage.

Many forwarders from abroad have "banded" their resources to form technology networks. They interface and exchange data to the benefit of their mutual clients. This gives them the capability to compete with larger forwarders and integrated carriers. Almost all transport carriers provide in-house computers to their clients, offering varying degrees of EDI capability interface.

> **Find substantive points, get referrals, and call them.**

In evaluating what serves you best, identify your needs and then your best scenario case. Don't be fooled by buzzwords and fancy names or slogans. Find substantive points, get referrals, and call them.

Management Information and Reports

Once all this information is available, has been recorded and saved, it can be made available to management to dissect, discuss, and draw conclusions. Once the quality of data has been qualified with acceptable degrees of accuracy, management needs to identify the usefulness of it in various formats. Most carriers, integrated companies, steamship lines, and truckers fall down in this area. It is the forwarders and logistics management companies that can deal with all the raw data and provide useful reports for management to evaluate. The following are some reports that utilize shipping data:

- Sales by carrier and mode.

- Shipper on-time performance.

- Volumes by customer, country, and mode of transit.

- Shipping costs by various units of measure, i.e., shipping to Asia costs $.20 per kilo compared to Europe where ther cost is $.17 per kilo. Why?

- Loss and damage reports by carrier and mode of transit.

- Shipping expenditures by carrier, mode, and areas of the world.

- Outturn reports showing differentials in shipped and received weights.

- Inventory and quality control reports.

The number and type of reports are endless. As long as the data is available and of an acceptable level of accuracy and can be captured, manipulated, and formatted, the value for management and operating personnel is extensive.

Exporting is a maturing industry in the United States. Compared to more mature industries EDI is in its infancy and has a long way to go. Fortunately, the support industries to exporting are recognizing the need to provide data in a timely and accurate manner, are reacting to this need immediately, and some interesting results are being provided by competitive forces . Five years from now the carrier, the forwarder, and the integrated transporter will be here and surviving if their EDI capability is vast, substantive, and 100 percent user-friendly.

The Automated Export System—a Logistics Professional's Opinion

Much has been said about AES in the media during the last four years. There has been much discussion outlining the attempts of several trade organizations, individual companies, and various exporting entities to curtail the combined efforts of customs, the BXA, and the Bureau of Census. There have also been inquiries made by other government agencies, representing Congress and the GAO, to determine the justification of customs efforts in AES.

I am very involved in AES as a user, proponent, and consultant, and I was a member of the Trade Resource Group (TRG) in Washington, D.C. with involvement in the NVOCC and exporter coalition groups. I represent several interests, including the Small Business Exporters Association (SBEA) and the National Association of Export Companies (NEXCO). The TRG was an attempt to allow commercial business to have input in the government's development of AES. In many ways this effort is successful and in others it fails.

The AES is the government's system for collecting timely, accurate, and comprehensive data on exports in an automated format in lieu of the paper SEDs, which are the source the government uses to make sure exporters do not export what they are not supposed to export.

There is also a desire to hold exporters, forwarders, and transportation providers more accountable to the government in export transactions. While there are many responsible American exporters and service providers, no one would argue that the current systems of control and quality of data is not flawed and could not be vastly improved.

Most professional exporters, associations, and entities involved in the process are proponents of the transfer of SED data electronically. The current "curtailing" is an attempt by industry to make sure this effort does not impede export trade and that there will be minimal repetition of work on the part of the exporter, i.e.,.that it does not create more work or greater expense!

Many, including the author, believe that the component of AES to control what is exported would best be served by increasing the systems at the point of export for checking, security, and surveillance. It would be a hands-on approach to checking freight with inspectors, sophisticated x-ray equipment, etc. that would best serve the interest of "control."

However, the main benefit of AES is being missed by most individuals. AES will be the catalyst for an entire industry in a global economy, which is hampered by "paper," to automate the entire export process from the United States and eventually the import process in most foreign countries. The cost efficiencies and systems for quality data and control for private commerce and government is the true benefit of the AES initiative. The future that allows an exporter to enter the export order, process it electronically, talk to its forwarder and carrier, book shipments, work with banks on letters of credit, track and trace shipments, communicate alerts, deal with foreign customs, and transfer documents electronically is the real benefit of the AES initiative. I believe the entities that currently serve the AES structure sometimes lose sight of this issue, which could significantly benefit global commerce.

All sides of the various issues are working and negotiating for a mutual resolve. We must have at the forefront of these discussions the concept that while the government is somewhat frustrated by the lack of and the poor quality of export data:

> *it must approach the AES initiative slowly, patiently, and with a sincere interest in listening and reacting to industry sources, making sure that the United States maintains a competitive advantage as an export source for goods and services and that no step, procedure, or law impedes this.*

The majority of exporters are and will continue to be responsible and develop better habits and systems for data reporting, but not at the expense of time, resources, or effort that would cause a competitive disadvantage. There is a compromise necessary that balance all points of view, but all the potential short-term consequences and the long-term benefits of the AES initiative must be kept in sight.

E-Commerce: Export Logistics

E-commerce has become a large phenomenon in global trade. The fulfillment and logistics segments for domestic sales have incorporated e-commerce successfully. But in international trade, statistics point to huge rates of failure in the attempt to incorporate e-commerce.

The following problems remain to be resolved:

1. While ordering can be achieved in e-commerce from almost anywhere in the world over the Internet, there is still the need to deliver the freight. All the exposures, this book has talked about in global trade exist for e-commerce, but perhaps more so.

2. Electronic ordering can be built into the system, but not electronic delivery.

3. Whatever system is structured for ordering, there is a basic premise in international business that you need to know who your customers are. Does e-commerce allow this? The BXA requires U.S.-based exporters to know who they are selling to, what the customers are using the product for, and to protect against transshipment. Does the e-commerce system afford this control?

Failure to comply has the consequences of not being able to export and/or heavy fines and penalties.

4. Payment needs to be made. Credit cards work up until the first dispute. Then you realize how useless credit cards can be in international sales, when you don't know the other party.

5. Someone must make sure the customer understands the risks, liabilities, and costs under INCO Terms. Professionals rarely understand them, how would the general public? Then who would be responsible for local clearance and delivery? Do they have local custom's representation? Has power of attorney been authorized?

6. Returns need to be handled correctly. How will the e-commerce system manage returns?

The questions are frightening. Thus far, no one company has successfully worked out <u>all of these issues</u> on a global basis with e-commerce. The bottom line is that the e-commerce supply chain in exports must be set up to respond to all these issues. It will require large EDI operating platforms of standard operating procedures (SOPs) by country, with compliance performance and all logistical concerns dealt with successfully.

A nuance to global trade is that successful logistics requires a lot of handholding and a lot of flexibility. I am not sure anyone involved in export e-commerce could achieve this without "mucho" tweaking.

Concluding Remarks

Technology controls the future of global commerce, and exporting is a major part of that formula. Taking the initiative to develop software solutions and manage the export supply chain with technology will go a long way in securing your export future. Following the guidelines and options in the use of technology in global trade from documentation to e-commerce provided in this chapter will support the exporter in achieving this goal.

12

Managing the Critical Geographic Areas of the World

Particular areas of the world present certain risks and obstacles, or at the very least, certain frustration for the U.S. exporter. Brazil, Mexico, China, and Russia are just a few of these areas. This chapter offers tried and proven solutions for making exporting to these areas run more smoothly. Much of the advice and counsel can be used in all new and difficult export markets.

Dealing with Customs in Foreign Countries

As the exporting business becomes more competitive, U.S. exporters are being asked to provide door-to-door service as a way of adding value. This often means providing the service of clearing freight in the customer's country and arranging local cartage to their door from the point of entry. This is often referred to as a "free domicile" shipment. Such arrangements present a number of problems, including the following:

- Exporters must arrange for an agent in the destination country to represent them for the clearance and the delivery. In some developing countries, this is more easily said than done.

- Local requirements regarding documentation, customs, duties, taxes, etc. must be dealt with. A lack of local expertise could prove disastrous.

- Additional costs must be added into the transaction. Clearance, handling, storage, delivery, duties, taxes, value-added tax (VAT), etc. must be dealt with. Each of these could be quite sizable, depending on the commodity, it's value, and the country you are dealing with. You could add additional costs of up to 60 percent of the traditional door-to-port shipment.

- Potential liabilities also exist, as the exporter now owns merchandise in a foreign country until title is released to the local customer. All sorts of insurance issues come up. General liability, property, marine, and product liability coverage all must be reviewed and addressed.

Forget about legal matters for a moment. When you agree to a door-to-door delivery or a free domicile shipment, you are representing in good faith that you have the wherewithal, knowledge, and resources to perform both on time and competitively. To maximize the potential for a safe, on time door-to-door delivery, take the following steps:

1. Make sure you and your customer fully understand what is being agreed to and who is going to pay for what. A lack of clarity in this regard, particularly regarding who must pay the clearance, delivery, duty, etc., is the cause of many disputes over money after a shipment has been delivered. Once this has been clarified, particularly if funding these additional costs are in the exporters purview, the cost of goods sold must take into account these additional expenses.

2. Establish a quality relationship with an agent in the importing country. Make sure the agent has the expertise to handle your needs. U.S.-based freight forwarders often can provide this service through their overseas offices and agency network. If you do business in many areas of the world, using two or three freight forwarders with expertise in certain regions will prove invaluable.

Because getting paid may depend on all aspects of the shipment cycle going according to plan, you must develop active resources with many entities to protect your interests. These include freight forwarders, customhouse brokers, international bankers and insurance brokers/underwriters, law offices, accounting firms, and local storage and cartage companies, etc. These entities will be key to protecting your interests and assets.

International insurance brokers and underwriters are excellent sources to manage the additional exposure on free domicile shipments. They have a staff of experts to review risk and offer means of cargo loss control and/or indemnification.

Proper documentation is integral to successful international trade, and for a free domicile shipment, it will be critical. Develop a checklist of the following:

Commercial invoice

Bills of lading

Packing lists

Inspection certificates (Societe Generali Surveillance Inspection Agency)

Export permits

Import licenses

Haz-mat paperwork

Quality certification

Certificates of insurance

The exporter also should consider:

> The number of copies necessary for each document
>
> Local language and translation issues
>
> Need for notarized, legalized, or consularized documents
>
> Who will need how many copies of which documents when
>
> Packing requirements, such as special marks or numbers
>
> Formatting of documents and signatories

It is likely that the customer has imported before and will have specific knowledge of local nuances in having shipments cleared. **Copies of documents should be faxed to the clearing agent and/or importer prior to shipment so they can be sure the documents are in compliance.** This will afford adequate time to make any necessary changes and avoid delays.

Close communication with your overseas customer regarding documentation requirements is critical. Unfortunately, in some countries, who you know and how much "black money" (a.k.a. bribes???) is offered are what will be required to get the job done. Time-sensitive deliveries often require this. Certain Latin American and African countries and countries of the former Soviet Union are currently the culprits in this regard. Most experienced international traders will tell you that it exists in all countries to a certain extent, but it is more prevalent in some countries. The bottom line is that "local knowledge" will assist greatly in the mitigation of customs issues.

The nature of the clearance process causes excess delays in some countries, which might present additional handling and storage charges. Imports in the United States typically will clear in twenty-four to forty-eight hours. Imports into many foreign ports such as Moscow, Bangkok, Bogota, Sao Paulo, and Lagos could take as much as ten days to clear, depending on a variety of circumstances. If perishables are being shipped, this delay must be anticipated and prepared for prior to shipping to prevent disastrous consequences.

Preparation and exact execution is a key ingredient to a free domicile shipment. U.S. exporters must be keenly aware that taking on this type of shipment results in greater responsibility with potentially significant costs and headaches associated with it. Following the steps outlined in this chapter will assist you in the preparation process, which will protect your interests as well as those of your overseas customers.

Europe and the New Euro

The world's many and varied markets offer untold opportunities to U.S. companies considering expansion through exporting. Not surprisingly, as markets mature and consumer demand changes, the potential opportunity within any given area rises and falls. In this section of the chapter, the forces currently at play that will help you consider entrance into some of the more rapidly changing markets, including Western and Eastern Europe and North America are discussed.

The European Community (EC)

The European Community (EC) is a group of countries that have joined together to establish a common market to enjoy the advantages that the combined powers of these nations provide. The EC represents an area of approximately 1,480,425 square miles and a population of roughly 350 million, the world's largest free market.

The overall purpose of the EC is to gradually achieve a community where the free movement of people, goods, services, and capital can be assured. However, in the early 1980s, it was clear to the members of the EC that fifteen years after they had amended the rules governing inter-EC trade, the EC was still far from being a free market. In 1985, after several summit meetings, the members of the EC formally instructed the European Commission to draft a detailed program for achieving a single, unified market by the end of 1992. While the EC generally did not develop a final plan for unification of the market by the close of 1992, it took another six years for the plan's implementation and resulting market unification. It is also certain that the plan, whatever its final form, will affect exporters to this vast European market.

Exports to the EC are subject to customs duties at the point of entry. Once the initial import formalities are completed and the duties are paid, the goods are considered to be in free circulation and subject to checks at internal borders.

The Euro

The most recent development within the EC is the Euro. While there are many issues to be resolved, effective January 1, 1999, a combined single currency, the Euro Dollar, went into effect, representing the following countries: Austria, Belgium, Finland, Ireland, Italy, Luxembourg, France, Germany, Spain, the Netherlands, and Portugal. Four EC members who will not participate as of January 1, 1999 are the United Kingdom, Denmark, Sweden, and Greece.

Exporters can trade in the local currency or utilize the Euro dollar, whichever the importer agrees to. This enables the exporter to take advantage of favorable exchange rates or banking costs.

In the long term, issues will extend to commonality among all trade-related matters, such as duties, VAT and taxes, trademarks, patents, intellectual property rights, operating standards, etc.

EC Duties, VAT, and Taxes

Customs Duties. Customs duties are charged under an EC-wide tariff system that establishes common rates regardless of point of entry into the EC. Most customs duties are *ad valorem*, i.e., expressed as a percentage of value. Additionally, the rates of duty to which goods are subject depend on which tariff classification affects them. Therefore, it is important for exporters to the EC to ensure that the tariff classification they report is correct. Wrong classification can lead to overpayment or underpayment of duties; either of which can be a costly error.

Excise taxes are levied on certain types of goods (e.g., alcohol, tobacco products, and gas), and the rates are determined by each member state. The commission is working on establishing uniform rates for excise duties throughout the EC.

Value-Added Tax (VAT). VAT is payable on import on the purchase price of goods. This price includes the actual product price plus any customs duty or excise tax and bans. VAT paid by a non-EC business may be reclaimed under the terms of the Thirteenth VAT Directive. Requests for refunds should be sent to the VAT Department of the member state where the expense was incurred. Note that the forms must be completed in the official language of that country. Your shipping agent should have the appropriate information.

Importers will not be charged income tax in the EC on imported goods if they have no establishment and no agent inside the EC. However, if there is a local agent, sales representative (resident or nonresident), or sales subsidiary, the situation may be different. Additionally, agents may be defined differently in the twelve member states. Often, unrelated agents (i.e., independents who represent several businesses) do not constitute a permanent establishment, and the foreign company is not subject to income tax in the EC. Taxes vary from one member state to another; it is best to seek the advice of an expert in these matters.

Product Standards, Testing, and Certification Manufacturers should be aware that the EC has its own product testing procedures, and technical regulations can differ from international standards. Where EC-wide standards do not exist, the member states typically establish and enforce national standards. Since 1992, all member states have been obliged to use EC standards when they exist. If standards do not exist for particular products, member states will recognize each other's standards.

During the last five years, I have witnessed several examples of local "product" requirements differing within "Euro" states.

Exporters to the EC also may find that they are required to repeat tests in the EC that have been performed (in some form) in their home country. These tests can cause delays and sometimes lead to product modifications in order to receive approval. Approval does not, however, guarantee a product's marketability. For instance, a product that meets all the technical requirements for sale in the EC may not be able to get local insurance or may not appeal to the European consumer. Exporters should be aware that the EC requires reciprocal access to markets of non-EC countries. It is essential that exporters fully examine the target market and their home country's policies toward the EC.

Antidumping and Antiavoidance

The EC has specific rules in place against dumping (the local price is higher than the exporter's price) and avoidance (a practice employed to circumvent the dumping rules).

Protecting the Public Consumer Health, Safety, and Labeling

The EC is approaching the issue of health and safety on a sectional basis. However, while the EC is establishing minimum standards to be enforced throughout the EC, the member states may set higher standards for their national markets. On the whole, however, the EC is setting strict standards.

Insurance and Product Liability

EC legislation requires member states to ensure that products do not present an "unacceptable risk" to consumers. Manufacturers, importers, and distributors can be held strictly liable for injury or harm if the consumer proves that the product caused the harm or injury.

Bidding on Public Contracts

Non-EC companies can bid for public contracts in the EC. Tender notices are published in the supplement to the official journal of the EC, which is available from the Office for Official Publications in Luxembourg or from any EC information office.

Non-EC businesses may bid on these contracts, but there are restrictions on local content and pricing that may be imposed by the contracting authority. It is important to read the tender notice carefully for special conditions.

ISO 9000, 9001, 9002

It is often necessary to make modifications to your product or process to make it sell internationally. Your product may need to obtain product approval, stating that it has been designed to certain standards and certifying that it meets the required standards.

Many certification alternatives related to quality assurance are available, but one in particular, ISO 9000 has become very popular in the EC. Issued by the International Organization for Standardization in 1987, ISO 9000 is a series of five international standards that establish requirements for the quality control systems of companies. It is being used to provide a universal framework for quality control. Some products already require ISO 9000 registration under EC legislation beginning January 1, 1993. High-risk products that come under greater levels of regulation are the most affected, including medical devices, gas appliances, telecommunications equipment, and personal protective equipment. ISO 9000 does not guarantee that a manufacturer produces a high-quality product, nor is it product-specific. Rather, the standards are generic and make an organization assure (through third party audits) that it has a quality assurance program in place that meets one of the published standards for a system of adequate quality.

Currently, registered companies display the EC mark as a seal of approval; nonconforming or unregistered companies cannot. Therefore, current interest in ISO 9000 is more a function of the marketplace than government regulations. It can provide a competitive advantage.

Find out early if your products must be certified and evaluate what your competitors are doing. If you must meet ISO 9000 standards to be competitive, it need not be a complicated process. You will need to document your operations, that you operate according to those procedures, and that you can produce the level of quality product that you have promised. Remember to factor the estimated costs of this process into your export equation.

Sources of Information

There are many sources of information on exporting to the European Community. The following is a brief list for consideration:

- Chambers, departments, or ministries of commerce
- European information centers
- Trade associations
- EC delegations located in many countries
- Member states' permanent representatives to the EC
- Commercial section of embassies
- Consultants and legal advisers

Eastern Europe

With all of the political and socioeconomic changes that took place in Eastern Europe in the late 1980s and 1990s, many entrepreneurs are evaluating the potential of this market. Tremendous challenges make operating in or exporting to Eastern Europe and the former Soviet Republics very difficult. These range from insufficient office space to unfamiliar business practices to complicated bureaucracies.

Each industry and nation has its own trade barriers, not the least of which is the changing geopolitical boundaries and governments of this rapidly changing region. The most demanding challenge, however, may well be communication.

Exports into the Former Soviet Union and Eastern Europe: Exporter Beware

Exports to the former Soviet Union and Eastern Europe are increasing despite the economic challenges. There are over a dozen new free economies that are starving for high-tech equipment, food equipment, and support. This new opportunity comes with a unique risk.

Following are three key elements to export success that the U.S. exporter needs to pay attention to:

- Knowing the customer
- Securing the transaction
- Quality logistics

Know the Buyer

Whether your initial contact has been made by phone, fax, or the Internet, once the lead looks like a customer, get into a plane and meet with the potential buyer/importer. While you're in Moscow, Prague, Gdansk, or elsewhere, you can visit other potential clients to increase the cost-effectiveness of a trip. The importance of a face-to-face relationship with the buyer cannot be overemphasized.

Secure the Transaction

Be assured you can collect your money. Hard currency, i.e.. U.S. dollars, is difficult to negotiate within these emerging economies. Secured means of financing, e.g., payment prior to shipping, may not be possible or may put you in a competitive disadvantage with Western European or Asian suppliers. Frequently the importer will need to sell the product before being able to pay for the goods or services.

Letters of credit are typically not readily available in the neophyte "westernized" banking system or may be too costly for the importer. If you choose to extend credit, you must take all the necessary precautions in establishing the creditworthiness of the buyer through international credit agencies, referrals, and diligent investigation. Alternatives include sight drafts, collection against documents or through Ex-Im Bank programs, or private sector options. Your international banker, freight forwarder, or insurance broker should be able to offer assistance with these alternative means of protecting the foreign receivable.

Quality Logistics

Logistics is critical to the bottom line. All of the freight considerations must be carefully planned prior to shipment. The transportation infrastructure in the former Soviet Union is poor. Movement from airport to port to final interior destinations is difficult and expensive. Theft and damage in transit is so common that many marine insurance companies will not extend coverage to these areas.

Getting freight into Moscow and St. Petersburg is less challenging than it is to interior points like Zaporozhye or Novosibirsk, which present greater difficulties. Many U.S. exporters are moving the freight through Western European cities such as Helsinki, Frankfurt, Vienna, or Rotterdam. Freight forwarders, carriers, and agents in these cities and other Western countries have found it more effective to move freight from their cities to interior points in lieu of utilizing gateways such as Moscow or St. Petersburg. Freight moves more expeditiously, mitigating some of the customs problems and providing a cost-effective option.

It is critical that when selling to Eastern Europe that the importer has a strong customs broker to deal with all of the complexities. The U.S. freight forwarder must be experienced and have a good responsive office or agency capability in this emerging area. Don't be part of their learning curve, make sure they are up to handling the job!

Communication systems are adequate but not consistent. As the distance increases from major cities, so do systems failures. Documentation must conform to local requirements and there are differences with local customs facilities from city to city, product to product, and importer to importer. Packaging, marking, and labeling must be sufficiently clear and adequate to withstand multiple handling, varying customs inspections, and poor storage facilities.

It may be wise to "hedge" on shipments to the former Soviet Union by allowing additional time and budgeting additional costs to the overall expense of logistics—an additional 3 to 8 percent above projected costs would be prudent. A greater focus on preshipment, alerting, tracking, and tracing also will be helpful.

Russia 2000 and Beyond

The current economic situation in Russia is characterized by the following:

- Shortage of foreign currency.

- Unreliability of Russian banks.

- De facto devaluation of the ruble.

- Russian banks delay or stop currency availability.

- Some banks have closed.

- Shortage of consumer goods, particularly food.

- Price increases as high as 40 percent.

- Retailers cannot or will not replace inventories.

- U.S. companies with staff in Russia relied on wire transfers to pay employees. This is becoming impossible to do making salary payments and cash available to staff difficult (no funds . . . no food).

- Theft and crime surrounding cargo shipments is great.

This tied into a stressful political situation with changes in the cabinet, inability to elect a prime minister, a new government, lack of support for current leadership, etc.

Bottom line: The political and economic situation is as bad as it has ever been. Some call it a time bomb ready to explode. The government continually has troops on alert. Most foreign companies are bringing personnel home and deferring investments. Cargo on route is being diverted or being held at the inbound gateways. Every day perishables are literally rotting at the piers. Numerous satellites have political difficulties bringing military initiatives from Moscow.

The short-term situation is bleak. Because of the size of the economy, the potential support from the West, the nature of the Russian people, and the potential for democracy to survive, the long-term situation is good.

Most consumer items are imported with very little manufactured or produced in Russia. German, Israeli, and Turkish firms are big competitors to U.S. companies.

The population is large, and the distribution infrastructure is good. All product imports are a definite potential for U.S. firms as Western tastes take hold.

Bigger than direct imports is development of the local production infrastructure of numerous manufacturing industries for local consumption and potential export sales.

Many U.S. companies have taken a path of direct foreign investment in the Russian manufacturing infrastructure, which has proved successful. There is skilled, industrious labor, a Russian government partner, and favorable funding sources from the Ex-Im Bank to the World Bank.

Packaging and food machinery, heavy equipment, and high-tech infrastructure industries are but a few of the industries that are badly needed in Russia. Current output cannot support local manufacturing.

Wherever one entity finds an obstacle, another can find opportunity, depending on the willingness to take risk and creative approaches to trade issues. The short-term recommendation is to wait six months or more to see what happens with the movement of foreign currency. Assuming these improve:

1. Do not trade with Russia without visiting and getting to know your trading partners well.

2. Many U.S. companies have done better by aligning with Russian partners or other European companies that have developed resources or infrastructure, mitigating the risks of trade. Experienced or on-site local partners can facilitate transactions more cost effectively, protecting your interests.

3. While Ex-Im Bank is currently delaying the processing of applications in support of financing and/or insuring U.S. shipments to Russia, it is likely that as the situation improves they will open up. I recommend that you look to the Ex-Im Bank programs for asset protection.

4. Many Russian-based companies trade into Russia, but have funds offshore to make payments outside of the Russian banking network.

5. Sell smaller size orders that can be handled easier in funds transfer and do not represent large exposures.

6. Do not skimp on packaging or cargo loss control procedures. Crime is up. Make sure your documentation, marking, and labeling is 100 percent accurate.

7. Contact your congressman. Lobby to make sure that the United States supports trade with Russia, keeps Ex-Im Bank open, and that the State Department and other departments continue to send aid and economic support.

8. Look to direct investment and participation in the building of their manufacturing infrastructure.

9. Use experienced consultants and service providers (freight forwarders, counsel, insurance, etc.) to guide you in developing and managing your interests in this market. The opportunities are great, but so are the risks—professional will help you mitigate the risks and maximize profits.

Shipping to Mexico Painlessly

It is almost impossible to ship to Mexico without some degree of difficulty and pain. What can be offered is some "Valium" type suggestions to mitigate the problems and maximize shipping effectiveness.

Problems in Profile

The Mexican transportation infrastructure is weak and logistics management is not developed. The country lacks state-of-the-art equipment, a communications network, proper warehousing, and truly intermodal capabilities. It is also sorely lacking a system for tracking and shipment status updates.

Communication can be an obvious problem. Technical jargon sometimes has no equivalent in Spanish or vice versa. The need for timely communication and to provide updates and status reports vary, but accomplishing this can be very discouraging. The telecommunications infrastructure in Mexico has vastly improved in the last five years, but there are still some weak spots and irregularities in service capabilities.

Customs inconsistencies and differences in operation from U.S. Customs can become a nightmare. The development of the North American Free Trade Agreement (NAFTA) has potentially caused more headaches and uncertainties than it has eased the Mexican clearance process.

Legal differences, as they relate to import licenses and permits, incorporations, and distribution agreements are cumbersome and difficult to accommodate. However, improvements have been made in the legal system.

Nine suggestions that if followed will mitigate some of the problems encountered when shipping to Mexico are now discussed.

1. Utilize only experienced carriers, agents, and forwarders who have a track record in shipping to Mexico. With increased trade development, there are a lot of new and less experienced players in the shipping business. The best method to determine experience level is to ask specific questions, require client referrals, and determine tenure of Mexican operation. Carriers with offices, personnel, or long-term agents in Mexico typically can provide the best services and overcome some of the inherent problems.

2. Establish relationship with the local Mexican clearance agents. These firms are key to timely and cost-effective customs clearance. Most U.S. shippers have sold to Mexico on FOB terms at various border points such as Laredo, Nogales, and El Paso. This puts the responsibility of clearance and local delivery in the hands of the Mexican importer. Even under these terms, the shipper is responsible for providing the importer's clearance agent with documentation and shipping details enabling them to do their job. A close working rapport will simplify and expedite the process.

Competitive pressures and the most recent developments with NAFTA have opened opportunities to sell door-to-door. This will force U.S. shippers to establish local clearance agents. Often, if a freight forwarder is being used to move the shipment, you will use their office or agent at the border. If you have arranged the shipping, however, you may need to obtain your own clearance agent.

The best agents have the capacity to operate throughout Mexico, can arrange local trucking, and have excellent working relationship with Mexican Customs and authorities to mitigate the clearance process. Establish preagreed pricing for their services, with all fees, taxes, etc. identified up-front to prevent hassles later.

3. As soon as each shipment is ready to go, the documentation for that shipment should be faxed to the clearance agent. One of the frustrations in shipping to Mexico is that local authorities can change the import documentation or process from one shipment to another or from one port of entry to another. Faxing the documentation for the shipment to the clearance agent as soon as it is ready to go will enable them to review the documents ahead of time and call in any changes before the shipment arrives. They have the opportunity to discuss the shipment with customs and call in changes while there still is time. This step will expedite the entire process by allowing the clearance process to start in advance.

4. It is imperative that U.S. exporters note that the NAFTA tariff rates apply ONLY to goods that qualify as North American. NAFTA rules have changed some marketing processes. NAFTA's benefit to the U.S. exporter is the competitive advantage of reduced tariffs. When marketing to Mexico, it is imperative that U.S. exporters note that the NAFTA tariff rates apply ONLY to goods that qualify as North American. Shippers cannot assume that products are eligible for preferential tariff treatment even if they were classified "Made in USA" prior to NAFTA. Exporters must examine the very specific NAFTA Rules of Origin to determine if their goods qualify. (See References for sources on this information). A NAFTA Certificate of Origin assumes a significance, as well as a legal implication, which shippers would not have encountered in Mexico prior to NAFTA. Use associates with experience in shipments to Mexico and appoint specific personnel in your office who will keep abreast of changes affecting origin eligibility.

5. With Mexico opening up, so have increased options in choice of mode. Typical volumes of freight into Mexico have been with truck and rail. Ocean carriers have begun to expand their service routes or open up entirely new segments. This can provide a cost-effective option to shippers who have greater access to ocean ports, inland rivers, etc. Carriers such as Crowley, Lykes, Mexican Line, Tecomar, and Transportes Navieros are examples of steamship lines with increasing services into various Mexican ports. Many European-based carriers also provide some levels of service into Mexico and can pick up U.S. freight at U.S. ports before going on to Mexico. The door-to-door, 40' and 20' are virtual realities to many points in Mexico, with enhanced geographic scope growing every day.

Patents for Certain Products

The U.S. and Canada have always been signatories to international patent protection treaties. Mexico, however, has been somewhat lax in protection for foreign patents. As part of NAFTA, Mexico is enhancing its protection standards, protecting patents for twenty years. Protection will also be accorded those that are still in the development stage. This gives Mexico the highest patent standards in Latin America.

Product Standards

NAFTA harmonizes standards in most areas, deferring to major multinational agreements for most. The agreement also prohibits any country from using technical standards to close its markets to companies from the other signatories. Disputes over standards are referred to a representative panel of experts for arbitration. However, the panel's findings are not binding.

Dispute Resolution

The dispute resolution process closely follows that of the Canada/U.S. Free Trade Agreement. A binational panel composed of trade experts will arbitrate conflicts. The panels will be empowered to issue nonbinding advisories. However, it is anticipated that in most cases the rulings will be adopted.

In dumping and government subsidy disputes, binational panels, whose rulings will be binding, will be convened. There will be an appeal process to a second panel that will come into effect in only limited circumstances; the rulings of this panel will be binding. There is a lingering dispute over duty drawback among the parties. The United States wants to eliminate duty drawback immediately upon implementation of NAFTA. Mexico and Canada want to continue it until 2001, but this issue has not been resolved. This has implications for shared production operations and could increase the costs of goods in the shared production process.

In addition, the U.S. plans to eliminate foreign trade zone benefits for shared production operations or other importation from Mexico and Canada.

U.S. Industry Benefits with NAFTA

There is no clear picture of which industry sectors will benefit and which will not fare well in each of the three countries. It does appear that middle-market and growing manufacturers in the U.S. will obtain greater access to Mexico almost immediately.

I did some research in Mexico for various U.S. interests, covering the period from the start of NAFTA in 1994 to the middle of 1998. U.S. manufacturers of food processing, packaging, and material management equipment experienced an increase of 7 to 9 percent in their product lines. There was also an increase in activity of refurbished and used equipment. Processed foods held their market share, but with local infrastructure being developed, this will likely decline.

In addition, some of the sectors that appear to be winners are automobile parts manufacturers, oil and gas service companies, certain agricultural sectors such as the beef cattle industry, trucking companies , U.S. steamship lines desiring to serve the Mexican interior, American companies willing to export their technology, including food, pharmaceutical, and medical equipment supply companies, among others.

Of course, there will also be losers in the process. Those that appear to suffer the most are already weak and subsidized industries, such as the U.S. sugar industry, orange juice concentrate producers, and certain other fruit and vegetable producers.

6. **International trade specialists can determine the proper tariff classification and transaction valuation to ensure that the exporter does not pay excessive customs duties.** Historical carriers in the rail industry have enhanced their services into Mexico with more railcars, faster transit times, better switching, and intermodal arrangements. Most railroads have made interline arrangements with companies such as Union Pacific and Southern Pacific to gain entry into Mexico.

Trucking companies are beginning to arrange door-to-door capabilities. They have begun to set up their own operations, but in more instances are forming partnerships with local Mexican companies with line haul agreements. Trucking companies such as Celadon, Roadway, Watkins, and Yellow Freight are examples of numerous companies with commitments of over the road capability and expansion into Mexico.

7. **The increased activity of U.S. exports into Mexico are molding new methods of logistics and distribution.** There is an increase of American companies looking to establish their own identity in Mexico that are incorporating and ultimately looking to ship product from U.S. origin points to their Mexican subsidiary to warehouse, and inventory the freight and distribute on a local basis.

More and more U.S. shipping firms in cooperation with Mexican agents and local trucking companies are providing these services. There is also local warehousing on the U.S. side of Mexican entry points, such as Brownsville, Laredo, and Nogales, with arrangements for expedited clearance and delivery to Mexican customers. As Mexican companies grow, they will demand just in time (JIT) inventory practices and capabilities from U.S. suppliers.

In 2001, the Bush administration is posturing to open the gateway for Mexican truckers to enter the United States. This should cause competition, which will reduce costs of importing and exporting, and improve freight times.

8. American firms that are establishing warehousing and distribution capabilities or are incorporating in Mexico should obtain local Mexican legal representation. The firms chosen should be affiliated with a major U.S. law entity that can interpret contracts and execute agreements combining both American and Mexican legal issues.

American companies that have utilized Mexican distributors and now will be setting this capability themselves should be keenly aware of how to obtain the import permits and licenses that are or were controlled by the distributor. This can be complicated and will be best served by quality counsel. Law firms such as Baker and McKenzie, Furman and Delcore, and Doyle and Doyle, which have offices/agents here and in Mexico, are an example of joint U.S./Mexican representation.

9. The amount of follow-up and strict compliance to knowing the status of shipments, inventories, etc. in international trade are vast, but for Mexico, the greatest diligence must be paid to these areas. Nothing can be assumed or taken for granted. Diligent shippers and forwarders track every shipment, every day until the Proof of Delivery is obtained. We recommend follow-up with customers to determine what condition the freight was in when it was received, how the carrier performed, etc.

We recommend when volumes warrant, that shippers visit with the local agents, warehouses, and carriers in Mexico to develop strong working relationships with a personal touch. This affords tighter control and goes a long way toward maximizing performance.

Resources

Obtaining resources on NAFTA issues starts within the following:

Department of Commerce

Department of Agriculture

Mexico Desk Office, National Technical Information Service (NAFTA Facts)

Major banks and accounting and law firms

Mexico provides many opportunities, and NAFTA in the long run will provide many benefits. But it will take many years for the infrastructure to mature. Until that happens the U.S. shipper will have to take many steps and invest additional expense and time into the transportation, distribution, and the logistics process. Management will have to be sharp, creative, and extremely diligent, particularly in establishing systems for follow-up and carrier performance. In almost every case there will be long learning curves. Mexico will sort out the strong from the weak, the persistent from the mellow. Where will you be?

Exporting to Brazil

As we enter the year 2001 in Brazil, inflation is a comparatively low 8 to 10 percent, while the country's 910 billion gross domestic product is expected to reach 5 percent this year. For the United States, the country's largest international investor and trading partner, there's a lot riding on the new political controlling party. In the last three years Brazil took in approximately $12.7 billion annually in U.S. computer products, telecommunications, medical supplies, foods, and other goods, a 44 percent jump from 1995. Brazil is pegged by the Commerce Department to collectively absorb more U.S. exports than Japan or Western Europe in the next few years. Brazil's economy is starting to grow again. Free trade is in, production is up, and exports are booming. This all sounds good for U.S. exporters. However, the new edict issued by the Brazil legislation may change that.

Government Restricts Exports

In an effort to restrict exports to Brazil the government has advised importers that with any purchase of $10,000 or more the credit terms must be extended to exceed 360 days. The shipper will have to accept these payment terms. The government has advised importers that if they do not agree with these terms they will be required to pay the invoices in full to The Central Bank Of Brazil within six months plus a penalty for the percentage of the value of the invoice. The restriction is intended to curb imports and reduce the country's growing trade deficit. It has drawn criticism from some of Brazil's trading partners. The office of the U.S. Trade Representative has announced it will investigate the restrictions. Therefore, it behooves all shippers and forwarders to be sure their invoices coincide with the Brazilian regulations or the importer faces extreme penalties and delays. It is the opinion of some brokers in Brazil that although this may discourage many shippers, it will also lead to alternative ways of invoicing and have results similar to the "unofficial exchange branches" that are labeled as corrupt.

Port Congestion

Port Congestion still exists in Brazil. Ports are controlled by union employees, who generally are not very cost-effective workers. They receive high salaries, work four hour days, and sometimes only three days a week. They are in control and cannot be forced to move things along unless someone is willing to pay a few dollars extra. These port workers also are prone to strike with little notification when they become the least bit dissatisfied. There is enough work to warrant the ports to be open 24 hours a day. However, the unions refused to let that happen and in 2000 authorized a strike that lasted two days. Port fees are high, congestion continues. These problems have pushed the administration to move toward privatization as quickly as possible, but it has not been easy. Lobbyists are fighting it. Foreign investment dollars are needed throughout Latin America. It is not surprising that 60 percent of the direct foreign investment went to Brazil, Mexico, and Argentina.

There is a lot of corruption. Companies are trying to receive goods quickly and are willing to pay to do it. There are government warehouses and also private warehouses. Both employ union workers. Cargo and documentation are expedited more quickly at the private warehouse, but the costs are higher. When a customs agent uncovers a discrepancy he assigns a code to the shipment. For example, code #44 might indicate the freight is to be removed to a public warehouse. He also assigns a docket number to the broker. If for example the docket is #56 then the customs agent will not review the corrected documents until he takes care of the fifty-five issues before this one. This means the freight remains in a public warehouse for as long as customs takes to resolve the problem. The importer is at the mercy of the customs agent. There is another option. The broker can move the goods to a private warehouse. Although the private warehouse also employs union workers the freight is expedited more quickly. The importer pays more for the private warehouse, however, because charges are based on a fifteen-day cycle most times it is less expensive. In addition to the costs and delays mentioned here, the importer also incurs excessive inland trucking charges. There are many truckers in the Sao Paulo area, but their insurance is extremely high and the cost is passed on to the customer. For example a 20-foot container hauled from Santos to Sao Paulo and returned, approximately 70 miles, can cost in the area of $700. Duties and taxes are based on cost, insurance, freight (CIF) values and are among the highest in the world. Under normal conditions shipping to Brazil is expensive and tedious. The government is taking measures to improve the congestion problems through privatization, but it is also passing legislation that discourages exports from the United States.

If there are any discrepancies in the documentation, your costs and delays are magnified even further. It is imperative that you communicate with your importer and broker and resolve all documentation requirements and government regulations before preparing documents. You should also fax the importer and broker copies of the invoice, ocean bill of lading, packing lists, etc. and have them examine them carefully prior to preparing originals.

Following are several suggestions for ocean freight in Brazil:

- Book with reputable forwarders and carriers who have experience in Brazil, with an existing infrastructure to deal with local problems.

- Dot your i's and cross your t's when preparing export documentation.

- Allow at least an extra two weeks for delivery time to deal with customs, port congestion, and local problems.

- Make sure you know and your Brazilian customer is aware of all the costs of shipping freight to Brazil. These costs should be identified prior to shipping, and all of costs from the various carriers, vendors, and service providers involved with the transaction should be in writing.

- Last, be patient and diligent, as it will take both qualities to assure a successful trade into Brazil.

Air Freight to Brazil

Those who have exported to Brazil would agree that it can be a frustrating experience. Exporters to Brazil are aware of the high import tariffs and
taxes that the Brazilian government imposes and the excessive clearance
costs charged locally. Also well known to the experienced exporter or
freight forwarder is that the simplest, minor error can drastically affect the
ability to clear customs in a timely manner. This delay in customs clearance will directly affect the ability to fulfill the product delivery deadline.
That can be costly!

Before some of the most common problem-causing examples are discussed, it needs to be said that Brazil holds great opportunity for
American manufacturers/exporters. Consumption of U.S. manufactured
products is increasing at a rapid rate. There is great potential for generating large revenues by exporting to Brazil. Brazil has one of the ten largest
economies in the Western world. You just need to do your homework,
cross your t's and dot your i's, and of course it is always helpful to consult someone who is experienced in this geographic area of global trade
to benefit from trade with Brazil.

A few of the most common problem-causing areas are documentation,
documentation, and documentation. The importance of perfect documentation cannot be stressed enough. Followings are just some of the most
simplest points to be aware of:

**1. Documentation must be exact to minimize any chance of problems
with Brazilian customs officials.** There should be no crossing out, typing
errors, or overtyping on any document. The Brazilian importer or consignee on the air waybill or bill of lading should have their CGC number
indicated along with their complete and full name and address. (CGC
stands for Cadastro Geral De Contribuintes and is equivalent to a U.S. importer's EIN or tax ID number.) This is critical to a successful Brazilian import.

2. At least one commercial invoice must have an original signature.
The commercial invoices should be on original letterhead of the exporter,
not just a photocopy of the letterhead. Only originals are accepted.

3. Shipping charges must be shown on the bill of lading/air waybill.
Brazil's tariffs and taxes are based on the CIF value of the shipment so the
Brazilian customs broker must have these charges on the documentation
to present the customs entry.

**4. If the shipment is going by airfreight, the buyer in Brazil should
advise the shipper of the specific airport the goods are to be shipped to.**
For example, let's assume the importer is located in Sao Paulo. Their registration (CGC number) has been lodged with the authorities in Viracopos
airport, but the air waybill shows the terminating airport as Guarulhos
(both airports service the city of Sao Paulo). The importer now faces fines,

long delays, and ultimately storage fees with the potential of additional costs in inland transit.

Marking, Labeling, and Packing

The process of receiving cargo at airports and seaports in Brazil exposes the cargo to extensive handling. As soon as cargo arrives at the airport/port, a customs official tends to the aircraft/vessel by taking the manifests and documentation from the carrier. The inspector then takes a copy of each document, both the master and house bills of lading/air waybills, and enters the data in the computer system called Mantra. If there are any discrepancies at this time (e.g., crossouts on documents, no CGC number) then it is marked by customs as being "unavailable." This means there is a problem with the shipment and customs entry cannot be submitted until an inspector gets around to dealing with the problem. This can take days, weeks, sometimes even months.

Once all data is entered into the Mantra system, the cargo is moved to a government warehouse system called Infraero. At this point, it is mandatory that the importer pay a five-day minimum storage fee to the government warehouse. If the goods are not cleared and picked up in five days, the importer will be charged an additional five days storage, and this continues until the cargo is released. One other option is to move the goods to a private warehouse. Although it is called private, it is under the rules of the government, similar to how bonded warehouses are set up in the United States. This private warehouse charges storage based on a fifteen-day cycle. Because of the fifteen-day cycle, it is most times less expensive to go with this option even when paying for the transportation from the government warehouse to the private warehouse. There are special Portuguese clauses that must be stated on the transportation documents to enable the importer to have goods sent to the private warehouse.

In this process, cargo is inspected and physically handled and moved numerous times before arriving at its final destination. The potential for damage and loss is obvious. For this reason, the exporter must be certain that the goods are packed well for export. It is worth the extra expense in packing and packaging—"an ounce of prevention is worth a pound of cure."

Labeling is another issue. Cargo should always be labeled by the shipper with the basic, obvious information (i.e., shippers name/address/phone number and consignee name/address/phone number). Each piece of the consolidated cargo on pallets should be individually marked and labeled in case the pallet is broken down prior to arrival at the consignees' facility. In addition, the freight forwarder must make sure the cargo is labeled wit the transportation information. This is a key factor. If the transportation information on the shipping documents is not marked on the cargo, heavy fines, delays, and storage fees imposed. This is critical to making a smooth transition from the Brazilian customs warehouse to the final door in Brazil.

There are many aspects of exporting to Brazil. The bottom line is that U.S. exporters should not allow these strict rules and regulations to deter their expansion into this lucrative market. If you are seriously considering exporting to Brazil, but have had too many problems to make it worth your while, you should consider consulting an expert in this area.

New Brazil Packing Regulations

The Brazilian ministers of Agriculture and Finance issued Interministerial Service Order 499 on November 3, 1999; effective date: January 5, 2000. This establishes severe restrictions on both timber imports and the utilization of wood in the transportation of cargo in the form of packages; i.e., cases, skids, pallets, etc. The text of order 499 mainly affects the importer as the responsible party, but eventually may involve shipowners or container lessors if there is wood flooring, etc. in containers. The main issues mentioned in this order are:

A. Preferably no wood would be used in the packing of cargo. If wood is used, it must be plywood or agglomerates (manufactured with wood, glue, heat, and pressure).

B. Any and all wood that is brought into the country must be free of bark, insects, or damage caused by such insects.

C. Any wooden packing that originates in or travels through China (including Hong Kong), Japan, Korea (North and South), or the United States must be incinerated, preferably in the primary clearance.

D. Incineration may be subject to review by the Ministry of Agriculture or the Ministry of Finance (or their agents). In case of noncompliance, the responsible party will be subject to any and all legal penalties.

E. The treated wooden packing used in the transportation of cargo must be protected from infestation from port to port. There must be a Sanitary Protection Certificate issued by the authorities of the country of origin, which guarantees that prior to loading the wood has been treated by heat, fumigation, or another form of preservation. The product, dosage, and exposure time to the temperature used for fumigation must be stated in the certificate. This must be presented in the place of entry of the country to officials of the Ministry of Agriculture.

F. The fumigation treatment must be done during a period that does not exceed fifteen days prior to the date of loading in the country of origin.

G. In the absence of an Official Sanitary Certificate, the packing shall be incinerated or fumigated prior to customs clearance by a specialized company. This company must be registered with the Ministry of Agriculture and operate under the agricultural officials at the expense of the importer.

H. Other countries may be added to the list or new determinations may be issued by a combined act of the Federal Revenue Department of the Ministry of Finance and/or the Secretariat of Agricultural Defense of the Ministry of Agriculture.

In its consideration for the restrictive measures to protect national forestry, the act mentions the outbreak of and the damage caused by the Chinese Beetle in the United States and the appearance of another high-risk insect in southern Brazil.

NAFTA Update: 2001 and Beyond

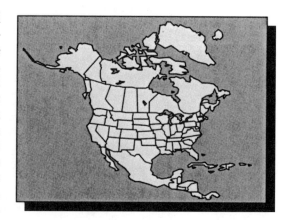

NAFTA was approved in 1994. It was undertaken to provide the economies of Mexico, Canada, and the United States with an economic base that would offer an enlarged market in each country that would provide an economic base that could compete around the world with the Europeans and Japanese. Specifically, the intent is to:

1. Provide a level playing field by standardizing the rules for conducting cross-border business among the three nations.

2. Provide assurance to businesses that the rules would not be changed in a capricious and arbitrary manner by any of the participating countries should there be changes in any of the participating governments.

3. Provide economies of scale for production throughout North America by allowing cross-border investment in production plants and facilities and by being able to access a unified market to build capacity to serve global markets.

4. Provide business and industry with a choice of technologies to compete more effectively around the world with Japan and Europe.

There is a lengthy process remaining before NAFTA is implemented. This process includes approval by each of the respective governments and a lengthy period of establishing regulations, standards, and procedures.

Although the agreement is in its early stages, there are some key issues that may be important for developing new business strategies. NAFTA includes several major industry provisions that would affect business in each of the three signatory countries. For example:

- Mexico will implement a phased elimination of tariffs on U.S. and Canadian textiles over a five- and six-year period.

- Mexico will phase out its 20 percent tariff on computers for the United States and Canada.

- There will be separate bilateral agreements among each of the signatory countries regarding the agricultural industry. Each country will eliminate its tariffs on many products and will undertake a phased reduction over five years. There will be some products that will continue to be protected for ten years and a few that will be protected for fifteen years.

- NAFTA will end restrictions that currently prevent U.S. and Mexican truckers from transporting cargo across the border. This will occur after a one- to three-year period of harmonizing the truck and cargo safety and regulatory standards.

- Manufactured goods offer the greatest potential for the middle market and growing company. The original objectives for entering into the agreement were designed to provide the greatest benefit to this industry sector.

- As a result of NAFTA, tariffs for most goods traded among the three countries will be eliminated over a ten-year period. Immediately upon implementation, tariffs on some 64 percent will be eliminated. An additional 15 percent will be removed at the end of five years. Most of the remaining tariffs will be phased out over a five- and ten-year period, although some will stay in effect for as long as fifteen years to provide adjustment periods for domestic industries.

- President Bush appears ready to open the border for Mexican trucks to enter the United States. This will significantly affect compliance, logistics costs, and safety concerns.

In addition to the industrial sector, NAFTA addresses the services industry to provide freer access to each of the signatories markets. Accords regarding patents and intellectual property were reached that provide standards of protection in accordance with international agreements. NAFTA documentation is outlined in the appendix.

Concluding Remarks

Many markets will present new opportunities for exporters and many existing markets present certain frustrations. How we proceed in dealing with these two circumstances will determine our export success.

The solutions discussed in this chapter provide valuable advice for the exporter to follow in managing exports to new markets, developing countries, the third world, and places like China, Brazil, and Mexico.

13

Global Personnel Deployment and Structure

Managing an export strategy is difficult enough without personnel issues, but they are inevitable. This chapter presents a review of how to maximize your personnel resources, attract quality personnel, and use developing seasoned international executives to their best advantage.

Successful International Sales: Future Managers Will Require Numerous Skill Sets

The global sales executives of the twenty-first century will require a vast arsenal of skill sets to make them the top in their fields. They will need to speak three to four languages and have a graduate degree in international marketing from an Ivy League school. In addition, they will need fifteen to twenty years of experience in all phases of global operations, cutting-edge negotiation skills, an understanding of the diversity of cultural and ethnic backgrounds in more than sixteen countries, and be able to function without any sleep. They will also need to be widely traveled, an expert in currency exchange rates, have a superman understanding of all legal issues in any one of the importing countries, be a mega-salesperson in the intimate marketing needs of all the global markets you sell in, willing to get up at all hours to coordinate sales activity in the Near and Far East, be inconvenienced during travel on three-week overseas adventures . . . and so forth.

That is all an exaggeration, but the reality is that at any one of the areas may be called upon at any time with the expectation that you will rise to the occasion and be all-knowing and all-showing.

International business is complicated and the international sales executive is the engine of the operations train, which leads to successful global trade. This means that to be successful the international sales executive must possess an array of skill sets, numerous talents, and varied resources.

Patience and Commitment

Most of the world works on a "relationship basis" first. This means that customers must want to buy from an individual who they have a relationship with before they buy from the company. This requires persistence and patience. Sales in the United States can be developed from a cold call and closed on the first visit. This does not happen in most overseas markets. The process of developing the relationship, over several meetings, over several months to years may be required to create the opportunity.

Commitment is one of the keys to success. The process takes time, traveling is costly, and all the related peripheral issues have cost and time associated with the process: sending samples, product registration data, answering questions, going back and forth in international communications and global courier services, etc. All take a toll. Only the executive who is committed and patient will survive this process.

Developing Resources and Networking Channels

Global sales is complicated, diverse and extensive, and no one can go it alone. There is no way one person could know all the cultural, political, logistical, and economic issues in all the countries they deal with. Complicating the issue is the fact that the situation is fluid and can change at any moment, i.e., the atomic bomb embargoes now in place in India and Pakistan, the renewed bombings in Iraq, the fall of Suharto in Indonesia, etc.

Developing relationships with quality service providers—bankers, attorneys, freight forwarders, air and ocean carriers, accountants, consultants, and trade associations, etc.—with expertise in world trade can be of support and assistance to global development efforts.

Understanding the Landed Cost

The terms of sale determine the extent of the costs associated with a foreign transaction. For example, an FOB plant sale minimizes costs and liabilities compared to a CIF sale, where the exporter bears most costs and liabilities associated with the transaction through to the port of entry.

However, irrespective of the terms of sale, the international executive needs to know that the importer (your customer) has numerous expenses associated with the transaction, in order to complete the entire supply chain process.

Inland freight and handling, air or ocean freight, import licensing and product registrations, warehousing/storage, freight insurance, customs clearance, VAT, duty and taxes, inland cartage are a few of the overall costs that the importer needs to calculate into the landed cost to determine the competitive pricing to the end-user.

Anything that the international salesman can do to affect any of these areas reduces the landed cost, thereby making the importer more competitive. This then becomes a competitive advantage for everyone.

Creative Marketing Skills

Global competition comes from many sources, including domestic companies to an array of sources from all four corners of the globe. Marketing is another key to maintaining or achieving a competitive edge. The following are some creative marketing ideas:

1. Using free trade zones to position products in local markets immediately ready for entry and delivery to the importing country, but not subject to duty and taxes until the order is processed. Reducing delivery time and differing entry costs can be a great advantage.

2. Offering credit terms can be a significant convenience. Selling on an open account, even at a higher price, can be a valuable tool in the marketing approach, and backed by export receivable insurance, can reduce overall exposure and provide entry into markets with current financial problems, such as those that exist in Africa, South America, and certain Asian countries.

Offering local country support in sales and marketing on behalf of the importer to the customer base can be very critical.

Running product seminars, sales campaigns, making time to go on sales calls, etc. can be invaluable to developing local knowledge, leading to more orders. This may mean producing a varied cadre of approaches, strategies, and plans tailored to the nuances of the culture, the economy, the logistics, and the politics of the market.

> *Developing the skill sets will be the key to allowing the international sales executive to navigate to the destinations of successful global trade.*

The Power of Networking in International Trade

One of the great advantages of membership and participation in the various export trade associations is the ability to interface with professionals who offer a wealth of information on international business.

One of the greatest challenges in international business is dealing with the array of exposures that are encountered compared to domestic sales. Forces of nature, customs authorities, political risks, currency adjustment factors, shipping logistics, legal, and insurance are but a few of the issues to be negotiated in the arena of international trade.

Each discipline requires expertise. It would be almost impossible for any individual to develop an expertise in all the disciplines. The better option is to develop a basic understanding of all areas and then align yourself with one or two experts in the field who you can call on once the specific need develops. These could be lawyers, air and ocean carriers, custom brokers, insurance brokers, accountants, freight forwarders, bankers, or other importers/exporters.

Networking in international business involves an investment in time, money, and resources. Successful people in international trade invest at least 5 percent of their time networking. International trade associations are great sources of networking. Every major city and gateway have associations involved in exporting, such as but not limited to: the District Export Council, World Trade Club, the National Institute for World Trade (NIWT), National Association of Export Companies (NEXCO), Small Business Exporters Association (SBEA)—all excellent options for international business networking.

Payback may not always be immediate. The need for a contact or resource may not occur for two years after a contact is made. Someone who needs council or assistance often calls a consultant who they met two or three years earlier.

The ability to get answers quickly can make you a hero, close the deal, and/or reduce some of the risks! Networking affords ease of access to timely resources and responses, which often can mean the difference between getting the order—or not. Power networking or maximizing resources can reduce liabilities and increase the opportunities for profit. Responsible and timely advice on international trade can mitigate all the inherent problems of global business.

International networking has other benefits. It provides the opportunity to meet interesting people who are world travelers and good social partners and friends. Many of the networking organizations sponsor social functions such as lunches, dinners, golf outings, seminars, and cocktail parties.

> *Networking can be a powerful discipline . . . ain't it so!!*

There is also a matter of altruism. By networking, we have the ability to contribute to everyone's advantage—in return you will receive the benefit of everyone else's contributions.

Matured Export Departments: Review and Analysis

Many corporations go through some difficult learning curves before structuring the export sales and operating units successfully. Some operate for more than twenty or thirty years without the proper structure.

Improper structure might not mean nonprofitability, but it does affect cost-effectiveness negatively, which leads to less than adequate results or a bottom line that could be better!

The starting point of a good export operation is senior management commitment. This is supported by an individual who is strong in international sales and operations and takes ownership of the entire export supply chain. They will have direct responsibility for or significant influence over all aspects of sales, marketing, production, inventory management, and logistics.

They will control the export supply chain. Like links in a chain, having control over all the aspects makes the chain strong. Not having control opens the door for possible weak links, making the entire supply chain ineffective.

- You can sell it right, pack it right—but if it doesn't get there on time, it may be of little value!

- You can do the right marketing and logistics, but if you don't get paid—all was for naught!

- You can have the best product, at the right price, but if the packing doesn't hold up and the freight is damaged there will be a dissatisfied customer—and no future orders!

The point is—everything has to be working correctly for the export supply chain to produce consistently high returns. The best chance at managing that is to give the entire process to one ownership. The "owner" may delegate many of the day-to-day responsibilities, but at the end of the day the responsibility rests with that person.

Another characteristic of a quality export operation is continuous staff education and training. Exporting is a fluid circumstance. The more growth and development—all the time—the better off you are.

> *Always taking the high ground comes back to you in the long run.*

A special characteristic of quality export operations is that of taking the high ground. Exporting leaves a lot of room to cut corners, take shortcuts, and be a little "shaky." And in the year 2001, with the Bureau of Export Administration (BXA), Department of Transportation (DOT), U.S. Food and Drug Administration (USFDA), U.S. Department of Agriculture (USDA), State Department, the Bureau of Alcohol, Tobacco, Firearms (ATF), and more in our faces, the high ground is a better place to be.

And it is in those circumstances, that I have observed the best export operations.

Attracting Quality Personnel

As we enter the new millennium, attracting quality personnel with international experience may be the greatest challenge. Corporations with successful export programs are doing their best to hold onto existing staff. "Golden Handcuffs" for senior executives and incentives for middle management tied into competitive compensation packages are the steps keeping most personnel loyal.

Following are several things a company can do to make it more attractive that its competitors:

- Offer compensation packages with tax free incentives.

- Offer overseas trips with families in tow, particularly in the summer months.

- Offer significant comp time to balance out the long overseas trips.

- Rotate personnel into different markets to prevent burnout and/or stagnation.

- Maintain high standards for continuing education, allotting proper time for responsible attendance.

- Encourage employees to learn several foreign languages.

- Develop compensation packages that offer incentives for profit sharing.

- Provide "ownership" of specific markets, products, or trade lanes, affording employees liberal freedoms and empowerment practices.

- Develop clear paths for growth, promotion, and advancement.

- Keep employees in the loop, with timely responsible communication so they know what's going on.

- Adopt a direct, straightforward, no-nonsense approach to performance and overall responsibilities.

Implementing all or some of these recommendations, combined with the specific nuances of your business, will not only maintain existing international personnel, but attract other professionals, as the word spreads about your career programs in export trade.

Concluding Remarks

The better we manage our corporate export infrastructure, the better we can export. The quality of our export business is directly related to the quality of the personnel we hire. This staff will require numerous skill sets in global business. We will have to find experienced staff or we will need to train them. In any case the entire personnel and deployment issue will need to be managed.

However, no matter how much training and education is provided, the staffs of international business will never know it all, partially because global trade is always changing. What it takes to clear and deliver freight in Laredo today, might be different tomorrow. Resources are needed to keep advised of current events in global trade and to find answers to the numerous questions that challenge us every day while managing our export affairs. This chapter provided many suggestions for good management based on the author's experience with hundreds of export companies.

14

Obtaining Export Assistance

This chapter focuses on the trade assistance that is available to exporters. In addition, the types of information that many organizations involved in trade assistance can provide is presented. Developing resource assistance in exporting is a critical step to successful export management.

Chambers of Commerce

Many chambers of commerce provide services for members interested in exporting. Services range from providing certificates of origin to supplying contacts with foreign companies and distributors. More active chambers of commerce are involved with international trade promotions and export workshops. They also provide access to business executives experienced in international trade.

The American Chambers of Commerce Abroad office is a valuable source of market information in any foreign country. It can supply leads on local trade opportunities, actual and potential competition, and periods of trading activity. Detailed service is supplied free to members of affiliated organizations; nonmembers usually are charged for some services.

A particularly active chamber, the U.S. Hispanic Chamber of Commerce has established a network of trade opportunities throughout Hispanic-speaking countries.

State Governments

Export development programs are rapidly increasing at the state level and, in some cases, county and city levels. The assistance these groups offer includes education, identification of potential markets and trade leads, and help with obtaining financing and vehicles to promote exporting, such as trade missions and trade shows.

U.S. Department of Commerce

The scope of services provided by this government agency is vast. The International Trade Administration (ITA) is a part of the Department of

Commerce and deals with U.S. exports. The ITA has many divisions, each with a variety of services and products to help companies planning to export. Working with the Department of Commerce used to be daunting, but the process has been streamlined. Now, all that is necessary is to contact the U.S. Foreign Commerical Service district office nearest you for information on everything from financing aid to sales leads. There are sixty-eight Department of Commerce district and branch offices throughout the United States and Puerto Rico.

U.S. businesses can participate in trade shows and trade missions sponsored or supported by the Department of Commerce. Trade missions target specific countries or groups of countries with promising export opportunities. For a description of the various trade shows and trade missions the Department of Commerce participates in, consult the *Export Programs Guide*, which can be obtained by calling the TIC. The TIC can also provide additional information on upcoming trade events.

Exporters can advertise U.S.-made products or services in *Commercial News USA*, a catalog/magazine published 10 times a year to promote U.S. products and services in overseas markets. *Commercial News USA* is disseminated to business readers worldwide via U.S. embassies and consulates and international electronic bulletin boards, and selected portions are reprinted in certain newsletters. Advertisement fees are based on the size of the listing. For more information call ABP International, visit the *Commercial News USA* web site at *http://www.cnewsusa.com*, or contact your local Department of Commerce District Office.

U.S. exporters can also advertise through the International Broadcasting Bureau (IBB), which is part of the United States Information Agency. IBB is the umbrella organization of Voice of America (VOA), Worldnet TV, and Radio Free Europe/Radio Liberty. Voice of America broadcasts almost 700 hours of programming to an estimated audience of 86 million each week. They can peg a company's ads to different language broadcasts about a particular subject, e.g., science and technology, health and medicine, or target the ads to a specific region or country. For additional information, contact the IBB.

The Department of Commerce's Trade Opportunities Program provides daily private and public trade leads from U.S. embassies abroad. These leads are printed in the *Journal of Commerce* and other private sector newspapers and are also available through the Economic Bulletin Board. Information on this bulletin board is accessible by Internet, modem, and fax. TIC fax retrieval document #7080 has detailed cost and ordering information for the Electronic Bulletin Board.

The *Country Directories of International Contacts* provides lists, categorized by country, of foreign directories of importers (showing name, address, telephone number, etc.), government agencies, trade associations and other organizations in countries where the Commercial Service maintains a presence. This list represents the primary sources of contact information that each Commercial Service post thought was useful and does not represent an endorsement of any of the services listed.

The Agent/Distributor Service is a customized search on behalf of U.S. companies seeking foreign representation. U.S. commercial officers abroad conduct the agent/distributor search based on requirements specified by the requesting firm. The search for agents and distributors takes sixty to ninety days and costs $250 per market. An order for this service can be placed through the local Department of Commerce District Office.

The Gold Key Service is custom-tailored for U.S. companies planning to visit a foreign country. It combines orientation briefings, market research, introductions to potential partners, interpreter service for meetings, and assistance developing a marketing strategy. The local Department of Commerce District Office can provide more information on this service.

The International Buyer Program supports major domestic trade shows featuring products and services of U.S. industries with high export potential. U.S. and Foreign Commercial Service officers worldwide recruit qualified foreign buyers to attend the shows. The shows are extensively publicized through embassy and regional commercial newsletters, catalog/magazines, foreign trade associations, chambers of commerce, travel agents, government agencies, corporations, import agents, and equipment distributors in targeted markets.

More information about the Agent/Distributor Service, Trade Opportunities Program, Gold Key Service, International Buyer Program, and other programs of the U.S. Commercial Service is available on the Commercial Service web site: *http://www.ita.doc.gov/tic* or by calling a trade specialist.

The Department of Commerce also organizes certain overseas events to promote U.S. businesses, including the following:

> **Trade Missions.** Focusing on one industry or service sector, trade missions provide detailed marketing information, advanced planning and publicity, logistical support to participants. They also arrange appointments with potential buyers, government officials, and others. Participants pay between $2,000 to $5,000 depending on locations and number of countries visited. The missions usually consist of five to twelve U.S. business executives.

> **Product Literature Center.** Trade Development industry specialists at ITA represent U.S. companies at various major international trade shows by distributing product or service literature. In addition, trade specialists at these centers identify potential customers for companies displaying their literature.

> **Reverse Trade Missions.** The United States Trade and Development Agency does not fund traditional trade missions to foreign countries, but it may fund visits to the United States by high-level foreign government officials to meet with U.S. industry and government representatives. These foreign officials represent procurement authorities of specific projects interested in purchasing U.S. equipment and services. The missions are usually co-funded by U.S. industry.

> **U.S. Pavilions.** About eighty to one hundred worldwide trade fairs are selected annually by the Commerce Department for re-

cruitment of a U.S. pavilion. Selection priority is given to events in viable markets that are suitable for new-to-export or new-to market "export ready" firms. Fees range from $2,500 to $12,000.

Small Business Administration (SBA)

The SBA's programs assists new and existing exporters who want to expand their operation. Through its field offices in cities throughout the United States, the SBA provides eligible companies with export information, financial assistance, legal advice, and training.

World Trade Centers

A world trade center brings together many kinds of businesses and government agencies involved in foreign trade and supplies a variety of services, from trade research and opportunities to information on government regulations and training programs. There are currently eighty world trade centers worldwide. For a nominal fee, you can obtain a directory of the centers from The World Trade Centers Association.

Commercial Banks

Approximately 300 large U.S. banks have international banking departments. Located in major U.S. cities, these banks maintain correspondent relationships with smaller banks throughout the country and with banks in foreign countries. Banks frequently provide consultation and guidance free of charge to clients, because their income is derived from loans to exporters and from fees for special services. Banks are sources of advice on export regulations, currency exchanges, collection of foreign receivables. In addition, they can assist with export financing and provide credit information on potential overseas buyers.

International World Trade Clubs

Clubs for those involved in international trade banks, traders, shippers, forwarders, customs brokers, and other service organizations conduct educational programs and organize promotional events to stimulate interest in world trade. Membership in a local association gives a company access to knowledgeable advice and benefits such as services, discounts, and contacts in affiliated foreign clubs.

Trading Companies

Trading companies can take full responsibility for the export end of the business, from market research to documentation. This can relieve you of all details except filling the orders.

Universities and Major State/Community Colleges

The databases maintained by state colleges and universities often are a valuable resource. Contact the international business department or the business school to inquire if it has information relevant to your situation. You may be able to hire a graduate student to help with market research, as many schools have programs that grant course credit to students involved in this type of extracurricular work.

Other Advisers

International trade consultants can advise and assist a company with all aspects of foreign marketing, from market identification to establishing contacts with necessary resources, such as advertising agencies, product service facilities, and local attorneys. Trade consultants usually specialize by product category and global area. When using a trade consultant, determine the consultant's level of experience, ask for references, and agree on the fee in advance.

Key International Web Sites

1999 Schedule B: *www.census.gov/foreign-trade/www*

1travel.com: *www.onetravel.com*

A UK service for small businesses that provides preliminary information on trade: *www.dti.uk/ots/esplorer/trade.html*

ACW *(Air Cargo Week): www.aircargoweek.com*

Addresses & Salutations: *www.bspage.com*

AES Direct (Automated Export System): *www.aesdirect.gov*

Africa Online: http://*www.africaonline.com*

AgExporter: *http://ffas.usda.gov/info/agexporter/agexport.html*

Air Cargo World: aircargoworld.com

AIRCARGO News: www.tabmag.com

Airforwarders Association: *http://www.logcity.com/airfwdrasn*

Airline Toll-Free Numbers and Websites: *http://www.princeton.edu/Main/air800.html*

American Association of Port Authorities (AAPA): *http://www.aapa-ports.org*

American Computer Resources, Inc.: *www.the-acr.com*

American Countertrade Association (ACA): *http://www.countertrade.org*

American Institute for Shippers' Associations (AISA): *http://www.shippers.org*

American Journal of Transportation (AJOT): http://www.ajot.com

American River International: *http://www.worldest.com*

American Shipper: *letters@shippers.com*

American Short Line and Regional Railroad Association (ASLRRA): *http://www.aslrra.org*

American Stock Exchange: *http://www.amex.com*

American Trucking Association (ATA): *http://www.trucking.org*

ASXTraders: *http://www.ASXTraders.com*

ATA Carnet (Merchandise Password):
http://www.uscib.org/frame5.htm
ATMs Around the World:
fita.org/marketplace/travel.html#atm
Aviation Consumer Action Project:
www.acap1971.org
Aviation Week: *http://www.aviationnow.com*
Bureau of Export Administration (BXA):
http://www.bxa.doc.gov
Bureau of National Affairs, *Int'l Trade
Reporter Export Reference Manual:*
www.bna.com
Business Advisor:
www.business.gov/Trade.html
Business Traveler Info Network:
*http://www.ultranet.com/%7Emes/
bt_links.htm*
Career China:
http://www.dragonsurf.com/careerwise
Cargo Systems: *http://www.cargosystems.net*
Cargovision: *editorial@cargovision.com*
Census Bureau, Foreign Trade Division:
www.census.gov/foreign trade/www
Central Europe Online:
http://centraleurope.com
Chicago Stock Exchange:
http://www.chicagostockex.com
Chinese News (in English):
http://www.insidechina.com
Classification Schedules:
*http://www.census.gov/ftp/pub/
foreign-trade/www/schedules.html*
Commerce Business Daily:
http://cbdnet.access.gpo.gov
Commercial Carrier Journal (CCJ):
http://www.ccjmagazine.com
Commercial Encryption Export Controls:
*http://www.bxa.doc.gov/Encryption/
Default.htm*
Compliance Consulting of
Importers/Exporters: *www.worldest.com*
Correct Way to Fill Out the Shipper's Export
Declaration:
*http://www.census.gov/ftp/pub/
foreign-trade/www/correct.way.html*
Country Risk Forecast: *www.controlrisks.com*
Create Your Own Newspapers:
http://unam.netgate.net/novedades
Culture and Travel:
http://ciber.bus.msu.edu/busres/culture.htm
Currency: www.oanda.com
Daily Intelligience Summary:
www.pinktertons.com

Database at the UN World Bank:
www.jepic.or.jp
DC-PRO: *www.iccbooks.com*
Department of Transportation:
www.dot.gov/airconsumer
Diverse languages of the modern world:
www.unicode.org
DOT's Office of Inspector General:
www.oig.dot.gov
Dr. Leanord's Healthcare Catalog:
www.drleornards.com
Dun & Bradstreet: *www.dnb.com*
Economic Times (India):
http://www.economictimes.com
Economist: *http://www.economist.com*
Electronic Embassy: *http://www.embassy.org*
Embassies & Consulates:
http://www.embassyworld.com
Embassy Web: *http://www.embassyweb.com*
Employment Resources Directory:
*http://www.highstreetcentral.com/
goemploy.htm*
European Union (EU):
http://www.europa.eu.int
Excite Travel: *http://www.excite.com/travel*
EXPOguide: *http://www.expoguide.com*
Export Administration Regulations (EAR):
http://www.ntis.gov/fcpc/cpn8543.htm
Export America: *www.nyuseac.org*
Export Assistant: *www.cob.ohio-state.edu*
Export Hotline: *www.exporthotline.com*
Export Legal Assistance Network (ELAN):
http://www.fita.org/elan
Export Practitioner (Export Regulations):
http://www.exportprac.com
Export Sales & Marketing Manual, Export Link:
www.export-link.com
Export Today magazine: www.exporttoday.com
Export-Import Bank of the United States (EX-
IMBANK): *http://www.exim.gov*
Far Eastern Economic Review:
http://www.feer.com
Federal Register Notice on the Status of AES
and AERP: *www.access.gpo.gov*
Federation of International Trade
Associations (FITA): *http://www.fita.org*
Financial Times: http://www.ft.com
For female travelers: *www.journeywoman.com*
Global Business:
www.globalbusiness.miningco.com
Global Business Information Network:
davidso@indiana.edu

Global Information Network for Small and Medium Enterprises: *www.gin.sme.ne.jp/intro.html*

Global Law & Business: *www.law.com/business.asp*

Glossary of Internalization and Localization terms: *www.bowneglobal.com/bowne.asp?page=9&language=1*

Glossary of Ocean Cargo Insurance Terms: *http://www.tsbic.com/cargo/glossary.htm*

Government Resources: *http://ciber.bus.msu.edu/busres/govrnmnt.htm*

Hong Kong Trade Development Counsel (TDC): *http://www.tdctrade.com*

iAgora Work Abroad: *http://www.iagora.com/pages/html/work/index.html*

IMEX Exchange: *www.imex.com*

Import Export Bulletin Board: *www.iebb.com*

Inbound Logistics: *www.inboundlogistics.com*

Incoterms 2000: *http://www.iccwbo.org/home/menu_incoterms.asp*

Independent Accountants International: *http://www.accountants.org*

Inexchange: *info@inexchange.net*

Information on Diseases Abroad: *www.cdc.gov*

Inside China Today: *http://www.insidechina.com*

Intellicast Weather (4-day forecast): *http://www.intellicast.com/LocalWeather/World*

Intermodal Association of North America (IANA): *http://www.intermodal.org*

International Air Transport Association (IATA): *http://www.iata.org*

International Association for Medical Assistance to Travelers (IAMAT): *~http://www.sentex.net/~iamat*

International Business: Strategies for the Global Marketplace Magazine: *www.internationalbusiness.com*

International Center for Canadian-American trade: *www.iccat.org*

International Chamber of Commerce (ICC): *http://www.iccwbo.org*

International Commercial Law Monitor: *http://www.lexmercatoria.org*

International Economics and Business: *http://dylee.keel.econ.ship.edu/intntl/index.html*

International Executive Service Corps (IESC): *http://www.iesc.org*

International Freight Association (IFA): *http://www.ifa-online.com*

International Law Check: *http://www.law.com/nav.asp?h=95*

International Maritime Organization (IMO): *http://www.imo.org*

International Monetary Fund (IMF): *http://www.imf.org*

International Society of Logistics (SOLE): *http://www.sole.org*

International Trade: *http://ciber.bus.msu.edu/busres/inttrade.htm*

International Trade Administration (ITA): *http://www.ita.doc.gov*

International Trade Shows and Business Events: *http://ciber.bus.msu.edu/busre*

International Trade/Import-Export Jobs: *http://www.internationaltrade.org/jobs.html*

International Trade/Import-Export Portal: *www.imakenews.com*

Intershipper: *www.intershipper*

IWLA: *www.warehouselogistics.org*

Journal of Commerce Online: http://www.joc.com

Kroll Travel Watch: *www.krollworld-wide.com*

Latin Trade: *http://www.latintrade.com*

Libraries: *http://www.libraryspot.com/librariesonline.htm*

Library of Congress: *www.loc.gov*

LLP Business and Trade Publishing: *http://www.llplimited.com*

Local Times Around the World: *http://times.clari.net.au*

Logistics: *LM@cahners.com*

Logistics Management & Distribution Report: *http://www.manufacturing.net/magazine/logistic*

London Stock Exchange: *http://www.londonstockexchange.com*

Mailing Lists: *http://ciber.bus.msu.edu/busres/maillist.htm*

Marine Digest: *http://www.marinedigest.com*

Market Research: *www.imakenews.com*

Matchmaker site: *www.ita.doc/exportmatch*

Medical Conditions Around the World: *www.cdc.gov/travel/blusheet.htm*

More Trade Leads: *www.ibrc.bschool.ukans.edu*

MTA-IC Air Cargo Newsgroup: *http://www.mta-ic.com*

NAFTA Customs: *http://www.nafta-customs.org*

National Association of Foreign Trade Zones:
www.NAFTZ.org

National Association of Purchasing
Management (NAPM):
http://www.napm.org

National Association of Rail Shippers
(NARS): *http://www.railshippers.com*

National Business Travel Assoc.:
www.biztraveler.org

National Customs Brokers & Forwarders
Association of America (NCBFAA):
http://www.ncbfaa.org

National Institute of Standards and
Technology (NIST): *http://www.nist.gov*

National Law Center For Inter-American
Free Trade: *http://www.natlaw.com*

National Motor Freight Traffic Association
(NMFTA): *http://users.erols.com/nmfta*

New Records Formats for Commodity Filing
and Transportation Filing:
www.customs.ustreas.gov/aes

New York Times: http://www.nyt.com

North American Industry Classification
System (NAICS): *http://www.census.gov/
epcd/www/naics.html*

Office of Anti-Boycott Compliance:
*http://www.bxa.doc.gov/
AntiboycottCompliance*

Online Chambers of Commerce:
http://www.online-chamber.com

Online Newspapers:
http://www.onlinenewspapers.com

Original notice /Bureau of Census re:a classification of the definition of the exporter
of record for SED rep. Purp.:
*www.access.gpo.gov/su_docs/fedreg/
a980806.html*

Overseas Private Investment Corp. (OPIC):
http://www.opic.gov

Pacific Dictionary of International Trade and
Business: *www.pacific.commerce.ubc.ca/
ditb/search.html*

Passenger Rights: *www.passengerrights.com*

PIERS (Port Import/Export Reporting
Service): *www.PIERS.com*

Ports and Maritime Service Directory:
http://www.seaportsinfo.com

Resources for International Job
Opportunities: *http://www.dbm.com/
jobguide/internat.html*

Reuters: *http://www.reuters.com*

Russia Export Import (REI):
http://www.users.globalnet.co.uk/~chegeo

Russia Today: *http://russiatoday.com*

SBA: *www.sbaonline.com*

SBA Office of International Trade:
http://www.sba.gov/oit

SBA Offices and Services:
http://www.sba.gov/services

Schedule B Export Codes:
*http://www.census.gov/foreign-trade/
schedules/b*

SEAL: *www.untpdc.org*

Search Engine: *http://www.google.com*

Service Corps of Retired Executives (SCORE):
http://www.score.org

Shipping International:
http://www.aajs.com/shipint

Shipping Times (Singapore): *http://business-
times.asia1.com.sg/shippingtimes*

SIC Codes:
www.trading.wmw.com/codes/sic.html

Small Business Administration (SBA):
http://www.sba.gov

Small Business Association:
www.sbaonline.gov

Small Business Development Centers
(SBDC): *http://www.sba.gov/sbdc*

Statistical Data Sources:
http://ciber.bus.msu.edu/busres/statinfo.htm

STAT-USA & NTDB: *http://www.stat-usa.gov*

Strategis: *http://www.strategis.ic.gc.ca*

Telephone Directories on the Web:
http://www.teldir.com/eng

The Expeditor: www.theexpeditor.com

The Exporter: http://www.exporter.com

The Global Business Forum:
www.w4pragmatix.com

The Import-Export Bulletin Board:
www.iebb.com/sell.html

The International Air Cargo Association
(TIACA): *http://www.tiaca.org*

The Times: http://www.londontimes.com

The Trading Floor: *www.trading/wmw.com*

Tokyo Stock Exchange: *http://www.tse.or.jp*

Trade: *www.host.scbbs.com/~tradewinds*

Trade and Development Agency (TDA):
http://www.tda.gov

Trade Compass: *www.tradecompass.com*

Trade Information Center (TIC):
http://infoserv2.ita.doc.gov/tic.nsf

Trade Law Website:
*www.anarse.irv.uit.no/trade_law/
documents/sales/incoterms/nav/inc.html*

Trade Net: *www.tradenet.gov*

Trade Point USA: *www.2pusa.com*

Trade Statistics: *www.ita.doc.gov/media*

Trading Floor Harmonized Code Search Engine: *www.trading.wmw.com/codes/codes/html*

Traffic world: *www.trafficworld.com*

Transportation Intermediaries Association (TIA): *http://www.tianet.org*

Transportation Jobs & Personnel: *http://www.quotations.com/trans.htm*

Travlang: *http://www.travlang.com*

UN Conference on Trade and Development: *www.uncad-trains.org*

UN International Trade Center (ITC): *http://www.intracen.org*

Unibex: *www.unibex.com*

United Nations (UN): *http://www.un.org*

United States-Mexico Chamber of Commerce: *http://www.usmcoc.org/nafta.html*

Universal Travel Protection Insurance (UTPI): *http://www.utravelpro.com*

U.S. Business Advisor: *http://www.business.gov*

U.S. Census Bureau: *www.census.gov*

U.S. Census Bureau Economic Indicators: *www.census.gov/econ/www*

U.S. Census Bureau Foreign Trade Division Harmonized Tariff Classification Schedule: *www.census.gov/foreign-trade/www/schedules.html*

U.S. Council for International Business (US-CIB): *http://www.uscib.org*

U.S. Customs Services: *http://www.customs.gov*

U.S. Department of Commerce (DOC): *http://www.doc.gov*

U.S. Department of Commerce Commercial Service: *www.ita.doc.gov/uscs*

U.S. Department of Commerce International Trade Administration: *www.ita.doc.gov*

U.S. Export Assistance Centers (USEAC): *http://www.sba.gov/oit/export/useac.html*

U.S. Export Portal: *www.export.gov*

U.S. Federal Maritime Commission (FMC): *http://www.fmc.gov*

U.S. Foreign Trade Zones: *http://ia.ita.doc.gov/ftzpage/ftzlist.html*

U.S. Government Glossary and Acronym of International Trade Terms: same as above

U.S. Patent and Trademark Office (USPTO): *http://www.uspto.gov*

U.S. State Department Travel Advisory: *http://travel.state.gov*

U.S. Trade Representative (USTR): *http://www.ustr.gov*

USA/Internet: *www.stat-usa.gov*

USDA Foreign Agricultural Service (FAS): *http://www.fas.usda.gov*

USDA Shipper and Export Assistance (SEA): *http://www.ams.usda.gov/tmd/tmdsea.htm*

USDOC Trade Information Center: *www.ita.doc.gov/tic*

Various Utilities and Useful Information: *http://ciber.bus.msu.edu/busres/utility.htm*

Wall Street Journal: *http://www.wsj.com*

Web Portal for International Business: *www.Quickport.com*

Wells Fargo: *http://www.wellsfargo.com*

World Bank Group: *http://www.worldbank.org*

World Chambers of Commerce Network: *http://www.worldchambers.com*

World Customs Organization (WCO): *http://www.wcoomd.org*

World Factbook: *http://www.odci.gov/cia/publications/factbook/index.html*

World Intellectual Property Organization (WIPO): *http://www.wipo.int*

World Newspapers On-line: *http://library.uncg.edu/news*

World Trade Analyzer: *www.tradecompass.com/trade_analyzer*

World Trade Centers Association (WTCA): *http://iserve.wtca.org*

World Trade Exchange: *www.wte.neta*

World Trade Magazine: *michael_white@link.freedom.com*

World Trade Organization (WTO): *http://www.wto.org*

World Wide Shipping: *www.ship.com*

Worldclass: *www.web.idirect.com/~tiger*

WorldPages: *http://www.worldpages.com*

15

Free Trade Zones (FTZs) and Bonded Warehouses

Making the Free Trade Zone (FTZ) Work for Your Export Program

Free Trade zones are economic free areas where goods can be inventoried without entering the commerce of the country they are in. More importantly, free trade zones allow a domiciled company to "work" on goods in these areas for various benefits.

One benefit is that taxes and duties are deferred until such time as the goods are cleared and entered into that country which could be months after initial arrival. Cash flow is the obvious advantage.

A secondary benefit of the FTZ is that local labor works on the goods, adding local content and value. For example, a manufacturer imports watch components, but the finished timepiece is assembled in the FTZ. The goods are ready for sale, quality controlled, packed, and shipped. In many countries that have FTZs, tax relief would be provided to the importer who added local value to the imported timepieces.

This could save the importer literally millions of dollars in tax liabilities, making the FTZ a significant cost-saving tool for lowering the landed cost for the imported goods.

All countries have different rules in how the FTZs operate. There are national and international free trade zone organizations that are conduits for information on worldwide locations and capabilities. Additional information can be obtained from the web sites listed in the appendix.

Another benefit is that the freight is positioned in the foreign market, which will shorten the delivery schedule in your global supply chain. This mitigates the advantages of local competition.

An additional benefit tied into local positioning is the ability to have showrooms. Touchy, feely on-site capabilities can prove advantageous with certain product lines, such as automobiles, cosmetics, computers, etc.

Areas in Europe, Asia, and Latin America are developing FTZ capabilities in numerous gateways, such as, but not limited to Monterey, Mexico; Singapore, Montevedio, Uruguay; Amsterdam, the Netherlands; and Panama City, Panama.

U.S. exporters, in working with their agents, distributors, direct customers, and subsidiary facilities are finding FTZs mean gaining competitive advantage, while providing local economic benefit. This has both short- and long-term political and economic advantages for the United States and the local country operating the FTZ.

Working with preferred FTZ organizations, such as the Rockefeller Group in Mt. Olive, New Jersey, is an excellent conduit into quality expertise and account management. The advice and counsel of these organizations combined with side development is *well* worth the effort.

What Exporter's Should Know about Custom Bonded Warehouses (CBW)

Custom bonded warehouses provide many of the same benefits as FTZs. The difference between FTZs and bonded warehouses is that in most countries bonded warehouses are more temporary and typically limit access to the freight. One cannot typically change the nature of the product in the bonded facility. One might be able to view the cargo, relabel or repack it, but its form, shape, or makeup cannot be changed.

There are a number of uses for CBWs for exporters. They can be made into a foreign consolidation center. Goods are held in bond, in that they have note entered the U.S. economy. A U.S.-based manufacturer/distributor may be selling to Latin America, but sourcing products from the USA and Europe. The U.S. company could import product from Europe into a bonded facility, say in Miami. The product would be held at this facility until it is combined with the domestic sourced/manufactured product and then shipped to Latin America with the cost benefits of a consolidated shipment.

A U.S.-based importer may bring in product with the eventual purpose of exporting a portion to Mexico, Canada, or the Caribbean. The bonded facility would be used as a storage warehouse until a decision is made to export. A CBW could be used as a warehouse to hold the freight, deferring tax/duty obligations until a decision is reached to import into the United States or export. The goods that are imported have the benefit of tax deferral until the time of actual import, and the exported goods never entered the United States economy, so no taxes/duties would be obligated. For the export—the goods would transit from the bonded facility to the outbound port by a bonded carrier, then by international carrier to the overseas market.

Custom facilities also can serve a "holding pens" during disputes with customs or until final determinations are made as to where and when the goods will be exported.

Exporter's need to look into CBWs in conjunction with their logistics departments, freight forwarders, third party providers, and carriers to determine the benefits applicable to their export operations.

16

Concluding Remarks

The people involved in exporting are intense, interesting, and intricate in-dividuals. I like being involved in this business because of the "exotic" people I meet and the many friendships I have established. I am always impressed by the "better" exporters who are very diverse, uniquely qual-ified, and intelligent executives. **I really believe good exporters are sharper, more demanding, and "raise the bar" of performing through hoops.**

The exporter of the new millennium requires comprehensive capabili-ties, which are elaborated in detail and brought to a functional value for everyday export transactions in this book. Consistently following my rec-ommendations and guidelines places the exporter in the best circumstance to gain competitive advantage in global sales, while remaining compliant and running a quality export operation.

I trust by now the reader has been impressed with the knowledge they have gained through the comprehensive contents of *The Ultimate Guide to Export Management*. The reader now should understand that there are an exorbitant amount of detail and skill sets required to manage exports cost effectively and prosper in international sales.

The book has also identified a "connectivity" between all aspects of ex-porting. Meaning that the exporter needs to have a series of events run correctly, in order for the export to be successful. From sales and market-ing, through to packing, marking and labeling, then logistics and getting paid. . . all have to be managed with great detail and diligence for the ex-port to be successful and profitable. For the exporter to get it all right, they must both develop a vast array of resources and quality service providers who will walk them through the maze of global issues and offer contin-ual advice and counsel.

Exporting clearly creates opportunity. With that opportunity comes significant risks, far greater than in domestic sales. The key focus is on tak-ing proactive management actions to mitigate the risks, which will open the door for serious profit potentials and long-term growth.

Middle management must obtain the commitment from senior man-agement to move ahead on handling exports in a proper fashion, because doing it correctly, takes time, money, and resources. Exports will only work well if senior management is fully informed of what it takes. Only then will they be fully supportive and fully committed. Half commitments are deadly in global trade.

While experience is ultimately the best guide, this book has identified a clear course and direction for an exporter to follow to find quality solutions to the numerous and complicated problems of moving freight on a global scale. The conscientious executive who methodically follows the steps outlined in this resource book will find it easier to perform and *"raise the bar"* of export excellence.

Exporters can manage their operations through good luck or good management practice. The choice is theirs to make. Most executives making the latter choice now have a comprehensive, single source of information to manage exports with stealth capability and cutting edge technology—*The Ultimate Guide to Export Management.*

Appendix

Contents

Glossary

Abandonment: Refusing delivery of a shipment that is so badly damaged in transit, it has little or no value.

Acceptance: An international banking instrument known as a time draft or bill of exchange that the drawee has accepted and is unconditionally obligated to pay at maturity.

Advising bank: A bank operating in the exporter's country that handles letters of credit for a foreign bank by notifying the exporter that the credit has been opened in their favor.

Agency for International Development (AID) shipments: The Agency for International Development is a U.S. Government agency created to provide relief to developing countries who must purchase products and services through U.S. companies. Specialized export documentation is necessary to complete the transactions.

Allowance: Typically afforded a consignee as a "credit" or "deduction" on a specific export transaction.

All-risk cargo insurance: A clause included in marine insurance policies to cover loss and damage from external causes during the course of transit within all the terms and conditions agreed to by the underwriters.

Arbitration: Wording included in export contracts introducing an independent third party negotiator into the dispute resolution in lieu of litigation.

Arrival notice: Advice to a consignee on inbound freight. Sometimes referred to as a prealert. Contains details of the shipments arrival schedule and bill of lading data.

"As is": An international term denoting that the buyer accepts the goods as is, it is a connotation there may be something wrong with the merchandise, and the seller limits their future potential liability.

Balance of trade: The difference between a country's total imports and exports. If exports exceed imports, a favorable balance of trade, or trade surplus, exists; if not, a trade deficit exists.

Barter: The direct exchange of goods and/or services without the use of money as a medium of exchange and without third party involvement.

Bill of lading: A document that establishes the terms of a contract between a shipper and a transportation company under which freight is to be moved between specified points for a specified charge. Usually prepared by the shipper on forms issued by the carrier, it serves as a document of title, a contract of carriage, and a receipt of goods.

Bond: A form of insurance between two parties obligating a surety to pay against a performance or obligation.

Bonded warehouse: A warehouse authorized by customs authorities for storage of goods on which payment of duties is deferred until the goods are cleared and removed.

Breakbulk cargo: Loose cargo that is loaded directly into a conveyance's hold.

Bretton Woods Conference: A meeting under the auspices of the United Nations at Bretton Woods, New Hampshire, in 1944, that was held to develop some degree of cooperation in matters of international trade and payments and to devise a satisfactory international monetary system to be in operations after World War II. The particular objectives intended were stable exchange rates and convertibility of currencies for the development of multilateral trade. The Bretton Woods Conference established the International Monetary Fund and the World Bank.

Carnet: A customs document permitting the holder to carry or send merchandise temporarily into certain foreign countries without paying duties or posting bonds.

Clingage: When shipping bulk liquids, the residue remaining inside the conveyance after discharge.

Combi: An aircraft with pallet or container capacity on its main deck and belly holds.

Commission agent: An individual, company, or government agent that serves as the buyer of overseas goods on behalf of another buyer.

Commodity specialist: An official authorized by the U.S. Treasury to determine proper tariff and value of imported goods.

Consignment: Delivery of merchandise from an exporter (the consignor) to an agent (the consignee) under the agreement that the agent sell the merchandise for the account of the exporter. The consignor retains the title to the goods until the consignee has sold them. The consignee sells the goods for commission and remits the net proceeds to the consignor.

Consolidator: An agent who brings together a number of shipments for one destination to qualify for preferential rates.

Cost, insurance, freight (CIF): A system of valuing imports that includes all costs, insurance, and freight involved in shipping the goods from the port of embarkation to the destination.

Countertrade: The sale of goods or services that are paid for in whole or part by the transfer of goods or services from a foreign country.

Credit risk insurance: Insurance designed to cover risks of nonpayment for delivered goods.

Currency: National form for payment medium: dollars, pesos, rubles, naira, pounds, etc.

Distributor: A foreign agent who sells for a supplier directly and maintains an inventory of the supplier's products.

Domestic International Sales Corporation (DISC): Established in 1971 by U.S. legislation, DISCs were designed to help exporters by offering income tax deferrals on export earnings. DISCs were phased out in 1984.

Dumping: Exporting or importing merchandise into a country below the costs incurred in production and shipment.

Duty: A tax imposed on imports by the customs authority of a country. Duties are generally based on the value of the goods (*ad valorem* duties), some other factor such as weight or quantity (specified duties), or a combination of value and other factors (compounded duties).

Embargo: A prohibition on imports or exports as a result of a political eventuality.

European Community (EC): The twelve nations of Europe that have combined to form the world's largest single market of more than 320 million consumers. The EC includes Belgium, Denmark, France, Greece, Ireland, Italy, Luxembourg, the Netherlands, Portugal, Spain, the United Kingdom, and West Germany.

Export: To send or transport goods out of a country for sale in another country. In international sales, the exporter is usually the seller or the seller's agent.

Export-Import Bank of the United States (Ex-Im Bank): Ex-Im Bank facilitates and aids the financing of exports of U.S. goods and services through a variety of programs created to meet the needs of the U.S. exporting community. Programs, which are tailored to the size of a transaction, can take the form of direct lending or loan guarantees.

Export management company: A private company that serves as the export department for several manufacturers, soliciting and transacting export business on behalf of its clients in return for a commission, salary or retainer plus commission.

Export trading company: An organization designed to facilitate the export of goods and services. It can be a trade intermediary that provides export-related services to producers or can be established by the producers themselves, though typically export trading companies do not take tittle to goods.

Ex Works (EXW) from Factory: The buyer accepts goods at the point of origin and assumes all responsibility for transportation of the goods sold. Also: Ex Warehouse, Ex Mine, Ex Factory as defined in Inco Terms, Chapter 6.

Fair trade: A concept of international trade in which some barriers are tolerable as long as they are equitable. When barriers are eliminated, there should be reciprocal action by all parties.

Force majeure: Expressed as "acts of God." Conditions found in some marine contracts exempting certain parties from liability for occurrences out of their control, such as earthquakes and floods.

Foreign Corrupt Practices Act of 1977: U.S. legislation with stringent antibribery provisions and guidelines for recordkeeping and internal accounting control requirements for all publicly held corporations. The act makes it illegal to offer, pay, or agree to pay money or any item of value to a foreign official for the purpose of getting or retaining business.

Foreign Credit Insurance Association (FCIA): An insurance program, previously government managed and underwritten, now privately held, that insures commercial and political risks for U.S. exporters.

Foreign sales agent: An individual or company that serves as the foreign representative of a domestic supplier and seeks sales abroad for the supplier.

Forfaiting: The selling, at a discount, of a longer-term receivable or promissory note of a buyer.

Franchising: A form of licensing by the service sector for companies that want to export their trademark, methods, or personal services.

Free along side (FAS): A system of valuing imports that includes inland transportation costs involved in delivery of goods to a port in the exporting country but excludes the cost of ocean shipping, insurance, and the cost of loading the merchandise on the vessel.

Free domicile: Terminology used for "door to door" deliveries.

Free on Board (FOB): A system of valuing imports that includes inland transportation costs involved in delivery of goods to a port in the exporting country and the cost of loading the merchandise on the vessel, but excludes the cost of ocean shipping and insurance.

Free port: An area such as a port city into which merchandise may legally be moved without payment of duties.

Free trade: A theoretical concept to describe international trade unhampered by governmental barriers such as tariffs or nontariff measures. Free trade typically favors the reduction or elimination of all tariff and nontariff barriers to trade.

Free trade zone (FTZ): A port designated by the government of a country for duty-free entry of any nonprohibited goods. Merchandise may be stored, displayed, or used for manufacturing within the zone, and re-exported without the payment of duties.

Freight all kinds (FAK): A mix of cargoes traveling as one.

General Agreement on Tariffs and Trade (GATT): A multilateral treaty to which 85 nations (or more than 80 percent of world trade) subscribe; it is designed to reduce trade barriers and promote trade through tariff concessions, thereby contributing to global economic growth and development.

Harter Act: Legislation protecting a shipowner from certain types of claims that are due to actions of the crew.

Haz-mat: Hazardous materials regulated by various government agencies, DOT/CFR Title 49, IATA, IMCO, Coast Guard, etc. Personnel who interface with Haz-mat cargoes need to be certified to do so.

Hedging: A mechanism that allows an exporter to take a position in a foreign currency to protect against losses due to wide fluctuations in currency exchange rates.

Hold: The space below deck inside an ocean-going vessel.

Irrevocable letter of credit: A letter of credit in which the specified payment is guaranteed by the bank if all terms and conditions are met by the drawee (buyer). *See also* Revocable letter of credit.

ISO 9000: Issued in 1987 by the International Organization for Standardization, ISO 9000 is a series of five international standards that establish requirements for the quality control systems of companies selling goods in the European Community. It now includes many additional countries and companies throughout the world.

Joint venture: A business undertaking in which more than one company shares ownership and control.

Letter of credit: A document is issued by a bank per instructions from a buyer of goods that authorizes the seller to draw a specified sum of money under specified terms, usually the receipt by the bank of certain documents within a given period of time.

Licensing: A business arrangement in which the manufacturer of a product (or a company with proprietary rights over certain technology, trademarks, etc.) grants permission to some other group or individual to manufacture that product (or make use of that proprietary material) in return for specified royalties or other payment.

Logistics: The science of transportation covering the planning and implementation of specific strategies to move materials at a desired cost.

Mala fide: Misrepresentation or in bad faith.

Maquiladora: A tax-free program allowing the import of materials into Mexico for manufacturing of goods for export back to the United States. Now declining in importance as a result of NAFTA.

Marine insurance: Insurance covering loss or damage of goods during transit. It covers all modes of transport.

Market research: Specific intelligence about the market in which a seller proposes to sell goods or services. This information is gathered through interviews, commissioned surveys, and direct contact with potential customers or their representatives.

Marks and numbers: The references made in writing to identify a shipment on the exterior packing, typically referenced in the documentation.

North American Free Trade Agreement (NAFTA): An agreement that creates a single unified market of the United States, Canada, and Mexico.

Open account: A trade arrangement in which goods are shipped to a foreign buyer without guarantee of payment. The obvious risk this method poses to the supplier makes it essential that the buyer's integrity be unquestionable.

Overseas Private Investment Corporation (OPIC): A government-sponsored organization that promotes investment in plans and equipment in less-developed countries by offering guarantees comparable to Ex-Im Bank.

Political risk: In exporting, the risk of loss due to such causes as currency inconvertibility, government action preventing entry of goods, expropriation, confiscation, or war.

Power of attorney: A document that authorizes a customs broker or freight forwarder to act on the exporter's/importer's behalf on issues relative to customs clearance, transportation, documentation, etc.

Premium: Insurance dollars paid to an underwriter to accept a transfer of risk.

Protectionism: The setting of trade barriers high enough to discourage foreign imports or to raise the prices sufficiently to enable relatively inefficient domestic producers to compete successfully with foreign producers.

Purchasing agent: An individual or company that purchases goods in their own country on behalf of foreign importers, such as government agencies or large private concerns.

Remarketers: Export agents, merchants, or foreign trading companies that purchase products from an exporter to resell them under their own name.

Revocable letter of credit: A letter of credit that can be cancelled or altered by the drawee (buyer) after it has been issued by the drawee's bank. Compared to a irrevocable letter of credit, which is totally binding without both parties written agreement.

Tariff: A tax on imports or the rate at which imported goods are taxed.

Time draft: A draft that matures in a certain number of days, either from acceptance or date of draft.

Tracking: A forwarder's or carrier's system of recording movement intervals of shipments from origin through to final destination.

Trade acceptance: *See* Acceptance.

Transfer risk: The risk associated with converting a local foreign currency into U.S. dollars.

Transmittal letter: Cover communication outlining details of an export transaction and accompanying documentation.

Twenty-foot equivalent (TEU): Twenty-foot equivalent or standard measure for a twenty-foot ocean freight container. Two TEUs represent one forty-foot standard container.

Ullage: Measuring the amount of liquid or dry bulk freight in the hold of a vessel by measuring the height of the stow from the opening on deck.

United States Agency for International Development (USAID): A U.S. Governmental agency that carries out assistance programs designed to help the people of certain lesser-developed countries develop their human and economic resources, increase production capacities, and improve the quality of human life as well as promote the economic or potential stability in friendly countries.

Value-added Tax (VAT): An indirect tax assessed on the increase in value of goods from the raw material stage through the production process to final consumption. The tax to processors or merchants is levied on the amount by which they have increased the value of items that were purchased by them for use or resale. This system is used in the European Community.

Weight breaks: Discounts to freight charges are given as the total weight increases at various weight breaks: 50 pounds, 100 pounds, 500 pounds, etc.

Wharfage: Charges assessed for handling freight near a dock or pier.

With average: A marine insurance term meaning that shipment is protected for partial damage whenever the damage exceeds an agreed percentage.

Zone: Freight tariffs are often determined by certain geographic areas called zones.

Credits and Support Reference Material

American River International
American Management
   Association
The Atlas Group
Bank of New York
Bureau of Export
   Administration
Chemical Bank
Chubb
CIGNA
Council of Logistics
   Management
Department of Commerce
Ex-Im Bank
Export America
Export Practitioner
Export/Import Procedures &
   Documentation
The Exporter
FSI Global Logistics

International Chamber of Commerce
Journal of Commerce
Institute of Management and
   Administration
Manufacturer's Hanover
Marine Midland Bank
NatWest
PriceWaterhouseCoopers
Rene Alston
RHDC
Sealand
Shipping Digest
Small Business Association
Unz & Co.
U.S. Customs
U.S. Council for International
   Business
World Trade Institute
World Trade Magazine
World Trade Press

Key Telephone Numbers

Organization and Number

Government Resources

Directory of Export Assistance Centers in the United States

Alabama
Birmingham (205) 731-1331

Alaska
Anchorage (907) 271-6237

Arizona
Phoenix (602) 640-2513
Tucson (520) 670-5540

California
Fresno (559) 325-1619
Inland Empire (909)
    466-4134
Long Beach Export
    Assistance Center (562)
    980-4550
Downtown Los Angeles
    (213) 894-8784
West Los Angeles (310)
    235-7206
Monterey (831) 641-9850
Novato (415) 883-1966
Oakland (510) 273-7350
Orange County (949)
    660-1688
Sacramento (916) 498-5155
Santa Clara (408) 970-4610
San Diego (619) 557-5395
San Francisco (415) 705-2300
San Jose U.S. Export
    Assistance Center (408)
    271-7300
Ventura County (805)
    676-1573

Colorado
Denver U.S. Export Center
    (303) 844-6623

Connecticut
Middletown (860) 638-6950

Delaware
Served by the Philadelphia
U.S. Export Assistance
    Center

Florida
Clearwater (727) 893-3738

Miami U.S. Export
    Assistance Center (305)
    526-7425
Ft. Lauderdale North
    Campus (954) 356-6640
Orlando (407) 648-6235
Tallahassee (850) 488-6469

Georgia
Atlanta U.S. Export
    Assistance Center (404)
    657-1900
Savannah (912) 652-4204

Hawaii
Honolulu (808) 522-8040

Idaho
Boise (208) 334-3857

Illinois
Chicago U.S. Export
    Assistance Center (217)
    466-5222
Peoria (309) 671-7815
Rockford (815) 987-8123

Indiana
Indianapolis (317) 582-2300

Iowa
Des Moines (515) 288-8614

Kansas
Wichita (316) 263-4067

Kentucky
Louisville (502) 582-5066
Somerset (606) 677-6160

Louisiana
Delta U.S. Export Assistance
    Center (504) 589-6546
Shreveport (318) 676-3064

Maine
Portland (207) 541-7400

Maryland
Baltimore U.S. Export
    Assistance Center (410)
    962-4539

Massachusetts
Boston U.S. Export
    Assistance Center (617)
    424-5990
Marlborough (508) 624-6000

Michigan
Detroit U.S. Export
    Assistance Center (313)
    226-3650
Ann Arbor (734) 741-2430
Grand Rapids (616) 458-3564
Pontiac (248) 975-9600

Minnesota
Minneapolis U.S. Export
    Assistance Center (612)
    348-1638

Mississippi
Mississippi (601) 857-0128

Missouri
St. Louis U.S. Export
    Assistance Center (314)
    425-3302
Kansas City (816) 410-9201

Montana
Missoula (406) 243-2098

Nebraska
Omaha (402) 221-3664

Nevada
Reno (702) 784-5203

New Hampshire
Portsmouth (603) 334-6074

New Jersey
Trenton (609) 989-2100
Newark (973) 645-4682

New Mexico
New Mexico (505) 827-0350

New York
Buffalo (716) 551-4191
Harlem (212) 860-6200
Long Island (516) 739-1765

New York U.S. Export Assistance/Westchester (914) 682-6712

North Carolina
Carolinas U.S. Export Assistance Center (704) 333-4886
Greensboro (336) 333-5345
Raleigh (919) 715-7373 x515

North Dakota
Served by the Minneapolis U.S. Export Assistance Center

Ohio
Cincinnati (513) 684-2944
Cleveland U.S. Export Assistance Center (216) 522-4750
Columbus (614) 365-9510
Toledo (419) 241-0683

Oklahoma
Oklahoma City (405) 608-5302
Tulsa (918) 581-6263

Oregon
Eugene (541) 484-1314
Portland (503) 326-3001

Pennsylvania
Harrisburg (717) 221-4510
Philadelphia U.S. Export Assistance Center (215) 597-6101
Pittsburgh (412) 395-5050

Puerto Rico
San Juan (787) 766-5555

Rhode Island
Providence (401) 528-5104

South Carolina
Charleston (843) 760-3794
Columbia (803) 765-5345
Upstate (864) 271-1976

South Dakota
Siouxland (605) 330-4264

Tennessee
Knoxville (865) 545-4637
Memphis (901) 323-1543
Nashville (615) 736-5161

Texas
Austin (512) 916-5939
Dallas U.S. Export Assistance Center (214) 767-0542
Fort Worth (817) 212-2673
Houston (713) 718-3062
San Antonio (210) 228-9878

Utah
Salt Lake City (801) 524-5116

Vermont
Montpelier (802) 828-4508

Virginia
Highland Park (847) 681-8010
Richmond (804) 771-2246

Washington
Seattle U.S. Export Assistance Center (206) 553-5615
Spokane (509) 353-2625
Tacoma (253) 593-6736

West Virginia
Charleston (304) 347-5123
Wheeling (304) 243-5493

Wisconsin
Milwaukee (414) 297-3473

Wyoming
Served by the Denver U.S. Export Assistance Center

General Export Sample with Definitions and Instructions

Export Transaction File

Pro Forma Invoice

Upon receiving a purchase order from a buyer overseas, a "pro forma" invoice is usually then prepared and sent to the buyer for approval. The buyer will check the pro forma to make sure only those items on the purchase order are listed. The approximate weights and value should be listed as well as terms and conditions of sale. In some cases, the buyer needs the pro forma to obtain import permits or foreign exchange permits.

Once the buyer approves the pro forma invoice, the seller (or exporter) begins to ready the order. Upon having the order completed, a commercial invoice and packing list is usually prepared.

Commercial Invoice

This document is a "bill" that the seller prepares for the buyer. It should contain all pertinent details of the sale, including the shipping terms and other information such as:

- Name, address, and phone number of export/shipper.
- Name and address of buyer, or "sold to" party.
- Name, address, and phone number of "ship to" party, if other than "sold to" party.
- Date.
- Invoice number.
- Buyer's purchase order number.
- Terms of payment.
- Terms of sale.
- Quantity, description of goods, unit price, and extended prices.
- Total value of goods (specify currency).
- Country of origin.
- Signature of exporter.

The commercial invoice travels with the air waybill (or ocean bill of lading).

Note: there may be certain countries that require additional specific information, so it is always best to check with the buyer for any documentation instructions.

Some countries require that the commercial invoice be "legalized" by the local chamber of commerce and the specific country's consulate. See page 348 for an example of a "legalized" commercial invoice.

Packing List

This document describes the physical packaging of the goods. It should list the following information:

- Date

- "Ship to" party

- Buyer purchase order number

- How many packages

- Type of packing (e.g., crate, drum, fiberboard box, cases)

- Contents of packages

- Gross and net weight

- Dimensions (length × width × height)

- Any marks or labels on the packages

Although not all countries require this document, it is certainly instrumental with regard to filing a cargo insurance claim. It is recommended that every cargo movement be accompanied by a packing list.

Certificate of Origin

Some countries require goods to be shipped with a certificate of origin. This document certifies the country of manufacture, and the manufacturer's name and address. This document is signed by the exporter, notarized by an official notary public, and usually is required to be certified by the local chamber of commerce.

Your freight forwarder can advise if your consignment needs a certificate of origin, but it is always recommended that the exporter check with the buyer for a list of all documents required to enable customs clearance in the country of destination.

When shipping between North America (Canada, Mexico, and the United States), there is a specific certificate of origin called North American Free Trade Agreement (NAFTA) that must be filled out by the manufacturer, or the seller if he has intimate knowledge of the product composition. This document allows preferential duty rates to be applied to the shipment.

Air Waybill

This document is a bill of lading for air transportation. It identifies the pieces, weight, commodity, shipper, and consignee.

This document must be tendered to the airline with the cargo. It also serves as a receipt of tender.

Shippers Export Declaration (SED)

This document is only required when:

a. Goods are valued at $2500.00 or more. (Exports from Canada do not require an SED.)

b. Goods are licensable by state or commerce department.

The main function of this document is to compile census information regarding trade and exports from the United States.

Insurance Certificate

Insurance certificates are used as evidence that the shipment has proper coverage. The standard is to insure for 110 percent of the cost-insurance-freight (CIF) value. This certificate is not always required so it is best to check the conditions and terms of sale and to see who the responsible party is.

Straight Bill of Lading Form

This document is used as a receipt of carriage for inland freight from the origin point to the airport or port of departure or the consolidation warehouse. It lists the pieces, weight, and a short description of the goods. Whoever is receiving goods against this inland freight form should always check the cargo they are receiving and sign any exceptions such as broken seals, crushed corners, tear in boxes etc

Ocean Bill of Lading

This document is issued by the ocean freight carrier as evidence that they acknowledge receipt of your goods and that they agree to transport it to the destination that is indicated and becomes the contract and agreement of carriage between the exporter and the carrier.

Quality Certificate

This document is used as evidence that the product complies with all U.S. Food and Drug Regulations, that it is offered for sale in the United States, and that it is fit for human consumption. Some products require more specific information regarding how the processing was done, etc

It cannot be stressed enough that you should always check with the buyer for their country's requirements.

Export License

There are certain commodities that cannot be exported from the United States without having those commodities licensed by the U.S. Department of State. These commodities are mainly technology and military end-use items. You can obtain information regarding your specific product by calling the Bureau of Export Administration in Washington, D.C. The license, after approval, must be validated by U.S. customs prior to export.

Air Freight Export

ABC EXPORT CORP.
123 PARK LANE
NEW YORK, N.Y. 10012
(212)-555-1234

<u>COMMERCIAL INVOICE</u>

DATE: FEBRUARY 12, 1999
INVOICE NUMBER: 990212

CUST PO#: 3265FD

SOLD TO / SHIP TO:
FOOD SERVICE SUPPLY STORES
AVENIDA 26 Y PALOMINA ASA #40
MEXICO CITY DF MEXICO

TERMS: C & F MEXICO CITY

ITEM#	*DESCRIPTION:*	*QTY:*	*UNIT PRICE:*	*TOTAL VALUE:*
NDX89	NON DAIRY COFFEE WHITENER	184 K	15.94/K	$2932.96

FREIGHT.. $ 467.00

TOTAL C & F VALUE:..........................$3399.96

MADE IN U.S.A.

**WE HEREBY CERTIFY THAT THE ABOVE INFORMATION IS TRUE AND CORRECT TO
THE BEST OF OUR KNOWLEDGE.**

RANDI
MANUFACTURING PLANT SUPERVISOR

ABC EXPORT CORP.
123 PARK LANE
NEW YORK, N.Y. 10012
(212)-555-1234

ORIGINAL

PACKING LIST

DATE: FEBRUARY 12, 1999
REFERENCE INVOICE NUMBER: 990212

CUST PO#: 3265FD

SOLD TO / SHIP TO:
FOOD SERVICE SUPPLY STORES
AVENIDA 26 Y PALOMINA ASA #40
MEXICO CITY DF MEXICO

ITEM#	*DESCRIPTION:*	*QTY:*
NDX89	NON DAIRY COFFEE WHITENER	184 K

ABOVE IS PACKED IN TWO FIBERBOARD BOXES.
GROSS WEIGHT: 220 KGS
NET WEIGHT: 186 KGS

MARKS:
AS ADDRESSED
#1/2

Accord de Libre-Échange Nord-Américain Certificat d'Origine
North American Free Trade Agreement Certificate of Origin

1. Nom et Adresse de l'Exportateur (Exporter Name and Address) ABC EXPORT CORP. 123 PARK LANE NEW YORK NY 10012 Numéro d'Identification aux Fins de l'Impôt (Tax I.D. Number)	2. Période Globale (Blanket Period) Du (AAMMJJ): (Effective Date YYMMDD) 99/02/15 Au (AAMMJJ): (Expiration Date YYMMDD) 00/02/14
3. Nom et Adresse du Producteur (Producer Name and Address) SAME Numéro d'Identification aux Fins de l'Impôt (Tax I.D. Number)	4. Nom et Adresse de l' Importateur (Importer Name and Address) FOOD SERVICE SUPPLY STORES AVENIDA 26 Y PALOMINA ASA #40 MEXICO CITY DF MEXICO Numéro d'Identification aux Fins de l'Impôt (Tax I.D. Number)

5. Description des Produits (Description of Goods)	6. Numéro de Classement Tarifaire S.H. (HS Tariff Classification)	7. Critère de Préférence (Preference Criterion)	8. Producteur (Producer)	9. Coût Net (Net Cost)	10. Pays d'Origine (Country of Origin)
NON DAIRY COFFEE WHITENER	210690	A	YES	NO	US

ORIGINAL

Certification d'Origine (Certification of Origin)
J'atteste Que (I Certify that):

- Les renseignements fournis dans le présent document sont exacts et je me charge de prouver, au besoin, ce qui y est avancé. Je comprends que je suis responsable de toutes fausses assertions ou omissions importantes faites dans le présent document ou s'y rapportant: (The information on this document is true and accurate and I assume the responsibility for proving such representations. I understand that I am liable for any false statements or material omissions made on or in connection with this document);

- Je conviens de conserver et de produire sur demande les documents nécessaires à l'appui du certificat et d'informer, par écrit, toute personne à qui il a été remis, des changements qui pourraient influer sur son exactitude ou sa validité; (I agree to maintain, and present upon request, documentation necessary to support this certificate, and to inform, in writing, all persons to whom the certificate was given of any changes that would affect the accuracy or validity of this certificate);

- Les marchandises sont originaires du territoire de l'une ou de plusieurs des parties et sont conformes aux exigences relatives à l'origine prévues dans l'Accord de libre échange nord-américain et, sauf exemption expresse à l'Article 411 ou à l'annexe 401, n'ont subi aucune production supplémentaire ou autre transformation à l'extérieur du territoire des parties; (The goods originated in the territory of one or more of the parties, and comply with the origin requirements specified for those goods in the North American Free Trade Agreement, and unless specifically exempted in Article 411 or Annex 401, there has been no further production or any other operation outside the territories of the Parties);

- Le présent certificat se compose de _____ pages, y compris les pièces jointes. (This certificate consists of __1__ pages, including all attachments).

11. Signature Autorisée (Authorized Signature):	Société (Company): ABC EXPORT CORP
Nom (Name): RANDI	Titre (Title): MANUFACTURING PLANT SUPERVISOR
Date (AAMMJJ) (Date YYMMDD): 99/02/15	Téléphone (Telephone): 212 555 1234	Télécopieur (Fax): 212 555 4321

Form No. 10-665 Printed and Sold by UNZ&CO 190 Baldwin Ave., Jersey City, NJ 07306 • (800) 631-3098

MINISTÈRE DU REVENU NATIONAL-DOUANES ET ACCISE
DEPARTMENT OF NATIONAL REVENUE-CUSTOMS AND EXCISE
B 232 (12/93)

ABC EXPORT COMPANY
123 PARK LANE
NEW YORK, NY 10012

SANITARY/QUALITY CERTIFICATE

We hereby certify that the products described on the attached invoices are manufactured in our own factory in the United States of America; that all ingredients contained in each of the products to be exported are approved for food use in a regulation of the United States Food and Drug Administration or appear on the GRAS list. Further, we hereby certify that each product is offered for sale and sold in the United States; that said product is perfectly fit and intended for human consumption when used in accordance with good manufacturing practices.

All of our products are free of heavy metals, radiation, and all kinds of DISEASE, including Cholera. The products shown on the attached invoices meet and/or exceed the food and sanitary regulations promulgated by all applicable federal and state authorities.

CODE DESCRIPTION:

NDX89 - NON DAIRY COFFEE WHITENER

JOHN JONES
DIRECTOR OF PROCESSING
ABC EXPORT COMPANY

DEPARTMENT OF THE TREASURY
UNITED STATES CUSTOMS SERVICE

AIR CARGO MANIFEST
19 CFR 122 48, 122 52, 122 54, 122 73, 122 113, 122 118

Form approved O.M.B. No. 1515-0001

1 PAGE NO
1 OF 1

| 2 OWNER/OPERATOR
AEROMEXPRESS | 3 MARKS OF NATIONALITY AND REGISTRATION
MEXICAN | 4 FLIGHT NO
123/15 |
|---|---|---|
| 5 PORT OF LADING
JFK NEW YORK | 6 PORT OF UNLADING
MEXICO CITY | 7 DATE
FEB. 15 1999 |

ITEMS 8 AND 9 FOR CONSOLIDATION SHIPMENTS ONLY

| 8 CONSOLIDATOR
FSI GLOBAL LOGISTICS | 9 DE CONSOLIDATOR
LINEA FEDERAL DE CARGA SA DE CV |
|---|---|

10 AIR WAYBILL TYPE (M=Master, H=House, S=Sub) / 11 AIR WAYBILL NO	12 NO OF PIECES	13 WEIGHT (Kg./Lb)	14 NO OF HAWBs	15 SHIPPER NAME AND ADDRESS	16 CONSIGNEE NAME AND ADDRESS	17 NATURE OF GOODS
M 976-1234 5678	2	220 K	1	FSI GLOBAL LOGISTICS
1229 OLD WALT WHITMAN RD
MELVILLE, NY 11747	LINEA FEDERAL DE CARGA SA DE CV
AVENIDA 602 Y CAMINO ASA #28
ADUANA DEL AEROPUERTO INTER-
NACIONAL ,COL.PENON DE LOS
BANOS DF MEXICO
PHONE#525-685-4567	CONSOLIDATION
H 900102	2	220 K		ABC EXPORT CORP.
123 PARK LANE
NEW YORK, NY 10012	FOOD SERVICE SUPPLY STORES
AVENIDA 26 Y PALOMINA ASA#40
MEXICO CITY DF MEXICO	NON PERISHABLE FOOD
PRODUCT

Customs Form 7509 (121289)

U.S. DEPARTMENT OF COMMERCE - BUREAU OF THE CENSUS - INTERNATIONAL TRADE ADMINISTRATION

FORM **7525-V** (1-1-88)   **SHIPPER'S EXPORT DECLARATION**   OMB No. 0607-0018

1a. EXPORTER *(Name and address including ZIP code)*

ABC EXPORT CORP.
123 PARK LANE
NEW YORK NY 10012   ZIP CODE

2. DATE OF EXPORTATION
02/12/99

3. BILL OF LADING/AIR WAYBILL NO.
976 1234 5678 900102

b. EXPORTER'S EIN (IRS) NUMBER
12-3456789

c. PARTIES TO TRANSACTION
☐ Related   ☒ Non-related

4a. ULTIMATE CONSIGNEE
FOOD SERVICE SUPPLY STORES AVENIDA 26 Y PALOMINA ASA#40
MEXICO CITY DF MEXICO

b. INTERMEDIATE CONSIGNEE

5. FORWARDING AGENT
FSI FREIGHT FORWARDERS, INC.
MELVILLE, N.Y. 11747

6. POINT (STATE) OF ORIGIN OR FTZ NO.
USA

7. COUNTRY OF ULTIMATE DESTINATION
MEXICO

8. LOADING PIER *(Vessel only)*

9. MODE OF TRANSPORT *(Specify)*
AIR

10. EXPORTING CARRIER
AEROMEXPRESS

11. PORT OF EXPORT
JFK AIRPORT

12. PORT OF UNLOADING *(Vessel and air only)*
MEXICO CITY

13. CONTAINERIZED *(Vessel only)*
☐ Yes   ☐ No

14. SCHEDULE B DESCRIPTION OF COMMODITIES,
15. MARKS, NOS, AND KINDS OF PACKAGES   *(Use columns 17-19)*

D/F (16)	SCHEDULE B NUMBER (17)	CHECK DIGIT	QUANTITY - SCHEDULE B UNIT(S) (18)	SHIPPING WEIGHT *(Kilos)* (19)	VALUE (U.S. dollars, omit cents) *(Selling price or cost if not sold)* (20)
D	2106.90.6575	0	KG	220 KG	$3400.00

21. VALIDATED LICENSE NO./GENERAL LICENSE SYMBOL
NLR

22. ECCN *(When required)*

23. ~~Randi Keenan~~ Duly authorized officer or employee   The exporter authorizes the forwarder named above to act as forwarding agent for export control and customs purposes.

24. I certify that all statements made and all information contained herein are true and correct and that I have read and understand the instructions for preparation of this document, set forth in the "Correct Way to Fill Out the Shipper's Export Declaration." I understand that civil and criminal penalties, including forfeiture and sale, may be imposed for making false or fraudulent statements herein, failing to provide the requested information or for violation of U.S. laws on exportation (13 U.S.C. Sec. 305; 22 U.S.C. Sec. 401; 18 U.S.C. Sec. 1001; 50 U.S.C. App. 2410).

Signature

Confidential - For use solely for official purposes authorized by the Secretary of Commerce (13 U.S.C. 301 (g).

Title

Export shipments are subject to inspection by U.S. Customs Service and/or Office of Export Enforcement.

Date
02/12/99   AGENT

25. AUTHENTICATION *(When required)*

The "Correct Way to Fill Out the Shipper's Export Declaration" is available from the Bureau of the Census, Washington, D.C. 20233.

976 JFK 1234 5678

Shipper's Name and Address / Shipper's Account Number

FSI GLOBAL LOGISTICS
1229 OLD WALT WHITMAN RD

MELVILLE , NY 11747

Not Negotiable

Air Waybill AEROMEXPRESS

AV. TEXCOCCO S/N ESQ. AV.
Issued by TAHEL COL PENON DE LOSBANOS

MAWB# 976 1234 5678

Copies 1, 2 and 3 of this Air Waybill are originals and have the same validity.

Consignee's Name and Address / Consignee's Account Number

LINEA FEDERAL DE CARGA, SA DE CV
AVENIDA 602 Y CAMINO ASA #28
ADUANA DEL AEROPUERTO INTERNACIONAL
COL. PENON DE LOS BANOS DF MEXICO

It is agreed that the goods described herein are accepted in apparent good order and condition (except as noted) for carriage SUBJECT TO THE CONDITIONS OF CONTRACT ON THE REVERSE HEREOF. ALL GOODS MAY BE CARRIED BY ANY OTHER MEANS INCLUDING ROAD OR ANY OTHER CARRIER UNLESS SPECIFIC CONTRARY INSTRUCTIONS ARE GIVEN HEREON BY THE SHIPPER, AND SHIPPER AGREES THAT THE SHIPMENT MAY BE CARRIED VIA INTERMEDIATE STOPPING PLACES WHICH THE CARRIER DEEMS APPROPRIATE. THE SHIPPER'S ATTENTION IS DRAWN TO THE NOTICE CONCERNING CARRIER'S LIMITATION OF LIABILITY. Shipper may increase such limitation of liability by declaring a higher value for carriage and paying a supplemental charge if required.

Issuing Carrier's Agent Name and City

FSI FREIGHT FORWARDERS, INC.
1229 OLD WALT WHITMAN ROAD
MELVILLE, N.Y. 11747

Accounting Information

FILE#900102

Agent's IATA Code / Account No.

01-1-9112/011

Airport of Departure (Addr. of First Carrier) and Requested Routing

JFK AIRPORT

To	By First Carrier	Routing and Destination	to	by	to	by	Currency	CHGS Code	WT/VAL PPD COLL	Other PPD COLL	Declared Value for Carriage	Declared Value for Customs
MEX	QQ						US$		X	X	N.V.D.	N.V.D.

Reference Number / Optional Shipping Information

Airport of Destination	Requested Flight/Date	Amount of Insurance	
MEXICO CITY	123/15	NIL	INSURANCE - If carrier offers insurance, and such insurance is requested in accordance with the conditions thereof, indicate amount to be insured in figures in box marked "Amount of Insurance".

Handling Information

NOTIFY IMMEDIATELY ON ARRIVAL TO PH#525-685-4567

SCI

These commodities, technology or software were exported from the United States in accordance with the Export Administration Regulations. Ultimate destination MEXICO

Diversion contrary to U.S. law prohibited.

No. of Pieces RCP	Gross Weight	kg lb	Rate Class / Commodity Item No.	Chargeable Weight	Rate / Charge	Total	Nature and Quantity of Goods (incl. Dimensions or Volume)
2	220 KG			220 KG	1.75	385.00	CONSOLIDATION AS PER ATTACHED MANIFEST DIMS IN INCHES: 2@ 24X28X22
2	220 KG					385.00	

Prepaid	Weight Charge	Collect	Other Charges
385.00			

Valuation Charge

Tax

Total Other Charges Due Agent

Total Other Charges Due Carrier

Shipper certifies that the particulars on the face hereof are correct and that insofar as any part of the consignment contains dangerous goods, such part is properly described by name and is in proper condition for carriage by air according to the applicable Dangerous Goods Regulations.

FSI FREIGHT FORWARDERS, INC.
Randi , as agent for shipper

Signature of Shipper or his Agent

Total Prepaid	Total Collect
385.00	

02/12/99   FSI FREIGHT FORWARDERS, INC.
Randi   JFK   , as agent for carrier

Executed on (date)   at (place)   Signature of Issuing Carrier or its Agent

Currency Conversion Rates	CC Charges in Dest. Currency

For Carriers Use only at Destination	Charges at Destination	Total Collect Charges

MAWB# 976 1234 5678

APPERSON PRINT MANAGEMENT SERVICES C5345 (11/98)   ORIGINAL 3 (FOR SHIPPER)

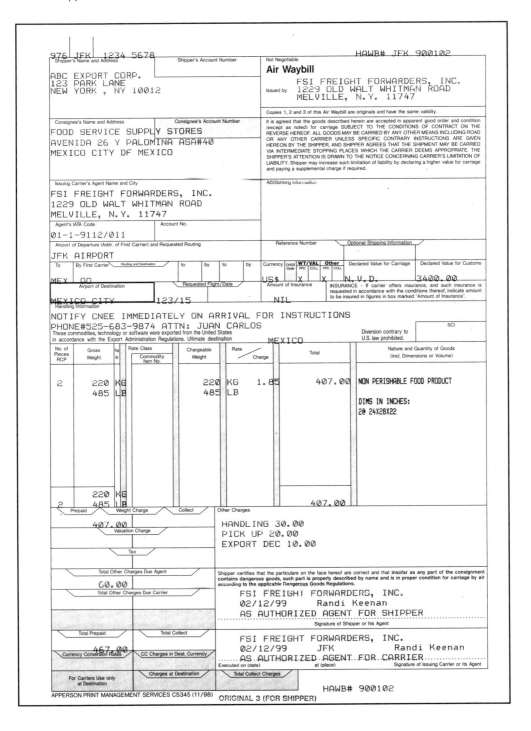

Air Freight Import

016	LHR	2355 4558		MAWB# 016 2355 4558

Shipper's Name and Address / Shipper's Account Number

WALDO MANUFACTURING CO.
UNIT 8 CAMBRIDGE PARK
SURREY, ENGLAND GU1 25X

Not Negotiable
Air Waybill UNITED AIRLINES
P.O. BOX 66100

Issued by
CHICAGO, IL 60666

Copies 1, 2 and 3 of this Air Waybill are originals and have the same validity.

Consignee's Name and Address / Consignee's Account Number

EMERSON SUPPLIES INC.
225 ELM DRIVE
BAYSHORE, NEW YORK 11706

It is agreed that the goods described herein are accepted in apparent good order and condition (except as noted) for carriage SUBJECT TO THE CONDITIONS OF CONTRACT ON THE REVERSE HEREOF. ALL GOODS MAY BE CARRIED BY ANY OTHER MEANS INCLUDING ROAD OR ANY OTHER CARRIER UNLESS SPECIFIC CONTRARY INSTRUCTIONS ARE GIVEN HEREON BY THE SHIPPER, AND SHIPPER AGREES THAT THE SHIPMENT MAY BE CARRIED VIA INTERMEDIATE STOPPING PLACES WHICH THE CARRIER DEEMS APPROPRIATE. THE SHIPPER'S ATTENTION IS DRAWN TO THE NOTICE CONCERNING CARRIER'S LIMITATION OF LIABILITY. Shipper may increase such limitation of liability by declaring a higher value for carriage and paying a supplemental charge if required.

Issuing Carrier's Agent Name and City

AMERICAN RIVER LOGISTICS, LTD.
1229 OLD WALT WHITMAN ROAD
MELVILLE, N.Y. 11747

Accounting Information

Agent's IATA Code 01-1-9112/0011   Account No.

Airport of Departure (Addr. of First Carrier) and Requested Routing

Reference Number   Optional Shipping Information

To	By First Carrier	Routing and Destination	to	by	to	by	Currency	CHGS Code	WT/VAL PPD COLL	Other PPD COLL	Declared Value for Carriage	Declared Value for Customs
JFK	UA						US$		X	X	N.V.D.	N.V.D.

Airport of Destination   Requested Flight/Date   Amount of Insurance

JFK NEW YORK   901/3   NIL

INSURANCE - If carrier offers insurance, and such insurance is requested in accordance with the conditions thereof, indicate amount to be insured in figures in box marked "Amount of Insurance".

Handling Information

NOTIFY CONSIGNEE UPON ARRIVAL.
These commodities, technology or software were exported from the United States in accordance with the Export Administration Regulations. Ultimate destination **USA**

Diversion contrary to U.S. law prohibited.   SCI

No. of Pieces RCP	Gross Weight	kg lb	Rate Class / Commodity Item No.	Chargeable Weight	Rate / Charge	Total	Nature and Quantity of Goods (incl. Dimensions or Volume)
4	206	KG		206	KG 2.20	453.20	
							MACHINERY PARTS
4	206	KG				453.20	

Prepaid	Weight Charge	Collect	Other Charges
	453.20		

Valuation Charge

Tax

Total Other Charges Due Agent

Total Other Charges Due Carrier

Shipper certifies that the particulars on the face hereof are correct and that insofar as any part of the consignment contains dangerous goods, such part is properly described by name and is in proper condition for carriage by air according to the applicable Dangerous Goods Regulations.

AMERICAN RIVER LOGISTICS, LTD.
Kelly Raia   ,as agent for shipper
Signature of Shipper or his Agent

Total Prepaid	Total Collect
453.20	

07/31/00   AMERICAN RIVER LOGISTICS, LTD.
Kelly Raia   LHR   ,as agent for carrier

Currency Conversion Rates   CC Charges in Dest. Currency

Executed on (date)   at (place)   Signature of Issuing Carrier or its Agent

For Carriers Use only at Destination   Charges at Destination   Total Collect Charges

MAWB# 016 2355 4558

APPERSON C9899 (5/00)   ORIGINAL 3 (FOR SHIPPER)

DEPARTMENT OF THE TREASURY
UNITED STATES CUSTOMS SERVICE

Form Approved
OMB No. 1515-0065

ENTRY/IMMEDIATE DELIVERY

American Brokers, Inc.
291 Whitman Avenue
Bayside, New York 22344

19 CFR 142.3, 142.16, 142, 22, 142.24

Page 1
Team 292
ABI Certified

1. ARRIVAL DATE	2. ELECTED ENTRY DATE	3. ENTRY TYPE CODE/NAME	4. ENTRY NUMBER
08/01/00		01 FORMAL/ID	275-2030392-1

5. PORT	6. SINGLE TRANS. BOND	7. BROKER/IMPORTER FILE NUMBER	
4701		237	

	8. CONSIGNEE NUMBER		9. IMPORTER NUMBER
	22-3335454		SAME

10. ULTIMATE CONSIGNEE NAME	11. IMPORTER OF RECORD NAME
EMERSON SUPPLIES INC. 225 ELM DRIVE BAYSHORE, NEW YORK 11706	SAME

12. CARRIER CODE	13. VOYAGE/FLIGHT/TRIP	14. LOCATION OF GOODS-CODE(S)/NAME(S)
UA	901	E111 UNITED AIRLINES

15. VESSEL CODE/NAME
UNITED AIRLINES

16. U.S. PORT OF UNLADING	17. MANIFEST NUMBER	18. G.O. NUMBER	19. TOTAL VALUE
4701			21508

20. DESCRIPTION OF MERCHANDISE
MACHINERY PARTS

21. IT/BL/AWB CODE	22. IT/BL/AWB NO.	23. MANIFEST QUANTITY	24. H.S. NUMBER	25. COUNTRY OF ORIGIN	26. MANUFACTURER ID.
M	016-2355-4558	4	8441.90.0000	GB	GBWALMAN8

27. CERTIFICATION	28. CUSTOMS USE ONLY
I hereby make application for entry/immediate delivery. I certify that the above information is accurate, the bond is sufficient, valid, and current, and that all requirements of 19 CFR Part 142 have been met.	☐ OTHER AGENCY ACTION REQUIRED, NAMELY:

SIGNATURE OF APPLICANT

X   AMERICAN BROKERS, INC.

PHONE NO.	DATE	
#631-565-7788	08/01/00	☐ CUSTOMS EXAMINATION REQUIRED.

29. BROKER OR OTHER GOVT. AGENCY USE	
	☐ ENTRY REJECTED, BECAUSE:

DELIVERY AUTHORIZED:	SIGNATURE	DATE

Paperwork Reduction Act Notice: This information is needed to determine the admissibility of imports into the United States and to provide the necessary information for the examination of the cargo and to establish the liability for payment of duties and taxes. Your response is necessary.

DEPARTMENT OF THE TREASURY
UNITED STATES CUSTOMS SERVICE

ENTRY SUMMARY

AMERICAN BROKRES, INC.
291 WHITMAN AVENUE
BAYSIDE, NEW YORK   22344

(1) Entry No.	(2) Entry Type Code	3. Entry Summary Date	
275-2030392-1	01 ABI/S	08/15/00	292
4. Entry Date	(5) Port Code		
08/01/00	4701		
6. Bond No.	7. Bond Type Code	8. Broker/Importer File No.	
089	8	237	

9. Ultimate Consignee Name and Address

10. Consignee No.

(11) Importer of Record Name and Address
EMERSON SUPPLIES INC.
225 ELM DRIVE
BAYSHORE, NEW YORK   11706

(12) Importer No.
22-3335454

(13) Exporting Country	14. Export Date
GB	07/31/00
(15) Country of Origin	16. Missing Documents
GB	
(17) I.T. No.	(18) I.T. Date

NY
State

(19) B L or AWB No.	20. Mode of Transportation	21. Manufacturer I.D.	22. Reference No.
016-2335-4558	40	GBWALMAN8	
(23) Importing Carrier		24. Foreign Port of Lading	25. Location of Goods/G.O. No.
UA UNITED AIRLINES 901			UNITED AIRLINES (UA)
26. U.S. Port of Unlading		(27) Import Date	E111
4701		08/01/00	

(28) Line No.	(29) Description of Merchandise			(33) A. Entered Value B. CHGS C. Relationship	34. A. T.S.U.S.A. Rate B. ADA/CVD Rate C. I.R.C. Rate D. Visa No.	(35) Duty and I.R. Tax	
	30. A. T.S.U.S.A. No. B. ADA CVD Case No.	31. A. Gross Weight B. Manifest Qty.	32. Net Quantity in T.S.U.S.A. Units			Dollars	Cents
			INVOICE #1	4 pcs			
001	MACHINERY PARTS			21508			
	8441.90.0000	395	x	C125	FREE	0	00
				N			
	MERCHANDISE PROCESSING FEE				0.21%	45	17
	INVOICE VALUE $ 21508						
	ENTERED VALUE $ 21508		DUTY =		+ 45.17 mpf		
			BLOCK 39 SUMMARY				
		MERCHANDISE PROCESSING FEE (499)			45.17		
			TOTAL		45.17		
	TEV=21508						

(36) Declaration of Importer of Record (Owner or Purchaser) or Authorized Agent	↓ U.S. CUSTOMS USE ↓	TOTALS	
I declare that I am the importer of record and that the actual owner, purchaser, or consignee for customs purposes is as shown above. OR [XX] owner or purchaser or agent thereof.	A. Liq. Code	(37) Duty	0 00
I further declare that the merchandise [XX] was obtained pursuant to a purchase or agreement to purchase and that the prices set forth in the invoice are true. OR [ ] was not obtained pursuant to a purchase or agreement to purchase and the statements in the invoice as to value or price are true to the best of my knowledge and belief.	B. Ascertained Duty		
	C. Ascertained Tax	(38) Tax	
I also declare that the statements in the documents herein filed fully disclose to the best of my knowledge and belief the true prices, values, quantities, rebates, drawbacks, fees, commissions, and royalties and are true and correct, and that all goods or services provided to the seller of the merchandise either free or at reduced cost are fully disclosed. I will immediately furnish to the appropriate customs officer any information showing a different state of facts.	D. Ascertained Other	(39) Other	45 17
	E. Ascertained Total	(40) Total	45 17
Notice required by Paperwork Reduction Act of 1980. This information is needed to ensure that importers/exporters are complying with U.S. Customs laws, to allow us to compute and collect the right amount of money, to enforce other agency requirements, and to collect accurate statistical information on imports. Your response is mandatory.	(41) Signature of Declarant, Title, and Date AS ATTY 08/02/00		

PART 3 - STATISTICAL

Customs Form 7501 (030984)

CARRIER CERTIFICATE

MAWB #016-2355-4558

UNITED AIRLINES
CUSTOMER SERVICE
JFK INTL. AIRPORT
JAMAICA, NEW YORK 11430

MASTER AIRWAY BILL

016-2355-4558

MARKS & NOS.	PIECES	WEIGHT	COMMODITY/DESCRIPTION	FROM
AS PER AWB	4	454 LBS.	MACHINERY PARTS	LONDON

ARRIVAL

FLIGHT NO.: UA 901

AIRCRAFT NO: N922FT

DATE OF ARRIVAL: 8/3/00

PICK UP ORDER AND TALLY

_____

TRUCKER NAME
Is authorized to pickup the Merchandise
Indicated

AUTHORIZED I.D. INDICATED BELOW:
1. **DRIVER'S LICENSE**
2. **U.S. CUSTOMS BOND CARD**
3. **AIRPORT SECURITY I.D. & POUCH**
4. **PASSPORT**

WALDO MANUFACTURING CO.
UNIT 8 CAMBRIDGE PARK
SURREY, ENGLAND   GU1 25X
TEL: 44 (0) 22 341 22 54
FAX: 44 (0) 22 341 22 78

INVOICE NO. :   300007

Emerson Supplies Inc.
225 Elm Drive
Bayshore, New York 11706

Your Order:
P15634

Part Number	Quantity	Unit Price	Total USD
2423 0211 99 Packaging Parts	395	54.45	USD $21507.75

Shipment
  Airfreight

Shipping Insurance
  Covered by you, to your charge

Terms of Payment
 60 Days from Invoice Date, Net

Country of Origin
  England

WALDO MANUFACTURING CO.
UNIT 8 CAMBRIDGE PARK
SURREY, ENGLAND   GU1 25X
TEL: 44 (0) 22 341 22 54
FAX: 44 (0) 22 341 22 78

PACKING LIST

Emerson Supplies Inc.
225 Elm Drive
Bayshore, New York 11706

Your Order: **Invoice Number:**
P15634   300007

Part Number   **Quantity**

2423 0211 99   395

Shipment
  Airfreight

Shipping Insurance
  Covered by you, to your charge

Terms of Payment
  60 Days from Invoice Date, Net

Country of Origin
  England

Ocean Freight Import

Shipper

HOLIDAY PRODUCTS SA
P.O. BOX 104
BASEL, SWITZERLAND

SAFCOMAR LINES LTD

Bill of Lading

For combined transport
and port to port shipments

Consignee

MATTHEW MANUFACTURING INC.
547 VERMONT AVENUE
NEW YORK, NEW YORK 11308

Notify Party

AMERICAN BROKERS, INC.
291 WHITMAN AVENUE
BAYSIDE, NEW YORK 22344

For release of goods apply to

SEASTAR INC.
202ROUTE 425
ELIZABETH, NEW JERSEY 08869
(980)867-9988

Combined transport - Place of receipt*

LE HAVRE

Ocean Vessel
EVER LEADING #100

Port of loading
LE HAVRE

Bill of Lading Number EISU540030075887

Port of discharge
NEW YORK

Combined transport - Place of delivery*
NEW YORK

Marks and Nos	Number and description of packages and goods	Gross weight, kos	Measurement, m3
CONTAINER #HXCL-258232-9 SEAL #008765	ONE (1) CASE STC TOASTER PARTS	1210 kgs	35CFT
	FREIGHT PREPAID		

As and according to the declaration of the merchant/shipper

*If not blank, shipment will be treated as Trough Combined Transport / Intermodal move

Freight payable at	Number of original Bills of Lading
LE HAVRE	THREE (3)

Place and date of issue

LE HAVRE 07/25/00

Freight and charges
FREIGHT PREPAID

Received by Safcomar Lines („carrier") from the merchant in apparent good order and condition (unless noted herein) the total number or quantity of containers or packages or units indicated, stated by the merchant to comprise the goods specified above, for the carriage subject to all the terms hereof (INCLUDING THE TERMS ON THE REVERSE HEREOF AND THE TERMS OF THE CARRIER'S APPLICABLE TARIFF) from the Place of receipt or the Port of loading, whichever is applicable, to the Port of discharge or the Place of delivery, whichever is applicable. In accepting this Bill of Lading, the merchant expressly accepts and agrees to all its terms, conditions and exceptions, whether printed, stamped or written, or otherwise incorporated, of which the merchant is fully aware notwithstanding the non-signing of the Bill of Lading by the Merchant. Goods in containers, vans or trailers or portable tanks may be carried on deck at the carrier's option.
IN WITNESS of the contract herein contained the number of original stated opposite have been issued each one being of the same contents and date, one which being accomplished the other(s) to be void.
For and on behalf of the Carrier. **SAFCOMAR LINES LTD.,**
SAFCOMAR SARL AS AGENT

SEASTAR INC.
202 Route 425
Elizabeth, New Jersey 08869

ARRIVAL NOTICE

For:

Matthew Manufacturing Inc.
547 Vermont Avenue
New York, New York 11308

Date: 8/3/00   Our Reference 548

Delivery Address:	CFS Location:
Matthew Manufacturing Inc.	HJD
547 Vermont Avenue	Building #242
New York, New York 11308	Avenel, New Jersey 07001

Importing Carrier:	Ever Leading	MBL #EISU540030075887
Port of Loading:	Le Havre	HBL #2077
Port of Discharge:	New York	O/O Container: HXCL258232-9
Shipper:	Holiday Products SA	
	P.O. Box 104	
	Basel, Switzerland	
Consignee Ref:	23566	

Local delivery or transfer by (Delivery order issued to)
ACS / Avenel, NJ 07001 (or their authorized agents)

Cargo Detail

Marks:	Pcs	Packing	Description	Weight
As Addressed	1	Case	Toaster Parts	1210 kgs
				2167 lbs

HOLIDAY PRODUCTS SA
P.O. BOX 1045
BASEL, SWITZERLAND
TEL: 41 33 2254 67
FAX: 41 33 2278 88

INVOICE #003511

Matthew Manufacturing Inc.
547 Vermont Avenue
New York, New York   11308

Your Order:
23566

Part Number	Quantity	Unit Price	Total USD
5566	5000	1.25	USD $ 6250.00
2387	2500	5.45	USD $ 13625.00

Housings for Toasters – Model #YK2

TOTAL USD $19,875.00

Shipment
  Oceanfreight

Shipping Insurance
  Covered by you, to your charge

Terms of Payment
  60 Days from Invoice Date, Net

Country of Origin
  Switzerland

HOLIDAY PRODUCTS SA
P.O. BOX 1045
BASEL, SWITZERLAND
TEL: 41 33 2254 67
FAX: 41 33 2278 88

PACKING LIST

Matthew Manufacturing Inc.
547 Vermont Avenue
New York, New York 11308

Your Order:
23566

Part Number	Quantity	Unit Price
5566	5000	1.25
2387	2500	5.45

Packed in One (1) Case

Housings for Toasters – Model #YK2

Shipment
  Oceanfreight

Shipping Insurance
  Covered by you, to your charge

Terms of Payment
  60 Days from Invoice Date, Net

Country of Origin
  Switzerland

DEPARTMENT OF THE TREASURY
UNITED STATES CUSTOMS SERVICE

ENTRY SUMMARY

AMERICAN BROKERS, INC.
291 WHITMAN AVENUE
BAYSIDE, NEW YORK 22344.

① Entry No. 275-2033495-1	② Entry Type Code 01 ABI/S	3. Entry Summary Date 08/18/00 245
4. Entry Date 08/03/00	⑤ Port Code 4601	
6. Bond No. 089	7. Bond Type Code 8	8. Broker/Importer File No. 267

9. Ultimate Consignee Name and Address	10. Consignee No.	⑪ Importer of Record Name and Address	⑫ Importer No. 22-3345567
		MATHEW MANUFACTURING INC. 547 VERMONT AVENUE NEW YORK, NEW YORK 11308	

⑬ Exporting Country CH	14. Export Date 07/25/00
⑮ Country of Origin CH	16. Missing Documents
⑰ I.T. No.	⑱ I.T. Date

NY
State

⑲ B L or AWB No. EISU540030075887	20. Mode of Transportation 10	21. Manufacturer I.D. CHHOLPRO104	22. Reference No.
㉓ Importing Carrier EVER LEADING 100	24. Foreign Port of Lading 42737	25. Location of Goods/G.O. No. HJD WAREHOUSE	
26. U.S. Port of Unlading 4601	㉗ Import Date 08/03/00	F226	

㉘ Line No.	㉙ Description of Merchandise 30. Ⓐ T.S.U.S.A. No. Ⓑ ADA CVD Case No.	31. Ⓐ Gross Weight Ⓑ Manifest Qty.	㉜ Net Quantity in T.S.U.S.A. Units	33. Ⓐ Entered Value Ⓑ CHGS Ⓒ Relationship	34. Ⓐ T.S.U.S.A. Rate Ⓑ ADA/CVD Rate Ⓒ I.R.C. Rate Ⓓ Visa No.	㉟ Duty and I.R. Tax Dollars	Cents
001	TOASTER PARTS 8516.9085.00		INVOICE #1 X	1 PC 19875 C575 N	3.9%	775	13
	MERCHANDISE PROCESSING FEE				0.21%	41	74
	INVOICE VALUE $ 19875 ENTERED VALUE $ 19875		DUTY =	+ 41.74mpf + 24.84hmf			
	HARBOR MAINTENANCE FEE			19875	0.125%	24	84
			BLOCK 39 SUMMARY MERCHANDISE PROCESSING FEE (499) HARBOR MAINTENANCE FEE (501) TOTAL		41.74 24.84 66.58		
	TEV=19875						

㊱ Declaration of Importer of Record (Owner or Purchaser) or Authorized Agent

I declare that I am the
☐ importer of record and that the actual owner, purchaser, or consignee for customs purposes is as shown above. **OR** ☒ owner or purchaser or agent thereof.

I further declare that the merchandise
☒ was obtained pursuant to a purchase or agreement to purchase and that the prices set forth in the invoice are true. **OR** ☐ was not obtained pursuant to a purchase or agreement to purchase and the statements in the invoice as to value or price are true to the best of my knowledge and belief.

I also declare that the statements in the documents herein filed fully disclose to the best of my knowledge and belief the true prices, values, quantities, rebates, drawbacks, fees, commissions, and royalties and are true and correct, and that all goods or services provided to the seller of the merchandise either free or at reduced cost are fully disclosed. I will immediately furnish to the appropriate customs officer any information showing a different state of facts.

Notice required by Paperwork Reduction Act of 1980. This information is needed to ensure that importers/exporters are complying with U.S. Customs laws, to allow us to compute and collect the right amount of money, to enforce other agency requirements, and to collect accurate statistical information on imports. Your response is mandatory.

㊶ Signature of Declarant, Title, and Date
AS ATTY 08/07/00

▼ U.S. CUSTOMS USE ▼		TOTALS	
A. Liq. Code	B. Ascertained Duty	㊲ Duty	775 13
	C. Ascertained Tax	㊳ Tax	
	D. Ascertained Other	㊴ Other	66 84
	E. Ascertained Total	㊵ Total	841 71

PART 2 - STATISTICAL

Customs Form 7501 (030984)

DEPARTMENT OF THE TREASURY
UNITED STATES CUSTOMS SERVICE

Form Approved
OMB No. 1515-0065

ENTRY/IMMEDIATE DELIVERY

AMERICAN BROKERS, INC.
291 WHITMAN AVENUE
BAYSIDE, NEW YORK 22344

PAGE 1
TEAM 245
ABI CERTIFIED

19 CFR 142.3, 142.16, 142, 22, 142.24

1. ARRIVAL DATE	2. ELECTED ENTRY DATE	3. ENTRY TYPE CODE/NAME	4. ENTRY NUMBER
08/03/00			275-2033495-1

5. PORT	6. SINGLE TRANS. BOND	7. BROKER/IMPORTER FILE NUMBER	
4601		267	

	8. CONSIGNEE NUMBER		9. IMPORTER NUMBER
	22-3345567		SAME

10. ULTIMATE CONSIGNEE NAME	11. IMPORTER OF RECORD NAME
MATHEW MANUFACTURING INC. 547 VERMONT AVENUE NEW YORK, NEW YORK 11308	SAME

12. CARRIER CODE	13. VOYAGE/FLIGHT/TRIP	14. LOCATION OF GOODS-CODE(S)/NAME(S)
EISU	100	F226 HJD WAREHOUSE

15. VESSEL CODE/NAME			
EVER LEADING			

16. U.S. PORT OF UNLADING	17. MANIFEST NUMBER	18. G.O. NUMBER	19. TOTAL VALUE
4601			19875

20. DESCRIPTION OF MERCHANDISE
TOASTER PARTS

21. IT/BL/AWB CODE 22. IT/BL/AWB NO.	23. MANIFEST QUANTITY	24. H.S. NUMBER	25. COUNTRY OF ORIGIN	26. MANUFACTURER ID.
M EISU540030075887	1	8516.9085.00	CH	CHHOLPRO104
H 2077				

27. CERTIFICATION

I hereby make application for entry/immediate delivery. I certify that the above information is accurate, the bond is sufficient, valid, and current, and that all requirements of 19 CFR Part 142 have been met.

SIGNATURE OF APPLICANT

X   AMERICAN BROKERS, INC.

PHONE NO.	DATE
#631-565-7788	08/03/00

29. BROKER OR OTHER GOVT. AGENCY USE

CTR #HXCL258232-9

28. CUSTOMS USE ONLY

☐ OTHER AGENCY ACTION REQUIRED, NAMELY:

☐ CUSTOMS EXAMINATION REQUIRED.

☐ ENTRY REJECTED, BECAUSE:

DELIVERY AUTHORIZED:	SIGNATURE	DATE

Paperwork Reduction Act Notice: This information is needed to determine the admissibility of imports into the United States and to provide the necessary information for the examination of the cargo and to establish the liability for payment of duties and taxes. Your response is necessary.

NAFTA Shipment
(Canada and Mexico)

976 JFK 0055 2833				MAWB# 976 0055 2833				
Shipper's Name and Address	**Shipper's Account Number**		Not Negotiable					
FRANKLIN PRODUCTS 215 MAIN STREET NEW CITY, NEW YORK 11203			Air Waybill **AEROMEXPRESS** AV. TEXCOCCO S/N ESQ. AV. Issued by **TAHEL COL PENON DE LOSBANOS**					
			Copies 1, 2 and 3 of this Air Waybill are originals and have the same validity.					
Consignee's Name and Address	**Consignee's Account Number**		It is agreed that the goods described herein are accepted in apparent good order and condition (except as noted) for carriage SUBJECT TO THE CONDITIONS OF CONTRACT ON THE REVERSE HEREOF. ALL GOODS MAY BE CARRIED BY ANY OTHER MEANS INCLUDING ROAD OR ANY OTHER CARRIER UNLESS SPECIFIC CONTRARY INSTRUCTIONS ARE GIVEN HEREON BY THE SHIPPER, AND SHIPPER AGREES THAT THE SHIPMENT MAY BE CARRIED VIA INTERMEDIATE STOPPING PLACES WHICH THE CARRIER DEEMS APPROPRIATE. THE SHIPPER'S ATTENTION IS DRAWN TO THE NOTICE CONCERNING CARRIER'S LIMITATION OF LIABILITY. Shipper may increase such limitation of liability by declaring a higher value for carriage and paying a supplemental charge if required.					
GRUPO PRODUCTOS SA DE CV KM. 23, CARRETA MEXICO CITY, MEXICO								
Issuing Carrier's Agent Name and City			Accounting Information					
AMERICAN RIVER LOGISTICS, LTD. 1229 OLD WALT WHITMAN ROAD MELVILLE, N.Y. 11747			NO SED REQUIRED SECTION 30.55 (H) FTSR					
Agent's IATA Code	**Account No.**							
01-1-9112/0011								
Airport of Departure (Addr. of First Carrier) and Requested Routing			Reference Number	Optional Shipping Information				
JFK AIRPORT								
To	**By First Carrier** Routing and Destination	**to** **by** **to** **by**	Currency CHGS Code	**WT/VAL** PPD COLL	**Other** PPD COLL	Declared Value for Carriage	Declared Value for Customs	
MEX	QO		US$	X	X	N.V.D.	N.V.D.	
Airport of Destination	**Requested Flight/Date**		Amount of Insurance	INSURANCE - If carrier offers insurance, and such insurance is requested in accordance with the conditions thereof, indicate amount to be insured in figures in box marked "Amount of Insurance".				
MEXICO CITY	9611/8		NIL					
Handling Information								
NOTIFY CONSIGNEE UPON ARRIVAL... These commodities, technology or software were exported from the United States in accordance with the Export Administration Regulations. Ultimate destination MEXICO						Diversion contrary to U.S. law prohibited.		SCI

No. of Pieces RCP	Gross Weight	kg lb	Rate Class Commodity Item No.	Chargeable Weight	Rate Charge	Total	Nature and Quantity of Goods (incl. Dimensions or Volume)
2	133 KG		SCR2340	133	KG 2.00	266.00	MACHINERY PARTS DIMS IN INCHES: (2) 22X23X22
2	133 KG					266.00	

Prepaid	Weight Charge	Collect	Other Charges		
	266.00				
	Valuation Charge				
	Tax				
Total Other Charges Due Agent			Shipper certifies that the particulars on the face hereof are correct and that insofar as any part of the consignment contains dangerous goods, such part is properly described by name and is in proper condition for carriage by air according to the applicable Dangerous Goods Regulations.		
Total Other Charges Due Carrier					
13.30			.Kelly......................,as agent for shipper............		
			AMERICAN RIVER LOGISTICS, LTD.		
			Signature of Shipper or his Agent		
Total Prepaid	Total Collect		08/05/00 AMERICAN RIVER LOGISTICS, LTD.		
279.30			.Kelly..............JFK.....,as agent for carrier....		
Currency Conversion Rates	CC Charges in Dest. Currency		Executed on (date) at (place) Signature of Issuing Carrier or its Agent		
Charges at Destination					
For Carriers Use only at Destination	Total Collect Charges		MAWB# 976 0055 2833		

APPERSON C9899 (5/00)   ORIGINAL 3 (FOR SHIPPER)

DEPARTMENT OF THE TREASURY
UNITED STATES CUSTOMS SERVICE

Approved through 12/31/96
OMB No. 1515-0204
See Back of form for Paper-
work Reduction Act Notice

NORTH AMERICAN FREE TRADE AGREEMENT
CERTIFICATE OF ORIGIN

Please print or type   **19 CFR 181.11, 181.22**

1. EXPORTER NAME AND ADDRESS	2. BLANKET PERIOD *(DD/MM/YY)*
Franklin Products Inc. 215 Main Street New City, New York 11203 TAX IDENTIFICATION NUMBER: 41-2060446	01/01/2000 FROM 01/01/2000 TO 12/31/2000

3. PRODUCER NAME AND ADDRESS	4. IMPORTER NAME AND ADDRESS
SAME TAX IDENTIFICATION NUMBER:	Grupo Products SA de CV Km. 23, Carreta Mexico City, Mexico TAX IDENTIFICATION NUMBER: AIN-987044 UR2

5. DESCRIPTION OF GOOD(S)	6. HS TARIFF CLASSIFICATION NUMBER	7. PREFERENCE CRITERION	8. PRODUCER	9. NET COST	10. COUNTRY OF ORIGIN
MACHINERY PARTS	5911.32	B	YES	NO	US

I CERTIFY THAT:

• THE INFORMATION ON THIS DOCUMENT IS TRUE AND ACCURATE AND I ASSUME THE RESPONSIBILITY FOR PROVING SUCH REPRESENTA-TIONS. I UNDERSTAND THAT I AM LIABLE FOR ANY FALSE STATEMENTS OR MATERIAL OMISSIONS MADE ON OR IN CONNECTION WITH THIS DOCUMENT;

• I AGREE TO MAINTAIN, AND PRESENT UPON REQUEST, DOCUMENTATION NECESSARY TO SUPPORT THIS CERTIFICATE, AND TO INFORM, IN WRITING, ALL PERSONS TO WHOM THE CERTIFICATE WAS GIVEN OF ANY CHANGES THAT COULD AFFECT THE ACCURACY OR VALIDITY OF THIS CERTIFICATE;

• THE GOODS ORIGINATED IN THE TERRITORY OF ONE OR MORE OF THE PARTIES, AND COMPLY WITH THE ORIGIN REQUIREMENTS SPECIFIED FOR THOSE GOODS IN THE NORTH AMERICAN FREE TRADE AGREEMENT, AND UNLESS SPECIFICALLY EXEMPTED IN ARTICLE 411 OR ANNEX 401, THERE HAS BEEN NO FURTHER PRODUCTION OR ANY OTHER OPERATION OUTSIDE THE TERRITORIES OF THE PARTIES; AND

• THIS CERTIFICATE CONSISTS OF [1] PAGES, INCLUDING ALL ATTACHMENTS.

11.	11a. AUTHORIZED SIGNATURE:	11b. COMPANY: FRANKLIN PRODUCTS INC.
	11c. NAME *(Print or Type)*: John Martin	11d. TITLE: Vice President
	11e. DATE *(DD/MM/YY)* 7/25/00	11f. TELEPHONE NUMBER ▷	*(Voice)* (566)555-1212	*(Facsimile)* (566)555-2212

Customs Form 434 (121793)

FRANKLIN PRODUCTS
215 MAIN STREET
NEW CITY, NEW YORK 11203
TEL: (212)221-3555
FAX: (212)221-3566

PACKING LIST

Grupo Productos SA de CV
Km. 23, Carreta
Mexico City, Mexico

Order #5222   **Item #2000**   **Quantity: 350 pcs**

Packed in Two (2) Cases

Shipment
  Airfreight

Terms of Payment
  60 Days from Invoice Date, Net

Country of Origin
  U.S.A.

FRANKLIN PRODUCTS
215 MAIN STREET
NEW CITY, NEW YORK 11203
TEL: (212)221-3555
FAX: (212)221-3566

INVOICE #27778

Grupo Productos SA de CV
Km. 23, Carreta
Mexico City, Mexico

Invoice Date: 8/1/00

Order #5222

Item #2000

Quantity: 350 pcs   @ $2.00 per piece = USD $700.00
Textile Machinery Part

Total Invoice Value USD $700.00

Shipment
  Airfreight

Terms of Payment
  60 Days from Invoice Date, Net

Country of Origin
  U.S.A.

SHARP INDUSTRIAL PRODUCTS
1075 WEST PARK AVENUE
LONG BEACH, NEW YORK 11561
(516)431-0299

PROFORMA INVOICE

CANADA PLASTICS CORP.
245 SOUTH ESPLANADE
TORONTO, CANADA Y7M 3H4
ATTN: ELLEN JOHNSTON

INVOICE DATE: 2/25/01

ORDER 8522

DESCRIPTION:

PRODUCT	QUANTITY	PRICE PER	TOTAL
HANDSAWS	400	25.45	$10180.00

VALUE FOR CUSTOMS PURPOSES ONLY: USD $10180.00

HTS #8202.1000.00

COUNTRY OF ORIGIN: U.S.A.

WE CERTIFY THIS INVOICE IS TRUE AND CORRECT AND THAT THE MERCHANDISE DESCRIBED
HEREIN IS OF U.S.A. ORIGIN. THESE COMMODITIES, TECHNOLOGY OR SOFTWARE WERE
EXPORTED FROM THE UNITED STATES IN ACCORDANCE WITH THE EXPORT ADMINISTRATION
REGULATIONS. DIVERSION CONTRARY TO U.S. LAW PROHIBITED.

_____

Henry Jones
Shipping Manager

SHARP INDUSTRIAL PRODUCTS
1075 WEST PARK AVENUE
LONG BEACH, NEW YORK 11561
(516)431-0299

PACKING LIST

CANADA PLASTIC CORP.
245 SOUTH ESPLANADE
TORONTO, CANADA Y7M 3H4
ATTN: ELLEN JOHNSTON

DATE: 2/25/01
ORDER: 8522

PRODUCT	QUANTITY
HANDSAWS	400

PACKED IN FOUR (4) CARTONS

DIMS IN INCHES: (4) 40 x 35 x 30

NET WEIGHT: 325 LBS.

GROSS WEIGHT: 350 LBS.

HTS #8202.1000.00

COUNTRY OF ORIGIN: U.S.A.

_____
Henry Jones
Shipping Manager

STRAIGHT BILL OF LADING— SHORT FORM   ORIGINAL – NOT NEGOTIABLE   Shipper's No. _____

Carrier's Name: PIB CARRIERS   Carrier's No. 499-2566

RECEIVED, subject to the classifications and tariffs in effect on the date of the issue of this Bill of lading.

at LONGBEACH, NEW YORK _____ (Date) 02/25/01 19 ____ FROM 1075 WEST PARK AVENUE, LONG BEACH, NY

SHARP INDUSTRIAL PRODUCTS

the property described below, in apparent good order, except as noted (contents and condition of contents of packages unknown), marked, consigned, and destined as shown below, which said company (the word company being understood throughout this contract as meaning any person or corporation in possession of the property under the contract) agrees to carry to its usual place of delivery at said destination, if on its own railroad, water line, highway route or routes, or within the territory of its highway operations, otherwise to deliver to another carrier on the route to said destination. It is mutually agreed, as to each carrier of all or any of said property over all or any portion of said route to destination, and as to each party at any time interested in all or any of said property, that every service to be performed hereunder shall be subject to all the terms and conditions of the Uniform Domestic Straight Bill of Lading set forth (1) in the Uniform Freight Classification in effect on the date hereof, if this is a rail or rail-water shipment, or (2) in the applicable motor carrier classification or tariff if this is a motor carrier shipment. Shipper hereby certifies that he is familiar with all the terms and conditions of the said bill of lading, including those on the back thereof, set forth in the classification or tariff which governs the transportation of this shipment, and the said terms and conditions are hereby agreed to by the shipper and accepted for himself and his assigns.

Consigned TO CANADA PLASTIC CORP., 245 SOUTH ESPLANADE, TORONTO, CANADA

(Mail or street address for purposes of notification only.)

On Collect on Delivery Shipments, the letters "COD" must appear before consignee's name or as otherwise provided in Item 430, Sec. 1.

Destination TORONTO, CANADA _____ Street 245 SOUTH ESPLANADE _____ City

TORONTO, CANADA County TORONTO, CANADA _____ State _____ Zip

                                    Delivery ★
Route _____   Address _____
                (★To be filled in only when shipper desires and governing tariffs provide for delivery thereat.)

Delivering Carrier _____ Car or Vehicle Initials and No. _____

Collect on Delivery $ _____ And Remit to _____

_____ Street _____ City _____ State

No. Packages	H.M.	Kind of Package, Description of Articles, Special Marks, and Exceptions	*Weight (Subject to Correction)	Class or Rate	Check Column
4		HANDSAWS	350 #	55	
		DELIVERY TO: CANADA PLASTIC CORP.			
		245 SOUTH ESPLANADE			
		TORONTO, CANADA Y7M 3H4			
		FREIGHT PREPAID			

Subject to Section 7 of conditions, if this shipment is to be delivered to the consignee without recourse on the consignor, the consignor shall sign the following statement:

The carrier shall not make delivery of this shipment without payment of freight and all other lawful charges.

_____
(Signature of consignor.)

C. O. D. Charges to be
                Paid by
□ Shipper   □ Consignee

If charges are to be prepaid, write or stamp here, "To be Prepaid."

TO BE PREPAID

Received $ _____ to apply in prepayment of the charges on the property described hereon.

_____
Agent or Cashier

Per _____
(The signature here acknowledges only the amount prepaid.)

Charges Advanced:

$ _____

† *The fibre containers used for this shipment conform to the specifications set forth in the box maker's certificate thereon, and all other requirements of Rule 41 of the Uniform Freight Classification and Rule 5 of the National Motor Freight Classification."

† Shipper's imprint in lieu of stamp; not a part of bill of lading approved by the Interstate Commerce Commission.

*If the shipment moves between two ports by a carrier by water, the law requires that the bill of lading shall state whether it is carrier's or shipper's weight.
NOTE — Where the rate is dependent on value, shippers are required to state specifically in writing the agreed or declared value of the property.

The agreed or declared value of the property is hereby specifically stated by the shipper to be not exceeding _____ per _____

_____ Shipper, Per _____   _____ Agent

Permanent post-office address of shipper. _____   Per _____

1

DEPARTMENT OF THE TREASURY
UNITED STATES CUSTOMS SERVICE

OMB No. 1515-0204
See Back of form for Paperwork Reduction Act Notice

NORTH AMERICAN FREE TRADE AGREEMENT

CERTIFICATE OF ORIGIN

Please print or type

19 CFR 181.11, 181.22

1. EXPORTER NAME AND ADDRESS	2. BLANKET PERIOD *(DD/MM/YY)*
SHARP INDUSTRIAL PRODUCTS 1075 WEST PARK AVENUE LONG BEACH, NEW YORK 11561 TAX IDENTIFICATION NUMBER: 22-6498132	FROM 01/01/2001 TO 12/31/2001
3. PRODUCER NAME AND ADDRESS	4. IMPORTER NAME AND ADDRESS
SAME TAX IDENTIFICATION NUMBER:	CANADA PLASTIC CORP. 245 SOUTH ESPLANADE TORONTO, CANADA Y7M 3H4 TAX IDENTIFICATION NUMBER: 57-6798833

5. DESCRIPTION OF GOOD(S)	6. HS TARIFF CLASSIFICATION NUMBER	7. PREFERENCE CRITERION	8. PRODUCER	9. NET COST	10. COUNTRY OF ORIGIN
HANDSAWS	8202.10	B	YES	10180.00	US

I CERTIFY THAT:

• THE INFORMATION ON THIS DOCUMENT IS TRUE AND ACCURATE AND I ASSUME THE RESPONSIBILITY FOR PROVING SUCH REPRESENTA-
TIONS. I UNDERSTAND THAT I AM LIABLE FOR ANY FALSE STATEMENTS OR MATERIAL OMISSIONS MADE ON OR IN CONNECTION WITH THIS
DOCUMENT;

• I AGREE TO MAINTAIN, AND PRESENT UPON REQUEST, DOCUMENTATION NECESSARY TO SUPPORT THIS CERTIFICATE, AND TO INFORM,
IN WRITING, ALL PERSONS TO WHOM THE CERTIFICATE WAS GIVEN OF ANY CHANGES THAT COULD AFFECT THE ACCURACY OR VALIDITY
OF THIS CERTIFICATE;

• THE GOODS ORIGINATED IN THE TERRITORY OF ONE OR MORE OF THE PARTIES, AND COMPLY WITH THE ORIGIN REQUIREMENTS
SPECIFIED FOR THOSE GOODS IN THE NORTH AMERICAN FREE TRADE AGREEMENT, AND UNLESS SPECIFICALLY EXEMPTED IN ARTICLE
411 OR ANNEX 401, THERE HAS BEEN NO FURTHER PRODUCTION OR ANY OTHER OPERATION OUTSIDE THE TERRITORIES OF THE
PARTIES; AND

• THIS CERTIFICATE CONSISTS OF [   ] PAGES, INCLUDING ALL ATTACHMENTS.

11.	11a. AUTHORIZED SIGNATURE:	11b. COMPANY: SHARP INDUSTRIAL PRODUCTS
	11c. NAME *(Print or Type)*: HENRY JONES	11d. TITLE: SHIPPING MANAGER
	11e. DATE *(DD/MM/YY)* 02/25/01	11f. TELEPHONE ▷ NUMBER	*(Voice)* (516)431-0299	*(Facsimile)* (516)430-9955

Customs Form 434 (121793)

| Canada Customs and Revenue Agency | Agence des douanes et du revenu du Canada | **CANADA CUSTOMS CODING FORM** **DOUANES CANADA - FORMULE DE CODAGE** | PROTECTED (WHEN COMPLETED) PROTÉGÉ (UNE FOIS REMPLI) |

1 IMPORTER NAME AND ADDRESS NOM ET ADRESSE DE L'IMPORTATEUR	NO. - N° 22-6498132	2 TRANSACTION NO. - N° DE TRANSACTION
CANADA PLASTIC CORP. 245 SOUTH ESPLANADE TORONTO, CANADA Y7M 3H4		1-6798

3 TYPE	4 OFFICE NO. N° DE BUREAU	5 GST REGISTRATION NO. N° DE TPS	6 PAYMENT CODE CODE DE PAIEMENT	7 MODE OF- DE TRANS.	8 PORT OF UNLOADING PORT DE	9 TOTAL VFD - TOTAL DE LA VD
AB	0497			1	0497	CAD $5025.00

10 SUB HDR NO. N° DE SOUS- EN-TÊTE	11 VENDOR NAME - NOM DU VENDEUR	NO. - N°	12 COUNTRY OF ORIGIN PAYS D'ORIGINE	13 PLACE OF EXPORT LIEU D'EXPORTATION	14 TARIFF TREATMENT TRAITEMENT TARIFAIRE	15 U.S. PORT OF EXIT BUREAU DE SORTIE DES É.-U.
	SHARP INDUSTRIAL PRODUCTS 1075 WEST PARK AVENUE LONG BEACH, NEW YORK 11561		UNY	UNY		0301

			16 DIRECT SHIPMENT DATE DATE D'EXPÉDITION DIRECTE	17 CRCY. CODE DEVISE	18 TIME LIMIT - DÉLAI	19 FREIGHT - FRET
				USD		350

	20 RELEASE DATE - DATE DE LA MAINLEVÉE

21 LINE LIGNE	22	DESCRIPTION DÉSIGNATION	23 WEIGHT IN KILOGRAMS POIDS EN KILOGRAMMES	PREVIOUS TRANSACTION - TRANSACTION ANTÉRIEURE		26 SPECIAL AUTHORITY AUTORISATION SPÉCIALE
		HANDSAWS		24 NUMBER NUMÉRO	25 LINE LIGNE	
27 CLASSIFICATION NO. N° DE CLASSEMENT	28 TARIFF CODE TARIFAIRE	29 QUANTITY QUANTITÉ	30 U - M	31 VFD CODE CODE VD	32 SIMA CODE CODE DE LMSI	33 RATE OF CUSTOMS DUTY TAUX DE DROIT DE DOUANE	34 E.T. RATE TAUX T.A.	35 RATE OF GST TAUX DE TPS	36 VALUE FOR CURRENCY CONVERSION CONVERSION VALEUR POUR CHANGE
8202.10		400					0	7	USD $4040.00
37 VALUE FOR DUTY VALEUR EN DOUANE		38 CUSTOMS DUTIES DROITS DE DOUANE		39 SIMA ASSESSMENT COTISATION DE LMSI		40 EXCISE TAX TAXE D'ACCISE		41 VALUE FOR TAX VALEUR POUR TAXE	42 GST TPS
CAD							CAD		$351

43 DEPOSIT - DÉPÔT		47 CUSTOMS DUTIES DROITS DE DOUANE	

DECLARATION - DÉCLARATION

I, JE   KELLY RAIA

PLEASE PRINT NAME - LETTRES MOULÉES S.V.P.

OF, DE   CANADA PLASTIC CORP.

IMPORTER / AGENT - IMPORTATEUR / AGENT

DECLARE THE PARTICULARS OF THIS DOCUMENT TO BE TRUE, ACCURATE AND COMPLETE.
DÉCLARE QUE LES RENSEIGNEMENTS CI-DESSUS SONT VRAIS ET COMPLETS.

DATE   SIGNATURE

| 44 WAREHOUSE NO. - N° D'ENTREPÔT |
| 45 CARGO CONTROL NO. - N° DE CONTRÔLE DU FRET |
| 46 CARRIER CODE AT IMPORTATION CODE DE TRANSPORTEUR À L'IMPORTATION |

| 48 SIMA ASSESSMENT COTISATION DE LMSI |
| 49 EXCISE TAX TAXE D'ACCISE |
| 50 GST TPS |
| 51 TOTAL |

B3 (00)

Printed in Canada - Imprimé au Canada

Canada

Truck Export

954572/028750

3-PART STOCK FORM NO. B-3876

STRAIGHT BILL OF LADING— SHORT FORM

ORIGINAL – NOT NEGOTIABLE

Shipper's No. ___233-4567___

Carrier's Name: VICTORY MOTOR CARRIERS   Carrier's No. _____

RECEIVED, subject to the classifications and tariffs in effect on the date of the issue of this Bill of lading,   MAX-SAM PET PRODUCTS, 17 MOUNTAINVIEW DR.

at FORT PARK, NEW YORK _____ (Date)___8/2/00___ 19___ FROM__FORT PARK, NEW YORK 11768

the property described below, in apparent good order, except as noted (contents and condition of contents of packages unknown), marked, consigned, and destined as shown below, which said company (the word company being understood throughout this contract as meaning any person or corporation in possession of the property under the contract) agrees to carry to its usual place of delivery at said destination, if on its own railroad, water line, highway route or routes, or within the territory of its highway operations, otherwise to deliver to another carrier on the route to said destination. It is mutually agreed, as to each carrier of all or any of said property over all or any portion of said route to destination, and as to each party at any time interested in all or any of said property, that every service to be performed hereunder shall be subject to all the terms and conditions of the Uniform Domestic Straight Bill of Lading set forth (1) in the Uniform Freight Classification in effect on the date hereof, if this is a rail or rail-water shipment, or (2) in the applicable motor carrier classification or tariff if this is a motor carrier shipment. Shipper hereby certifies that he is familiar with all the terms and conditions of the said bill of lading, including those on the back thereof, set forth in the classification or tariff which governs the transportation of this shipment, and the said terms and conditions are hereby agreed to by the shipper and accepted for himself and his assigns.

Consigned **TO** SINGH MANUFACTURING CANADA, 552 REX STREET STATION

(Mail or street address for purposes of notification only.)

On Collect on Delivery Shipments, the letters 'COD' must appear before consignee's name or as otherwise provided in Item 430, Sec. 1.

Destination ___TORONTO, ONTARIO L4V 1W1___ Street_552 REX STREET STATION___City

___TORONTO, ONTARIO___ County___TORONTO, ONTARIO___ State__L4V 1W1___ Zip

Delivery
Route _____ Address ★_____

(★To be filled in only when shipper desires and governing tariffs provide for delivery thereat.)

Delivering Carrier _____ Car or Vehicle Initials and No._____

Collect on Delivery $_____ And Remit to _____

_____ Street _____ City_____ State____

Subject to Section 7 of conditions, if this shipment is to be delivered to the consignee without
recourse on the consignor, the consignor shall
sign the following statement:
    The carrier shall not make delivery of this
shipment without payment of freight and all
other lawful charges.

_____
(Signature of consignor.)

C. O. D. Charges to be
Paid by
☐ Shipper   ☐ Consignee

If charges are to be prepaid, write or
stamp here, "To be Prepaid."

TO BE PREPAID

No. Packages	H.M.	Kind of Package, Description of Articles, Special Marks, and Exceptions	*Weight (Subject to Correction)	Class or Rate	Check Column
25		25 SKIDS PET SUPPLIES	3575 #		
		DELIVERY TO: SINGH MANUFACTURING CANADA			
		552 REX STREET STATION			
		TORONTO, ONTARIO, CANADA L4V 1W1			
		FREIGHT PREPAID			

Received $_____ to apply
in prepayment of the charges on the
property described hereon.

_____
Agent or Cashier

Per _____
(The signature here acknowledges only
the amount prepaid.)
Charges Advanced:

$_____

† The fibre containers used for this shipment
conform to the specifications set forth in the
box maker's certificate thereon, and all other
requirements of Rule 41 of the Uniform Freight
Classification and Rule 5 of the National Motor
Freight Classification."
† Shipper's imprint in lieu of stamp; not a part
of bill of lading approved by the Interstate
Commerce Commission.

*If the shipment moves between two ports by a carrier by water, the law requires that the bill of lading shall state whether it is carrier's or shipper's weight.
NOTE — Where the rate is dependent on value, shippers are required to state specifically in writing the agreed or declared value of the property.
The agreed or declared value of the property is hereby specifically stated by the shipper to be not exceeding _____ per _____

_____ Shipper, Per_____   Agent

Permanent post-office
address of shipper, _____   Per _____

1

AMERICAN RIVER LOGISTICS
1 800 524-2493

STRAIGHT BILL OF LADING

PRO #233-4567

CARRIER NAME:
VICTORY MOTOR CARRIERS

DATE:
8/2/00

FROM:
MAX-SAM PET PRODUCTS
17 MOUNTAINVIEW DRIVE
FORT PARK, NEW YORK 11768

SHIP TO:
SINGH MANUFACTURING CANADA
552 REX STREET STATION
TORONTO, ONTARIO L4V 1W1

NO PCS	DESCRIPTION	WEIGHT
25 SKIDS	PET SUPPLIES	3575 #

FREIGHT PREPAID

DEPARTMENT OF THE TREASURY
UNITED STATES CUSTOMS SERVICE

Approved through 12/31/96
OMB No. 1515-0204
See Back of form for Paper-
work Reduction Act Notice

NORTH AMERICAN FREE TRADE AGREEMENT
CERTIFICATE OF ORIGIN

Please print or type   19 CFR 181.11, 181.22

1. EXPORTER NAME AND ADDRESS	2. BLANKET PERIOD *(DD/MM/YY)*
MAX-SAM PET PRODUCTS 17 MOUNTAINVIEW DRIVE FORT PARK, NEW YORK 11768 TAX IDENTIFICATION NUMBER: 22-4453632	FROM 01/01/2000 TO 12/31/2000
3. PRODUCER NAME AND ADDRESS SAME TAX IDENTIFICATION NUMBER:	4. IMPORTER NAME AND ADDRESS SINGH MANUFACTURING CANADA 552 REX STREET STATION TORONTO, CANADA L4V 1W1 TAX IDENTIFICATION NUMBER: AIN-983452 RS1

5. DESCRIPTION OF GOOD(S)	6. HS TARIFF CLASSIFICATION NUMBER	7. PREFERENCE CRITERION	8. PRODUCER	9. NET COST	10. COUNTRY OF ORIGIN
DOG LEASHES, COLLARS	4201.00	B	YES	NO	US
OTHER ARTICLES OF WOOD	4421.90	B	YES	NO	US

I CERTIFY THAT:

• THE INFORMATION ON THIS DOCUMENT IS TRUE AND ACCURATE AND I ASSUME THE RESPONSIBILITY FOR PROVING SUCH REPRESENTA-TIONS. I UNDERSTAND THAT I AM LIABLE FOR ANY FALSE STATEMENTS OR MATERIAL OMISSIONS MADE ON OR IN CONNECTION WITH THIS DOCUMENT;

• I AGREE TO MAINTAIN, AND PRESENT UPON REQUEST, DOCUMENTATION NECESSARY TO SUPPORT THIS CERTIFICATE, AND TO INFORM, IN WRITING, ALL PERSONS TO WHOM THE CERTIFICATE WAS GIVEN OF ANY CHANGES THAT COULD AFFECT THE ACCURACY OR VALIDITY OF THIS CERTIFICATE;

• THE GOODS ORIGINATED IN THE TERRITORY OF ONE OR MORE OF THE PARTIES, AND COMPLY WITH THE ORIGIN REQUIREMENTS SPECIFIED FOR THOSE GOODS IN THE NORTH AMERICAN FREE TRADE AGREEMENT, AND UNLESS SPECIFICALLY EXEMPTED IN ARTICLE 411 OR ANNEX 401, THERE HAS BEEN NO FURTHER PRODUCTION OR ANY OTHER OPERATION OUTSIDE THE TERRITORIES OF THE PARTIES; AND

• THIS CERTIFICATE CONSISTS OF [1] PAGES, INCLUDING ALL ATTACHMENTS.

11a. AUTHORIZED SIGNATURE:	11b. COMPANY: MAX-SAM PET PRODUCTS
11c. NAME *(Print or Type):* MARTIN SMITH	11d. TITLE: VICE PRESIDENT
11e. DATE *(DD/MM/YY)* 08/02/00	11f. TELEPHONE NUMBER ▷ *(Voice)* 632-445-7878	*(Facsimile)* 632-445-7879

Customs Form 434 (121793)

MAX-SAM PET PRODUCTS
17 MOUNTAINVIEW DRIVE
FORT PARK, NEW YORK 1768

INVOICE #MSP345

SOLD TO: SINGH MANUFACTURING CANADA
            552 REX STREET STATION
            TORONTO, ONTARIO LV4 1W1

Order #	Description	Quantity	Price Per Unit	Total
2010	Pet Collars	500	USD $ 2.50	USD $1250.00
567A	Leashes	500	USD $ 1.00	USD $ 500.00
3555	Wooden Birdcages	150	USD $15.00	USD $2250.00
	Total			USD $4000.00

Shipment
 Truck via Victory Motor Carriers

Shipping Insurance
 Covered by you, to your charge

Terms of Payment
 30 Days from Invoice Date, Net

Country of Origin
 U.S.A.

Ocean Freight Export

PK Industrial Products Inc.
1017 Amanda Drive
Sloan, New York 11706
Tel: (631)754-1054 Fax: (631)754-1055

Invoice No. 126

INVOICE

Customer

Name	Ricardo Keating GMBH	Date	6/15/00
Address	AM Weiher 7, 65452 Frankfurt Germany	Order No.	4736
City	Frankfurt Country DE	Rep	
Phone		FOB	

Qty	Description	Unit Price	TOTAL
350	Metal Side Tables - #JFQ5433	$555.00	$194,250.00
		SubTotal	$194,250.00
		Shipping & Handling	
		Taxes State	
		TOTAL	$194,250.00

Payment Details

- ◉
- ○
- ○

Office Use Only

PACKING LIST

SUPPLIER: PK INDUSTRIAL PRODUCTS INC.
1017 AMANDA DRIVE
SLOAN, NEW YORK 11706

SOLD TO: RICARDO KEATING GMBH
AM WEIHER 7
65452   FRANKFURT GERMANY

QUANTITY	DESCRIPTION	STYLE NO.
350	Metal Side Tables	#JFQ5433

COVER LETTER.........

AMERICAN RIVER LOGISTICS
OFFICES & AGENTS WORLDWIDE
CORPORATE OFFICE: 1229 OLD WALT WHITMAN RD MELVILLE NY 11747
1-800-524-2493 TEL# 631-396-6809 FAX# 631-396-6801 EMAIL: michael@worldest.com

AMERICAN RIVER LOGISTICS LTD.
ASSOCIATED WITH... Sea Lion Shipping, LTD.

TO: PK INDUSTRIAL PRODUCTS INC.
  T/631-754-1054   F/631-754-1055
ATTN: MR. PK

FROM: MICHAEL
DATE: July 20, 2000

RE: BOOKING#123456789 FOR 1 X 20' TO GERMANY

1. ATTACHED PLEASE FIND OUT THE BOOKING CONFIRMATION AND DOCK
    RECEIPT FOR ABOVE SHIPMENT.

2. TRUCKER WILL CONTACT WITH YOU FOR THE LIVE LOAD ON 07/24/00 .

3. AFTER LOADING OF CONTAINER, PLEASE FILL IN THE CONTAINER
    NUMBER, SEAL NUMBER, NUMBER OF PACKAGES LOADED AND THE
    GROSS WEIGHT AND FAX ME BACK A COPY OF THE COMPLETED DOCK
    RECEIPT.

4. ANY QUESTION, PLEASE FEEL FREE TO CALL ME DIRECTLY.

TKS N B RGDS.

OUR COMPETITIVE ADVANTAGE IN INTERNATIONAL TRADE!!!!!!

COVER LETTER.........

AMERICAN RIVER LOGISTICS

OFFICES & AGENTS WORLDWIDE
CORPORATE OFFICE: 1229 OLD WALT WHITMAN RD MELVILLE NY 11747
1-800-524-2493 TEL# 631-396-6809 FAX# 631-396-6801 EMAIL: michael@worldest.com

AMERICAN RIVER LOGISTICS LTD.
ASSOCIATED WITH... Sea Lion Shipping, LTD.

TO: EXPRESS
   T/516-371-5110   F/516-371-5107
ATTN: JOHN, TOMMY

FROM: MICHAEL
DATE: July 20, 2000

RE: BOOKING# 123456789 FOR 1 X 20'

1. ATTACHED PLEASE FIND OUT THE DOCK RECEIPT.

2. PLEASE ARRANGE PICK UP EMPTY CONTAINER FROM P&O TERMINAL
    AND DELIVERY TO SHIPPER'S WAREHOUSE ON 07/24/2000. PLEASE
    RETURN THE FULL CONTAINER BACK TO M&H TERMINAL BEFORE
    07/26/2000 12:00 NOON.

3. IF THERE IS ANY QUESTION, PLEASE FEEL FREE TO CALL ME DIRECTLY.

TKS N B RGDS.

OUR COMPETITIVE ADVANTAGE IN INTERNATIONAL TRADE!!!!!!

American River Logistics, Ltd.

1229 Old Walt Whitman Road
Melville, New York 11747
Tel:1-(516)-396-6800 Fax:1-(516)-396-6801

BOOKING CONFIRMATION

TO   : PK INDUSTRIAL PRODUCTS INC.   ATTN   : MR. PK

FROM : ARI, NY   DATE   : Jul 20, 2000

We are pleased to provide the following booking confirmation and details:

SHIPPER   : PK INDUSTRIAL PRODUCTS INC.   BOOKING #: 123456789

CONTAINER

COMMODITY	: METAL SIDE TABLES
LINE	: ROSE CONTAINERLINE
VESSEL	: SHENZHEN BAY
VOYAGE	: 28
	:

PICKUP DATE	: 07/24/2000
PICKUP ORIG	: SLOAN, NEW YORK
ETD	: 07/28.2000
EXPORT PORT	: PORT NEWARK

ETA   : 08/16/2000
ULT DEST : GERMANY

CUT OFF   : 07/26/2000

PORT   : FRANKFURT

PACKAGES	COMMODITY DESCRIPTION	WEIGHT LBS	MEASURE CBM	OVERSIZE LxWxH
1	20' STD CONTAINER. STC 350 METAL SIDE TABLES STYLE NO. #JFQ5433	15432	875 CFT	

CONTAINER NO. _____

SEAL# _____   ARI# N007999

Any questions regarding this booking, please notify us at the number below immediately.

Very truly yours,

Michael
Phone:5163966800

```
                        D O C K   R E C E I P T
           T R U C K E R  /  L O A D   I N S T R U C T I O N S
```

TO: COUGAR EXPRESS.   ATTN: JOHN,TOMMY,JOE,TED
FROM: AMERICAN RIVER LOGISTICS, LTD.   DATE: Jul 20, 2000

Please arrange trucking for the account of American River Int'l (800) 524-2493
as per the following:

          SHIPPER: PK INDUSTRIAL PRODUCTS INC.
          PICKUP @: PK INDUSTRIAL PRODUCTS INC.
                   1017 AMANDA DRIVE   PICK-UP DATE : 07/24/2000
                   SLOAN, NEW YORK 11706
                   MR. PK/631-754-1054
  STEAMSHIP LINE: ROSE CONTAINERLINE   BOOKING NUMBER: 123456789
     DEST PORT: FRANKFURT
  CUT OFF AT PIER: 07/26/2000   VESSEL: SHENZHEN BAY
                                       VOYAGE: 28

  COMMODITY: METAL SIDE TABLES
  CONTAINERS: SIZE: TYPE:

Packages Commodity Description   Weight   Measure   Oversize LxWxH
      1 20' STD CONTAINER. STC   15432 875 CFT
         350 METAL SIDE TABLES
         STYLE NO. #JFQ5433

CONTAINER NO. _____

SEAL# _____   ARI# N007999

PICKUP AND DELIVERY INSTRUCTIONS:
PLEASE P/UP EMPTY CONTAINER FROM P&O TERMINAL AND
RETURN FULL CONTAINER TO M&H TERMINAL BEFORE 07/26/2000
12:00 NOON
BOOKING# 123456789
REF# N007999

LOADED CONTAINERS TO BE DRAYED TO:
THIS IS TO CERTIFY THAT THE ABOVE NAMED MATERIAL ARE PROPERLY CLASSIFIED,
DESCRIBED, PACKAGED, MARKED AND LABELED AND ARE IN PROPER CONDITION FOR
TRANSPORTATION ACCORDING TO THE APPLICABLE REGULATION OF THE DEPARTMENT OF
TRANSPORTATION.
Very Truly Yours
Michael
AMERICAN RIVER LOGISTICS, LTD.
MELVILLE, NY 11747

(631) 396-6800
(631) 396-6801

COVER LETTER.........

AMERICAN RIVER LOGISTICS

OFFICES & AGENTS WORLDWIDE
CORPORATE OFFICE: 1229 OLD WALT WHITMAN RD MELVILLE NY 11747
1-800-524-2493 TEL# 631-396-6809 FAX# 631-396-6801 EMAIL: michael@worldest.com

AMERICAN RIVER LOGISTICS LTD.
ASSOCIATED WITH... Sea Lion Shipping, LTD.

TO: ROSE CONTAINERLINE
   T/212-966-0084 F/212-966-5141
ATTN: CLAIRE

FROM: MICHAEL
DATE: July 20, 2000

RE: BOOKING# 123456789

1. **ATTACHED PLEASE FIND THE B/L INSTRUCTION AND SED.**

2. **PLEASE FAX A COPY TO US FOR OUR APPROVAL BEFORE SENDING THE**
    ORIGINAL B/L TO US.

3. **ANY QUESTION, PLEASE CALL ME DIRECTLY.**

TKS N B RGDS.

OUR COMPETITIVE ADVANTAGE IN INTERNATIONAL TRADE!!!!!!

PK INDUSTRIAL PRODUCTS INC.   123456789
1017 AMANDA DRIVE
SLOAN, NEW YORK 11706

                                        Export File#:N007999

RICARDO KEATING GMBH
AM WEIHER 7   AMERICAN RIVER INT'L LTD. FMC#4124
65452 FRANKFURT   GERMANY   1229 WALT WHITMAN ROAD
                                 MELVILLE , NY 11747

SAME AS ABOVE   SLOAN, NEW YORK

                              SLOAN, NEW YORK
SHENZHEN BAY 28   PORT NEWARK

FRANKFURT

   CONTAINER NO.   1 20' STD CONTAINER. STC   15432#   875 CFT
   ABCD-987654-3   350 METAL SIDE TABLES   7000K
   SEAL# 88888   STYLE NO. #JFQ5433

                     "FREIGHT PREPAID"

"THESE COMMODITIES, TECHNOLOGY OR SOFTWARE WERE EXPORTED FROM THE
UNITED STATES IN ACCORDANCE WITH THE EXPORT ADMINISTRATION
REGULATIONS. DIVERSION CONTRARY TO U.S. LAW PROHIBITED".

FORM **7525-V** (1-1-88)

U.S. DEPARTMENT OF COMMERCE—BUREAU OF THE CENSUS—INTERNATIONAL TRADE ADMINISTRATION
SHIPPER'S EXPORT DECLARATION

OMB No. 0607-0018

1a. EXPORTER *(Name and address including ZIP code)*
PK INDUSTRIAL PRODUCTS INC.
1017 AMANDA DRIVE
SLOAN, NEW YORK 11706

ZIP CODE

2. DATE OF EXPORTATION
07/28.2000

3. BILL OF LADING/AIR WAYBILL NO.

b. EXPORTER'S EIN (IRS) NO.
55-1017630

c. PARTIES TO TRANSACTION
☐ Related X X ☐ Non-related

BOOKING #: 123456789
A.R.L. REF #: N007999

4a. ULTIMATE CONSIGNEE RICARDO KEATING GMBH
AM WEIHER 7
65452 FRANKFURT   GERMANY

b. INTERMEDIATE CONSIGNEE

5. FORWARDING AGENT
FMC#:4124
AMERICAN RIVER INTERNATIONAL
1229 WALT WHITMAN ROAD
MELVILLE, NY 11747

6. POINT (STATE) OF ORIGIN OR FTZ NO.

7. COUNTRY OF ULTIMATE DESTINATION

8. LOADING PIER *(Vessel only)*

9. MODE OF TRANSPORT *(Specify)*

NY — USA

GERMANY

10. EXPORTING CARRIER

11. PORT OF EXPORT
OCEAN VESSEL

12. PORT OF UNLOADING *(Vessel and air only)*
SHENZHEN BAY

13. CONTAINERIZED *(Vessel only)*
PORT NEWARK
☐ Yes   ☐ No

FRANKFURT

11

14. SCHEDULE B DESCRIPTION OF COMMODITIES.

15. MARKS, NOS., AND KINDS OF PACKAGES

(Use columns 17 - 19)

VALUE (U.S. dollars, omit cents)
(Selling price or cost if not sold)
(20)

D/F (16)	SCHEDULE B NUMBER (17)	CHECK DIGIT	QUANTITY SCHEDULE B UNIT(S) (18)	SHIPPING WEIGHT (Kilos) (19)	
D	9403.20.0010		7000	7000KG	194,250.00
	20' STD CONTAINER. STC		NET WGT — KGS.		
	350 METAL SIDE TABLES				
	STYLE NO. #JFQ5433				
	"FREIGHT PREPAID"				

21. VALIDATED LICENSE NO./GENERAL LICENSE SYMBOL
NLR

22. ECCN *(When required)*

23. Duly authorized officer or employee

The exporter authorizes the forwarder named above to act as forwarding agent for export control and customs purposes.

24. MICHAEL HSU
I certify that all statements made and all information contained herein are true and correct and that I have read and understand the instructions for preparation of this document, set forth in the "Correct Way to Fill Out the Shipper's Export Declaration." I understand that civil and criminal penalties, including forfeiture and sale, may be imposed for making false or fraudulent statements herein, failing to provide the requested information or for violation of U.S. laws on exportation (13 U.S.C. Sec. 305: 22 U.S.C. Sec. 401: 18 U.S.C. Sec. 1001: 50 U.S.C. App. 2410).

Signature

Confidential - For use solely for official purposes authorized by the Secretary of Commerce (13 U.S.C. 301 ig))

Title

Export shipments are subject to inspection by U.S. Customs Service and/or Office of Export Enforcement

AGENT

Date 07/20/00

25. AUTHENTICATION *(When required)*

This form may be printed by private parties provided it conforms to the official form. For sale by the Superintendent of Documents, Government Printing Office, Washington, D.C. 20402, and local Customs District Directors. The **"Correct Way to Fill Out the Shipper's Export Declaration"** is available from the Bureau of the Census, Washington, D.C. 20233.

COVER LETTER.........

AMERICAN RIVER LOGISTICS

OFFICES & AGENTS WORLDWIDE
CORPORATE OFFICE: 1229 OLD WALT WHITMAN RD MELVILLE NY 11747
1-800-524-2493 TEL# 631-396-6809   FAX# 631-396-6801   EMAIL: michael@worldest.com

AMERICAN RIVER LOGISTICS LTD.
ASSOCIATED WITH... Sea Lion Shipping, LTD.

TO:PK INDUSTRIAL PRODUCTS INC.
   T/631-754-1054   F/631-754-1055
ATTN: MR. PK

FROM: MICHAEL
DATE: JULY 28, 2000

RE: BOOKING# 123456789 FOR 1 X 20' TO GERMANY

ATTACHED PLEASE FIND :

a. B/L COPY
b. CERTIFICATE OF ORIGIN COPY
c. CERTIFICATE OF INSURANCE COPY
d. OUR INVOICE COPY

THE ORIGINAL DOCUMENTS WILL BE SEND TO YOU BY FEDEX TODAY.
PLEASE ACKNOWLEDGE.

ANY QUESTION, PLEASE CALL ME DIRECTLY.

TKS N B RGDS.

OUR COMPETITIVE ADVANTAGE IN INTERNATIONAL TRADE!!!!!!

CERTIFICATE OF ORIGIN for general use and for the following countries

ARGENTINA AUSTRIA BRAZIL COLOMBIA CYPRUS ECUADOR EGYPT ERITREA GERMANY (Western)
GREECE INDIA IRAN ITALY KUWAIT LIBYA NETHERLANDS PAKISTAN SAUDI ARABIA VIET-NAM

The undersigned MICHAEL AS AGENT
                  (Owner or Agent, or DC)
for PK INDUSTRIAL PRODUCTS INC., 1017 AMANDA DRIVE SLOAN, NEW YORK 11706 declares
               (Name and Address of Shipper)
that the following mentioned goods shipped on S/S SHENZHEN BAY VOYAGE 28
                          (Name of Ship)
on the date of 07/28.2000 consigned to RICARDO KEATING GMBH, AM WEIHER 7

65452 FRANKFURT GERMANY are the product of the United States of America.

MARKS AND NUMBERS	NO. OF PKGS., BOXES OR CASES	WEIGHT IN KILOS		DESCRIPTION
		GROSS	NET	
CONTAINER NO. ABCD-987654-3 SEAL# 88888	1	7000		20' STD CONTAINER. STC 350 METAL SIDE TABLES STYLE NO. #JFQ5433 "FREIGHT PREPAID"
				CERTIFIED TRUE AND CORRECT

Sworn before me

this _____ 28th _____ day of JULY _____ 20 00

Dated at NEW YORK on the 28th day of JULY, 2000

_____

(Signature of Owner or Agent)

The _____, a recognized Chamber of Commerce under the laws of the State of

_____, has examined the manufacturer's invoice or shipper's affidavit concerning the origin of the merchandise and,
according to the best of its knowledge and belief, finds that the products named originated in the United States of North America.

Secretary _____

* $ 213,675.00
(sum insured)

CERTIFICATE OF MARINE INSURANCE

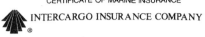

INTERCARGO INSURANCE COMPANY

No. 10

This is to Certify, *That on the* 20TH *day of* JULY   20 00 , *this Company*

insured under Policy No. 307027   *made for* AMERICAN RIVER LOGISTICS FOR A/C: PK INDUSTRIAL PRODUCTS INC.

for the sum of TWO HUNDRED THIRTEEN THOUSAND SIX HUNDRED SEVENTY-FIVE &00/100   U.S. *Dollars,*

on 1 X 20'CONTAINER STC 350 METAL SIDE TABLES **************

*(Amounts in excess of $1,000,000.00 cannot be insured under this Certificate)

Valued at sum insured. Shipped on board the S/S or M/S SHENZHEN BAY V.28

at and from PORT NEWARK   , *via*   *and/or following*
                                                                        steamer or steamers
                    (Initial Point of Shipment)   *(Port of Shipment)*

to FRANKFURT, GERMANY   *and it is understood and agreed, that in case of loss, the same*
                    (Port of Places of Destination)

is payable to the order of THE ASSURED   *on surrender of the Certificate which*
conveys the right of collecting any such loss as fully as if the property were covered by a special policy direct to the holder hereof, and free from any liability for unpaid premiums. This certificate is issued subject to the INTERCARGO INSURANCE COMPANY open cargo policy issued in conjunction with this certificate and which is incorporated herein by reference. To the extent that any terms or conditions in this certificate are inconsistent with the policy, the policy shall govern the rights and duties of all parties subject to the contract of insurance. Copies of the policy are available, upon request, from INTERCARGO INSURANCE COMPANY, 1450 E. American Lane, 20th Floor, Schaumburg, Illinois 60173-5458. If you would like more information about INTERCARGO or would like to file a claim electronically, INTERCARGO INSURANCE COMPANY'S website is www.intercargo.com.

SPECIAL CONDITIONS	MARKS & NUMBERS

Approved merchandise per policy except while under an ON DECK bill of lading insured -
  Against all risks of physical loss or damage from any external cause, irrespective of percentage, excepting those excluded by the F.C. & S and S.R. & C.C. Warranties, arising during transportation between the points of shipment and of destination named herein.
  Bagged commodities-insured as above but subject to a deductible of 5% of the insured value ($500 minimum deductible).
  Automobiles, household goods, personal effects-insured as above but subject to a deductible of 3% of the insured value ($500 minimum deductible).

CONTAINER NO.
ABCD-987654-3
SEAL#88888

ON DECK SHIPMENTS (with an ON DECK bill of lading) and/or shipments of used merchandise and/or returned or defective merchandise and/or refrigerated, frozen or perishable merchandise insured:
  Warranted free of particular average unless caused by the vessel being stranded, sunk, burnt, on fire or in collision, but including risk of jettison and/or washing overboard, irrespective of percentage.
FOR SHIPMENTS TO RUSSIA, CIS AND/OR FORMER EASTERN BLOC COUNTRIES - SEE ALSO BACK HEREOF

	SCHEDULE B CODE *(commodity)*	SCHEDULE C-E CODE *(country)*

TERMS AND CONDITIONS - SEE ALSO BACK HEREOF

WAREHOUSE TO WAREHOUSE: This insurance attaches from the time the goods leave the Warehouse and/or Store at the place named in the Policy for the commencement of the transit and continues during the ordinary course of transit, including customary transhipment if any, until the goods are discharged overside from the overseas vessel at the final port. Thereafter the insurance continues whilst the goods are in transit and/or awaiting transit until delivered to final warehouse at the destination named in the Policy or until the expiry of 15 days (or 30 days if the destination to which the goods are insured is outside the limits of the port) whichever shall first occur. The time limits referred to above to be reckoned from midnight of the day on which the discharge overside of the goods hereby insured from the overseas vessel is completed. Held covered at a premium to be arranged in the event of transhipment, if any, other than as above and/or in the event of delay in excess of the above time limits arising from circumstances beyond the control of the Assured.
  NOTE – IT IS NECESSARY FOR THE ASSURED TO GIVE PROMPT NOTICE TO THESE ASSURERS WHEN THEY BECOME AWARE OF AN EVENT FOR WHICH THEY ARE "HELD COVERED" UNDER THIS POLICY AND THE RIGHT TO SUCH COVER IS DEPENDENT ON COMPLIANCE WITH THIS OBLIGATION. FAILURE TO DO SO WILL VOID COVERAGE.
  PERILS CLAUSE: Touching the adventures and perils which this Company is contented to bear, and takes upon itself, they are of the seas, fires, assailing thieves, jettisons, barratry of the master and mariners, and all other like perils, losses and misfortunes (illicit or contraband trade excepted in all cases), that have or shall come to the hurt, detriment or damage of the said goods and merchandise, or any part thereof.
  SHORE CLAUSE: Where this insurance by its terms covers while on docks, wharves or elsewhere on shore, and/or during land transportation, it shall include the risks of collision, derailment, overturning or other accident to the conveyance, fire, lightning, sprinkler leakage, cyclones, hurricanes, earthquakes, floods (meaning the rising of navigable waters), and/or collapse or subsidence of docks or wharves, even though the insurance be otherwise F.P.A.
  BOTH TO BLAME CLAUSE: Where goods are shipped under a Bill of Lading containing the so-called "Both to Blame Collision" Clause, these Assurers agree as to all losses covered by this insurance, to indemnify the Assured for this Policy's proportion of any amount (not exceeding the amount insured) which the Assured may be legally bound to pay to the shipowners under such clause. In the event that such liability is asserted the Assured agree to notify these Assurers who shall have the right at their own cost and expense to defend the Assured against such claim.
  MACHINERY CLAUSE: When the property insured under this Policy includes a machine consisting when complete for sale or use of several parts, then in case of loss or damage covered by this insurance to any part of such machine, these Assurers shall be liable only for the proportion of the insured value of the part lost or damaged, or at the Assured's option, for the cost and expense, including labor and forwarding charges, of replacing or repairing the lost or damaged part; but in no event shall these Assurers be liable for more than the insured value of the complete machine.
  LABELS CLAUSE: In case of damage affecting labels, capsules or wrappers, these Assurers, if liable therefor under the terms of this policy, shall not be liable for more than an amount sufficient to pay the cost of new labels, capsules or wrappers, and the cost of reconditioning the goods, but in no event shall these Assurers be liable for more than the insured value of the damaged merchandise.
  DELAY CLAUSE: Warranted free of claim for loss of market or for loss, damage or deterioration arising from delay, whether caused by a peril insured against or otherwise, unless expressly assumed in writing hereon.
  AMERICAN INSTITUTE CLAUSES: This insurance, in addition to the foregoing, is also subject to the following American Institute Cargo Clauses, current forms:

1. CRAFT, ETC.	4. GENERAL AVERAGE	8. INCHMAREE	12. WAR RISK INSURANCE
2. DEVIATION	5. EXPLOSION	9. CONSTRUCTIVE TOTAL LOSS	13. SOUTH AMERICAN 60 DAY CLAUSE
3. LANDING WAREHOUSING	6. BILL OF LADING, ETC.	10. CARRIER	
	7. MARINE EXTENSION CLAUSES	11. S.R. & C.C. ENDORSEMENT	

  PARAMOUNT WARRANTIES: THE FOLLOWING WARRANTIES SHALL BE PARAMOUNT AND SHALL NOT BE MODIFIED OR SUPERSEDED BY ANY OTHER PROVISION INCLUDED HEREIN OR STAMPED OR ENDORSED HEREON UNLESS SUCH OTHER PROVISION REFERS SPECIFICALLY TO THE RISKS EXCLUDED BY THESE WARRANTIES AND EXPRESSLY ASSUMES THE SAID RISKS:
  F.C. & S. (a) Notwithstanding anything herein contained to the contrary, this insurance is warranted free from capture, seizure, arrest, restraint, detainment, confiscation, preemption, requisition or nationalization, and the consequences thereof or any attempt thereat, whether in time of peace or war and whether lawful or otherwise; also warranted free, whether in time of peace or war, from all loss, damage or expense caused by any weapon of war employing atomic or nuclear fission and/or fusion or other reaction or radioactive force or matter or by any mine or torpedo, also warranted free from all consequences of hostilities or warlike operations (whether there be a declaration of war or not), but this warranty shall not exclude collision or contact with aircraft, rockets or similar missiles or with any fixed or floating object (other than a mine or torpedo), stranding, heavy weather, fire or explosion unless caused directly (and independently of the nature of the voyage or service which the vessel concerned or, in the case of a collision, any other vessel involved therein, is performing) by a hostile act by or against a belligerent power; and for the purposes of this warranty 'power' includes any authority maintaining naval, military or air forces in association with a power.
  Further warranted free from the consequences of civil war, revolution, rebellion, insurrection, or civil strife arising therefrom, or piracy.
  S.R. & C.C. (b) Warranted free of loss or damage caused by or resulting from strikes, lockouts, labor disturbances, riots, civil commotions or the acts of any person or persons taking part in any such occurrence or disorder.

This Certificate is issued in Original and Duplicate, one of which being accomplished the other to stand null and void. To support a claim local Revenue Laws may require this Certificate to be stamped.

Not transferable unless countersigned

Countersigned _____   *Stanley Alan Galanski*
OM 41 12/99   *President*
ADDITIONAL CONDITIONS AND

Air Freight Export

PACKING LIST

SUPPLIER: PK INDUSTRIAL PRODUCTS INC.
               1017 AMANDA DRIVE
               SLOAN, NEW YORK 11706

SOLD TO: RICARDO KEATING GMBH
               AM WEIHER 7
               65452   FRANKFURT GERMANY

QUANTITY	DESCRIPTION	STYLE NO.
5	Metal Tables	#JFQ2454

PK Industrial Products Inc.
1017 Amanda Drive
Sloan, New York 11706
Tel: (631)754-1054 Fax: (631)754-1055

Invoice No.   303

INVOICE

Customer

Name	Ricardo Keating GMBH
Address	AM Weiher 7, 65452 Frankfurt Germany
City	Frankfurt Country DE ###
Phone	

Date	7/18/00
Order No.	6819
Rep	
FOB	

Qty	Description	Unit Price	TOTAL
5	Metal Tables - JFQ2454	$2,950.00	$14,750.00
		SubTotal	$14,750.00
		Shipping & Handling	
	Taxes State		
		TOTAL	$14,750.00

Payment Details

⦿
○
○

Office Use Only

CERTIFICATE OF ORIGIN for general use and for the following countries

ARGENTINA AUSTRIA BRAZIL COLOMBIA CYPRUS ECUADOR EGYPT ERITREA GERMANY (Western)
GREECE INDIA IRAN ITALY KUWAIT LIBYA NETHERLANDS PAKISTAN SAUDI ARABIA VIET-NAM

The undersigned KELLY RAIA, AS AGENT

(Owner or Agent, or DC)

for PK INDUSTRIAL PRODUCTS INC., 1017 AMANDA DRIVE, SLOAN, NEW YORK 11706,, declares

(Name and Address of Shipper)

that the following mentioned goods shipped on S/S LUFTHANSA CARGO AG 020 3122 4524

(Name of Ship)

on the date of 07/17/2000 consigned to RICARDO KEATING GMBH, AM WEIHER 7

65452 FRANKFURT GERMANY are the product of the United States of America.

MARKS AND NUMBERS	NO. OF PKGS., BOXES OR CASES	WEIGHT IN KILOS		DESCRIPTION
		GROSS	NET	
ADDR:	5	205	189	FURNITURE
				CERTIFIED TRUE AND CORRECT

Sworn before me

Dated at NEW YORK on the 17th day of JULY, 2000

this 17th day of JULY 20 00

_____

(Signature of Owner or Agent)

The _____ , a recognized Chamber of Commerce under the laws of the State of

_____ , has examined the manufacturer's invoice or shipper's affidavit concerning the origin of the merchandise and, according to the best of its knowledge and belief, finds that the products named originated in the United States of North America.

Secretary _____

U.S. DEPARTMENT OF COMMERCE – BUREAU OF THE CENSUS – INTERNATIONAL TRADE ADMINISTRATION

FORM **7525-V** (1-1-88)

SHIPPER'S EXPORT DECLARATION

OMB No. 0607-0018

1a. EXPORTER *(Name and address including ZIP code)*

PK INDUSTRIAL PRODUCTS INC.
1017 AMANDA DRIVE
SLOAN, NEW YORK 11706

ZIP CODE	2. DATE OF EXPORTATION	3. BILL OF LADING/AIR WAYBILL NO.
	07/17/2000	020 3122.4524 N631017

b. EXPORTER'S EIN (IRS) NO.

55-1017630

c. PARTIES TO TRANSACTION

☐ Related ₓₓ   ☐ Non-related

4a. ULTIMATE CONSIGNEE

RICARDO KEATING GMBH AM WEIHER 7

65452 FRANKFURT   GERMANY

b. INTERMEDIATE CONSIGNEE

5. FORWARDING AGENT

AMERICAN RIVER LOGISTICS, LTD.
1229 OLD WALT WHITMAN ROAD
MELVILLE, N.Y. 11747

6. POINT (STATE) OF ORIGIN OR FTZ NO.	7. COUNTRY OF ULTIMATE DESTINATION
USA	GERMANY

8. LOADING PIER *(Vessel only)*

9. MODE OF TRANSPORT *(Specify)*

AIR

10. EXPORTING CARRIER

LUFTHANSA CARGO AG

11. PORT OF EXPORT

JFK AIRPORT

12. PORT OF UNLOADING *(Vessel and air only)*

FRANKFURT

13. CONTAINERIZED *(Vessel only)*

☐ Yes   ☐ No

14. SCHEDULE B DESCRIPTION OF COMMODITIES.

15. MARKS, NOS., AND KINDS OF PACKAGES

(Use columns 17 - 19)

VALUE (U.S. dollars, omit cents)
(Selling price or cost if not sold)
(20)

D/F (16)	SCHEDULE B NUMBER (17)	CHECK DIGIT	QUANTITY SCHEDULE B UNIT(S) (18)	SHIPPING WEIGHT *(Kilos)* (19)	
D	9403.20.0010		XXX	204 KG	$14750.00

21. VALIDATED LICENSE NO./GENERAL LICENSE SYMBOL

NLR

22. ECCN *(When required)*

23. Duly authorized officer or employee

Kelly Raia

The exporter authorizes the forwarder named above to act as forwarding agent for export control and customs purposes.

24. I certify that all statements made and all information contained herein are true and correct and that I have read and understand the instructions for preparation of this document, set forth in the "**Correct Way to Fill Out the Shipper's Export Declaration**." I understand that civil and criminal penalties, including forfeiture and sale, may be imposed for making false or fraudulent statements herein, failing to provide the requested information or for violation of U.S. laws on exportation (13 U.S.C. Sec. 305; 22 U.S.C. Sec. 401; 18 U.S.C. Sec. 1001; 50 U.S.C. App. 2410).

Signature

Title AGENT

Date 07/17/2000

Confidential - For use solely for official purposes authorized by the Secretary of Commerce (13 U.S.C 301 (g))

Export shipments are subject to inspection by U.S. Customs Service and/or Office of Export Enforcement.

25. AUTHENTICATION *(When required)*

This form may be printed by private parties provided it conforms to the official form. For sale by the Superintendent of Documents, Government Printing Office, Washington, D.C. 20402, and local Customs District Directors. The "**Correct Way to Fill Out the Shipper's Export Declaration**" is available from the Bureau of the Census, Washington, D.C. 20233.

```
020  JFK  3122 4524                                    MAWB# 020 3122 4524
```

Shipper's Name and Address			No. Negotiable Air Waybill	
PK INDUSTRIAL PRODUCTS INC. 1017 AMANDA DRIVE SLOAN, NEW YORK 11706			LUFTHANSA CARGO AG LANGER KORNWEG 341 D-65451 KELSTERBACH	

Consignee's Name and Address / Consignee's Account Number:

RICARDO KEATING GMBH
AM WEIHER 7
65452 FRANKFURT   GERMANY

It is agreed that the goods described herein are accepted in apparent good order and condition (except as noted) for carriage SUBJECT TO THE CONDITIONS OF CONTRACT ON THE REVERSE...

Issuing Carrier's Agent Name and City

AMERICAN RIVER LOGISTICS, LTD.
1229 OLD WALT WHITMAN ROAD
MELVILLE, N.Y. 11747

Agent's IATA Code: 01-1-9112/0011

Airport of Departure (Addr. of First Carrier) and Requested Routing

JFK AIRPORT

To	By First Carrier	to	by	to	by	Currency	WT/VAL		Other		Declared Value for Carriage	Declared Value for Customs
FRA	LH					USS	X		X		N.V.D.	N.V.D.

Airport of Destination	Requested Flight/Date	Amount of Insurance	
FRANKFURT	404/18	NIL	INSURANCE - If carrier offers insurance...

Handling Information:
NOTIFY CONSIGNEE UPON ARRIVAL...

These commodities, technology or software were exported from the United States in accordance with the Export Administration Regulations. Ultimate destination **GERMANY**. Diversion contrary to U.S. law prohibited.

No. of Pieces RCP	Gross Weight	kg/lb	Rate Class / Commodity Item No.	Chargeable Weight	Rate / Charge	Total	Nature and Quantity of Goods (incl. Dimensions or Volume)
5	204 KG			204	KG 2.15	438.60	FURNITURE DIMS IN INCHES: (5) 33X23X16
5	204 KG					438.60	

Prepaid	Weight Charge	Collect	Other Charges	
438.60				

Valuation Charge	

Tax	

Total Other Charges Due Agent		Shipper certifies that the particulars on the face hereof are correct and that insofar as any part of the consignment contains dangerous goods, such part is properly described by name and is in proper condition for carriage by air according to the applicable Dangerous Goods Regulations.

Total Other Charges Due Carrier	
20.40	Kelly Raia

AMERICAN RIVER LOGISTICS, LTD.
,as agent for shipper
Signature of Shipper or his Agent

Total Prepaid	Total Collect	07/17/00	AMERICAN RIVER LOGISTICS, LTD.
459.00		Kelly Raia JFK	,as agent for carrier

Executed on (date)   at (place)   Signature of Issuing Carrier or its Agent

Currency Conversion Rates	CC Charges in Dest. Currency		

For Carriers Use only at Destination	Charges at Destination	Total Collect Charges	MAWB# 020 3122 4524

APPERSON PRINT MANAGEMENT SERVICES C9501 (3/00)   ORIGINAL 2 (FOR CONSIGNEE)

Miscellaneous Export Documents

POWER OF ATTORNEY

Check appropriate box:
- [ ] Individual
- [ ] Partnership
- [ ] Corporation
- [ ] Sole Proprietorship

KNOW ALL MEN BY THESE PRESENTS: That, _____

(Full Name of person, partnership, or corporation, or sole proprietorship (Identify)

a corporation doing business under the laws of the State of _____ or a _____

doing business as _____ residing at _____

having an office and place of business at _____, hereby constitutes and appoints each of the following persons

_____

(Give full name of each agent designated)

as a true and lawful agent and attorney of the grantor named above for and in the name, place, and stead of said grantor from this date and in all Customs Districts, and in no other name, to make, endorse, sign, declare, or swear to any entry, withdrawal, declaration, certificate, bill of lading, carnet or other document required by law or regulation in connection with the importation, transportation, or exportation of any merchandise shipped or consigned by or to said grantor; to perform any act or condition which may be required by law or regulation in connection with such merchandise; to receive any merchandise deliverable to said grantor;

To make endorsements on bills of lading conferring authority to transfer title, make entry or collect drawback, and to make, sign, declare, or swear to any statement, supplemental statement, schedule, supplemental schedule, certificate of delivery, certificate of manufacture, certificate of manufacture and delivery, abstract of manufacturing records, declaration of proprietor on drawback entry, declaration of exporter on drawback entry, or any other affidavit or document which may be required by law or regulation for drawback purposes, regardless of whether such bill of lading, sworn statement, schedule, certificate, abstract, declaration, or other affidavit or document is intended for filing in any customs district;

To sign, seal, and deliver for and as the act of said grantor any bond required by law or regulation in connection with the entry or withdrawal of imported merchandise or merchandise exported with or without benefit of drawback, or in connection with the entry, clearance, lading, unlading or navigation of any vessel or other means of conveyance owned or operated by said grantor, and any and all bonds which may be voluntarily given and accepted under applicable laws and regulations, consignee's and owner's declarations provided for in section 485, Tariff Act of 1930, as amended, or affidavits in connection with the entry of merchandise;

To sign and swear to any document and to perform any act that may be necessary or required by law or regulation in connection with the entering, clearing, lading, unlading, or operation of any vessel or other means of conveyance owned or operated by said grantor;

To authorize other Customs Brokers to act as grantor's agent; to receive, endorse and collect checks issued for Customs duty refunds in grantor's name drawn on the Treasurer of the United States; if the grantor is a nonresident of the United States, to accept service of process on behalf of the grantor;

And generally to transact at the customhouses in any district any and all customs business, including making, signing, and filing of protests under section 514 of the Tariff Act of 1930, in which said grantor is or may be concerned or interested and which may properly be transacted or performed by an agent and attorney, giving to said agent and attorney full power and authority to do anything whatever requisite and necessary to be done in the premises as fully as said grantor could do if present and acting, hereby ratifying and confirming all that the said agent and attorney shall lawfully do by virtue of these presents; the foregoing power of attorney shall remain in full force and effect until the _____ day of _____, 19_____, or until notice of revocation in writing is duly given to and received by a District Director of Customs. If the donor of this power of attorney is a partnership, the said power shall in no case have any force or effect after the expiration of 2 years from the date of its execution.

IN WITNESS WHEREOF, the said _____

has caused these presents to be sealed and signed: (Signature) _____

(Capacity) _____   (Date) _____

WITNESS: _____

_____   (Corporate seal)

NCR BUSINESS FORMS, INC. (718) 244-7777   (SEE OVER)

INDIVIDUAL OR PARTNERSHIP CERTIFICATION *(Optional)

CITY _____
COUNTY _____ } SS.
STATE _____

On this _____ day of _____, 19___, personally appeared before me _____

residing at _____, personally known or sufficiently identified to me, who certifies that

_____ (is) (are) the individual(s) who executed the foregoing instrument and acknowledge it to be _____ free act and deed.

CORPORATE CERTIFICATION *(Optional)
(To be made by an officer other than the one who executes the power of attorney)

I, _____, certify that I am the _____

of _____, organized under the laws of the State of _____

that _____, who signed this power of attorney on behalf of the donor, is the _____

of said corporation ; and that said power of attorney was duly signed, sealed, and attested for and behalf of said corporation by authority of its governing body as the same appears in a resolution of the Board of Directors passed at a regular meeting held on the _____ day of _____, now in my possession or custody. I further certify that the resolution is in accordance with the articles of incorporation and bylaws of said corporation.

IN WITNESS WHEREOF, I have hereunto set my hand and affixed the seal of said corporation, at the City of _____ this _____ day of _____, 19_____

_____ (Signature)   _____ (Date)

If the corporation has no corporate seal, the fact shall be stated, in which case a scroll or adhesive shall appear in the appropriate, designated place.

Customs powers of attorney of residents (including resident corporations) shall be without power of substitution except for the purpose of executing shipper's export declaration. However, a power of attorney executed in favor of a licensed customhouse broker may specify that the power of attorney is granted to the customhouse broker to through any of its licensed officers or any employee specifically authorized to act for such customhouse broker by power of attorney.

*NOTE: The corporate seal may be omitted. Customs does not require completion of a certification. The grantor has the option of executing the certification or omitting it.

Power of Attorney

1.　POWER OF ATTORNEY TO PREPARE, EXECUTE, AND
FILE SHIPPER'S EXPORT DECLARATIONS

Know all men by these presents, that Account Corporation ("Account"), organized and doing business under the laws in the State of Delaware and having an office and place of business in_____, hereby authorizes Sea Lion from this day forward to act as its forwarding agent for the limited purpose of preparing, executing, and filing Shipper's Export Declarations as required by law or regulations for goods sold by Account to _____, which are exported from the United States.

For this limited purpose, and in this limited capacity, Sea Lion is authorized to act on behalf of Account in the following manner.

1.　Prepare, sign, and file the Shipper's Export Declarations based on any information obtained from Account, the U.S. Principal Party in Interest (or from other parties involved in the transaction if such information is not available from Account).

2.　Maintain documentation to support the information reported on the Shipper's Export Declaration.

3.　Provide the appropriate copies of the documentation to Account to verify that the information Account provided was accurately reported on the SED.

4.　Provide all information in its possession necessary to complete the Shipper's Export Declaration, including the information specified below:

a.　Date of exportation;
b.　Bill of lading/airway bill number;
c.　Ultimate consignee;
d.　Intermediate consignee (if any);
e.　Forwarding or other agent name and address;
f.　Country of ultimate designation;
g.　Loading pier;
h.　Method of transportation;
i.　Export carrier;
j.　Port of export;
k.　Port of unlading;
l.　Containerized;
m.　Weight;
n.　ECCN (is applicable);
o.　License authority (if applicable); and
p.　Signature in the certification block on the Shipper's Export Declaration;

This power of attorney will terminate one (1) year from its date of the execution.

IN WITNESS WHEREOF, Account, the U.S. Principal Party in Interest, has caused these presents to be sealed and signed by its duly authorized representative,
_____this_____14th_____day of September, 2000.

ACCOUNT CORPORATION
(Principal Party In Interest)

By: _____
　　Title: Officer?

POWER OF ATTORNEY TO PREPARE, EXECUTE, AND

Power of Attorney

License is hereby granted to the applicant for the described commodity to be permanently exported from the United States. This license may be revoked, suspended or amended by the Secretary of State without prior notice whenever the Secretary deems such action advisable.

Signature

6 42 7   LICENSE NO.

'97
VALID
XXXXX
X IXXXXX VAL
MONTHS FROM

UNITED STATES OF AMERICA   DEPARTMENT OF STATE

APPLICATION/LICENSE FOR PERMANENT EXPORT OF UNCLASSIFIED DEFENSE ARTICLES AND RELATED UNCLASSIFIED TECHNICAL DATA

1. Date Prepared	2. PM/DTC Applicant/Registrant Code	3. Country of Ultimate Destination	4. Probable Port of
12/24/96	079 -53	Italy	New York,

5. Applicant's Name, Address, ZIP Code, Tel. No.
Applicant is: ☐ Government ☒ Manufacturer ☐ Exporter/freight forwarder

ABC EXPORT COMPANY
123 PARK AVENUE
NEW YORK, NY 10012

TELEPHONE NUMBER:

6. Names, agency and telephone numbers of U.S. Government person (not PM/DTC) familiar with the commodity
☐ Army   ☐ Air Force
☒ Navy   ☐ Other

7. Name and telephone number of applicant contact if U.S. Government additional information.

MARY SMITH   (212) 343-3020

8. Description of Transaction
a. This application represents: ☒ ONLY completely new shipment; ☐ ONLY the unshipped balance of license no. _____
b. The IDENTICAL commodity ☐ was licensed to the country in block 3 under license no._____ ; ☐ was licensed to other country license no. ____ ☐ was returned without action under voided license no._____ ; ☐ was denied to the country in block voided license no. _____ ; ☐ was never licensed for this applicant.
c. If commodity is being financed under ☐ Foreign Military Sale (FMS); ☐ Foreign Military Financing (FMF) or; ☐ Grant Aid Program (GAD), give the number: _____

9. QUANTITY	10. COMMODITY ☒ Hardware ☐ Technical Data	11. USML CAT	12. VAL
THREE(3)	HIGH TECH INFRA-RED TRACKING DEVICE		$95,6
		13. TOTAL VALUE: $	

14. Name and address of foreign end-user

ITALIAN IMPORT CO.
TORINO, ITALY

15. ☐ :Source or ☒ Manufacturer of Commodity

Export License

Drop Shipment Certificate

When one Canadian company sells to another Canadian company, this form is filled out and kept on file to avoid paying the GST.

- These goods are eventually exported.
- Rarely used because most companies apply for a refund.
- Is used when there are hugh amounts of taxes to be paid.

DROP-SHIPMENT CERTIFICATE

TO:

Name of Consignee: _____ (the "Consignee")

I, the [authorized officer/agent of the Consignee]/[the Consignee (if an individual)], hereby certify and acknowledge [on behalf of the Consignee (if agent or officer of a corporation)] as follows:

1. (a) The Consignee has or will receive physical possession of [describe tangible personal property in sufficient detail to identify specific shipment of tangible personal property] (the "Property") ordered from you by [name of unregistered non-resident]; **OR**

   (b) During the period from _____ to _____ the Consignee has or will receive physical possession of [describe tangible personal property in sufficient detail to identify specific shipment of tangible personal property] (the "Property") ordered from you by unregistered non-residents.

2. The Consignee is acquiring possession of the Property for the purpose of supplying a commercial service(s) (as defined in the *Excise Tax Act and the Québec Sales Tax Act*) in respect of the Property, or for consumption, use or supply in the course of its commercial activities.

3. If the Consignee subsequently transfers physical possession of the Property to a person who is not registered for the purposes of the Goods and Services Tax, otherwise than for export, or to another person who is registered for purposes of the Goods and Services Tax who does not provide to the Consignee a drop-shipment certificate under subsection 179(2) of the *Excise Tax Act*, and section 327.1 of the *Québec Sales Tax Act,* the Consignee will be required to account for the Goods and Services Tax and the Québec Sales Tax on the fair market value of the Property at that time.

4. If the Consignee is not acquiring the Property for consumption, use or supply exclusively in the course of its commercial activities, or if the Property is a passenger vehicle that is acquired for use as capital property, where the cost of the vehicle exceeds the vehicle's capital cost for income tax purposes, the Consignee is required to self-assess the Goods and Services Tax and the Québec Sales Tax.

DATE: _____   _____
                                                                    (Signature of individual who is
GST/QST REG. NO._____   Consignee of officer of Consignee)

NOTE: Part 1(a) is for use in the case of one or more deliveries relating to orders by the same unregistered non-resident.

Part 1(b) is for general use in the case of shipments, over a specified period of time, of tangible personal property of a particular description or class — not necessarily restricted to orders placed by the same unregistered non-resident.

CERTIFICAT DE LIVRAISON DIRECTE

À: (Nom du fournisseur)

Nom du consignataire : _____ (le "consignataire")

Je, [le mandataire ou le représentant du consignataire]/[le consignataire (s'il s'agit d'un particulier)], certifie et reconnaît par le présent certificat [au nom du consignataire (s'il est le mandataire ou le représentant d'une personne morale)] ce qui suit :

1. a) le consignataire a ou aura la possession matérielle du [décrire le bien meuble corporel avec suffisamment de détails pour que puisse être identifiée une livraison précise de ce bien] (le "bien") commandé auprès de vous par [nom de la personne non résidante qui n'est pas inscrite]; OU

   b) pendant la période du _____ au _____, le consignataire a ou aura la possession matérielle du [décrire le bien meuble corporel avec suffisamment de détails pour que puisse être identifiée une livraison précise de ce bien] (le "bien") commandé auprès de vous par des personnes non résidantes qui ne sont pas inscrites.

2. Le consignataire acquiert la possession du bien en vue de fournir un service commercial (défini dans la *Loi sur la taxe de vente du Québec*) à l'égard de ce bien, ou pour le consommer, l'utiliser ou le fournir dans le cadre de ses activités commerciales.

3. Si le consignataire transfère par la suite la possession matérielle du bien à une personne qui n'est pas inscrite sous le régime de la taxe de vente du Québec, sauf en ce qui concerne l'exportation, ou à une autre personne qui est inscrite sous le régime de la taxe de vente du Québec et qui ne fournit pas au consignataire un certificat de livraison directe aux termes du paragraphe 327.1 de la *Loi sur la taxe de vente du Québec*, le consignataire est tenu de déclarer la taxe de vente du Québec sur la juste valeur marchande du bien à ce moment.

4. Si le consignataire n'acquiert pas le bien pour le consommer, l'utiliser ou le fournir exclusivement dans le cadre de ses activités commerciales, ou si le bien est une voiture de tourisme achetée pour servir d'immobilisation, si le coût de la voiture dépasse le coût en capital de la voiture aux fins de l'impôt sur le revenu, le consignataire est tenu d'établir lui-même le montant de la taxe de vente du Québec en application de la *Loi sur la taxe de vente du Québec*.

DATE: _____   _____

                                 (Signature du particulier qui est

NO. INSCRIPT. TVQ_____   consignataire ou mandataire du

                                 consignataire)

NOTE : La partie 1a) sert lorsqu'il y a une ou plusieurs livraisons relatives à des commandes effectuées par la même personne non résidante qui n'est pas inscrite.

La partie 1b) sert à des fins plus générales dans le cas de livraisons, au cours d'une période précise, d'un bien meuble corporel d'une description ou d'une catégorie particulière - sans être nécessairement limitée aux commandes passées par la même personne non résidante qui n'est pas inscrite.

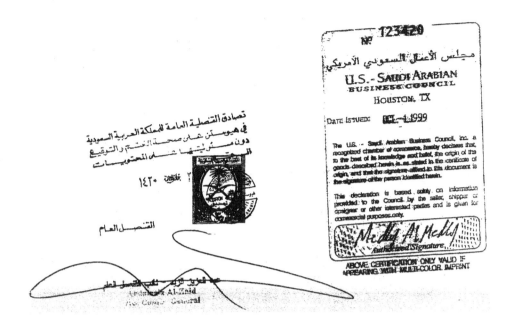

Sample of Consularization Stamp on the Back of the Invoice

USFWS Form 3-177
(revised 9/90)

Form Approved O.M.B. No. 1018-0012
Approval Expires: 07/31/93

U.S. FISH AND WILDLIFE SERVICE

Name of Carrier:
British Airways

Airway Bill or Bill of Lading No.:
125 -6987-5344

Imported or Exported Via:
☒ air cargo ☐ ocean cargo ☐ truck
☐ rail ☐ mail ☐ personal baggage
☐ automobile: License no._____
state _____

Indicate One:
☐ import ☒ export

Port of:
JFK, NEW YORK

Date:
3/5/01

☒ Commercial ☐ Non-commercial

Customs Identification No.:

DECLARATION FOR IMPORTATION

OR EXPORTATION OF

FISH OR WILDLIFE

Location where wildlife is available for inspection:
BRITISH AIRWAYS

Package or Bale Marks and Nos.:
ADDR:

Please Type or Print Legibly

☐ U.S. Importer of Record
☒ U.S. Exporter GILES COMPANY
(name)

Foreign Consignor TANKER COMMODITIES LTD.
or Consignee
(name)

Customs Broker
or Agent

32 CARRAIGE COURT, RIVERHEAD, NEW YORK 22344
(address—street, city, state, zip code)

567 DRIVE ROAD, LONDON, ENGLAND RH5 78W
(address—street, city, country)

Shipping Agent or AMERICAN RIVER LOGISTICS
Freight Forwarder

Furnish All Information Below (invoices or lists providing required information may be attached)

QUANTITY	SCIENTIFIC NAME Genus Species	COMMON NAME	DESCRIPTION If live, so state. If product, describe.	DOMESTIC VALUE	COUNTRY OF ORIGIN
ONE	Genius Specious	Hides of Cow	Hides of Cow	$450.00	U.S.A.

U.S. License and/or Permit Nos.:
US 23589

Foreign License and/or Permits:
Country No.

I certify the information contained nerein is true and complete to the best of my knowledge and belief.

signature   date

Action Taken: Date:
☐ cleared
☐ clearance refused
☐ seized

_____ % of Wildlife Inspected:

Officer Signature and Badge No.:

FOR OFFICIAL USE ONLY

Control Number

SEE REVERSE OF THIS FORM FOR INSTRUCTIONS AND PRIVACY ACT NOTICE

Fish and Wildlife Form for Export

USFWS Form 3–177
(revised 8/90)

Form Approved O.M.B. No. 1018–0012
Approval Expires: 07/31/93

U.S. FISH AND WILDLIFE SERVICE

Name of Carrier:
LUFTHANSA

Airway Bill or Bill of Lading No.:
020–1017–1963

Indicate One:

☒ import   ☐ export

Imported or Exported Via:

☒ air cargo ☐ ocean cargo ☐ truck
☐ rail ☐ mail ☐ personal baggage
☐ automobile: License no._____
state _____

Port of:
JFK, NEW YORK

Date:
3/1/01

DECLARATION FOR IMPORTATION

OR EXPORTATION OF

FISH OR WILDLIFE

Location where wildlife is available for inspection:
LUFTHANSA CARGO

☒ Commercial   ☐ Non-commercial

Package or Bale Marks and Nos.:
ADDR:

Customs Identification No.:
395–0015693–2

Please Type or Print Legibly

(indicate one)

☒ U.S. Importer of Record   ANIMAL IMPORTS
☐ U.S. Exporter_____
(name)

23 JOHNSON ROAD, MELVILLE, NY 11747
(address — street, city, state, zip code)

Foreign Consignor
or Consignee   TIGRESS EXPORT GMBH

DE 2, HAMBURG ALEN, HAMBURG, GERMANY

(name)

(address — street, city, country)

Customs Broker
or Agent   AMERICAN BROKERS, INC.

Shipping Agent or
Freight Forwarder   AMERICAN BROKERS, INC.

Furnish All Information Below (invoices or lists providing required information may be attached)

QUANTITY	SCIENTIFIC NAME Genus Species	COMMON NAME	DESCRIPTION If live, so state. If product, describe.	DOMESTIC VALUE	COUNTRY OF ORIGIN
2	Psittacus Erithacus	African Grey Parrot	Two (2) Live Birds	$500.00	Germany

U.S. License and/or Permit Nos.:

Foreign License and/or Permits:
Country   No.

I certify the information contained nerein is true and complete to the best of my knowledge and belief.

signature   date

FOR OFFICIAL USE ONLY

Action Taken: Date:
☐ cleared
☐ clearance refused
☐ seized

_____ % of Wildlife Inspected:

Officer Signature and Badge No.:

Control Number

SEE REVERSE OF THIS FORM FOR INSTRUCTIONS AND PRIVACY ACT NOTICE

Fish and Wildlife Form for Import

FILING INSTRUCTIONS

File original declaration only. Copies may be retained by importer or broker if desired. Print or type legibly. Provide all relevant information. Declared value need not be shown for scientific specimens, game or game trophies not imported or exported for a commercial purpose.

"Country of Origin" means the country where the animal was taken from the wild or the country of natal origin of the animal.

When And Where To File.

At Designated Ports: File with the U.S. Fish and Wildlife Service office serving the designated port. For imports, file declarations when requesting wildlife clearance. For exports, file declaration in sufficient time in advance of actual departure of wildlife from the United States to allow reasonable time for inspection.

At Nondesignated Ports: File with U.S. Customs. For imports, file declaration prior to removal of wildlife from Customs custody. For exports, file prior to departure of wildlife from the United States.

Note To Customs Officers. Mail all Form 3–177's collected to the Assistant Regional Director for Law Enforcement, U.S. Fish and Wildlife Service, for your district at the end of each month.

Regulations concerning the importation and exportation of wildlife may be found in 50 CFR Part 14. Specific regulations concerning the filing of declarations for the importation and exportation of wildlife may be found in 50 CFR 14.61–14.64.

Failure to file a declaration for importation or exportation of fish or wildlife when required by the regulations in 50 CFR 14.61–14.64 is a violation of the Endangered Species Act of 1973 as amended (16 U.S.C. 1531 et seq.).

Knowingly making a false statement in a Declaration for Importation or Exportation of Fish or Wildlife may subject the declarant to the penalty provided by 18 U.S.C. 1001.

NOTICE

In accordance with the Privacy Act of 1974 (Pub. L. 93–579) and the Paperwork Reduction Act of 1980 (Pub. L. 96–511), please be advised that:

1. The gathering of information on the importation or exportation of wildlife, including any wild mammal, bird, fish, amphibian, reptile, mollusk, or crustacean, is authorized by the Endangered Species Act of 1973 as amended (16 U.S.C. 1531 et seq.) and Parts 14 and 17 of Title 50 of the Code of Federal Regulations.

2. The disclosure of the requested information is required to provide information about wildlife imports or exports, including products and parts, to facilitate enforcement of the Act and to carry out the provisions of the Convention on International Trade in Endangered Species of Wild Fauna and Flora. Failure to provide all of the requested information is sufficient cause for the U.S. Fish and Wildlife Service to deny you permission to import or export wildlife.

3. In the event there is indicated a violation of a statute, regulation, rule, order, or license, whether civil, criminal, or regulatory in nature, the requested information may be transferred to the appropriate Federal, State, local, or foreign agency charged with investigating or prosecuting such violations.

4. In the event of litigation involving the records or the subject matter of the records, the requested information may be transferred to the U.S. Department of Justice.

5. The requested information may be subject to disclosure under provisions of the Freedom of Information Act (5 U.S.C. 552).

6. Public reporting burden for this form is estimated to vary from 10 to 15 minutes per response. Direct comments regarding the burden estimate or any other aspect of this form to the Service Information Collection Clearance Officer, Fish and Wildlife Service, U.S. Department of the Interior, 1849 C Street, N.W., Washington, D.C. 20240, and the Interior Desk Officer, Office of Management and Budget, Washington, D.C. 20503.

U.S. GOVERNMENT PRINTING OFFICE : 1990 O - 273-888

U.S. DEPARTMENT OF COMMERCE — U.S. CENSUS BUREAU – Economics and Statistics Administration — BUREAU OF EXPORT ADMINISTRATION

FORM **7525-V** (7-25-2000)   **SHIPPER'S EXPORT DECLARATION**   OMB No. 0607-0152

1a. U.S. PRINCIPAL PARTY IN INTEREST (USPPI) *(Complete name and address)*

ZIP CODE   **2.** DATE OF EXPORTATION   **3.** TRANSPORTATION REFERENCE NO.

b. USPPI EIN (IRS) OR ID NO.   **c.** PARTIES TO TRANSACTION
☐ Related   ☐ Non-related

4a. ULTIMATE CONSIGNEE *(Complete name and address)*

b. INTERMEDIATE CONSIGNEE *(Complete name and address)*

5. FORWARDING AGENT *(Complete name and address)*

6. POINT (STATE) OF ORIGIN OR FTZ NO.   **7.** COUNTRY OF ULTIMATE DESTINATION

8. LOADING PIER *(Vessel only)*   **9.** METHOD OF TRANSPORTATION *(Specify)*   **14.** CARRIER IDENTIFICATION CODE   **15.** SHIPMENT REFERENCE NO.

10. EXPORTING CARRIER   **11.** PORT OF EXPORT   **16.** ENTRY NUMBER   **17.** HAZARDOUS MATERIALS
☐ Yes   ☐ No

12. PORT OF UNLOADING *(Vessel and air only)*   **13.** CONTAINERIZED *(Vessel only)*   ☐ Yes   ☐ No   **18.** IN BOND CODE   **19.** ROUTED EXPORT TRANSACTION   ☐ Yes   ☐ No

20. SCHEDULE B DESCRIPTION OF COMMODITIES *(Use columns 22–24)*

D/F or M (21)	SCHEDULE B NUMBER (22)	QUANTITY – SCHEDULE B UNIT(S) (23)	SHIPPING WEIGHT (Kilograms) (24)	VIN/PRODUCT NUMBER/ VEHICLE TITLE NUMBER (25)	VALUE (U.S. dollars, omit cents) (Selling price or cost if not sold) (26)

27. LICENSE NO./LICENSE EXCEPTION SYMBOL/AUTHORIZATION   **28.** ECCN *(When required)*

29. Duly authorized officer or employee   The USPPI authorizes the forwarder named above to act as forwarding agent for export control and customs purposes.

30. I certify that all statements made and all information contained herein are true and correct and that I have read and understand the instructions for preparation of this document, set forth in the **"Correct Way to Fill Out the Shipper's Export Declaration."** I understand that civil and criminal penalties, including forfeiture and sale, may be imposed for making false or fraudulent statements herein, failing to provide the requested information or for violation of U.S. laws on exportation (13 U.S.C. Sec. 305; 22 U.S.C. Sec. 401; 18 U.S.C. Sec. 1001; 50 U.S.C. App. 2410).

Signature   **Confidential** – For use solely for official purposes authorized by the Secretary of Commerce (13 U.S.C. 301 (g)).

Title   Export shipments are subject to inspection by U.S. Customs Service and/or Office of Export Enforcement.

Date   **31.** AUTHENTICATION *(When required)*

Telephone No. *(Include Area Code)*   E-mail address

2001 Revised Shipper's Export Declaration

```
.------------------------------------------------------------------
                    CORRECT WAY TO COMPLETE THE
                    SHIPPER'S EXPORT DECLARATION
                          FORM 7525-V


         Title 15 Code of Federal Regulations, Part 30
                (www.census.gov/foreign-trade)

--------------------------------------------------------------------
```

                                    U.S. Department of Commerce
                                        Donald L. Evans, Secretary

                                    Bureau of the Census
                                        (Vacant), Director

                                    Foreign Trade Division
                                    Bureau of the Census
                                            C. Harvey Monk, Jr., Chief

Issued: February 14, 2001

```
------------------------------------------------------------------------
------------------------------------------------------------------------
```

                        THE CORRECT WAY TO COMPLETE
                                    THE
                    SHIPPER'S EXPORT DECLARATION (SED)

This booklet explains how to properly complete the
SED and contains references to the major rules,
regulations, and guidelines to assist you in preparing
the SED. If, at any time, you have a question
regarding the completion of the SED please contact
the Regulations, Outreach, & Education Branch on
301-457-2238 or visit our website at
<www.census.gov/foreign-trade>

```
------------------------------------------------------------------------
```

TABLE OF CONTENTS

THE CORRECT WAY TO COMPLETE THE SED

(Follow these instructions carefully to avoid delay at shipping point.
Refer to the Foreign Trade Statistics Regulations (FTSR) for specific details on these
provisions, 15 CFR Part 30)

1a.   Shipper's Export Declarations (SEDs) are Required in the Following Instances

From	To	No. of Copies
United States	Canada	1 (only if a license is required)
United States (Postal & Non-Postal)	Foreign Countries	Postal (1), Non-Postal (2)
United States	Puerto Rico	1
United States	U.S. Virgin Islands	1
Puerto Rico	United States	1
Puerto Rico	Foreign Countries	1
Puerto Rico	U.S. Virgin Islands	1
U.S. Virgin Islands	Foreign Countries	1

1b. Shipper's Export Declarations ARE NOT REQUIRED in the Following Instances:

From	To
United States	Canada (unless an export license is required)
U.S. Virgin Islands	United States
U.S. Virgin Islands	Puerto Rico
United States/Puerto Rico	Other U.S. Possessions**
Other U.S. Possessions	United States

** American Samoa, Baker Island, Commonwealth of the Northern Mariana Islands, Guam, Howland Island, Jarvis Island, Johnston Atoll, Kingmen Reef, Midway Islands, Navassa Island, Palmyra Atoll, Wake Island.

2. Purpose of the SED

The Shipper's Export Declaration (SED), Commerce Form 7525-V, is used for compiling the official U.S. export statistics for the United States and for export control purposes. The regulatory provisions for preparing, signing and filing the SED are contained in the foreign Trade Statistics Regulations (FTSR), Title 15 Code of Federal Regulations (CFR) Part 30.

3. Form or Method of Data Collection

      (a)   Paper

The Commerce Form 7525-V and its continuation sheet may be purchased from the Government Printing Office, (202) 512-1800, local Customs District Directors, or can be privately printed. Privately printed SEDs must conform in every respect to the official form. The SED Form 7525-V can also be downloaded from the Foreign Trade Division website at <www.census.gov/foreign-trade> on buff (yellow) or goldenrod colored paper. Customs will not accept SEDs on white paper.

      (b) Electronic: Automated Export System (AES)

The U.S. Census Bureau and the U.S. Customs Service jointly offer an electronic method for filing shipper's export declaration information known as the Automated Export System (AES). Participants in the AES include exporters (U.S. principal party in interest), forwarding or other agents, carriers, non-vessel operating common carriers (NVOCCs), consolidators, port authorities, software vendors, or service centers. Once certified by the Census Bureau, participants may file shipper's export data electronically using the AES in lieu of filing an individual paper SED for each shipment. The Census Bureau also offers a free Internet service for filing SED information through the AES called AESDirect. For additional information on AES and AESDirect go to the Foreign Trade Division web sites at <www.census.gov/foreign-trade > or <www.aesdirect.gov>.

For regulatory requirements on filing shipper's export information electronically AES refer to the FTSR, Sections 30.60 through 30.66.

4.   Preparation and Signature of the SED

The SED must be prepared in English, be typewritten or in other non-erasable medium. The original should be signed (signature stamp acceptable) by the exporter (U.S. principal party in interest) or its authorized forwarding or other agent. In all cases where a forwarding or other agent is preparing a SED or AES record on behalf of a principal party in interest i.e., US or foreign), the principal party in interest must authorize the forwarding or other agent to prepare and sign and file the SED or transmit the AES record on its behalf through a formal power of attorney, written authorization, or, for USPPIs only, by signing block 29 on the paper SED.

5. Requirement for Separate SEDs

A separate SED is required for each shipment per USPPI, including each rail car, truck, or vessel, airplane, or other vehicle.

A shipment is defined as - All merchandise sent from one exporter (U.S. principal party in interest) to one foreign consignee, to a single foreign country of ultimate destination, in a single carrier, on the same day.

The exporter (U.S. principal party in interest) may list more than one Commerce Department (BXA) license or license exception or a combination of licenses and license exceptions on the same SED or AES shipment. In addition, the exporter may combine "No License Required" (NLR) items with licensed items and license exceptions on the same SED or AES shipment. To avoid confusion when preparing the paper SED, goods licensed by other U.S. agencies such as the State Department, should be reported on a separate SED from goods licensed by the Commerce Department. For AES transactions, multiple licenses can be reported on 1 shipment.

Where two or more items are classified under the same Schedule B number, the Schedule B number should appear only once on the SED with a single quantity, shipping weight, and value, unless a validated license requires otherwise or, the shipment consists of a combination of foreign and domestic merchandise classified under the same Schedule B number.

Shipments involving multiple invoices or packages should be reported on the same SED.

6. Presentation of the SED

(a)   Postal (mail) Shipments - the SED must be delivered to a Post Office official with the package at the time of mailing. (See the U.S. Postal Service's International Mail Manual). All mail shipments valued at $2,500 or over, or that require an export license, require a SED.

(b)   All other shipments - the SEDs shall be delivered to the exporting carrier with the merchandise.

(c)   Exporting carriers are required to file the SED and manifest with Customs at the port of export.

The SED may accompany the merchandise or it may be delivered directly to the exporting carrier at the port of exportation.

In cases where a shipment does not require a SED based on the FTSR, a reference to the applicable section of the FTSR that exempts the merchandise from the requirement to file a SED, must be noted on the bill of lading, air waybill, or other loading document. Detailed exemption provisions for when a SED is not required are contained in the FTSR, Subpart D, sections 30.50 through 30.58. For acceptable SED exemption statements refer to Foreign Trade Statistics Letter 168 (amendment 1). Also, see Section 8 below.

7. Correction to a SED

Corrections or amendments of data to a previously filed SED should be made on a copy of the originally filed SED. Mark "CORRECTED COPY" on the top of the SED, line through the appropriate field(s) requiring correction and insert the correction. File the corrected SED with the Customs Director at the port of export.

For mail exports, corrections must be sent directly to the U.S. Census Bureau, National Processing Center. Attention: Foreign Trade Section, 1201 East 10th Street, Jeffersonville, Indiana 47132 as soon as the need to make such correction or cancellation is determined.

8. A SED is not Required In the Following Instances (SED Exemptions):
   (Reference Sections 30.50 thru 30.58 of the FTSR)

A. Shipments where the value of commodities classified under each individual Schedule B number is $2,500 or less and for which an export license is not required, except that a SED is required for exports destined to Cuba, Iran, Iraq, Libya, North Korea, Serbia (excluding Kosovo), Sudan, and Syria. (See 30.55(h))

If a shipment contains a mixture of individual Schedule B numbers valued at $2,500 or less and individual Schedule B numbers valued at over $2,500, only those valued at $2,500 or more should be reported on the SED. (See 30.55(h)(1))

When either all or part of the shipment does not require a SED, one of the following statements must appear on the bill of lading, air waybill, or other loading documents for carrier use:

    1. "No SED required, FTSR Section 30.55 (h)".

2. "No SED required - no individual Schedule B number valued over $2,500".

3. "Remainder of shipment valued $2,500 or less per individual Schedule B number".

[Note: Refer to FTSR Letter 168 (amendment 1) for more detailed information on acceptable SED exemption statements.]

B. Shipments from the United States to Canada, except those: (See 30.58)

(1) Requiring a Department of Commerce export license.

(2) Subject to the Department of State, International Traffic in Arms Regulations regardless of license requirements.

(3) Subject to Department of Justice, Drug Enforcement Administration, export declaration requirements.

[Note: For merchandise transhipped from the United States through Canada for ultimate destination to a foreign country, other than Canada, a SED or AES record is required.

C. Shipments through the U.S. Postal Service that do not require an export license and the shipment is valued at $2500 or under.

D. Shipments from one point in the United States to another point in the United States by routes passing through Mexico, and shipments from one point in Mexico to another point in Mexico by routes passing through the United States.

E. Shipments to the U.S. Armed Services

(1) All commodities consigned to the U.S. Armed Service, including exchange systems. (See 30.52)

(2) Department of Defense Military Assistance Program Grant-Aid shipments being transported as Department of Defense cargo. (See 30.52)

F. Shipments to U.S. Government agencies and employees for their exclusive use. (See 30.53)

G. Other miscellaneous shipments. (See 30.55)

(1) Diplomatic pouches and their contents.

(2) Human remains and accompanying receptacles and flowers.

(3) Shipments of gift parcels moving under General License GFT.

(4) Shipments of interplant correspondence and other business records from a US firm to its subsidiary or affiliate.

(5) Shipments of pets as baggage, accompanying or not accompanying persons leaving the United States.

H. Merchandise not moving as cargo under a bill of lading or air waybill and not requiring a validated export license.

(1) Baggage and household effects of persons leaving the United States when such are owned by the person, in his possession at the time of departure and not intended for sale.

(2) Carriers' stores, supplies, equipment, bunker fuel, and so forth, when not intended for unlading in a foreign country.

(3) Usual and reasonable kinds and quantities of dunnage necessary to secure and stow cargo. (For sole use on board the carrier)

If the above shipments are moving under a bill of lading or air waybill, a SED is required, but Schedule B numbers should not be shown, and the SED should include a statement that the shipment consists of baggage, personal effects, and so forth.

If these shipments require a validated export license, the SED must identify the shipment as baggage, personal effects, and so forth, and must contain all of the information required on the SED.

I. SED for Personal Effects and Household Goods

(1) A SED is required for personal effects and household goods only when the value of such items is $2,500 or over. A schedule B number is not required for such items.

(2) Personal effects and household goods destined for Canada do not require a SED regardless of value.

9. Retention of Shipping Documents

Exporters or their agents must maintain copies of shipping documents for a period of 5 years for statistical purposes. Additional record retention requirements for licensed shipments appear in the Export Administration Regulations. Exporters or their agents must also be aware of the record retention policies of other Government agencies.

10. Administration Provisions

The SED and its content is strictly confidential and used solely for official purposes authorized by the Secretary of Commerce in accordance with 13 U.S.C. Section 301(g). Neither the SED nor its contents may be disclosed to anyone except the exporter or its agent by those having possession of or access to any official copy. (See 30.91)

Information from the SED (except common information) may not be copied to manifests or other shipping documents. The exporter (U.S. principal party in interest) or the forwarding or other agent may not furnish the SED or its content to anyone for unofficial purposes

Copies of the SED may be supplied to the exporter (U.S. principal party in interest) or its agent only when such copies are needed to comply with official U.S. Government requirements.

A SED presented for export constitutes a representation by the exporter (U.S. principal party in interest) that all statements and information are in accordance with the export control regulations. The commodity described on the declaration is authorized under the particular license as identified on the declaration, all statements conform to the applicable licenses, and all conditions of the export control regulations have been met.

It is unlawful to knowingly make false or misleading representation for exportations. This constitutes a violation of the Export Administration Act, 50, U.S.C. App. 2410. It is also a violation of export control laws and regulations to be connected in any way with an altered SED to effect export.

Commodities that have been, are being, or for which there is probable cause to believe they are intended to be exported in violation of laws or regulations are subject to seizure, detention, condemnation, or sale under 22 U.S.C. Section 401.

To knowingly make false or misleading statements relating to information on the SED is a criminal offense subject to penalties as provided for in 18 U.S.C. Section 1001.

Violations of the Foreign Trade Statistics Regulations are subject to civil penalties as authorized by 13 U.S.C. Section 305. (See 30.95)

11. Regulations

Detailed legal and regulatory requirements regarding the SED and its preparation are contained in the Foreign Trade Statistics Regulations (FTSR) (15 CFR, Part 30). Questions concerning the FTSR may be directed to the Regulations, Outreach, & Education Branch Foreign Trade Division, U.S. Census Bureau on (301) 457-2238. Up to date copies of regulations, FTSR Letters, Federal Register Notices, and other current information can also be accessed on the Foreign Trade Division's web site at <www.census.gov/foreign-trade>

Information concerning export control laws and regulations including additional SED requirements is contained in the Export Administration Regulations (EAR) (15 CFR Parts 730 - 774) which may be purchased from the Superintendent of Documents, U.S. Government Printing Office, Washington, DC 20402. The EAR can also be accessed on the Bureau of Export Administration (BXA) web site at <www.bxa.doc.gov>

12. Office of Management and Budget Response Burden Paragraph

Public reporting burden for this collection of information is estimated to average slightly more than 11 minutes (.186 hour) per response for the paper SED, Commerce Form 7525-V, and approximately 3 minutes (.05 hour) per response for the Automated Export System, including the time for reviewing instructions, searching existing data sources, gathering and maintaining the data needed, and completing and reviewing the collection of information. Send comments regarding this burden or any other aspect of this collection of information, including suggestions for reducing this burden to the Associate Director for Administration, Room 3104, Federal Office Building 3, Bureau of the Census, Washington, DC 20233-0001; and to the Office of Management and Budget, Washington, DC 20503.

13. References

Schedule B - Statistical Classification of Domestic and Foreign Commodities Exported from the United States. For sale by the Superintendent of Documents, U.S. Government, U.S. Government Printing Office, Washington, DC 20402 and local U.S. Customs District Directors. A Schedule B search engine is also available on the FTD web site. (www.census.gov/foreign-trade)

Schedule C - Classification of Country and Territory Designations for U.S. Foreign Trade Statistics. Free from the Bureau of the Census, Washington, DC 20233-0001. Also included as part of Schedule B. Schedule C codes are also available on the FTD web site. (www.census.gov/foreign-trade)

Schedule D - Classification of Customs Districts and Ports for U.S. Foreign Trade Statistics Free from the Bureau of the Census, Washington, DC 20233-0001. Also included as part of the Schedule B. The Schedule D codes are also available on the FTD web site. (www.census.gov/foreign-trade)

Foreign Trade Statistics Regulations (FTSR). Free from the Bureau of the Census, Washington, DC 20233-0001. The FTSR is also available for downloading on the FTD web site. (www.census.gov/foreign-trade)

Export Administration Regulations (EAR). For sale by the Superintendent of Documents, U.S. Government Printing Office, Washington, DC 20402 and U.S. Department of Commerce and District Offices. The EAR is also available on the BXA web site (www.bxa.doc.gov)

Note: This is an instructional pamphlet summarizing the preparation of the SED. It is no way intended as a substitute for either the Foreign Trade Statistics Regulations, the Export Administration Regulations, or the regulations of any other agency.

See the Appendix for a List of Telephone Contacts Providing Additional Information

----

INFORMATION TO BE REPORTED ON THE
SHIPPER'S EXPORT DECLARATION
FORM 7525-V

Block Number and Data Required

1(a)   U.S. Principal Party In Interest (USPPI) - Provide the name and address of the U.S. exporter (U.S. principal party in interest). The USPPI is the person in the United States that receives the primary benefit, monetary or otherwise, of the export transaction. Generally that person is the U.S. seller, manufacturer, order party, or foreign entity. The foreign entity must be listed as the USPPI if in the United States when the items are purchased or obtained for export. Report only the first five digits of the ZIP Code (See 30.4, 30.7)

1(b) USPPI Employer Identification Number (EIN) or ID Number- Enter the USPPI's Internal Revenue Service Employer Identification Number (EIN) or Social Security Number (SSN) if no EIN has been assigned. Report the 9-digit numerical code as reported on your latest Employer's Quarterly Federal Tax Return, Treasury Form 941. The EIN is usually available from your accounting or payroll department. If an EIN or SSN is not available a border crossing number, passport number, or a Customs identification number must be reported. (See 30.7(d)(2))

1(c) Parties To Transaction - Indicate if this is a related or non-related party transaction. A related party transaction is a transaction between a USPPI and a foreign consignee, (e.g., parent company or sister company), where there is at least 10 percent ownership of each by the same U.S. or foreign person or business enterprise.

2   Date of Exportation - Enter the date the merchandise is scheduled to leave the United States for all methods of transportation . If the actual date is not known, report the best estimate of departure. The date format should be indicated by MM/DD/YYYY.

3   Transportation Reference Number - Report the booking number for ocean shipments. The booking number is the reservation number assigned by the carrier to hold space on the vessel for the cargo being shipped. For air shipments the airway bill number must be reported. For other methods of transportation leave blank.

4(a) Ultimate Consignee - Enter the name and address of the foreign party actually receiving the merchandise for the designated end-use or the party so designated on the export license. For overland shipments to Mexico, also include the Mexican state in the address.

4(b) Intermediate Consignee - Enter the name and address of the party in a foreign country who makes delivery of the merchandise to the ultimate consignee or the party so named on the export license.

5   Forwarding Agent - Enter the name and address of the forwarding or other agent authorized by a principal party in interest.

6   Point (State) of Origin or Foreign Trade Zone (FTZ) Number

   (a)   If from a FTZ enter the FTZ number for exports leaving the FTZ, otherwise enter the:

   (b)   two-digit U.S. Postal Service abbreviation of the state in which the merchandise actually starts its journey to the port of export, or

   (c)   State of the commodity of the greatest value, or

   (d)   State of consolidation.

7   Country of Ultimate Destination - Enter the country in which the merchandise is to be consumed, further processed, or manufactured; the final country of destination as known to the exporter at the time of shipment; or the country of ultimate destination as shown on the export license. Two-digit (alpha character) International Standards Organization (ISO) codes may also be used.

8   Loading Pier - (For vessel shipments only) Enter the number or name of the pier at which the merchandise is laden aboard the exporting vessel.

9   Method of Transportation - Enter the method of transportation by which the merchandise is exported (or exits the border of the United States). Specify the method of transportation by name, such as, vessel, air, rail, truck, etc. Specify "own power" if applicable.

10   Exporting Carrier - Enter the name of the carrier transporting the merchandise out of the United States. For vessel shipments, give the name of the vessel.

11   Port of Export

    (a) For Overland Shipments - Enter the name of the U.S. Customs port at which the surface carrier (truck or railcar) crosses the border.

    (b) .For Vessel and Air Shipments - Enter the name of the U.S. Customs port where the merchandise is loaded on the carrier (airplane or ocean vessel) that is taking the merchandise out of the United States.

    (c) For Postal (mail) Shipments - Enter the U.S. Post Office from which the merchandise is mailed.

12   Foreign Port of Unloading - For vessel shipments between the United States and foreign countries, enter the foreign port and country at which the merchandise will be unloaded from the exporting carrier. For vessel and air shipments between the United States and Puerto Rico, enter the Schedule C code, "U.S. Customs District and Port Code".

13   Containerized - (For vessel shipments only) Check the YES box for cargo originally booked as containerized cargo and for cargo that has been placed in containers at the vessel operator's option.

14   Carrier Identification Code - Enter the 4-character Standard Carrier Alpha Code (SCAC) of the carrier for vessel, rail and truck shipments, or the 2- or 3-character International Air Transport Association (IATA) Code of the carrier for air shipments. In a consolidated shipment, if the ultimate carrier is unknown, the consolidators carrier ID code may be reported. The National Motor Freight Traffic Association (703) 838-1831 or www.nmfta.org issues the SCAC's for ocean carriers, trucking companies and consolidators. The American Association of Railroads, Railing (919)651-5006 issues the SCAC codes for rail carriers. The International Air Transportation Association (IATA) issues the air carrier codes. The IATA codes are available on the Foreign Trade Division web site under "Air Carrier Codes" at <www.census.gov/foreign-trade>.

15   Shipment Reference Number - Enter the unique reference number assigned by the filer of the SED for identification purposes. This shipment reference number must be unique for five years. For example, report an invoice number, bill of lading or airway bill number, internal file number or so forth.

16   Entry Number - Enter the Import Entry Number when the export transaction is used as proof of export for import transactions, such as In-Bond, Temporary Import Bond or Drawback's and so forth. Also, an Entry Number is required for merchandise that is entered as an import (CF 7501 or Automated Broker Interface (ABI) entries) and is then being exported out of the United States.

17   Hazardous Materials - Check the appropriate "Yes" or "No" indicator that identifies the shipment as hazardous as defined by the Department of Transportation.

18   In Bond Code - Report one of the 2 - character In-Bond codes listed in Part IV of Appendix C of the FTSR (15 CFR Part 30) to include the type of In-Bond or not In-Bond shipment.

19   Routed Export Transaction - Check the appropriate "Yes" or "No" indicator that identifies the transaction as a routed export transaction. A routed export transaction is where the foreign principal party in interest authorizes a U.S. forwarding or other agent to export the merchandise out of the United States.

20   Schedule B Description of Commodities - Use columns 22 - 24 to enter the commercial

description of the commodity being exported, its schedule B number, the quantity in schedule B units, and the shipping weight in kilograms. Enter a sufficient description of the commodity as to permit verification of the Schedule B Commodity Number or the commodity description as shown on the validated export license. Include marks, numbers, or other identification shown on the packages and the numbers and kinds of packages (boxes, barrels, baskets, etc.)

21   "D" (Domestic) , "F" (Foreign) or M (Foreign Military Sales)

   (a)   Domestic exports (D) - merchandise that is grown, produced, or manufactured in the United States (including imported merchandise which has been enhanced in value or changed from the form in which imported by further manufacture or processing in the United States).

   (b)   Foreign exports (F) - merchandise that has entered the United States and is being re-exported in the same condition as when imported.

   (c)   Foreign Military Sales (M) - exports of merchandise that are sold under the foreign military sales program.

22   Schedule B Number - Enter the commercial description of the commodity being exported and the ten-digit commodity number as provided in Schedule B - Statistical Classification of Domestic and Foreign Commodities Exported from the United States. See item 5 (page 2) for a discussion of not repeating the same Schedule B numbers on the SED. If necessary, the Harmonized Tariff Schedule (HTS) number can be reported on the SED. See the Appendix showing a list of telephone numbers for assistance with Schedule B numbers.

23   Quantity (Schedule B Units) - Report whole unit(s) as specified in the Schedule B commodity classification code. Report also the unit specified on the export license if the units differ. See the Appendix showing a list of telephone numbers for assistance with units of quantity.

24   Shipping Weight (kilograms) - (For vessel and air shipment only) Enter the gross shipping weight in kilograms for each Schedule B number, including the weight of containers but excluding carrier equipment. To determine kilograms use pounds (lbs) Multiplied by 0.4536 = kilograms (report whole units.)

25   VIN/Product Number/Vehicle Title Number - (For used self-propelled vehicles only). Report the following items of information for used self-propelled vehicles as defined in Customs regulations 19 CFR 192.1: (1) Report the unique Vehicle Identification Number (VIN) in the proper format; (2) Report the Product Identification Number (PIN) for those used self propelled vehicles for which there are no VINs; and (3) the Vehicle Title Number.

26   Value (U.S. dollars) - Enter the selling price or cost if not sold, including freight, insurance, and other charges to U.S. port of export, but excluding unconditional discounts and commissions (nearest whole dollar, omit cents). The value to be reported on the SED is the exporter's (U.S. principal party in interest) price or cost if not sold to the foreign principal party in interest. Report one value for each Schedule B number.

27   License No./License Exception Symbol/Authorization - Whenever a SED or AES record is required:

   (a)   Enter the license number on the SED or AES record when you are exporting under the authority of a Department of Commerce, Bureau of Export Administration (BXA) license, a Department of State, Office of Defense Trade Controls (ODTC) license, a Department of the Treasury, Office of Foreign Assets Control (OFAC) license (enter either the general or specific OFAC license number), a Department of Justice, Drug Enforcement Agency (DEA) permit, or any other export license number issued by a Federal government agency. For the BXA license the expiration date of the license must be entered on the paper version of the SED only.

   (b)   Enter the correct License Exception symbol (e.g. LVS, GBS, CIV) on the SED or AES record when you are exporting under the authority of a License Exception.

See 740.1, 740.2, and 758.1 of the Export Administration Regulations (EAR).

(c) Enter the "No License Required" (NLR) designator when you are exporting items under the NLR provisions of the EAR:

(1) When the items being exported are subject to the EAR but not listed on the Commerce Control List (CCL) (i.e. items that are classified as EAR99); and

(2) When the items being exported are listed on the CCL but do not require a license.

28 Export Control Classification Number (ECCN) - Whenever a SED or AES record is required, you must enter the correct Export Control Classification Number (ECCN) on the SED or AES record for all exports authorized under a license or License Exception, and items being exported under the "No License Required" (NLR) provisions of the EAR that are listed on the CCL and have a reason for control other than anti-terrorism (AT).

29 Duly authorized officer or employee - Provide the signature of the exporter (U.S. principal party in interest) authorizing the named forwarding or agent to effect the export when such agent does not have a formal power of attorney or written authorization.

30 Signature/Certification - Provide the signature of the exporter (U.S. principal party in interest) or authorized forwarding or other agent certifying the truth and accuracy of the information on the SED, the title of exporter (U.S. principal party in interest) or authorized agent, the date of signature, the telephone number of the exporter (U.S. principal party in interest) or authorized agent preparing the SED and who can best answer questions for resolving problems on the SED, and the email address of the exporter (U.S. principal party in interest) or authorized agent.

31 Authentication - For Customs use only.

APPENDIX

List of telephone Numbers Providing Additional Assistance in Filling Out the Shipper's Export Declaration (SED)

(Census Bureau) Foreign Trade Division Contacts

Commodity Classification (Schedule B Number)	Assistance	Schedule B
Food, Animal and Wood Products	301-457-3484	Chapters 1-24; 41; 43-49
(Including paper and printed matter)		
Minerals	301-457-3484	Chapters 25-27; 68-71
Metals	301-457-3259	Chapters 72-83
Textiles and Apparel	301-457-3484	Chapters 41-43; 50-67
Machinery and Vehicles	301-457-3259	Chapters 84-85; 86-89
(including computers, other electronic equipment and transportation)		
Chemical and Sundries	301-457-3259	Chapters 28-40; 90-98

Foreign Trade Statistics Regulations   301-457-2238

Automated Export System (AES)   1-800-549-0595

Other Agency Export Control Telephone Contacts

Bureau of Export Administration, Department of Commerce   <www.bxa.doc.gov>
Washington, DC   Newport Beach, CA   San Jose, CA
202-482- 4811 or   949-660-0144   408-998-7402
202-482-2642

International Trade Administration, Export Assistance Center 1-800-872-8723

```
<www.ita.doc.gov>

Department of State, Office of Defense Trade Controls (ODTC)
(International Traffic In Arms Regulations (ITAR))    202-663-2714    <www.pmdtc.org>

Department of the Treasury, Office of Foreign Assets Control (OFAC)
(Sanctioned countries and trade restrictions)    202-622-2490    <www.treas.gov/ofac>

U.S. Customs Import (Inbound) Questions (Summary Management Office)  202-927-0625
<www.customs.treas.gov>

U.S. Customs Export (Outbound) Questions (Outbound Programs)   202-927-6060
<www.customs.treas.gov>

NAFTA (hotline)  972-574-4061       <www.mac.doc.gov/nafta/nafta2.htm>

----------------------------------------------------------------------

To Order Paper SEDs Contact the:   Government Printing Office (GPO)
                                    Publication Order & Information Office
                                    202-512-1800

----------------------------------------------------------------------
```

DEPARTMENT OF THE TREASURY
UNITED STATES CUSTOMS SERVICE

Form Approved.
OMB No. 1515-0014

CERTIFICATE OF REGISTRATION

NO.

19 CFR 10.8, 10.9, 10.68,
148.1, 148.8, 148.32, 148.37

(NOTE: Number of copies to be submitted varies with type of transaction.
Inquire at District Director's office as to number of copies required.)

VIA (Carrier)	B/L or INSURED NO.	DATE
American Airlines	016 6547 8907	3 March 1998

NAME, ADDRESS, AND ZIP CODE TO WHICH CERTIFIED FORM IS TO BE MAILED (If Applicable)	ARTICLES EXPORTED FOR:
XYZ News 321 23rd St NYC, NY 10098	☐ ALTERATION* ☐ PROCESSING* ☐ REPAIR* ☒ OTHER, (specify) ☐ USE ABROAD ~~News event coverage~~ ☐ REPLACEMENT

* NOTE: The cost or value of alterations, repairs, or processing abroad is subject to Customs duty.

LIST ARTICLES EXPORTED

Number Packages	Kind of Packages	Description
1	Computer Case	TV Monitor
2	Crates	TV Cables

SIGNATURE OF OWNER OR AGENT (Print or Type and Sign)	DATE
John Francis	3 March 1998

The Above-Described Articles Were:

	EXAMINED	LADEN under my supervision
DATE		DATE PORT
SIGNATURE OF CUSTOMS OFFICER		SIGNATURE OF CUSTOMS OFFICER

CERTIFICATE ON RETURN

Duty-free entry is claimed for the described articles as having been exported without benefit of drawback and are returned unchanged except as noted. (use reverse if needed)

SIGNATURE OF IMPORTER (Print or Type and Sign)	DATE

NOTE: Certifying officers shall draw lines through all unused spaces with ink or indelible pencil.

PAPERWORK REDUCTION ACT NOTICE: The Paperwork Reduction Act of 1980 says we must tell you why we are collecting this information, how we will use it, and whether you have to give it to us. We ask for the information to carry out the Customs Service laws of the United States. We need the information to ensure that importers/exporters are complying with these laws in claiming duty free entry for exported articles which are then returned into the United States. Your response is mandatory and to your benefit.

Export Certificate of Registration

SHIPPER'S DECLARATION FOR DANGEROUS GOODS

Shipper	Air Waybill No. 041 5543 6788
Don Manufacturing 32 West St Avon, CT 21345	Page of Pages
	Shipper's Reference Number D909 *(optional)*

Consignee	
Subaroo Tractor Company 1500 Rue du Goiytee Rio, del mar Brazil 7892	

Two completed and signed copies of this Declaration must be handed to the operator.

WARNING

Failure to comply in all respects with the applicable Dangerous Goods Regulations may be in breach of the applicable law, subject to legal penalties. This Declaration must not, in any circumstances, be completed and/or signed by a consolidator, a forwarder or an IATA cargo agent.

TRANSPORT DETAILS

This shipment is within the limitations prescribed for: *(delete non-applicable)*	Airport of Departure: BDL Hartford
PASSENGER AND CARGO AIRCRAFT	CARGO AIRCRAFT ONLY XXX

Airport of Destination:
RIO de Janiero   Brazil   RIO

Shipment type: *(delete non-applicable)*

| NON-RADIOACTIVE | ~~RADIOACTIVE~~ |

NATURE AND QUANTITY OF DANGEROUS GOODS

Proper Shipping Name	Dangerous Goods Identification				Quantity and type of packing	Packing Inst.	Authorization
	Class or Division	UN or ID No.	Pack-ing Group	Subsi-diary Risk			
Acrylamide	6.1	UN2074	III		2 kg/ 4g x 1	619	

Additional Handling Information   International –1–510–744–2000

X ☐ ICAO/IATA   ☐ 49 CFR

24 HR. Emergency Contact Telephone 1–800–333–3333

I hereby declare that the contents of this consignment are fully and accurately described above by the proper shipping name, and are classified, packaged, marked and labelled/placarded, and are in all respects in proper condition for transport according to applicable international and national governmental regulations.

Name/Title of Signatory   ED Edwards
Export Mgr
Place and Date
3 March 1998   New York
Signature
(see warning above)

Form 30-065 Printed and Sold by UNZCO 700 Central Ave., New Providence, NJ 07974 • (800) 631-3098

Restricted Articles Declaration

Francis Food Services
45 Denver Ave.
Detroit, California 00987

Health & Sanitary Certificate

To whom it may concern,

We herby certify that the products described on the attached invoices are manufactured in our factory in the USA; that all of the ingredients contained in each of the products to be exported are approved for food use in a regulation of the United States FDA or appear on the GRAS List. Further, we hereby certify that each product is offered for sale and sold in the USA; that said product is perfectly fit and intended for human consumption when utilized in accordance with good manufacturing practices.

All our products are free of heavy metals, radiation and all kinds of disease including cholera.

The products shown on the attached invoices meet and/or exceed the Food and Sanitary regulations promulgated by all applicable all federal and state authorities.

This product was inspected and certified by FFS internal quality control personnel, as identified below and meet or exceed all internal quality control standards.

Bob Bobbo
3 March 1998

Health & Sanitary Certificate

The Export Finance Matchmaker (EFM)

Website at:
www.doc.gov/td/efm helps you:

Match with financing firms that are likely to facilitate your overseas sales.

Understood export financing terminology and techniques.

Link to other U.S. Government and State export finance websites.

Contact other U.S. Government agencies for more information.

Provides a variety of financial products:

Pre-export capital: Financing to fill export orders.

Direct loans to foreign buyers: Financing the overseas buyer.

Forfaiting: Converting a foreign buyer's medium and long-term receivables to cash.

Export factoring: Converting short-term foreign account receivables to cash.

Documentary products: Facilitating collections from overseas buyers using various bank products.

Export credit insurance: Reducing an exporter's credit and political risk with insurance.

Miscellaneous types: Offering collection activity, foreign exchange, purchase order financing, and structured trade finance/offsets, among others.

EFM's five simple steps to financing:

GO TO: www.ita.doc.gov/td/efm.

Click "ENTER".

Click "EXPORTERS" on the left menu.

Complete the "exporter query" and click "SUBMIT".

Review the results and choose the option to have EFM send an e-mail to all, a select few, or only one matched firm!

Export Management Systems (EMS) and BXA Guidelines

Contents

Background—History of Export Management System (EMS)

The events of the early 1990s in Europe and the former Soviet Union have resulted in a significant easing of the U.S. and multilateral export controls on West-East trade. At the same time, developments in other areas of the world, such as the Middle East, have underscored the importance of non-proliferation controls on chemical, biological, and nuclear weapons and missile technology.

The Commerce Department's Bureau of Export Administration (BXA) has responded to the changing world events by focusing much of its attention on items and services that could be used to develop or deliver weapons of mass destruction. Regulations issued pursuant to the President's Enhanced Proliferation Control Initiative (EPCI) were published in 1991 and place greater emphasis on the end-use or end-user of exported items. As a result, exporters need to be more vigilant in screening their customers and transactions.

Before the EPCI regulation changes, license requirements were identified primarily by checking the item and country of destination against the Commerce Control List (CCL). Items not specifically identified on the CCL as controlled to a given destination could, in most instances, be exported under a General License. The export of General License eligible items did not require prior approval from the Department of Commerce except for certain nuclear end-uses and persons denied export privileges.

Under the EPCI controls, a third element, the end-use or end-user, has become critical in determining whether an export requires a license. Under the nonproliferation regulations, items that might not otherwise require a license based on a review of the CCL and country requirements, could require a license from the Department of Commerce because of the nature of the end-use/user.

The first EMS Guidelines were published in September 1992 to assist companies with the establishment of internal procedures for screening exports. The Guidelines provided steps for exporters to determine whether a license is required because of item/country identification on the CCL. The Guidelines also focused on screening mechanisms that a company could use to determine whether an export required a license because of the nature of the end-use or end-user.

In March 1996, BXA published a complete rewrite of the Export Administration Regulations (EAR), which restructured and reorganized the EAR. While the old EAR had a binary structure, requiring either a "General License" or a "Validated License" for every transaction, the new EAR has a decision tree format. The simplification dropped the term "General License." Items previously exported under the broadest of the old General License, General Destination or G-DEST, may now be exported under "No License Required" (NLR). Those General Licenses that allowed export of items that would otherwise have required a license became "License Exceptions." The 1997 revised EMS Guidelines incorporate changes necessary to be consistent with the 1996 publication of the Export Administration Regulations.

In response to requests from the business community, BXA has prepared these detailed Export Management System Guidelines to assist firms wishing to establish an internal procedure for screening exports. The information contained in the Guidelines is not meant to modify or interpret the Export Administration Regulations, and no action should be taken based solely on what is contained in the EMS Guidelines.

What Is an EMS?

An EMS is an optional program a company can consider establishing to ensure that their exports and export decisions are consistent with the EAR. An EMS is based on a corporate philosophy that says: "We want to maximize our export sales while ensuring that we comply with the U.S. export laws and regulations." Just as it is vital for a firm to have a system that ensures its tax returns are submitted accurately and on time, an EMS can be an important part of an exporting firm's operation to be sure that it complies with export control requirements. A vital part of an EMS is the establishment of mechanisms within the company that provide checks and safeguards at key steps in the order processing system, helping to better manage the overall export process. Such checks and safeguards help to ensure that the right questions are being asked to preclude exporters from making shipments that are contrary to U.S. export controls and therefore inconsistent with the company's best interests.

How Can an EMS Be Helpful?

An EMS can be a useful tool to help companies comply with export control requirements. The implementation of EPCI and the changing world situation have increased the need for such systems.

The regulations require the exporter to assume greater responsibility in screening export transactions against the prohibitions of exports, re-exports, and selected transfers to certain end-users and uses:

- Denied persons list (General Prohibition Four): Engaging in actions prohibited by a denial order.

- End-use/users (General Prohibition Five): Export or re-export to prohibited end-uses or end-users.

- Activities of U.S. persons (General Prohibition Seven): Activities of U.S. persons in relation to proliferation activities.

Exporters should also have a procedure in place to screen transactions to ensure that they do not conduct business with persons/firms where BXA has "informed" the exporter or the public at large that the transaction involves an unacceptable risk of use in, or diversion to, prohibited proliferation activities anywhere in the world.

Firms/Persons that act contrary to General Prohibitions could lose their export privileges, be fined, or even be criminally prosecuted.

An EMS is *not* a U.S. Government mandated requirement. However, in a changing export control environment, it is a program that companies should consider establishing to ensure their actions are handled in a way that is consistent with the EAR.

The establishment of an EMS, in and of itself, will not relieve an exporter of criminal and administrative liability under the law if a violation occurs. However, the implementation of an EMS, coupled with good and sound judgment, can greatly reduce the risk of inadvertently exporting to an unauthorized party or for an unauthorized end-use.

Preliminary Steps in Developing an EMS

There are certain steps that companies will need to address as they begin to develop an EMS.

Know the customer. A key objective of an effective EMS is to be able to detect and react to information that raises questions about the legitimacy of a customer or transaction. The "Know Your Customer Guidance" help all persons avoid an illegal activity under the EAR. The EAR also prohibits specific activities with "knowledge" that a violation is about to occur. These duties require a certain standard of care. The optional screening suggestions in the Guidelines can help the exporter understand his/her responsibilities.

BXA's "Know Your Customer" Guidance as defined in Supplement 1 to Part 732 of the EAR is included in the booklet as appendix II. This Guidance refers to the provisions in the regulations that require a license when an exporter "knows" that a proscribed end-use, end-user, destination, activity, or other violation is involved. It is important that the exporter have an established procedure for reviewing proposed transactions in accordance with this Guidance. For your convenience, a Checklist of the Red Flag indicators is included with Element 3.

Understanding the EAR. Companies should have a clear understanding of the EAR. Exporters, as well as firms that facilitate exports or engage in other controlled activities, need a working knowledge of the regulations and their applications. It is strongly recommended that to develop such an understanding you send company personnel responsible for export controls to one of the many seminars offered by BXA. (For further information, contact the Export Seminar Staff at (202) 482-6031).

Identifying the factors that will form the foundation for the system. Each firm should provide examples, i.e., steps, scope, prohibitions, recordkeeping, etc. of the export regulations that apply to the firm's specific activities. The company's management team should look at a number of factors as it plans the development of its EMS.

A company's EMS should be appropriate to the scope of its export and re-export markets and to its business situation. Several factors can affect how an EMS can be structured. All of the factors that follow are important to consider, however, the most significant are exporter size, location of customers, product sensitivity or restrictions, and order processing system.

    A. Exporter type
      –Manufacturer
      –Trading company
      –Purchasing agent
      –Original equipment manufacturer (OEM)
      –Systems integrator
      –Servicing Agent
      –Other (i.e., banks, transportation, freight forwarder, etc.)

    B. U.S. person participation
      –Direct export

–Financing
–Shipping
–Service
–Employment
–Other assistance or facilitation

C. Nature of item exported
–Production material or capital equipment
–Part or component
–End item:
 for retail consumption
 for use by customer
–Software
–Technical data
–Service (i.e., financing, freight forwarding, legal, technical, engineering, architectural assistance, etc.)

D. Source of item exported
–Own manufacture:
 at one location
 at multiple locations
–Purchase from manufacturer(s)
–Purchase from distributor(s)

E. Item sensitivity of restrictions
–Authorized for export/re-export to all destinations (except embargoed or terrorist countries)
–License exception eligibility or likelihood of approval under a license to Country Group D (Supp. 1 Part 740)
–Subject to the missile technology restrictions
–Subject to the nuclear restrictions
–Subject to the chemical and biological weapons restrictions
–Potential for use by restricted nuclear, missile technology, and chemical and biological weapon end-uses/users

F. Exporter size
–Small
–Medium
–Large

G. Customer type
–Reseller:
 Distributor
 Sales agent
 Systems integrator
 Original equipment manufacturer (OEM), i.e., assembler
–End-use:
 Government entity
 Manufacturer
 OEM
 Purchaser of capital equipment regardless of nature
 Banks

H. Use of product by customer
  –Capital or other equipment exclusively for own use
  –Resale to retail customers
  –Resale to manufacturers or OEMs for own use
  –Incorporation into new product of manufacture for resale
  –Support equipment for foreign product for resale
  –Servicing
  –Warehousing for further distribution
  –Systems integration activities
  –Assembling finished product from kit form
  –Other

I. Location of customers
  –Country group A (see Part 740, Supplement No. 1, to the
   EAR)
  –Country group B
  –Country group D:1
  –Country group D:2
  –Country group D:3
  –Country group E

J. Activity of customers
  –Disposition in country in which located
  –Re-exports to countries listed in Section I
  –Exports of foreign manufactured products incorporating U.S.
   origin parts and components
  –Exports of foreign manufactured products produced using
   U.S. origin technical data

K. Exporter/customer relationships
  –Customer is a foreign branch of a U.S. company
  –Customer is a foreign subsidiary or affiliate under effective
   control of U.S. company
  –U.S. exporter is the subsidiary/branch of customer
  –Independent relationship
  –Company is a new customer

L. Product flow
  –Exported from U.S. manufacturing site(s)
  –Exported/re-exported from off-shore manufacturing site(s)
  –Direct shipments to an end-customer
  –Shipments direct from a nonaffiliated manufacturing entity to
   a customer

M. Order processing system
  –Order received at:
    One location
    Several locations
    Regional international sales or headquarters office
  –Records maintained at:
    One central location
    Several locations

The various elements described in the Guidelines, and as noted in the Menu of EMS Elements with specific Objectives identified in appendix III, constitute compliance options. The elements are *not* minimum requirements that every exporting company must follow regardless of its size, products, destinations, and methods of distribution. Rather, the Guidelines provide a "menu" of options a company may choose from to shape a compliance program uniquely suited to its particular operational features. No one compliance program will be appropriate for every company. Referring to the factors described previously can help a company select elements it believes are appropriate. Some examples may help to illustrate this point.

> A small company with only two or three employees will probably not need a list with the names, phone numbers, and responsibilities of all persons involved in export control issues. However, such a list may be very useful for large firms.

> Likewise, a small company will not necessarily develop its own formalized training program. Rather, the company's employees or owners may familiarize themselves with the EAR and one of the employees will take on export compliance duties in addition to several other duties. In contrast, a large company might find it extremely valuable to develop its own ongoing training program to educate a large number of employees on evolving export control requirements.

> A company that exports bacterial agents may develop a compliance program that includes an extensive screen of end-uses. The company would want to ensure that no exports/re-exports of the bacterial agents will be used in any of the prohibited end-uses described in Section 744.4. However, a compliance program for such an exporter need not necessarily include a screen to identify, for instance, nuclear end-uses, because their transactions do not involve prohibited nuclear end-uses.

> A firm may have determined that no end-uses/end-users activities described in Part 744 apply to its transactions. Therefore, it does not need to include extensive nuclear, missile, or chemical, and biological screens. However, it should still set up a procedure for Denied Persons screening and Diversion Risk screening.

> A bank or other financial institution need only be concerned with end-use and end-user screens to avoid prohibited financing or other participation in the design, development, production, stockpiling, and use of missiles or chemical/biological weapons and financing certain transactions with Denied Persons.

The size, organizational structure, and production/distribution network of a company will determine the location of activities required to implement and maintain an EMS. In small companies, one individual at one location may perform almost all of the activities. In large or medium-size companies, these activities may be performed in different organizational areas (comptroller, accounting, sales, marketing, contracts, general counsel, customer service, traffic, corporate audits, order processing, etc.) and/or at different geographical locations (product center, regional office, headquarters, shipping points, etc.).

Some companies choose to designate a single employee as responsible for the administration, performance, and coordination of these activities (e.g., EMS Administrator). Some large companies decentralize export control responsibilities throughout the organization, but with corporate oversight to ensure essential standards are set and maintained.

Regardless of the method of export control coordination or the size of the exporting company, the person or entity responsible should be sufficiently high in the management hierarchy to maintain and impose a strong commitment to export control activities for the entire company. In instances where export control activities are decentralized, it is paramount to have knowledgeable staff trained in export control issues at each location or in each function where orders are received and from which items are shipped.

Many companies centralize the administration of training, recordkeeping, dissemination of regulatory material, notification of noncompliance, and internal reviews. However, the actual screening activities in some companies of the denied persons lists, end-use and end-user activities, and diversion-risk may be performed by personnel throughout the company, (e.g., sales and marketing, order entry, or shipping) where first-hand knowledge and information on the consignee is available.

If a company decides to adopt an EMS, BXA recommends that the export control program be formalized into a written format. This format, an EMS Manual, should describe what elements the company has identified as necessary to include in its program. Further, it should address "who," "how," "when," and "where," export control checks are conducted.

An exporter clearly benefits from an EMS that:

- Protects employees through training and awareness programs from inadvertently violating the EAR.

- Protects the company through on-going control and review systems against inadvertent violations of the EAR.

- Demonstrates to the U.S. Government, and a company's employees, a strong commitment to comply with U.S. export laws and regulations.

- Instills confidence that the company is complying with the letter of the law.

How Do I Develop an EMS?

Sometimes the toughest part of any job is getting started. This section is intended to offer you a starting point that has worked for many companies and to give you steps to proceed with the development of your EMS.

The following five types of facts determine how your EMS should be crafted:

1. What is it (the item)?

2. Where is it going (country)?

3. Who will receive it (end-user)?

4. What will they do with it (end-use)?

5. What else do they do (activity)?

Developing Administrative Elements

The administrative elements are considered to be the foundation of the EMS. These elements may be developed simply by answering questions about your company and the company personnel.

Step One. Determine which employees are involved in the day-to-day export functions and identify specific responsibilities of each employee.

Step Two. Identify the most experienced employee(s) in the area of export controls and appoint an export control administrator.

Step Three. Evaluate any training programs that you currently have in place and formally detail the type of training that is being done.

Step Four. Review export control documents (records) and evaluate how they are kept and specifically what is kept.

Step Five. Refer to the specific elements within the EMS guidelines for a more detailed description of the administrative elements. Formalize your written procedures including the necessary details that apply to your company.

Developing Screening Elements

An ideal place to start in developing the screening elements necessary to perform export control functions is with the order processing element. This screen will assist companies in combining all of the various screens into a comprehensive flow chart and will allow a company to demonstrate what screens are addressed during order processing.

Starting with the order processing element is like building the foundation of a puzzle. Once the order processing system (foundation) has been established and formalized, it will be easy to fit all of the other pieces in their appropriate place. The following steps should help you place the screening elements into your written procedures/EMS manual:

Step One. In narrative form, describe each step of the company's order entry operation to the point of shipment.

Step Two. Create a flow chart that visually displays company's order processing system narrative (see step one).

Step Three. On the flow chart, fill in any missing pieces with the screening elements described in the EMS, identifying at what point(s) the various screenings take place. Keep in mind that Companies should adapt those elements necessary to meet their particular exporting requirements. Screening elements include the following:

1. Denied persons screen/entities list screening.
2. Product classification/licensing determination screen.
3. Diversion-risk screen.
4. Nuclear screen.
5. Missile screen.
6. Chemical and biological weapons screen.
7. Anti boycott screen (if performed).

Step Four. Ensure consistent processing of all orders with appropriate "Hold" and "Release" functions.

Step Five. Once all relevant screening elements have been placed on the flow chart, a more detailed description of those elements may be described and formalized within the individual element of the EMS.

Assistance for Developing an EMS

Due to the wide diversity of export transactions, companies may still have questions after studying the EAR and reading these guidelines. BXA's Office of Exporter Services (OEXS) seminars may provide assistance in gaining proficiency in the regulations and valuable insights into developing and refining an EMS. Finally, where additional guidance is desired, OEXS's Special License and Compliance Division should be consulted. For additional guidance, or one-on-one counseling, telephone or send your EMS program to one of the following offices for review to:

The Office of Exporter Services
Attention: SLCD
P.O. Box 273
Washington, D.C. 20044
(202) 482-4524 or (202) 482-3541 phone
(202) 501-6750 fax

    or

Western Regional Office
3300 Irvine Avenue
Suite 345
Newport Beach, CA 92660-3198
(714) 660-0144 phone
(714) 660-9347 fax

    or

Northern California Office
101 Park Center Plaza
Suite 1001
San Jose, CA 95113
(408) 998-7402 phone
(408) 998-7470 fax

Administrative Elements: Introduction

The administrative elements have been developed to assist companies to ensure that documents attesting to the completion of the various checks are maintained along with other pertinent records. These elements also ensure that the personnel responsible for compliance are given authority commensurate with their responsibilities and receive all necessary training.

The content of these elements can be incorporated easily into a company's existing office procedures. Such elements help establish a concept that export control issues play an important role in company's day-to-day operation.

Although the implementation of an EMS is entirely optional, as are most of the administrative elements, any exporting company is required to maintain records relevant to all its export transactions. Consequently, the objective of Administrative Element 3: Recordkeeping is a regulatory *requirement* for all exporters. The administrative elements consist of the following:

1. Management policy

2. Responsible officials

3. Recordkeeping

4. Training

5. Internal reviews

6. Notification

Element 1: Management Policy

A clear statement of management policy communicated to all levels of the firm involved in export/re-export sales, traffic and related functions, emphasizing the importance of compliance with the Export Administration Regulations.

Objective. To convey a clear commitment of compliance with the EAR from senior management to all employees involved with U.S. export controls. An important component of this commitment consists of providing sufficient time, money, and personnel to make the compliance program effective.

Procedure. One way of demonstrating strong management support of compliance with export control regulations is to prepare and distribute a policy statement. If a company decides to adopt an EMS, the written statement should convey a clear commitment to comply with the EAR. This formal statement should be included in the EMS manual and disseminated to all employees who work in export-related functions.

Senior management, preferably the president, owner of the company, or the chief executive officer, should be the responsible party for issuance of the statement. Senior management is also responsible for providing the relevant corporate policies, organizational structure, and resources to carry out an effective EMS.

The policy statement of commitment to export controls may include the following types of policies:

- Under no circumstances will sales be made contrary to U.S. export regulations. Special care should be taken to prevent transactions with entities involved in the proliferation of weapons of mass destruction.

- Any question concerning the legitimacy of a transaction or potential violations should be referred to: (responsible official).

- A description of penalties (corporate, criminal, and administrative) applied in instances of compliance failure.

The policy statement can be reinforced through a continuing education program. (See Administrative Element 4.) Other important vehicles for the communication of the policy statement of commitment to export controls are:

- New employee orientation

- In-house publications

- Training and/or procedures manuals

Important recipients of the policy statement of commitment to export controls are all employees of the company, specifically those dealing with:

- International sales

- Customer service

- Marketing

- Contracts

- Finance and accounting

- Legal counsel

- Field services

- Export administration

- Order entry

- Shipping

- Traffic

- Engineering (those involved in item classifications)

Comments. To be effective, the policy statement included in any EMS manual should be communicated to employees on a regular basis and would:

- Be prepared on company letterhead.

- Be dated.

- Be signed (including the name and title of the signer).

- Include policy statements referring to those factors in the preceding list.

If the names of any other individuals identified in the management policy statement change, the statement should be reissued. However, one way to avoid constant reissuing of the policy statement due to personnel changes is to use the title of the "responsible official" within the statement and refer all export control personnel to a company web page that posts current names and phone numbers.

Issuance of a policy statement by management or owners of even a small company shows employees the importance of complying with export control requirements. For exporting companies of all sizes, it highlights the fact that compliance with export regulations is essential to protecting a company's future.

Element 2: Responsible Officials

Identification of positions and specific individuals responsible for compliance with the Export Administration Regulations.

Objective: To ensure that all compliance-related functions, duties, and responsibilities in the company are clearly identified and assigned, the positions and incumbents are known, and the list is routinely updated.

Procedure: Initially, each company involved in the export or re-export of controlled items may wish to analyze its current organizational structure and operations to determine the effective placement of these functions. Effort should be made, where practicable, to assign export responsibility separately from the sales function to prevent a conflict of objectives. However, sales staff should communicate, to the export control staff, information on the end-user, intended end-use, or end destination of the export. Where possible, the organizational structure of the company should centralize the key export functions and coordinate export activities with other departments that may become involved in export-related issues (e.g., legal counsel, credit, shipping, or contracts).

Personnel assigned export control functions should be given authority commensurate with their responsibilities. Formal lines of communication between the key personnel and others with export-related functions should be established.

Once the export control responsibilities have been assigned, the company adopting an EMS may want to document the following information:

- A list and/or organizational chart identifying the employee(s) responsible for each export and export-related function. General export control responsibilities should be listed in brief and the formal coordination between the various functions clearly set forth.

- A list of the personnel responsible, identified by name, title, and telephone number or extension. To ensure ongoing compliance in cases of absence, backup personnel should be formally assigned for all key export control-related functions. Telephone numbers or extensions should also be provided for these individuals.

- The list or chart of personnel with export and export-related functions should be distributed throughout the organization.

- A list identifying the EMS administrator (or persons with equivalent responsibilities) at the firm's consignees or customers. This may prove especially useful in instances where customers receive a variety of items or are authorized to resell controlled items in approved re-export territories. If this information is maintained, procedures can be developed to ensure that this list of contacts is updated promptly when changes occur.

Comments: The exporter may accomplish these objectives in a variety of ways. The following is provided to assist in development:

- At large or medium-size companies, the initial analysis of positions and individuals responsible for export compliance may include the development of an Export Control Unit.

- Information should be maintained in the form of lists and/or organizational charts. Use of lists are superior for presenting specific export control duties, while organizational charts are preferable for illustrating reporting lines and structures. A combination may be most practical. Responsible individuals should be identified by name and/or title.

- Policies, procedures, and job descriptions should be written to ensure smooth transitions during personnel turnover. Of key importance during these events is the assignment of backup personnel. A backup should be identified for each position with export-related responsibilities. This information should be promptly updated and disseminated when changes occur.

- Consignees and customers should also be made aware of the name and position of the exporter's EMS administrator. These companies should be encouraged to direct questions or problems to the administrator as they arise.

The amount of detail provided in the list of responsible officials may depend on the size of the exporting company. At a small company, it is probably not necessary to go into a great amount of detail. However, at a large company that has many players involved in export control issues, it is very important to clearly identify responsible parties in detail.

Introduction to the Order Processing System Element

This optional element has been developed to assist companies in combining all of the various screens into a comprehensive flow chart or narrative.

This will allow a company to demonstrate what screens are addressed during order processing.

Order Processing System

An order processing system that documents employee clearance of transactions in accordance with the requirements of the firm's EMS.

Objective. To set forth in written procedures the order processing system used to screen and document the checks required by the firm's EMS.

Procedure. The EMS administrator should determine the nature and frequency of export checks through the use of these guidelines and analysis of the company's operational system. This should be completed prior to designing a company's particular order processing flow chart or narrative.

An EMS should contain a formal flow chart or narrative description of the order processing system. The flow chart or narrative should include export checks equivalent to those listed in the optional screening elements that determine the type(s) of license(s) to be used by the company. The order processing system should be supported by documentation to leave a trail to verify export control compliance.

It is recommended that the flow chart or narrative include descriptions for the processing of the following shipping documents:

- Commercial/billing invoices

- Shipper's export declarations/shipper's letter of instructions (SED/SLI)

- Air waybills (AWB) and/or bills of lading

Comments. The order processing system, whether it is manual or automated, should have "hold" functions that ensure adherence to sign-off procedures and prevent the preparation of commercial invoices and shipping documents prior to review and sign-off. Each individual with responsibility for performing a control check(s) should be held accountable for orders processed. All special transactions should receive supervisory sign-off.

The EMS administrator and all order processing personnel should be aware that the chosen optional screening elements should be performed on all intermediate parties involved in a transaction. This is particularly true for denied persons screening. This is to ensure that items exported under in-transit shipments and shipments to bonded warehouses and free trade zones are disposed of as authorized, thereby reducing the possibility of diversion. The company should determine whether any of its transactions with its consignees involve these types of activities.

The party with control over the items should be assigned responsibility for monitoring the items. For example, control over items that are in-transit remains the responsibility of the company until such time that the title is transferred to the customer.

However, control over shipments to bonded warehouses or free trade zones may not rest with the exporter. The question of control therefore depends on the point at which title passes from the company to the ultimate customer. The export clearance and retention of records requirements for these types of shipments are no different from any ordinary export transaction.

Menu of EMS Elements with Objectives

Administrative Elements

The administrative elements are designed to help exporters establish a foundation upon which the Export Management System (EMS) is built. All of the following elements are optional with the exception of Administrative Element # 3-Recordkeeping.

1. Management Policy. A clear statement of management policy communicated to all levels of the firm involved in export/re-export sales, traffic and related functions, emphasizing the importance of compliance with the Export Administration Regulations (EAR).

Objective. To convey a clear commitment of compliance with the EAR from senior management to all employees involved with U.S. export controls. An important component of this commitment consists in providing sufficient time, money, and personnel to make the compliance program effective.

2. Responsible Officials. Identification of positions and specific individuals responsible for compliance with the EAR.

Objective. To ensure that all compliance-related functions, duties, and responsibilities in the firm are clearly identified and assigned, and that the positions and incumbents are known.

3. Recordkeeping. A program for recordkeeping as required by the EAR.

Objective. To ensure documents are maintained in an accurate and consistent manner and are available for inspection as required by the EAR.

4. Training. A continuing program for educating people who require knowledge of the EAR.

Objective. To ensure training and education are provided on a regular basis to all employees involved in export-related activities.

5. Internal Reviews. An internal review program to verify compliance with the company's EMS and the EAR.

Objective. To ensure compliance at all the company's export-related locations with the EMS and EAR.

6. Notification. A system for consulting the BXA when questions arise regarding the propriety of specific export transactions.

Objective. To ensure that all exports and re-exports are conducted in accordance with the EAR.

Order Processing System Element

An optional order processing element is recommended to help clarify when and where exports are appropriately screened.

Order Processing System. An order processing system that documents employee clearance of transactions in accordance with the requirements of the company's EMS.

Objective. To set forth in written procedures the order processing system used to screen and document the checks required by the firm's EMS.

Screening Elements

The optional screening elements are designed to provide a mechanism to help exporters evaluate export transactions.

1. Denied Persons Screen. A system for screening all customers against the most current list of denied persons.

Objective. To ensure that transactions involving U.S. origin items covered by the EAR do not involve persons or entities whose export privileges have been denied by the U.S. Department of Commerce.

2. Product Classification/License Determination Screen. A system for classifying products by Export Control Classification Number (ECCN) to determine what export authorization may potentially be used for the intended destination.

Objective. To ensure that the export license or license exception to be used authorizes the transfer of the items to the intended country.

3. Diversion-Risk Screen. A system for assessing proposed transactions against a diversion risk profile (DPL) that takes into account the factors outlined in Screening Element 3 of the EMS.

Objective. To establish procedures to adequately screen orders for "red flag" indicators using the diversion-risk profile (DRP).

4. Nuclear Screen. A system for assuring compliance with the restrictions on prohibited nuclear end-uses/end-users.

Objective. To ensure that transactions do not involve prohibited nuclear end-uses/end-users without authorization from the U.S. Government.

5. Missile Screen. A system for assuring compliance with the restrictions on prohibited missile end-uses/end-users.

Objective. To ensure that transactions do not involve prohibited missile end-uses/end-users without authorization from the U.S. Government.

6. Chemical and Biological Weapons Screen. A system for assuring compliance with the restrictions on prohibited chemical and biological weapons end-uses/end-users.

Objective. To ensure that transactions do not involve prohibited chemical or biological weapons end-uses/end-users without authorization from the U.S. Government.

Commerce Control List Overview and the Country Chart

Supplement No. 1 to Part 738   page 1

Commerce Country Chart
Reason for Control

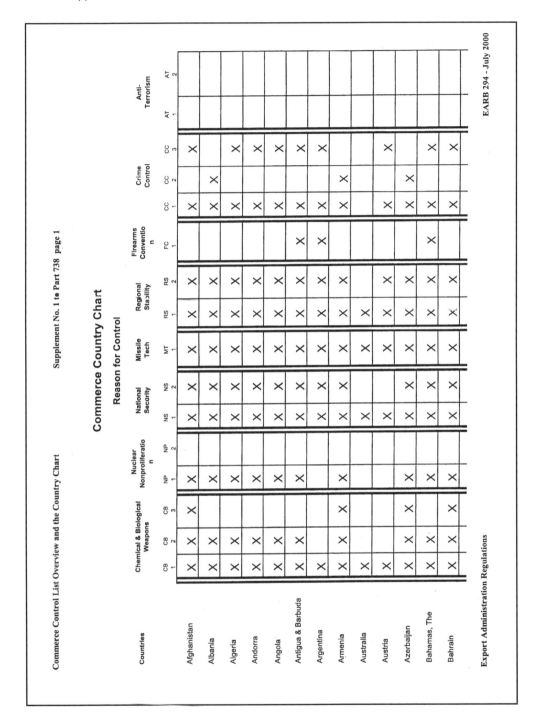

Countries	Chemical & Biological Weapons			Nuclear Nonproliferation		National Security		Missile Tech	Regional Stability		Firearms Convention	Crime Control			Anti-Terrorism	
	CB 1	CB 2	CB 3	NP 1	NP 2	NS 1	NS 2	MT 1	RS 1	RS 2	FC 1	CC 1	CC 2	CC 3	AT 1	AT 2
Afghanistan	X	X	X	X		X	X	X	X	X		X		X		
Albania	X	X		X		X	X	X	X	X		X	X			
Algeria	X	X		X		X	X	X	X	X		X		X		
Andorra	X	X		X		X	X	X	X	X		X		X		
Angola	X	X				X	X	X	X	X		X		X		
Antigua & Barbuda	X	X		X		X	X	X	X	X	X	X		X		
Argentina	X					X	X	X	X	X	X	X		X		
Armenia	X		X	X		X		X	X	X		X	X			
Australia	X					X		X	X	X		X				
Austria	X					X	X	X	X	X	X	X	X	X		
Azerbaijan	X	X	X	X		X	X	X	X	X		X		X		
Bahamas, The	X	X				X	X	X	X	X	X	X		X		
Bahrain	X	X	X	X		X	X	X	X	X		X		X		

Export Administration Regulations

EARB 294 - July 2000

Commerce Control List Overview and the Country Chart

Supplement No. 1 to Part 738 page 2

Commerce Country Chart

Reason for Control

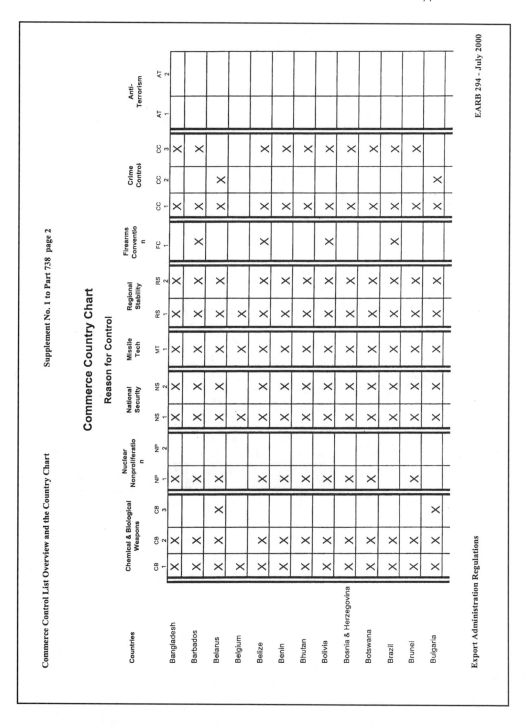

Countries	Chemical & Biological Weapons			Nuclear Nonproliferation		National Security		Missile Tech	Regional Stability		Firearms Convention	Crime Control			Anti-Terrorism	
	CB 1	CB 2	CB 3	NP 1	NP 2	NS 1	NS 2	MT 1	RS 1	RS 2	FC 1	CC 1	CC 2	CC 3	AT 1	AT 2
Bangladesh	X	X		X		X	X	X	X	X		X		X		
Barbados	X	X		X		X	X	X	X	X	X	X		X		
Belarus	X	X	X	X		X	X	X	X	X		X	X			
Belgium	X	X				X		X	X							
Belize	X	X		X		X	X	X	X	X	X	X		X		
Benin	X	X				X	X	X	X	X		X		X		
Bhutan	X	X		X		X	X	X	X	X		X		X		
Bolivia	X	X		X		X	X	X	X	X	X	X		X		
Bosnia & Herzegovina	X	X				X	X	X	X	X		X		X		
Botswana	X	X		X		X	X	X	X	X		X		X		
Brazil	X	X				X	X	X	X	X	X	X		X		
Brunei	X	X		X		X	X	X	X	X		X		X		
Bulgaria	X	X	X			X	X	X	X	X		X	X			

Export Administration Regulations

EARB 294 - July 2000

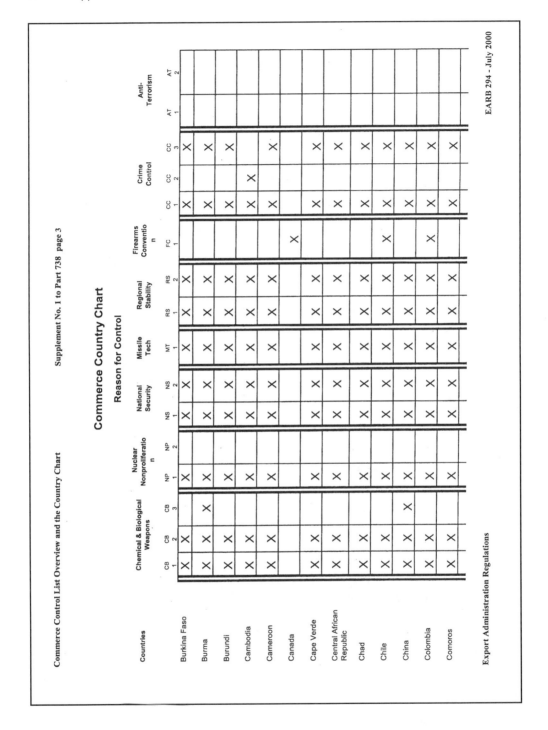

Commerce Control List Overview and the Country Chart

Supplement No. 1 to Part 738 page 4

Commerce Country Chart

Reason for Control

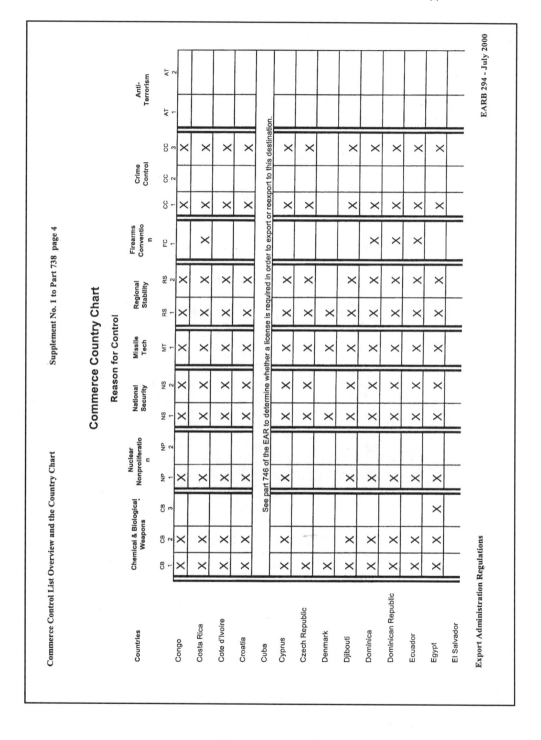

Countries	Chemical & Biological Weapons CB 1	CB 2	CB 3	Nuclear Nonproliferation NP 1	NP 2	National Security NS 1	NS 2	Missile Tech MT 1	Regional Stability RS 1	RS 2	Firearms Convention FC 1	Crime Control CC 1	CC 2	CC 3	Anti-Terrorism AT 1	AT 2
Congo	X	X		X		X	X	X	X	X		X		X		
Costa Rica	X	X		X		X	X	X	X	X	X	X		X		
Cote d'Ivoire	X	X		X		X	X	X	X	X		X		X		
Croatia	X	X		X		X	X	X	X	X		X		X		
Cuba	See part 746 of the EAR to determine whether a license is required in order to export or reexport to this destination.															
Cyprus	X	X		X		X	X	X	X	X		X		X		
Czech Republic	X					X	X	X	X	X		X		X		
Denmark	X			X		X		X	X							
Djibouti	X	X		X		X	X	X	X	X		X		X		
Dominica	X	X		X		X	X	X	X	X	X	X		X		
Dominican Republic	X	X		X		X	X	X	X	X	X	X		X		
Ecuador	X	X		X		X	X	X	X	X	X	X		X		
Egypt	X	X		X		X	X	X	X	X		X		X		
El Salvador			X													

Export Administration Regulations

EARB 294 - July 2000

Commerce Control List Overview and the Country Chart

Supplement No. 1 to Part 738   page 5

Commerce Country Chart

Reason for Control

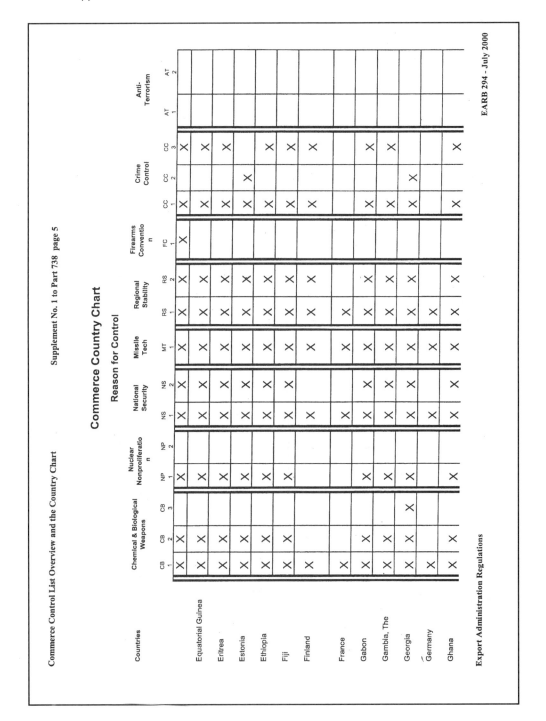

Countries	CB 1	CB 2	CB 3	NP 1	NP 2	NS 1	NS 2	MT 1	RS 1	RS 2	FC 1	CC 1	CC 2	CC 3	AT 1	AT 2
	Chemical & Biological Weapons			**Nuclear Nonproliferation**		**National Security**		**Missile Tech**	**Regional Stability**		**Firearms Convention**	**Crime Control**			**Anti-Terrorism**	
Equatorial Guinea	X	X		X		X	X	X	X	X	X	X		X		
Eritrea	X	X		X		X	X	X	X	X		X		X		
Estonia	X	X		X		X	X	X	X	X		X	X	X		
Ethiopia	X	X		X		X	X	X	X	X		X		X		
Fiji	X	X		X		X	X	X	X	X		X				
Finland	X	X				X	X	X	X	X		X				
France	X	X				X		X	X			X		X		
Gabon	X	X		X		X	X	X	X	X		X		X		
Gambia, The	X	X		X		X	X	X	X	X		X		X		
Georgia	X	X	X	X		X	X	X	X	X		X	X	X		
Germany	X	X				X		X	X			X				
Ghana	X	X		X		X	X	X	X	X		X		X		

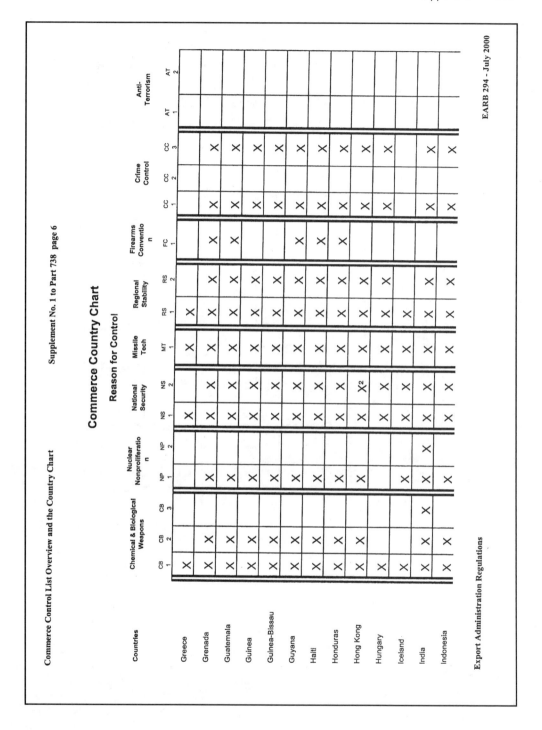

Commerce Control List Overview and the Country Chart

Supplement No. 1 to Part 738 page 6

Commerce Country Chart

Reason for Control

Export Administration Regulations

EARB 294 - July 2000

Commerce Control List Overview and the Country Chart

Supplement No. 1 to Part 738 page 7

Commerce Country Chart

Reason for Control

Countries	Chemical & Biological Weapons			Nuclear Nonproliferation		National Security		Missile Tech	Regional Stability		Firearms Convention	Crime Control			Anti-Terrorism	
	CB 1	CB 2	CB 3	NP 1	NP 2	NS 1	NS 2	MT 1	RS 1	RS 2	FC 1	CC 1	CC 2	CC 3	AT 1	AT 2
Iran	See part 746 of the EAR to determine whether a license is required in order to export or reexport to this destination.															
Iraq[1]	See part 746 of the EAR to determine whether a license is required in order to export or reexport to this destination.															
Ireland	X	X		X		X		X	X							
Israel	X	X	X	X	X	X	X	X	X	X		X		X		
Italy	X	X		X		X		X	X							
Jamaica	X	X		X		X	X	X	X	X	X	X		X		
Japan	X	X		X		X		X	X							
Jordan	X	X		X		X	X	X	X	X		X		X		
Kazakhstan	X	X	X	X		X	X	X	X	X		X	X			
Kenya	X	X		X		X	X	X	X	X		X		X		
Kiribati	X	X		X		X	X	X	X	X		X		X		
Korea, North	X	X	X	X	X	X	X	X	X	X		X	X	X	X	X

Export Administration Regulations

EARB 294 – July 2000

Commerce Control List Overview and the Country Chart

Supplement No. 1 to Part 738 page 8

Commerce Country Chart

Reason for Control

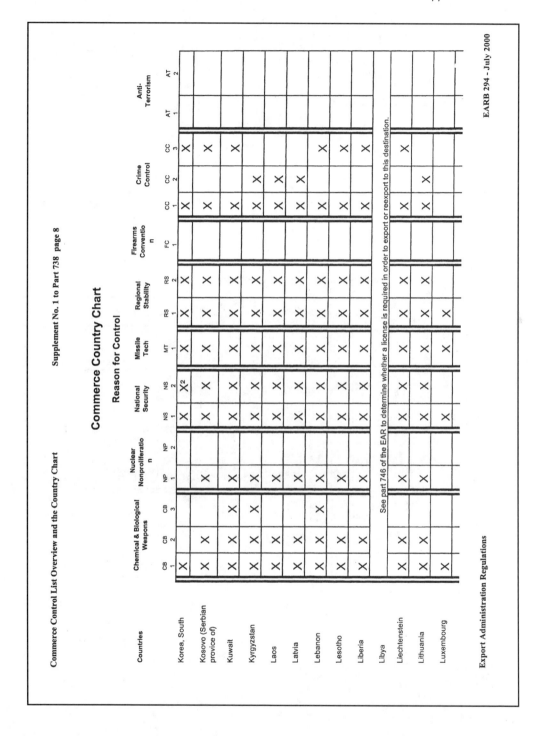

Countries	Chemical & Biological Weapons			Nuclear Nonproliferation		National Security		Missile Tech	Regional Stability		Firearms Convention	Crime Control			Anti-Terrorism	
	CB 1	CB 2	CB 3	NP 1	NP 2	NS 1	NS 2	MT 1	RS 1	RS 2	FC 1	CC 1	CC 2	CC 3	AT 1	AT 2
Korea, South	X	X				X	X²	X	X	X		X		X		
Kosovo (Serbian province of)	X	X				X	X	X	X	X		X		X		
Kuwait	X	X	X	X		X	X	X	X	X		X				
Kyrgyzstan	X	X	X	X		X	X	X	X	X		X		X		
Laos	X	X		X		X	X	X	X	X		X	X			
Latvia	X	X		X		X	X	X	X	X		X	X			
Lebanon	X	X	X	X		X	X	X	X	X		X	X			
Lesotho	X	X		X		X	X	X	X	X		X		X		
Liberia	X	X		X		X	X	X	X	X		X		X		
Libya	See part 746 of the EAR to determine whether a license is required in order to export or reexport to this destination.															
Liechtenstein	X	X		X		X	X	X	X	X		X		X		
Lithuania	X	X		X		X	X	X	X	X		X	X			
Luxembourg	X					X		X	X							

Export Administration Regulations

EARB 294 - July 2000

Commerce Control List Overview and the Country Chart

Supplement No. 1 to Part 738 page 9

Commerce Country Chart

Reason for Control

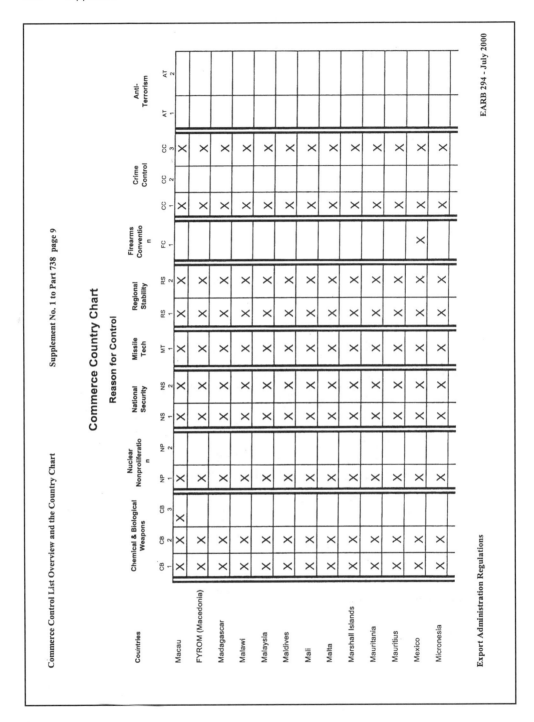

Countries	Chemical & Biological Weapons			Nuclear Nonproliferation		National Security		Missile Tech	Regional Stability		Firearms Convention	Crime Control			Anti-Terrorism	
	CB 1	CB 2	CB 3	NP 1	NP 2	NS 1	NS 2	MT 1	RS 1	RS 2	FC 1	CC 1	CC 2	CC 3	AT 1	AT 2
Macau	X	X	X	X		X	X	X	X	X		X		X		
FYROM (Macedonia)	X	X		X		X	X	X	X	X		X		X		
Madagascar	X	X		X		X	X	X	X	X		X		X		
Malawi	X	X		X		X	X	X	X	X		X		X		
Malaysia	X	X		X		X	X	X	X	X		X		X		
Maldives	X	X		X		X	X	X	X	X		X		X		
Mali	X	X		X		X	X	X	X	X		X		X		
Malta	X	X		X		X	X	X	X	X		X		X		
Marshall Islands	X	X		X		X	X	X	X	X		X		X		
Mauritania	X	X		X		X	X	X	X	X		X		X		
Mauritius	X	X		X		X	X	X	X	X		X		X		
Mexico	X	X		X		X	X	X	X	X	X	X		X		
Micronesia	X	X		X		X	X	X	X	X		X		X		

Export Administration Regulations

EARB 294 - July 2000

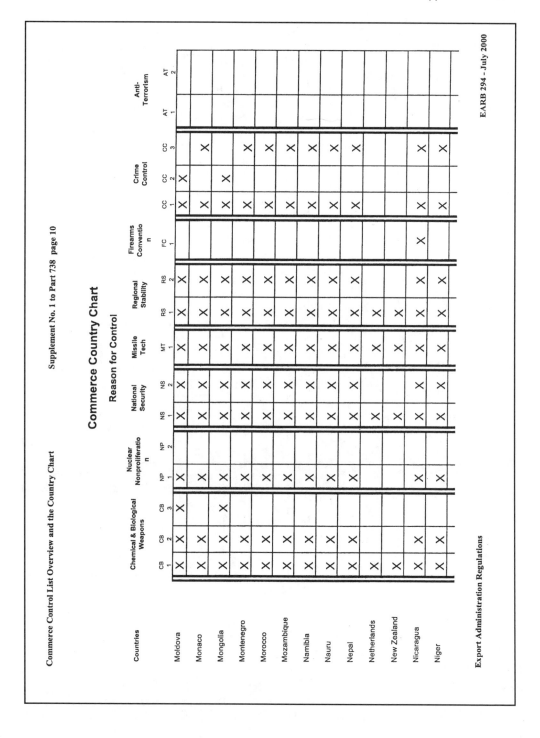

Commerce Control List Overview and the Country Chart

Supplement No. 1 to Part 738 page 10

Commerce Country Chart

Reason for Control

Countries	Chemical & Biological Weapons			Nuclear Nonproliferation		National Security		Missile Tech	Regional Stability		Firearms Convention	Crime Control			Anti-Terrorism	
	CB 1	CB 2	CB 3	NP 1	NP 2	NS 1	NS 2	MT 1	RS 1	RS 2	FC 1	CC 1	CC 2	CC 3	AT 1	AT 2
Moldova	X	X	X	X		X	X	X	X	X		X	X			
Monaco	X	X		X		X	X	X	X	X		X		X		
Mongolia	X	X	X	X		X	X	X	X	X			X			
Montenegro	X	X		X		X	X	X	X	X		X		X		
Morocco	X	X		X		X	X	X	X	X		X		X		
Mozambique	X	X		X		X	X	X	X	X		X		X		
Namibia	X	X		X		X	X	X	X	X		X		X		
Nauru	X	X		X		X		X	X	X		X		X		
Nepal	X	X		X		X		X	X	X		X				
Netherlands	X					X		X	X	X		X				
New Zealand	X	X		X		X	X	X	X	X	X	X		X		
Nicaragua	X	X		X		X	X	X	X	X		X		X		
Niger	X	X		X		X	X	X	X	X		X		X		

Export Administration Regulations

EARB 294 - July 2000

Commerce Control List Overview and the Country Chart

Supplement No. 1 to Part 738   page 11

Commerce Country Chart
Reason for Control

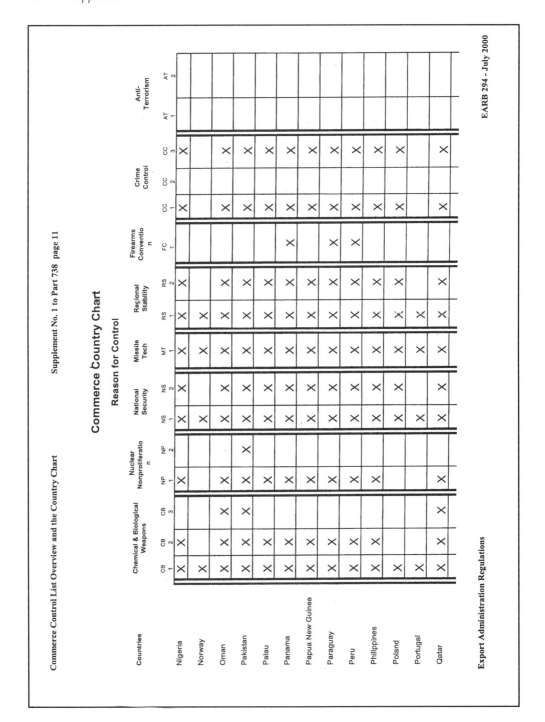

Countries	CB 1	CB 2	CB 3	NP 1	NP 2	NS 1	NS 2	MT 1	RS 1	RS 2	FC 1	CC 1	CC 2	CC 3	AT 1	AT 2
	Chemical & Biological Weapons			Nuclear Nonproliferation		National Security		Missile Tech	Regional Stability		Firearms Convention	Crime Control			Anti-Terrorism	
Nigeria	X	X		X		X	X	X	X	X		X		X		
Norway	X					X			X							
Oman	X	X	X	X		X	X	X	X	X		X		X		
Pakistan	X	X	X	X	X	X	X	X	X	X		X		X		
Palau	X	X		X		X	X	X	X	X		X		X		
Panama	X	X		X		X	X	X	X	X		X		X		
Papua New Guinea	X	X		X		X	X	X	X	X	X	X		X		
Paraguay	X	X		X		X	X	X	X	X	X	X		X		
Peru	X	X		X		X	X	X	X	X	X	X		X		
Philippines	X	X		X		X	X	X	X	X		X		X		
Poland	X					X	X	X	X	X		X		X		
Portugal	X					X		X	X			X		X		
Qatar	X	X		X		X	X	X	X	X		X		X		

Export Administration Regulations

EARB 294 – July 2000

Commerce Control List Overview and the Country Chart Supplement No. 1 to Part 738 page 12

Commerce Country Chart

Reason for Control

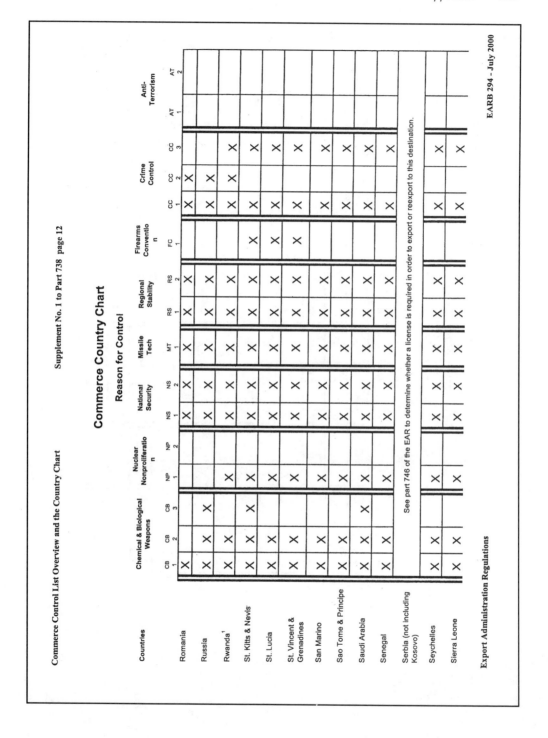

Countries	Chemical & Biological Weapons CB 1	CB 2	CB 3	Nuclear Nonproliferation NP 1	NP 2	National Security NS 1	NS 2	Missile Tech MT 1	Regional Stability RS 1	RS 2	Firearms Convention FC 1	Crime Control CC 1	CC 2	CC 3	Anti-Terrorism AT 1	AT 2
Romania	X	X				X	X	X	X	X		X	X			
Russia	X	X	X			X	X	X	X	X		X	X			
Rwanda¹	X	X		X		X	X	X	X	X		X		X		
St. Kitts & Nevis	X	X	X	X		X	X	X	X	X	X	X	X	X		
St. Lucia	X	X		X		X	X	X	X	X		X		X		
St. Vincent & Grenadines	X	X		X		X	X	X	X	X	X	X		X		
San Marino	X	X		X		X	X	X	X	X		X		X		
Sao Tome & Principe	X	X		X		X	X	X	X	X	X	X		X		
Saudi Arabia	X	X	X	X		X	X	X	X	X		X		X		
Senegal	X	X		X		X	X	X	X	X		X		X		
Serbia (not including Kosovo)	See part 746 of the EAR to determine whether a license is required in order to export or reexport to this destination.															
Seychelles	X	X		X		X	X	X	X	X		X		X		
Sierra Leone	X	X		X		X	X	X	X	X		X		X		

Export Administration Regulations EARB 294 - July 2000

Commerce Control List Overview and the Country Chart

Supplement No. 1 to Part 738   page 13

Commerce Country Chart

Reason for Control

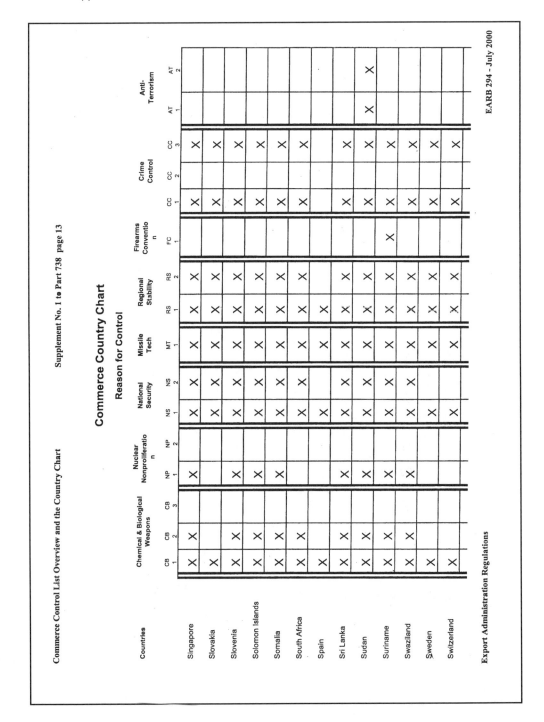

Countries	Chemical & Biological Weapons			Nuclear Nonproliferation		National Security		Missile Tech	Regional Stability		Firearms Convention	Crime Control			Anti-Terrorism	
	CB 1	CB 2	CB 3	NP 1	NP 2	NS 1	NS 2	MT 1	RS 1	RS 2	FC 1	CC 1	CC 2	CC 3	AT 1	AT 2
Singapore	X	X		X		X	X	X	X	X		X		X		
Slovakia	X					X	X	X	X	X		X		X		
Slovenia	X	X		X		X	X	X	X	X		X		X		
Solomon Islands	X	X		X		X	X	X	X	X		X		X		
Somalia	X	X		X		X	X	X	X	X		X		X		
South Africa	X	X				X	X	X	X	X		X		X		
Spain	X					X		X	X							
Sri Lanka	X			X		X	X	X	X	X		X		X		
Sudan	X	X		X		X	X	X	X	X		X		X	X	X
Suriname	X	X		X		X	X	X	X	X	X	X		X		
Swaziland	X	X		X		X	X	X	X	X		X		X		
Sweden	X					X			X	X		X		X		
Switzerland	X					X		X	X	X		X		X		

Export Administration Regulations

EARB 294 - July 2000

Commerce Control List Overview and the Country Chart

Supplement No. 1 to Part 738 page 14

Commerce Country Chart

Reason for Control

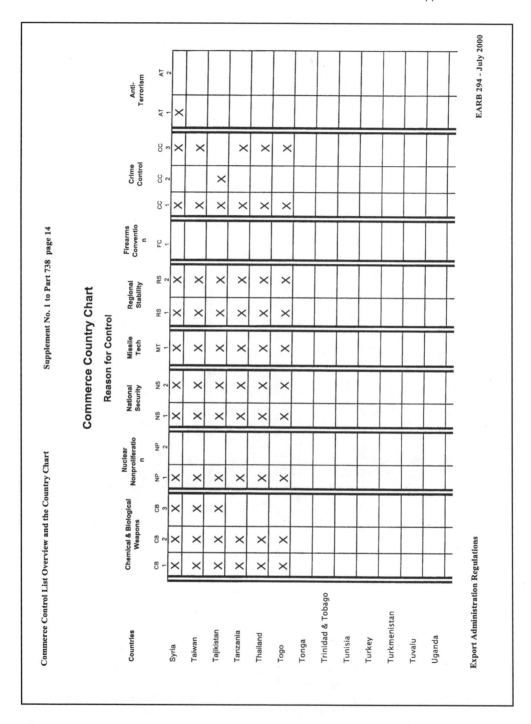

Countries	Chemical & Biological Weapons			Nuclear Nonproliferation		National Security		Missile Tech	Regional Stability		Firearms Convention	Crime Control			Anti-Terrorism	
	CB 1	CB 2	CB 3	NP 1	NP 2	NS 1	NS 2	MT 1	RS 1	RS 2	FC 1	CC 1	CC 2	CC 3	AT 1	AT 2
Syria	X	X	X	X		X	X	X	X	X		X		X	X	
Taiwan	X	X		X		X	X	X	X	X		X		X		
Tajikistan	X	X	X	X		X	X	X	X	X			X			
Tanzania	X	X		X		X	X	X	X	X		X		X		
Thailand	X	X		X		X	X	X	X	X		X		X		
Togo	X	X		X		X	X	X	X	X		X		X		
Tonga																
Trinidad & Tobago																
Tunisia																
Turkey																
Turkmenistan																
Tuvalu																
Uganda																

EARB 294 - July 2000

Export Administration Regulations

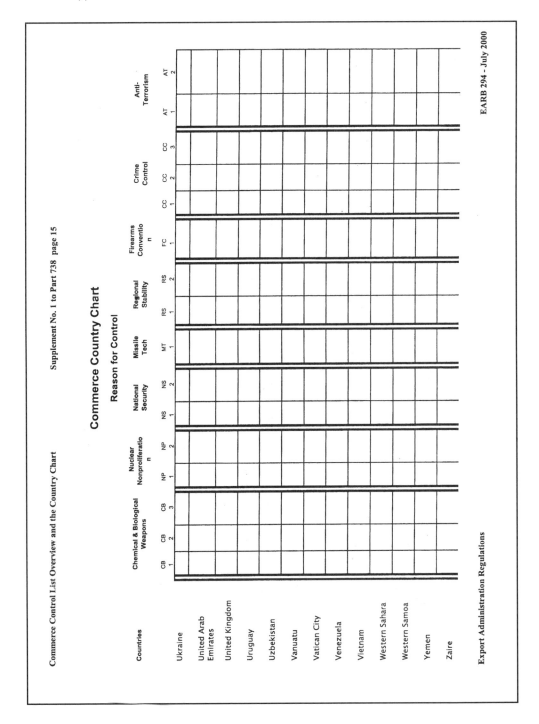

Commerce Control List Overview and the Country Chart

Supplement No. 1 to Part 738   page 15

Commerce Country Chart
Reason for Control

Countries	Chemical & Biological Weapons			Nuclear Nonproliferation		National Security		Missile Tech	Regional Stability		Firearms Convention	Crime Control			Anti-Terrorism	
	CB 1	CB 2	CB 3	NP 1	NP 2	NS 1	NS 2	MT 1	RS 1	RS 2	FC 1	CC 1	CC 2	CC 3	AT 1	AT 2
Ukraine																
United Arab Emirates																
United Kingdom																
Uruguay																
Uzbekistan																
Vanuatu																
Vatican City																
Venezuela																
Vietnam																
Western Sahara																
Western Samoa																
Yemen																
Zaire																

Export Administration Regulations

EARB 294 - July 2000

Commerce Control List Overview and the Country Chart

Supplement No. 1 to Part 738 page 16

Commerce Country Chart

Reason for Control

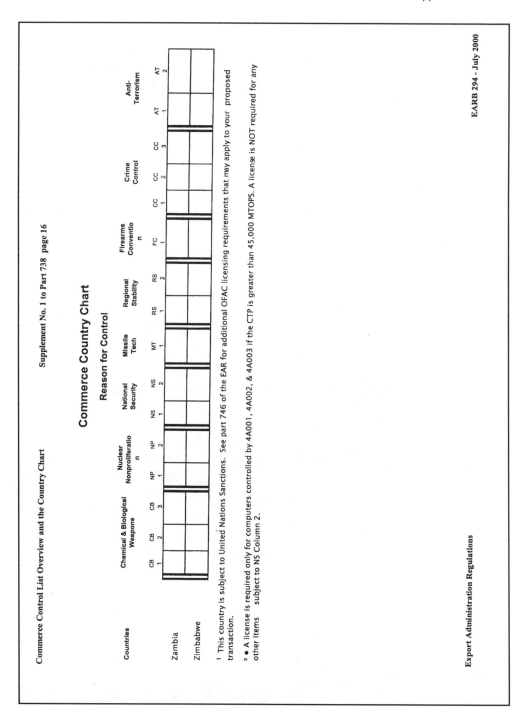

Countries	Chemical & Biological Weapons			Nuclear Nonproliferation		National Security		Missile Tech	Regional Stability		Firearms Convention	Crime Control			Anti-Terrorism	
	CB 1	CB 2	CB 3	NP 1	NP 2	NS 1	NS 2	MT 1	RS 1	RS 2	FC 1	CC 1	CC 2	CC 3	AT 1	AT 2
Zambia																
Zimbabwe																

[1] This country is subject to United Nations Sanctions. See part 746 of the EAR for additional OFAC licensing requirements that may apply to your proposed transaction.

[2] ● A license is required only for computers controlled by 4A001, 4A002, & 4A003 if the CTP is greater than 45,000 MTOPS. A license is NOT required for any other items subject to NS Column 2.

Export Administration Regulations

EARB 294 - July 2000

Import Compliance Issues Review and U.S. Customs Guidelines

Three Major Players in the Import Process

1. Importer of Record. Person or party who is responsible for duties and penalties to U.S. Customs

2. U.S. Customs Service. Division of the U.S. Department of Treasury responsible for protecting the U.S. borders against illegal importation of commodities, persons, and contraband. Revenue collection agency.

3. Customs Broker. Person or party licensed by the Department of Treasury to conduct "customs business" on behalf of an importer of record.

U.S. customs is collecting less and less funds each year in the form of duties and taxes due to special tariff treatment programs and yearly rate reductions of general duties and taxes. To offset this reduction in funds collected, customs is aggressively pursuing fines and penalties from importers through the customs audit process.

The Customs Modernization Act of 1993 was passed to encourage the following:

1. Reasonable care standards

2. Informed compliance standards

3. Supervision and control standards

4. Recordkeeping standards

5. Proper valuation of imported goods

Every U.S. importer will be audited by U.S. Customs. There is no importer that is totally compliant. Most importers do not understand their responsibility to U.S. Customs and their total liability pending a customs audit.

Most importers rely on their customs broker for compliance standards. However, most customs brokers do not have the operational expertise to properly operate in a compliant manner themselves. As a result, most customs brokers give improper advice to importers.

Reasonable Care

The Modernization Act mandated and passed into law the concept of reasonable care, so defined as. . . .

That degree of care which a person of ordinary prudence would exercise in the same or similar circumstances.

Reasonable care is the "legal responsibility" to fix the final classification and value.

Meeting Reasonable Care Standards

Customs Brokers

A broker shall not withhold information relative to any "customs business" from a client who is entitled to the information.

A broker shall exercise due diligence to ascertain the correctness of any and all information which he or she imparts to a client.

A broker shall not knowingly impart to a client false information relative to any customs business.

Importers of Record

Following are some of the responsibilities of importers of record:

Should seek guidance from customs for proper compliance through the formal rulings program.

Should consult with **qualified experts** such as a customs broker, customs consultant, or customs attorney who specializes in customs law.

If using a broker, must provide such broker with full and complete information sufficient enough for the broker to make an entry properly or for the broker to provide advice on how to make an entry.

When appropriate, obtain analyses from accredited labs to determine the technical qualities of imported merchandise.

Use in-house employees such as counsel, customs administrators, and customs managers who have experience in customs law proceedings.

Follow any customs binding rulings requested and received from customs.

Cannot classify own identical merchandise in different ways.

Notify customs when receiving different treatment by customs for the same goods in different ports of entry.

To examine Import Declarations CF 3461 prepared by the broker to determine the accuracy of information in relation to classification and valuation.

Customs Bonds

A customs bond is a contract that obligates the importer to perform certain functions in the importing process. These, among others, include:

1. The obligation to pay duties and related charges on a timely basis

2. To pay as demanded by customs, all additional duties, taxes, and charges subsequently found due

3. To file complete entries

4. To produce documents where customs releases merchandise conditionally

5. To hold the merchandise at the place of examination until the merchandise is properly released

6. To redeliver merchandise in a timely fashion to customs custody; where, for example, the merchandise is inadmissible (e.g., product of convict labor, non-compliance automobile, etc) or, more commonly, where it does not comply with the country-of-origin marking rules

The requirement for a bond is found in 19 U.S.C1623. This section of the U.S. code gives the Secretary of the Treasury the authority to allow the U.S. Customs Service to take bonds or other security (other security meaning cash deposits, U.S. bonds (except saving bonds), treasury notes, or treasury bills) in an amount equal to the amount of the bond.

Parties to a Bond

- Principal (importer)

- Surety (insurance company)

- The beneficiary–U.S. Customs Service

A bond is not designed or intended to protect the importer (rather it protects the government of the United States), nor does it relieve the importer of any of their obligations.

The surety (insurance) company by bonding the importer assumes the same duties and responsibilities of the importer. If an importer fails to honor any condition of the bond, surety can be compelled to do so in their place.

Types of Bonds

1. *Single Transaction.* Covers a particular entry (declaration) at a particular port.

2. *Continuous.* Covers all entries (declarations) at all ports in the United States.

Amount of Bond

1. *Single transaction.*

   - *Unrestricted Merchandise.* Entered value, plus all duties, taxes, fees.

   - *Restricted Merchandise.* Entered value ×3. (Restricted merchandise is that subject to other government agency requirements where failure to redeliver could pose a threat to the public health and safety).

2. *Continuous Bond.* Ten percent of all duties, taxes, and fees paid in the preceding calendar year. If no duties, taxes, and fees were paid in the preceding calendar year, then 10 percent of all duties, taxes, and fees, estimated to be paid in the current calendar year.

Breach of Bond (Failure to comply with bond conditions)

Liquidated damages assessed in the following amounts:

- *Unrestricted Merchandise.* Entered value, plus all duties, taxes, and fees.

- *Restricted Merchandise.* Three (3) times the entered value.

Requirements to Issue

Because the bond is a guarantee by surety (insurance company) of performance by the importer, prior approval from surety must be obtained in the following situations:

1. For importers who previously have not paid estimated duties timely.

2. For foreign principals (individuals and corporations).

3. For importers in bankruptcy or any insolvency proceedings.

4. For bond covering the importation of an automobile.

5. For bond covering merchandise subject to food and drug regulations.

6. Financial statement may be required.

Invoice Requirements

Invoice requirements as set forth in the CFR 19 Pt 141.86 are crucial element of the customs clearance process. Many penalty case situations develop and stem from incorrect invoices submitted on behalf of imported merchandise. It is the importer's responsibility to present to the broker a proper invoice as established in the mentioned customs regulations.

It is the broker's responsibility to ensure that a proper invoice is received from the importer for presentation purposes to U.S. Customs. If the invoice is incomplete or in violation of the rules and regulatory standards in Pt 141.86 of the CFR, the broker is to request from the importer a corrected invoice. Failure to do so is a violation of lack of reasonable care on behalf of the broker. The broker then would possibly face a penalty for the submission of incomplete or incorrect documentation in connection to an import clearance.

Carefully review CFR 141.86 to ensure all levels of understanding of the proper and regulatory invoicing requirements. You will note that most invoices used on a common practice basis are incomplete or contain a basic error. Avoid future penalties and correct this situation immediately.

MOORE™ SPEEDISET™ MCP™ - PATENTED 226

CODE	PROD ACCT #		RATING CODE			

2529281

CHB REF #

1. INFORMATION REQUIRED—CHB MUST COMPLETE

RATING CODE

0. SCH 3/4S SECTION-XI	6. SCHB PT 1/4S
1. TIB	CHAPTER 98
2. WHSE	SUB CHAPTER I, II, III
3. AUTO	7. CBI/GSP
4. AD/CVD	8. OTHER—NOT
5. FDA	LISTED ABOVE

CHB READ BEFORE FILING BOND
- VERIFY YOUR U/W AUTHORITY AND SURETY GUIDELINES BEFORE EXECUTING THIS BOND
- UNRATED BONDS WILL BE BILLED AT HIGHEST RATE
- REPORT THIS BOND TO SURETY AGENT PROMPTLY —PART 4 OF EXECUTED BOND WITH APPLICABLE SECURITY —PARTS 1, 2, 3, 4 OF VOIDED BOND (DO NOT DESTROY)
- REMOVE THIS TAB BEFORE FILING PARTS 1-3 WITH CUSTOMS

In order to secure payment of any duty, tax or charge and compliance with law or regulation as a result of activity covered by any condition referenced below, we, the below named principal(s) and surety(ies), bind ourselves to the United States in the amount or amounts, as set forth below.

Execution Date

SECTION I—Select Single Transaction OR Continuous Bond (not both) and fill in the applicable blank spaces.

SINGLE TRANSACTION BOND	Identification of transaction secured by this bond (e.g., entry no., seizure no., etc.)		Date of transaction	Transaction district & port code

CONTINUOUS BOND	Effective date	This bond remains in force for one year beginning with the effective date and for each succeeding annual period, or until terminated. This bond constitutes a separate bond for each period in the amounts listed below for liabilities that accrue in each period. The intention to terminate this bond must be conveyed within the time period and manner prescribed in the Customs Regulations.

SECTION II—This bond includes the following agreements.² (Check one box only, except that, 1a may be checked independently with or without 1, and 3a may be checked independently with or without 3. Line out all other parts of this section that are not used.)

Activity Code	Activity Name and Customs Regulations in which conditions codified	Limit of Liability	Activity Code	Activity Name and Customs Regulations in which conditions codified	Limit of Liability
1	Importer or broker 113.62		☐ 5	Public Gauger 113.67	N/A
☐ 1a	Drawback Payment Refunds 113.65		☐ 6	Wool & Fur Products Labeling Acts Importation (Single Entry Only) 113.68	N/A
2	Custodian of bonded merchandise .... 113.63 (includes bonded carriers, freight forwarders, cartmen and lightermen, all classes of warehouses, container station operators)	N/A	☐ 7	Bill of Lading (Single Entry Only) 113.69	N/A
			☐ 8	Detention of Copyrighted Material (Single Entry Only) 113.70	N/A
3	International Carrier 113.64	N/A	☐ 9	Neutrality (Single Entry Only) 113.74	N/A
☐ 3a	Instruments of International Traffic 113.66		☐ 10	Court Costs for Condemned Goods (Single Entry Only) 113.72	N/A
	Foreign Trade Zone Operator 113.73	N/A			

SECTION III—List below all tradenames or unincorporated divisions that will be permitted to obligate this bond in the principal's name including their Customs Identification Number(s).³ (If more space is needed, use Section III (Continuation) on back of form.)

Importer Number	Importer Name	Importer Number	Importer Name
N/A	N/A	N/A	N/A

Total number of importer names listed in Section III: N/A

Principal and surety agree that any charge against the under any of the listed names is as though it was by the principal(s).

Principal and surety agree that they are bound to the extent as if they executed a separate bond for each set of conditions incorporated by reference Customs Regulations into this bond.

If the surety fails to appoint an agent under Title 6, United States Code, Section 7, surety consents to service on the Clerk of any United States District Court or the U.S. Court of International Trade, where suit is brought on this bond. That clerk is to send notice of the service to the surety at:

Mailing Address Requested by the Surety

WASHINGTON INTERNATIONAL INSURANCE COMPANY
1930 THOREAU DRIVE   SUITE 101
SCHAUMBURG, IL 60173

Name and Address	Importer No.³	
	SIGNATURE⁴	SEAL

Name and Address	Importer No.³	
	SIGNATURE⁴	SEAL

Name and Address⁴	Surety No.⁷	
WASHINGTON INTERNATIONAL INSURANCE COMPANY (AN ARIZONA CORPORATION) 1930 THOREAU DRIVE SUITE 101 SCHAUMBURG, IL 60173	891 SIGNATURE⁵ *Karen Muck* Attorney-in-Fact POWER OF ATTORNEY LIMITED TO $300,000	CORPORATE SEAL

Name and Address⁴	Surety No.⁷	
	SIGNATURE⁵	SEAL

(f) Advices of the Port Director (—) _____.   (g) Other (—) _____.

A—Case marks numbers	B—Manufacturer's item No. symbol or brand	C—Quantities and full description	D—Unit purchase price (currency)	E—Total purchase price (currency)	F—Unit foreign value	G—Total foreign value
....	....	....	....	....	....	....
....	....	....	....	....	....	....

Check which of the charges below are, and which are not included in the prices listed in columns "D" and "E":

Amount	Included	Not included
Packing	....	....
Cartage	....	....
Inland freight	....	....
Wharfage and loading abroad ...	....	....
Lighterage	....	....
Ocean freight	....	....
U.S. duties	....	....
Other charges (identify by name and amount)	....	....
Total	....	....

· Country of origin _____
If any other invoice is received, I will immediately file it with the Port Director.

_____
(Signature of person making invoice)

_____
(Title and firm name)

Date _____

[T.D. 73–175, 38 FR 17447, July 2, 1973, as amended by T.D. 85–39, 50 FR 9612, Mar. 11, 1985; T.D. 95–78, 60 FR 50032, Sept. 27, 1995]

§ 141.86 Contents of invoices and general requirements.

(a) *General information required on the invoice.* Each invoice of imported merchandise, shall set forth the following information:

(1) The port of entry to which the merchandise is destined;

(2) The time when, the place where, and the person by whom and the person to whom the merchandise is sold or agreed to be sold, or if to be imported otherwise than in pursuance of a purchase, the place from which shipped, the time when and the person to whom and the person by whom it is shipped;

(3) A detailed description of the merchandise, including the name by which each item is known, the grade or quality, and the marks, numbers, and symbols under which sold by the seller or manufacturer to the trade in the country of exportation, together with the marks and numbers of the packages in which the merchandise is packed;

(4) The quantities in the weights and measures of the country or place from which the merchandise is shipped, or in the weights and measures of the United States;

(5) The purchase price of each item in the currency of the purchase, if the merchandise is shipped in pursuance of a purchase or an agreement to purchase;

(6) If the merchandise is shipped otherwise than in pursuance of a purchase or an agreement to purchase, the value for each item, in the currency in which the transactions are usually made, or, in the absence of such value, the price in such currency that the manufacturer, seller, shipper, or owner would have received, or was willing to receive, for such mer-

chandise if sold in the ordinary course of trade and in the usual wholesale quantities in the country of exportation;

(7) The kind of currency, whether gold, silver, or paper;

(8) All charges upon the merchandise itemized by name and amount, including freight, insurance, commission, cases, containers, coverings, and cost of packing; and if not included above, all charges, costs, and expenses incurred in bringing the merchandise from alongside the carrier at the port of exportation in the country of exportation and placing it alongside the carrier at the first United States port of entry. The cost of packing, cases, containers, and inland freight to the port of exportation need not be itemized by amount if included in the invoice price, and so identified. Where the required information does not appear on the invoice as originally prepared, it shall be shown on an attachment to the invoice;

(9) All rebates, drawbacks, and bounties, separately itemized, allowed upon the exportation of the merchandise;

(10) The country of origin of the merchandise; and,

(11) All goods or services furnished for the production of the merchandise (e.g., assists such as dies, molds, tools, engineering work) not included in the invoice price. However, goods or services furnished in the United States are excluded. Annual reports for goods and services, when approved by the port director, will be accepted as proof that the goods or services were provided.

(b) *Nonpurchased merchandise shipped by other than manufacturer.* Each invoice of imported merchandise shipped to a person in the United States by a person other than the manufacturer and otherwise than pursuant to a purchase or agreement to purchase shall set forth the time when, the place where, the person from whom such merchandise was purchased, and the price paid therefor in the currency of the purchase, stating whether gold, silver, or paper.

(c) *Merchandise sold in transit.* If the merchandise is sold on the documents while in transit from the port of exportation to the port of entry, the original invoice reflecting the transaction under which the merchandise actually began its journey to the United States, and the resale invoice or a statement of sale showing the price paid for each item by the purchaser, shall be filed as part of the entry, entry summary, or withdrawal documentation. If the original invoice cannot be obtained, a pro forma invoice showing the values and transaction reflected by the original invoice shall be filed together with the resale invoice or statement.

(d) *Invoice to be in English.* The invoice and all attachments shall be in the English language, or shall have attached thereto an accurate English translation containing adequate information for examination of the merchandise and determination of duties.

(e) *Packing list.* Each invoice shall state in adequate detail what merchandise is contained in each individual package.

(f) *Weights and measures.* If the invoice or entry does not disclose the weight, gage, or measure of the merchandise which is necessary to ascertain duties, the consignee shall pay the expense of weighing, gaging, or measuring prior to the release of the merchandise from Customs custody.

(g) *Discounts.* Each invoice shall set forth in detail, for each class or kind of merchandise, every discount from list or other base price which has been or may be allowed in fixing each purchase price or value.

(h) *Numbering of invoices and pages*—(1) *Invoices.* When more than one invoice is included in the same entry, each invoice with its attachments shall be numbered consecutively by the importer on the bottom of the face of each page, beginning with No. 1.

(2) *Pages.* If the invoice or invoices filed with one entry consist of more than two pages, each page shall be numbered consecutively by the importer on the bottom of the face of each page. The page numbering shall begin with No. 1 for the first page of the first invoice and continue in a single series of numbers through all the invoices and attachments included in one entry.

(3) *Both invoices and pages.* When applicable, both the invoice number and the page number shall be shown at the bottom of each page. For example, if an entry covers one invoice of one page and a second invoice of two pages, the numbering at the bottom of the pages shall be as follows:

Inv. 1, p. 1.
Inv. 2, p. 2.
Inv. 2, p. 3.

(i) *Information may be on invoice or attached thereto.* Any information required on an invoice by any provision of this subpart may be set forth either on the invoice or on an attachment thereto.

(j) *Name of responsible individual.* Each invoice of imported merchandise shall identify by name a responsible employee of the exporter, who has knowledge, or who can readily obtain knowledge, of the transaction.

[T.D. 73–175, 38 FR 17447, July 2, 1973, as amended by T.D. 79–221, 44 FR 46820, Aug. 9, 1979; T.D. 85–39, 50 FR 9612, Mar. 11, 1985; T.D. 95–78, 60 FR 50032, Sept. 27, 1995]

§ 141.87   Breakdown on component materials.

Whenever the classification or appraisement of merchandise depends on the component materials, the invoice shall set forth a breakdown giving the value, weight, or other necessary measurement of each component material in sufficient detail to determine the correct duties.

§ 141.88   Computed value.

When the port director determines that information as to computed value is necessary in the appraisement of any class or kind of merchandise, he shall so notify the importer, and thereafter invoices of such merchandise shall contain a verified statement by the manufacturer or producer of computed value as defined in § 402(e), Tariff Act of 1930, as amended by the Trade Agreements Act of 1979 (19 U.S.C. 1401a(e)).

[T.D. 87–89, 52 FR 24445, July 1, 1987; T.D. 95–78, 60 FR 50032, Sept. 27, 1995]

§ 141.89   Additional information for certain classes of merchandise.

(a) Invoices for the following classes of merchandise, classifiable under the Harmonized Tariff Schedule of the United States (HTSUS), shall set forth the additional information specified: [75–42, 75–239, 78–53, 83–251, 84–149.]

Aluminum and alloys of aluminum classifiable under subheadings 7601.10.60, 7601.20.60, 7601.20.90, or 7602.00.00, HTSUS (T.D. 53092, 55977, 56143)—Statement of the percentages by weight of any metallic element contained in the article.

Articles manufactured of textile materials, Coated or laminated with plastics or rubber, classifiable in Chapter(s) 39, 40, and 42—Include a description indicating whether the fabric is coated or laminated on both sides, on the exterior surface or on the interior surface.

Bags manufactured of plastic sheeting and not of a reinforced or laminated construction, classified in Chapter 39 or in heading 4202—Indicate the gauge of the plastic sheeting.

Ball or roller bearings classifiable under subheading 8482.10.50 through 8482.80.00, HTSUS (T.D. 68–306)—(1) Type of bearing (i.e. whether a ball or roller bearing); (2) If a roller bearing, whether a spherical, tapered, cylindrical, needled or other type; (3) Whether a combination bearing (i.e. a bearing containing both ball and roller bearings, etc.); and (4) If a ball bearing (not including ball bearing with integral shafts or parts of ball bearings), whether or not radial, the following: (a) outside diameter of each bearing; and (b) whether or not a radial bearing (the definition of radial bearing is, for Customs purposes, an antifriction bearing primarily designed to support a load perpendicular to shaft axis).

Beads (T.D. 50088, 55977)—(1) The length of the string, if strung; (2) The size of the beads expressed in millimeters; (3) The material of which the beads are composed, i.e. ivory, glass, imitation pearl, etc.

Bed linen and Bedspreads—Statement as to whether or not the article contains any embroidery, lace, braid, edging, trimming, piping or applique work.

Chemicals—Furnish the use and Chemical Abstracts Service number of chemical compounds classified in Chapters 27, 28 and 29, HTSUS.

Colors, dyes, stains and related products provided for under heading 3204, HTSUS—The following information is required: (1) Invoice name of product; (2) Trade name of product; (3) Identity and percent by weight of each component; (4) Color Index number (if none, so state); (5) Color Index generic name (if none so state); (6) Chemical Abstracts Service number of the active ingredient; (7) Class of merchandise (state whether acid type dye, basic dye, disperse dye, fluorescent brightener, soluble dye, vat dye, toner or other (describe); (8) Material to which applied (name the material for which the color, dye, or toner is primarily designed).

Copper (T.D. 45878, 50158, 55977) articles classifiable under the provisions of Chapter 74, HTSUS—A statement of the weight of articles of copper, and a statement of percentage of copper content and all other elements—by weight—to articles classifiable according to copper content.

Copper ores and concentrates (T.D. 45878, 50158, 55977) classifiable in heading 2603, and subheadings 2620.19.60, 2620.20.00, 2620.30.00, and heading 7401—Statement of the percentages by weight of the copper content and any other metallic elements.

Cotton fabrics classifiable under the following HTSUS headings: 5208, 5209, 5210, 5211, and 5212—(1) Marks on shipping packages; (2) Numbers on shipping packages; (3) Customer's call number, if any; (4) Exact width of the merchandise; (5) Detailed description of the merchandise; trade name, if any; whether bleached, unbleached, printed, composed of yarns of different color, or dyed; if composed of cotton and other materials, state the percentage of each component material by weight; (6) Number of single threads per

Invoice Requirements

General Information

Each invoice of imported merchandise must set forth the following information:

1. The port of entry to which the merchandise is destined.

2. If merchandise is sold or agreed to be sold, the time, place, names of buyer and seller. If consigned, the time and origin of shipment, and names of shipper and receiver.

3. A detailed description of the merchandise including:
   - The name by which each item is known
   - The grade or quality
   - Marks, numbers, and symbols under which sold by the seller or manufacturer to the trade in the country of exportation
   - Marks and numbers of the packages in which the merchandise is packed

4. The quantities in weights and measures.

5. If sold or agreed to be sold, the purchase price of each item in the currency of the sale.

6. If the merchandise is shipped on consignment, the value of each item in the currency in which the transactions are usually made or, in the absence of such value, the price in such currency that the manufacturer, seller, shipper, or owner would have received or was willing to receive, for such merchandise if sold in the ordinary course of trade and in the usual wholesale quantities in the country of exportation.

7. The kind of currency (yen/U.S. dollars, etc.).

8. All charges upon the merchandise, itemized by name and amount including:
   - Actual amount of freight
   - Actual amount of insurance
   - Actual amount of any commission paid
   - Actual cost of packing
   - All charges, costs, and expenses incurred in bringing the merchandise from alongside the carrier at the port of exportation in the country of exportation and placing it alongside the carrier at the first U.S. port of entry

9. All rebates, drawbacks, and bounties, separately itemized, allowed upon the exportation.

10. The country of origin (manufacture).

11. All cost for goods or services furnished for the production of the merchandise not included in the invoice price. These costs

are termed "assists" and defined as dies, molds, tooling, printing plates, artwork, engineering work, design, and development, financial assistance, etc.

12. Must state in adequate detail the packing information (what merchandise is contained in each individual package).

13. Set forth in detail for each class or kind of merchandise every discount from list or other base price that has been or may be allowed in fixing each price or value.

14. Must be in the English language or shall have attached thereto an accurate English translation containing adequate information for examination of the merchandise and determination of duties.

15. Shall identify by name a responsible employee of the exporter who has knowledge or who can readily obtain knowledge of the transaction.

Additional Information

Special information is required on certain goods or classes of goods in addition to the general information outlined previously.

Frequent Errors in Invoicing

The fundamental rule is that the shipper and importer must furnish customs with all pertinent information with respect to each import transaction to assist customs in determining the tariff status of the goods. Some examples of omissions and inaccuracies to be avoided are:

1. On CIF transactions, actual prepaid amounts for freight and insurance are not shown. In many situations only estimated amounts are shown. In others, none are shown.

2. The shipper assumes that a commission, royalty, or other charges against the goods is a so-called nondutiable item and omits it from the invoice.

3. A foreign shipper who purchases goods and sells them to a U.S. importer at a delivered price shows on the invoice the cost of the goods to him instead of the delivered price.

Valuation Verifications

Transaction value

Transaction value of identical or similar value

Deductive value

Computed value

Derived value

Methods of valuation are contained in the preceeding hierarchy. Knowledge of this order is essential in the comprehension of proper valuation concepts as outlined in CFR 152.

All transactions contain a term of sale:

CIF duty paid

CIF

CF

FOB

FAS

Ex-Works

Verifications must be made to determine the correct term of sale for every invoice and every import declaration of merchandise.

Proper deductions from price can only be calculated after categorizing the proper term of sale through solid identification from the commercial or proforma invoice. For example, prepaid freight, insurance, duty paid calculations, are nondutiable charges. Foreign loading and foreign inland freight and packing are subject to duty charges.

COMMERCIAL INVOICE

04-10-93

INVOICE #001

MANUFACTURER/SHIPPER

MAXIMUM COMPUTER COMPANY
300 AVENUE SEELES
STUTTGART, GERMANY

IMPORTER OF RECORD

ABC COMPUTER COMPANY OF AMERICA
100 CENTER STREET
PRINCETON, NJ 00675

FIFTY (50) CARTONS CONTAINING: COMPUTER PARTS   C.I.F. VALUE: $15,775.00

INSURANCE: $75.00

PREPAID FREIGHT: $700.00

GROSS WEIGHT: 250 KGS   NET WEIGHT: 200 KGS

SERIAL NUMBER: 2354667

TRUE AND CORRECT

DAVID SINCLAIR
MAXIMUM COMPUTER COMPANY

U.S. Customs Service Regulatory Audit General Compliance Assessment Questionnaire for Importer Audits

A. General Organizational Information.

Please provide the following information on the organization of your company:

1. Description of overall organization structure, organization charts, and similar information.
2. Company's full name and IRS identification number(s).
3. Name and title of the company's officers.
4. Name, title, and telephone number of the person who will be the U.S. Customs contact during the review.
5. Name, title, and telephone number of the official(s) preparing information for this questionnaire.
6. General information on company operations such as a description of business operations, number of employees, location of facilities and related operations, products, divisions, and customers.
7. Names and addresses of any other U.S. and foreign-related companies (as defined in section 152.102(g) of the Customs Regulations).
8. Similar material as items 1 through 6 for the company's parent, sister, subsidiary, and joint venture organizations and relationships.
9. Name and contact person for internal preparer of year end financial statements.
10. Name and contact person for external financial auditors, such as a certified public accountant, and authorization to contact those auditors.

B. Customs-Related Activities.

1. Identify the organizational element (departments, divisions, subsidiaries, etc.) involved in customs-related operations.
2. List names under which the company imports. Does the company import under a broker's bond?
3. List customs identification numbers and suffixes (importer ID numbers) applicable to customs-related business and the organizational element that imports under each number or suffix.
4. List the names and locator information for key individuals associated with customs-related operations.
5. List the name(s) and addresses of broker(s) your company uses.
6. Provide the names and addresses of all foreign sellers and suppliers.
7. Describe the disposition of imported products (manufacturing, resale, etc.).
8. Identify and explain situations in which the company *exports* merchandise from the United States.

9. Identify situations in which the company *imports* merchandise in accordance with binding rulings received from customs.

C. Recordkeeping System.

The Tariff Act of 1930 as amended (Title 19 USC 1508) establishes recordkeeping requirements for organizations dealing in customs operations. Organizations conducting customs-related operations are required to maintain and produce records that are normally kept in the ordinary course of business. During the audit, specific recordkeeping requirements that are being defined in accordance with the Customs Modernization Act will be discussed.

Describe the recordkeeping system supporting customs-related operations, including accounting and financial recordkeeping systems, documents, and information. This information may be available in the company's internal procedures manuals. Include the following:

1. The identity of the source records and information used to prepare customs information. Please explain how they are created, maintained, and transferred to and from originating, using, and storing organizations. Please provide other information necessary to understand operating procedures and associated internal controls over record production and retention.
2. Location of records. If records are maintained at multiple locations, list each location by address and identify documents and information at each. Include the name and telephone number of the contact person at each location.
3. Procedures or techniques to link records and information to customs entry submissions.
4. Retention period. Length of time records are retained within department before moving to storage and length of time retained in storage.
5. Storage medium.
6. Retrieval procedures with contact names and phone numbers.
7. Description of alternative storage procedures (conversion and maintenance of information in other than original formats), if applicable.
8. Internal and management controls concerning recordkeeping practices.
9. Other appropriate information.
10. A description of the company's accounting and financial system as it relates to and supports customs-related operations.
11. The company's fiscal year.
12. General ledger accounts typically used to record customs-related transactions.

D. Internal Controls.
1. Provide the company's formal policies and procedures manuals or other written directives related to the handling of customs matters and documents. If there are no formal written procedures, provide a written summary of your procedures for ensuring compliance with customs laws, regulations, and rulings.
2. If transaction value is the method of appraisement, explain procedures to ensure that import values reported to customs accurately reflect the price actually paid or payable for the imported merchandise. Explain procedures to assure that indirect and additional payments are included in the transaction value.
3. Explain procedures to ensure that assists, commissions, royalties, license fees, freight, and other dutiable costs are correctly reported to customs.
4. Explain procedures to ensure that import quantities reported to customs are accurate. Include procedures for reporting overages and shortages of merchandise receipts.
5. Explain procedures to ensure that nondutiable costs such as international freight and insurance are accurate and fully supported by documentation.
6. Explain procedures to ensure that harbor maintenance fees and merchandise processing fees are accurately calculated and timely paid on imports. Explain procedures to ensure that harbor maintenance fees are accurately calculated and timely paid on admissions to the foreign trade zones, domestic shipments, and exports. See section 24.24 of the Customs Regulations.
7. Explain procedures to ensure that imported merchandise is accurately classified and all admissibility requirements are met. List other agencies for which compliance requirements on importations must be met.
8. If different procedures are used for nonrelated and related foreign sellers, explain the procedures used for each.
9. Explain the company's merchandise entry procedures. For example, does the company rely exclusively on a customs broker to fulfill all of the company's responsibilities related to customs, or does the company maintain an internal staff responsible for conducting customs entry operations? If an internal staff is maintained, provide the names of the individuals, a description of the job performed by each, and identify those who have a customs license and provide the license number.
10. Provide and explain results of evaluations of the effectiveness of the company's system of internal controls, particularly with respect to customs-related operations. Please include evaluations by internal or independent parties.

E. Customs Value Information and Company Internal Procedures for Import-Related Operations

1. Identify the method of appraisement, as prescribed in sections 152.103 through 152.108 of the Customs Regulations, used to value imported merchandise from each of your major suppliers (consider any supplier who provides 10 percent or more of the total value of your importations as a major supplier).

2. If transaction value is used for importations from related parties, do the importations qualify for transaction value based on the circumstances of the sale or on the basis of test values? Provide an explanation and support documentation for the method that you use to support transaction value.

3. Describe how prices for imported merchandise from major suppliers are determined.

4. If the company is an exclusive U.S. importer of merchandise from foreign suppliers, explain the circumstances of sale and relationships with the foreign suppliers. Provide written agreements, if applicable.

5. If applicable, identify situations in which foreign *related* suppliers sell the same or similar merchandise to other U.S. companies.

6. Explain how and when the company takes title to the imported merchandise. Explain differences that may exist between different importing situations.

7. Explain transportation procedures and responsibilities for foreign, international, and domestic transportation of merchandise from the foreign plant to the place of international shipment, to the port of importation, and to the final U.S. destination. Include explanations and information concerning responsibilities for foreign inland freight charges. For example, is foreign inland freight included on the invoice with the merchandise or is it invoiced separately? If included on the invoice with the merchandise, is it separately identified or included with the charge for international freight? Identify general ledger accounts used to record the various freight charges.

8. Explain contractual agreements between the company or foreign suppliers with shippers or freight forwarders. Identify and explain any rebates received by the company or foreign affiliate from shippers or freight forwarders. Identify general ledger accounts used to record rebates, if any.

9. Identify and explain loans payable to or receivable from foreign suppliers and sellers.

10. Identify situations in which the merchandise price from the foreign seller does not include all costs plus a profit.

11. Identify and explain retroactive price increases or adjustments for imported merchandise at the end of the accounting period or other times that are paid to or accrue to the

company and/or the foreign supplier. Identify the general ledger accounts used to record the transactions.

12. Explain procedures and accounting for foreign currency fluctuations. Identify general ledger accounts used to record the fluctuations.

13. Identify and explain situations in which the company receives price adjustments, variances, rebates, or allowances directly or indirectly from foreign exporters or sellers. Identify the general ledger accounts used to record the transactions.

14. Identify and explain payments to foreign companies for expenses other than imported merchandise, such as management fees, research and development, tooling, and similar matters. Identify general ledger accounts used to record the transactions.

15. Identify and explain situations in which the foreign seller influences or controls the resale price of merchandise imported into the United States.

16. Identify and explain situations in which prices for imported merchandise are subject to restrictions or conditions as explained in sections 152.103(j)(1)(i–iv) of the Customs Regulations.

17. Describe how packing costs are calculated and declared to customs in accordance with section 152.103(b)(1)(i) of the Customs Regulations. Identify general ledger accounts where packing costs are recorded.

18. Identify and explain situations in which the company uses the services of foreign selling agents. Explain procedures for declaring selling commissions on entries in accordance with section 152.103(b)(1)(ii) of the Customs Regulations. Provide names and addresses of agents and agency agreements, and identify the general ledger accounts used to record commissions and related transactions.

19. Identify and explain situations in which the company provides assists to foreign suppliers in accordance with 152.103(b)(1)(iii) and 152.103(d) of the Customs Regulations. Describe the form of any assists (tools, molds, fabrics, loans, design and engineering costs, machinery used in production, etc.), their values, and identify general ledger accounts used to record the transactions.

20. Identify and explain situations in which *third parties* provide assists to foreign suppliers in accordance with 152.103(b)(1)(iii) and 152.103(d) of the Customs Regulations. Describe the form of any assists (tools, molds, fabrics, loans, design and engineering costs, machinery used in production, etc.), their values, and identify general ledger accounts in which the transactions are recorded.

21. Identify and explain situations in which royalties or license fees were paid for importer merchandise. Provide copies of

the royalty or license agreement. Identify the general ledger accounts used to record the transactions.

22. Identify and explain situations in which proceeds of any subsequent resale, disposal, or use of the imported merchandise accrue directly or indirectly to the seller. Identify the general ledger accounts used to record the transaction and provide documentation on how the proceeds are calculated.

23. Identify and explain situations in which the company makes indirect payments to foreign sellers as covered by section 152.103(a)(2) of the Customs Regulations? Include supporting documentation, agreements, and the identity of general ledger accounts used to record the transactions.

24. Identify and explain the company's usual form of payment (e.g., letters of credit, wire transfers, checks, open accounts, etc.) for imported merchandise. Explain whether the payment is made in U.S. dollars or in a foreign currency, frequency of payments made to foreign sellers, and the identity of general ledger accounts used to record the payments.

25. If applicable, explain circumstances and responsibilities for obtaining and paying for quota, visa, and licenses. Identify general ledger accounts used to record the payments.

ATTACHMENT 3

U.S. CUSTOMS SERVICE
REGULATORY AUDIT
EDP QUESTIONNAIRE

Please provide the following information regarding your Electronic Data Processing equipment and system.

<u>EDP Department Contact Person and Phone Number:</u>

_____

<u>Equipment:</u>

Computer Manufacturer:_____

Model:_____

Type of Equipment (LAN/WAN, Mini, Mainframe, IBM/Apple PC): _____

_____

<u>Peripheral Devices:</u>

Tape Drives:_____(Density)

Disk Drives:_____(Model)

Operating System(s):_____

Program Development Environment (TSO/ISPF, Roscoe, Etc.): _____

Current Version of COBOL Compiler: _____

Retrieval Software Available (Easytrieve, DYL280, SQL, RPG, SAS, Etc.): _____

Utilities (SyncSort, DFSort, IBM OS Utilities, Etc.): _____

Accounting Software Package: _____

Management Information System:

    Contact Name: _____

    Phone Number: _____

IRS Record Retention Agreement: _____ Yes _____ No _____ Pending

What Records are Kept Electronically (accounts payable, cash disbursements, inventory

records of receipts, withdrawals, and balances, etc.): _____

_____

_____

For Each Record System, provide the following information:
    Record layout
    Field identification
    Period of active retention on electronic media
    Period of retrievable retention on electronic media
    Established key fields for data base queries

Please provide a copy of your internal control procedures for EDP operations.

Harmonize Tariff Schedule of the United States (HTSUS)

Explanation and Use Exercise

The HTSUS is a very thick reference and guide to proper classification of merchandise upon entry into the United States. All articles subject to customs clearance needs to be properly classified prior to such clearance. The customs service takes great care in the annual preparation and update of this book and expects reasonable care to be used in referencing this book for classification purposes.

Book Format

The HTSUS has many key components to assist you in obtaining proper harmonize classifications. Lets take a look at these components now!

General Rules of Interpretation (GRI)

The GRI is found at the front of the book and is relied upon greatly in the determination of proper classification techniques. Classification itself is not an exact science. In many cases, an entry writer is asked to interpret the determining factors of what is being imported to properly classify the imported goods. Because different individuals may "interpret" imported items of description and usage in many different ways as to effect the classification, customs uses the GRI as a formal guide of interpretation. Read the GRI carefully and memorize them. It is essential to proper classification to do so.

General Notes

General Notes are located next in the HTSUS to provide ease in the usage of the book as well as provide a definitive explanation and analysis to special tariff treaty programs. It is important to be familiar with these notes to ensure proper classification techniques. Each general note is essential to classification clarity and understanding.

Chapters and Chapter Notes

The HTSUS is formatted in numerical order by chapters. Each chapter deals with a specific class of commodities. Each chapter is preceded by

chapter notes, which provide a more defined level of understanding on individual chapters, for classification purposes. Inclusions to and exclusions from a chapter are found here. Key definitions to terms and descriptions are also outlined in the chapter notes. Prior to selecting any HT-SUS ten-digit number it is essential to read the related chapter note for any required reference to the imported or classifiable items.

Alphabetical Index

The alphabetical index is located in the back of the book and is the guide to quickly and correctly access the proper chapter for classification purposes. The index contains commodity descriptions of everything that you could possible think of. To classify an item, look in this index to reference the description. The index provides at least the first two letters of the ten-digit HTSUS number. In most cases the first four digits are provided.

Techniques of Usage of the HTSUS

The most difficult task in proper HTSUS classification is to determine what it is that you are classifying. In that determination, one must consider the GRI for interpretation. Once you have decided what you are classifying, reference the alphabetical index for a "hint or clue" (the first four digits of the HTSUS). This will direct you to the the numerical chapter in the HTSUS where the goods are described. Next, reference the chapter notes to verify any exclusions or inclusions to the chapter. The HTSTS number is a ten-digit number. You have not properly classified something until you have reached a tenth digit in its classification.

HTSUS Page Outline/Description

Heading and subheading = the first eight digits of the HTSUS number.

Statistical suffix = the last two digits in the HTSUS number.

Article description = A detailed description of articles for classification purposes.

Rates of duty
General column = rate of duty originating in a most-favored nation (see the general notes for a detailed analysis).
Special column = rate of duty originating in a county under a special tariff treaty program.
Column 2 = rate of duty on goods originating in an unfavored nation (see the General notes for detailed analysis).

Gen.Rs.Int.

GENERAL RULES OF INTERPRETATION

Classification of goods in the tariff schedule shall be governed by the following principles:

1. The table of contents, alphabetical index, and titles of sections, chapters and sub-chapters are provided for ease of reference only; for legal purposes, classification shall be determined according to the terms of the headings and any relative section or chapter notes and, provided such headings or notes do not otherwise require, according to the following provisions:

2. (a) Any reference in a heading to an article shall be taken to include a reference to that article incomplete or unfinished, provided that, as entered, the incomplete or unfinished article has the essential character of the complete or finished article. It shall also include a reference to that article complete or finished (or falling to be classified as complete or finished by virtue of this rule), entered unassembled or disassembled.

    (b) Any reference in a heading to a material or substance shall be taken to include a reference to mixtures or combinations of that material or substance with other materials or substances. Any reference to goods of a given material or substance shall be taken to include a reference to goods consisting wholly or partly of such material or substance. The classification of goods consisting of more than one material or substance shall be according to the principles of rule 3.

3. When, by application of rule 2(b) or for any other reason, goods are, *prima facie*, classifiable under two or more headings, classification shall be effected as follows:

    (a) The heading which provides the most specific description shall be preferred to headings providing a more general description. However, when two or more headings each refer to part only of the materials or substances contained in mixed or composite goods or to part only of the items in a set put up for retail sale, those headings are to be regarded as equally specific in relation to those goods, even if one of them gives a more complete or precise description of the goods.

    (b) Mixtures, composite goods consisting of different materials or made up of different components, and goods put up in sets for retail sale, which cannot be classified by reference to 3(a), shall be classified as if they consisted of the material or component which gives them their essential character, insofar as this criterion is applicable.

    (c) When goods cannot be classified by reference to 3(a) or 3(b), they shall be classified under the heading which occurs last in numerical order among those which equally merit consideration.

4. Goods which cannot be classified in accordance with the above rules shall be classified under the heading appropriate to the goods to which they are most akin.

5. In addition to the foregoing provisions, the following rules shall apply in respect of the goods referred to therein:

    (a) Camera cases, musical instrument cases, gun cases, drawing instrument cases, necklace cases and similar containers, specially shaped or fitted to contain a specific article or set of articles, suitable for long-term use and entered with the articles for which they are intended, shall be classified with such articles when of a kind normally sold therewith. This rule does not, however, apply to containers which give the whole its essential character;

    (b) Subject to the provisions of rule 5(a) above, packing materials and packing containers entered with the goods therein shall be classified with the goods if they are of a kind normally used for packing such goods. However, this provision is not binding when such packing materials or packing containers are clearly suitable for repetitive use.

6. For legal purposes, the classification of goods in the subheadings of a heading shall be determined according to the terms of those subheadings and any related subheading notes and, *mutatis mutandis*, to the above rules, on the understanding that only subheadings at the same level are comparable. For the purposes of this rule, the relative section, chapter and subchapter notes also apply, unless the context otherwise requires.

HARMONIZED TARIFF SCHEDULE of the United States (1999)

Annotated for Statistical Reporting Purposes

Add.U.S.Rs.Int.

ADDITIONAL U.S. RULES OF INTERPRETATION

1. In the absence of special language or context which otherwise requires--

    (a) a tariff classification controlled by use (other than actual use) is to be determined in accordance with the use in the United States at, or immediately prior to, the date of importation, of goods of that class or kind to which the imported goods belong, and the controlling use is the principal use;

    (b) a tariff classification controlled by the actual use to which the imported goods are put in the United States is satisfied only if such use is intended at the time of importation, the goods are so used and proof thereof is furnished within 3 years after the date the goods are entered;

    (c) a provision for parts of an article covers products solely or principally used as a part of such articles but a provision for "parts" or "parts and accessories" shall not prevail over a specific provision for such part or accessory; and

    (d) the principles of section XI regarding mixtures of two or more textile materials shall apply to the classification of goods in any provision in which a textile material is named.

HARMONIZED TARIFF SCHEDULE of the United States
Annotated for Statistical Reporting Purposes

GNs 1–3(a)(iv)(B)

GENERAL NOTES

1. <u>Tariff Treatment of Imported Goods and of Vessel Equipments, Parts and Repairs</u>. All goods provided for in this schedule and imported into the customs territory of the United States from outside thereof, and all vessel equipments, parts, materials and repairs covered by the provisions of subchapter XVIII to chapter 98 of this schedule, are subject to duty or exempt therefrom as prescribed in general notes 3 through 14, inclusive, and general note 16.

2. <u>Customs Territory of the United States</u>. The term "customs territory of the United States", as used in the tariff schedule, includes only the States, the District of Columbia and Puerto Rico.

3. <u>Rates of Duty</u>. The rates of duty in the "Rates of Duty" columns designated 1 ("General" and "Special") and 2 of the tariff schedule apply to goods imported into the customs territory of the United States as hereinafter provided in this note:

   (a)   Rate of Duty Column 1.

   (i)   Except as provided in subparagraph (iv) of this paragraph, the rates of duty in column 1 are rates which are applicable to all products other than those of countries enumerated in paragraph (b) of this note. Column 1 is divided into two subcolumns, "General" and "Special", which are applicable as provided below.

   (ii)   The "<u>General</u>" subcolumn sets forth the general most-favored-nation (MFN) rates which are applicable to products of those countries described in subparagraph (i) above which are not entitled to special tariff treatment as set forth below.

   (iii) The "<u>Special</u>" subcolumn reflects rates of duty under one or more special tariff treatment programs described in paragraph (c) of this note and identified in parentheses immediately following the duty rate specified in such subcolumn. These rates apply to those products which are properly classified under a provision for which a special rate is indicated and for which all of the legal requirements for eligibility for such program or programs have been met. Where a product is eligible for special treatment under more than one program, the lowest rate of duty provided for any applicable program shall be imposed. Where no special rate of duty is provided for a provision, or where the country from which a product otherwise eligible for special treatment was imported is not designated as a beneficiary country under a program appearing with the appropriate provision, the rates of duty in the "General" subcolumn of column 1 shall apply.

   (iv)   <u>Products of Insular Possessions</u>.

   (A)   Except as provided in additional U.S. note 5 of chapter 91 and except as provided in additional U.S. note 2 of chapter 96, and except as provided in section 423 of the Tax Reform Act of 1986, goods imported from insular possessions of the United States which are outside the customs territory of the United States are subject to the rates of duty set forth in column 1 of the tariff schedule, except that all such goods the growth or product of any such possession, or manufactured or produced in any such possession from materials the growth, product or manufacture of any such possession or of the customs territory of the United States, or of both, which do not contain foreign materials to the value of more than 70 percent of their total value (or more than 50 percent of their total value with respect to goods described in section 213(b) of the Caribbean Basin Economic Recovery Act), coming to the customs territory of the United States directly from any such possession, and all goods previously imported into the customs territory of the United States with payment of all applicable duties and taxes imposed upon or by reason of importation which were shipped from the United States, without remission, refund or drawback of such duties or taxes, directly to the possession from which they are being returned by direct shipment, are exempt from duty.

   (B)   In determining whether goods produced or manufactured in any such insular possession contain foreign materials to the value of more than 70 percent, no material shall be considered foreign which either—

   (1)   at the time such goods are entered, or

   (2)   at the time such material is imported into the insular possession,

HARMONIZED TARIFF SCHEDULE of the United States
Annotated for Statistical Reporting Purposes

GN 3(c)(ii)(A)—3(iv)

(A) if a rate of duty for which the article may be eligible is set forth in the "Special" subcolumn in chapter 99 followed by one or more symbols described above, such rate shall apply in lieu of the rate followed by the corresponding symbol(s) set forth for such article in the "Special" subcolumn in chapters 1 to 98; or

(B) if "No change" appears in the "Special" subcolumn in chapter 99 and subdivision (c)(ii)(A) above does not apply, the rate of duty in the "General" subcolumn in chapter 99 or the applicable rate(s) of duty set forth in the "Special" subcolumn in chapters 1 to 98, whichever is lower, shall apply.

(iii) Unless the context requires otherwise, articles which are eligible for the special tariff treatment provided for in general notes 4 through 14 and which are subject to temporary modification under any provision of subchapters III or IV of chapter 99 shall be subject, for the period indicated in chapter 99, to the rates of duty in the "General" subcolumn in such chapter.

(iv) Whenever any rate of duty set forth in the "Special" subcolumn in chapters 1 to 98 is equal to or higher than, the corresponding rate of duty provided in the "General" subcolumn in such chapters, such rate of duty in the "Special" subcolumn shall be deleted; except that, if the rate of duty in the "Special" subcolumn is an intermediate stage in a series of staged rate reductions for that provision, such rate shall be treated as a suspended rate and shall be set forth in the "Special" subcolumn, followed by one or more symbols described above, and followed by an "s" in parentheses. If no rate of duty for which the article may be eligible is provided in the "Special" subcolumn for a particular provision in chapters 1 to 98, the rate of duty provided in the "General" subcolumn shall apply.

HARMONIZED TARIFF SCHEDULE of the United States
Annotated for Statistical Reporting Purposes

ALPHABETICAL INDEX

HARMONIZED TARIFF SCHEDULE of the United States
Annotated for Statistical Reporting Purposes

XVI
84-80

Heading/ Subheading	Stat. Suf- fix	Article Description	Units of Quantity	Rates of Duty 1 General	Rates of Duty 1 Special	2
8472		Other office machines (for example, hectograph or stencil duplicating machines, addressing machines, automatic banknote dispensers, coin-sorting machines, coin-counting or wrapping machines, pencil-sharpening machines, perforating or stapling machines):				
8472.10.00	00	Duplicating machines...........................	No......	2.6%	Free (A,CA,E,IL,J, MX)	25%
8472.20.00	00	Addressing machines and address plate embossing machines...........................	No......	3.4%	Free (A,CA,E,IL,J, MX)	25%
8472.30.00	00	Machines for sorting or folding mail or for inserting mail in envelopes or bands, machines for opening, closing or sealing mail and machines for affixing or canceling postage stamps...............................	No......	2.9%	Free (A,CA,E,IL,J, MX)	35%
8472.90 8472.90.20		Other: Automatic banknote dispensers and other coin or currency handling machines.......	....	2.9%	Free (A,CA,E,IL,J, MX)	35%
	10	Automatic banknote dispensers....... Other:	No.			
	20	Coin and currency handling machines......................	No.			
	30	Other...........................	No.			
8472.90.40	00	Pencil sharpeners......................	No......	4.2%	Free (A,CA,E,IL,J, MX)	40%
8472.90.60	00	Numbering, dating and check-writing machines...............................	No......	Free		25%
8472.90.70	00	Accessory and auxiliary machines which are intended for attachment to an electrostatic photocopier and which do not operate independently of such photocopier........	No......	Free		35%
8472.90.90	00	Other...................................	No......	2.9%	Free (A,CA,E,IL, J,MX)	35%

ATA Carnet

ATA
Carnet
USA

Carnet De Passage En Douane For Temporary Admission

Where to Sign an ATA Carnet

Definitions

Certificate: A yellow, white, or blue perforated sheet used to enter, exit, or transit a Carnet country. Certificates consist of a counterfoil and voucher. USE ALL CERTIFICATES IN NUMBER SEQUENCE.
Counterfoil: The section of the certificate above the perforation.
Holder: A corporation or individual on whose behalf the Carnet has been issued.
Voucher: The section of the certificate below the perforation.

Holder	Customs Inspector
Front Green Cover	
Holder must sign in the lower right hand box, on the line between the two "X's, marked "Signature of Holder."	U.S. Customs should complete and stamp the lower left hand box, "Certificate by Customs Authorities."
Yellow Exportation Certificate	
On the voucher, complete sections D–F, located on the left hand column, as well as the lower right corner, below the shaded box.	U.S. Customs should complete and stamp the counterfoil and the "For Customs Use Only" section of the voucher. Generally, USCS does **not** remove the voucher.
White Importation Certificate	
On the voucher, the Holder must complete sections D–F, located on the left hand column, as well as the lower right corner, below the shaded box.	Foreign Customs should complete and stamp the counterfoil and the "For Customs Use Only," secton of the voucher. The customs inspector should then remove the voucher. **Note:** Be sure to comply with "Final Date for Re-exportation" on the counterfoil.
White Re-Exportation Certificate	
On the voucher, the Holder must complete sections D–F, located on the left hand column, as well as the lower right corner, below the shaded box.	Foreign Customs should complete and stamp the counterfoil and the "For Customs Use Only," section of the voucher. The customs inspector should then remove the voucher.
Blue Transit Certificates	
Holders must complete sections D–F, located on the left hand column, as well as the lower right corner, below the shaded box.	**At the time of Entry** Foreign Customs will complete and stamp the sections of the counterfoil and voucher entitled, "Clearance for Transit," indicating which goods have entered, the port to which the goods are being dispatched, final date that the goods must exit that port. The customs inspector will then remove the voucher. **At the time of Departure** Foreign Customs at the port of discharge will complete and stamp the sections of both the counterfoil and voucher entitled, "Certificate of Discharge." The customs inspector will then remove the second voucher.
Yellow Re-Importation Certificate	
On the voucher, the Holder must complete sections D–F, as well as the lower right corner below the shaded box.	U.S. Customs will complete the counterfoil and the section of the voucher entitled"For Customs Use Only." The customs inspector should then remove the voucher.

Complete details on the handling of a Carnet are located on the inside of the blue jacket of the ATA Carnet.

For more information contact:
USCIB ATA Carnet Customer Service Department
212-354-4480 or atacarnet@uscib.org

INTERNATIONAL GUARANTEE CHAIN ·················· ·············· INTERNATIONAL GUARANTEE CHAIN
CHAINE DE GARANTIE INTERNATIONALE *CHAINE DE GARANTIE INTERNATIONALE*

GENERAL LIST / *LISTE GENERALE*
(May be used for Continuation Sheets / *Feuille Supplementaire*)

X.. X

Signature of Holder / *Signature du titulaire*

....
Signature of authorized official and stamp of the Issuing Association /
Signature du delegué et timbre de L'association emettrice

VOUCHER No.	CONTINUATION SHEET No.	A.T.A. Carnet No.
VOLET DE No.	*FEUILLE SUPPLEMENTAIRE No.*	*Carnet A.T.A. No.*

Item No./ *No. d'ordre*	Trade description of goods and marks and numbers, if any/ *Désignation commerciale des marchandises et, le cas échéant, marques et numéros*	Number of Pieces/ *Nombre de Pièces*	Weight or Volume/ *Poids ou Volume*	**Country of origin/ *Value/ *Valeur*	For Customs Use/ *Pays d'origine*	Réservé à la douane
1	2	3	4	5	6	7
TOTAL CARRIED OVER / *REPORT*						

General List includes ———(number) "Continuation Sheets".

TOTAL or CARRIED OVER / *TOTAL ou A REPORTER*						

*Commercial value in country of issue and in the currency, unless stated differently. / *Valeur commerciale dans le pays d'émission et dans sa monnaie sauf indication contraire.*
**Show country of origin if different from country of issue of theCarnet, using ISO country codes. / *Indiquer le pays d'origine s'il est différent du pays d'émission du Carnet en utilisant le code international des pays ISO.*
6/99

General List Instructions

The General List is an itemized list of *all* the items covered by the Carnet. Careful completion of this form is essential to ensure entry and exit from foreign countries with a minimum of time and trouble.

Each item must be accurately described and accompanied by a stated value. Be sure to include serial numbers whenever appropriate. If your General List exceeds one page then use Continuation Sheets. (Continuation Sheets may be obtained by photocopying a blank General List.) Make sure to put the total number of Continuation Sheets in the space provided at the bottom of the first General List page. Individuals applying for the Carnet, or applying on behalf of a corporation must sign the original General List page and all Continuation Sheets in the space marked Holder's Signature. *Only typed lists will be accepted*! Do not list such consumable items as bottle fluids, food, paper goods, pamplets, or giveaways. **Carnets cannot be issued for consumables.**

To Complete the General List

Column 1—Item No.: Each item of the shipment must be given an item number. Items answering to the same description may be grouped togheter.

Column 2—Trade Description of Goods: This column must contain a complete and specific description of each line item of merchandise, including the manufactuers's name, serial number, and/or model number.

Column 3—Number of Pieces: Indicate the quantity of each particular item.

Column 4—Weight or Volume: This column should include the total weight for each item number. (Example: if an item consists of three pieces each weighing five pounds, then a total weight of fifteen pounds be shown.) Make sure to indicate the correct unit of measure, e.g., pounds, ounces, kilograms.

Column 5—Value: Show total cost for each line item. Example: Four pieces with a value of $400 each should be listed at a total value of $1,600. Be sure to use the insured value of the goods.)

Column 6—Country of Origin: Country in which the goods were *originally* manufactured.

Note: In order to close the General List, columns 3 and 5 *must* be totaled.

Temporary Importation and the Benefits of an ATA Carnet

All countries have procedures allowing for the temporary importation of goods across their borders. Such importations are generally valid for less than 12 months.

Importers may choose from three options when considering a temporary importaton: (1) duty drawback, (2) temporary importation under bond (TIB), and (3) ATA Carnet.

1. Duty drawback is the process by which an importer registers the goods at the time of entry, and deposits the applicable duties and taxes. In Europe, duty and taxes range from 20–30 percent of the value of the goods. At the time of departure, the exporter presents the goods and appropriate paperwork to the customs inspector. Exporters can expect to receive a full refund of the duties and taxes posted at some future point. (For Europe, refunds are generally made two to six months after departure.)

2. To use a TIB, importers are required to secure the TIB from a customhouse broker at the time of entry into the foreign country. The purchase of a TIB is required for each country visited on every trip. Fees for TIBS vary widely.

3. The ATA Carnet was created by international convention thirty years ago. ATA Carnets:

   - May be used for **unlimited exits** from and entries into the U.S. and foreign countries. (Carnet are valid for one year.)

   - Are **accepted in** over 50 countries and territories.

   - **Eliminate** value-added taxes (VAT), duties, and the posting of security normally required at the time of importation.

   - **Simplify** customs procedures. Carnets allow a temporary exporter to use a single document for all customs transactions, make arrangements in advance and at a predetermined cost.

   - **Facilitate** reentry into the United States by eliminating the need to register goods with U.S. Customs at the time of departure.

Merchandise Covered by ATA Carnets

Virtually all goods, including commercial samples, professional equipment, and goods for tradeshows and exhibitions.

Ordinary goods such as computers, tools, cameras and video equipment, industrial machinery, automobiles, gems and jewelry, and wearing apparel. **Extraordinary items,** for example, Van Gogh Self-portrait, Ringling Brothers tigers, Cessna jets, Paul McCartney's band instruments, World Cup class yachts, satellites, human skulls, and the New York Philharmonic.

Carnets do not cover consumable goods (food and agriculture products), disposable items, or postal traffic.

Carnet Countries

ATA Carnet are accepted in:

Algeria	Hong Kong	New Zealand
Andorra	Hungary	Norway
Australia	Iceland	Poland
Austria	India	Portugal
Belgium	Ireland	Romania
Bulgaria	Israel	Senegal
Canada	Italy	Singapore
China	Ivory Cost	Slovakia
Croatia	Japan	Slovenia
Cypress	Korea	South Africa
Czech Republic	Lebanon	Spain
Denmark	Luxembourg	Sri Lanka
Estonia	Malaysia	Sweden
Finald	Macedonia	Switzerland
France	Malta	Thailand
Germany	Mauritius	Tunisia
Gibralter	Morocco	Turkey
Greece	Netherlands	United Kingdom

Countries are added to the ATA system periodically. Call to determine if the country to which you are traveling accepts Carnets.

Fees and Processing Time

There are **three basic components to the Carnet application** process:

1. Preparation of the *General List*

2. Completion of the *Carnet application*

3. Provision of a *security deposit*

The normal processing time for a Carnet is five working days. Basic processing fees ($120–$250) are determined by the value of the shipment. Expedited service ($35–$150). Payment can be made in the form of a check or money order.

For more information contact:

USCIB ATA Carnet Customer Service Department
212-354-4480 or atacarnet@uscib.org

All Contents 1996–1998 U.S. Council for International Business. All Rights Reserved. (With permission from USCIB/NYC.)

ATA Carnet Service Bureaus

The first point of contact should be the New York office.

ATA Carnet Headquarters and Service Bureau:
1212 Avenue of the Americas
New York, NY 10036
Tel: (212) 354-4480
Fax: (212) 944-0012

Regional Service Bureaus:
New England
185 Devonshire Street, Suite 800
Boston, MA 02110
Tel: (800) 233-3620/(617) 728-9199
Fax: (617) 728-9830

Mid-Atlantic

61 Broadway, Suite 2700
New York, NY 10006
Tel: (888) 571-1675/(212) 747-1800
Fax: (212) 747-1948

Executive Plaza I, Suite 105
11350 McCormick Road
Hunt Valley, MD 21031
Tel: (800) 422-9944/(410) 771-6100
Fax: (410) 771-6104

Southeast
7205 N.W. 19th Street, Suite 104
Miami, FL 33126
Tel: (800) 468-5467/(305) 592-6929
Fax: (305) 592-9537

Mid-West

1501 East Woodfield Road,
Suite 302N
Schaumburg, IL 60173
Tel: (800) 762-6653/(847) 969-8211
Fax: (847) 969-8200

118 Barrington Commons Plaza,
Suite 236
Barrington, IL 60010
Tel: (800) ATA-2900/(847) 381-1558
Fax: (847) 381-3857

Southwest
5112Morningside Drive
Houston, TX 77005
Tel: (800) 227-6387
Fax: (281) 847-0700

Northern California
425 California Street, Suite 700
San Francisco, CA 94104
Tel: (800) 255-4994/(415) 765-6636
Fax: (415) 391-2716

Southern California
100 West Broadway, Suite 100
Long Beach, CA 90802
Tel: (800) 421-9324/(562) 628-9306
Fax: (562) 590-8523

For more information contact:
USCIB ATA Carnet Customer Service Department
(212) 354-4480 or atacarnet@uscib.org

All Contents 1996–1998 U.S. Council for International Business. All Rights Reserved. (With permission from USCIB/NYC.)

Options in Export Finance

Exporters control the options for their payment. Often, the option chosen will determine the exporter's competitiveness.

The terms of sale in an export transaction are arranged between the buyer and the seller prior to shipment. Typically, the actual collection of payments internationally is accomplished through the facilities of a commercial bank. The payment method, or financial instrument used, is dependent on such factors as the credit standing of the buyer (importer), any existing exchange restrictions in the buyer's country, competitive pressure that the seller faces, and the political and economic condition of the country of import.

Most merchandise sales by U.S. exporters to overseas buyers are made on the basis of one of the following methods of payment:

1. Cash in advance

2. Open account

3. Documentary collection

4. Letter of credit

A. Open Account

Open account sales in international trade may be defined as one in which no financial institutions act as intermediaries between buyer and seller. This mode of payment is usually dictated by custom and competitive terms. The seller must be confident of the buyer's creditworthiness and ability to pay promptly.

In an open account transaction, the seller is sending the buyer goods without any negotiable instrument evidencing the obligation and is dependent soley upon the buyer to make payment. The advantages of selling on an open account basis are simplicity and reduced banking charges. The seller has little legal recourse in cases of dishonored transactions and typically has a harder time getting dollar exchange from a defaulted buyer. For these reasons, this sales method is used primarily when sellers are dealing with buyers they know well, to established markets, and for sales to foreign branches or subsidiaries.

B. Documentary Collection

Export collections require that the seller forward documents and instructions to his bank which will pass them to a foreign bank for collection. Various banks provide a direct collection service to their customers. Under this method, the exporter or his or her forwarder sends collection instructions directly to the buyer's bank and a copy to their bank for follow-up.

A collection does not eliminate the market risk associated with the buyer (failure of buyer to take title of material purchased; not uncommon in a period of falling market prices) or the country risk associated with the buyer's country. When asked for payment by a bank, the buyer could refuse. The bank or banks involved in the collection assumes no liability for payment requested on a collection basis. A sight draft ensures that documents do not pass to the buyer until payment is made. Neither a time draft nor a clean draft provides this protection.

C. Letter of Credit

Except for cash in advance, the letter of credit affords the seller the highest degree of protection. A letter of credit is issued by the opening bank assuring that certain payments will be made under specified conditions. Normally, letter of credit transactions involve two banks: one in the exporter's country and one in the buyer's.

An irrevocable letter of credit replaces the commercial risk associated with the Buyer with that of the bank issuing the letter of credit. Hence, the seller is no longer relying on the buyer's promise to pay; he or she is relying on the promise and the ability to pay of a bank located in a foreign country. If the seller wishes to reduce the risk of nonpayment further, he or she can request that the bank confirm the letter of credit. From the seller's viewpoint, this eliminates the foreign country risk and replaces the commercial risk of the buyer's bank with that of the confirming bank. Payment against a confirmed letter of credit is assured by the confirming bank when documents in good order are submitted.

It is crucial to understand that a letter of credit is not an unconditional guarantee of payment; rather, payment will be made only after the terms of the letter of credit have been precisely fulfilled. Anyone using collections or letters of credit have been precisely fulfilled. Anyone using collections or letters of credit should very carefully read the segment on documents, "How a Letter of Credit Works" because discrepancies that can delay payment often arise upon inspection of the documents.

Foreign trade normally presents the following uncertainties:

A. Country Risk

   Country risk is the risk associated with the buyer's country. This covers the country's financial condition, stability of currency, social and political climate, and availability of foreign exchange.

B. Commercial Risk

   Commercial risk is the risk associated with the individual or institution responsible for payment. Because the purchase is in another country, the seller generally not only has less reliable information regarding his financial condition and integrity, but also typically has few avenues of redress should the buyer fail to pay or otherwise violate the agreed upon terms of sale.

The existence of greater commercial and country risk explains why few international transactions are made on an open account or consignment basis.

Completing the Export Transaction

The initial step in a foreign sales transaction may be taken by the buyer or the seller. A buyer may approach the seller with a request for a quotation, or he may dispatch an offer to buy at stipulated prices and on certain terms and conditions, or the seller may extend his quotation to potential buyers on his own initiative. Regardless of the approach and the formality of such exchanges, once an offer has been accepted by the other party, a contract, known as a sales contract, has been created.

Given the complexities that arise in a foreign transaction where language, cutstom, and practices may differ, the importance of the sales contract is readily apparent. Hence, companies engaged in foreign trade should have a sales contract form fitted to their basic requirements encompassing all the necessary details to assure a satisfactory conclusion to the transaction. Following is a list of some of the more important items that should be included in such a form:

Merchandise. A complete description specifying standards of grade or quality, catalog numbers or other descriptive terms.

Quantity. The exact number in units or specific weight, measurement or volume. Care should be taken as to different weight and measurement systems.

Price. Unit price specifying the currency in which the unit price is expressed.

Terms of Sale (INCO). Normally are expressed as FOB, CIF, etc., with named points or ports to which they apply. These terms indicate the duties and responsibilities of both buyer and seller with respect to point of delivery, costs, and risks to be assumed by each.

Packing. The type of packing is usually determined by the nature of the merchandise, conditions at sea, at the ports, and in transit in the interior as well as by customs regulations.

Marking. Usually are dictated by the customs regulations of the importing country and the requirements of the buyer.

Insurance. The extent of coverage required and who is to provide it should be stated.

Shipping Instructions. Method of transportation and consignment, documents required, and time of shipment should be explicit.

Method of Payment. Whether payment will be effected against cash in advance, on open account, on a collection basis, against a letter of credit, etc.

This list should not be considered complete, but rather used as as guide that can be adapted to fit the needs of individual transactions.

Letters of Credit

For new trading entities, a letter of credit is often an excellent means to arrange payment. It compromises the exposures on both sides of the trade.

A letter of credit is used to reduce the risk in international trade. It is a contract in letter form, written by a bank (issuing bank) on behalf of the buyer (applicant). The issuing bank then forwards the letter of credit, which is transmitted through a bank. If you are the exporter, you must have your foreign buyer specify your bank to be the advising bank. Similarly, if you want to have the letter of credit confirmed, you should have your buyer include the request for confirmation on the application for the letter of credit.

Because the advising bank has no contact with the buyer but takes the instructions from the issuing bank, it is, therefore, important that the seller (beneficiary) examine the letter of credit carefully to ensure that it is consistent with the agreed upon terms of sale and that the seller can comply with its terms and conditions. If changes are needed, the seller should contact the buyer immediately to request an amendment to the letter of credit. A credit cannot be amended without the agreement of both parties.

The documents required under letters of credit may vary, but most often call for the presentation of a draft, commercial invoices, packing lists, and bills of lading. It is the responsibility of the bank making payments to examine those documents with care to be certain that they appear on their face to comply with the terms and conditions of the credit. It must be understood that in documentary credit operations all parties concerned deal in documents and not in goods. Because credits advised by the bank are subject to the Uniform Customs and Practice for Documentary Credit, its provisions will be applied to documents presented under such credits in determining whether payment will be made.

It is important to remember that all terms and conditions should be consistent with the sales contracts, since an irrevocable letter of credit cannot be modified or canceled without the consent of all parties concerned. If a situation arises where a letter of credit has to be amended, the buyer submits a written request, whereupon the credit may be amended. Once the amendment is accepted by the seller, the amendment will become an integral part of the credit.

A letter of credit may be payable at sight against presentation of documents in accordance with the credit or at a future date.

Letters of credit may be issued in U.S. dollars or foreign currency. The credit may also be transmitted by full text teletransmission, short cable/telex, and airmail or courier.

Terms of Sale (INCO)

Sending goods from one country to another as part of a commercial transaction can be a risky business. If they are lost or damaged, or if the delivery does not take palce for some other reason, the climate of confidence between parties may degenerate to the point where a lawsuit is initiated.

However, if when drawing up the contract, buyer and seller specifically refer to one of the following common international trade terms, they can be sure of defining their respective responsibilities, simply and safely. In doing so, they eliminate any possibility of a misunderstanding and subsequent dispute.

Ex Works (named place). Under this term, the price quoted applies only at the point of origin, and the seller agrees to place the goods at the disposal of the buyer at the agreed place on the date or within the period fixed.

Free alongside Ship (FAS) or FAS Vessel (named port of shipment). Under this term, the seller quotes a price including delivery of the goods alongside the overseas vessel and within reach of its loading tackle.

Free on Board (FOB) or FOB Vessel (named port of shipment). Under this term, the seller quotes a price covering all expenses up to and including delivery of the goods upon the overseas vessel provided by or for the buyer at the named port of shipment.

Cost and Freight (CFR) or CFR (named port of destination). Under this term, the seller quotes a price including the cost of transportation to the named point of destination.

Cost, Insurance, Freight (CIF) or CIF (named port of destination). Under this term, the seller quotes a price including the cost of the goods, the insurance, and all transportation charges to the named point of destination.

Delivered, Duty, Paid (DDP). Under this term, the seller assumes responsibility for all aspects of the transaction, cost of goods, insurance transportation charges, clearance costs, and duties to the final destination.

Types of Letters of Credit

Documentary Credits

Irrevocable Letter of Credit. One in which the issuing bank irrevocably undertakes to pay or accept drafts presented with documents in compliance with the credit terms. Can only be modified/canceled with the agreement of all parties concerned. Virtually all import credits are issued irrevocably by the bank.

Irrevocable Unconfirmed Letter of Credit. The same as an irrevocable letter of credit, except it is being advised through another bank that does not add any obligation of its own. Most import credits are advised by foreign banks on an unconfirmed basis.

Irrevocable Confirmed Letter of Credit. A credit that adds the obligation of the second (confirming) bank to the irrevocable undertaking of the first (issuing) bank. The beneficiary has protection to two banks, however, protection is only as good as the banks giving it.

Revocable Letter of Credit. Contains the undertaking of no one and can be revoked anytime prior to payment being effected. Rarely issued.

Red Clause Credit. A special notation that the beneficiary may draw advances up to a stipulated amount to purchase and pay for the merchandise before shipping against presentation of "Undertaking to Ship" or of a similar document. When issuing a red clause credit, the issuing bank, on behalf of applicant, undertakes to repay the foreign bank for advances made even if shipment did not take place.

Revolving Credit. Allows the beneficiary to make multiple shipments and draw a specific amount of money on a specified periodic basis. The amount drawn becomes available to the beneficiary as the shipments and drawings are made and continues up to the expiration of the letter of credit.

Transferable Letter of Credit. One that expressly authorizes transfers to be made to other parties by a bank as directed by the beneficiary. The transfer credit must contain the identical conditions as the original letter of credit except that the amount transferred may be less and the dates indicated may be earlier.

Back to Back Letter of Credit Arrangement. One in which a beneficiary under an original confirmed letter of credit utilizes this letter of credit issued in his or her favor as collateral to open another letter of credit in favor of a supplier. A back to back letter of credit must contain the same conditions, merchandise, and documents as the original letter of credit with the exception of the invoice, unit prices, amount of drawing and shipping, and validity dates that must be prior to the dates stipulated in the original letter of credit.

Time or Usance Credit. Allows payment at a future specified time.

Stand by Letter of Credit. Does not involve the direct purchase of merchandise or the presentation of title documents. Rather, it is similar to performance or bid bonds. The bank's obligation to pay should arise only upon the presentation of a draft or other documents as specified in the letter of credit, and the bank must not be called upon to determine questions of fact or law at issue between the applicant and the beneficiary. The applicant for a standby letter of credit must trust the beneficiary. If the beneficiary presents documents in accordance with the terms of the standby credit, the bank must pay irrespective of any extenuating circumstances brought to its attention. The applicant is legally bound to reimburse the bank. Standby letters of credit are versatile instruments and can be used for the following:

- Payments for merchandise shipped on open account

- Bid and performance bonds

- Advance payment guarantees

- Other financial obligations

Assignments under Letters of Credit. The beneficiary of a letter of credit may, at his or her discretion, assign the proceeds of a letter of credit to another party. An assignment of a credit should not be construed as a transfer of the instrument. By an assignment, the beneficiary does not transfer the credit, but only directs the bank involved in the payment or negotiation of documents to pay the assignee a certain portion of the beneficiary's proceeds. An assignment of proceeds may be made against any letter of credit; it need not be designated as "transferable." The assignment of proceeds has no monetary value until the proceeds come into existence. In other words, receipt of an assignment does not guarantee payment; it ensures payment only if the beneficiary presents the documents against the credit, and the credit terms are satisfied. For the assignee to receive payment directly from the bank, the assignment of proceeds must be made directly through the bank.

Letter of Credit Checklist

On receipt of the letters of credit, the beneficiary should check the following:

1. Name and address of beneficiary and applicant. All documents presented under the credit must show names and addresses consistent with those in the credit

2. The type of credit and its terms and conditions conform to the sales contract or purchase order, if not, request amendment

3. All conditions are acceptable

4. The documents can be obtained in the form stated

5. The description of the merchandise or commodity and any unit price conforms with the sales contract

6. The amount of the credit is sufficient to cover all costs permitted by the terms of the contract

7. The shipping and expiration dates and the period of time allowed for presentation of the shipping documents following their date of issuance and making presentation of the documents to the bank for payment, acceptance, or negotiation

8. The points of shipment and destination are as agreed

9. The provision for insurance is in accordance with the terms of the sale

10. Country in which credit is payable

11. The credit is subject to Uniform Customs and Practice for Documentary Credits, International Chamber of Commerce, Paris, France, that are in effect on the issue date

Parties to Commercial Credits

1. *Direct Parties*

   The Buyer—Bank Customer/Applicant/Importer

   - Applies for letter of credit from bank.
   - Creditworthiness must be satisfactory to bank.

   The Beneficiary—Party to Be Paid/Seller/Exporter/Shipper

   - Party to whom letter of credit is issued/addressed.
   - Party who arranges compliance with terms and presentation of documents to the paying bank.

   Issuing Bank

   - Buyer's bank that issues the letter of credit to the beneficiary.
   - Examines documents to insure conformity to letter of credit.
   - Arranges for financing of transactions, if requested.
   - Releases documents to buyer and charges his or her account.

   Advising Bank

   - Bank that advises the beneficiary of the opening of the credit. May be the issuing bank, negotiating bank, or a third bank.

   Confirming Bank

   - The advising bank, which adds its obligation to that of the issuing bank.

   Negotiating Bank

   - Bank, usually unnamed in credit, that agrees to purchase draft of beneficiary.
   - Pays beneficiary immediately, usually with recourse.

2. *Indirect Parties*

   Steamship Company

   - Receives merchandise from exporter/shipper/forwarder and arranges for transport of merchandise.
   - Issues bills of lading that serve as the title document, receipt of goods, contract between shipper and steamship company.

   Air Carrier

   - Receives merchandise from exporter/shipper/forwarder and arranges for transport of merchandise.

- Issues airway bill that serves as the receipt of goods and the contract between shipper and carrier.

Freight Forwarder

- Acts as the agent for exporter.

- Assists exporter to expedite shipments.

- Prepares necessary documents and makes other arrangements for the movement of merchandise.

Customs Broker

- Acts as the agent for the importer.

- Receives shipping documentation from the bank or importer.

- Clears merchandise upon arrival.

- Arranges for delivery of merchandise to the importer.

Insurance Company

- Insures shipment for value requested.

- Issues policy/certificate covering risks requested.

- Settles claims, if any.

Comparison Method of Export Payment Options

Method	Goods Available to Buyer	Usual Time of Payment	Risk to Exporter	Risk to Importer
Cash in advance	After payment	Before shipment	None	Maximum, relies on exporter to ship goods
Letter of credit: Confirmed Unconfirmed	After payment	When documents are available at shipment	Virtually none	Assured of quantity and other particulars
Documentary collection sight draft documents against acceptance	After payment	On presentation of draft to importer	If draft unpaid, goods must be returned or disposed of	Assured of quantity and quality
Documentary collection time draft documents against acceptance	Before payment	On maturity of draft	Relies on importer to pay draft if unpaid goods must be returned or disposed of	Minimal, can check shipment for quantity and quality before payment
Consignment	Before payment exporter retains title until goods are sold or used	After use	Substantial risk	None
Open	Before payment	As agreed	Relies on importer to pay account as agreed. Complete risk	None

Examples of Volume Weight vs. Gross Weight

Transportation carriers will charge a shipper for the gross weight or the volume weight, whichever is greater. The formula for international volume calculations is length × width × height (divided by) 166. For the purpose of the following examples, assume the air freight cost is $1.50 per pound.

Example # 1 (cargo that is voluminous)
One (1) skid @ 660 pounds gross weight
Dimensions in inches: l 48 × w 48 × h 63
Calculation: 48 × 48 × 63 divided by 166 = 874 pounds
***Volume weight: 874 pounds
***Chargeable weight: 874 pounds
874 pounds × 1.50 per pound = $1,311 = air freight

Example # 2 (cargo that is not voluminous)
One (1) skid @ 660 pounds gross weight
Dimensions in inches: l 48 × w 48 × h 35
Calculation: 48 × 48 × 35 divided by 166 = 486
***Volume weight: 486 pounds
***Chargeable weight: 660 pounds
660 pounds × 1.50 per pound = $990 = air freight

Differences in freight
Example #1: $1,311
Example #2: $990
Difference in freight charges: $321
(Difference is only because of change in dimensions.)

Resources for Export Credit Insurance

Export-Import Bank of the United States (U.S. Ex-Im Bank)
811 Vermont Avenue NW
Washington DC 20571 USA
Tel: (+1) 202-565-3946
Fax: (+1) 202-565-3380
Internet: http://www.exim.gov
Ownership structure: 100 percent sovereign.

Overview: Provides medium- and long-term guarantees and loans and short- and medium-term insurance.

General Description: The Export-Import Bank of the United States (U.S. Ex-Im Bank) provides guarantees, insurance, and loans. The main programs offered are short-term supplier credit and medium- and long-term buyer credit. Policies cover up to 100 percent for political and commercial risks. The CIRR is offered for loans. Overseas investment insurance is not offered. The U.S. Ex-Im Bank carries the full faith and credit of the U.S. Government. The bank is bound by OECD consensus and has a dedicated project finance department. Commercial banks provide a source for lending. The bank works with many institutions, including commercial banks, insurance brokers, and state and local governments and organizations.

Overseas Private Investment Corporation (OPIC)
1100 New York Avenue NW
Washington, DC 20527 USA
Tel: (+1) 202-336-8484
Fax: (+1) 202-218-0235
Contact for guarantee information: Alfredo M Rodriguez. Fax: (+1) 202-408-9866.
Contact for insurance information: Julie Martin. Tel: (+1) 202-336-8586; Fax: (+1) 202-408-5142.
Ownership structure: 100 percent sovereign.

Overview: Provides medium- and long-term guarantees, insurance, and finance to support U.S. investment in emerging markets.

General Description: The Overseas Private Investment Corporation (OPIC) is a self-sustaining federal agency that operates at no net cost to taxpayers. The agency sells investment services to U.S. businesses of all sizes. OPIC-backed projects strengthen the U.S. economy by promoting investment by American companies and American-made exports that support and create American jobs. OPIC only supports projects that take steps to protect the local environment and respect workers rights. OPIC provides insurance and guarantees. The agency is not bound by OECD consensus, except in certain instances when it insures loans tied to the U.S. government. OPIC carries the full faith and credit of the government and has a dedicated project finance department.

American International Group Inc. (AIG)
70 Pine Street
New York, NY 10270 USA
Tel: (+1) 212-770-7261
Fax: (+1) 212-269-3387
Contact for trade credit: Des DeSwart (New York); Ed Brittenham (AIG Europe-London).
Contact for political risk: John Hegeman (New York); Julian Edwards (AIG Europe-London).
Ownership structure: 100 percent private.

Overview: Provides short-term export credit and political risk insurance.

General Description: American International Group, Inc. (AIG) members underwrite property, casualty, marine, life, and financial services insurance in approximately 130 countries and jurisdictions and are involved in a range of financial services businesses. AIG is rated AAA by Standard & Poor's and AAA by Moody's. AIG Global Trade and Political Risk Insurance comprises the trade credit division and the political and commercial risks. AIG is not bound by the OECD consensus. No interest support is offered. AIG is a member of the Berne Union.

C N A Credit Insurance (C N A)
1100 Cornwall Road
PO Box 905
Monmouth Junction, NJ 08852 USA
Tel: (+1) 732-398-4463
Fax: (+1) 732-398-5106
Contact: Jim Higgins.
Internet: http://www.CAN-CREDIT.com
E-mail: James.Higgins@CAN.com
Ownership structure: 100 percent private.

Overview: Provides short-term insurance.

General Description: C N A Credit is a division of C N A, one of the largest insurance groups in the United States. C N A is the second largest commercial insurer in the United States, providing a variety of insurance products to business. Policies cover up to 90 percent for political and commercial risks. C N A is not bound by OECD consensus, does not carry the full faith and credit of the government, and does not have a project finance department.

Exporters Insurance Company (Exporters)
30 Woodbourne Avenue
Hamilton, HM 08 Bermuda
Tel: (+1) 441-296-1745
Fax: (+1) 441-292-8682
Contact: Bob Svensk, President.
Internet: http://www.exporters.bm
E-mail: RSVENSK@EFSGROUP.com
Exporters Services
37/39 Lime Street, 9th Floor
London, EC3M 7AY, UK
335 Madison Avenue
New York, NY 10017, USA
Tel: (+1) 212-370-6000
Fax: (+1) 212-370-0357
Ownership structure: 100 percent private.

General Description: Exporters Insurance Company (Exporters) is a group captive insurance company. Its policies cover up to 90 percent for political and commercial risks. Interest support is offered, but the CIRR is not. Exporters insurance is not bound by OECD consensus, does not carry the full faith and credit of any government, and does not have a separate project finance department.

FCIA Management Company Inc. (FCIA)
40 Rector Street
New York, NY 10006 USA
Tel: 212-306-5000
Fax: 212-306-5218
Contact: Lindley Franklin.
Ownership structure: 100 percent private.

Overview: Provides credit and political risks insurance.

General Description: FCIA Management Company, Inc. provides the underwriting and administrative services for the worldwide credit insurance businesses of Great American Insurance Company and Foreign Credit Insurance Association. FCIA offers a broad line of credit insurance and political risks products. Great American insurance Company heads one of the largest property/casualty groups in the United States, and provides a wide variety of specialty coverages to U.S. customers. Foreign Credit Insurance Association was established in 1961 and has continuously provided export credit insurance to U.S. companies since that time—longer than any other insurer.

Local Contacts of the Export Import Bank

Northeast Region
New York City, New York
6 World Trade Center, Suite 635
New York, NY 10048
Tel: (212) 466-2950
Fax: (212) 466-2959

Mid-Atlantic Region
Washington, DC
Ex-Im Bank Headquarters
811 Vermont Ave., NW, Suite 911
Washington, DC 20571
Tel: (800) 565-3946, ext. 3908
(202) 565-3940
Fax: (202) 565-3932

Southeast Region
Miami, Florida
777 NW 72nd Ave., Suite 3M2
Miami, FL 33126
Tel: (305) 526-7436
Fax: (305) 526-7435

Midwest Region
Chicago, Illinois
55 W. Monroe St., Suite 2440
Chicago, IL 60603
Tel: (312) 353-8081
Fax: (312) 353-8098

Southwest Region
Houston, Texas
1880 South Dairy Ashford II,
Suite 585
Houston, TX 77077
Tel: (281) 721-0465
Fax: (281) 679-0156

West Region
Long Beach, California
1 World Trade Center, Suite 1670
Long Beach, CA 90831
Tel: (562) 980-4580
Fax: (562) 980-4590
Orange County Satellite Office
3300 Irvine Ave., Suite 305
Newport Beach, CA 92660
Tel: (949) 660-1688 ext. 150
Fax: (949) 660-8039
San Francisco Satellite Office
250 Montgomery Street,
    14th Floor
San Francisco, CA 94104
Tel: (415) 705-2285
Fax: (415) 705-1156

Or contact Michael J. Spivey, Director Business Development, at
(202) 565-3459; E-mail: mike.Spivey@exim.gov.; www.exim.gov/
contacts.html
Local contacts of the Export Import Bank can also be found at
www.exim.gov/regional.gtml

Countries Requiring Legalization and Consularization

	Minimum Documents Required	Minimum Charges, Including Handling and Chamber Fees	Cost Per Page of FA Additional Documents	Estimated Time in Consulate
Consulate				
Argentina	1 C/O (send 1 and 3)	$65.00	$30.00	Depends on jurisdiction of consulate office—24 to 48 hours.
Bahrain	1 C/O and 1 C/I (send 2 and 3)	$72.00	$24.00	24 to 48 hours.
Costa Rica	1 C/O and 1 C/I	$135.00	$55.00	Two to three working days.
Cyprus	1 C/O and 1 C/I (send 1 and 3)	The bottom line grand total of your invoice × 0.004 (round up to nearest $1.00) plus $72.00. The minimum cost for one set of documents is $86.00.	Depends on whether the document is an invoice or a certificate. Please call 1-800-468-3627.	Same day to three working days.
Dominican Republic	1 AWB or B/L and 1 C/I (send 1 and 5)	$161.00 all ports of loading but Miami. $241.00 for Miami port of landing.	Please call 1-800-468-3627.	Same day all ports of landing but Miami. 48 hours for Miami.
Egypt	1 C/O and 1 C/I (send 1 and 3)	$179.00	$75.00	24 hours.
Guatemala	1 B/L and 1 C/I (send 1 and 4)	$65.00 Houston port of landing, $95.00 for all others.	$30.00	24 to 48 hours.
Jordan	1 C/O and 1 C/I (send 1 and 3)	Based on bottom line "grand total" of your invoice: Invoice total — Cost up to $1,500 — $83.00 $1,500.01–7,500.00 — 123.00 $7,500.01–15,000.00 — 163.00 $15,000.01–37,500.00 — 183.00 $37,500.01–75,000.00 — 223.00 $75,000.01–150,000.00 — 263.00 over $150,000.01 — please call	Depends on whether the document is an invoice or a certificate. Please call 1-800-468-3627.	24 hours.
Kuwait	1 C/O and 1 C/I (send 1 and 3)	$107.00	$39.00	Two to three working days.
Lebanon	1 C/O and 1 C/I (send 1 and 3)	The bottom line grand total of your invoice × 0.004 (round up to the nearest $1.00) plus $72.00. The minimum cost for one set of documents is $86.00.	Depends on whether the document is an invoice or a certificate. Please call 1-800-468-3627.	Four to five working days.

Legalization Prices and Requirements

Legalization Prices and Requirements (*Continued*)

Consulate	Minimum Documents Required	Minimum Charges, Including Handling and Chamber Fees	Cost Per Page of FA Additional Documents	Estimated Time in Consulate
Nicaragua	1 AWB or 3 B/Ls and 1 C/I (send 3 and 4)	Based on bottom line grand total of your invoice: Invoice total — Cost up to $49.00 — $75.00 $49.01–500.00 — $85.00 $500.01–1,000.00 — $90.00 $1,000.01–10,000.00 — $105.00 $10,000.01–100,000.00 — $125.00 over $100,000.01 — please call	Please call 1-800-468-3627.	24 hours.
Oman	1 C/O and 1 C/I Plus AWB or B/L (send 1 and 5)	Cost is $121.00 for invoices under $10,000.00 and $136.00 for invoices over $10,000.	Depends on whether the document is an invoice or a certificate. Please call 1-800-468-3627.	Two to three working days.
Paraguay	1 C/O and 1 C/I (send 1 and 4)	$125.00	$24.00	Two to three working days.
Qater	1 C/O and 1 C/I (send 1 and 4)	Based on bottom line grand total of your invoice: Invoice total — Cost up to $1,373.00 — $125.00 $1,373.01–4,120.00 — $152.00 $4,120.02–13,736.00 — $235.00 $13,736.01–27,472.00 — $345.00 $27,472.01–41,208.00 — $454.00 $41,208.01–68,681.00 — $592.00 $68,681.01–137,362.00 — $702.00 $137,362.01–274,725.00 — $922.00 over $274,725.01 — please call	Depends on whether the document is an invoice or a certificate. Please call 1-800-468-3627.	24 hours.
Saudi Arabia	1 C/O and 1 C/I (send 1 and 3)	$72.00	$24.00	24 hours.
Spain	1 Spanish C/O and 1 C/I (send 1 and 3)	$124.00–includes Spanish C/O and preparation.	Please call 1-800-468-3627.	24 to 48 hours.
Syria	1 C/O and 1 C/I (send 1 and 3)	The bottom line grand total of your invoice × 0.004 (round up to the nearest $1.00) plus $72.00. The minimum cost for one set of documentation is $86.00.	Depends on whether the document is an invoice or certificate. Please call 1-800-468-3627.	Same day to three working days.
Tunleta	1 C/O and 1 C/I (send 1 and 3)	$86.00	$30.00	Two to three working days.
Turkey	1 C/O and 1 C/I (send 1 and 3). Please do NOT notarize documents.	The bottom line grand total of your invoice × 0.005 (round up to the nearest $1.00) plus $80.00. The minimum cost for one set of documents is $99.00.	Depends on whether the document is an invoice or a certificate. Please call 1-800-468-3627.	Three to four working days.

(continued)

Legalization Prices and Requirements (*Continued*)

Consulate	Minimum Documents Required	Minimum Charges, Including Handling and Chamber Fees	Cost Per Page of FA Additional Documents	Estimated Time in Consulate
United Arab Emirates	1 C/O and 1 C/I (send 1 and 3) C/I (send 1 and 3)	Based on bottom line grand total of your invoice: Invoice total Cost up to $2,702.00 $99.00 $2,702.01–8,108.00 $130.00 $8,108.01–16,216.00 $190.00 $16,216.01–24,324.00 $250.00 $24,324.01–40,540.00 $310.00 $40,540.01–67,567.00 $370.00 $67,567.01–135,135.00 $460.00 $135,135.01–270,270.00 $520.00 over $270,270.01 please call	Depends on whether the document is an invoice or a certificate. Please call 1-800-468-3627. $45.00	Three to four working days. 24 to 48 hours.
Yamen	1 C/O and 1	$115.00		

(Provided by RHDC, who can be contacted at 1-800-468-3627.)

SGS Inspection Countries

**SGS Government Programs Inc. New York, New York
Preshipment Inspection Countries**

Countries Currently Mandating SGS Preshipment Inspection

Angola	Democratic Republic of the Congo	Rwanda
Burkina Faso	Guinea	Senegal
Burundi	Ivory Coast	Surinam***
Cambodia	Malawi	Uganda***
Cameroon	Mali	Zambia
Central African Republic	Mauritania	Zanzibar
Republic of the Congo	Philippines	

Countries Currently Mandating Preshipment Inspections Shared Among SGS and Other Inspection Companies

Argentina	Kenya
Bangladesh***	Mexico
Bolivia	Paraguay
Ecuador	Peru
Ghana	Tanzania

Countries Currently Mandating Preshipment Inspections by Companies Other Than SGS

Benin

Colombia***

Sierra Leone

Somalia

Zimbabwe

*Selected Mexican Government Purchases only.
**Voluntary participation by importers.
***Presently suspended but may activate at any time.
SGS is pleased to furnish this information as an accomodation, but without responsibility, as countries frequently update their requirements.

International Commercial (INCO) Terms

INCO Terms are internationally recognized terms of sale used to determine responsibility for shipping arrangements and transfer of goods shipped in international trade. These standard terms help eliminate or reduce legal disputes and misinterpretation of responsibilities to the export transaction. There are four term categories:

E Terms. The seller makes the goods available at the seller's facility.

F Terms. The seller is required to deliver the goods to a carrier specified by the buyer.

C Terms. The seller contracts for carriage, but does not assume the risk of loss or damage to the goods after delivery to the carrier.

D Terms. The seller is responsible for all costs and risks required to bring the shipment to the destination country.

INCO Terms 1990: Responsibilities to the Export Transaction

Ex-Works

Seller. Goods made available at seller's premises.
Buyer. Inland transportation to port of exit, ocean carriage, applicable documentation and forwarding fees, marine insurance, and inland transit at destination.

Free Carrier

Seller. Inland transit to the exporting carrier or freight forwarder.
Buyer. Inland move to port of exit, ocean carriage, forwarding and documentation fees, insurance, and overland move at destination.

Free alongside Ship

Seller. Inland move to the port of exit.
Buyer. Ocean carriage, forwarding and documentation, insurance, and overland move at destination.

Free on Board

Seller. Inland move to port of export, loading of cargo on vessel, and applicable forwarding/documentation fees.
Buyer. Ocean carriage, insurance, and overland move at destination.

Cost and Freight

Seller: Inland move to the pier, ocean carriage, and forwarding/documentation fees.
Buyer: Marine insurance and overland move at destination.

Cost Insurance, and Freight

Seller: Inland move to the pier, ocean carriage, forwarding/documentation fees and marine insurance.
Buyer: Overland move at destination.

Carriage Paid To

Seller. Inland move to the pier, ocean carriage, forwarding/documentation fees, and inland move from port to consignee.
Buyer. Marine insurance.

Carriage Insurance Paid To

Seller. Inland move to the pier, ocean carriage, forwarding/documentation fees, marine insurance, and inland move from port to consignee.
Buyer: Possible inland move to facility.

Delivered at Frontier

Seller. All aspects of move, but before the custom border of the adjoining control.
Buyer: Customs clearance and inland move to facility.

Delivered Ex Ship

Seller. All aspects of move to vessel arrival in port of discharge.
Buyer. Unloading, customs clearance, and delivery.

Delivered Ex Quay

Seller. All aspects of move to discharge of cargo on the wharf
Buyer. Customs clearance and delivery to facility.

Delivered Duty Unpaid

Seller. All physical aspects of the move.
Buyer. Customs clearance (duties, taxes, and other official charges).

Delivered Duty Paid

Seller. All physical aspects of the move, including customs clearance.
Buyer. No responsibility to make shipment or customs clearance arrangements.

WTO Agreement on Rules of Origin

What is this Agreement and what does it do?

Who benefits from this Agreement?

How can this Agreement help my company?

Can the U.S. Government help me if I have a problem?

How can I get more information?

What is this Agreement and what does it do?

The Rules of Origin Agreement of the World Trade Organization (WTO) requires that WTO members apply their rules of origin in an impartial, transparent, and consistent manner. The Agreement also requires that rules of origin not restrict, distort, or disrupt international trade.

Rules of origin are the laws, regulations, and administrative guidelines that governments use to determine an imported product's country of origin; not always an easy matter when the raw materials, manufacturing, processing, or assembly of a product can be provided in several different countries. Rules of origin have many applications—for example in setting duty rates (including antidumping and countervailing duties), granting tariff preferences, administering government procurement policies, and applying safeguards.

All WTO members are parties to this Agreement.

The Agreement entered into force on January 1, 1995. It has no expiration date.

Who benefits from this Agreement?

Any company involved in international trade can benefit from clear and predictable rules of origin.

How can this Agreement help my company?

The Agreement requires WTO members to permit companies interested in exporting a product requiring an origin determination to request an assessment of the origin of the product, normally from that country's customs service. Requests must be accompanied by the appropriate documentation. Under the WTO Rules of Origin Agreement, the importing country must issue its origin assessment within 150 days. Assessments are valid for three years, and changes in origin rules cannot be applied retroactively. Information of a confidential nature that is provided to government officials for the purpose of assessing origin must be treated as confidential by the authorities concerned.

If you need further information on whether your product requires an origin determination and how to obtain one, you can contact the Trade Information Center at the U.S. Department of Commerce.

The WTO Agreement provides for the establishment of a Committee on Rules of Origin, where member countries consult on matters relating to the operation of the Agreement. This Committee and a Technical Committee on Rules of Origin of the World Customs Organization (WCO) have been charged with developing a permanent, harmonized set of product-specific origin rules that will apply to all trade in goods—except preferential trade—among WTO members. (Preferential trade is trade that is carried out within free trade areas or other regional trading arrangements, such as the North American Free Trade Agreement, or trade preference programs like the U.S. Generalized System of Preferences.) Both Committees are still working on this project. Once it is completed, exporters will be able to determine exactly which origin criteria will be applied to their product lines when exporting to any WTO member country.

Can the U.S. Government help me if I have a problem?

Yes, but first, if you disagree with an importing country's origin determination, or if that country is not complying with the provisions of the WTO Agreement, you or your importer should contact the customs service of that country and try to resolve the problem. If this attempt fails, the Agreement requires WTO member countries to permit a prompt review by an independent judicial or administrative tribunal in the importing country, which would have the authority to modify or reverse a customs official's ruling.

If these courses of action prove fruitless, then contact the U.S. Commerce Department's Trade Compliance Center hotline, which can provide you with the information and assistance you need to understand your rights under this Agreement. The Center can also activate the U.S. Government to help you resolve your exporting problem. If appropriate, U.S. officials can make official inquiries with the government of the other country involved. The World Trade Organization's dispute settlement process, which is described in the Exporter's Guide to the WTO Understanding on the Settlement of Disputes, can also be used by the U.S. Government, in certain circumstances, when WTO member countries fail to comply with a WTO Agreement.

How can I get more information?

The complete text of the WTO Rules of Origin Agreement is available from the Trade Compliance Center's web site.

If you have questions about this Agreement or how to use it, you can e-mail the Trade Compliance Center which will forward your message to the Commerce Department's Designated Monitoring Officer for the

Agreement. You can also contact the Designated Monitoring Officer at the following address:

Designated Monitoring Officer
WTO Rules of Origin Agreement
Office of Multilateral Affairs
International Trade Administration
Room 3027
U.S. Department of Commerce
14th Street & Constitution Avenue, N.W.
Washington, D.C. 20230
Tel: (202) 482-3681
Fax: (202) 482-5939

WTO Agreement on Anti-Dumping

What is this Agreement and what does it do?

Who benefits from this Agreement?

How can this Agreement help my company?

Can the U.S. Government help me if I have a problem?

How can I get more information?

What is this Agreement and what does it do?

The Anti-Dumping Agreement of the World Trade Organization (WTO), commonly known as the AD Agreement, governs the application of anti-dumping measures by WTO member countries.

A product is considered to be "dumped" if it is exported to another country at a price below the normal price of a like product in the exporting country. Anti-dumping measures are unilateral remedies (the imposition of anti-dumping duties on the product in question) that the government of the importing country may apply after a thorough investigation has determined that the product is, in fact, being dumped, and that sales of the dumped product are causing material injury to a domestic industry that produces a like product.

All members of the WTO are parties to this Agreement, whose full name is the "Agreement on Implementation of Article VI of the General Agreement on Tariffs and Trade 1994". It went into effect on January 1, 1995. It has no expiration date.

Who benefits from this Agreement?

Any company involved in international trade can benefit from clear and predictable rules for the application of anti-dumping measures.

How can this Agreement help my company?

The AD Agreement ensures that WTO members will not apply anti-dumping measures arbitrarily. It provides detailed substantive requirements for determining whether dumping and injury are, in fact, taking place, and sets forth elaborate procedures that governments must follow when they conduct anti-dumping investigations and impose anti-dumping duties. The Agreement ensures that all proceedings will be transparent and that all interested parties have a full opportunity to defend their interests.

Substantive Requirements

Since a determination of dumping requires a comparison between the export price of a product and its normal value in the exporting country, the AD Agreement sets forth rules for the calculation of export price and normal value. It then explains how a "fair comparison" is made between the two. The government conducting an anti-dumping investigation uses this fair comparison as the basis for determining the "margin of dumping."

The Agreement then sets forth rules for determining whether dumped imports are causing injury to a domestic industry that produces a like product. Injury is defined to mean material injury itself, the threat of material injury or material retardation in the establishment of a domestic industry. The government authorities must establish injury to the domestic industry and that the dumped imports are a cause of that injury. The AD Agreement provides for "cumulative assessments" of the effects of imports on a domestic industry when imports of a product from more than one country are simultaneously subject to anti-dumping investigations.

Investigations

A government normally initiates an anti-dumping investigation on the basis of a written application by a domestic industry, although in special circumstances the government itself can initiate the investigation on the industry's behalf. The application must provide evidence of dumping, injury and a causal link between the two. It must include a complete description of the allegedly dumped product, infomation on the like product produced by the applicant, evidence regarding export price and normal value, an assessment of the impact of the imports on the domestic industry, and information concerning industry support for the application.

The rules set forth in the Agreement for the collection of evidence state that as soon as government authorities initiate an investigation, they must provide the full text of the written application to all known exporters. All interested parties are given access to nonconfidential information and the opportunity to meet with the parties that have adverse interests, so that opposing views can be presented and rebuttal arguments offered. Before they make a final determination of whether dumping has occurred, the government authorities must inform all interested parties of the essential facts under consideration, giving them sufficient time to defend their interests.

An application will be rejected, according to the Agreement, and an investigation promptly terminated if the government authorities conclude that there is insufficient evidence of either dumping or injury. The Agreement provides that unless there are special circumstances, investigations will be concluded within one year and will continue in no case more than 18 months after their initiation.

Price Undertakings

The Agreement provides that goverment authorities can suspend or terminate an anti-dumping proceeding if they receive voluntary undertakings from an exporter that it will revise its prices or cease exporting to the area in question at dumped prices. Investigating authorities have the option of accepting price increases that are less than the margin of dumping if they are adequate to remove the injury to the domestic industry.

Imposition of Anti-Dumping Duties

Under the Agreement, it is up to the government of the importing country to decide whether or not to impose anti-dumping duties. (The Agreement provides an option of not imposing duties in cases where all requirements for imposing such duties have been fulfilled, but not all authorities allow such an option.) The amount of the duty set by the government cannot exceed the margin of dumping, but the Agreement permits it to be lower if it is adequate to remove the injury to the domestic industry.

Normally anti-dumping duties are applied to all imports of the subject merchandise made on or after the date on which their is a preliminary determination of dumping, injury, and causality.

The Agreement states that an anti-dumping duty shall remain in force as long as necessary to counteract dumping that is causing injury. It contains a "sunset" provision that provides that the duty will be terminated five years from the date of its imposition unless the government authorities determine in a review that termination of the duty would lead to continuation or recurrence of dumping and injury.

The Committee; Notifications

The Agreement established a Committee on Anti-dumping Practices, composed of representatives of each WTO member country. This Committee meets not less than twice a year and affords members the opportuniy to consult on any matters relating to the operation of the Agreement. Member countries are required to notify this Committee of their anti-dumping legislation and/or regulations, their anti-dumping actions, and the names, addresses and contact numbers of officials responsible for anti-dumping matters.

Can the U.S. Government help me if I have a problem?

Yes. If your export business is being adversely affected because another WTO member country is not complying with the Anti-Dumping Agreement, contact the Trade Compliance Center's hotline at the U.S. Department of Commerce. The Center can help you understand your rights under this Agreement and can alert the relevant U.S. Government officials to make inquiries, if appropriate, with the other country involved that could help you resolve your exporting problem.

Disputes under the Anti-dumping Agreement can also, in certain circumstances, be resolved by the U.S. Government through the WTO's dispute settlement process, which is described in the *Exporter's Guide to the WTO Understanding on the Settlement of Disputes*.

How can I get more information?

The complete text of the WTO Anti-Dumping Agreement is available from the Trade Compliance Center's web site.

If you have questions about this Agreement or how to use it, you can e-mail the Trade Compliance Center, which will forward your message to the Commerce Department's Designated Monitoring Officer for the Agreement. You can also contact the Designated Monitoring Officer at the following address:

Designated Monitoring Officer—
WTO Anti-Dumping Agreement
Office of Policy—Import Administration
International Trade Administration
Room 3713
U.S. Department of Commerce
14th Street & Constitution Avenue, N.W.
Washington, D.C. 20230
Tel: (202) 482-4412
Fax: (202) 482-2308

Correct Way to Complete the Shipper's Export Declaration Form 7525-V

CORRECT WAY TO COMPLETE THE SHIPPER'S EXPORT DECLARATION FORM 7525-V

Title 15 Code of Federal Regulations, Part 30
(www.census.gov/foreign-trade)

U.S. Department of Commerce
Donald L. Evans, Secretary

Bureau of the Census
(Vacant), Director

Foreign Trade Division
Bureau of the Census
C. Harvey Monk, Jr., Chief

Issued: February 14, 2001

Table of Contents

The Correct Way to Complete the Shipper's Export Declaration (SED)
This booklet explains how to properly complete the SED and contains references to the major rules, regulations, and guidelines to assist you in preparing the SED. If, at any time, you have a question regarding the completion of the SED please contact the Regulations, Outreach, & Education Branch on 301-457-2238 or visit our website at <www.census.gov/foreign-trade>.

The Correct Way to Complete the SED

Follow these instructions carefully to avoid delay at shipping point. Refer to the Foreign Trade Statistics Regulations [FTSR] for specific details on these provisions, 15 CFR Part 30)

1a. Shipper's Export Declarations (SEDs) are required in the following instances:

From	To	No. of Copies
United States	Canada	1 (only if a license is required)
United States (Postal & Non-postal)	Foreign Countries	Postal (1), Nonpostal (2)
United States	Puerto Rico	1
United States	U.S. Virgin Islands	1
Puerto Rico	United States	1
Puerto Rico	Foreign Countries	1
Puerto Rico	U.S. Virgin Islands	1
U.S. Virgin Islands	Foreign Countries	1

1b. Shipper's Export Declarations <u>ARE NOT REQUIRED</u> in the following instances:

From	To
United States	Canada (unless an export license is required)
U.S. Virgin Islands	United States
U.S. Virgin Islands	Puerto Rico
United States/ Puerto Rico	Other U.S. Possessions**
Other U.S. Possessions	United States

** American Samoa, Baker Island, Commonwealth of the Northern Mariana Islands, Guam, Howland Island, Jarvis Island, Johnston Atoll, Kingmen Reef, Midway Islands, Navassa Island, Palmyra Atoll, Wake Island.

2. Purpose of the SED. The Shipper's Export Declaration (SED), Commerce Form 7525-V, is used for compiling the official U.S. export statistics for the United States and for export control purposes. The regulatory provisions for preparing, signing, and filing the SED are contained in the Foreign Trade Statistics Regulations (FTSR), Title 15 Code of Federal Regulations (CFR) Part 30.

3. Form or method of data collection. (a) Paper—The Commerce Form 7525-V and its continuation sheet may be purchased from the Government Printing Office, (202) 512-1800, local Customs District Directors, or can be privately printed. **Privately printed SEDs must conform in every respect to the official form.** The SED Form 7525-V can also be downloaded from the Foreign Trade Division website at *<www.census.gov/foreign-trade>* on buff (yellow) or goldenrod colored paper. Customs will not accept SEDs on white paper. (b) Electronic: Automated Export System (AES)—The U.S.

Census Bureau and the U.S. Customs Service jointly offer an electronic method for filing shipper's export declaration information known as the Automated Export System (AES). Participants in the AES include exporters (U.S. principal party in interest), forwarding or other agents, carriers, nonvessel operating common carriers (NVOCCs), consolidators, port authorities, software vendors, or service centers. Once certified by the Census Bureau, participants may file shipper's export data electronically using the AES in lieu of filing an individual paper SED for each shipment. The Census Bureau also offers a free Internet service for filing SED information through the AES called AES*Direct*. For additional information on AES and AES*Direct* go to the Foreign Trade Division web sites at <*www.census.gov/foreign-trade*> or <*www.aesdirect.gov*>.

For regulatory requirements on filing shipper's export information electronically through the AES refer to the FTSR, Sections 30.60 through 30.66.

4. Preparation and signature of the SED. The SED must be prepared in English, be typewritten or in other nonerasable medium. The original should be signed (signature stamp acceptable) by the exporter (U.S. principal party in interest) or its authorized forwarding or other agent. In all cases where a forwarding or other agent is preparing a SED or AES record on behalf of a principal party in interest (i.e., U.S. or foreign), the principal party in interest must authorize the forwarding or other agent to prepare and sign and file the SED or transmit the AES record on its behalf through a formal power of attorney, written authorization, or, for USPPIs only, by signing block 29 on the paper SED.

5. Requirement for separate SEDs. A separate SED is required for each shipment per USPPI, including each rail car, truck, ocean vessel, airplane, or other vehicle.

A shipment is defined as: All merchandise sent from one exporter (U.S. principal party in interest) to one foreign consignee, to a single foreign country of ultimate destination, on a single carrier, on the same day.

The exporter (U.S. principal party in interest) may list more than one Commerce Department (BXA) license or license exception or a combination of licenses and license exceptions on the same SED or AES shipment. In addition, the exporter may combine "No License Required" (NLR) items with licensed items and license exceptions on the same SED or AES shipment. To avoid confusion when preparing the paper SED, goods licensed by other U.S. agencies, such as the State Department, should be reported on a separate SED from goods licensed by the Commerce Department. For AES transactions, multiple licenses can be reported on one shipment.

Where two or more items are classified under the same Schedule B number, the Schedule B number should appear only once on the SED with a single quantity, shipping weight, and value, unless a validated license requires otherwise or the shipment consists of a combination of foreign and domestic merchandise classified under the same Schedule B number.

Shipments involving multiple invoices or packages should be reported on the same SED.

6. Presentation of the SED. (a) Postal (mail) shipments—the SED must be delivered to a Post Office official with the package at the time of mailing. (See the *U.S. Postal Services's International Mail Manual*.) All mail shipments valued at $2,500 or over, or that require an export license require a SED. (b) All other shipments—the SEDs shall be delivered to the exporting carrier with the merchandise. (c) Exporting carriers are required to file the SED and manifest with Customs at the port of export.

The SED may accompany the merchandise or it may be delivered directly to the exporting carrier at the port of exportation.

In cases where a shipment does not require a SED based on the FTSR, a reference to the applicable section of the FTSR that exempts the merchandise from the requirement to file a SED must be noted on the bill of lading, air waybill, or other loading document. Detailed exemption provisions for when a SED is not required are contained in the FTSR, Subpart D, sections 30.50 through 30.58. For acceptable SED exemption statements refer to Foreign Trade Statistics Letter 168 (amendment 1). Also, see Section 8.

7. Correction to a SED. Corrections or amendments of data to a previously filed SED should be made on a copy of the originally filed SED. Mark "**CORRECTED COPY**" on the top of the SED, line through the appropriate field(s) requiring correction, and insert the correction. File the corrected SED with the Customs Director at the port of export.

For mail exports, corrections must be sent directly to the U.S. Census Bureau, National Processing Center. Attention: Foreign Trade Section, 1201 East 10th Street, Jeffersonville, Indiana 47132 as soon as the need to make such correction or cancellation is determined.

8. A SED is not required in the following instances (SED exemptions). (Reference Sections 30.50 through 30.58 of the FTSR)

A. Shipments where the value of commodities classified under each individual Schedule B number is $2,500 or less and for which an export license is not required, except that a SED is required for exports destined to Cuba, Iran, Iraq, Libya, North Korea, Serbia (excluding Kosovo), Sudan, and Syria. (See §30.55(h))

If a shipment contains a mixture of individual Schedule B numbers valued at $2,500 or less and individual Schedule B numbers valued at over $2,500, only those valued at $2,500 or more should be reported on the SED. (See §30.55(h)(1))

When either all or part of the shipment does not require a SED, one of the following statements must appear on the bill of lading, air waybill, or other loading documents for carrier use:

1. "No SED required, FTSR Section 30.55(h)"
2. "No SED required—no individual Schedule B number valued over $2,500"

3. "Remainder of shipment valued $2,500 or less per individual Schedule B number"

(Note: Refer to FTSR Letter 167 [amendment 1] for more detailed information on acceptable SED exemption statements.)

B. Shipments from the **United States to Canada, except those:** (See §30.58)
   1. Requiring a Department of Commerce export license
   2. Subject to the Department of State, International Traffic in Arms Regulations regardless of license requirements
   3. Subject to Department of Justice, Drug Enforcement Administration, export declaration requirements

(Note: For merchandise transshipped from the United States through Canada for ultimate destination to a foreign country, other than Canada, a SED or AES record is required.)

C. Shipments through the U.S. Postal Service that do not require an export license and the shipment is valued at $2500 or under

D. Shipments from one point in the United States to another point in the United States by routes passing through Mexico, and shipments from one point in Mexico to another point in Mexico by routes passing through the United States

E. Shipments to the U.S. Armed Services
   1. All commodities consigned to the U.S. Armed Service, including exchange systems. (See §30.52)
   2. Department of Defense Military Assistance Program Grant-Aid shipments being transported as Department of Defense cargo. (See §30.52)

F. Shipments to U.S. Government agencies and employees for their exclusive use (See §30.53)

G. Other miscellaneous shipments (See §30.55)
   1. Diplomatic pouches and their contents
   2. Human remains and accompanying receptacles and flowers
   3. Shipments of gift parcels moving under General License GFT
   4. Shipments of interplant correspondence and other business records form a U.S. firm to its subsidiary or affiliate
   5. Shipments of pets as baggage, accompanying or not accompanying persons leaving the United States

H. Merchandise not moving as cargo under a bill of lading or air waybill and not requiring a validated export license
   1. Baggage and household effects of persons leaving the United States when such are owned by the person, in his possession at the time of departure and not intended for sale
   2. Carriers' stores, supplies, equipment, bunker fuel, and so forth, when not intended for unlading in a foreign country

3. Usual and reasonable kinds and quantities of dunnage necessary to secure and stow cargo (for sole use on board the carrier)

If the above shipments are moving under a bill of lading or air waybill, a SED is required, but Schedule B numbers should **not** be shown, and the SED should include a statement that the shipment consists of baggage, personal effects, and so forth.

If these shipments require a validated export license, the SED must identify the shipment as baggage, personal effects, and so forth, and must contain all of the information required on the SED.

I. SED for personal effects and household goods
   1. A SED is required for personal effects and household goods only when the value of such items is $2,500 or over. A Schedule B number is not required for such items.
   2. Personal effects and household goods destined for Canada do not require a SED regardless of value.

9. Retention of shipping documents. Exporters or their agents must maintain copies of shipping documents for a period of 5 years for statistical purposes. Additional record retention requirements for licensed shipments appear in the Export Administration Regulations. Exporters or their agents must also be aware of the record retention policies of other government agencies.

10. Administration provisions. The SED and its content is strictly confidential and used solely for official purposes authorized by the Secretary of Commerce in accordance with 13 U.S.C. Section 301(g). Neither the SED nor its contents may be disclosed to anyone except the exporter or its agent by those having possession of or access to any official copy. (See §30.91)

Information from the SED (except common information) may not be copied to manifests or other shipping documents. The exporter (U.S. principal party in interest) or the forwarding or other agent may not furnish the SED or its content to anyone for unofficial purposes.

Copies of the SED may be supplied to the exporter (U.S. principal party in interest) or its agent only when such copies are needed to comply with official U.S. Government requirements.

A SED presented for export constitutes a representation by the exporter (U.S. principal party in interest) that all statements and information are in accordance with the export control regulations. The commodity described on the declaration is authorized under the particular license as identified on the declaration, all statements conform to the applicable licenses, and all conditions of the export control regulations have been met.

It is unlawful to knowingly make false or misleading representation for exportation. This constitutes a violation of Export Administration Act, 50, U.S.C. App. 2410. It is also a violation of export control laws and regulations to be connected in any way with an altered SED to effect export.

Commodities that have been, are being, or for which there is probable cause to believe they are intended to be exported in violation of laws or regulations are subject to seizure, detention, condemnation, or sale under 22 U.S.C. Section 401.

To knowingly make false or misleading statements relating to information on the SED is a criminal offense subject to penalties as provided for in 18 U.S.C. Section 1001.

Violations of the Foreign Trade Statistics Regulations are subject to civil penalties as authorized by 13 U.S.C. Section 305. (See §30.95)

11. Regulations. Detailed legal and regulatory requirements regarding the SED and its preparation are contained in the Foreign Trade Statistics Regulations (FTSR) (15 CFR, Part 30). Questions concerning the FTSR may be directed to the Regulations, Outreach, & Education Branch Foreign Trade Division, U.S. Census Bureau on (301) 457-2238. Up-to-date copies of regulations, FTSR Letters, *Federal Register* Notices, and other current information can also be accessed on the Foreign Trade Division's web site at <*www.census.gov/foreign-trade*>

Information concerning export control laws and regulations including additional SED requirements is contained in the Export Administration Regulations (EAR) (15 CFR Parts 730-774) which may be purchased from the Superintendent of Documents, U.S. Government Printing Office, Washington, DC 20402. The EAR can also be accessed on the Bureau of Export Administration (BXA) website at <*www.bxa.doc.gov*>

12. Office of Management and Budget Response burden paragraph. Public reporting burden for this collection of information is estimated to average slightly more than 11 minutes (.186 hour) per response for the paper SED, Commerce Form 7525-V, and approximately 3 minutes (.05 hour) per response for the Automated Export System, including the time for reviewing instructions, searching existing data sources, gathering and maintaining the data needed, and completing and reviewing the collection of information. Send comments regarding this burden or any other aspect of this collection of information, including suggestions for reducing this burden to the Associate Director for Administration, Room 3104, Federal Office Building 3, Bureau of the Census, Washington, DC 20233-0001; and to the Office of Management and Budget, Washington, DC 20503.

13. References
Schedule B—Statistical Classification of Domestic and Foreign Commodities Exported from the United States. For sale by the Superintendent of Documents, U.S. Government, U.S. Government Printing Office, Washington, DC 20402 and local U.S. Customs District Directors. A Schedule B search engine is also available on the FTD web site. (*www.census.gov/foreign-trade*)

Schedule C—Classification of Country and Territory Designations for U.S. Foreign Trade Statistics. Free from the Bureau of the Census, Washington, DC 20233-0001. Also included as part of Schedule B. Schedule C codes are also available on the FTD web site. (*www.census.gov/foreign-trade*)

Schedule D—Classification of Customs Districts and Ports for U.S. Foreign Trade Statistics. Free from the Bureau of the Census, Washington, DC 20233-0001. Also included as part of Schedule B. The Schedule D codes are also available on the FTD web site. (*www.census.gov/foreign-trade*)

Foreign Trade Statistics Regulations (FTSR). Free from the Bureau of the Census, Washington, DC 20233-0001. The FTSR is also available for downloading on the FTD web site. (*www.census.gov/foreign-trade*)

Export Administration Regulations (EAR). For sale by the Superintendent of Documents, U.S. Government Printing Office, Washington, DC 20402 and U.S. Department of Commerce District Offices. The EAR is also available on the BXA web site (*www.bxa.doc.gov*)

Note: This is an instructional pamphlet summarizing the preparation of the SED. It is in no way intended as a substitute for the Foreign Trade Statistics Regulations, the Export Administration Regulations, or the regulations of any other agency.

See the Appendix for a list of telephone contacts providing additional information.

Information to Be Reported on the Shipper's Export Declaration Form 7525-V

Block Number and Data Required

1(a) **U.S. Principal Party In Interest (USPPI).** Provide the name and address of the U.S. exporter (U.S. principal party in interest). The USPPI is the person in the United States that receives the primary benefit, monetary or otherwise, of the export transaction. Generally that person is the U.S. seller, manufacturer, order party, or foreign entity. The foreign entity must be listed as the USPPI if in the United States when the items are purchased or obtained for export. Report only the first five digits of the Zip code. (See §30.4, 30.7)

1(b) **USPPI Employer Identification Number (EIN) or ID Number.** Enter the USPPI's Internal Revenue Service Employer Identification Number (EIN) or Social Security Number (SSN) if no EIN has been assigned. Report the 9-digit numerical code as reported on your latest Employer's Quarterly Federal Tax Return, Treasury Form 941. The EIN is usually available from your accounting or payroll department. If an EIN or SSN is not available a border crossing number, passport number, or a Customs identification number must be reported. (See §30.7(d)(2).)

1(c) **Parties to transaction.** Indicate if this is a *related* or *nonrelated* party transaction. A related party transaction is a transaction between a USPPI and a foreign consignee, (e.g., parent company or sister company), where there is at least 10 percent ownership of each by the same U.S. or foreign person or business enterprise.

2 **Date of exportation.** Enter the date the merchandise is scheduled to leave the United States for all methods of transportation. If the actual date is not known, report the best estimate of departure. The date format should be indicated by MM/DD/YYYY.

3 **Transportation reference number.** Report the booking number for ocean shipments. The booking number is the reservation number assigned

by the carrier to hold space on the vessel for the cargo being shipped. For air shipments the airway bill number must be reported. For other methods of transportation leave blank.

4(a) **Ultimate consignee.** Enter the name and address of the foreign party actually receiving the merchandise for the designated end-use or the party so designated on the export license. For overland shipments to Mexico, also include the Mexican state in the address.

4(b) **Intermediate consignee.** Enter the name and address of the party in a foreign country who makes delivery of the merchandise to the ultimate consignee or the party so named on the export license.

5 **Forwarding agent.** Enter the name and address of the forwarding or other agent authorized by a principal party in interest.

6 **Point (State) of origin or foreign trade zone (FTZ) number.**
   a. If from a FTZ enter the FTZ number for exports leaving the FTZ, otherwise enter the:
   b. Two-digit U.S. Postal Service abbreviation of the state in which the merchandise actually starts its journey to the port of export, or
   c. State of the commodity of the greatest value, or
   d. State of consolidation

7 **Country of ultimate destination.** Enter the country in which the merchandise is to be consumed, further processed, or manufactured; the final country of destination as known to the exporter at the time of shipment; or the country of ultimate destination as shown on the export license. Two-digit (alpha character) International Standards Organization (ISO) codes may also be used.

8 **Loading pier.** (For vessel shipments only.) Enter the number or name of the pier at which the merchandise is laden aboard the exporting vessel.

9 **Method of transportation.** Enter the method of transportation by which the merchandise is exported (or exits the border of the United States). Specify the method of transportation by name, such as, vessel, air, rail, truck, etc. Specify "own power" if applicable.

10 **Exporting carrier.** Enter the name of the carrier transporting the merchandise out of the United States. For vessel shipments, give the name of the vessel.

11 **Port of export.**
   a. For overland shipments—Enter the name of the U.S. Customs port at which the surface carrier (truck or railcar) crosses the border.
   b. For vessel and air shipments—Enter the name of the U.S. Customs port where the merchandise is loaded on the carrier (airplane or ocean vessel) that is taking the merchandise out of the United States.
   c. For postal (mail) shipments—Enter the U.S. Post Office from which the merchandise is mailed.

12 **Foreign port of unloading.** For vessel shipments between the United States and foreign countries, enter the foreign port and country at which the merchandise will be unloaded from the exporting carrier. For vessel and air shipments between the United States and Puerto Rico, enter the Schedule C code, "U.S. Customs District and Port Code."

13 **Containerized.** (For vessel shipments only.) Check the **YES** box for cargo originally booked as containerized cargo and for cargo that has been placed in containers at the vessel operator's option.

14 **Carrier identification code.** Enter the 4-character Standard Carrier Alpha Code (SCAC) of the carrier for vessel, rail, and truck shipments or the two- or three-character International Air Transport Association (IATA) Code of the carrier for air shipments. In a consolidated shipment, if the ultimate carrier is unknown, the consolidators carrier ID code may be reported. The National Motor Freight Traffic Association (703) 838-1831 or *www.nmfta.org* issues the SCACs for ocean carriers, trucking companies, and consolidators. The American Association of Railroads, Railinc (919) 651-5006 issues the SCAC codes for rail carriers. The International Air Transportation Association (IATA) issues the air carrier codes. The IATA codes are available on the Foreign Trade Division web site under "Air Carrier Codes" at *<www.census.gov/foreign-trade>*.

15 **Shipment reference number.** Enter the unique reference number assigned by the filer of the SED for identification purposes. This shipment reference number must be unique for five years. For example, report an invoice number, bill of lading or airway bill number, internal file number or so forth.

16 **Entry number.** Enter the Import Entry Number when the export transaction is used as proof of export for import transactions, such as In-Bond, Temporary Import Bond, or Drawback's and so forth. Also, an Entry Number is required for merchandise that is entered as an import (CF 7501 or Automated Broker Interface (ABI) entries) and is then being exported out of the United States.

17 **Hazardous materials.** Check the appropriate "Yes" or "No" indicator that identifies the shipment as hazardous as defined by the Department of Transportation.

18 **In bond code.** Report one of the two-character In-Bond codes listed in Part IV of Appendix C of the FTSR (15 CFR Part 30) to include the type of In-Bond or not In-Bond shipment.

19 **Routed export transaction.** Check the appropriate "Yes" or "No" indicator that identifies the transaction as a routed export transaction. A routed export transaction is where the foreign principal party in interest authorizes a U.S. forwarding or other agent to export the merchandise out of the United States.

20 **Schedule B description of commodities.** Use columns 22-24 to enter the commercial description of the commodity being exported, its schedule B number, the quantity in schedule B units, and the shipping

weight in kilograms. Enter a sufficient description of the commodity as to permit verification of the Schedule B Commodity Number or the commodity description as shown on the validated export license. Include marks, numbers, or other identification shown on the packages and the numbers and kinds of packages (boxes, barrels, baskets, etc.)

21 **"D" (Domestic), "F" (Foreign), or "M" (Foreign Military Sales)**

    a. Domestic exports (D)—merchandise that is grown, produced, or manufactured in the United States (including imported merchandise which has been enhanced in value or changed from the form in which imported by further manufacture or processing in the United States).

    b. Foreign exports (F)—merchandise that has entered the United States and is being re-exported in the same condition as when imported.

    c. Foreign military sales (M)—exports of merchandise that are sold under the foreign military sales program.

22 **Schedule B Number.** Enter the commercial description of the commodity being exported and the ten-digit commodity number as provided in Schedule B—Statistical Classification of Domestic and Foreign Commodities Exported from the United States. See item 5 for a discussion of not repeating the same Schedule B numbers on the SED. If necessary, the Harmonized Tariff Schedule (HTS) number can be reported on the SED. See the Appendix showing a list of telephone numbers for assistance with Schedule B numbers.

23 **Quantity (Schedule B units).** Report whole unit(s) as specified in the Schedule B commodity classification code. Report also the unit specified on the export license if the units differ. See the Appendix showing a list of telephone numbers for assistance with units of quantity.

24 **Shipping weight (kilograms).** (For vessel and air shipment only.) Enter the gross shipping weight in kilograms for each Schedule B number, including the weight of containers but excluding carrier equipment. To determine kilograms use pounds (lbs) multiplied by 0.4536 = kilograms (report whole units).

25 **VIN/product number/vehicle title number.** (For used self-propelled vehicles only.) Report the following items of information *for used self-propelled vehicles* as defined in Customs regulations 19 CFR 192.1: (1) report the unique vehicle identification number (VIN) in the proper format; (2) report the product identification number (PIN) for those used self propelled vehicles for which there are no VINs; and (3) the vehicle title number.

26 **Value (U.S. dollars).** Enter the selling price or cost if not sold, including freight, insurance, and other charges to U.S. port of export, but excluding unconditional discounts and commissions (nearest whole dollar, omit cents). The value to be reported on the SED is the exporter's (U.S.

principal party in interest) price or cost if not sold to the foreign principal party in interest. Report one value for each Schedule B number.

27 License no./license exception symbol/authorization—*whenever a SED or AES record is required:*

    a. Enter the license number on the SED or AES record when you are exporting under the authority of a Department of Commerce, Bureau of Export Administration (BXA) license, a Department of State, Office of Defense Trade Controls (ODTC) license, a Department of the Treasury, Office of Foreign Assets Control (OFAC) license (enter either the general or specific OFAC license number), a Department of Justice, Drug Enforcement Agency (DEA) permit, or any other export license number issued by a Federal government agency. For the BXA license the expiration date of the license must be entered on the paper version of the SED only.

    b. Enter the correct License Exception symbol (e.g., LVS, GBS, CIV) on the SED or AES record when you are exporting under the authority of a License Exception. See §740.1, §740.2, and §758.1 of the Export Administration Regulations (EAR).

    c. Enter the "No License Required" (NLR) designator when you are exporting items under the NLR provisions of the EAR:

        1. When the items being exported are subject to the EAR but not listed on the Commerce Control List (CCL) (i.e. items that are classified as EAR99); and

        2. When the items being exported are listed on the CCL but do not require a license.

28 Export Control Classification Number (ECCN). Whenever a SED or AES record is required, you must enter the correct Export Control Classification Number (ECCN) on the SED or AES record for all exports authorized under a license or License Exception, and items being exported under the "No License Required" (NLR) provisions of the EAR that are listed on the CCL and have a reason for control other than antiterrorism (AT).

29 Duly authorized officer of employee. Provide the signature of the exporter (U.S. principal party in interest) authorizing the named forwarding or agent to effect the export when such agent does not have a formal power of attorney or written authorization.

30 Signature/Certification. Provide the signature of the exporter (U.S. principal party in interest) or authorized forwarding or other agent certifying the truth and accuracy of the information on the SED, the title of exporter (U.S. principal party in interest) or authorized agent, the date of signature, the telephone number of the exporter (U.S. principal party in interest) or authorized agent prepating the SED and who can best answer questions for resolving problems on the SED, and the e-mail address of the exporter (U.S. principal party in interest) or authorized agent.

31 Authentication. For Customs use only.

Appendix

List of telephone numbers providing additional assistance in filling out the Shipper's Export Declaration (SED)

(Census Bureau) Foreign Trade Division Contacts

Commodity Classification (Schedule B Number) Assistance		*Schedule B*
Food, animal, and wood products (Including paper and printed matter)	301-457-3484	Chapters 1–24; 41; 43–49
Minerals	301-457-3484	Chapters 25–27; 68–71
Metals	301-457-3259	Chapters 72–83
Textiles and apparel	301-457-3484	Chapters 41–43; 50–67
Machinery and vehicles (including computers, other electronic equipment and transportation)	301-457-3259	Chapters 84–85; 86–89
Chemical and sundries	301-457-3259	Chapters 28–40; 90–98

Foreign Trade Statistics Regulations   301-457-2238

Automated Export System (AES)   1-800-549-0595

Other Agency Export Control Telephone Contacts

Bureau of Export Administration, Department of Commerce:
<www.bxa.doc.gov>
Washington, D.C.: 202-482-4811 or 202-482-2642
Newport Beach, California 949-660-0144
San Jose, California 408-998-7402

International Trade Administration, Export Assistance Center
1-800-872-8723; <www.ita.doc.gov>

Department of State, Office of Defense Trade Controls (ODTC)
(International Traffic in Arms Regulations (ITAR)) 202-663-2714;
<www.pmdtc.org>

Department of the Treasury, Office of Foreign Assets Control (OFAC)
(Sanctioned countries and trade restrictions) 202-622-2490;
<www.treas.gov/ofac>

U.S. Customs Import (Inbound) Questions (Summary Management Office) 202-927-0625; <www.customs.treas.gov>

U.S. Customs Export (Outbound) Questions (Outbound Programs)
202-927-6060; *<www.customs.treas.gov>*

NAFTA (hotline) 972-574-4061; *<www.mac.doc.gov/nafta/nafta2.htm>*

To order paper SEDs contact the: Government Printing Office (GPO), Publication Order & Information Office: 202-512-1800

U.S. DEPARTMENT OF COMMERCE — U.S. Census Bureau – Economics and Statistics Administration — BUREAU OF EXPORT ADMINISTRATION

SHIPPER'S EXPORT DECLARATION

FORM **7525-V** (7-25-2000)

OMB No. 0607-0152

1a. U.S. PRINCIPAL PARTY IN INTEREST (USPPI) *(Complete name and address)*		
Willis and Company 4052 Jodie Lane Toledo, OH		

ZIP CODE: 12345

2. DATE OF EXPORTATION: 10-01-00

3. TRANSPORTATION REFERENCE NO.: 00-333-3838

b. USPPI EIN (IRS) OR ID NO.: 12-3456789

c. PARTIES TO TRANSACTION: ☐ Related ☒ Non-related

4a. ULTIMATE CONSIGNEE *(Complete name and address)*
Brandy, Inc.
38 Windy Lane
London, England WB32LB

b. INTERMEDIATE CONSIGNEE *(Complete name and address)*
Hercule Movers
33 Airport Road
London, England WB32LB

5. FORWARDING AGENT *(Complete name and address)*
Export Services
10 Parcel Express Way
New York, NY 10001

6. POINT (STATE) OF ORIGIN OR FTZ NO.: OH

7. COUNTRY OF ULTIMATE DESTINATION: England

8. LOADING PIER *(Vessel only)*

9. METHOD OF TRANSPORTATION *(Specify)*: AIR

14. CARRIER IDENTIFICATION CODE: PEGA

15. SHIPMENT REFERENCE NO.: SED1001-01

10. EXPORTING CARRIER: Peg Airlines

11. PORT OF EXPORT: JFK International Airport

16. ENTRY NUMBER

17. HAZARDOUS MATERIALS: ☐ Yes ☒ No

12. PORT OF UNLOADING *(Vessel and air only)*: Gatwick, England

13. CONTAINERIZED *(Vessel only)*: ☐ Yes ☐ No

18. IN BOND CODE

19. ROUTED EXPORT TRANSACTION: ☐ Yes ☒ No

20. SCHEDULE B DESCRIPTION OF COMMODITIES *(Use columns 22–24)*

D/F or M (21)	SCHEDULE B NUMBER (22)	QUANTITY – SCHEDULE B UNIT(S) (23)	SHIPPING WEIGHT (Kilograms) (24)	VIN/PRODUCT NUMBER/ VEHICLE TITLE NUMBER (25)	VALUE (U.S. dollars, omit cents) (Selling price or cost if not sold) (26)
D	3406.00.0000 Candles	15 KG	18 KG	USE ONLY FOR USED VEHICLES	3000.00
D	3405.10.0000 Shoe Polish	20 KG	21 KG		2900.00

27. LICENSE NO./LICENSE EXCEPTION SYMBOL/AUTHORIZATION: AO12345

28. ECCN *(When required)*: 2A225

29. Duly authorized officer or employee

The USPPI authorizes the forwarder named above to act as forwarding agent for export control and customs purposes.

30. I certify that all statements made and all information contained herein are true and correct and that I have read and understand the instructions for preparation of this document, set forth in the "**Correct Way to Fill Out the Shipper's Export Declaration**." I understand that civil and criminal penalties, including forfeiture and sale, may be imposed for making false or fraudulent statements herein, failing to provide the requested information or for violation of U.S. laws on exportation (13 U.S.C. Sec. 305; 22 U.S.C. Sec. 401; 18 U.S.C. Sec. 1001; 50 U.S.C. App. 2410).

Signature

Title: President

Date: 10-01-00

Telephone No. *(Include Area Code)*: (111) 555-1111

E-mail address: your.name@your.company

Confidential – For use solely for official purposes authorized by the Secretary of Commerce (13 U.S.C. 301 (g)).

Export shipments are subject to inspection by U.S. Customs Service and/or Office of Export Enforcement.

31. AUTHENTICATION *(When required)*

NOTE: If no license is required put 'NLR' in block 27 and EAR 99 in block 28.

This form may be printed by private parties provided it conforms to the official form. For sale by the Superintendent of Documents, Government Printing Office, Washington, DC 20402, and local Customs District Directors. The "**Correct Way to Fill Out the Shipper's Export Declaration**" is available from the U.S. Census Bureau, Washington, DC 20233.

U.S. DEPARTMENT OF COMMERCE — U.S. CENSUS BUREAU – Economics and Statistics Administration — BUREAU OF EXPORT ADMINISTRATION

FORM **7525-V** (7-25-2000)   **SHIPPER'S EXPORT DECLARATION**   OMB No. 0607-0152

1a. U.S. PRINCIPAL PARTY IN INTEREST (USPPI) *(Complete name and address)*

ZIP CODE

2. DATE OF EXPORTATION

3. TRANSPORTATION REFERENCE NO.

b. USPPI EIN (IRS) OR ID NO.

c. PARTIES TO TRANSACTION
__ Related   __ Non-related

4a. ULTIMATE CONSIGNEE *(Complete name and address)*

b. INTERMEDIATE CONSIGNEE *(Complete name and address)*

5. FORWARDING AGENT *(Complete name and address)*

6. POINT (STATE) OF ORIGIN OR FTZ NO.

7. COUNTRY OF ULTIMATE DESTINATION

8. LOADING PIER *(Vessel only)*

9. METHOD OF TRANSPORTATION *(Specify)*

14. CARRIER IDENTIFICATION CODE

15. SHIPMENT REFERENCE NO.

10. EXPORTING CARRIER

11. PORT OF EXPORT

16. ENTRY NUMBER

17. HAZARDOUS MATERIALS
Yes   __ No

12. PORT OF UNLOADING *(Vessel and air only)*

13. CONTAINERIZED *(Vessel only)*
Yes   No

18. IN BOND CODE

19. ROUTED EXPORT TRANSACTION
__ Yes   __ No

20. SCHEDULE B DESCRIPTION OF COMMODITIES *(Use columns 22–24)*

D/F or M (21)	SCHEDULE B NUMBER (22)	QUANTITY – SCHEDULE B UNIT(S) (23)	SHIPPING WEIGHT (Kilograms) (24)	VIN/PRODUCT NUMBER/ VEHICLE TITLE NUMBER (25)	VALUE (U.S. dollars, omit cents) (Selling price or cost if not sold) (26)

27. LICENSE NO./LICENSE EXCEPTION SYMBOL/AUTHORIZATION

28. ECCN *(When required)*

29. Duly authorized officer or employee

The USPPI authorizes the forwarder named above to act as forwarding agent for export control and customs purposes.

30. I certify that all statements made and all information contained herein are true and correct and that I have read and understand the instructions for preparation of this document, set forth in the **"Correct Way to Fill Out the Shipper's Export Declaration."** I understand that civil and criminal penalties, including forfeiture and sale, may be imposed for making false or fraudulent statements herein, failing to provide the requested information or for violation of U.S. laws on exportation (13 U.S.C. Sec. 305; 22 U.S.C. Sec. 401; 18 U.S.C. Sec. 1001; 50 U.S.C. App. 2410).

Signature

Confidential – For use solely for official purposes authorized by the Secretary of Commerce (13 U.S.C. 301 (g)).

Title

Export shipments are subject to inspection by U.S. Customs Service and/or Office of Export Enforcement.

Date

31. AUTHENTICATION *(When required)*

Telephone No. *(Include Area Code)*

E-mail address

This form may be printed by private parties provided it conforms to the official form. For sale by the Superintendent of Documents, Government Printing Office, Washington, DC 20402, and local Customs District Directors. The **"Correct Way to Fill Out the Shipper's Export Declaration"** is available from the U.S. Census Bureau, Washington, DC 20233.

Sample Fines and Penalties on Export Transactions from the Bureau of Export Administration (BXA) Archives

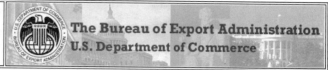

Contacts:

Eugene Cottilli
(202) 482-2721
Email

For Immediate Release
October 23, 2000

New York Customs Broker Pays Fine
for Dealing With a Denied Person

(WASHINGTON) The Commerce Department announced today that it has imposed a $40,000 civil penalty on Worchell Transport Inc., doing business as Prime Transport, a freight forwarder and customs broker, in Springfield Garden, New York.

The civil penalty resolves allegations that on eight separate occasions Prime Transport engaged in export transactions with a person whose U.S. export privileges had been denied. In this case, Prime Transport shipped U.S.-origin commodities to Cosmotrans AG in Switzerland. The Department denied Cosmotrans's U.S. export privileges in 1988 for 20 years. The transactions that led to the penalty on Prime Transport took place in 1995 and 1996. As part of the settlement, the Department will suspend $7,000 of the $40,000 fine for one year, and will waive that amount provided that Prime Transport commits no further violations.

Special agents from the Bureau of Export Administration's Export Enforcement field office in New York investigated the case.

The Department of Commerce through its Bureau of Export Administration administers and enforces export controls for reasons of national security, foreign policy, nonproliferation, and short supply. Criminal penalties, as well as administrative sanctions can be imposed for violations of the Regulations.

BXA Home > BXA Press Page

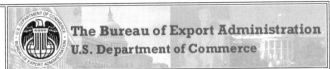

The Bureau of Export Administration
U.S. Department of Commerce

Contacts:

Eugene Cottilli
(202) 482-2721
Email

**For Immediate Release
September 29, 2000**

Michigan Firm Settles Charges of Illegal Export

Washington - The Department of Commerce's Bureau of Export Administration (BXA) today imposed a $64,000 civil penalty on Trijicon, Inc., a Michigan company, to settle allegations that it illegally exported U.S.- origin optical sighting devices for firearms, F. Amanda DeBusk, Assistant Secretary for Export Enforcement, announced.

BXA alleged that on four separate occasions between 1994 and 1998 Trijicon, Inc., exported U.S. - origin optical sighting devices for firearms from the United States to Argentina and South Africa without the licenses that it knew were required by the Export Administration Regulations. While neither admitting nor denying the allegations, Trijicon, Inc. agreed to settle the allegations.

Special agents from Commerce's Chicago Office of Export Enforcement investigated the case. A portion of the fine, $19,500, has been suspended for one year.

The Department of Commerce, through its Bureau of Export Administration, administers and enforces export controls for reasons of national security, foreign policy, nonproliferation and short supply. Criminal penalties, as well as administrative sanctions, can be imposed for violations of the regulations.

United States
Department of
Justice

11th Floor, Federal Building
450 Golden Gate Avenue
Box 36055
San Francisco, California 94102
(415) 436-7200
FAX:(415) 436-

FOR IMMEDIATE RELEASE

**Commerce
Department
Contacts:**
Eugene Cottilli
Steve Jacques
(202) 482-2721
Email

The United States Attorney's Office for the Northern District of California announced today that Optical Associates, Inc. has pled guilty to the charge that it made an unlawful export to a prohibited entity in violation of 50 U.S.C. § 1705(b). The Company pled guilty today in court proceedings in San Francisco before the Honorable Phyllis J. Hamilton, United States District Judge.

In pleading guilty, the Company admitted that on September 30, 1998, it exported a mask aligner and related parts from the United States to the State Bank of India. The Company admitted that the value of this export was $93,360, and that the Company did not seek or obtain a license for this export. The Company further admitted that the intended end-user for this export was Bhaba Atomic Research Center, an entity also known as BARC.

The Company admitted that its export to BARC was illegal. The Company also admitted that at the time it exported the mask aligner, it knew the export was illegal.

According to the indictment, the mask aligner is controlled for anti-terrorism under the Export Administration Regulations issued by the United States Department of Commerce. BARC is a division of the Department of Atomic Energy of the Government of India. Unlicensed exports to Bhaba Atomic Research Center have been prohibited since June 30, 1997.

Optical Associates, Inc. is a California corporation with offices in Milpitas, California.

Optical Associates, Inc. will appear for sentencing on January 17, 2000 at 1:30 PM before Judge Hamilton. Judge Hamilton's courtroom is located at 450 Golden Gate Avenue, San Francisco, California.

The maximum statutory penalty for a violation of 50 U.S.C. § 1705(b) is five years probation and a maximum fine of $500,000. The actual sentence will be dictated by the Federal Sentencing Guidelines, which take into account a number of factors, and will be imposed in the discretion of the Court.

The conviction is the result of an investigation by the United States Department of Commerce and the United States Customs Service. Dave Anderson is the Assistant U.S. prosecuting the case with the assistance of legal technician Helen Yee.

All press inquiries to the United States Attorney's Office should be directed to Assistant U.S. Attorney Matthew J. Jacobs at 415-436-7181.

BXA Home > BXA Press Page

United States Department of Justice

United States Attorney
Northern District of Georgia

Suite 1800 Richard Russell Building
75 Spring Street, S.W.
Atlanta, Georgia 30335
Telephone (404)581-6000
Fax (404)581-6181

Commerce Department Contacts:
Eugene Cottilli
Steve Jacques
(202) 482-2721
Email

NORCROSS, GEORGIA, COMPANY SENTENCED FOR VIOLATING EMBARGO BY SELLING $600,000 IN GOODS TO IRAN

Richard H. Deane, Jr., United States Attorney for the Northern District of Georgia and Amanda DeBusk, Assistant Secretary for Export Enforcement, United States Department of Commerce, announce that FEDERAL PARTS INTERNATIONAL, INC., a Norcross, Georgia, based corporation, has been sentenced on charges of conspiracy to violate the United States' embargo against Iran, and MEDHI a/k/a "Michael" AZARIN, 58, of Atlanta, Georgia, the owner of FEDERAL PARTS INTERNATIONAL, and the company's manager, FARHAD AZARIN, 33, of Norcross, Georgia, have been sentenced on charges of making false statements to federal investigators. According to Deane:

FEDERAL PARTS INTERNATIONAL was sentenced to pay a fine of one quarter of a million dollars. MEDHI a/k/a "Michael" AZARIN, the owner of FEDERAL PARTS INTERNATIONAL, was sentenced to 6 months in federal prison, and an additional 5 months of home confinement, and the company's manager, FARHAD AZARIN, was sentenced to 6 months in federal prison, and an additional 5 months of home confinement.

MEDHI a/k/a "Michael" AZARIN, the owner of FEDERAL PARTS INTERNATIONAL, and the company's manager, FARHAD AZARIN, pleaded guilty before United States District Judge Orinda D. Evans on May 8, 2000, which had been the first scheduled day of trial on the charges.

On December 2, 1998, a federal grand jury returned an indictment against the corporation and the two men. The indictment charged that from May, 1995, through June, 1996, FEDERAL PARTS INTERNATIONAL conspired with German and Iranian companies to export automobile parts from the U.S. to companies in Iran in violation of an Executive Order issued by the President of the United States in May, 1995. The order imposed an embargo against Iran which prohibited virtually all exports of goods from the U.S. to Iran and also prohibited persons in the U.S. from conducting transactions with the purpose of evading and avoiding the embargo's prohibitions.

Between October 1995, and June, 1996, FEDERAL PARTS INTERNATIONAL conspired to export auto parts to Iran using a German company as an intermediary to complete the transactions.

Approximately $600,000 worth of auto parts were shipped from the FEDERAL PARTS INTERNATIONAL warehouse for this purpose, and the government alleged that FEDERAL PARTS INTERNATIONAL was preparing to make additional shipments valued at $5-6 million when the scheme was discovered and stopped by the United States Department of Commerce, Office of Export Enforcement.

During the Commerce Department's investigation, MEHDI AZARIN, the owner of Federal Parts International, and FARHAD AZARIN, his nephew, were both questioned as to whether the German company was forwarding the auto parts it had received from FEDERAL PARTS INTERNATIONAL to companies in Iran. Both MEHDI AZARIN and FARHAD AZARIN falsely denied that they knew what the German company was doing with those parts.

The case was investigated by Special Agents of the Office of Export Enforcement, United States Department of Commerce.

Assistant United States Attorneys Daniel P. Griffin and Randy S. Chartash are prosecuting the case.

For further information please contact Richard H. Deane, Jr., United States Attorney or F. Gentry Shelnutt, Criminal Chief, through Patrick Crosby, Public Affairs Officer, U.S. Attorney's Office, at (404) 581-6016.

BXA Home > BXA Press Page

BXA HOME
WHAT'S NEW
SITE SEARCH

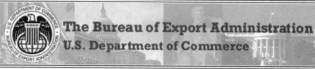

The Bureau of Export Administration
U.S. Department of Commerce

Contacts:

Eugene Cottilli
(202) 482-2721
Email

**For Immediate Release
August 18, 2000**

Commerce Reaches Settlement with Dexin International, Inc. for Illegal Exports to China

WASHINGTON -- Commerce Assistant Secretary of Export Enforcement F. Amanda DeBusk today announced that the Department has imposed a $50,000 penalty on Dexin International, Inc., of West Covina, CA, for alleged violations of the Export Administration Regulations (EAR) involving shipments to China.

The Department alleged that on two separate occasions in 1994 and 1995, Dexin International, Inc., exported thermal video systems to China without obtaining the export licenses it knew or had reason to know were required under the EAR. Commerce also alleged that the company made a false and misleading statement of material fact on a Shipper's Export Declaration filed with the U.S. government in connection with one export.

Dexin International, Inc., agreed to pay the penalty to settle the charges. The Department suspended payment of $35,000 of the civil penalty for one year. It will then be waived as long as the company does not violate the EAR. The company neither admitted nor denied the allegations.

The Department of Commerce, through its Bureau of Export Administration, administers and enforces export controls for reasons of national security, foreign policy, nonproliferation and short supply. Criminal penalties, as well as administrative sanctions, can be imposed for violations of the regulations.

BXA Home > BXA Press Page

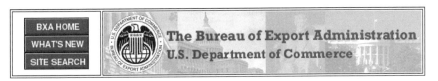

Contact
BXA Public Affairs:
Eugene Cottilli
(202) 482-2721
Email

For Immediate Release
August 10, 2000

Federal Express Settles Charges of Illegal Exports

WASHINGTON -- Commerce Assistant Secretary for Export Enforcement F. Amanda DeBusk today imposed $15,000 in civil penalties on Federal Express (FedEx), of Memphis, Tenn., for allegedly facilitating the export of U.S.-origin equipment to a Denied Person and failure to maintain records of the subject transaction. A person or company may not participate, directly or indirectly, in an export-related transaction subject to the Export Administration Regulations with a Denied Person.

The Department alleged that FedEx, in 1996, facilitated the export of semiconductor equipment from the United States to Taiwan. The export was destined to a Denied Person, Realtek Semiconductor Co., Ltd., of Taipei, Taiwan. The Department also alleged that FedEx failed to maintain a proper record of the transaction.

The penalties were imposed as a result of an investigation conducted by the Office of Export Enforcement's Boston Field Office.

The Department of Commerce, through its Bureau of Export Administration, administers and enforces export controls for reasons of national security, foreign policy, nonproliferation and short supply. Criminal penalties, as well as administrative sanctions, can be imposed for violations of the regulations.

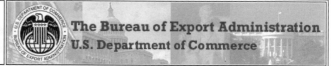

BXA HOME
WHAT'S NEW
SITE SEARCH

Contacts:

Eugene Cottilli
(202) 482-2721
Email

**For Immediate Release
August 9, 2000**

Washington Company Settles Charges of Illegal Exports

WASHINGTON -- Commerce Assistant Secretary for Export Enforcement F. Amanda DeBusk today imposed a $5,000 civil penalty on Expeditors International, Inc., through its San Francisco office, for facilitating the export of U.S.-origin equipment to a Denied Party. It is a violation of the Export Administration Regulations for a person to take any action that facilitates the acquisition or attempted acquisition by a denied person of any item subject to the Regulations.

The Department alleged that Expeditors International, in 1995, facilitated the export of semiconductor test equipment from the United States to Taiwan. The export was destined to a Denied Person, Realtek Semiconductor Co., Ltd., of Taipei, Taiwan.

Commerce's Boston Office of Export Enforcement investigated the case.

The Department of Commerce, through its Bureau of Export Administration, administers and enforces export controls for reasons of national security, foreign policy, nonproliferation and short supply. Criminal penalties, as well as administrative sanctions, can be imposed for violations of the regulations.

BXA Home > BXA Press Page

BXA HOME
WHAT'S NEW
SITE SEARCH

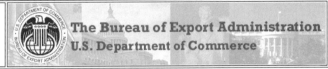

The Bureau of Export Administration
U.S. Department of Commerce

Contacts:

Eugene Cottilli
(202) 482-2721
Email

For Immediate Release
August 3, 2000

Texas Firm Settles Charges of Export Control Violations

WASHINGTON -- Commerce Assistant Secretary for Export Enforcement F. Amanda DeBusk today announced a $10,000 civil penalty imposed on Texas-based S.R. Traffic Service for alleged exports of U.S.-origin potassium flouride from United States to Mexico without the proper licenses.

Potassium fluoride is controlled for export by multilateral agreement with the 30-nation Australia Group of chemical producers because, in addition to its legitimate commercial uses, the chemical has the potential to serve as a precursor in a chemical weapons program.

The Department of Commerce, through its Bureau of Export Administration, administers and enforces export controls for reasons of national security, foreign policy, nonproliferation and short supply. Criminal penalties, as well as administrative sanctions, can be imposed for violations of the regulations.

BXA Home > BXA Press Page

BXA HOME
WHAT'S NEW
SITE SEARCH

Contacts:

Eugene Cottilli
(202) 482-2721
Email

**For Immediate Release
August 3, 2000**

Mass. Firm Settles Charges of Export Control Violations

Washington -- U.S. Department of Commerce Assistant Secretary for Export Enforcement F. Amanda DeBusk today imposed a $13,000 civil penalty on EMC Corporation on behalf of its Data General Division (formerly the Data General Corporation), Westboro, MA. The penalty was imposed to settle allegations that Data General exported computer equipment to Israel in 1995 without the required authorization. The Department also alleged that Data General made a false statement on an export control document related to the shipment of computer equipment to Mexico.

Commerce's Office of Export Enforcement Boston Field Office investigated the case.

The Department of Commerce, through its Bureau of Export Administration, administers and enforces export controls for reasons of national security, foreign policy, nonproliferation and short supply. Criminal penalties, as well as administrative sanctions, can be imposed for violations of the regulations.

BXA Home > BXA Press Page

BXA HOME
WHAT'S NEW
SITE SEARCH

The Bureau of Export Administration
U.S. Department of Commerce

Contacts:

Eugene Cottilli
(202) 482-2721
Email

For Immediate Release
July 25, 2000

Texas Freight Forwarder Settles Antiboycott Violations

WASHINGTON -- Commerce Assistant Secretary for Export Enforcement F. Amanda DeBusk announced today that Bailey International, Inc., a Houston, Texas freight forwarder, has agreed to pay a $4,000 civil penalty to settle four alleged violations of the antiboycott provisions of the Export Administration Regulations.

The Department alleged that on one occasion in 1992, Bailey violated the Regulations when it furnished a statement that the goods being shipped to Kuwait did not contain materials from Israel. The Department also alleged that Bailey, in three instances, failed to report its receipt of boycott requests as required by the Regulations. The Regulations prohibit companies and individuals from furnishing information about business relationships with or in boycotted countries, including Israel, and requires recipients to report such requests to the Department.

The antiboycott provisions of the Export Administration Regulations prohibit companies and individuals from complying with certain aspects of unsanctioned foreign boycotts maintained against any country friendly to the United States that is not itself the object of any form of boycott by the United States. Through its Office of Antiboycott Compliance, the Commerce Department investigates alleged violations, provides support in administrative or criminal litigation of cases and prepares cases for settlement.

BXA Home > BXA Press Page

BXA HOME
WHAT'S NEW
SITE SEARCH

Contacts:

Eugene Cottilli
(202) 482-2721
Email

For Immediate Release
June 14, 2000

Assistant Secretary DeBusk
to be Honored

Assistant Secretary of Commerce for Export Enforcement F. Amanda DeBusk has been selected by Women in Federal Law Enforcement, Inc. (WIFLE, INC.) to receive their First Honorable Mention for Outstanding Advocate for Women in Law Enforcement Award.

According to WIFLE, INC., "This award honors an individual who has made a substantial contribution having broad impact for women in law enforcement and who also acts as an advisor, advocate and leader in the continued support of women in law enforcement." The award will be presented to Assistant Secretary. DeBusk at a ceremony on August 3, 2000 in Washington, DC.

DeBusk was appointed assistant secretary for Export Enforcement by President Clinton and sworn-in on November 10, 1997. The office of Export Enforcement protects national security and foreign policy interests safeguarded by the Export Administration Act, the Export Administration Regulations and the antiboycott regulations. As assistant secretary, she oversees offices responsible for preventative enforcement, investigations and anitboycott matters. She supervises eight field offices located in the major exporting centers of the United States.

Prior to joining the Department of Commerce, DeBusk was a partner in the international trade department of the law firm of O'Melveny & Meyers, LLP. She received a B.A. from the University of Richmond and a J.D. from Harvard University.

BXA Home > BXA Press Page

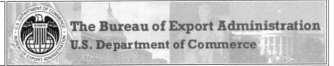

The Bureau of Export Administration
U.S. Department of Commerce

BXA HOME
WHAT'S NEW
SITE SEARCH

Contacts:

Eugene Cottilli
(202) 482-2721
Email

For Immediate Release
June 15, 2000

California Company Settles Antiboycott Charges

WASHINGTON -- Commerce Assistant Secretary for Export Enforcement, F. Amanda DeBusk, today announced a $104,000 civil penalty imposed on Kenclaire (West) Electrical Agencies, Inc., a Fresno, California, wholesaler of lighting supplies, to settle allegations that Kenclaire violated the antiboycott provisions of the Export Administration Regulations on 30 occasions.

According to allegations made by the Department, Kenclaire committed 11 violations of the antiboycott regulations when it agreed not to do business with manufacturers banned under the Arab boycott rules. The antiboycott regulations prohibit, among other things, refusals to do business or agreements to refuse to do business with companies that are banned under the Arab boycott of Israel. The Department also alleged that Kenclaire committed 19 additional violations when it failed to report, to the Department, its receipt of 19 requests to comply with this boycott related condition. The regulations also require U.S. companies to report their receipt of such boycott requests.

The antiboycott provisions of the Export Administration Act and Regulations prohibit U.S. companies and individuals from complying with certain aspects of unsanctioned foreign boycotts maintained against any country friendly to the United States that is not itself the object of any form of U.S. sanctioned boycotts. Through its Office of Antiboycott Compliance, the Commerce Department investigates alleged violations, provides support in administrative or criminal litigation of cases and prepares cases for settlement.

BXA Home > BXA Press Page

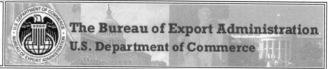

BXA HOME
WHAT'S NEW
SITE SEARCH

Contacts:

Eugene Cottilli
(202) 482-2721
Email

**For Immediate Release
May 10, 2000**

Massachusetts Company Settles Charges of Illegal Finger Print Machine Exports

WASHINGTON -- Commerce Assistant Secretary for Export Enforcement F. Amanda DeBusk today announced a $25,000 civil penalty, with $10,000 suspended, on NEC Technologies, Inc., of Boxborough, MA, to settle allegations that NEC illegally shipped automated finger print identification systems to several countries in violation of the Export Administration Regulations (EAR).

The Commerce Department alleged that on five separate occasions in 1996, NEC Technologies, Inc., exported U.S.-origin automated finger print identification systems, to Argentina, Peru, Singapore, South Africa and Taiwan, without obtaining the required Commerce licenses. Commerce also alleged that the company made false and misleading statements of material fact on Shipper's Export Declarations filed with the U.S. government in connection with the exports. NEC voluntarily disclosed the alleged violations.

Commerce's Boston Office of Export Enforcement investigated the case.

The Department of Commerce, through its Bureau of Export Administration, controls and licenses exports and reexports of dual-use commodities, technology, and software for reasons of national security, foreign policy, nonproliferation and short supply. Criminal penalties, as well as administrative sanctions, can be imposed for violations of the Export Administration Regulations.

BXA Home > BXA Press Page

BXA HOME
WHAT'S NEW
SITE SEARCH

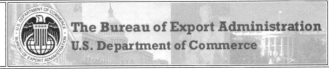

The Bureau of Export Administration
U.S. Department of Commerce

Contacts:

Eugene Cottilli
(202) 482-2721
Email

For Immediate Release
May 2, 2000

Illinois Company Settles Charges
of Unlawful Exports of Chemicals

WASHINGTON, D.C.-- Commerce Assistant Secretary for Export
Enforcement F. Amanda DeBusk today announced a $142,000 civil
penalty imposed on Illinois Tool Works, Inc. of Glenview, Illinois,
to settle allegations that the company illegally exported chemicals
to Brazil.

The Commerce Department alleged that on seven separate
occasions between March 1994 and October 1997, the Magnaflux
Division of Illinois Tool Works, Inc. exported U.S.-origin chemicals
to Brazil without the required Commerce Department licenses. The
Department also alleged that Magnaflux made false or misleading
statements on Shipper's Export Declarations in connection with
these shipments.

The Commerce Department controls the export of certain U.S.-
origin chemicals as part of a multilateral agreement with 30
chemical producing countries known as the Australia Group. The
controlled chemicals have legitimate commercial uses but also
have the potential to be used as precursors in chemical weapons.

Illinois Tool Works neither confirmed nor denied the allegations
but agreed to pay the penalty, $37,000 of which was suspended
as part of today's settlement. Commerce's Export Enforcement
Chicago Field Office investigated the case.

The Department of Commerce, through its Bureau of Export
Administration, controls and licenses exports and reexports of
dual-use commodities, technology, and software for reasons of
national security, foreign policy, nonproliferation and short supply.
Criminal penalties, as well as administrative sanctions, can be
imposed for violations of the Export Administration Regulations.

Bureau of Export Administration
U. S. Department of Commerce

For Immediate Release
April 24, 2000

Houston Marketing Company Settles
Antiboycott Charge

Contacts:
Eugene Cottilli
(202) 482-2721
Email

BXA HOME
WHAT'S NEW
SITE SEARCH

WASHINGTON -- Commerce Assistant Secretary for Export Enforcement, F. Amanda DeBusk today announced that Itochu Project Management Corp., a Houston, Texas marketing agent, has agreed to pay a $4,000 civil penalty for an alleged violation of the antiboycott provisions of the Export Administration Regulations.

The Department alleged that Itochu Pipe and Tube Company, now merged with Itochu Project Management, in a transaction involving a sale to Syria in 1994, furnished information regarding another company's business relationship with or in Israel, by certifying that the goods did not contain Israeli materials. Furnishing such information is prohibited by the Regulations. While neither admitting nor denying the allegations, Itochu Project Management agreed to pay the civil penalty.

The antiboycott provisions of the Export Administration Act and Regulations prohibit U.S. companies and individuals from complying with certain aspects of unsanctioned foreign boycotts maintained against any country friendly to the United States that is not itself the object of any form of U.S. sanctioned boycott. Through its Office of Antiboycott Compliance, the Commerce Department investigates alleged violations, provides support in administrative or criminal litigation of cases and prepares cases for settlement.

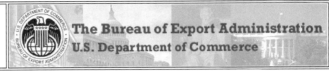

BXA HOME
WHAT'S NEW
SITE SEARCH

Contacts:

Eugene Cottilli
(202) 482-2721
Email

For Immediate Release
April 11, 2000

Hong Kong Company
Settles Charges of Illegal Transfer

WASHINGTON -- Commerce Assistant Secretary for Export Enforcement

F. Amanda DeBusk today announced a $20,000 civil penalty imposed on Haneflex Sales and Services Ltd., a Hong Kong trading and distribution company, for alleged violations of the Export Administration Regulations.

The Commerce Department alleged that in January 1995 Haneflex sold and transferred U.S. origin diffusion pumps to Shun Fat Metal and Iron Works in Hong Kong in violation of conditions in a Commerce license that had authorized the original export of the equipment from the United States to Hong Kong. The Department also alleged that Haneflex acted with knowledge that a violation of the Export Administration Regulations would occur.

Haneflex has also agreed to a 5 year denial of export privileges (suspended) as part of today's settlement. Commerce's San Jose Office of Export Enforcement investigated the case.

The Department of Commerce, through its Bureau of Export Administration, administers and enforces export controls for reasons of National Security, Foreign Policy, Nonproliferation and Short Supply. Criminal penalties, as well as administrative sanctions, can be imposed for violations of the Regulations.

BXA Home > BXA Press Page

Bureau of Export Administration
U. S. Department of Commerce

For Immediate Release
March 23, 2000

Contacts:
Eugene Cottilli
(202) 482-2721
Email

BXA HOME

WHAT'S NEW

SITE SEARCH

The National Defense Stockpile Market Impact Committee requests Public Comment on the Potential Market Impact of Proposed Stockpile Material Sales

(WASHINGTON) - The National Defense Stockpile Market Impact Committee (the Committee), co-chaired by the Departments of Commerce and State, today announced it published a Federal Register Notice (65 FR 15613) requesting public comment on the potential market impact of the proposed sale by the Department of Defense (DOD) of certain excess materials from the National Defense Stockpile.

The Committee provides advice to DOD on the projected domestic and foreign economic effects of all acquisitions and disposal of materials from the Stockpile that are to be included in an Annual Materials Plan (AMP). The AMP must be approved by Congress.

The Committee is seeking public comment on the potential market impact of the DOD proposed revisions to the disposal levels for columbium concentrates, mica (All Forms), palladium, tantalum minerals, and sebacic acid for Fiscal Year 2000 and proposed Fiscal Year 2001 AMPs. Public comment on these proposed revisions, reprinted in Attachment 1 (see attachment), must be received by April 24, 2000 to ensure full consideration by the Committee.

The material quantities listed in Attachment 1 are the proposed maximum disposal quantities for each material that may be sold in a particular fiscal year. They are not sales target disposal quantities. The actual quantity of each material offered for sale will depend on the market for the material at the time of the offering as well as on prior Congressional approval.

Under the authority of the Strategic and Critical Materials Stock Piling Act, as amended, DOD maintains a stockpile of strategic and critical materials to supply the military, industrial, and essential civilian needs of the United States for national defense. In selling and acquiring Stockpile materials, DOD has a statutory obligation to refrain from causing undue market disruption, while at the same time protecting the U.S. Government against avoidable loss.

To obtain a copy of, or more information about, the Federal Register Notice, please contact either Richard V. Meyers, Office of Strategic Industries and Economic Security, U.S. Department of Commerce, Tel: (202) 482-3634, FAX (202) 482-5650, or E-Mail RMEYERS@bxa.doc.gov; or Stephen H. Muller, Office of International Energy and Commodity Policy, U.S. Department of State, Tel.: (202)

647-3423 or FAX: (202) 647-8758; (co-chairs of the National Defense Stockpile Market Impact Committee).

Proposed Revisions to FY 2000 and Proposed FY 2001 Annual Material Plans

Material	Units	Current FY 2000 and Proposed FY 2001 Quantity	Revised FY 2000 and Proposed FY 2001 Quantity
Columbium Concentrates	LB Cb	FY 2000 200,000 FY 2001 250,000	375,000
Mica (All Forms)	LB	2,260,000	4,000,000
Palladium	TR Oz	200,000	300,000
Sebacic Acid	LB	400,000	600,000
Tantalum Minerals	LB Ta	200,000	300,000

The Bureau of Export Administration
U.S. Department of Commerce

Contacts:

Eugene Cottilli
(202) 482-2721
Email

For Immediate Release
March 22, 2000

Chicago Area Freight Forwarder
Settles Antiboycott Charges

WASHINGTON -- Commerce Assistant Secretary for Export Enforcement F. Amanda DeBusk today announced a $4,000 civil penalty on BDP International Inc., for one alleged violation of the antiboycott provisions of the Export Administration Regulations by its Des Plaines, Illinois branch. BDP International Inc. is a freight forwarder with headquarters in Philadelphia, Pennsylvania.

The Department alleged that BDP, in a transaction involving a shipment to Saudi Arabia in 1997, furnished information regarding another company's business relationship with or in Israel by certifying that the goods were not of Israeli origin, did not contain Israeli materials and were not exported from Israel. Furnishing such information is prohibited by the Regulations. While neither admitting nor denying the allegations, BDP agreed to pay the civil penalty.

The antiboycott provisions of the Export Administration Act and Regulations prohibit U.S. companies and individuals from complying with certain aspects of unsanctioned foreign boycotts maintained against any country friendly to the United States that is not itself the object of any form of a U.S. sanctioned boycott. Through its Office of Antiboycott Compliance, the Commerce Department investigates alleged violations, provides support in administrative or criminal litigation of cases and prepares cases for settlement.

BXA Home > BXA Press Page

Bureau of Export Administration
U. S. Department of Commerce

For Immediate Release
March 20, 2000

California Freight Forwarder
Settles Charges of
Illegal Computer Exports to China

Contact:
Eugene Cottilli
(202) 482-2721
Email

BXA HOME
WHAT'S NEW
SITE SEARCH

WASHINGTON - Commerce Assistant Secretary for Export Enforcement F. Amanda DeBusk today announced a $20,000 civil penalty imposed on U-Freight, Inc., a freight forwarder in South San Francisco, CA., to settle allegations that the company arranged for a shipment of computers to the People's Republic of China, in violation of a condition on the Commerce export license.

The Department alleged that in September 1993, U-Freight arranged for a shipment of Sun Microsystems computers to the People's Republic of China when it knew or had reason to know that the shipment was contrary to a condition on the validated export license. While neither admitting nor denying the allegations, U-Freight, Inc. agreed to pay the penalty; a portion of which, $10,000, was suspended.

The Department of Commerce, through its Bureau of Export Administration, administers and enforces export controls for reasons of National Security, Foreign Policy, Nonproliferation and Short Supply. BXA's Office of Export Enforcement Washington Field Office investigated this case. Criminal penalties, as well as administrative sanctions, can be imposed for violations of the Regulations.

**United States
Department of
Justice**

FOR IMMEDIATE RELEASE:
Friday, March 10, 2000

Contact: Channing D. Phillips
(202)514-6933
Judiciary Center
555 Fourth Street NW
Washington, DC 20001

Department of Justice Website:
www.usdoj.gov

Chinese National and His Corporation
Plead Guilty to Illegal Shipment of Riot
Control Vehicle with a Pressurized Pepper Gas System

Washington, D.C. - United States Attorney Wilma A. Lewis, U.S. Department of Commerce Assistant Secretary for Export Enforcement F. Amanda DeBusk, and United States Customs Service Assistant Commissioner Bonnie Tischler, Office of Investigations, jointly announced that A & C International Trade, Inc., 350 5th Ave., New York, New York, and Yufeng Wang, age 36, also known as Alan Wang, a Chinese National currently living in Ft. Lee, N.J., and the president of A & C International Trade, Inc., entered pleas of guilty today before U.S. District Judge Emmet G. Sullivan to violating U.S. export control laws and making a false statement related to the shipment of a 60-ton riot control vehicle equipped with a pressurized pepper gas dispensing system to the People's Republic of China (PRC) in late November of 1995.

A & C International Trade, Inc., entered a plea of guilty to an Information charging it with a felony violation of 22 U.S. Code § 2778 for the November 30, 1995 export, without a license as required by law, of a police riot control vehicle equipped with a pressurized pepper gas system to the People's Republic of China, and defendant WANG entered a plea of guilty to a separate count of the Information charging him with a misdemeanor violation of 26 U.S. Code §7207, for the filing of a false document with the United States Customs Service and the Secretary of the Treasury in connection with the export of the police riot control vehicle.

Based on the violation of 22 U.S.C. § 2778, A & C International Trade, Inc., is subject to a fine of not more than $1,000,000, possible probation of five years and a mandatory special assessment of $100, while defendant Wang, based on a violation of 26 U.S.C. § 7207, is subject to a fine of up to $100,000, and imprisonment of not more than one year, or both, and a mandatory special assessment of $25. Sentencing has been scheduled for June 26, 2000.

The vehicle, sold by Moore Custom Trucks of Hernando, MS, was sold under the name of MCT Blueshield Riot Control Vehicle. It contained a pressurized system capable of spraying tear and pepper gas from the truck in several directions and would have required a State Department license for shipment to the PRC.

U.S. Attorney Lewis noted that "these unlawful transactions constitute serious violations of export control laws designed to further the security and foreign policy of the United States."

The Department of Commerce, through its Bureau of Export Administration, and the United States Customs Service administer and enforce export controls for reasons of national security, foreign policy, nonproliferation, and short supply. Criminal penalties, as well as administrative sanctions, can be imposed for violations.

"This case illustrates our strong commitment to the enforcement of our nation's export control laws," said Commerce Assistant Secretary for Export Enforcement F. Amanda Debusk.

In announcing the guilty pleas, U.S. Attorney Lewis, Assistant Secretary for Export Enforcement Debusk, and Assistant Commissioner Tischler commended the cooperative effort of the United States Attorney's Office, the Department of Commerce of Export Enforcement and the U.S. Customs Service, Office of Investigations, in handling this investigation. They also commended the efforts of the Commerce Department's Boston Office of Export Enforcement and the U.S. Customs Services which originally investigated the case. Commended also was the work of Assistant United States Attorney Joseph B. Valder and Mariclaire Rourke, Trial Attorney, Internal Security Section, U.S. Department of Justice, who jointly prosecuted the case, and Department of Commerce Bureau of Export Administration Special Agent David Poole and United States Customs Service Special Agent John M. Kennedy who investigated the case.

Bureau of Export Administration
U. S. Department of Commerce

For Immediate Release
March 8, 2000

Contact:
Eugene Cottilli
(202) 482-2721
Email

BXA HOME
WHAT'S NEW
SITE SEARCH

Massachusetts Company
Settles Charge of Illegal Exports

WASHINGTON -- Assistant Secretary of Commerce for Export Enforcement, F. Amanda DeBusk, today announced a $15,000 civil penalty imposed on LTX Corporation of Westwood, MA, for allegedly exporting U.S.-origin semiconductor test equipment to a Denied Person.

The Commerce Department alleged that in two separate shipments, one in 1995 and the other in 1996, LTX Corporation exported semiconductor test equipment to a Denied Person, Realtek Semiconductor Co., Ltd., Taipei, Taiwan, in violation of the Export Administration Regulations. Denied Persons are specific individuals or businesses that are prohibited from exporting or receiving exports of U.S.-origin goods.

Commerce's Office of Export Enforcement's Boston Field Office conducted the investigation.

The Department of Commerce, through its Bureau of Export Administration, administers and enforces export controls for reasons of national security, foreign policy, nonproliferation and short supply. Criminal penalties, as well as administrative sanctions, can be imposed for violations of the regulations.

Bureau of Export Administration
U. S. Department of Commerce

For Immediate Release
March 2, 2000

Seattle Businessman Settles Charges of Unlawful Exports of Shotguns to Russia

Contact:
Eugene Cottilli
(202) 482-2721
Email

BXA HOME
WHAT'S NEW
SITE SEARCH

WASHINGTON, D.C. -- Assistant Secretary of Commerce for Export Enforcement F. Amanda DeBusk today announced an $18,000 civil penalty and three-year denial of export privileges on Ronald O. Brown of Seattle, Wash., in connection with the unauthorized exports and attempted export of U.S. origin shotguns to Russia.

The Department alleged that Brown, individually and formerly doing business as Mirazh Ltd., aided and abetted on six occasions in 1994 in the export of shotguns to Russia without obtaining the required Commerce licenses. Brown is also alleged to have aided and abetted in the attempted export of one shotgun to Russia and for having on two occasions made false and misleading statements of material fact to a federal government agency. The three-year denial and $9,000 of the civil penalty were suspended.

The Bureau of Export Administration's San Jose Field Office investigated the case.

The Department of Commerce, through its Bureau of Export Administration, administers and enforces export controls for reasons of national security, foreign policy, nonproliferation and short supply. Criminal penalties, as well as administrative sanctions, can be imposed for violations of the regulations.

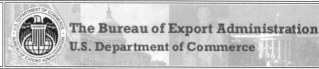

BXA HOME
WHAT'S NEW
SITE SEARCH

The Bureau of Export Administration
U.S. Department of Commerce

Contacts:

Eugene Cottilli
(202) 482-2721
Email

For Immediate Release
March 2, 2000

Texas Freight Forwarder
Settles Antiboycott Charges

WASHINGTON -- U.S. Department of Commerce Assistant Secretary for Export Enforcement, F. Amanda DeBusk, today announced a $20,000 civil penalty imposed on Panalpina, Inc., a Humble, Texas, freight forwarder, to settle allegations that Panalpina committed 10 violations of the antiboycott provisions of the Export Administration Regulations (EAR).

Panalpina is a U.S. subsidiary of a Swiss company. The Department of Commerce alleged that on ten occasions during 1996, Panalpina furnished, to persons in Saudi Arabia, information concerning other persons' business relationships with Israel. Furnishing such information for boycott purposes is prohibited by the EAR.

The antiboycott provisions of the Export Administration Act and Regulations prohibit U.S. companies and individuals from complying with certain aspects of unsanctioned foreign boycotts maintained against any country friendly to the United States that is not itself the object of any form of U.S. sanctioned boycotts. Through its Office of Antiboycott Compliance, the Commerce Department investigates alleged violations, provides support in administrative or criminal litigation of cases and prepares cases for settlement.

BXA Home > BXA Press Page

The Bureau of Export Administration
U.S. Department of Commerce

Contacts:

Eugene Cottilli
(202) 482-2721
Email

For Immediate Release
March 1, 2000

Commerce Department Imposes $200,000 Penalty on U.S. Firm for Unlicensed Exports

WASHINGTON -- U.S. Assistant Secretary of Commerce for Export Enforcement, F. Amanda DeBusk today announced a $200,000 civil penalty on Bayer Corporation, Tarrytown, NY, to settle allegations that the company's Diagnostics Division exported U.S.-origin glucose and other reagents to several destinations.

The Department alleged that on 57 occasions between October 1994 and January 1997, Bayer Corporation exported glucose and other reagents from the United States to Hong Kong, Malaysia, Mexico, Singapore, South Africa, South Korea, and Taiwan, without obtaining the required validated export licenses. The U.S. government controls glucose and other reagents because of concerns that they may be used for chemical or biological weapons.

The Department of Commerce, through its Bureau of Export Administration, administers and enforces export controls for reasons of national security, foreign policy, nonproliferation and short supply. Criminal penalties, as well as administrative sanctions, can be imposed for violations of the regulations.

BXA Home > BXA Press Page

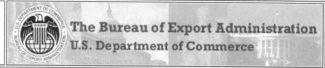

Contacts:

Eugene Cottilli
(202) 482-2721
Email

**For Immediate Release
February 28, 2000**

**Pennsylvania Company Settles Charges
of Unlawful Exports of Chemicals**

WASHINGTON -- Assistant Secretary of Commerce for Export Enforcement F. Amanda DeBusk today announced a $150,000 civil penalty imposed on Houghton International Inc., Valley Forge, PA, a manufacturer of specialty chemical products, to settle allegations that the company illegally exported chemicals to South Korea.

Today's settlement resolves allegations that on 20 separate occasions Houghton International Inc., exported chemicals to South Korea without the required U.S. Department of Commerce licenses. The shipments occurred during the period of August 1994 through August 1996.

The Department controls the export of certain U.S.-origin chemicals as part of a multilateral agreement with 30 chemical producing countries known as the Australia Group. The controlled chemicals have legitimate commercial uses but also have the potential to serve as precursors in chemical weapons.

The Bureau of Export Administration's Office of Export Enforcement, New York Field Office, investigated this case.

The Department of Commerce through its Bureau of Export Administration administers and enforces export controls for reasons of national security, foreign policy, nonproliferation, and short supply. Criminal penalties, as well as administrative sanctions can be imposed for violations of the regulations.

BXA Home > BXA Press Page

Bureau of Export Administration
U. S. Department of Commerce

For Immediate Release
December 21, 1999

Hong Kong Firm Settles Charges of Illegal Shipments

WASHINGTON - The Commerce Department's Bureau of Export Administration (BXA) today imposed a $20,000 civil penalty on Gold Valley Technology Company to settle allegations that it violated a term of an export license involving a shipment of computers to the People's Republic of China, Commerce Assistant Secretary for Export Enforcement F. Amanda DeBusk announced.

BXA alleged that in September 1993, the company, located in Hong Kong, arranged for a shipment of computers to the People's Republic of China although it knew or had reason to know that it would violate a condition on the validated BXA license issued for the export. While neither admitting nor denying the allegations, Gold Valley Technology Company agreed to pay the penalty. A portion of the penalty, $10,000, was suspended.

The Department of Commerce, through its Bureau of Export Administration, administers and enforces export controls for reasons of National Security, Foreign Policy, nonproliferation and short supply. BXA's Office of Export Enforcement Washington Field Office investigated this case. Criminal penalties, as well as administrative sanctions, can be imposed for violations of the regulations.

Bureau of Export Administration
U. S. Department of Commerce

For Immediate Release
July 28, 1999

Contacts:
Eugene Cottilli
Susan Hofer
(202) 482-2721
Email

Go to: Press Page

BXA Home Page

BXA What's New

BXA Site Search

Staten Island Man Sentenced For Illegally Shipping Auto Parts to Iran

(NEW JERSEY)-- Hadi Shalchi, a Staten Island, N.Y. businessman, has been sentenced to six months' imprisonment and fined $30,000 as a result of his guilty plea to making false statements in connection with the illegal export of auto parts to Iran, F. Amanda DeBusk, Commerce assistant secretary for Export Enforcement, announced. Shalchi was also sentenced to four months' home confinement and 3 years' probation to be served following his prison time.

Shalchi's business, Continental A. P. Company, of Hopelawn, New Jersey, was sentenced to a criminal fine of $200,000 after pleading guilty to charges that it illegally exported auto parts to Iran. The sentencings occurred in the U.S. District Court for New Jersey before District Court Judge William H. Walls. The cases were the result of investigations by the Department of Commerce's Office of Export Enforcement New York field office.

The Department of Commerce controls and licenses the export and re-export of dual-use commodities and technical data. Commerce's Bureau of Export Administration maintains and enforces these controls for reasons of national security, foreign policy, nonproliferation and short supply.

Bureau of Export Administration
U. S. Department of Commerce

For Immediate Release
September 30, 1999

Contact:
Eugene Cottilli
(202) 482-2721
Email

BXA Home
What's New
Site Search

Connecticut Firm Settles
Charges of Illegal Exports

WASHINGTON -- The U.S. Department of Commerce today imposed a $5,000 civil penalty on Gilbert & Jones, Inc. of New Britain, to settle allegations that the company exported potassium cyanide to Taiwan without the licenses required by the Export Administration Regulations, Assistant Secretary for Export Enforcement F. Amanda DeBusk announced.

The Commerce Department's Bureau of Export Administration (BXA) alleged that on two occasions in 1994 and 1995, Gilbert & Jones, Inc. exported U.S. origin potassium cyanide to Taiwan without obtaining the required export licenses. BXA's Office of Export Enforcement Boston Field Office investigated the case.

The Department of Commerce, through its Bureau of Export Administration, administers and enforces export controls for reasons of national security, foreign policy, nonproliferation and short supply. Criminal penalties, as well as administrative sanctions, can be imposed for violations of the regulations.

Bureau of Export Administration
U. S. Department of Commerce

For Immediate Release
September 30, 1999

Contact:
Eugene Cottilli
(202) 482-2721
Email

BXA Home

What's New

Site Search

California Exporter Fined
in Connection with
Attempted Taiwan Export

WASHINGTON -- The U.S. Department of Commerce today imposed a $10,000 civil penalty on Laser Devices, Inc., a Monterey, California exporter, to settle allegations that the company attempted to illegally ship laser gun aimer/sights to Taiwan, Commerce Assistant Secretary for Export Enforcement F. Amanda DeBusk announced.

The Department alleged that in March, 1995 Laser Devices attempted to export U.S.-origin laser gun aimer/sights to Taiwan without the required Commerce authorizations. Commerce's Office of Export Enforcement, San Jose Field Office and the U.S. Customs Service, RAC/San Jose investigated the case.

The Department of Commerce, through its Bureau of Export Administration, administers and enforces export controls for reasons of national security, foreign policy, nonproliferation and short supply. Criminal penalties, as well as administrative sanctions, can be imposed for violations of the Regulations.

Bureau of Export Administration
U. S. Department of Commerce

For Immediate Release
September 30, 1999

Contact:
Eugene Cottilli
(202) 482-2721
Email

BXA Home

What's New

Site Search

Illinois Firm Fined in Connection with Shipment to Iran

WASHINGTON -- The U.S. Department of Commerce Department Bureau of Export Administration (BXA) today imposed a $10,000 civil penalty on Illinois-based Varlen Corporation for a false statement made by its former wholly-owned subsidiary, Precision Scientific, Inc. on an export control document in connection with a shipment to Iran, Commerce Assistant Secretary for Export Administration F. Amanda DeBusk announced.

The Department alleged that Precision Scientific shipped a U.S.-origin incubator to Iran through an independent distributor in The Netherlands. Precision Scientific identified The Netherlands as the country of ultimate destination on the Shipper's Export Declaration, when in fact the intended destination was Iran. Varlen self-disclosed the violation and agreed to accept responsibility for the actions of Precision Scientific. BXA's Chicago Office of Export Enforcement investigated the case.

The U.S. government maintains a comprehensive economic sanctions program against the government of Iran and prohibits virtually all commercial transactions involving U.S.-origin goods or U.S. persons, or both, with the government of Iran.

The Department of Commerce, through its Bureau of Export Administration, administers and enforces export controls for reasons of national security, foreign policy, nonproliferation and short supply. Criminal penalties, as well as administrative sanctions, can be imposed for violations of the Regulations.

Bureau of Export Administration
U. S. Department of Commerce

For Immediate Release
December 22, 1999

Contact:
Eugene Cottilli
(202) 482-2721
Email

BXA HOME
WHAT'S NEW
SITE SEARCH

Two Hong Kong Companies and a New Jersey Company Settle Charges of Export Violations

WASHINGTON - The Commerce Department's Bureau of Export Administration today imposed a $174,000 civil penalty on Hua Ko Electronics Co. Ltd., a Hong Kong company which had previously been denied export privileges, for ordering and receiving U.S.-origin goods in violation of its denial order, Commerce Assistant Secretary for Export Enforcement F. Amanda DeBusk announced.

The allegations involve shipments that occurred between August 1994 and May 1997. Hua Ko was also denied export privileges for five years. The denial and $87,000 of its fine were both suspended.

The Department imposed a $38,500 civil penalty on Nanshing Color & Chemical Co., Ltd., also a Hong Kong company, for transferring U.S.-origin goods to Hua Ko Electronics Co. Ltd. The lesser civil penalty imposed was due in large part to Nanshing's cooperation in the investigation. A third company, General Chemical Corporation of New Jersey, agreed to a $77,000 civil penalty to settle allegations that it exported U.S.-origin goods to Nanshing while knowing or having reason to know that the Nanshing would transfer the goods to Hua Ko Electronics Co. Ltd.

Export denials prohibit a person from exporting such goods or technical data to a denied party, whether directly or indirectly.

BXA's Office of Export Enforcement Washington Field Office conducted the investigation. The Commerce Department administers and enforces export controls for reasons of national security, foreign policy, nonproliferation and short supply. Criminal penalties, as well as administrative sanctions, can be imposed for violations of the regulations.

Bureau of Export Administration
U. S. Department of Commerce

For Immediate Release
September 30, 1999

Contact:
Eugene Cottilli
(202) 482-2721
Email

BXA Home
What's New
Site Search

Virginia Non-Profit Settles Charges
of Illegal Exports

WASHINGTON -- The Commerce Department's Bureau of Export Administration (BXA) and the American Type Culture Collection of Manassas, Virginia, today resolved allegations that the non-profit organization exported US-origin microorganisms to various destinations without obtaining the required export licenses, Commerce Assistant Secretary for Export Enforcement F. Amanda DeBusk announced.

American Type Culture Collection voluntarily disclosed the activity to BXA, but agreed to pay a $290,000 civil penalty, which was suspended, and to collaborate with BXA on educational efforts designed to improve compliance with export controls on biological agents. The alleged violations occured on 58 separate occasions between 1993 and 1996. BXA's Office of Export Enforcement Washington Field Office investigated the case.

The Department of Commerce, through its Bureau of Export Administration, administers and enforces export controls for reasons of national security, foreign policy, nonproliferation and short supply. Criminal penalties, as well as administrative sanctions, can be imposed for violations of the Regulations.

U. S. Department of Commerce
Bureau of Export Administration

FOR IMMEDIATE RELEASE:
April 13, 1999

CONTACTS:
Eugene Cottilli
Susan Hofer
(202) 482-2721
E-Mail

Massachusetts Firm Penalized by Commerce Dept.

Go to:
Press Page
BXA Home Page
What's New
Site Search

WASHINGTON -- The Department of Commerce's Bureau of Export Administration today imposed a $50,000 civil penalty on Schott Fiber Optics, Inc. (Schott), of Southbridge, MA, for alleged illegal exports of fiber optic image inverters from the United States to the Netherlands, Commerce Assistant Secretary of Export Enforcement F. Amanda DeBusk announced.

Fiber optic inverters are used in the manufacture of night vision equipment and are controlled for national security, foreign policy and missile technology reasons. The Department alleged that Schott made 20 exports of inverters to the Netherlands without obtaining the required validated licenses. The shipments took place between November 1993 and April 1994.

Commerce's Office of Export Enforcement Boston field office investigated the case. Schott voluntarily disclosed the alleged violations to the Department. A portion of the penalty, $10,000, is suspended for one year, provided Schott does not commit any export control violations during that period.

The Commerce Department's Bureau of Export Administration enforces export controls for reasons of national security, foreign policy, nonproliferation and short supply. Criminal penalties, as well as administrative sanctions, can be imposed for violations of regulations.

U. S. Department of Commerce

Bureau of Export Administration

FOR IMMEDIATE RELEASE: February 1, 1999

CONTACTS: Eugene Cottilli | Susan Hofer (202) 482-2721| E-Mail
Go to: Press Page | BXA Home Page | What's New | Site Search

Freight Forwarder Settles Antiboycott Charges

WASHINGTON-- Fritz Companies, Inc. agreed to pay a $12,000 civil penalty to settle charges that its Houston, Texas office, Fritz Air Freight, Inc., committed six violations of the antiboycott provisions of the Export Administration Regulations, the Commerce Department's Assistant Secretary for Export Enforcement, F. Amanda DeBusk, announced today. Fritz Companies, Inc. is a freight forwarding company with headquarters in San Francisco.

The Department's Office of Antiboycott Compliance alleged that the Houston, Texas based freight forwarder, in six transactions involving shipments to Qatar in 1995, furnished information regarding another person's business relationships with or in a boycotted country by certifying that the goods shipped were not of Israeli origin, were not shipped from Israel and did not contain any material from Israel.

The company voluntarily disclosed the alleged violations to the Department. While neither admitting nor denying the allegations, the company agreed to pay the civil penalty.

The antiboycott provisions prohibit U.S. companies and individuals from complying with certain aspects of unsanctioned foreign boycotts against any country friendly to the United States that is not, itself, the object of any U.S. boycott. Through its Office of Antiboycott Compliance, the Commerce Department investigates alleged violations, provides support in administrative or criminal litigation of cases, and prepares cases for settlement.

Return to Press Page

Bureau of Export Administration
U. S. Department of Commerce

For Immediate Release
June 11, 1999

Louisiana Man Convicted for Illegal Exports

WASHINGTON -- A U.S. District Court jury for the Western District of Louisiana has found Dien Duc Huynh and his corporation, Dien's Auto Salvage, guilty of ten counts of violating U.S. export laws, Commerce Assistant Secretary for Export Enforcement, F. Amanda DeBusk announced.

Dien Duc Huynh and Dien's Auto Salvage were convicted of one count of conspiracy to violate the Export Administration Act, seven counts of violating the Export Administration Act, two counts of violating the Trading with the Enemy Act and one count of conspiracy to commit theft of government property. Following his conviction, Dien Duc Huynh agreed to plead guilty to two forfeiture counts and pay $250,000 in lieu of forfeiting his property to the government.

The conviction results from a joint investigation by the Commerce Dept. Dallas Office of Export Enforcement, the U.S. Customs Service and the Department of Defense. Investigators found evidence that the defendants were purchasing surplus military vehicles from Army bases in the U.S. and Europe and exporting them to Vietnam through Singapore in violation of U.S. export control laws.

The vehicles are controlled for national security, antiterrorism and regional stability reasons and an export license is required for export to Vietnam. Several of the violations occurred during the period when the United States maintained a comprehensive trade embargo against Vietnam.

The Department of Commerce, through its Bureau of Export Administration, administers and enforces export controls for reasons of national security, foreign policy, nonproliferation and short supply. Criminal penalties, as well as administrative sanctions, can be imposed for violations of the Regulations.

Bureau of Export Administration
U. S. Department of Commerce

For Immediate Release
August 5, 1999

Contact:
Eugene Cottilli
(202) 482-2721
Email

BXA Home

What's New

Site Search

Chicago Company Settles Charges of Unlawful Exports of Chemicals

WASHINGTON, D.C. -- The Commerce Department's Bureau of Export Administration today imposed a $25,000 civil penalty on Starlite Technical Service, Inc. of Chicago, Illinois, in connection with the unauthorized exports of U.S.-origin chemicals to Lebanon and Colombia, Commerce Assistant Secretary for Export Enforcement F. Amanda DeBusk announced.

The Department alleged that Starlite Technical Service, Inc. was responsible for exporting the chemicals without the required Commerce Department licenses on five separate occasions between January 1994 and December 1996. The company neither admitted nor denied the charges, but agreed to pay the penalty.

The Department controls certain U.S.-origin chemicals for export to implement a multilateral agreement with the 30-nation Australia Group of chemical producers because, in addition to their legitimate commercial uses, these chemicals have the potential to serve as precursors in chemical weapons.

Special agents from the Bureau of Export Administration's Chicago Field Office investigated the case.

The Department of Commerce, through its Bureau of Export Administration, administers and enforces export controls for reasons of national security, foreign policy, nonproliferation and short supply. Criminal penalties, as well as administrative sanctions can be imposed for violations of the regulations.

Bureau of Export Administration
U. S. Department of Commerce

For Immediate Release
August 24, 1999

Canadian Businessman Pleads Guilty to Illegal Trade with Iran and Iraq

Contact:
Eugene Cottilli
(202) 482-2721
Email

BXA Home
What's New
Site Search

WASHINGTON -- Abdulamir Mahdi, a Canadian businessman, pleaded guilty today in U.S. District Court, in Orlando, Florida, to a criminal indictment charging him with violating U.S. export controls by diverting industrial equipment to Iran and Iraq, Commerce Assistant Secretary for Export Enforcement F. Amanda DeBusk announced.

Mahdi, 47, used two Canadian companies, OTS Refining Equipment Corporation and Tech-Link Development Corporation, which he operated, to buy U.S. oil-field and industrial equipment for diversion to Iran and Iraq. U.S. export laws prohibit the export of industrial equipment to Iran and Iraq because of their sponsorship of international terrorism.

U.S. District Court Judge Anne Conway scheduled Mahdi's sentencing for November 19, 1999. Mahdi faces a maximum sentence of five years imprisonment and a fine of up to $250,000.

Mahdi's guilty plea is the result of a three year investigation by BXA's Export Enforcement office in Miami. DeBusk also credited the shut down of Mahdi's diversion network to an alert manufacturer who reported a suspicious inquiry, federal prosecutors A. B. Phillips and Ana Escobar of the U.S. Attorney's Office in Orlando, the U.S. Customs Service, and the Royal Canadian Mounted Police.

The Department of Commerce, through its Bureau of Export Administration, administers export controls for reasons of national security, foreign policy, nonproliferation and short supply. BXA's Office of Export Enforcement assists U.S. industry in complying with U.S. export laws and investigates violations of those laws.

U. S. Department of Commerce
Bureau of Export Administration

FOR IMMEDIATE RELEASE:
February 26, 1999

CONTACTS:
Eugene Cottilli
Susan Hofer
(202) 482-2721
E-Mail

Go to:
Press Page
BXA Home Page
What's New
Site Search

Commerce Department Penalizes Mexican Firm to Settle Charges of Illegal Exports

WASHINGTON -- The Commerce Department's Bureau of Export Administration today imposed a $60,000 civil penalty on a Mexican chemical company to settle charges it violated Export Administration Regulations in connection with the export of potassium fluoride from the United States to Mexico, Assistant Secretary for Export Enforcement F. Amanda DeBusk announced.

The Department alleged that PPG Industries de Mexico, S.A. de C.V., was responsible for exporting the chemical without the required Commerce Department licenses on eight separate occasions between July 1993 and March 1995. The Department also alleged that, on two of those occasions, PPG Mexico knew that violations would occur. The company neither admitted nor denied the charges, but agreed to pay the penalty to settle the allegations. A portion of the penalty, $20,000, will be suspended for one year, then waived if PPG Mexico commits no violations during that time.

Potassium fluoride is controlled for export by multilateral agreement with the 30-nation Australia Group of chemical producers because, in addition to its legitimate commercial uses, the chemical has the potential to serve as a precursor in a chemical weapons program.

The Bureau of Export Administration's Chicago Field Office conducted the investigation.

The Department of Commerce, through its Bureau of Export Administration , administers and enforces export controls for reasons of national security, foreign policy, nonproliferation and short supply. Criminal penalties, as well as administrative sanctions, can be imposed for violations of the Regulations.

Return to Press Page

Bureau of Export Administration
U. S. Department of Commerce

For Immediate Release
December 8, 1999

Indiana Company Agrees to
Pay $10,000 to Settle Allegation of
Violating License Terms in Sale to China

Contact:
Eugene Cottilli
(202) 482-2721
Email

BXA Home

What's New

Site Search

WASHINGTON --The Commerce Department's Bureau of Export Administration (BXA) today imposed a $10,000 civil penalty on Lafayette Instrument Company, Inc. of Lafayette, Indiana, to settle an allegation that Lafayette violated the terms of an export license when a shipment of its polygraph machines was reexported without authorization from Hong Kong to the People's Republic of China.

"This settlement demonstrates the importance of knowing your customer and underlines the serious responsibility an exporter undertakes when it becomes the licensee on an export license. Since Hong Kong reverted to China in 1997, it is more important than ever to know your customer and be sure about the transaction before you proceed," said Commerce Assistant Secretary for Export Enforcement F. Amanda DeBusk who made the announcement.

BXA alleged that Lafayette was the licensee on a validated license dated September 25, 1993 which authorized the export of U.S.-origin Factfinder polygraph machines to Hong Kong, but which prohibited the resale, transfer, or reexport of the machines without prior Commerce authorization. As the licensee, Lafayette was responsible for all license terms and provisions. The polygraph machines were reexported from Hong Kong to the People's Republic of China in violation of those terms. Crime control and detection instruments such as polygraph machines are controlled by the United States for foreign policy reasons.

Commerce, through its Bureau of Export Administration, administers and enforces export controls for reasons of national security, foreign policy, nonproliferation and short supply. Criminal penalties, as well as administrative sanctions, can be imposed for violations of the regulations.

U. S. Department of Commerce
Bureau of Export
Administration

FOR IMMEDIATE RELEASE:
February 19,1999

CONTACTS:
Eugene Cottilli
Susan Hofer
(202) 482-2721
E-Mail

Go to:
Press Page
BXA Home Page
What's New
Site Search

ALCOA Fined $750,000 by Commerce Department
For Illegal Chemical Shipments

WASHINGTON -- The Commerce Department's Under Secretary for Export Administration, William A. Reinsch, imposed a civil penalty of $750,000 on Aluminum Company of America (ALCOA) for 100 violations of U.S. export regulations involving shipments of potassium fluoride and sodium fluoride.

The penalty results from Reinsch's affirming an administrative law judge's (ALJ) recommended findings in the case. The ALJ found that ALCOA exported potassium fluoride and sodium fluoride from the United States to Jamaica and Suriname on 50 separate occasions without obtaining the required Commerce Department export licenses. The violations occurred between June 1991 and December 1995. The ALJ also found that the company made false statements on export control documents in each shipment.

Potassium fluoride and sodium fluoride are controlled because they can be used to make chemical weapons. These chemicals were added to the Department's control list in March 1991, but ALCOA's export compliance program failed to recognize and incorporate the change. There was no indication that in this case the chemicals were used for weapons purposes.

Reinsch observed, "This penalty should send the

message that there are significant advantages to having an internal compliance program that catches and reports problems quickly."

Reinsch's action imposes the maximum civil penalty of $10,000 for each of the 50 shipping without a license violations. He also imposed a penalty of $5,000 for each false statement.

Commerce's Export Administration Regulations provide that an administrative law judge administrative enforcement proceedings be conducted by who recommends an appropriate resolution of the case to the Under Secretary for Export Administration. The Under Secretary may affirm, modify, or vacate the ALJ's recommendation. In this case, Reinsch agreed with the findings but modified the penalties recommended by the ALJ.

Reinsch's order and the ALJ's recommendations will be printed in the Federal Register.

Return to Press Page

International Traffic in Arms (ITAR) Regulations Overview

What Is ITAR? (and General Information Covered by ITAR)

ITAR stands for the International Traffic in Arms Regulations.

The Arms Export Control Act authorizes the President to control the export and import of defense articles and defense services. The President shall designate which articles shall be deemed to be defense articles and defense services.

License or other approval may be granted only to U.S. persons and foreign government entities in the U.S. Application for license or requests for other approval will generally be considered only if the applicant is registered with the Office of Munitions Control.

Defense articles:

Technical data recorded or stored in any physical form, models, mock-ups, and other such items which reveal technical data relating to items such as:

Significant military equipment	Launch vehicles
Firearms	Vessels of war and special naval equipment
Ammunition	
Explosives, propellants	Tanks and military vehicles
Aircraft and associated equipment	Protective personnel equipment
Military training equipment	Optical and guidance control equipment
Military electronics	
Toxicological agents/equipment	Radiological equipment
Spacecraft systems	Auxiliary military equipment i.e., cameras
Submersible vessels	
Missile technology	Nuclear weapons, design and test equipment
Artillery projectors	

Defense services:

- Furnishing assistance to foreign persons, whether in the United States or abroad in the design, development, engineering, manufacture, production, assembly, testing, repair, maintenance, modification, operation, demilitarization, destruction, processing, or use of defense articles

- Furnishing to foreign persons any technical data such as classified information, software, information for the design, development, production, including blueprints, drawings, photographs, plans

U.S. person:

Lawful permanent resident, also means any corporation, organization, trust, entity that is incorporated to do business in the United States.

Foreign person:

Not a lawful permanent resident, also means any foreign corporation, organization, trust, entity that is not incorporated or organized to do business in the United States.

Export:

- Sending or taking a defense articles out of the United States

- Transferring registration, control or ownership to a foreign person of any aircraft, vessel or satellite covered by the U.S. Munitions List whether in the United States or abroad

- Disclosing/transferring in the United States defense articles to an embassy, agency, or diplomatic mission

- Disclosing/transferring technical data to a foreign person whether in the United States or abroad

- Performing a defense service on behalf of or for the benefit of a foreign person whether in the United States or abroad

How Does ITAR Affect Exports? (Registration with Office of Defense Trade and Obtaining an Export License)

Any person in the United States who engages in the business of either manufacturing or exporting defense articles or furnishing defense services is required to register with the Office of Defense Trade Controls. Manufacturers who do not engage in exporting must nevertheless register. Registration is a means to provide the U.S. Government with necessary information on who is involved in certain manufacturing and exporting activities. Registration does not confer any export rights or privileges. It is generally a precondition to the issuance of any license or other approval.

Exemptions:

- Officers and employees of the U.S. Government acting in an official capacity

- Persons whose pertinent business activity is confined to the production of unclassified technical data only

- Persons all of whose manufacturing and export activities are licensed under the Atomic Energy Act of 1954

- Persons who engage only in the fabrication of articles for experimental or scientific purpose, including research and development

Any person in the United States who intends to export or to import temporarily a defense article must obtain the approval of the Office of Defense Trade prior to the export or temporary import, unless the export or temporary import qualifies for an exemption.

Applications for export or temporary import to be made as follows:

- Applications for permanent export (Form DSP-5)

- Applications for licenses for temporary export (Form DSP-73)

- Applications for licenses for temporary import (Form DSP-61)

- Applications for export or temporary import of classified defense articles or Classified technical data (DSP-85)

Applications for Department of State export licenses must be confined to proposed exports of defense articles including technical data.

Office of Defense Trade Control requires all pertinent documentary information regarding the proposed transaction and proper completion of the application form, also including:

- Attachments and supporting technical data or brochures

- Freight forwarders' lists

- Certification letter signed by an empowered official must accompany all applications submitted

- Purchase order, letter of intent, etc.

Problems/Consequences of Not Following ITAR

Seizure, Forfeiture, Criminal Penalties, Civil Penalties

Seizure and forfeiture of materials and carriers: Whenever an attempt is made to export or ship from or take out of the United States any arms or munitions of war or other articles in violation of law or where there is probable cause to believe that any arms or munitions of war or other articles are intended to be or are being or have been exported or removed from the United States in violation of law, duly authorized personnel may seize and detain such articles and may seize and detain any vessel, vehicle, or aircraft containing the same or which has been used or is being used in exporting or attempting to export such arms or munitions of war.

Any willful violation of any provision of the Arms Export Control Act and in a registration, license application including omission of material fact or issuing an untrue statement of a material fact:

Customs Seizure

Policy of denial: Department of State will not approve any exports (unless there is overriding proof the shipment is in the best interest of protecting national security)

Three-year debarment

Criminal Penalties
- Fine not to exceed $1,000,000.00 per violation
- Imprisonment not to exceed ten years per violation
- Or both

Civil Penalties: Not to exceed $500,000.00 per violation

How Does ITAR Differ from BXA?

ITAR regulations are administered by the Department of State, Office of Defense Controls. ITAR regulations specifically cover defense articles and defense services under the Arms Export Control Act.

BXA is a Department of Commerce agency responsible for administering and enforcing export controls on "dual-use" items. BXA administers the Export Administration Act by developing export control policies, issuing export licenses, and prosecuting violators. In addition, the BXA enforces the anitboycott provisions of the EAA.

Note: BXA/Antiboycott provisions: Antiboycott laws were adopted to encourage/require U.S. firms to refuse to participate in foreign boycotts that the United States does not sanction. They have the effect of preventing U.S. firms from being used to implement the foreign policies of other nations which run counter to U.S. policy, i.e., boycott of Israel by Arab League of Nations.

Code of Federal Regulations [EXERPTS]
International Traffic in Arms Regulations (ITAR)

International Traffic in Arms Regulations

Title 22–Foreign Relations;

Chapter I–Department of State

Subchapter M–International Traffic in Arms Regulations

[Revised as of April 1, 1992]

Part 120

Purpose, Background and Definitions

Sec. 120.1 General.

(a) Purpose. Section 38 of the Arms Export Control Act (22 U.S.C. 2778) authorizes the President to control the export and import of defense articles and defense services. It is the purpose of this subchapter to implement this authority. The statutory authority of the President to promulgate regulations with respect to exports of defense articles and defense services was delegated to the Secretary of State by Executive Order 11958, as amended (42 FR 4311). By virtue of delegations of authority by the Secretary of State, these regulations are primarily administered by the Director of the Office of Munitions Control, Bureau of Politico-Military Affairs, Department of State (35 FR 5422).

(b) Eligibility. Licenses or other approvals (other than approvals obtained pursuant to Sec. 123.9 of this subchapter) may be granted only to U.S. persons (as defined in Sec. 120.23) and foreign governmental entities in the United States. Foreign persons (as defined in Sec. 120.11) other than governments are not eligible. U.S. persons who have been convicted of violating the U.S. criminal statutes enumerated in Sec. 120.24, or who have been debarred pursuant to part 127 of this subchapter, are also generally ineligible (see Sec. 127.6(c) of this subchapter). Applications for licenses or requests for other approvals will generally be considered only if the applicant has registered with the Office of Munitions Control pursuant to part 122 of this subchapter. All applications and requests for approval must be signed by a responsible official who is a U.S. person and who has been empowered by the registrant to sign such documents.

SOURCE: [49 FR 47684, Dec. 6, 1984; 50 FR 12787, Apr. 1, 1985, as amended at 53 FR 11496, Apr. 7, 1988; 54 FR 42497, Oct. 17, 1989]

AUTHORITY: Sec. 38, Arms Export Control Act, 90 Stat. 744 (22 U.S.C. 2778); E.O. 11958, 42 FR 4311; 22 U.S.C. 2658.

Sec. 120.2 Designation of defense articles and defense services.

The Arms Export Control Act also provides (22 U.S.C. 2778(a) and 2794(7)) that the President shall designate which articles shall be deemed to be defense articles and defense services for purposes of this subchapter. The items so designated constitute the United States Munitions List, and are specified in part 121 of this subchapter. Such designations are made by the Department of State with the concurrence of the Department of Defense.

Sec. 120.3 Policy on designating defense articles and services.

Designations of defense articles and defense services are based primarily on whether an article or service is deemed to be inherently military in character. Whether it has a predominantly military application is taken into account. The fact that an article or service may be used for both military and civilian purposes does not in and of itself determine whether it is subject to the export controls of this subchapter. (Narrow exceptions to this general policy exist with respect to exports of certain spare parts and components in Categories V(d); VIII (e) and (g); XI(e); XII(c); and XVI(b).) The intended use of the article or service after its export (i.e., for a military or civilian purpose) is also not relevant in determining whether the export is subject to the controls of this subchapter.

Sec. 120.4 Relation to Department of Commerce regulations.

If an article or service is placed on the United States Munitions List, its export is regulated exclusively by the Department of State. Exports which are not subject to the controls of this subchapter are generally under the regulatory jurisdiction of the Department of Commerce pursuant to the Export Administration Act of 1979, as amended (50 U.S.C. App. 2401 through 2420) and the implementing Export Administration Regulations (15 CFR parts 368 through 399).

Sec. 120.5 Commodity jurisdiction procedure.

The Office of Munitions Control will provide, upon written request, a determination on whether a particular article is included on the United States Munitions List. Such requests should be accompanied by five copies of the letter requesting a determination and any brochures or other documentation or specifications relating to the article. A "commodity jurisdiction" procedure is used if a doubt exists within the U.S. Government on whether an article is on the Munitions List. The procedure entails consultations among the Departments of State, Commerce and Defense.

Sec. 120.6 General.

The definitions contained in this part (listed alphabetically) apply to the use of the defined terms throughout this subchapter unless a different meaning is specified. See also Sec.Sec. 130.2 through 130.8 for definitions applicable to Part 130.

Sec. 120.7 Defense articles.

Defense article means any item designated in Sec. 121.1. This term includes models, mockups, and other such items which reveal technical data directly relating to items designated in Sec. 121.1.

Sec. 120.8 Defense services.

Defense service means:

(a) The furnishing of assistance, including training, to foreign persons in the design, engineering, development, production, processing, manufacture, use, operation, overhaul, repair, maintenance, modification, or reconstruction of defense articles, whether in the United States or abroad; or

(b) The furnishing to foreign persons of any technical data, whether in the United States or abroad. . . .

Sec. 120.10 Export.

Export means, for purposes of this subchapter:

(a) Sending or taking defense articles out of the United States in any manner; or . . .

(c) Sending or taking technical data outside of the United States in any manner except by mere travel outside of the United States by a person whose personal knowledge includes technical data; or

(d) Disclosing or transferring technical data to a foreign person, whether in the United States or abroad; or

(e) The performance of a defense service on behalf of, or for the benefit of, a foreign person, whether in the United States or abroad. . . .

Sec. 120.11 Foreign person.

Foreign person means any person (Sec. 120.16) who is not a citizen or national of the United States unless that person has been lawfully admitted for permanent residence in the United States under the Immigration and Naturalization Act (8 U.S.C. 1101, section 101(a)20, 60 Stat. 163) (i.e., individuals referred to as "immigrant aliens" under previous laws and regulations). It includes foreign corporations (i.e., corporations that are not incorporated in the United States), international organizations, foreign governments, and any agency or subdivision of foreign governments (e.g., diplomatic missions). . . .

Sec. 120.13 License.

License means a document bearing the word "license" which when issued by the Director, Office of Munitions Control, or his authorized designee, permits the export or intransit shipment of a specific defense article, defense service, or technical data.

Sec. 120.14 Manufacturing license agreement.

An agreement (e.g., contract) whereby a U.S. person grants a foreign person an authorization or a license to manufacture defense articles abroad and which involves or contemplates (a) the export of technical data (as defined in Sec. 120.21) or defense articles or the performance of defense services, or (b) the use by the foreign person of technical data or defense articles previously exported by the U.S. person.

Sec. 120.15 Office of Munitions Control.

Office of Munitions Control means the Office of Munitions Control, Bureau of Politico-Military Affairs, Department of State, Washington, D.C. 20520.

Sec. 120.16 Person.

Person means a natural person as well as a corporation, business association, partnership, society, trust, or any other entity, organization or group, including governmental entities. If a provision in this subchapter does not refer exclusively to a foreign person (Sec. 120.11) or U.S. person (Sec. 120.23), then it refers to both.

. . .

Sec. 120.18 Public domain.

Public domain means information which is published and which is generally accessible or available to the public:

(a) Through sales at newsstands and bookstores;

(b) Through subscriptions which are available without restriction to any individual who desires to obtain or purchase the published information;

(c) Through second class mailing privileges granted by the U.S. Government; or,

(d) At libraries open to the public.

Sec. 120.19 Significant military equipment.

(a) Significant military equipment means articles, as identified in paragraph (b) of this section, for which special export controls are warranted because of their capacity for substantial military utility or capability.

(b) Articles designated as significant military equipment under the criterion specified in paragraph (a) of this section include all classified articles and the articles enumerated in Sec. 121.1 in Categories I (a) and (c) (in quantity); II (a) and (b); III(a) (excluding ammunition for firearms in Category (I)) and (d); IV (a), (b), (d), (e), (f) and (g); V (a) (in quantity) and (b); VI (a), (b) ... and (e); VII (a), (b), (c), (e), (f) and (g); VIII (a), (b)(1), (c), (d), (g), (h), and (i). GEMS as defined in (i), and inertial systems as defined in (j); XI (a)(1), (b)(1), (c); XII (a) and (b); XIV (a), (b), (c) and (d); XVI; XVII; and XX (a) and (b).

(c) Items in Sec. 121.1 which are preceded by an asterisk are "significant military equipment."

(d) Section 47(6) of the Arms Export Control Act (22 U.S.C. 2794(6) note) provides a definition of "major defense equipment" and refers to certain significant combat equipment on the U.S. Munitions List. The terms "significant military equipment" and "significant combat equipment" are considered to be equivalent for purposes of that section of the Arms Export Control Act and this subchapter.

Sec. 120.20 Technical assistance agreement.

An agreement (e.g., contract) for the performance of defense services or the disclosure of technical data, as opposed to an agreement granting a right or license to manufacture defense articles.

Sec. 120.21 Technical data.

Technical data means, for purposes of this subchapter:

(a) Classified information relating to defense articles and defense services;

(b) Information covered by an invention secrecy order;

(c) Information, in any form, which is directly related to the design, engineering, development, production, processing, manufacture, use, operation, overhaul, repair, maintenance, modification, or reconstruction of defense articles. This includes, for example, information in the form of blueprints, drawings, photographs, plans, instructions, computer software and documentation. This also includes information which advances the state of the art of articles on the U.S. Munitions List. This definition does not include information concerning general scientific, mathematical or engineering principles commonly taught in academia. It also does not include basic marketing information on function or purpose or general system descriptions of defense articles. . . .

Sec. 120.24 U.S. criminal statutes.

For purposes of this subchapter, the phrase U.S. criminal statutes means:

(a) Section 38 of the Arms Export Control Act (22 U.S.C. 2778);

(b) Section 11 of the Export Administration Act of 1979 (50 U.S.C. App. 2410);

(c) Sections 793, 794, or 798 of Title 18, United States Code (relating to espionage involving defense or classified information);

(d) Section 16 of the Trading with the Enemy Act (50 U.S.C. App. 16);

(e) Section 206 of the International Emergency Economic Powers Act (relating to foreign assets controls; 50 U.S.C. 1705); . . .

(l) Section 371 of Title 18, United States Code (when it involves conspiracy to violate any of the above statutes).

. . .

Part 121

The United States Munitions List Enumeration of Articles

Sec. 121.1 General. The United States Munitions List. (a) The following articles, services and related technical data are designated as defense articles and defense services pursuant to sections 38 and 47(7) of the Arms Export Control Act (22 U.S.C. 2778 and 2794(7)). Changes in designations will be published in the Federal Register. Information and clarifications on whether specific items are defense articles and services under this subchapter may appear periodically in the Defense Trade News published by the Center for Defense Trade.

(b) Significant Military Equipment. An asterisk precedes certain defense articles in the following list. The asterisk means that the article is deemed to be "significant military equipment" to the extent specified in Sec. 120.19. The asterisk is placed as a convenience to help identify such articles. . . .

Category XI–Military [and Space] Electronics

(a) Electronic equipment not included in Category XII of the U.S. Munitions List which is specifically designed, modified or configured for military application. This equipment includes but is not limited to: . . .

(6) Computers specifically designed or developed for military application and any computer specifically modified for use with any defense article in any category of the U.S. Munitions List.

(7) Any experimental or developmental electronic equipment specifically designed or modified for military application or specifically designed or modified for use with a military system.

*(b) Electronic systems or equipment specifically designed, modified, or configured for intelligence, security, or military purposes for use in search, reconnaissance, collection, monitoring, direction-finding, display, analysis and production of information from the electromagnetic spectrum and electronic systems or equipment designed or modified to counteract electronic surveillance or monitoring. A system meeting this definition is controlled under this subchapter even in instances where any individual pieces of equipment constituting the system may be subject to the controls of another U.S. Government agency. Such systems or equipment described above include, but are not limited to, those:

(1) Designed or modified to use cryptographic techniques to generate the spreading code for spread spectrum or hopping code for frequency agility. This does not include fixed code techniques for spread spectrum.

(2) Designed or modified using burst techniques (e.g., time compression techniques) for intelligence, security or military purposes.

(3) Designed or modified for the purpose of information security to suppress the compromising emanations of information-bearing signals. This covers TEMPEST suppression technology and equipment meeting or designed to meet government TEMPEST standards. This definition is not intended to include equipment designed to meet Federal Communications Commission (FCC) commercial electro-magnetic interference standards or equipment designed for health and safety. . . .

(e) Technical data (as defined in Sec. 120.21) and defense services (as defined in Sec. 120.8) directly related to the defense articles enumerated in paragraphs (a) through (d) of this category. (See Sec. 125.4 for exemptions.) Technical data directly related to the manufacture or production of any defense articles enumerated elsewhere in this category that are designated as Significant Military Equipment (SME) shall itself be designated as SME. . . .

Category XIII—Auxiliary Military Equipment . . .

(b) Information Security Systems and equipment, cryptographic devices, software, and components specifically designed or modified therefore, including:

(1) Cryptographic (including key management) systems, equipment, assemblies, modules, integrated circuits, components or software with the capability of maintaining secrecy or confidentiality of information or information systems, except cryptographic equipment and software as follows:

(i) Restricted to decryption functions specifically designed to allow the execution of copy protected software, provided the decryption functions are not user-accessible.

(ii) Specially designed, developed or modified for use in machines for banking or money transactions, and restricted to use only in such transactions. Machines for banking or money transactions include automatic teller machines, self-service statement printers, point of sale terminals or equipment for the encryption of interbanking transactions.

(iii) Employing only analog techniques to provide the cryptographic processing that ensures information security in the following applications:

a. Fixed (defined below) band scrambling not exceeding 8 bands and in which the transpositions change not more frequently than once every second;

b. Fixed (defined below) band scrambling exceeding 8 bands and in which the transpositions change not more frequently than once every ten seconds;

c. Fixed (defined below) frequency inversion and in which the transpositions change not more frequently than once every second;

d. Facsimile equipment;

. . .

(iv) Personalized smart cards using cryptography restricted for use only in equipment or systems exempted from the controls of the USML.

(v) Limited to access control, such as automatic teller machines, self-service statement printers or point of sale terminals, which protects password or personal identification numbers (PIN) or similar data to prevent unauthorized access to facilities but does not allow for encryption of files or text, except as directly related to the password of PIN protection.

(vi) Limited to data authentication which calculates a Message Authentication Code (MAC) or similar result to ensure no alteration of text has taken place, or to authenticate users, but does not allow for encryption of data, text or other media other than that needed for the authentication.

(vii) Restricted to fixed data compression or coding techniques.

(viii) Limited to receiving for radio broadcast, pay television or similar restricted audience television of the consumer type, without digital encryption and where digital decryption is limited to the video, audio or management functions.

(ix) Software designed or modified to protect against malicious computer damage, e.g., viruses.

(2) Cryptographic (including key management) systems, equipment, assemblies, modules, integrated circuits, components or software which have the capability of generating spreading or hopping codes for spread spectrum systems or equipment.

(3) Cryptanalytic systems, equipment, assemblies, modules, integrated circuits, components or software.

(4) Systems, equipment, assemblies, modules, integrated circuits, components or software providing certified or certifiable multi-level security or user isolation exceeding class B2 of the Trusted Computer System Evaluation Criteria (TCSEC) and software to certify such systems, equipment or software.

(5) Ancillary equipment specifically designed or modified for paragraphs (b) (1), (2), (3), (4) and (5) of this category; ...

Category XVII–Classified Articles, Technical Data and Defense Services Not Otherwise Enumerated

*(a) All articles, technical data (as defined in Sec. 120.21) and defense services (as defined in Sec. 120.8) relating thereto which are classified in the interests of national security and which are not otherwise enumerated in the U.S. Munitions List. ...

Category XXI–Miscellaneous Articles

(a) Any article not specifically enumerated in the other categories of the U.S. Munitions List which has substantial military applicability and which has been specifically designed or modified for military purposes. The decision on whether any article may be included in this category shall be made by the Director of the Office of Defense Trade Controls.

(b) Technical data (as defined in Sec. 120.21) and defense services (as defined in Sec. 120.8) directly related to the defense articles enumerated in paragraphs (a) of this category. ...

Sec. 121.2 Interpretations of the United States Munitions List.

The following interpretations (listed alphabetically) explain and amplify the terms used in Sec. 121.1. These interpretations have the same force as if they were a part of the United States Munitions List category to which they refer. ...

Sec. 121.8 End-items, components, accessories, attachments, parts, firmware, software and systems.

(a) An "end-item" is an assembled article ready for its intended use. Only ammunition, fuel or another energy source is required to place it in an operating state.

(b) A "component" is an item which is useful only when used in conjunction with an end-item. A major component includes any assembled element which forms a portion of an end-item without which the end-item is inoperable. (Example: airframes, tail sections, transmissions, tank treads, hulls, etc.) A minor component includes any assembled element of a major component.

(c) "Accessories" and "attachments" are associated equipment for any component, end-item or system, and which are not necessary for their operation, but which enhance their usefulness or effectiveness. (Examples: riflescopes, special paints, etc.)

(d) A "part" is any single unassembled element of a major or a minor component, accessory, or attachment which is not normally subject to disassembly without the destruction or the impairment of design use. (Examples: rivets, wire, bolts, etc.)

(e) Firmware and any related unique support tools (such as computers, linkers, editors, test case generators, diagnostic checkers, library of functions and system test diagnostics) specifically designed for equipment or systems covered under any category of the United States Munitions List are considered as part of the end-item or component. "Firmware" includes but is not limited to circuits into which software has been programmed.

(f) "Software" includes but is not limited to the system functional design, logic flow, algorithms, application programs, operating systems and support software for design, implementation, test, operation, diagnosis and repair. A person who intends to export software only should, unless it is specifically enumerated in Sec. 121.1, apply for a technical data license pursuant to part 125 of this subchapter.

(g) A "system" is a combination of end-items, components, parts, accessories, attachments, firmware or software, specifically designed, modified or adapted to operate together to perform a specialized military function. . . .

Part 122

Registration of Manufacturers and Exporters

Sec. 122.1 Registration requirements.

(a) General. Any person who engages in the United States in the business of either manufacturing or exporting defense articles or furnishing defense services is required to register with the Office of Munitions Control. Manufacturers who do not engage in exporting must nevertheless register.

(b) Exemptions. Registration is not required for: . . .

(2) Persons whose pertinent business activity is confined to the production of unclassified technical data only. . . .

(4) Persons who engage only in the fabrication of articles for experimental or scientific purposes, including research and development.

(c) Purpose. Registration is primarily a means to provide the U.S. Government with necessary information on who is involved in certain manufacturing and exporting activities. Registration does not confer any export rights or privileges. It is generally a precondition to the issuance of any license or other approval under this subchapter.

Sec. 122.2 Submission of registration statement.

(a) General. The Department of State Form DSP-9 (Registration Statement) and the transmittal letter required by paragraph (b) of this subsection must be submitted by an intended registrant with a payment by check or money order payable to the Department of State of one of the fees prescribed in Sec. 122.3(a) of this subchapter. The Registration Statement and transmittal letter must be signed by a senior officer who has been empowered by the intended registrant to sign such documents. The intended registrant shall also submit documentation that demonstrates that it is incorporated or otherwise authorized to do business in the United States. The Office of Munitions Control will return to sender any Registration Statement that is incomplete, or that is not accompanied by the required letter or payment of the proper registration fee. . . .

Sec. 122.5 Maintenance of records by registrants.

(a) A person who is required to register must maintain records concerning the manufacture, acquisition and disposition of defense articles and the provision of defense services by the registrant. All such records must be maintained for a period of 6 years. The Director, Office of Munitions Control, may prescribe a longer or shorter period in individual cases.

(b) Records maintained under this section shall be available at all times for inspection and copying by the Director, Office of Munitions Control or a person designated by the Director (the Director of the Diplomatic Security Service or a person designated by the Director of the Diplomatic Security Service or another designee), or the Commissioner of the U.S. Customs Service or a person designated by the Commissioner.

Part 123

Licenses for the Export of Defense Articles

Sec. 123.1 Requirement for export licenses.

(a) Any person who intends to export a defense article must obtain a license from the Office of Munitions Control prior to the export unless the export qualifies for an exemption under the provisions of this subchapter.

(b) As a condition to the issuance of a license or other approval, the Office of Munitions Control may require all pertinent documentary information regarding the proposed transaction.

(c) An application for a license under this part for the permanent export of defense articles sold commercially must be accompanied by a copy of a purchaser order, letter of intent or other appropriate documentation. In cases involving the U.S. Foreign Military Sales program, three copies of the relevant Department of Defense Form 1513 are required, unless the procedures of Sec. 126.4(c) or Sec. 126.6 are followed. . . .

Sec. 123.2 Imports.

No defense article may be imported into the United States unless (a) it was previously exported temporarily under a license issued by the Office of Munitions Control; or (b) it constitutes a temporary import/intransit shipment licensed under Sec. 123.3; or (c) its import is authorized by the Department of the Treasury (see 27 CFR parts 47, 178 and 179).

. . .

Sec. 123.9 Country of ultimate destination.

(a) The country designated as the country of ultimate destination on an application for an export license, or on a shipper's export declaration where an exemption is claimed under this subchapter, must be the country of ultimate end-use. The written approval of the Department of State must be obtained before reselling, diverting, transferring, transshipping, or disposing of a defense article in any country other than the country of ultimate destination as stated on the export license, or on the shipper's export declaration in cases where an exemption is claimed under this subchapter. Exporters must ascertain the specific end-user and end-use prior to submitting an application to the Office of Munitions Control or claiming an exemption under this subchapter. End-use must be confirmed and should not be assumed.

. . .

Sec. 123.10 Non-transfer and use assurances and Congressional notification.

(a) An application for a license (Form DSP-5) to export significant military equipment defined in Sec. 120.19 must be accompanied by a nontransfer and use certificate (Form DSP-83) at the time of submission to the Office of Munitions Control. This form is to be executed by the foreign consignee and foreign end-user. The certificate stipulates that, except as specifically authorized by prior written approval of the Department of State, the foreign consignee and foreign end-user will not reexport, resell or otherwise dispose of the significant military equipment enumerated in the application outside the country named as the location of the foreign end-use.

. . .

Part 124

Manufacturing License Agreements, Technical Assistance Agreements, and Other Defense Services

Sec. 124.1 Manufacturing license agreements and technical assistance agreements.

(a) General. The approval of the Office of Munitions Control must be obtained before the defense services described in Sec. 120.8(a) of this subchapter may be furnished. In order to obtain such approval, the U.S. person must submit a proposed agreement with the foreign person concerned to the Office of Munitions Control. Such agreements are generally characterized as either "Manufacturing license agreements" or "technical assistance agreements" as defined in Sec. 120.14 and Sec. 120.20, and may not enter into force without the prior written approval of the Office of Munitions Control. Once approved, the defense services described in the agreements may generally be provided without further licensing in accordance with Sec. 124.3 and Sec. 125.4(b)(2). The requirements of this section apply whether or not technical data is to be disclosed or used in the performance of the defense services described in Sec. 120.8(a) (e.g., all the information relied upon by the U.S. person in performing the defense service is in the public domain or is otherwise exempt from the licensing requirements of this subchapter pursuant to Sec. 125.4). This requirement also applies to the training of foreign military forces, both regular and irregular, in the use of defense articles. Technical assistance agreements must be submitted in such cases. (In exceptional cases, the Office of Munitions Control, upon written request, will consider approving the provision of defense services described in Sec. 120.8(a) by granting a license under part 125. Also, see Sec. 126.8 for the requirements for prior approval of proposals relating to significant military equipment.)

(b) Amendments. Proposed amendments, including extensions, to agreements subject to the requirements of this part must also be submitted for approval. The amendments may also not enter into force until approved by the Office of Munitions Control. Amendments which only alter delivery or performance schedules, or other minor administrative amendments which do not affect in any manner the duration of the agreement or the clauses or information which must be included in such agreements because of the requirements of this part, do not have to be submitted for approval. One copy of all such minor amendments must be submitted to the Office of Munitions Control within thirty days after they are concluded.

. . .

Sec. 124.3 Exports of technical data in furtherance of an agreement.

(a) Unclassified technical data. District directors of customs or postal authorities may permit the export without a license of unclassified technical data if the export is in furtherance of a manufacturing license or technical assistance agreement which has been approved in writing by the Office of Munitions Control. The export is not authorized without a license if it exceeds the scope or limitations of the relevant agreement. The U.S. party to the agreement must certify that the export does not exceed the scope of the agreement and any limitations imposed pursuant to this part. The approval of the Office of Munitions Control must be obtained for the export of any unclassified technical data which may exceed the terms of the agreement.

. . .

Sec. 124.13 Procurement by United States persons in foreign countries (offshore procurement).

Notwithstanding the other provisions in part 124, the Office of Munitions Control may authorize by means of a license (DSP-5) the export of unclassified technical data to foreign persons for offshore procurement of defense articles, provided that:

(a) The contract or purchase order for offshore procurement limits delivery of the defense articles to be produced only to the person in the United States or to an agency of the U.S. Government; and

(b) The technical data of U.S. origin to be used in the foreign manufacture does not disclose the details of the design, development, production or manufacture of defense articles; and

(c) The contract or purchase order between the person in the United States and the foreign person:

(1) Limits the use of the technical data to the manufacture of the defense articles required by the contract or purchase order only; and

(2) Prohibits the disclosure of the data to any other person except duly qualified subcontractors within the same country; and

(3) Prohibits the acquisition of any rights in the data by any foreign person; and

(4) Provides that any subcontracts between foreign persons in the approved country for manufacture of equipment for delivery pursuant to the contract or purchase order contain all the limitations of this paragraph (c); and

(5) Requires the foreign person, including subcontractors, to destroy or return to the person in the United States all of the technical data exported pursuant to the contract or purchase order upon fulfillment of their terms; and

(6) Requires delivery of the defense articles manufactured abroad only to the person in the United States or to an agency of the U.S. Government; and

(d) The person in the United States provides the Office of Munitions Control with a copy of each contract, purchase order or subcontract for offshore procurement at the time it is accepted. Each such contract, purchase order or subcontract must clearly identify the article to be produced and must identify the license number or exemption under which the technical data was exported; and

(e) Licenses issued pursuant to this section must be renewed upon their expiration if offshore procurement is to extend beyond the period of validity of the license.

If the technical data involved in an offshore procurement arrangement is otherwise exempt from the licensing requirements pursuant to Sec. 126.4 or Sec. 126.5, the DSP-5 referred to in the first sentence of this section is not required. However, the exporter must comply with the other requirements of this section.

Sec. 124.14 Exports to warehouses or distribution points outside the United States.

(a) General. Agreements (e.g., contracts) between U.S. persons and foreign persons for the warehousing and distribution of defense articles must be approved by the Office of Munitions Control before they enter into force. Such agreements will be limited to unclassified defense articles and must contain conditions for special distribution, end-use and reporting. Licenses for exports pursuant to such ageements must be obtained prior to exports of the defense articles (see Sec. 123.7).

(b) Required information. Proposed warehousing and distribution agreements (and amendments thereto) shall be submitted to the Office of Munitions Control for approval. The following information must be included in all such agreements:

(1) A precise description of the defense articles involved. This shall include when applicable the military nomenclature, the Federal stock number, nameplate data, and any control numbers under which the defense articles were developed or procured by the U.S. Government.

(2) A detailed statement of the terms and conditions under which the defense articles will be exported and distributed;

(3) The duration of the proposed agreement;

(4) Specific identification of the country or countries that comprise the distribution territory. Distribution must be specifically limited to the governments of such countries or to private entities seeking to procure defense articles pursuant to a contract with a government within the distribution territory. Consequently, any deviation from this condition must be fully explained and justified. A nontransfer and use certificate (DSP-83) will be required to the same extent required in licensing agreements under Sec. 124.10(b).

(c) Required statements. The following statements must be included in all warehousing and distribution agreements:

(1) "This agreement shall not enter into force, and may not be amended or extended, without the prior written approval of the Department of State of U.S. Government."

(2) "This agreement is subject to all United Sates laws and regulations related to exports and to all administrative acts of the United States Government pursuant to such laws and regulations.

(3) "The parties to this agreement agree that the obligations contained in this agreement shall not affect the performance of any obligations created by prior contracts or subcontracts which the parties may have individually or collectively with the U.S. Government."

(4) "No liability will be incurred by or attributed to the U.S. Government in connection with any possible infringement of privately owned patent

or proprietary rights, either domestic or foreign by reason of the U.S. Goverment's approval of this agreement."

(5) "No export, sale, transfer, or other disposition of the defense articles covered by this agreement is authorized to any country outside the distribution territory without the prior written approval of the Office of Munitions Control of the U.S. Department of State."

(6) "The parties to this agreement agree that an annual report of sales or other transfers pursuant to this agreement of the licensed articles, by quantity, type, U.S. dollar value, and purchaser or recipient shall be provided by (applicant or licensee) to the Department of State." This clause must specify which party is obligated to provide the annual report. Such reports may be submitted either directly by the licensee or indirectly through the licensor, and may cover calendar or fiscal years. Reports shall be deemed proprietary information by the Department of State and will not be disclosed to unauthorized persons. (See Sec. 126.10(b)).

(7) "(Licensee) agrees to incorporate the following statement as an integral provision of a contract, invoice or other appropriate document whenever the articles covered by this agreement are sold or otherwise transferred:

These commodities are authorized for export by the U.S. Government only to (country of ultimate destination or approved sales territory). They may not be resold, diverted, transferred, transshipped, or otherwise be disposed of in any other country, either in their original form or after being incorporated through an intermediate process into other end-items, without the prior written approval of the U.S. Department of State."

(8) "All provisions in this agreement which refer to the United States Government and the Department of State will remain binding on the parties after the termination of the agreement."

(d) Special clauses for agreements relating to significant military equipment. With respect to agreements for the warehousing and distribution of significant military equipment, the following additional provisions must be included in the agreement:

(1) A completed nontransfer and use certificate (DSP-83) must be executed by the foreign end-user and submitted to the U.S. Department of State before any transfer may take place.

(2) The prior written approval of the U.S. Department of State must be obtained before entering into a commitment for the transfer of the licensed article by sale or otherwise to any person or government outside the approved distribution territory.

(e) Transmittal letters. Requests for approval of warehousing and distribution agreements with foreign persons must be made by letter. The original letter and seven copies of the letter and seven copies of the proposed agreement shall be submitted to the Office of Munitions Control. The letter shall contain:

(1) A statement giving the applicant's Munitions Control registration number.

(2) A statement identifying the foreign party to the agreement.

(3) A statement identifying the defense articles to be distributed under the agreement.

(4) A statement identifying any U.S. Government contract under which the equipment may have been generated, improved, developed or supplied to the U.S. Government, and whether the equipment was derived from any bid or other proposal to the U.S. Government.

(5) A statement that no classified defense articles or classified technical data are involved.

(6) A statement identifying any patent application which discloses any of the subject matter of the equipment or related technical data covered by an invention secrecy order issued by the U.S. Patent and Trademark Office.

(f) Additional clause. Unless the articles covered by the agreement are in fact intended to be distributed to private persons or entities (e.g., sporting firearms for commercial resale, cryptographic devices and software for financial and business applications), the following clause must be included in all warehousing and distribution agreements: "Sales or other transfers of the licensed article shall be limited to governments of the countries in the distribution territory and to private entities seeking to procure the licensed article pursuant to a contract with a government within the distribution territory, unless the prior written approval of the U.S. Department of State is obtained."

PART 125

LICENSES FOR THE EXPORT OF TECHNICAL DATA AND CLASSIFIED DEFENSE ARTICLES

Sec. 125.1 Exports subject to this part.

(a) The export controls of this part apply to the export of technical data and the export of classified defense articles. Information which is in the "public domain" (see Sec. 120.18) is not subject to the controls of this subchapter.

(b) A license for the export of technical data and the exemptions in Sec. 125.4 may not be used for foreign production purposes or for technical assistance unless the approval of the Department of State has been obtained. Such approval is generally provided only pursuant to the procedures specified in part 124 of this subchapter.

(c) Technical data authorized for export may not be diverted or transferred from the country of ultimate end-use (as designated in the license or approval for export) or disclosed to a national of another country without the prior written approval of the Department of State.

(d) The export controls of this part apply to the exports referred to in paragraph (a) of this section regardless of whether the person who intends to export the technical data produces or manufactures defense articles if the technical data is determined by the Office of Munitions Control to be subject to the controls of this subchapter.

(e) The provisions of this subchapter do not apply to technical data related to articles in Category VI(e) and Category XVI. The export of such data is controlled by the Department of Energy and the Nuclear Regulatory Commission pursuant to the Atomic Energy Act of 1954, as amended, and the Nuclear Non-Proliferation Act of 1978.

Sec. 125.2 Exports of unclassified technical data.

(a) General. A license issued by the Department of State is required for the export of unclassified technical data unless the export is exempt from the licensing requirements of this subchapter.

(b) Patents. A license issued by the Department of State is required for the export of technical data whenever the data exceeds that which is used to support a domestic filing of a patent application or to support a foreign filing of a patent application whenever no domestic application has been filed. The export of technical data to support the filing and processing of patent applications in foreign countries is subject to regulations issued by the U.S. Patent and Trademark Office pursuant to 35 U.S.C. 184.

(c) Disclosures. Unless otherwise expressly exempted in this subchapter, a license is required for the oral, visual or documentary disclosure of technical data to foreign nationals in connection with visits by U.S. persons to foreign countries, visits by foreign persons to the United States, or otherwise. A license is required regardless of the manner in which the technical data is transmitted (e.g., in person, by telephone, correspondence, electronic means, telex, etc.). A license is required for such disclosures in connection with visits by U.S. persons to foreign diplomatic missions and consular offices.

...

Sec. 125.4 Exemptions of general applicability.

(a) The following exemptions apply to exports of technical data for which no license or other approval is needed from the Office of Munitions Control. These exemptions, except for paragraph (b)(13) of this section, do not apply to exports to proscribed destinations under Sec. 126.1. Transmission of classified information must comply with the requirements of the Department of Defense Industrial Security Manual and the exporter must certify to the transmittal authority that the technical data does not exceed the technical limitation of the authorized export. A person who determines that an export is not subject to this subchapter should review the Department of Commerce regulations to ensure that the export is not subject to its export jurisdiction.

(b) The following exports are exempt from the licensing requirements of this subchapter:

...

(2) Technical data, including classified information, in furtherance of a manufacturing license or technical assistance agreement approved by the Department of State under part 124 of this subchapter and which meet the requirements of Sec. 124.3;

. . .

(4) Copies of technical data, including classified information, previously authorized for export to the same recipient. Revised copies of such technical data are also exempt if they pertain to the identical defense article, and if the revisions are solely editorial and do not add to the content of technology previously exported or authorized for export to the same recipient;

(5) Technical data in the form of basic operations, maintenance, and training information relating to a defense article lawfully exported or authorized for export to the same recipient. This exemption applies only to exports by the original exporter. Intermediate or depot-level repair and maintenance information may be exported only under a license or agreement approved specifically for that purpose;

. . .

(7) Technical data, including classified information, being returned to the original source of import;

. . .

(9) Technical data, including classified information, sent by a U.S. corporation to a U.S. person employed by that corporation overseas or to a U.S. Government agency. This exemption is subject to the limitations of Sec. 125.1(b) and may be used only if (i) the technical data is to be used overseas solely by U.S. persons and (ii) if the U.S. person overseas is an employee of the U.S. Government or is directly employed by the U.S. corporation and not by a foreign subsidiary;

(10) Disclosures of technical data in the U.S. by U.S. institution of higher learning to foreign persons who are their bona fide and full time regular employees. This exemption is available only if (i) the employee's permanent abode throughout the period of employment is in the United States; (ii) the employee is not a national of a country to which exports are prohibited pursuant to Sec. 126.1; and (iii) the institution informs the individual in writing that the technical data may not be transferred to other foreign persons without the prior written approval of the Office of Munitions Control; . . .

(12) Technical data which is specifically exempt under part 126 of this subchapter; or

(13) Technical data approved for public release (i.e., unlimited distribution) by the cognizant U.S. Government department or agency. This exemption is applicable to information approved by the cognizant U.S. Government department or agency for public release in any form (e.g.,

publications, speeches, conference papers, movies, etc.). It does not require that the information be published in order to qualify for the exemption. . . .

Sec. 125.6 Certification requirements.

To claim an exemption for the export of technical data under the provisions of Sec. 125.4 and Sec. 125.5, an exporter must certify that the proposed export is covered by a relevant paragraph of that section. This certification is not required if the technical data is only disclosed orally or visually. The certification referred to in this section consists of marking the package or letter containing the technical data: "22 CFR 125. (identify subsection) applicable" and identifying the specific paragraph under which the exemption is claimed. In the case of unclassified technical data, district directors of customs may require that the certification be made on a shipper's export declaration.

Sec. 125.7 Exports of unclassified technical data.

(a) General. Unless an export is exempt from the licensing requirements of this subchapter, an application for the permanent export of unclassified technical data must be made to the Office of Munitions Control on Form DSP-5. If the technical data is to be returned to the United States, Form DSP-73 should be used instead. In the case of a visit, sufficient details of the proposed discussions must be transmitted for an adequate appraisal of the data. Seven copies of the data or the details of the discussions must be provided. Only one copy must be provided if a renewal of the license is requested.

(b) Patents. Requests for the filing of patent applications in a foreign country and requests for the filing of amendments, modifications or supplements to such patents must be directed to the U.S. Patent and Trademark Office in accordance with 37 CFR part 5. If an applicant complies with the regulations of that office, the approval of the Office of Munitions Control is required only in the circumstance described in Sec. 125.2(b). In such cases, an application must be submitted in accordance with the provisions of paragraph (a) of this section.

. . .

Sec. 125.9 Filing of licenses for exports of unclassified technical data.

Licenses for the export of unclassified technical data must be deposited with the appropriate district director of customs or postmaster at the time of shipment or mailing. The district director of customs or postmaster will endorse and transmit the licenses to the Office of Munitions Control in accordance with the instructions contained on the reverse side of the license. If a license for the export of unclassified technical data is used but not endorsed by U.S. Customs or a postmaster for whatever reason, the person exporting the data must self-endorse the license and return it promptly to the Office of Munitions Control.

. . .

PART 126

Sec. 126.1 Prohibited exports and sales to certain countries.

(a) General. It is the policy of the United States to deny licenses and other approvals with respect to defense articles and defense services destined for or originating in certain countries or areas. This policy also applies to exports to and imports from these countries or areas. This policy applies to Albania, Bulgaria, Cambodia, Cuba, Estonia, Latvia, Lithuania, North Korea, Outer Mongolia, Romania, the Soviet Union and Vietnam. This policy also applies to countries or areas with respect to which the United States maintains an arms embargo (e.g., Angola) or whenever an export would not otherwise be in furtherance of world peace and the security and foreign policy of the United States. The exemptions provided in the regulations in this subchapter, except Sec. 123.17 and Sec. 125.4(b)(13) of this subchapter, do not apply with respect to exports to or originating in any of such proscribed countries or areas.

(b) Shipments. A defense article licensed for export under this subchapter may not be shipped on a vessel, aircraft or other means of conveyance which is owned or operated by, or leased to or from, any of the proscribed countries or areas.

. . .

(d) Terrorism. Exports to countries that have repeatedly provided support for acts of international terrorism are contrary to the foreign policy of the United States and are thus subject to the policy specified in paragraph (a) of this section and the requirements of section 40 of the Arms Export Control Act (22 U.S.C. 2780). The countries in this category are Cuba, Iran, Iraq, Libya, Syria, and North Korea. These are the same countries identified pursuant to section 6(j) of the Export Administration Act, as amended (50 U.S.C. App. 2405(j)).

(e) Proposed Sales. No sale or transfer and no proposal to sell or transfer any defense articles, defense services or technical data subject to this subchapter may be made to any country referred to in this section (including the embassies or consulates of such a country), or to any person acting on its behalf, whether in the United States or abroad, without first obtaining a license or other written approval from the Office of Munitions Control. (See Sec. 120.10(f) of this subchapter), in accordance with paragraph (a) of this section, it is the policy of the Department of State to deny licenses and approvals in such cases. Any person who knows or has reason to know of such a proposed or actual sale, or transfer, of such articles, services or data must inform the Office of Munitions Control.

Sec. 126.2 Temporary suspension or modification of this subchapter.

The Director, Office of Munitions Control, may order the temporary suspension or modification of any or all of the regulations of this subchapter in the interest of the security and foreign policy of the United States.

. . .

Sec. 126.5 Canadian exemptions.

(a) General. District directors of customs and postmasters may permit the export without a license of any unclassified defense article or any unclassified technical data to Canada for end-use in Canada or return to the United States, with the exception of the articles or technical data listed in paragraph (b) of this section.

. . .

Sec. 126.7 Denial, revocation, suspension, or amendment of licenses and other approvals.

(a) Policy. Licenses or approvals shall be denied or revoked whenever required by any statute of the United States (see Sec. 127.6 and Sec. 127.10 of this subchapter). Any application for an export license or other approval under this subchapter may be disapproved, and any license or other approval or exemption granted under this subchapter may be revoked, suspended, or amended without prior notice whenever:

(1) The Department of State deems such action to be in furtherance of world peace, the national security or the foreign policy of the United States, or is otherwise advisable; or

(2) The Department of State believes that 22 U.S.C. 2778, any regulation contained in this subchapter, or the terms of any U.S. government export authorization (including the terms of a manufacturing license or technical assistance agreement, or export authorization granted pursuant to the Export Administration Act, as amended) has been violated by any party to the export or other person having significant interest in the transaction; or. . . .

Sec. 126.9 Advisory opinions.

A U.S. person desiring information as to whether the Office of Munitions Control would be likely to grant a license or other approval for the export of particular defense articles or defense services to a particular country may use the Office of Munitions Control's informal "Advisory Opinions" procedure. These opinions are advisory only. They are not binding on the Department of State and are revocable. A request for an advisory opinion must be by letter. It must outline in detail the equipment, its usage, the security classification, if any, of the articles or related technical data, and the country or countries involved. An original and seven copies of the letter must be provided along with seven copies of suitable descriptive information concerning the defense article or defense service. If a request for an advisory opinion involves more than one country, the letter should address only those countries in the same geographic area.

Sec. 126.10 Disclosure of information to the public.

(a) General. Subchapter R of this title of CFR contains regulations on the availability to the public of information and records of the Department of State. The provisions of Subchapter R apply to such disclosures by the Office of Munitions Control.

(b) Determinations required by law. Section 38 of the Arms Export Control Act (22 U.S.C. 2778) provides that certain information required by the Department of State in connection with the licensing process may generally not be disclosed to the public unless certain determinations relating to the national interest are made in accordance with the procedures specified by that provision. Any determinations required by section 38(e) shall be made by the Under Secretary for Security Assistance, Science, and Technology.

(c) Information required under part 130. Part 130 of this subchapter contains specific provisions on the disclosure of information described in that part.

Sec. 126.12 Continuation in force.

All determinations, authorizations, licenses, approvals of contracts and agreements and other action issued, authorized, undertaken, or entered into by the Department of State pursuant to section 414 of the Mutual Security Act of 1954, as amended, or under the previous provisions of this subchapter, continue in full force and effect until or unless modified, revoked or superseded by the Department of State.

. . .

PART 127

VIOLATIONS AND PENALTIES

Sec. 127.1 Violations in general.

(a) It is unlawful (1) to export or attempt to export from the United States any defense article or technical data or to furnish any defense service for which a license or written approval is required by this subchapter without first obtaining the required license or written approval from the Office of Munitions Control (2) to import or attempt to import any defense article whenever a license is required by this subchapter without first obtaining the required license or written approval from the Department of State; or (3) to violate any of the terms or conditions of licenses or approvals granted pursuant to this subchapter.

. . .

(d) No person may willfully cause, or aid, abet, counsel, demand, induce, procure or permit the commission of any act prohibited by, or the omission of any act required by 22 U.S.C. 2778, 22 U.S.C. 2779, or any regulation, license, approval, or order issued thereunder.

. . . .

Sec. 127.3 Penalties for violations.

Any person who willfully:

(a) Violates any provision of section 38 or section 39 of the Arms Export Control Act (22 U.S.C. 2778 and 2779), or any undertaking specifically required by part 124 of this subchapter; or

(b) In a registration, license application or report required by section 38 or section 39 of the Arms Export Control Act (22 U.S.C. 2778 and 2779) or by any rule or regulation issued under either section, makes any untrue statement of a material fact or omits a material fact required to be stated therein or necessary to make the statements therein not misleading, shall, upon conviction, be subject to fine or imprisonment, or both, as prescribed by 22 U.S.C. 2778(c).

Sec. 127.4 Authority of U.S. Customs Service officers.

(a) U.S. Customs Service officers may take appropriate action to ensure observance of this subchapter as to the export or the attempted export of any defense article or technical data, including the inspection of loading or unloading of any vessel, vehicle, or aircraft. This applies whether the export is authorized by license or by written approval issued under this subchapter.

(b) Upon the presentation to a customs officer of a license or written approval authorizing the export of any defense article, the customs officer may require the production of other relevant documents and information relating to the proposed export. This includes an invoice, order, packing list, shipping document, correspondence, instructions, and the documents otherwise required by the U.S. Customs Service.

Sec. 127.5 Seizure and forfeiture in attempts at illegal exports.

(a) An attempt to export from the United States any defense articles in violation of the provisions of this subchapter constitutes an offense punishable under section 401 of Title 22 of the United States Code. Whenever it is known or there is probable cause to believe that any defense article is intended to be or is being or has been exported or removed from the United States in violation of law, such article and any vessel, vehicle or aircraft involved in such attempt is subject to seizure, forfeiture and disposition as provided in section 401 of Title 22 of the United States Code.

. . .

Sec. 127.9 Civil penalty.

(a) The Assistant Secretary for Politico-Military Affairs, Department of State is authorized to impose a civil penalty in an amount not to exceed that authorized by 50 U.S.C. App. 2410(c) for each violation of 22 U.S.C. 2778, or any regulation, order, license or approval issued thereunder. This civil penalty may be either in addition to, or in lieu of, any other liability or penalty which may be imposed.

(b) The Office of Munitions Control may make (1) the payment of a civil penalty under this section or (2) the completion of any administrative action pursuant to part 127 or 128 of this subchapter a prior condition for the issuance, restoration, or continuing validity of any export license or other approval.

. . .

Index